ECONOMICS AS WORLDLY PHILOSOPHY

Also by Edward J. Nell

BEYOND THE STEADY STATE (*editor with Joseph Halevi and David Laibman*)
NICHOLAS KALDOR AND MAINSTREAM ECONOMICS (*co-editor with Willi Semmler*)
TRANSFORMATIONAL GROWTH AND EFFECTIVE DEMAND

Professor Robert L. Heilbroner (*circa* 1980)

Economics as Worldly Philosophy

Essays in Political and Historical Economics in Honour of Robert L. Heilbroner

Edited by

Ron Blackwell
Assistant to the President for Economic Affairs
Amalgamated Clothing and Textiles Union, USA

Jaspal Chatha
Lecturer in Economics
Lehmann College of the City University of New York

and

Edward J. Nell
Professor of Economics
New School for Social Research, New York

St. Martin's Press

First published in Great Britain 1993 by
THE MACMILLAN PRESS LTD
Houndmills, Basingstoke, Hampshire RG21 2XS
and London
Companies and representatives
throughout the world

A catalogue record for this book is available
from the British Library.

ISBN 0–333–49477–6

Printed in Hong Kong

First published in the United States of America 1993 by TP
Scholarly and Reference Division,
ST. MARTIN'S PRESS, INC.,
175 Fifth Avenue,
New York, N.Y. 10010

ISBN 0–312–07982–6

Library of Congress Cataloging-in-Publication Data
Economics as worldly philosophy : essays in political and historical
economics in honour of Robert L. Heilbroner / edited by Ron Blackwell,
Jaspal Chatha, and Edward J. Nell.
p.   cm.
ISBN 0–312–07982–6
1. Economics.   I. Heilbroner, Robert L.   II. Blackwell, Ron.
III. Chatha, Jaspal.   IV. Nell, Edward J.
HB34.E2729   1993
330.1—dc20   92–2547
                                                        CIP

For Robert L. Heilbroner

Over the years Robert L. Heilbroner has been a helpful and kindly, yet critical, teacher, mentor, guide and colleague to us and to all the authors of this book. All of us have been inspired by, and in large part have come to share, his vision of what economics could and should be – an analytical, yet philosophical, dissection of the nature and logic of an evolving system, in order to devise policies to improve it, and thereby improve our world. We dedicate this book to him, as the very model of a worldly philosopher.

Contents

Notes on Contributors

Ronald Blackwell is Assistant to the President for Economic Affairs at the Amalgamated Clothing and Textiles Union (ACTWU). Formerly he taught economics as a Member of the Faculty of the Seminar College at the New School, where he also served as an academic dean.

Martha Campbell received her Ph.D. from the New School for Social Research in 1992.

Richard Castellana is Assistant Professor in Social Sciences at Edward Williams College, Fairleigh Dickinson University. He is currently completing a book on Marx's concept of justice and its relation to economic life.

Jaspal Chatha teaches economics at Lehmann College of the City University of New York.

Patrick Clawson is Editor of *Orbis* and Resident Scholar at the Foreign Policy Research Institute in Philadelphia. He was previously a Senior Economist at the World Bank and the IMF.

David R. Howell received his Ph.D. in economics from the Graduate Faculty in 1982. From 1981–4 he worked at NYU's Institute for Economic Analysis, directed by W. Leontief, on an input–output study of the employment effects of technical change. He is currently on the faculty of the Graduate School of Management and Urban Policy at the New School.

Elias L. Khalil is Assistant Professor of Economics at Ohio State University, Mansfield. He is the author of 'Rationality and Social Labor in Marx'. (*Critical Review*, 1990), 'Beyond Self-Interest and Altruism: A Reconstruction of Adam Smith's theory of Human Conduct' (*Economics and Philosophy*, 1990), and 'Entropy Law and Exhaustion of Natural Resources' (*Ecological Economics*, 1990).

Chidem Kurdas is Assistant Professor of Economics at Pennsylvania State University. Her publications focus on investment spending, growth, and technical change. Her current research is concerned with technical change in the health care sector.

Richard McGahey is Economics Policy Advisor to Senator Edward M. Kennedy, and Chief Economist for the US Senate Committee on Labor and Human Resources.

Thomas Michl received his Ph.D. in economics from the New School for Social Research. He is currently Associate Professor of Economics at Colgate University.

Scott Moss is Nuffield Social Science Research Fellow at Manchester Polytechnic. He is the editor of *Artificial Intelligence and Economic Analysis: Problems and Prospects*.

Edward J. Nell is Professor of Economics at the Graduate Faculty of the New School for Social Research. He is the author of *Transformational Growth and Effective Demand: Economics after the Capital Critique*, *Keynes After Sraffa: The Reconstruction of Political Economy*, editor (with Willi Semmler) of *Nicholas Kaldor and Mainstream Economics: Confrontation or Convergence?*, and editor (with Joseph Halevi and David Laibman) of *Beyond the Steady State: A Revival of Growth Theory*.

Robert Pollin received his Ph.D. from the New School in 1982. He is Associate Professor of Economics at the University of California at Riverside, specializing in money and banking, macroeconomics, and political economy. He is co-director of the Financial Restructuring Working Group of the Economic Policy Institute, and an editorial associate of *Dollars and Sense*.

Steven Pressman is Associate Professor of Economics and Finance at Monmouth College in West Long Branch, New Jersey and Associate Editor of the Eastern Economic Journal. He is currently working on a book, *Keynes and Public Policy*.

Frank Roosevelt is Professor of Economics and Chair of the Social Science faculty at Sarah Lawrence College. He has written on market socialism in the *Journal of Economic Issues* and on the economics of the Cambridge School in Edward J. Nell (ed.): *Growth, Profits, and Property: Essays in the Revival of Political Economy*.

Robert Urquhart received his Ph.D. from the New School for Social Research. He is an Assistant Professor of Economics at the University of Denver.

Acknowledgements

It is a special pleasure for the editors to acknowledge the help of the New School Economics Department. Karin Ray and Julie Barnes handled innumerable chores. Susan Pashkoff helped with some particularly difficult editing, and Ross Thomson with measured advice and support. Mathew Forstater undertook the assembling and management of the papers and efficiently oversaw the proofreading. Marsha Lasker Nell helped to keep us on track and provided encouragement. And finally, everyone involved in the project would like to acknowledge the example and inspiration provided by Robert Heilbroner.

RON BLACKWELL
JASPAL CHATHA
EDWARD J. NELL

1 Introduction: History and Vision in Economics

Edward J. Nell

In a famous essay a few years ago, at a time when her admirers had perhaps hoped for answers, Joan Robinson asked instead, 'What Are the Questions?' Her list provided a catalogue of the ills of economics: unsatisfactory definitions at the heart of the subject – in regard to equilibrium, production, and the firm; inappropriate methodology for considering time and history; confused and unsatisfactory theories of capital, distribution, prices, growth and trade; ideology rather than analysis guiding policy; and, above all, no clear idea of what it is all about – no adequate answer to the question, what is more wealth *for*?

Many, perhaps most, of Joan's questions and complaints would appear on Heilbroner's list, too. But they would be further down the page. Her questions remain firmly in the field of economics. For Heilbroner, 'what are the questions?' is indeed the question, but unlike Joan, who provided a shopping list, he reformulates the problem as a meta-question, a quest for the source of questions, and for him this will not be found in economics. The question of questions arises in History; this is what is to be explained. And it provides the organizing principle for inquiry into economic matters. Economics provides Answers to questions generated by history, or rather, it gives us a part of the answers, an indispensable – though incomplete – basis for explaining the course of history. Joan's shopping list can be given an order, ranked by both subject matter and importance.

Joan Robinson attacked neo-classical theory and in the process contributed to its development; in a sense she always remained its prisoner. Heilbroner, for the most part, has stood aside from it and, as a result, has not only remained largely free of its influence but has been able to fit some of its questions and approach into a larger scheme. To be sure, Heilbroner wrote a textbook, a very successful one, but its success arose not from its fairly conventional treatment of elementary macro and micro – though these were presented very clearly – but from its outstanding encapsulation of the centuries-long rise and development of capitalism – a part, but only a small part, of which conventional theory helps us to understand. Growth and development, and the emergence of accompanying problems, are the focus of Heilbroner's economic analysis.

1.1 THE GRAND TRADITION

In this way, Heilbroner falls clearly into that set of economists, mostly classical, but including the leading American institutionalists, who see economics as the analysis of the engine that drives the progress of history (though, as we shall see, his analysis in important respects is at once more confined and more universal than most others). Capital accumulation is the power source, the drive – but the transmission, as it were, is the social institution of the market, equally fundamental but different. Economics therefore has two tasks, both prefigured in Adam Smith: to understand the logic of capital accumulation, and to comprehend the nature of markets – and to show how the two are related. Smith, indeed, embodies most of the later themes of economics but on accumulation he is significantly in error – he thinks accumulation will, one day, come to an end when as much capital as is required will be employed in every trade. He simply did not appreciate the importance and ubiquity of technological change. By contrast, he did understand the role of the market not only in coordinating diverse activities, but also in promoting the division of labour, and thereby the transformation of work. Smith is regarded by Heilbroner as the first great expositor of 'the nature and logic of capitalism', an exposition limited, to be sure, by the still undeveloped capitalism of his own day, but nevertheless the first systematic attempt at 'worldly philosophy'.

By contrast, the conventional view focuses on only one of the issues above, and treats only part of that, taking the object of economics to be the analysis of the working of markets in given conditions, where markets are considered to perform the social function of allocating scarce resources – more or less optimally as the markets are more or less competitive.

It might seem that there need be no conflict between Heilbroner and conventional economics; if markets allocate scarce resources, their success or failure in doing so will affect the political and social arena, and so eventually influence the movement of history. Capital accumulation can be treated simply as another scarcity problem – the allocation of savings. Conventional thinking concentrates on the particular problems; whereas Heilbroner prefers to consider the general implications, taking the long view. Surely, the two could be reconciled?

But if markets do not, or do not primarily, allocate scarce resources, or if they perform other functions as well, concentrating on allocative questions will not adequately explain the role of markets in the working of the system, particularly in relation to the creation and distribution of the surplus. This could quite possibly lead to a misinterpretation of the real development of the market system, and even worse, to an approach that may actually assign markets the wrong role in the march of history. For in Heilbroner's view, while the market is the medium through which accumulation takes place, the study of the market itself will explain neither the production of the surplus nor the waves of creative destruction inherent in accumulation. Focusing on savings and allocation provides an anaemic picture that tells us little or nothing about the power structure inherent in capital or the transformational dynamics of accumulation. Concentrating on the market alone, we will never fully understand either work or wealth.

Indeed, it will be hard to understand the market if we focus on it alone. For it is not at all easy to say just what 'markets are'. The concept of the 'market' (like that of 'capital') is a 'theory-laden' term; the question of what something is, when the object is as complicated and multifaceted as the institution of the market (in what society, what century, what culture?), presents a surprisingly difficult problem. The answers seem easy until we are asked to justify or, even worse, prove them; then we realize that we have nowhere to turn, for we have arrived back at our starting point. The reason why it is difficult to justify these answers is that we have reached the point on which the whole of our picture of the economic world rests. We find it hard to justify this point because it is the basis of our justifications.

1.2   A QUESTION OF VISIONS

Heilbroner, following Schumpeter, terms this the 'pre-analytic vision' which colours and shapes all our theoretical thinking. Yet, unlike Schumpeter, he does think that these pre-analytic visions are capable of analysis and to a certain extent of being criticized and justified or rejected; proof or disproof may not be possible, but certainly critical analysis is in order.

Indeed, he subjects Schumpeter to just such a critique, for what especially interests Heilbroner is the fact that Schumpeter's theory is built on *two* 'visions', which on the face of it appear to be incompatible. Moreover, they are the visions which give shape to the two main threads making up the fabric of the history of economics as a discipline – the turbulent dynamics of the classical approach – Smith, Ricardo and Marx, and the smooth equilibrium of neo-classical allocation theory – Walras, Marshall, and Arrow–Debreu. For Schumpeter, the normal working of the system is described by the smoothly equilibrated 'circular flow' – the market system as portrayed by neo-classical theory. But innovations are introduced by entrepreneurs, disrupting this equilibrium and creating the turbulent dynamics of the classics. How successfully can two such differing visions be mixed? Schumpeter's mix depends on an arbitrary assignment of roles to the businessman and the entrepreneur, reflecting an élitist view of the social order – and perhaps of human nature. Businessmen are ordinary and act following a routine, resulting in equilibrium; entrepreneurs, a self-selected élite, rising like cream to the top, disrupt this with the innovations that transform the world. And this role assignment is echoed in Schumpeter's treatment of economics and history – economics is the sphere of smooth adjustment to equilibrium, the working of the circular flow. But history is the parade of social forms and structures – capitalism emerges from mercantilism, flowers, develops and eventually decays, undermined by the very rationalist critique of problems and institutions that gave impetus to its birth, thus giving way to socialism. History, then, is the stage on which the intellectual élite acts out its destiny; economics just keeps the machine of everyday life ticking over. It has little or nothing to contribute to history, which is made by the élite, by the innovators, the entrepreneurs and scientists who invent and introduce the new technologies that periodically change the world.

For Heilbroner, this will not do. The neo-classical vision of crystalline equilibrium just does not describe the way markets actually work. Where is the truck and barter of Smith, the deceitful practices and conspicuous consumption of Veblen, the conflict between capitalists and workers of Marx (and between masters and journeymen in Smith); what about the booms and busts, the 'general gluts' that worried Malthus in his debates with Ricardo? Do machines sometimes drive men out of work, as Ricardo finally conceded? If there are compensating employment opportunities, will the new industries require the same skills? And so on. For Heilbroner, the idea that markets accomplish allocation and reach equilibrium just sweeps too much under the carpet. Perhaps . . . perhaps . . . Heilbroner never totally rejects the neo-classical idea. Markets may sometimes, in part, perform an allocative function; but markets also do many other things – and these other functions are more important, for they are part of what drives history.

1.3   THE ROLE OF MARKETS

So what do markets do? For one thing they structure work, the way we make and distribute the things of everyday life; and this determines not only what people do, but what they need to know. Who people are, depends, in our society, in large part, on what they do. So a society's structure of work tells a great deal about what kinds of people inhabit that society. And markets establish this structure by setting up a game, a competitive race, so that the institutions of work are constantly scrambling for advantage. Contrary to Schumpeter, it is not the élite entrepreneurs who transform the world. It is the struggle that arises from the ordinary working of ordinary markets for ordinary things. And the result is extraordinary change. Moreover, the benefits are quite unequally, often inequitably, distributed; and changes in this distribution, resulting from booms and busts, often unforeseen, can occur at times with great rapidity. When work is organized through competitive markets workers are formally, i.e. contractually, free (although in fact while at work they are under strict discipline), but they are subject to the dictates of the system itself, a system in which the winds of creative destruction are constantly blowing.

Markets also make possible the accumulation of wealth. The surplus is produced through the employment of labour, hired in the free market, and the goods produced are sold on the market for more money than the business laid out in wages and materials, etc. Thus capital revolves in the circuit described by Marx: $M - C - P - C' - M'$, money is exchanged for commodities, inputs and labour, which produce a new set of commodities, outputs, which are then exchanged again for money, realizing the surplus in cash. This process, once established, destroys the old feudal and mercantile systems and both creates and supports a new class structure, with owners and managers of capital at the top, then lesser managers, professionals and white collar workers, and finally, blue collar workers of various categories at the bottom. A class structure? Well, a hierarchy, certainly;

and, yes, classes. The system reproduces itself; but it also changes. It is in constant flux, and it is uncommonly hard to identify a *ruling class*. A power élite, definitely. But a ruling class – the trouble is, the two words do not quite fit together. The élite are not able to rule, in the sense of controlling the destiny of the system. First, even if the upper class were united, the system would still behave according to its own logic. Second, power tends to move around. It follows the market, and the market follows the money. Power, in fact, seems to be tied more closely to institutions than to families. And institutions are driven to change by the developmental logic of the system.

But markets themselves, when fully developed, constitute a dramatic change in the form of social coordination, compared to earlier systems. Based on free contractual relations, they define a realm of vitally important behaviour, production and distribution, from which government has been largely excluded, and not least, they have significantly legitimated acquisitive behaviour as a norm in this realm. Smith was not wrong to celebrate what he called 'the system of perfect liberty'; it is a dramatic force for increasing wealth. (Nor was he blind to the inequality in property on which it is based.)

Markets, then, are part of the stuff of history. Their emergence and development signals and encourages, even compels, major social changes. They are not smooth-working, sparkling crystals of equilibrium; they are the forms that contain and channel the energy of social conflict, directing it towards creative destruction. But, in and of themselves, they do not generate the energy that forces social change. That comes from capital accumulation.

1.4 HEILBRONER'S VISION: CAPITALISM AS A REGIME

The driving force of capitalism is the pressure to accumulate – not just to produce, but to expand the power to produce, to extend control over productive processes, to expand them and create new ones. But the drive of capitalism is not just to expand production; capitalism requires realizing the gains in monetary terms. So it requires simultaneous expansion of the power to produce and the ability to sell – markets must be extended *pari passu* with the transformation of the powers of production. Financial markets have to keep pace also; accumulation therefore creates pressure for expansion and innovation in all aspects of economic life.

Nor is this expansion a simple process. Economists sometimes portray growth, usually for mathematical convenience, as a kind of equiproportional 'swelling-up'. Heilbroner knows better, and has no bag of mathematical tools to weigh him down. Accumulation means, on the one hand, to extend the sway of capitalist control over processes formerly controlled and directed by earlier or more primitive methods; on the other, it means ploughing back earnings to expand present processes, and open new markets. Capital accumulation is an active force; it is an attack on our present ways of living and doing things, an attack that will rationalize and improve the lives of many – and make some people rich in the process, while ruining others.

Capital is a way of organizing production and is therefore a form of social control. The owners or, latterly, the managers of capital determine what is to be produced, how and by whom. Workers, whose ability to support themselves and their families depends on getting and holding a job, do as they are told when working. When at work, therefore, labour is subordinated; it obeys the dictates of capital. But workers are nevertheless, in an important sense, free; free, that is, in dimensions unknown to serfs or slaves or apprentices, even journeymen, in earlier societies. Workers are free to quit, to find other jobs, to move about geographically, even to set up shop for themselves and try to become capitalists. But on the job they do as they are told.

It is a striking and historically innovative feature of capitalism that it divides society into two realms, in one of which the traditional authority of the state is exercised, while in the other the exercise of authority follows as the consequence of contracts between free agents, who, however, are characterized by unequal status in regard to property. In this second sphere the state is largely excluded, apart from its role as the ultimate enforcer of contract and protector of property. Yet it is in this 'private' realm, expanded far beyond the traditional boundaries of the household to encompass the greater part of marketable production, that most members of modern society spend most of their time and in which they lodge their fondest hopes and greatest fears. This division of realms creates both the distinctive freedom and the sometimes appalling commercialization of so many aspects of personal and cultural life, characteristic of the modern world.

1.5   PARTICULAR DYNAMICS AND UNIVERSAL FOUNDATIONS

Heilbroner then not only shares but develops the classical 'grand tradition' of historical dynamics. But unlike many of the classics, and especially unlike some of their modern followers, he sees the patterns of development of different social formations as unique to each. General laws of development, transcending social formations, are not to be found. Ancient society, feudalism and capitalism each develop according to their own logic, the study of which is the proper basis of economic analysis, though only in the latter are we able to isolate a realm – that of the market – in which behavioural regularities covering a broad range of activities can be reliably defined.

Nevertheless, this is not the end of the matter. For the nature and logic of social formations itself must be grounded in something. Part of the answer will be found in the environment, the general material conditions in which a society subsists. But the environment is simply there; to shape the formation of a society it has to enter into the actions and reactions of people. Hence the other and more significant term of the relationship is that elusive philosopher's stone of social thought, 'human nature'.

A universal condition of mankind, inherent in our biology, is prolonged infant dependency, and this, Heilbroner feels, lies at the root of the power relationships in human societies. 'Infancy is . . . the great readying experience that prepares us for the adult world and conditions(s)' of domination and subordination. Being the condition from which we must all escape, it provides the unconscious source for the drive for emancipation, while remaining at the same time 'the prototype of the existential security that we also seek'. It is therefore a condition that leaves in our unconscious a willingness to accept relations of dominance and subordination as wholly natural. By itself, however, this will not explain the emergence of stratification and dominance in conditions of equality and free access to resources – that, Heilbroner feels, must be left to *ad hoc* conjectures. But once an organized, stratified society emerged it could easily conquer its egalitarian neighbours, and spread.

1.6 SCEPTICISM

Perhaps his picture of the 'nature and logic' of capitalism is Heilbroner's most carefully drawn analytical portrait, receiving far more attention than, for example, the 'principles' of economics, upon which the mainstream accounts of market equilibrium rest. These do not interest Heilbroner, by and large, not only because they concern less fundamental questions and have been exhaustively treated by others, but in addition, because he regards their status with a jaundiced eye. Do the 'principles' of supply and demand hold always and everywhere? Are they a pure expression of the rational mind facing choices under constraint? Obviously not, for there are many different and inconsistent models of rational choice. And as Adam Smith knew, self-interest itself – as well as the way we pursue it – will be in part defined by the prevailing views as to what is right and wrong. Even the preferred models may give rise to multiple and/or unstable equilibria. But if many models are possible, how do we know which ones apply here and now? Especially when they screen out institutional content, on the one hand, and provide an account of markets that is admittedly 'unrealistic', on the other. No doubt the basic principles of mainstream economics can be stated with elegance and rigour, but sometimes it seems to be *fin de siècle* elegance and rigor mortis.

The mainstream principles stem, Heilbroner argues, from a basic vision – a vision that is itself seldom articulated, but can be seen to be a form of individualism. For Heilbroner this cannot be acceptable; individuals are shaped and moulded from their earliest years by the pressures of family, class, education and work – they are the products of their societies. They cannot be the foundation stone as well.

So the 'principles of economics' are left hanging for Heilbroner. They are not eternal; derived from choice, they depend on the characteristics of the choosers, and the contexts in which the choices exist, both of which depend on the more basic 'nature and logic' of the system. And systems change.

1.7   FROM CAPITALISM TO . . . SOCIALISM?

Heilbroner's scepticism extends from economics and philosophy to the system itself. He regards not only the claims of capitalism but its foundations and actual working with a systematic suspension of belief. The claims are made, for the most part, by hired help. Heilbroner believes in the efficacy of material incentives; academics and publicists will not usually bite the hand that feeds them – and those that do are likely to go hungry. The foundations, on the other hand, appear solid and the workings effective – yet even these appearances may be deceptive.

This is where his scepticism can be seen. He gives a careful account of the foundations, and a reasonable sketch of the workings – but . . . but . . . Just how solid is this system? Yes, it has succeeded in establishing its legitimacy, something the now largely defunct socialist systems never did. And after correcting what led to the fiasco of the Great Depression, it has delivered the goods. And it offers a mixture of individual choice and responsibility that seems to have an almost universal appeal. But it has a distinctly unpleasant and tyrannical side, too. It 'commodifies' and commercializes, turns everything into a commodity for sale, and thereby inverts civilized values. It is a system with built-in uncertainty and fear that provides undeserved rewards to the few and unwarranted punishments to many, that systematically skews the distribution of wealth and power, and that grinds on relentlessly churning out private consumable goods long after the needs of those who can afford them have been met, while neglecting the more pressing needs of those who cannot, on the one hand, and the unmarketable collective aspects of civilized life, on the other. It is a system that works, but it doesn't work well or fairly.

Is it likely to be overthrown? Or replaced, through reform? Overthrown by a revolution, certainly not. Even in the headiest days of the late 1960s, Heilbroner was certain that the system would readily survive any challenge the Left could mount. Not only did no alternative form of organization exist, nothing that could command allegiance had even been conceived. And certainly not the regimes of 'socialism on earth', who failed not only to win – or deserve – the allegiance of their people, but also never succeeded in establishing an efficient system of incentives to work. Its recent failures can be traced in part to a kind of gigantic, system-wide go-slow, a massive strike.

Reform, however, is another story. Heilbroner has always believed in 'Sweden', not so much in actual Sweden, but in a semi-mythical Sweden, that combines the best of all the democratic reforms proposed for capitalism: a full-employment, price-controlled, sensibly regulated, progressively taxed and egalitarian, capitalist welfare state, with a large well-managed public sector, and progressive, technologically innovative private industries in which labour and capital share the profits through collective bargaining. (Actual Sweden, of course, has a drab side, some serious social problems, and a large defence industry – but its achievements, compared for example to US social problems, nevertheless do almost warrant its near-mythic status.)

Is 'Sweden' capitalist? If all the desirable democratic reforms listed above were put into practice, including profit sharing, would the resulting system still be capitalist? Or is this what we mean by 'feasible' socialism? On the one hand, it is no longer driven by the pursuit of exclusively private wealth, for wealth will now be shared. Yet it is still a system of accumulation through the market, driven by market incentives, i.e. by profit, even if that profit is no longer private, in the same sense. Such a feasible system may not be ideal but it may be, practically speaking, the best we can attain. This does not, however, exempt intellectuals from the task of analytical criticism. There is something rotten at the core of any system of market-driven accumulation. The original aspirations of socialism went far beyond this mythical 'Sweden', imagining a social order in which work would be fulfilling, done because it gave form to people's creative impulses, not because it put bread on the table.

1.8 PROSPECTS FOR THE FUTURE: THE ENVIRONMENT AND BEYOND

Yet the strength and resilience of capitalism, even democratically reformed capitalism, may be reaching a breakpoint, a challenge it cannot meet – without changes so great that we must acknowledge that the nature and logic of the system has become different. The accumulated impact of modern industry on the environment has created a situation in which a degree of interdependence now exists, between different production processes, between production and consumption, and between different geographical areas, that was inconceivable even a few decades ago. My production can injure your enjoyment of your consumption; your consumption can affect mine. Both of us can be damaged or, more rarely, benefited, by activities in another country undertaken without thought of us. And none of these effects is transmitted through the market – nor do they seem to be controllable through the market, certainly not without extensive state intervention, including major redefinitions of property rights.

The foundation of capitalism is accumulation – which works through the market. Yet this interdependence, this environmental interlocking of activities occurs outside the market and cannot, at present or in the foreseeable future, be regulated or controlled through the market. Worse, it undermines the market, for the signals given are no longer reliable. But if the market is no longer reliable, can no longer coordinate the activities of capital accumulation, what is to replace it?

Even worse, a projection of the consequences of air and water pollution, global warming, hazards from solid waste, and associated difficulties makes it clear that industrial growth, following present patterns, can neither be extended to the Third World, nor even continued for another generation in the First, without the likelihood of catastrophic disorders. But if we must abandon industrial growth – and by implication industrial methods of production, what is to replace this? What new relationship will we have with the natural and material world?

Capitalism is doomed, not as the stagnationists thought, by its failure to deliver on its promise of material plenty, nor as Marx would have it, by the polarization and class conflict it creates, but by its actual success, or rather, by the narrowness of its definition of success – it delivers private wealth, at the expense of creating public ills, which now seem to be accumulating faster than our ability to deal with them can grow. Capital accumulation, in its present form, is likely soon to undermine prosperity faster than it can create it. Unfortunately, this is not likely to promote the development of a more desirable or more fulfilling social order. From this perspective the human prospect is bleak:

> . . . a few elements of the society of the post-industrial era can be discerned. Although we cannot know on what technical foundation it will rest, we can be certain that many of the accompaniments of an industrial order must be absent. To repeat once again . . . the societal view of production and consumption must stress parsimonious, not prodigal, attitudes. Resource-consuming and heat-generating process must be regarded as necessary evils, not as social triumphs, to be relegated to as small a portion of economic life as possible. This implies a sweeping reorganization of the mode of production in ways that cannot be foretold, but that would seem to imply the end of the giant factory, the huge office, perhaps of the urban complex . . .
>
> In these half-blind gropings there is, however, one element in which we can place credence, although it offers uncertainty as well as hope. This is our knowledge that some human societies have existed for millennia, and that others can probably exist for future millennia, in a continuous rhythm of birth and coming of age and death, without pressing toward those dangerous ecological limits, or engendering those dangerous social tensions, that threaten present-day 'advanced' societies. In our discovery of 'primitive' cultures, living out their timeless histories, we may have found the single most important object lesson for future man.
>
> What we do not know, but can only hope, is that future man can rediscover the self-renewing vitality of primitive culture without reverting to its levels of ignorance and cruel anxiety . . .
>
> The question, then, is how we are to summon up the will to survive – not perhaps in the distant future, where survival will call on those deep sources of imagined human unity, but in the present and near-term future, while we still enjoy and struggle with the heritage of our personal liberties, our atomistic existences . . . [a] figure from Greek mythology comes to mind. It is that of Atlas bearing with endless perseverance the weight of the heavens in his hands. If mankind is to rescue life, it must first preserve the very will to live, and thereby rescue the future from the angry condemnation of the present. The spirit of conquest and aspiration will not provide the inspiration it needs for this task. It is the example of Atlas, resolutely bearing his burden, that provides the strength we seek (from Robert L. Heilbroner, *An Inquiry into the Human Prospect*, 1991, New York: W.W. Norton & Co., pp. 165–70)

1.9   CONCLUSION

Such, in outline, is Heilbroner's vision of the system in which we live, and of the proper role of economics in understanding it, a role that the mainstream has not filled at all adequately. Mainstream economics is not so much wrong as blinkered and anaemic, parochial in its concerns and lacking what George Bush, in another but related context, with typical eloquence, termed 'the vision thing'. Heilbroner has dedicated his life's work not only to developing a vision of the nature and evolution of capitalism, relating this picture to the deepest levels of social philosophy, but also to expressing it in judicious and carefully crafted prose, writing that is both clear and direct, yet elegantly forceful, putting his work in a class by itself. His project cannot be described better than in his own words, in the Preface to *The Worldly Philosophers*:

> Economics is an engrossing chapter in the history of human self-understanding in its own right, but it is not a chapter that stands entirely by itself. Economic philosophizing gains its ultimate fascination because its complex analyses of gain and loss are the vehicles for still deeper-lying dramas – morality plays, contests of power, and at some very profound level, the ultimate tensions of social bonding. What is perhaps most astonishing in the history of economic thought is that neither its authors nor its audience are usually aware of these fundamental aspects of the inquiry they are pursuing.

To bring these aspects to light, in elegant and memorable writings, has been his greatest achievement.

*   *   *

Robert Heilbroner's first book in economics was *The Worldly Philosophers*, written while he was a graduate student at the New School for Social Research, studying with Adolph Lowe, whom he later joined as a colleague. Together they shaped a department that became justly famous for its wide-ranging yet profound approach to economics, emphasizing the Classics and historical dynamics. The essays in this volume, contributed by a selection of Heilbroner's former students at the Department of Economics at the Graduate Faculty of the New School, have been chosen for their originality in illuminating characteristic themes running through his work. The book begins with two very different essays on the methods and approach of economic analysis, then moves to a discussion of stages of technological development, followed by three examinations of characteristic issues in political economy and policy. Next we have four essays in the history of thought, and the book concludes with four papers that relate issues in the history of thought to contemporary theory and current problems.

Part I
Method and Approach

Scott Moss, 'The Economics of Positive Methodology'

Elias Khalil, 'Neo-classical Economics and Neo-Darwinism'

At first glance these two papers, so unlike each other, may seem far removed from Heilbroner's chief concerns, too. But on closer inspection the connections become evident. Moss applies a neo-classical approach to the question of its own applicability; he does a cost–benefit analysis of the conditions of the applicability of a 'positive' approach to neo-classical theory – and finds that the test will be hard to pass. The results have a nice air of paradox about them, yielding the conclusion that applicability will very likely have to be decided in a continuous process of learning and modification. The theory will not be independent of its conditions of application. The orthodox approach is used to undermine itself – an argument much in the spirit of Heilbroner.

Khalil's essay – almost an outline for a treatise – attacks the ahistorical nature of the neo-classical enterprise, comparing its methods and results with those of the neo-Darwinians, whose work he finds to rest on similar and equally fundamental defects, also stemming from the lack of historical vision. What is particularly interesting is the *way* the lack of history manifests itself in each case, and the light this sheds on the meaning of taking a historical perspective in economics.

2 The Economics of Positive Methodology

Scott Moss

2.1 INTRODUCTION

In what I believe to have been the first year (c. 1969) that Robert Heilbroner ran his graduate seminar in political economy, he was clearly wrestling with his own ideas on methodology and, in particular, Friedman's (1953) essay on 'The Methodology of Positive Economics'. Heilbroner argued that the essential problem with Friedman's rejection of the importance of the realism of assumptions was that it denied any historical dimension to economic theory.

That same year saw the arrival of Edward Nell at the New School. Nell at the time was working with Martin Hollis on the manuscript of *Rational Economic Man*. In 1971, he ran his own graduate seminar on the methodological issues on which *Rational Economic Man* was centred. One of the prime concerns of that book was the importance of the conditions in which a theory can be tested and, in particular, whether the descriptive accuracy of the assumptions can or should constitute the conditions of testing of the theory. The Hollis-Nell approach was steeped in formal logic. Heilbroner's concern with the ahistorical nature of positivist economics was apparently quite different.

In this chapter, I attempt to bring Nell's formal approach together with Heilbroner's humanist and intuitive approach to the methodological question which concerned them both. I have tried to couch the argument in terms which will open up rational discussion rather than to establish an immovable posture. I think this is in line with Heilbroner's expositional method.

For the purposes of the present argument, I will ignore the boundedness of human rationality and adopt the mainstream definition of rationality as the constrained maximization of some net benefit. I will make the further assumption that economic policy analysts are rational according to the mainstream criterion. Following Hollis and Nell, the central issue to which the argument will be addressed is the determination of the conditions in which a theory can be applied. Unlike Hollis and Nell, however, I will consider the conditions in which a theory can be applied for purposes of policy prescription rather than the conditions in which it can be tested and, if disconfirmed, rejected. Consequently, the implications of the present argument are less broad, though perhaps more clearly defined, than the Hollis–Nell argument. It may serve to make clear the relatively limited nature of the present argument, if I refer to the conditions of application of a theory rather than the conditions of testing.

In line with the foregoing remarks, I will take it for granted that a theory should be used for policy prescription only when that application maximizes the policy analyst's subjective expectation of policy benefit. In effect, a standard cost–benefit approach is applied to methodological issues.

Section 2.2 sets out the positions of Friedman (1953) and Machlup (1967) in relation to the cost–benefit arguments. A formal cost–benefit analysis of alternative procedures for policy prescription is presented in section 2.3. An economic interpretation of the implications of the model is developed in section 2.4. The paper concludes with an outline of possible extensions along both neo-classical and non-neo-classical lines.

2.2   CONDITIONS OF APPLICATION IN POSITIVE ECONOMICS

The philosophical validity of the various methodological propositions of economists is not of concern here. The purpose of this section is only to demonstrate that, as a matter of history, the main exponents of positive economics have accepted the general importance of conditions of application. Methodological controversies in economics have concentrated on the importance of a specific condition of application: the descriptive accuracy of the theory's assumptions.

In his seminal essay on the subject, Friedman (1953, pp. 36–9) argued that it is entirely legitimate to employ different models to study different aspects of the behaviour of the same industries, even when the assumptions underlying one of those models directly contradicts the assumptions underlying the others.

Quoting Friedman (ibid., p. 36) directly:

> Everything depends on the problem; there is no inconsistency in regarding the same firm as if it were a perfect competitor for one problem and a monopolist for another . . . An example may help to clarify this point. Suppose that the problem is to determine the effect on retail prices of an increase, expected to be permanent, in the federal cigarette tax. We venture to predict that broadly correct results will be obtained by treating cigarette firms as if they were producing an identical product and were in perfect competition . . . On the other hand the hypothesis that cigarette firms would behave as if they were perfectly competitive would have been a false guide to their reactions to price control in World War II, *and this would doubtless have been recognized before the event.* (Emphasis added)

The italicized phrase – 'and this would doubtless have been recognized before the event' – demonstrates that some sort of cost–benefit analysis is essential for rational application of theory to public policy.

The purpose of prescribing any policy is to generate some benefit. If one is concerned with public policy, the benefit will be some improvement in employment figures, inflation rates, growth rates, trade balances or other indicators of social welfare. If business policies are being prescribed, then the intended benefits will include improvements in profits, market share, asset growth or whatever business criteria are held by the firm's managers. Policy analysts must have some reason to expect that such benefits will result from specific policy acts. The relationship between benefits and acts could be expected simply as a result of experience or because the relationship is predicted by some theory. The present argument is concerned only with the theory-based prediction – as was Friedman's argument. A policy prescription is one kind of prediction: if act *a* then benefit *b*. Accordingly, Friedman's assertion that the appropriate model to use 'would doubtless have been recognized before the event' amounts to the presumption that the conditions in which to apply one model or the other will always be known before the benefit-maximizing policies implied by the chosen model are implemented. Unfortunately, Friedman never indicates the basis on which the policy analyst recognizes the correct model to apply in any given set of circumstances.

Fritz Machlup (1967) was altogether more careful in specifying the conditions in which marginalist perfect competition theory could be applied to policy analysis and the conditions in which behavioural or managerial-discretion theories would be more appropriate. Machlup differentiated the marginalist theory from the others in relation to the assumption of profit-maximization. He argued that profit maximization alone motivates the decisions of entrepreneurs in the marginalist but not in the other theories. Consequently, the marginalist theory will be applicable in those empirical circumstances in which the value of profits is the only argument of the objective function of the firm.

Machlup identified these conditions with 'heavy, vigorous or effective competition' (ibid., p. 18). Such competition, Machlup argued, will compel any actual firm constantly 'to react to actual or potential losses in sales and/or reductions in profits, so much so that the firm will not be able to pursue any objectives other than the maximization of profits – for the simple reason that anything less than the highest attainable profits would be below the rate of return regarded as normal at the time'. Since profits below 'what is regarded as normal at the time' imply firm failure (i.e. exit from the industry) in marginalist theory, Machlup must have meant that firms can exist in competitive industries only if they are strict profit maximizers.

Machlup's argument is important in the present context because he defined the empirical conditions in which competition would be effective and so the marginalist theory apposite to policy prescription. As defined by Machlup (ibid.), 'competition is effective if it continually depresses profits to the level regarded as the minimum tolerable. *What makes it effective has to be explained by the conditions of entry, aggressive attitudes on the part of existing firms, or imports from abroad*' (emphasis added). Machlup was arguing that the effects of policy acts will be those predicted by the marginalist theory of the firm for those industries that are subject to easy entry and import competition, and in which firms aggressively seek to increase their market shares. These characteristics of industries are all measurable in one way or another. At least, psychologists do measure aggressiveness and industrial economists do measure ease of entry and openness – however imperfect these measures might be in practice. It might well be, of course, that one or another of these measures will be more costly to determine and some will be less reliable than others.

Taking these points together, we are led naturally to the proposition that the rational policy analyst will prescribe measures that maximize the expected benefits from the implementation of the policies net of all costs. The costs must include the costs of verifying conditions of application of the theory, and the expectation of benefit must give due recognition to the reliability of evidence regarding the conditions of application. The simplest means of bringing these aspects of the methodological position together is elementary probability theory.

2.3   MAXIMIZING NET POLICY BENEFIT

Define a policy as a set of individual acts **P**. We suppose the set of acts to be implied by a theory whenever all of its conditions of application are satisfied.

If there are n conditions of application of the theory k, then represent the ith condition by $C : \in \{true, false\}$. Define C as the mapping $[C : \bigcap_{i=1}^{n} C \rightarrow \{true, false\}]$. C takes the value $true$ if $\bigcap_{i=1}^{n} C = true$ and $false$ otherwise.

Let B be the image of the mapping $[P \mid C] \rightarrow R$, the value of the benefits expected from the set of policy actions **P**.

The 'observation marker' for the ith condition is $\phi_i : \in \{true, false\}$ which takes the value $true$ if it is *intended* to observe the ith condition and false otherwise. The intentions of the policy analyst to observe conditions of application is captured by the set $\Phi = \{\phi : \mid i = 1 \dots n\} \cap true$. In addition, we denote by $c(\Phi)$ the cost of observing all conditions $\phi : \in \Phi$.

To complete our notation we require some means of representing degrees of prior belief in the satisfaction of the conditions of application which it is intended to observe. In a chapter intended to demonstrate that Friedman's view of conditions of application fails on the most mainstream professional criteria, the natural representation is in terms of subjective probabilities. For this reason, we adopt the mapping $[\Psi(\Phi) : \Phi \rightarrow [0.1]]$. For the present purpose, we interpret $\Psi(\Phi)$ as the subjective probability that all conditions of application which it is intended to observe will be satisfied.

Since all the conditions of application of the theory must be true if the acts in **P** are to yield the expected benefit and some different benefit will result otherwise, we note that the prior expected benefit of act **P** under the Friedman regime – i.e. when the set of conditions to be observed is empty – is

$$E(B \mid \Phi = \emptyset) = E(B \mid C) E(C) + E(B \mid -C) [1 - E(C)] \qquad (2.1)$$

More generally, the expected benefit given any arbitrary set of conditions to be observed will be

$$
\begin{aligned}
E\,(B \mid \Phi) = \Psi\,(\Phi) \cdot \{ &E\,(C \mid \Psi\,(\Phi)) \cdot E\,(B \mid C) \\
&-[1 - E\,(C \mid \Psi\,(\Phi)) \cdot E\,(B \mid -C) - c\,(\Phi)\} \\
&-[1 - \Psi\,(\Phi)] \cdot c\,(\Phi)
\end{aligned}
\tag{2.2}
$$

Expanding and simplifying this expression, we get

$$
\begin{aligned}
E\,(B \mid \Phi) = \{ &E\,(C \mid \Psi\,(\Phi)\} \cdot \Psi\,(\Phi) \cdot E\,(B \mid C) \\
&-\Psi\,(\Phi) \cdot E\,(B \mid -C) - E\,(C \mid \Psi\,(\Phi)) \cdot \Psi\,(\Phi) \cdot E\,(B \mid -C) \\
&- c\,(\Phi)
\end{aligned}
\tag{2.3}
$$

Since $E\,(C \mid \Psi\,(\Phi)) \cdot E\,(\Psi\,(\Phi) = E\,(\Psi\,(\Phi) \mid C) \cdot E\,(C)$ and, from the definition of C, $E\,(\Psi\,(\Phi) \mid C) = 1$, equation (2.3) can be written

$$
E\,(B \mid \Phi) = E\,(B \mid C)\,E\,(C) + [1 - E(C)]\,E\,(B \mid -C) - [1 - \Psi\,(\Phi)]
$$
$$
E\,(B \mid -c) - c\,(\Phi)
\tag{2.4}
$$

Substituting into equation (2.4) from equation (2.1), we have

$$
E\,(B \mid \Phi) = E\,(B \mid \Phi = \varnothing) - \{1 - \Psi\,(\Phi)] \cdot E\,(B \mid -c) + c\,(\Phi)\}
\tag{2.5}
$$

For the Friedman regime in which no conditions of application are observed to entail rationality, it must be the case that the negative term in the right side of equation (2.5) is positive. That is, the Friedman regime is efficient if and only if

$$
[1 - \Psi\,(\Phi)] \cdot E\,(B \mid -c) + c\,(\Phi) \geq 0
\tag{2.6}
$$

for every possible set Φ – i.e. for every possible combination of conditions of application of the theory.

2.4   THE ECONOMIC MEANING OF RATIONALITY IN THE FRIEDMAN REGIME

The discussion in this section turns on the meaning of condition (2.6) as a representation of the state of mind of the policy analyst.

For example, presuming that there is some cost to observing conditions of application, condition (2.6) will always be satisfied if $[1 - \Psi\,(\Phi)] = 0$. This would be the case if the policy analyst were convinced that all the conditions of application of the theory were always satisfied. As a result, any subset of those conditions will also always be satisfied. This is the 'blind-faith' condition.

A more open-minded and no less rational policy analyst might allow for the possibility that his theory does not apply, while believing at the same time that, in the worst-case scenario, the policies implied by the theory yield substantial and positive benefits even when the conditions of application of the theory are violated. Formally, E (B | – C) is so high that allowing for the probability of –C, the benefit when conditions of application are known not to be fulfilled swamp the cost of observation. Presumably, some alternative theory supports that belief.

The more general possibility is that even if conditions of application might be violated and, if they are, negative benefits might result from the implied policies, the cost of observing the conditions of application could in principle be so great that they exceed the expected disbenefits associated with the inapplicability of the theory. This possibility seems reasonable when observation requires detailed and expensive investigations which themselves yield no collateral benefits. What does not seem reasonable is to assume that observation is never sufficiently cheap, that error is never sufficiently costly, and that the world is never sufficiently risky as to make it *a priori* worthwhile to investigate the validity of some conditions of application of some theory. If, in effect, condition (2.6) can be unsatisfied in non-trivial cases, then we must turn more seriously to the issue of what constitutes a condition of application.

Friedman's position is well known: conditions of application are not to be identified with the descriptive accuracy of any of the assumptions of a theory. Whatever the conditions of application might be, their validity 'will doubtless be recognized before the event'. This is a position which offers no practical guidance.

Machlup's position is more helpful – provided that we can recognize effective and vigorous competition and aggressive managerial attitudes in advance. Of course, these conditions are part and parcel of the assumption of perfect competition and so could amount to the requirement that at least some of the assumptions of marginalist theory be descriptively accurate. I do not believe that Machlup actually rejected descriptive accuracy of assumptions as possible conditions of application, though he did reject the notion that all the assumptions must be descriptively accurate.

2.5   POSSIBLE EXTENSIONS OF THE ANALYSIS

The assumptions underlying the analysis reported above are more restrictive than is necessary. It ought to be a relatively straightforward matter to allow the expectation of benefit to vary with the particular composition of satisfied conditions of application. This relaxation involves the further relaxation of the assumption that C is true if and only if all of the C_t take the value *true*.

Further extensions would either involve the maintenance of the assumption that all relevant probabilities are mutually exclusive and exhaustive or the relaxation of that assumption, too. The former strategy would be more in accord with mainstream economics while the latter would involve a more Keynesian approach. A neo-classical economist would doubtless order the combinations of conditions of application according to their respective costs of observation or, if benefits were assumed to vary with satisfied conditions, the combinations of conditions could be ordered according to net benefits. Then observation would proceed until the net benefits of the marginal observation were non-positive.

A non-neo-classical approach might follow the work of artificial intelligence scientists such as Herbert Simon (e.g. 1977). The value of Ψ (Φ) could be treated as a confidence factor rather than a probability. In that case, we could not rely on any form of Bayes' Theorem and so would lose the simplicity of condition (2.6). The concern would then shift from outcomes to the process of learning associated with continuing policy prescription and evaluation. That, I think, would be more in keeping with the example set by Bob Heilbroner's teaching and writing.

References

Friedman, Milton (1953), 'Essay on the Methodology of Positive Economics', in *Essays on Positive Economics* (Chicago: University of Chicago Press).

Machlup, Fritz (1967), 'Theories of Firm: Marginalist, Behavioral, Managerial', *American Economic Review*, vol. 57, pp. 1–33.

Hollis, Martin and Edward Nell (1975), *Rational Economic Man* (Cambridge: Cambridge University Press).

Simon, Herbert (1977), 'On How to Decide What to Do', *Bell Journal of Economics*, vol. 8, pp. 494–507.

3 Neo-classical Economics and Neo-Darwinism: Clearing the Way for Historical Thinking

Elias L. Khalil*

> [E]conomics has never interested me primarily as a 'kit of tools' for the examination or repair of the existing social mechanism. Perhaps because my first serious work plunged me into the worlds of Adam Smith, David Ricardo, John Stuart Mill, and Karl Marx, I have always found the greatest attraction of economics to lie elsewhere, in the astonishing capabilities of the discipline to elucidate the problem of large-scale historical . . . change. (Heilbroner, 1970, p. xii)

3.1 INTRODUCTION

In his contributions to different fields of economics, Professor Robert L. Heilbroner has advanced many arguments, but the one which made the most lasting impression on me is his call to exploit the capabilities of economics for the study of large-scale historical change. His advice as a teacher was unambiguous: one should not seek guidance from neo-classical economics, since it is ahistorical. The great worldly philosophers of the not too distant past are the proper guides to follow. This calls for a return to an older tradition of grand visions of historical evolution.

Putting my central argument succinctly, the neo-classical (hereafter: NC) paradigm[1], in its textbook version at least, is ahistorical because it is the progeny of reductionist and efficient modes of conception. Although these two complement each other, they are distinct. Reductionist economics ignores organization of production on the ground of having no bearing on the analysis of the constitutive economic agents. Agents are assumed independent and defined prior to the constitution of the organization. Albeit, the disavowal of reductionism by itself, as in the cases of behavioural economics of Herbert Simon and Harvey Leibenstein,

---

* This chapter was presented as a paper at the meeting of the International Society for the History, Philosophy and Social Studies of Biology, University of Western Ontario, London, Ontario, Canada, 22 June 1989. I appreciate the response of the audience at that meeting. I thank also Stanley Sâlthe, Jeffrey Wicken, David Depew for safeguarding my ventures into biology, and also Edward Nell, Roger D. Masters, and Jack Hirshleifer. I thank Kamel Merarda and Carole Brown for some technical help. The usual disclaimer applies.

is insufficient for historical thinking. One still has to address the question whether the organization or agent behaves according to purpose or efficient cause.

Economics emphasizes efficient causality (in the Aristotelian sense) at the expense of final causality (purposeful behaviour). Agents are assumed passive and unimaginative within the model. That is, initiative and creativity are viewed as exogenous. However, the repudiation of efficient reasoning by itself, as in the case of Austrian economics, is insufficient for historical thinking. One still has to answer the question as to whether organization is a congeries of sub-agents or an integral, organic unit.

Put tersely, historical thinking calls for the replacement of reductionism with an organic view, and efficient thinking with teleological reasoning. One should note that historical thinking involves more than theorizing about the business cycle and market dynamics. It deals with large-scale economic change – a topic which has enthralled Heilbroner. The mark of large-scale change is irreversibility. Otherwise, it is a form of business cycle. Examples of processes which usually do not proceed backwards include the development or evolution of consumer needs, major technological innovations, and the exhaustion of the carrying capacity of an environmental niche. They are as much irreversible as the processes of aging and the evolution of species.

In order to qualify as history, a process's reversibility should be pronounced impossible on theoretical rather than statistical grounds. To illustrate, heat always moves from hot to cold masses, not because the opposite motion is theoretically impossible, but because it is highly improbable. Thus, the motion of heat is *not* historically irreversible – which Boltzmann's version of the entropy law acknowledges (Khalil, 1990c).

Thus, to submit that a certain type of economic change is historical means that it is, like aging, irreversible at the theoretical, not the statistical level. A great part of the core conception of NC theory needs to be repudiated since it conceives economic phenomena exclusively according to efficient causality. That is, it fails to treat economic phenomena differently from the motion of heat. In order to disavow efficient reasoning, one has to recognize that households, firms and governments pursue goals like accumulation of wealth and growth, and act to maintain their integrity for the sake of it. This entails the adoption of – to use a much disdained term – teleological reasoning.

I need not repeat the familiar story of how modern science in general had originated as a revolution against the teleological thought of the scholastic and Aristotelian traditions. While that thought has been justly criticized, the anti-teleological zeal has gone to excess. The observation that economic agents pursue reproduction and the accumulation of capital for its own sake, need not be grounded on an extravagant teleological cosmology or theology. Teleological reasoning can be much humbler, enough to recognize phenomena like the striving of economists to publish in order to achieve respect, and that firms grow in order to attain power. Purposeful behaviour is copious; it arises from duty, ambition, self-respect, and less lofty values like status, wealth, and even includes negative drives like envy and self-aggrandizement.

Englis (1986) was not afraid to call economics a teleological inquiry since one has to specify the values which economic means are supposed to meet. Adam Smith (1976a) considered human conduct to be prompted by – beside the sentiments – the desire to do what is praiseworthy. Praiseworthiness cannot be explained by the want for public applause *à la* the stimulus–response framework (see Khalil, 1990a). Duty and responsibility prompt humans to do what is right. This principle is reminiscent of John Locke's much neglected concept of *fides*, 'the duty to observe mutual undertakings and the virtue of consistently discharging this duty' (quoted by Dunn in Gambetta, 1988, p. 81).

One way to attain satisfaction is to act according to duty and praiseworthiness. This goes beyond the NC modelling of human behaviour as a series of responses to stimuli, governed by the utility function. To Adam Smith, satisfaction is not a function of the absolute, but relative size of goods in regard to expectations (Khalil, n.d.; cf. Frank, 1989). When a student, for example in an exam attains the expected C grade, it is more satisfying than achieving a B grade when an A grade was expected. The fact that a person with limited means is more likely to be satisfied than a rich person, a favourite theme of Smith (1976a, pp. 149–53), indicates that satisfaction is not the product of a mechanistic utility, but of the proximity of actual achievement to specified goals.

Thus, the pursuit of satisfaction, at a basic level, should not be conceived as a response to a stimulus *à la* B.F. Skinner's behaviourism. The stimulus–response framework may explain some categories of behaviour, but not all. Satisfaction is, for the greater part, the fulfilling of self-made, multilayered final goals, which are not rigidly defined. Final goals are normally the result of an on-going fusion of individual and communal values of what is the proper ends to pursue during the irreversible process of growth.

Such innocuous observations go, for the most part, unremarked in the mainstream enterprise, in order for it to attain its dubious scientific precision. This enterprise amounts to producing pen-and-paper models about utility maximization, which resemble Byzantine theology and pre-Copernican astronomy. But 'precision' is not the fish I want to fry.[2] Rather, I am concerned with the truth content of NC economics.

When under fire, NC theorists seek other sciences. Darwinism, and neo-Darwinism (hereafter ND) have been a favourite haven. Yet, the Darwinian shelter, in the textbook version at least, suffers from deep faults, not different from the ones that permeate the NC edifice. The parallel is astounding – given that both have evolved independently.

It is true that Darwin was influenced by Malthus's principles of population, but NC economics was still to be born at the time of the publication of *The Origins of Species* in 1859. Moreover, the progenitors of NC economics – Menger, Walras, and Jevons – were oblivious to Darwinism and more interested in utilitarianism and engineering. This has prompted Veblen (1898) to admonish economics for not being evolutionary. Furthermore, it is true that NC and ND paradigms have been involved in cross-fertilization in the past decade, but the love has struck too late to conceive new core concepts.

Thus, the similarity of the core of both orthodoxies must be attributed to the circumambient scientific milieu within which both disciplines were incubated. The milieu has been dominated by the Newtonian framework, which, as Appendix 3.1 argues, is underpinned by efficient and reductionist conceptions. These two conceptions underlie the Darwinian approach. It is no surprise that NC economics finds Darwinism a haven.

Despite its metamorphosis over the past century (Depew and Weber, 1989), Darwinism is still a reductionist and efficient scheme, which postulates an ahistorical view of events.[3] Darwinism is praised for that reason (Ghiselin, 1969). The modern version, neo-Darwinism, has perfected that irony:

> 'new Darwinism' has been able to displace the historical perspective from the center stage of evolutionary science . . . It [evolution] is but the tailings of the instantaneous selective process much as the pile of sawdust is the accumulated residue of the cutting action of a saw blade upon logs in a saw mill. (Campbell, in Weber *et al.*, 1988, p. 275)

Similar judgements have been articulated by increasing numbers of scholars. Depew and Weber (in Weber *et al.*, 1988) view the ND approach as a progeny of the Newtonian framework; Wicken (1986, 1987) calls for the injection of ND with thermodynamics to attain historical directionality (see Matsuno and Ho, in Ho and Saunders, 1984). These indictments do not stem from the mystical cosmologies of Bergson (1913) and Teilhard de Chardin (1959).[4]

The anomalies, which have been budding and chipping at the edges of NC and ND paradigms, have emboldened heterodox approaches recently. The platform which the critics of both orthodoxies share is the advocacy of a historical paradigm.[5] It is no surprise that heterodox biology parallels heterodox economics. Each heterodoxy may fortify the other.

Given the similarity of their core theoretical approaches, it was natural for the two orthodoxies to exchange support once they met. An increasing number of articles have appeared in the past decade that apply the tools of NC economics – concepts like maximization of utility, work/leisure trade-off, and transaction–cost analysis – to study how rats, pigeons, and honeybees supposedly supply labour, reveal preferences for goods, and enter cooperative behaviour (*inter alia*, Battalio *et al.*, 1979, 1981a, 1981b; Kagel *et al.*, 1975, 1980a, 1980b; Landa and Wallis, 1988; cf. Rapport and Turner, 1977). Likewise, NC economists (Alchian, 1950; Becker, 1976; Hirshleifer, 1977, 1978a, 1978b, 1982; Ursprung, 1988) borrow heavily from ND concepts like natural selection and survival of the fittest.

No one can object *per se* to cross-fertilization between the disciplines. There are insights, beyond metaphors, to be learned from each other. For instance, Marshall's theory of the aging of firms and industries is conceived after biological senescence. But I have reservations about the cross-fertilization between the NC and ND orthodoxies. If each is defective at the core, the progeny are likely to be freakish!

This chapter has two main parts. The first part, in four sections, explains the conceptual cores of NC and ND paradigms. The second part recounts, in the same order, the heterodox challenges in both disciplines. At the end I reflect on how the challenges of different schools of heterodox economics can be synthesized.

3.2   THE CONCEPTUAL CORES

3.2.1   Overview

In his classic work, Robbins (1932, p. 38) views economics as concerned with efficient means and given ends. Means have to be selected efficiently since they are scarce. For the NC scheme, if there were no scarcity, there would be no economic problem. The NC approach expresses the economic problem in a four-word tenet, *maximization subject to constraints*. The maximized variable is the utility derived from goods; the constraints are resources. The NC tenet assumes that the scarcity constraints are fungible: there is more than one way to skin a cat. The economic problem is about the best way to rearrange the fungibles, so that output maximizes the given utility function (Walsh and Gram, 1980).[6]

The fundamental problem facing organisms, according to ND, is scarcity – similar to the contention of neo-classical economics. The amount of nutrients/prey is supposed to be given; otherwise, natural selection would not work.[7] Nature has to select (disregarding the animistic connotation) efficient traits which make the best use of given nutrients/prey. That is, nature encourages the maximization of a fitness function which is indicated in the reproductive success. This may also be expressed by the four-word tenet, *maximization subject to constraints*. The maximized variable is fitness of traits;[8] the constraints are nutrients/prey. The ND tenet assumes that nutrients/prey and gene frequency are fungible, i.e. can produce a variety of traits. In this manner, evolution is about producing the best composition of traits which, given the niche, maximizes the fitness function.

Sociobiologists (e.g. Wilson, 1975) have expanded the meaning of trait to include behaviour, ranging from selfishness to altruism.[9] Behaviour is subject to fitness pressure which causes 'evolutionary stable strategy' (ESS). The term 'strategy' denotes preprogrammed behaviour not consciously worked out. The word 'stable' means equilibrium. That is, fitness pressure engenders behaviour which, *ceteris paribus*, cannot be improved: no gene which alters the genetic ratios can successfully invade a population at ESS – reminiscent of Nash equilibrium in economics.

The parallelism between NC and ND paradigms is unmistakable. Both postulate the maximization of a variable, utility or fitness, via selection. For NC, the selected set of products determines the set of efficient firms. For ND, the selected set of traits ascertains the set of fit organisms. Albeit, selection would not occur if there were no constraints and exogenous variables. The variables which are specified as exogenous by both orthodoxies are remarkably analogous. Similarly, the endogenous variables, firms and organisms, are highly parallel. Causality runs in one direction: a change in the equilibrium product compositions or trait frequency is the result of a change of exogenous variables. Both orthodoxies give an *ad hoc* account of why exogenous variables change; they usually explain the change away as fortuitous in origin.

Before going into detail, let me sketch the conceptual cores. The given 'resources' in NC theory include primordial labour, materials, and land. Similarly, the exogenous 'nutrients' in ND theory include prey (in the broad sense) and territory. In Table 3.1, I place these constraints in the first column under the general heading 'factors'. Recalling Aristotle's categories of causation, factors can be identified with material cause. The second constraint in NC scheme is 'technology', and in ND paradigm is 'genotype' (as opposed to phenotype).[10] I locate these constraints in the second column under the general heading 'information', which can be identified with formal cause. Factors and information are put together in NC theory to generate product and through it to maintain the firm, or in short 'product/firm'. Equivalently, factors and information are put together in the ND approach to generate trait and through it to sustain the organism, or in short 'trait/organism'. I set these outputs in the third column under the general heading 'yield/thing', which can be identified with material cause since it is a mere rearrangement of factors. Moreover, there would be no maximization of utility or fitness without selectors. The screening device in the NC scheme is 'preferences' of consumer and in ND theory is 'nature'. I situate them in the fourth column under the general heading 'selector', which can be identified with efficient cause.

Instructive though such parallelism is, we need to go further. In one case, resources are ordered by technology to produce a product/firm which is subjected to selection by preferences. In another case, nutrients are ordered by genotype to produce a trait/organism which is subjected to selection by nature. Put in general terms, factors are ordered by information to produce a yield/entity which is screened by the selector. In both cases, the yield is under direct selection pressure, while the entity is selected indirectly as a result. The firm or organism is treated as a passive object; its existence is contingent on external causes. Moreover, the

Table 3.1   Parallelism of NC and ND conceptual cores

Factors *(Material* *cause)*	+	*Information* *(Formal* *cause)*	→	*Yield/Thing* *(Material* *cause)*	←	*Selector* *(Efficient* *cause)*
Given NC resources	+	Given technology	→	Passive product/firm	←	Given preferences
Given ND nutrients	+	Given genotype	→	Passive trait/organism	←	Given nature

firm or organism amounts to a patch of well-defined, independent products or traits. Thus, from the perspective of historical thinking NC and ND paradigms have two conceptual flaws: they deny that the firm or organism acts according to purpose; they deny that the firm or organism is an integral, organic whole.

There are some differences between the two orthodoxies. However, they stem from the dissimilarity of the subject of study, rather than the mode of conception. One difference is related to the constitution of the selector. The selector in the NC approach, preferences, is carried by agents who also make up the producer, the firm. In contrast, the selector in ND theory, nature, is segregated from the producer, the organism. This difference is superficial, however. The preferences are assumed by NC theory to be independent of producers. This difference calls for a qualification which neutralizes it. In the economy, according to NC theory, the rules of justice (property rights) are observed. There are no such observances in the jungle.

The second difference is related to awareness. Nature obviously does not select traits consciously, while agents calculate what products to consume. This difference is also more apparent than real. Agents in the economy, with respect to NC theory, are dormant rather than vigorous, passive rather than active, and inert rather than entrepreneurial. That is, agents act 'as if' they are conscious, but in fact it does not matter; they are the dummies and the pre-determined preferences are the ventriloquists. NC economics expunges creativity, initiative, and purposeful behaviour from its tool kit. This resembles the crux of the ND paradigm, where no room is allowed for teleological explanations of evolution. As Table 3.1 shows, the fact that economic agents are aware has not prompted NC orthodoxy to recognize final cause.

The third difference is related to the unit of evolution. According to ND, the organism does not evolve but the population does. It occurs as a result of the failure of the relatively unfit organisms to leave proportionate scion behind. In contrast, NC theory recognizes that inefficient firms need not perish if they adjust. This difference, though, is non-substantive.

Given these differences, one can assert that the parallelism of the two mainstreams is striking. It is the outcome of disregarding teleological and organic conceptions. Certainly, many phenomena should not be explained through such conceptions, for example the gyration of stocks or ecological change. But other phenomena, like the firm or the organism, require teleological and organic views.[11] The orthodox rejection of these views has made economic or biological organization look no different from chaotic forms. In fact, the theoretical core of both orthodoxies resembles the mechanical gas law and entropy law. The gas law, as expressed by J.D. van der Waals, states:

$$\{p + a(n/V)^2\} \ (V - nb) = nRT$$

Where p, V, T are the state variables of pressure, volume, absolute temperature, R the universal gas constant, and n the number of molecules (moles) (Fenn, 1982,

p. 43–7). A good illustration is the balloon. As temperature and/or pressure increase, the volume of the balloon expands. This equation depicts real gases since the parameters *a* and *b* specify its identity.

Rosen (1987) argues that the equation, on one hand, masquerades as the difference between parameters and state variables and, on the other, camouflages the functional relationship between exogenous (pressure and temperature) and endogenous (volume) variables. Thus, he rewrites it as:

$$\Phi_{abR}, n \mid (T, p) \rightarrow (V)$$

Where the parameters *a*, *b*, *R* act as coordinates in the functional space Φ, given *n*. They specify the function of a particular gas from a range of functions. The variable *V* is rewritten to show clearly that it is a function of *T* and *p*. In Table 3.2, I show the mechanical core of the gas law, using Aristotle's categories of causation. The gas law turns out to be no different from the cores of NC and ND paradigms. The number of molecules (the factors which make up the system) can be identified with material cause, parameters (the informational identity of the system) with formal cause, volume (the entity under focus) with material cause since it is the form which molecules take, and temperature and pressure (the conditioning selector) with efficient causes. Final cause is fittingly absent since volume changes for an efficient, not purposeful reason.

Moreover, as shown in Table 3.2, the mechanical entropy law repeats the cores of NC and ND theories. The law observes that a closed system tends towards equilibrium like an ice cube in a glass of water where the ice melts. The variable that measures the degree of melting is dubbed entropy. Each system has its individuality specified by the parameters. In Table 3.2, I demonstrate the entropy law in thermodynamic terms (not statistical ones). The number of molecules can be identified with material cause, parameters with formal cause, entropy with

Table 3.2   Parallelism of gas law, entropy law, NC, and ND conceptual cores

	Factors (*Material cause*)	+	*Information* (*Formal cause*)	→	*Yield/Thing* (*Material cause*)	←	*Selector* (*Efficient cause*)
Gas law:	Molecules	+	Parameters	→	Volume	←	Temp./Pres.
Entropy law:	Molecules	+	Parameters	→	Entropy	←	Temp./Heat
NC:	Resources	+	Technology	→	Product/firm	←	Preferences
ND:	Nutrients	+	Genotype	→	Trait/organism	←	Nature

material cause since it is the form which molecules take, and temperature and heat with efficient causes. For the same fitting reason, final cause is absent.[12]

Table 3.2 shows that the core of NC and ND theories is no different from the law which describes chaotic gases. This is not accidental but the outcome of conscious attempt to purge teleology from scientific reasoning. Teleological conception need not be alarming, however. It does not have to be derived from vitalist conceptions. That is, final cause need not be the character of some strange force in living matter. With aid of quantum mechanics, physicists like David Bohm trace teleology to the behaviour of subatomic matter.

Quantum mechanics has raised troubling questions about the classical view of nature. David Bohm views matter as an organic, integral unit (Khalil, 1989g). Matter is a potential with penumbral boundaries. The 1982 experiment by Alain Aspect and his colleagues at the University of Paris-South confirmed that matter does not occupy the ordinary space we are familiar with. To Bohm, matter constantly moves from the realm of abstract space to the concrete.[13] This movement implies purpose. Rosen (1987; see also 1985a, 1985b) finds this idea relevant to living matter. Thus, one need not whimsically introduce *vita* to living matter to explain purpose.[14] Hence one need not apologize for teleology. Teleological reasoning is materialist, after all.

Before presenting the critique, I discuss the three variables which ND considers as given. The treatment of factors, information, and selector as given underpins the 'efficient' conception of NC and ND. I seldom take notice of auxiliary qualifications. I present orthodoxy in its virgin or textbook form in order to sharpen the image of the core. That is, I take public choice and new household economics as the purest forms of the NC paradigm (Khalil, 1987b). Similarly, I find socio-biology and Dawkins's approach the quintessence of ND. In this manner, I can focus on the meta-theoretical questions.

3.2.2 Factors: Given

The NC paradigm

Factors of production are called 'resources'. NC models usually stipulate that resources are scarce endowments, like manna fallen from heaven. Robinson Crusoe or a nation faces given resources, consisting of an X amount of labour, Y quantity of raw materials, and Z measure of land. They are the material cause which could be formed into alternative products at the production possibility frontier. The economic question is limited to determining the position on the frontier, not the quantity of resources. A change of the quantity of resources is considered an external shock, not an endogenous event.

The view of resources does not change when we move to the level of one producer among others, the firm. The firm is faced with the challenge of choosing the correct combination of resources in such a manner that, given their relative prices, its budget constraint generates maximum output. This is the idea behind the tangency of the firm's output isoquants with the budget constraint: the tangency point is the equality of the resources' relative marginal product with their relative prices. In this way, the firm is maximizing its output given its total budget constraint and the scarcity prices of the resources.

The concept of scarcity in the NC scheme is not the niggardliness of nature which purposeful agents face in production, but rather it is a mathematical constraint. In this manner, the model is concerned with how the exogenously given constraint is allocated in order to maximize satisfaction. In this sense, the NC term 'scarcity' has no relation to the common meaning. In day-to-day usage, a commodity is scarce if quantity demanded is greater than quantity supplied at a certain price, while in NC theory the price is restricted to zero. This appears an innocuous linguistic innovation. It implies, though, that a commodity is essentially free; if its price is not zero, it is in order to attenuate quantity demanded and bring it to equal given quantity supplied. Thus, the cost of purposeful production does not enter the picture at first approximation, as if resources are handed on a silver platter.

This abstract mode of conceptualization is not without practical consequences. The national income accounts treat resources as if, indeed, they were handed on a silver platter. While it has a provision for depreciation, it is restricted for man-made assets, such as tools and buildings. The provision does not cover rivers and soil which are polluted and exhausted as a result of production. The depreciated natural capital is not written off against the *gross* national products. As a result, the rate of growth of *net* national product is inflated. More seriously, growth and prosperity would suffer greatly if resources were actually replaced at the same rate of replenishment.

The ND paradigm

Organisms obviously do not possess resources like raw materials and land. They have, though, something equivalent dubbed 'nutrients', like prey and territory. In this manner, prey is equivalent to raw materials. Besides hunted rabbits and deer, prey includes plants and what they depend on like solar energy, minerals in the ground, and compounds in the air, without which no organism can survive (Ricklefs, 1979, pp. 780 ff.). Likewise, territory is equivalent to land, which most organisms need and defend to secure prey and sexual partners. Nutrients are the material cause in Aristotle's categories.

Similar to the treatment of resources by NC theory, nutrients are figured by ND to be given, not altered by the organism. Otherwise, the selection by nature is nullified. The given nutrients correspond to the concept of budget constraint in economics (Rapport and Turner, 1977, p. 368). The organism's 'budget constraint' is determined by a variety of ecological parameters. In comparison to orthodox economics, the time and energy allocated to foraging corresponds to the total budget, and the relative ease of capturing fungible nutrients/prey to relative prices. The relative ease is determined by the relative scarcity of nutrients/prey, accentuated by the intensity of competition among predators for prey.

According to orthodox biology (e.g. MacArthur, 1972), the given nutrients determine the organism's foraging strategy, since it attempts to maximize the captured nutrients/prey. Put differently, the organism chooses the correct combination of preys in a way which maximizes its fitness function. In such manner, a unit of captured prey is produced with minimal energy expenditure. For insect societies, the fitness function is the production of queens. Wilson (1975) explains division of labour in insect colonies using neo-classical linear programming. The number of castes and their relative size in a colony is similar to the number of factors of production and their relative size in a firm. If the environment does not change, castes and their relative sizes stay stable. That is, there is a substitution among factors of production of queens, depending on their relative availability.

In such manner, scarce nutrients are used efficiently to maximize output and fitness. This means maximum net energy gain. The gain could either be translated into current growth of bio-mass or investment in reproduction – future growth of one's descendants – or a combination of both. This is similar to maximum output in economics, which is the surrogate of maximum profit. The profit could either be translated into current consumption or investment, or a combination of both (Rapport and Turner, 1977).

R. Levins (1967) calls the fitness function 'adaptive function', since the selector of nature determines which organism, and hence genotype, is relatively more fit in transforming scarce nutrients into phenotypes. Stated differently, natural selection determines which organisms score best in the employment of given nutrients. If organisms could create new nutrients, Darwinian selection would not work, and the mathematical exercise of fitness maximization would be void.

3.2.3 Information: Given

The NC paradigm

Information is called 'technology'. It is the formal cause behind the production of tools, upgrading of labour skills, and improvement of land. NC economics sees technology as information, i.e. given, distinct rules about how to attain definite products. They are precisely grafted in human capital, the capital stock, and improved land. This view consists of two relatively independent theses: technology as exogenous; technology as definite.

Technology as exogenous. Instructions on how to assemble a product from resources run in one way: from the given technology to the product. Feedback is not allowed. The thesis that information is exogenous rules out improvement of know-how as a result of practice. Production does not entail the generation of new technology, but the execution of what is given.

NC economists recognize technological innovations. They are, however, treated as external shocks to the system. The theory fails to incorporate technological change as an endogenous feature. Of course, when NC-trained economists roll up their sleeves to do empirical work, some of these assumptions are revised, and sometimes played with to generate more sophisticated models. This should not blind us to the fact that technological improvements are essentially viewed as exogenous. Discovery is considered idiosyncratic or serendipitous, and hence cannot be subjected to theoretical inquiry. Technological change is not considered the result of feedbacks from experience. Hence there is no surprise that NC theorists resist the idea that change is usually an irreversible process.

Technology as definite. Once technology is considered given and not influenced by the purposeful process of production, it is deemed rigid and self-defined. Technology is assumed to be analyzable into self-contained parts, whose contributions could be calculated precisely. This is the origin of the concept of marginal productivity and the production function.

The production function is a mathematical formula whose variables could vary independently of each other. Technology is represented as another feature of production, independent of labour and raw materials. Technology is deemed to be an exact commodity, like traffic signals and computational codes. In this capacity, technology is capable of specifying each step of production, insulated from the process itself. Instances through time are seen as reversible since technology is assumed to be self-defined, unaffected by past experience.

The ND paradigm

Information is called 'genotype'. It is the formal cause behind organs and their function. Similar to the NC view, ND sees genotype as information, i.e. given, distinct rules on how to attain definite traits. Rules are exactly grafted on organs and behaviour. This view consists of two relatively separate theses: genotype as exogenous; genotype as definite.

Genotype as exogenous. According to ND, the mutation of genotype rules arises from random causes. Jacques Monod (1972) has established himself as biologist-turned-philosopher in his forceful defence of the view that chance lies behind mutation. According to him, mutations give rise to more or less complex organisms. If there is a rise of complexity during evolution, it is the result of natural selection, which indicates that greater complexity confers greater fitness.

The doctrine of random mutation is concomitant with the belief that genotype is a set of passive rules like traffic regulation, not a set of self-seeking, self-defining principles. As rules, they are inert; they do not determine their own mutation. Rules are the starting point which determine the phenotype: genotype → phenotype. The claim that the phenotype does not react and affect the genotype in a loop-fashion is the basic citadel of the ND programme. Any physical alteration which arises from experience, will, or accident does not affect the genotype, and most certainly cannot be passed on to progeny. That is, the germ (sex) cells are supposedly insulated from somatic (body) cells.

This came to be called Weismann's barrier, after August Weismann. It postulates that acquired characteristics cannot penetrate germ (sex) cells. That is, germ cells, while giving rise to a variety of organisms, are passed on to progeny intact. The Weismann barrier is at the core of the ND programme. This makes Lamarck (1984), who postulated the inheritance of acquired characteristics, the archpriest of heresy in the temples of orthodoxy.[15]

With regard to ND, the genetic code spells out the differentiation of cells into different positions and functions during development. The synthesis of proteins proceeds according to instructions sent by the DNA. There is no feedback which alters the DNA of cells. It is recognized that enzymes suppress and activate certain genes. Albeit, the activity of enzymes is dictated by the genetic code and it does not alter, after all, the DNA.

If Weismann's barrier is made of steel, what gives rise to new proteins and traits? Darwin struggled with an explanation. In later editions of *Origin* (1959), particularly the last (sixth) edition, he conceded to the Lamarckian notion of the inheritance of acquired characteristics. Modern genetics, as first introduced by Dobzhansky (1982), Mayr (1982), and Simpson (1984), came to the rescue by proposing random mutation of germ cells as the basis of new traits.[16] This addition came to be called the modern synthesis or ND.

Parallel to the NC view of technological innovation, the idea of random mutation presents the genotype as insulated from the process of maintaining the organism. Any change which occurs is fortuitous in origin, not the result of feedbacks from experience. Not surprisingly, ND theorists resist the idea that evolution is usually an irreversible process.

Genotype as definite. The view of genotype as exogenous implies that it is self-defined and explicit. That is, the genotype sends unambiguous messages, not subject to interpretation. Otherwise, the environment might influence the genotype, and make it endogenous.

The assumed explicitness of the DNA makes it available for slicing into tidbits. Each tidbit is supposed to be a precise instruction for the 'machinery' of the cell and the organism. Genes are seen as bits of information which transmit unclouded messages, like a computer programme. In fact, a huge cottage industry has sprung up around likening the genetic code to C. Shannon's information theory, designed initially to transmit intelligence signals. These signals, measured by bits of information, became more than a metaphor. Genes became conceived as self-contained bits of information. The organism became a mere vehicle for genetic rules (see Dawkins, 1976). A genetic message, like the NC view of technology, is capable of specifying each step of production, insulated from the process itself. Instances through time are seen as reversible since genes are presumably unaffected by experience.

3.2.4 Selector: Given

The NC paradigm

The pertinent selector is called 'preferences'. It is the efficient cause which solves the economic problem, the position along the production frontier. Thus, preferences of consumers are designated as the sovereign of the economy. Given the distribution of endowments, the composition of GNP, as selected by consumers, represents maximum allocative efficiency.

Once consumers determine the product composition, allocation of resources is determined indirectly. Consumers' tastes are not determined endogenously, especially not by firms. Otherwise, the maximum efficiency criterion would be undermined. Stigler and Becker (1977) offer the classic defence of this posture. To them, economists need not be concerned with preferences since they originate from eccentric sources. They call them 'tastes' in order to underline their whimsical nature. It is possible that consumers, for no economic reason, start favouring horse-pulled carriages over cars and ice-boxes over electric refrigerators. To wit, there is no *a priori* reason why needs should be considered irreversible. As a corollary, technological change is also viewed as reversible since products are subject to consumers' tastes. Put differently, technological change is not necessarily unidirectional since the sovereign, preferences, could reverse itself.

This highlights the arbitrary link between goods and the consumer as portrayed by the NC approach. This is expressed by the NC utility function, where goods are represented as fungible: there is no endurable connection between particular goods and the consumer; all goods serve equally a homogeneous utility function. In this fashion, consumers have no particular attachments arising from habit or consistency of personality. Consumers are ready to switch among fungible goods in order to maximize the utility function. This presumes that consumers act optimally; i.e. they choose among goods in such a way which equalizes the relative prices with the subjective marginal rate of substitution. Furthermore, this presumes that they have perfect knowledge, even in the form of statistical expectation, of all opportunities and prices in the present and future markets.

Given these perfectly prudent consumers, inefficient producers are not spared. The assumption that goods are fungible is essential to the view that preferences is an efficient selector.

The ND paradigm

The relevant selector is called 'nature'. Nature, as an efficient selector, allows the relatively fit organisms to increase their share; the propitious organisms validate their genotype via differential copulation. Given external conditions, the frequency of traits of organisms adjust accordingly; i.e. nature makes population fit.

Selectors include abiotic and biotic nature. In relation to the biotic nature, predators, MacArthur (1972) argues that they are efficient selectors in two senses

– resembling the NC assumptions about consumer behaviour. First, they act optimally; that is, no predator expends more energy on capturing a prey than opportunity cost. Although MacArthur does not use the term 'opportunity cost', he postulates that predators maximize the returns in terms of grams of captured prey per unit of time. Second, predators have perfect knowledge; that is, they have a clear statistical expectations of the location of prey. With these assumptions at hand, a predator is made into a prudent selector.

The selector is not influenced by the fitness process. In other words, the selector is not manipulated by the organism, since the organism is seen as a helpless entity. Otherwise, nature would be incapable of acting as an arbitrator; it would be unable to maximize the fitness function. That does not imply that the environment does not change, but the change is exogenous in origin. The change might be reversed, which allows, with random mutations, for the return of old gene frequencies. Although the statistical likelihood of reversals is nil, as stated by Dollo's Law, reversals are not ruled out at the theoretical level. Thus, according to ND, genetic change is not theoretically irreversible, since the sovereign, nature, could reverse itself.

3.3   A CRITIQUE OF THE CONCEPTUAL CORES

3.3.1   Overview

I have attempted to show that NC economics is ahistorical. An appeal to ND provides no consolation, since it is also ahistorical. Both treat time as a backdrop for events rather than a thread in the fabric of events. Non-conventional approaches in economics may be emboldened by their counterparts in biology.

The ahistorical conception is the outcome of treating factors of production, information, and selector as given. The handling of these key variables as exogenous should not come as a surprise. It is expected after treating the organism or the firm as exclusively governed by efficient causes. Such an explanation strips the agent of purposefulness since it accents efficient cause, at the expense of final cause. It should not come as a revelation that the critiques levelled at them have great affinities.

Within each discipline, the critics are not monolithic. Each critic may question one or another key orthodox concept. Once purposeful behaviour is admitted, it might be feasible to reach a synthesis among the critics. Factors, information, and selector would be seen as determined by purposeful behaviour. Heterodoxies within each discipline would appear to match like mortise and tenon.

Put together, heterodoxies treat factors of production, information and selector as partially endogenously determined. Table 3.3 sums up such findings. In comparison to Table 3.2, there are two major related departures: final cause is recognized and the other categories of causes are not taken as exogenous, but partially (as shown by the arrows) determined by the final cause. In Table 3.3, resources and nutrients in the first column are called 'inputs' to signify their continuous flux. Inputs are still identified with material cause. In the second column, technology and genotype are dubbed 'knowledge' to denote their penumbral organizational quality. Knowledge is still identified with formal cause. In the third column, the firm and organism are named 'organization', which is no longer subsumed to the product or the trait. This signifies that it is a purposeful agent and hence identified with final cause. Consumers' preferences and nature are flexible and labelled 'environment'. The environment is still identified with efficient cause.

The critical exposition below is divided into three parts. The axioms about factors, information and selector are examined in turn.

3.3.2 Inputs: Not Given Factors

Heterodox economics

People make choices. This phenomenon is taken by NC theory as the only behavioural imperative, since the economic problem is exclusively identified with scarcity, i.e. given factors. This makes the economy a closed system, and the only price is scarcity price or opportunity cost. Those who use real cost instead are usually taunted as accountants.

The opportunity cost concept is counter-intuitive; first, it implies that the cost of production is zero – as if goods are given by a cornucopia; second, profit is not considered a return above the cost of production, but rather a specific kind of opportunity cost. A major assumption underlies the opportunity cost concept: all goods are fungible, i.e. could be substituted for each other. As a corollary, orthodoxy ignores limits to growth posed by natural resources, since depleted resources could easily be substituted. This is one of the greatest ironies in the history of ideas: the NC idea of scarcity leads to the postulate that there is no ecological limits to growth.[17]

The opportunity cost concept is alien to classical economists. From Adam Smith to Karl Marx, they recognize real cost – the effort it takes to procure

Table 3.3 Parallelism of the critiques of NC and ND conceptual cores

	Inputs *(Material cause)*	+	*Knowledge* *(Formal cause)*	↔	*Organization* *(Final cause)*	↔	*Environment* *(Efficient cause)*
Heterodox economics	Resource influx	+	Organizational technology	↔	Purposeful firm	↔	Flexible preferences
Heterodox biology	Nutrient influx	+	Organizational genotype	↔	Purposeful organism	↔	Flexible nature

resources. According to them, the economic problem is the securing of returns which at least offset effort and, if possible, secure a surplus for reproduction on a greater scale. This surplus is not seen as part of cost, as NC economists postulate, the 'cost of capital'.

Thus, there is a behavioural imperative beside making choices, since at a more fundamental level humans do not deal with scarce, given resources. To the contrary, they deal with a multilayered, underdetermined amount of resources, which become available only upon the expenditure of effort. Thus, the economic problem is not scarce resources, but securing the appropriation of resources at steady and even extended scales.

This calls for a distinction which is usually overlooked by conventional analyses. The actor and the tools of labour must be distinguished from what is acted upon. As an actor, the agency of production expends effort to procure inputs, both exhaustible and renewable, from the biophysical environment. The agency of production is the potential and the drive behind the processing of raw inputs. The drive to work is a purposeful action, and the inputs are ingredients to be worked on.

Thus, the agency of labour should not be part of resource input, the first column in Table 3.3. But rather, the agency of labour is constitutive of the organization of production, since it is a final cause. After all, the organization of labour and its tools determines the continuous influx of resources.

This amounts to stating that the economic problem is not about scarce inputs. I may add that it is not about the scarce agency of labour either. Labour, though, is not scarce for a different reason. While inputs are not scarce because they are sought out by the agency of production, labour is not scarce because of procreation. This means that the purposeful agency of production has a longer life than the lifespan of the individual. That may explain why humans do not see their effort is wasted in vain. Future generations are counted to enjoy the fruits of the effort – as if the time horizon is infinite and mortality is irrelevant.

A person would consider the agency of production scarce if work is seen, in a fundamental sense, as an alien tool to attain higher indifference curves. The view of labour as scarce is epitomized by new household economics, spearheaded by Gary Becker (1981). At first examination, it is true that work is drudgery, but at a higher level, work is part of an endless chain of projects. Thus, work is not a mere tool but the life process itself.

The non-scarcity view of inputs and labour has been articulated lately by a new heterodox school called ecological economics (Christensen, 1989; Daly, 1977; Jansson, 1984; Perrings, 1987; Proops, 1989). The heterodox view has come of age with the initiation in 1989 of a new journal, *Ecological Economics*. It acknowledges the role of the ecosystem in renewing inputs by absorbing pollution and waste (Faber *et al.*, 1987). It repudiates the NC representation of the GNP as the circular flow of goods and services, insulated from the biophysical sphere. The NC model implies that the ecosystem either does not exist or its capacity is large enough to be of no concern to economics. The non-scarcity view argues that the capacity of the ecosystem is fragile beyond a critical point. Thus, it rectifies the ironic orthodox position, which, on one hand, asserts scarcity as the perennial problem and, on the other, ignores the capacity of the ecosystem.

Ecological economists can seek inspiration from classical theorists, since they, beside rejecting the scarcity theory of price, have recognized input limits to growth. Malthus, Ricardo and Mill have realized the niggardliness of land fertility and the constraint it places on accumulation. They did not portray a rosy picture of the prospects of commercial society. Technological innovations cannot, in the final analysis, reverse the downhill slide. This is the origin of the cliché about economics as the 'the dismal science'.

In Georgescu-Roegen's (1971) work, the dismal science reaches its acme; he predicts doomsday since the dowry of earth's resources are on an irreversible course of dispersion. His premonition of doldrums is based on the concept of resources as self-defined in the abstract, independent of the particular agency of production. Inputs, though, cannot be defined in the abstract. For example, oil companies find different resources in Alaska from what the Eskimo tribes did. Minerals on Mars are not inputs for human society since the organizational capacity and technology is not yet created. The rub is that the ecosystem capacity is not given, but demarcated by the complexity of the purposeful agency of production. I show elsewhere (Khalil, 1990c) that Georgescu-Roegen's misuse of the entropy law has contributed to his erroneous view of ecosystem capacity as an absolutely defined dowry.[18]

Another erroneous extension of the entropy law follows the work of the chemist Ilya Prigogine (1980). Prigogine uses the entropy law to explain spontaneously emerging patterns, 'dissipative structures', in far-from-equilibrium systems. He and others (e.g. Schneider, Dyke, Wiley, Brooks in Weber *et al.*, 1988; Allen, in Dosi *et al.*, 1988; Artigiani, 1987) extend dissipative structures to analyze biological and social organization. The project amounts to explaining the constitution of organization, its irreversible development and evolution after the explanation of the structure of storm systems or ocean currents. This is an erroneous explanation since dissipative structures are chaotic systems, while organizations are purposeful complexes (Khalil, 1990b, 1989f).

To explain irreversibility of biological and social processes, there is no need to seek help from Prigogine's notions of entropy.[19] The observation made above about the limitations posed by ecosystem capacity is adequate to explain – in conjunction with other variables discussed below – irreversibility of historical change. Wicken (1986) weaves a scenario of socio-economic evolution as the result of the drive to reverse the degradation of the capacity of the ecological niche. With each fresh regime of institutional and technological infrastructure, a new gate is opened to a more vigorous carrying capacity. Thus, change is driven by the exhaustion of ecological niches. Since exhausted niches cannot be reused, evolution cannot be reversed.

Heterodox biology

Parallel to the view of ecological economists, heterodox biologists (e.g. Harrison, Johnson, Depew and Weber, Schneider, Wicken, in Weber *et al.*, 1988) introduce input influx to evolutionary theory. Although they retain Darwin's idea of natural selection, they introduce a major theoretical consideration: the ability to process input influx is more important than passive traits in determining fitness.

Inputs are not given nutrients which the organism is obliged to endure while selection activity is taking place. Rather, the organism actively manipulates the influx of inputs. This challenges the ND axiom of given nutrients. According to Wicken (1986, 1987), inputs are not given in nature in a ready form. Except for parasites, all others have to work. Expenditure of effort is essential for, on the one hand, obtaining nutrients and, on the other hand, altering them by the body's digestive system into goods ready for consumption.

Lotka (1925) and Odum (1971) propose the concept 'maximum power principle' to complete Darwin's natural selection. Organisms attempt to maximize the rate of transformation of given input into useful output by minimizing waste. Waste cannot be eliminated totally – analogous to the case of heat engines – but there is a pressure to minimize it.

Beside the drive for greater efficiency, organisms attempt to muster materials and energy as much as they can by penetrating larger portions of the environment, which Ulanowicz (1986) calls 'ascendancy'. That is, beside minimizing waste, there is a need to increase the influx of inputs. In order to increase the input influx, the organism has to prolong the search or hunting period. There are strong grounds for the thesis that ascendancy is more pertinent for survival and evolution than efficiency. In either case, organisms are under pressure to attain greater efficiency and ascendancy. Otherwise, they will be swept away, since they are afflicted with the Red Queen Paradox (although the metaphor was first expressed by Van Valen, 1973, it is put to better use by Campbell, in Depew and Weber, 1985). The Queen, in Alice's Wonderland, has to to keep running in order to stay in the same place.

Put differently, nature selects the more *efficient* in transforming given input, and the more *productive* in harnessing inputs from the environment.[20] The fact that organisms work to transform and harness nutrients from a territory highlights the isomorphism of the economic problem. Organisms have to expend effort since they, like humans, cannot find what is needed immediately available, placed on a silver platter. The effort to produce are aided with tools, not too dissimilar from human tools. Spiders, for example, build webs, beavers construct dams, and higher primates use twigs. Most organisms, though, do not employ tools in the strict sense; rather they use tools like eyes, legs, skin, claws, teeth, wings, etc. They are part of the agency of purposefully directed effort, and hence are capital tools in the broader sense. Lotka (1945) calls them 'endosomatic instruments', to separate them from 'exosomatic instruments' like webs, nets, wheels, arrows, etc.

Endosomatic instruments should not be lumped together with inputs. It amounts to the confusion of the actor with what is acted upon – reminiscent of the confusion committed by conventional economics. For example, the claws of a vulture belong to the vulture and should not be lumped with the prey. The size of inputs is contingent on the capability of the actor, its degree of experience, and its territory. Any improvements of those variables assist the organism to process greater amounts of input, attaining greater ascendancy. With ascendancy, eco-logical connections (nodes) become more stable. Stability cannot endure, since the carrying capacity of the environment is finite to some extent. Pertinent nutrients in the ecological niche eventually deplete by the sheer fact of production activity, even though it is conducted at the same scale. Ironically, when the carrying capacity is expanded as a result of the employment of more sophisticated instruments, i.e. evolution, the deterioration of the environment is accelerated.

Wicken (1986, 1987) views the rise of more complex instruments a remedy to the on-going deterioration of the input influx. Greater complexity allows the organism to appropriate more food than others and makes some nutrients useful when they were not before; i.e. the carrying capacity of the environment is expanded. Wicken (in Ho and Saunders, 1984) calls this phenomenon anagenesis to indicate that evolution favours the more complex. That is, evolution is the irreversible process of the rise of complexity. The depletion of input influx necessitates evolutionary change to favour the more complex. Otherwise, a population becomes unable to explore deeper resources in the environment. This goes against the ethos of ND which cannot assert that evolution is irreversible theoretically.[21]

3.3.3 Knowledge: Not Given Information

Heterodox economics

Economists, throughout the history of the discipline, have levelled criticisms at the axiom of given technological information. To recapitulate, the orthodox view involves two fairly distinguishable statements: technology as exogenous; tech-nology as definite.

Technology as non-exogenous. Heterodox economists assert that technological innovation, and so productivity, is normally endogenous. They appeal to Smith's postulate that innovation is a function of learning-by-doing and the growth of demand, i.e. production and the market at large.

Smith (1976b, chapter 1) argues that division of labour heightens productivity gains. It engenders greater labour dexterity, time saving, and replacement of monotonous tasks with tools. The productivity gain allows external economies; unit cost drops as output rises. This rebuts the NC law of supply (Young, 1928; Kaldor, 1972; Kurdas, 1988).[22]

While productivity is a function of division of labour, the latter is a function of the extent of the market facing a firm. Smith (1976b, chapter 3) argues that the greater the demand for a certain good, the more the firm can afford further division of labour – which enhances its innovation and productivity. Thus, the growth of demand facing a firm indirectly induces innovation.

The growth of demand facing a firm need not be exogenously induced. As innovative activity of a firm rises, it expands further. As a result of vertical linkages, this has unintended spill-over effects – the expansion of one firm spurs demand facing other firms (Levine, 1981). I call this macroexternality 'asymmetry of demand' (Khalil, 1987c). As other firms expand, demand facing the original firm may rise, and hence *ex post* confirm the initial expansion. Thus, growth of demand is endogenously induced (Nell, 1992).

To sum up the story of one firm, growth of demand which indirectly encourages innovation is itself induced initially by innovation. Figure 3.1 depicts the virtuous circle: growth of specific demand induces division of labour, which in turn invite innovation, productivity, and expansion of the firm. Expansion of one firm enhances growth of aggregate demand. The latter may spill over and stir specific demand facing the firm. This envelops the circle and shows that innovation is endogenous.[23]

Likewise, Karl Marx conceived innovative activity to be endogenous in the sense of being the product of the purposeful activity of capital to accumulate. In *Capital*, Marx presented technical innovation in volume 1 as part of accumulation, prior to the presentation of circulation of capital in volume 2, and competition in volume 3. This indicates that, for Marx, innovation is not primarily the outcome of market structure as NC theory claims, but which empirical findings by and large fail to corroborate (Coombs, in Dosi *et al.*, 1988b). For Marx, innovation is sought after even by monopolistic firms, since it generates absolute surplus value (increased productivity independent of intensified effort).

Despite the unbridgeable ideological divide, Marx was admired by Joseph Schumpeter (1949), who also elevated accumulation and innovation to the centre of theory. In his work, technological innovation and product innovation are not desultory, competition-driven, or serendipitous activities. Innovative activities are rather purposeful endeavours, pursued earnestly by the entrepreneur. Schumpeter postulated that the ebbs and flows of accumulation are punctuated by the introduction of major technological innovations. Without innovations and the entrepreneurial spirit behind them, capitalism would perish.

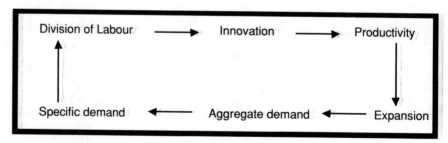

Figure 3.1   Endogenously determined innovations

Schumpeter is a good representative of Austrian economics. Austrian economics, at least the strand which emphasizes subjective human behaviour, views the economy as a process of creation and discovery (O'Driscoll and Rizzo, 1985). It emphasizes purposeful human action (von Mises, 1966). It faults NC theory for ignoring entrepreneurship. The idea of entrepreneurship is also advanced by evolutionary economists like Nelson and Winter (1982). They propose a theory of the firm which includes purposeful innovative activity, which are embodied in R & D departments (Nelson, in Dosi *et al.*, 1988b).

Dosi (1988a, and in Dosi *et al.*, 1988b, p. 221 ff.) argues likewise that innovations are pursued by the firm independently of market structure. To him, technological improvements proceed according to a well-recognized trajectory, which is discerned from antecedent historical events. The general outline is specified by what he calls the 'technological paradigm', which defines the range of innovations. Improvements are not pulled out of a hat, but rather out of solving puzzles generated and outlined by the paradigm (Nell, 1992, esp. Ch. 16).

Rosenberg (1976b) calls the paradigm a set of 'focusing devices', which identify the problems and their solution. Similarly, the French regulation school (Boyer, in Dosi *et al.*, 1988b) calls it an 'accumulation regime', which stabilizes and provides impetus to accumulation. The accumulation regime does not change continuously, but is transformed in the face of punctuated economic doldrums. Radical institutionalists (Gordon *et al.*, in Cherry *et al.*, 1987) give a similar version and call it the 'social structure of accumulation'. Nell (1988 and 1992) explains the same phenomenon under the name 'transformational growth'. Freeman and Perez (in Dosi *et al.*, 1988b) call it 'techno-economic paradigm', and distinguish it from innovations sponsored by it. These accumulation paradigms are probably behind Kondratieff's finding about long waves (van Duijn, 1983).

Most of these ideas fail in one regard – they lack coherent theoretical account. This failing, though, pales next to the disregard from which these findings suffer at the hand of NC economists. Given the NC tool kit, long waves and regime change stand as stubborn thorns – reminiscent of the difficulty hard-core neo-Darwinian theorists have with punctuated evolutionary change. In contrast, such large-scale changes are the bread and butter for approaches which embrace innovative activity as endogenous.

Technology as non-definite. NC economists view technology as discrete bits of information, like signals in communication theory. Heterodox economists challenge such reductionism. While some techniques are discrete rules, the rest are integral organizations who function in light of to the environment. As a corollary, the firm should not be viewed as a black box.

At the bottom of this reductionism is the conflation between knowledge and information. While knowledge is fuzzy and made of contingent principles, information is precise and composed of self-defined rules (Khalil, 1989d). There are certain canons which are bits of information, like engineering rules and codes of computer programmes. Others should be considered as knowledge, like the technological know-how to make an axe or bread.

According to Jean Piaget (see Russell, 1978), the acquisition of knowledge is a biological process. The person has to maintain a harmonious field to make sense of new acquisitions. The nervous system is not a bag of potatoes which can be stuffed with information, but a coherent organizer. For accumulated knowledge to function, the components have to blend well together. Similarly, Gestalt psychology describes perception and thoughts as attempts to build holistic forms of the sensory fields (Kohler, 1969). In the essay on the history of astronomy, Smith (1980) argues that knowledge amounts to making links between the familiar and unfamiliar to ease the tension of the imagination (Khalil, 1989e).

As the mind reaches a new harmony among acquired experiences, the components of knowledge coexist in a flexible balance. While each component complements the other, insightful reorganization may lead to improvements, since the meaning of each part is not self- but topologically-defined. This makes knowledge a versatile potential, taking different forms depending on the context. By contrast, information is context free, not open for interpretation, since its units are self-defined. If the bits are reassembled, the message is destroyed since each bit is rigid, cannot be defined by other bits.

Given this distinction, most technical know-how is not composed of self-defined bits of information, but formed of fuzzy principles of abstract potential which are organically connected. This makes technology susceptible to the environment of consumers' needs. Homologous to how Waddington's epigenetic landscape explains environmental shaping of the organism, discussed below, consumers' needs shape the development of technology in unique ways. Technology takes shape through unique producer–consumer interaction, which Lundvall (in Dosi *et al.*, 1988b) calls 'organized market'. Unique surroundings shape the way technology grows. The actual product is contingent upon the particular and personal way an agent applies the technology.

Dosi (ibid., pp. 221 ff.) expounds a similar thesis. He views technical know-how as personal knowledge – reminiscent of Michael Polanyi's (1958) central proposition. It cannot be made fully explicit through the transmission of self-defined information. In fact, knowledge loses effectiveness when it is broken down for transmission.

That explains, according to Fagerberg (in Dosi *et al.*, 1988b), the failure of the developing countries to import technology. He shows that growth rate differentials among nations are a function of nationally induced technological activity, which cannot be transplanted. He argues that the key to unlock the vicious cycle of underdevelopment is a national policy that encourages innovative activity at the local level. Local experiences need to develop in an authentic fashion with the help of the government. Modern Japan is a case in point, according to Freeman (ibid.).

Thus, for technology to work it has to be at least partly home-grown. Technology is the outcome of historically accumulated, particular experiences. Thus, it is part of the 'personality' of a firm. To treat technology as mere transferable information amounts to viewing the firm as a black box with no character (Rosenberg, 1982). In the NC approach the firm is treated as an entity that simply transforms, according to a production function, given resources with the help of given information into a precise output.

Within the NC view, it is anomalous to observe two firms with identical information but different productivities. This is not anomalous according to Leibenstein (1987; see Khalil, 1989a). He rejects the view of the firm as an informational blueprint. While two firms may have identical production functions, it does not establish that effort expended on the part of labour is identical. The extraction of effort, which Marx calls relative surplus value, can be impeded by workers disgruntled by unfulfilled expectations promised by the firm.[24]

Cultural heritage also explains divergent productivities. Maurice *et al.* (1986) have shown amply how the difference in industrial relations between France and Germany untangles the conspicuous difference in the productivity performance, although there is no difference in the quantity and quality of investment. Performance by a nation or a firm depends on its historical record; each producing agency has a personality developed through unique conventions. The firm is the embodiment of its particular experiences and specific technological tradition. This, to some extent, insulates, in an unrestricted market, inefficient firms or nations from competition; their unique personality may have developed committed consumers. According to Metcalfe (in Dosi *et al.*, 1988b), diffusion of innovations, even under competitive pressure, is not as homogeneous and rapid as NC theory make us expect. It is rather erratic, since each nation or firm has its own personal conditions which cause it to ignore new technologies.

This suggests that technology is not an extraneous shirt. What is at stake is the identity of the firm. Technology is not only capital goods, but also the organization of the division of labour, the break-up of tasks, the accumulated technical experience by the labour force, and even includes the marketing apparatus (Levine, 1981). Technology permeates the producing agency and makes it into an organic whole. Thus, according to heterodox theorists (see Robinson, 1953, 1970; Pasinetti, 1966), it is ludicrous to suggest *à la* NC theory of capital that, within a certain technological organization, the relative composition of labour, capital and land is fungible. That is, they cannot be rearranged according to changes in relative prices. This is the origin of the reswitching of technique debate between Cambridge, USA and Cambridge, UK (see Moss, in Nell, 1980). Most critics of orthodoxy have focused on the logical and mathematical inadequacies of NC capital theory. Meanwhile, the conceptual failing was almost lost in the tussle. Factors, within certain limits, are not substitutable, since technological know-how permeates and unites the firm as an organic whole (Nell, 1992).

The basis of the view of factors of production as fungible is the conception of the firm as a mere contractual entity, a black box. This reductionist conception sees the firm as contingently premised on the independent will of owners of factors (Coase, 1937; Alchian and Demsetz, 1972). Owners of factors are assumed to form firms to avoid relatively higher transaction costs (Williamson, 1985). While this question is legitimate, it should not be the whole story – particularly when the concern is with the nature of organization. In this regard, vertically dependent firms should be considered as a single organization since their technologies are locked in, even when subcontracting is not explicitly evident. Although vertical transactions are conducted via the market, firms form an organic organization. They produce products according to the specification of others (see Lorenz, in Gambetta, 1988).

This signifies that a firm is more than the negation of the market. The firm is part of the vertical division of labour which expresses technological know-how. The firm, in a profound sense, cannot be severed into factors. These factors are not preconstituted, and hence cannot replace each other according to relative prices. They are organically joined by knowledge.

One cannot simply rearrange technology. It is not a congeries of self-defined bits of information. A mechanical reorganization of the components of technology may well generate undesired outcomes. Technology should be handled carefully if one intends to create an improved product or process of production. Components of technology are fuzzy know-how that engender products only through historical interaction between producer and environments.

Heterodox biology

Darwin's theory was rescued from decline by injecting it with modern genetics in the 1940s. The synthesis, ND, postulates that the genotype is given. To recapitulate, this axiom consists of two relatively separate statements: the genotype as exogenous; the genotype as definite.

Genotype as non-exogenous. The tenet that genotype is exogenous entails that genes are insulated from experience and purposeful will. If a gene mutates, it presumably occurs for random and extraneous reasons. The heterodox idea that gene mutation is directed (non-random), epitomized by the work of Lamarck, became something of a pariah in the hallways of ND orthodoxy.

One implication of the random mutation idea is that species evolve gradually. It is, however, unsupported by the fossil record unearthed by paleontologists. The record shows that species remain largely stable for long periods of time. Periods of prolonged stasis are interrupted by sudden appearances of new species in relatively short periods. The new species are usually more elaborate and complex forms of their lineage – reminiscent of technological regime change in economics. The rhythmic character of change suggests that the genotype does not mutate randomly or exogenously.[25]

A second implication of the random mutation idea is that the outcome of genetic mutation is open: anything goes. The soft-core version of ND, however, recognizes that genes operate within families, which confine the range of outcomes (Bateson, in Gambetta, 1988). In this light, Gould (in Milkman, 1982) has redefined the meaning of randomness: it does not mean that outcomes are equally probable but that they occur in disregard to expected benefit.

This redefinition of randomness, to Grasse (1977, p. 245), does not save ND. It does not matter how long the genome is shuffled, the DNA of bacteria does not have enough components to engender the DNA of mice. Random mutations are simply rearrangements of what already exists. Complex organisms require complex gene families which cannot be constructed from simpler ones by random mutations. Furthermore, random mutations are rare; there is a chemical 'proof-reader' which ensures that newborn cells carry the same genes as parent cells. Moreover, if a random mutation occurs, it would most likely be fatal. If it is not fatal, it would more probably be neutral, since there is no one–to–one correlation between genetic change and phenotypic change. The probability of a propitious mutation dwindles even further in light of the fact that most traits require the cooperation of multitudes of genes. That is, the chance of apropos genes randomly mutating in complementary fashion is astronomically low (Noda, 1982; Schoffeniels, 1976, *passim*; Moorhead and Kaplan, 1987).[26]

Furthermore, random mutation, as the origin of substantial and evolutionary change, is highly unlikely. The work of Cairns *et al.* (1988) suggests an altern-ative. He and his collaborators cultured a strain of bacteria that cannot digest lactose, in a dish with only lactose in it. Most cells starved to death; a few managed to develop the proper enzyme to digest lactose. The likelihood of this mutation occurring randomly is reckoned to be ludicrously small. More surpris-ingly, the mutation was passed on to daughter cells. They concluded that not only did the bacteria seem to have directed their mutation, but they also managed to pass the acquired character to progeny.[27] This challenges the orthodox idea of mutation as exogenous – similar to the case nurtured by heterodox economics in respect to innovations.

Other workers (e.g. Cullis, Steele *et al.*, Temin and Engels, in Pollard, 1984) extend the directed mutation and Lamarckian inheritance ideas to multicellular organisms. In multicellular organisms, cells may direct their genetic mutation through the enzymatic machinery. The idea of directed mutation should not sound radical, since it is the normal way of life for sexually reproducing species. Sexual organisms usually exercise power over the progeny through sexual selection. Humans assist such sexual selection through breeding and domestication of animals (Campbell, in Depew and Weber, 1985, p. 150).

Matsuno (in Ho and Saunders, 1984) shows that studies on the origin of life suggests an 'active agent' behind the assembly of non-living into living matter. To Campbell (in Milkman, 1982, pp. 200–1), the active agent is present at the lowest levels of hierarchy, the gene. Genes are crafty agents which modify their own structure according to circumstances. They team together and form families which shield members, even when they are defective. Families also help transport members anywhere, even to other species (Pollard, in Ho and Saunders, 1984). This 'colonialism' could change gene expression drastically if high ranking genes are involved (Hunkapillar *et al.* in Milkman, 1982).

A problem still needs to be confronted: how directed mutations are transferred from somatic (body) cells to germ (sex) cells, so that they can be passed on to progeny. This is discussed in Appendix 3.2. Meanwhile, I have shown that heterodox biologists, like their counterpart in economics, argue that change of know-how is at least partially directed by agents to promote their survival.

Genotype as non-definite. As explained above, orthodox biologists conceive genes as definite bits of information, similar to signals in communication theory. Heterodox biologists challenge such reductionism; while some genes are definite, the rest are organizations with somewhat flexible functions. As a corollary, heterodoxy does not conceive the organism as a black box. These ideas are reminiscent of heterodox views on technology and the firm.

Surroundings which influence genes include other genes, the cytoplasm (the protoplasm encircling the cell's nucleus), and, to a lesser extent, the organism, population, and natural habitat at large. Here, I am dealing with a different type of influence from the one I discussed in the previous subsection, where I argued that genes in many cases undergo directed rather than random mutations, as ND claims. The source of these mutations is learning feedbacks and the purposeful determination to survive. In this subsection, I am not dealing with genetic mutation but with genetic ambiguity, which allows the surroundings to interpret genetic messages in a liberal fashion.

As all interpretative activity has proven, the product depends, to some extent, on the interpreter. That is, interpreters with different contexts interpret the same genetic message differently; the circumstance of the interpreter matters to an extent. This is similar to what hermeneutics claims with respect to classic texts: there is no definite, precise meaning in biblical or Aristotelian texts (Gadamer, 1975). Likewise, genes are not definitive in themselves; they do not have precise messages. In order for a genetic message actually to become precise, it needs an interpreter to make sense of it.

Ptashne (1989) shows how the surroundings shape the messages of genes. This signifies that the DNA, for the most part, is not a self-defined entity, but, according to Wright (1988), is an organizational knowledge that possesses 'meaning'. The idea of DNA as possessing 'meaning' is iconoclastic, supposing that genes have, within reason, many ways of manifesting themselves. This may explain to baffled scientists how the immune system is capable of producing a large variety of antigens whose number could well surpass the number of genes. This versatility shows that the DNA is a supple organization capable of diverse behavioural strategies.[28] The RNA has been found to exhibit such diversity as well.[29]

The behaviour strategy of an organism is also versatile. It involves flexible actions ranging from self-promotion to mutual aid. It suggests that at least some genes do not emit self-defined rules, but fuzzy principles. The inclusive fitness hypothesis of sociobiology may be the last bulwark against such a suggestion; it insists that behaviour, following genes, is rigid. It expounds that mutual aid is disguised selfishness. An organism aids only relatives, in order to promote its own genes. Some empirical findings are not supportive of such an explanation. Queller *et al.* (1988), for example, have shown that members of a species of wasps undertake altruistic behaviour with no regard to kin.

Such flexibility of behaviour suggests that genes are not a blueprint. The fuzziness of some genes invites the participation of environments to shape the development of the organism. Wolterick (Ho and Saunders, 1984, p. 269) calls the confrontation a 'norm of reaction', since the organism is not defined until it confronts the environment. Waddington's (1957) metaphor of epigenetic landscape highlights the role of milieu in embryogenesis. He uses the metaphor to depict the development of a trait as a ball rolling down a genetically fixed path. Given gradient heights, the ball skirts the path when external factors exceed certain thresholds. In this manner, external, environmental factors participate in shaping the organism, which indicates that the genotype is fuzzy.[30]

Likewise, Lovtrup (in Ho and Saunders, 1984) views ontogeny (the development of organism to adult form) as the historical unfolding of abstract body plan into particular organisms. In this sense, according to von Baer's Law, phylogeny (the evolution of a lineage), like ontogeny, is the unfolding of the general into the particular. That is, ontogeny, broadly speaking, does not recapitulate phylogeny as asserted by Ernst Haeckel's biogenetic law (Gould, 1977). The earliest embryonic stages of related species are identical since they share the same abstract body plan before distinguishing features emerge during development. This suggests, as elaborated in Appendix 3.3, that evolution is highly related to development (ibid.).

Thus, ontogeny and phylogeny, from the heterodox view, show that the organism is not exclusively the product of a genetic blueprint. Besides the genotype, the organism is shaped by pressures from a multitude of environments. The consequent acquired characteristics are different from the ones prompted by the Lamarckian will. Regardless, traits changed by milieu also amount to nothing without evidence of their inheritance, as discussed in Appendix 3.2.

In light of this, the organism and its traits are not epiphenomena of some well-defined genotype. Contrary to Dawkins's (1976) view, the organism is not a black box for the genome to make another genome, a medium between genes and environment (Ho and Fox, 1988, *passim*). Some soft neo-Darwinists have conceded as much; they point out that genotype and phenotype may not correspond one to one (e.g. Eldredge, in Khalil and Boulding, 1993). They have failed, though, to draw the conclusion that activity of genes is to some extent a function of the organization of which they are members.

Campbell (in Milkman, 1982; in Depew and Weber, 1985; in Weber *et al.*, 1988; cf. Khalil, 1989f) emphasizes the integrity of organization running from multigene families to the organism (see also Hunkapillar *et al.*, in Milkman, 1982). Likewise, Varela (1979; cf. Kauffman, in Depew and Weber, 1985) views the organism as an 'autopoiesis', a self-reproducing, integral organization. Similarly, Edelman's (1988, 1989) idea of topobiology attempts to recover the organism from reductionism. According to him, current interactions of any cell depend on its current and past positions. Past history is important in the life of a cell since the kind of neighbours a cell used to have affects its current individuality and uniqueness. Such place-dependent interactions are most crucial in embryonic development, and continue throughout the organism's life.[31]

An earlier attempt to save the organism from the black-box conception is the work of D'Arcy Thompson (1961), an inspiration for many modern cladists (Janvier, in Pollard, 1984). Thompson charges that Darwin explained away the remarkable persistence of organizational form throughout evolution as a result of common origin (Kauffman, in Depew and Weber, 1985; Goodwin, in Pollard, 1984). Thompson's work is given a respectful, albeit lukewarm, attention in the history of biological thought. In most cases, it is misunderstood as highlighting physical forces in shaping the plan of the body (e.g. O'Grady and Brooks, in Weber *et al.*, 1988). Thus, it is assumed to complement ND. It is, however, an alternative to ND and suggests that evolution is the variation of the same body plan – which still needs to be explained.

A similar non-reductionist view of the organism and evolution is expressed by Webster and Goodwin (1982; in Ho and Saunders, 1984; in Pollard, 1984). Although their approach may have problems, they advance the unique conception of the organism as a field that cannot be reduced to insulated bits of information. Like Thompson, they do not attempt to explain diversity, but homological invariance. Universal homology suggests a generative field underlying all processes (cf. Ho, Saunders, in Ho and Saunders, 1984).[32] The field idea was first proposed by the arch-vitalist Hans Driesch in response to the remarkable ability of sea-urchin embryos to recover parts after being severed (see Sheldrake, 1988, pp. 79–80). Webster and Goodwin call their approach 'structuralism' since it rejects the genetic reductionism of ND and emphasizes the role of the cytoplasm.

The notion of the organism as a generative field which unfolds from the abstract to the concrete indicates that the genotype is not completely self-defined. Instead, the genotype is a form of organizational knowledge, defined partially through the assimilation of historical experience.

3.3.4   Environment: Not Given Selector

Heterodox economics

Alchian (1950) employed the neo-Darwinian notion of natural selection to expound the view that extant firms, by virtue of survival, signify efficiency.[33] The selector, made up of preferences, must be assumed to be given in order for the efficiency thesis to work. If agents manipulate the selector, less than optimal efficiency would persist. The axiom of a given selector has two untenable parts – similar to the neo-Darwinian view of nature: first, selectors are perfectly efficient because of perfect knowledge and hyper-rationality. Second, selectors are unyielding to the manipulations of firms because their preferences are well-defined before entering the market.

Under attack, NC theorists opted for the notion that agents have statistical rather than perfect knowledge of the prices of goods in all markets, spatially and temporally spread. The statistical qualification (even the subjective variety) is no response to critics like Frank Knight (1971; see O'Driscoll and Rizzo, 1985) and G.L.S. Shackle (1970) who insist that subjective or objective uncertainty cannot be reduced to probabilistic risk. No one denies that agents actually do not know all the opportunities and prices of goods in current markets, not to mention future markets. When this thesis is incorporated theoretically, the clout of agents as efficient selectors is clipped.

Furthermore, the hyper-rationality tenet comes under heavy fire from Simon (1978). He calls it 'substantive' rationality, in distinction to his view of rationality as 'procedural'. Regarding the NC substantive view, information is processed to generate an unambiguous, single-exit solution (Latsis, in Latsis, 1976). It presumes that agents are hyper-rational, capable of superseding their habits, historical uniqueness, and pragmatic rules of thumb. According to Simon's procedural view, information is knowledge which carries meaning and subject to interpretation. Agents are not automata but carry tacit, personal knowledge.

Thus, agents make decisions according to past knowledge; they are not exempt from the recency effect or inertia. According to Simon, their behaviour over time is more or less consistent; it is not erratically determined by an extraneous utility function. Decisions are part of a chain of events, from which agents cannot extricate themselves at the whim of price gyrations. Agents do not stand on suprahistorical grounds. They are defined by biological, cultural, and individual habits, which it is possible to overthrow, but not instantaneously.

Classical institutional thinkers, like Veblen (see Coats, in Latsis, 1976), have likewise emphasized the role of habits and tradition in moulding agents. Despite the new avenues they have opened, by neo-institutionalists (Langlois, 1986), arrive at conclusions reached by classical institutionalists, but through NC axioms. The neo-institutionalists postulate the ineluctability of rules from the perspective of hyper-rationality. Heiner (in Dosi *et al.*, 1988), for instance, reasons that rules arise because agents lack the competence to make prudent decisions.

Classical institutional economics and Simon's behaviouralism stand for the thesis that agents exhibit satisficing behaviour. That is, agents choose the first opportunity or course of action which satisfies their minimum requirement, rather than optimize an imagined utility function. Agents act according to inertia and habit, and are not ready to change behaviour in response to marginal stimuli. Habits emerge because agents' satisfaction arises from the act of consumption.

Thus, goods are not perfectly fungible. Consumers develop attachments to particular goods which express their personality (see Levine, 1988, chapter 1) as it develops biological and socially. That is, consumers relate to goods in a non-arbitrary manner. The array of goods exhibits some coherence which reflects the integrity of consumers. Consequently, consumers, within reason, do not substitute goods as relative prices change. Thus, preferences of consumers cannot act as the efficient selector as envisaged by NC theory. Preferences do not put the underachiever out of business. This explains the anomalous coexistence of firms with diverse rates of profit. The environment is multilayered, and hence inefficient firms can survive in the long run.

The fact that preferences are hypoefficient permits producers to mould and manipulate them. Preferences, after all, are not rigid enough; they yield to the manipulation of firms and are not absolutely sovereign as claimed. The environment is not an ironclad selector. Consumers are usually not precisely aware of their preferences, which are ductile enough to be moulded by advertisement and socialization forces.

Moreover, because preferences are hyporational and flexible explains the ability of most firms to develop special connections with their clients. Each firm carves a niche in the economy. This permits firms producing the same good to coexist, despite long-term profit rate gradients – reminiscent of the wide intra-population genetic frequency. As Galbraith argues (1958), firms have power to shape preferences (and even politics), rather than the other way around. Firms cultivate specific tastes that can be almost exclusively met by them.

Consequently, preferences are not the guardian angels that screen out the inefficient. The term 'efficiency' is non-operational and hazy in a world of hyporationality and flexible consumers' preferences. The fact that preferences are not given undermines the thesis that the satisfaction of consumers is the gauge of economic efficiency. There cannot be such a neutral criterion, since the environment can never be exogenously given. The environment is like an intaglio impressed upon by the cameo of purposefully acting producers.

Heterodox biology

The axiom that nature is given underlies the ND term 'adaptation', which denotes the act of fitting organisms to given habitats. The axiom involves two parts: first, nature is a hyperefficient selector (similar to the idea of hyper-rationality in economics); second, nature is unyielding (coinciding with the idea of well-defined preferences in economics). If nature is less than hyperefficient, and yields to agents' manoeuvres, it could not make an organism adapt to its habitat. Heterodoxy challenges the idea of adaptation and its underlying axiom that nature is given.

Heterodox biologists highlight the fact that intra-population frequency of a gene allele is wider than ND leads us to expect. This would not be the case if nature were a hyperefficient selector. The excessive intra-population variability is explained away by ND as the result of meiotic division and sexual recombination. This did not, however, stop some workers from questioning the efficiency of nature. Large differences among organisms of the same population were taken as serious anomalies, implying that nature is not a rigid selector. Organisms of various abilities could coexist for long periods of time – similar to the coexistence of firms with different rates of profit. This indicates that nature is a multilayered habitat, which allows diverse abilities to live side by side.

Specifically in relation to predators, studies have shown that these animals do not have perfect knowledge, even in the statistical form. They look for prey in a trial and error or iterative process. Furthermore, they do not forage in an optimal fashion, but rather pursue a course which seems to satisfy their minimum requirement. Thus, the selector, after all, is not hyperefficient.

This allows the organism to mould and manipulate native to an extent. The agent, within limits, may carve certain habitats after its own image rather than adapt to what is given. The common example, and sometimes mistaken to be the exclusive one, is the transfiguring of nature by humans. In fact, almost all living forms carve their own niche and exercise some power over the environment (Lewontin, 1984). The most primordial form of such power is the motion of animals and the roots of plants, which allow the organism to seek nutrients. More obvious examples of the manipulation of habitat include nests, dens, burrows, and colonies.

Thus, the environment yields to 'persuasion'; it is flexible in the face of the potency of organisms. This repudiates the orthodox thesis that nature is given. Nature is not the absolute arbiter of the fate of organisms, since nature is, to some extent; manipulated by organisms.

3.4   REFLECTIONS

When economists appeal to the core of ND in order to buttress the axioms of orthodoxy, they open a can of worms. ND is hard pressed to offer any help since it is under attack for the same reasons that the axioms of NC economics are under attack. The umbrella tenet which unites these attacks in both disciplines is the principle of purposeful behaviour. The principle puts non-conventional ideas in context and provides a deeper rationale for them.

The rejection of the precept of given material cause implies that the agent partially determines input influx. The repudiation of the tenet of given formal cause signifies that initiative and need to some extent determine technological and genetic innovations. The renunciation of the axiom of given efficient cause suggests that producers are somewhat able to redefine the environment. Put succinctly, the different challenges to NC and ND axioms are underpinned by the principle of purposeful action.

Orthodox theorists recognize purposeful behaviour, of course. But they do not really include it at the theoretical level in the textbook version of their approaches. The outcome is a theory which relies exclusively on efficient causality: phenomena like institutional arrangements are presented as contingent on exogenous causes, not a function of purposeful action. To NC theory, such arrangements are theoretically reversible since they depend on capriciously given variables. Orthodoxy, at the first level of approximation, is not equipped to discern temporal continuity.

To clear the way for historical theorizing, variables like resources, technology, and preferences must be treated as partially endogenous, determined to some extent by purposeful action. This makes theoretical endeavours more difficult. The gain, though, is worth the effort. Then, one can conceive historical trends theoretically: availability of resources, the evolution of technology, and development of preferences are the outcomes (some unintended) of irreversible purposeful action. These three moments contribute differently to the irreversible historical process. The detailed blend of these variables can be expressed in diverse scenarios. This chapter is not the place to develop them. But for a scenario to be historical, it must conceive one kind of action as self-seeking, purposeful behaviour.

Conventional theory finds teleology unpalatable. It does not need to be. Teleology is not necessarily the brainchild of wild metaphysics. Purposeful behaviour simply *completes* the organizational framework of humans:

> Humans are self-organizing and self-constructing. Committing oneself to goals not yet accomplished creates incomplete organization. Incomplete organization or disorganization elicits efforts to transform it into some coherent organizational form. When progress towards, or accomplishment of, a set of current concerns is not occurring, an incomplete behavior episode (i.e. incomplete organization) exists. A person will try to create organizational coherence, either by increased striving to accomplish current goals or abandonment of them (at least temporarily). (Ford, 1987, p. 408)

Organization, like household, firm, or government agency, is essentially incoherent. In order to eradicate incoherence, the agent has to pursue goals: 'The drama of real life reveal (sic) the importance of human purpose in ways sterile laboratory conditions cannot' (ibid., p. 394). If there are no goals to pursue, the organization would degenerate and perish. The absence of purpose is the most frequent cause of suicide and, to some extent, sickness. Purpose does not need to be fully attained. What matters is its presence:

> Without the direction which purposes give to life, there can be no coherent organization and no reference against which to evaluate one's activities and experiences. Without direction, life is meaningless. Like a ship on a stormy sea without someone steering it, one gets pushed around by the winds and waves of life until one capsizes and sinks to oblivion. Given the fundamental importance of the directive function in human life, it is sad that science has for so long treated it as an epiphenomenon. (ibid., p. 395)

The function of purpose in life is to end incoherence and incompleteness of organization – which really cannot be willed (Elster, 1983). This suggests that organization is not a self-constituted, well-defined agency – similar to technological knowledge discussed above. That is, the worth of an agent of production cannot be determined independently of the actual pursuit of production. The agent acquires different attributes depending on the greater organizational context. Thus, when incomplete, fuzzy organizations of production join hands to form a greater organiza-tion, the productivity of labour, for example, is *not* the sum of independent productivities. The productivity of each agent cannot be determined in isolation from the organic context. An agent's productivity is a potential with diverse actualities, depending on how the agent relates to others. Thus, the firm's productivity is not the sum of the productivity of its agents'.

Therefore, the whole organization has to be specified in order to know the actual productivity of the constitutive agents. This sheds doubt on the other conceptual pillar of NC economics, reductionism. For that matter, it is also the pillar of ND. The firm is not a black box, an entity. It is not a congeries of agents; the way agents are connected is a crucial matter. Heterodox biologists have registered similar ideas in regard to the organism.

The upshot is that NC theory, at the first theoretical approximation, not equipped to handle organization. The way agents are connected, in the NC world, is capricious, the function of relative prices. The fungibility of inputs, as stipulated by the NC production function, indicates that the firm lacks an organizational integrity. The idea of fungibility makes job differentiation or the rise of complexity contingent on relative prices, and hence reversible.[34]

Williamson (1985) tries to remedy the situation. However, the picture does not improve much, since his concern is still the NC emphasis on the size of the firm. He adds a twist to the NC explanation. The size is a function of transaction cost. While market structure is a sound inquiry, it is insufficient.

One needs to combine the organic idea of organization with the earlier assertion, the teleological idea of action, in order to clear the way for historical thinking. Each idea complements the other. Purposeful action means the agent is incomplete, and incomplete organization drives the agent to act purposefully. Unfortunately, most heterodox views have incorporated one idea at the expense of the other. Some have recognized the organic idea, but retained the efficient view; others have accepted teleology, but kept reductionism. Consequently, these traditions have only produced partial historical thinking.

The first type includes Leibenstein's (1987; see Khalil, 1989a) theory of the firm. He holds organic views, but does not entertain teleology. To him, the agent is not a purposeful actor that defines the influx of resources, technology, and preferences. It is not surprising that Leibenstein's study of the inefficiency of US firms relative to Japanese firms lacks a historical perspective. He blames hierarchy and the individualist ethos (which generates prisoner dilemma outcomes) for inefficiency in US industry, rather than seeing the expenditive of effort as the subject of historical development.[35]

The second type of heterodox traditions includes Austrian economics. It advocates teleology, but fails to subscribe to organic views.[36] In fact, the Austrian school is a forceful proponent of reductionism. Schumpeter's work is a good representative. His analysis of purposeful entrepreneurship is not complemented with an organic view of organization. There could be only one type of correct organization, namely, the small, independent entrepreneur. History for him hence is not an on-going process of evolution of organization, but a motion which terminates with the society of small entrepreneurs. His prognostication of the appearance of large firms and socialism leads him to pessimism, which further substantiates my point: Schumpeter's view of history is ahistorical (cf. Heilbroner, 1986, chapter 10).

In another paper (Khalil, 1992; cf. Khalil 1990d), I show in detail that Marx's view of the agent is similar to the Austrian programme: Marx's conception of action is teleological, but falls short of organic views. He is not, though, a reductionist. His vision is non-organic in another sense: he advocates a functionalist view of organization which amounts to portraying it as a mere entity. This is clearest in Marx's writings on abstract labour and the dominance of capital.

The concept of abstract labour means that labour-power is fungible; there is no irreversible technical division of labour. Dominance of capital for Marx is a moment which subsumes all others. Organization of production is totally subsumed under the yoke of capital. The firm is portrayed as a unidimensional agent which is only interested in the valorization of capital. There are, though, other dimensions to the firm. The firm is interested in its reputation, satisfying different sectors – like consumers and owners – and maintaining its constitutive suborganizations. This multi-faceted complexity is ignored by Marx at the first level of approximation. For him, there could be only one type of correct organization, namely, the association of producers who are free from the yoke of capital. Similar to Schumpeter, Marx sees history not as an endless process of development of organization, but as a motion which terminates with the society of free producers. Thus, Marx's view of history is ahistorical as well.

Thus, for clear historical thinking, organic conception should be combined with teleology. If the organic view is infused into Schumpeter's and Marx's analyses, history would be seen as an endless process of evaluation, not as an ideal telos to reach. If teleological reasoning is infused into Leibenstein's analysis, X-efficiency would be seen in a historical context.

While teleological conception has been repudiated for its mystical connotations, the organic conception has been rebuked for its imprecision. I may add that there might be a common rationale for the castigation of teleological and organic conceptions. Namely, it is the commitment to crude, pre-quantum materialism, which seems to be the ethos of mainstream scientific milieu. It is crude since it portrays itself as committed mainly to tangible objects, which excludes 'ghostly' things like final cause and organic interaction. In the light of quantum mechanics, matter after all is neither located in space in a point-like way nor bounded by sharp edges.

Such crude materialism is supposed to save us from teleology, which is usually identified with mystical speculations. The teleological conception has been castigated as non-scientific since it opens a Pandora's box of theology, metaphysics, and mysticism. With reference to the above discussion, I hope that I have demonstrated that teleological thinking need not be extravagant speculation. Furthermore, teleology should not be identified with an enigmatic, predestined telos which presumably guides development and evolution from an Olympian height.

Another promise made by the crude materialist ethos is the delivery of precise prediction. Precise prediction, however, has not been the silver lining of orthodoxy. So, why champion precision, and pay the high expense of relevance? If one champions relevance instead, its price – imprecision – is not too high, given the need of the intellect to understand and for public policy to be sagacious.

Action and organization should not, respectively, be reasoned in exclusively efficient and reductionist frameworks. As things stand now, those who try to shake the scales off their eyes and explain large-scale historical change are seen by the majority of on-lookers as peculiar. The audience, however, changes in the larger theatre of human ideas.

Appendix 3.1 The Newtonian Framework

The Newtonian framework is reductionist and efficient. The Newtonian law of gravity is the epitome of reductionism. The law is underpinned by the apparently innocuous assumptions that matter is independent of space, and both are analytically conceived apart from time and force. Thus, the movement of terrestrial and celestial masses is explained, when there is no contiguous force, as an action at-a-distance between objects, while the spatial/temporal matrix serves as a mere background. This allows the break-up of a phenomenon into its constitutive parts, as if the parts are independent and self-constituted. In this manner, the Newtonian framework has no room for the concept of organization as an integral, organic unit.

Newton's three laws of motion – inertia, acceleration, and action/reaction – are the quintessence of efficient conception. They relate mobility to contiguous forces, like pushing. Aristotle's efficient causality is emphasized at the expense of final causality. Classical, pre-twentieth-century physics perceives the world as a colossal machine or a huge billiard table which is mechanically determined. Along these lines, the behaviour of organization is conceived exclusively as a response to stimulus, similar to the response to contiguous force in the Newtonian world. In this manner, the Newtonian framework has no room for the concept of action as self-seeking, purposeful behaviour.

The Cartesian strategy is also reductionist and efficient. It reduces phenomena to kinematic and geometrical quantities, like mobility, impenetrability, and extension. It views the organism as a machine, and hence cannot be the basis of purposeful action. Any intentional action must have a separate ground that can be appended to the machine.

Appendix 3.2   The Inheritance of Acquired Characteristics

Characteristics may be acquired through purposeful will or the moulding of experience. They would amount to nothing, as far as evolutionary theory is concerned, if they cannot be inherited. That is, it has to be shown that Weismann's barrier is permeable.

To recapitulate, the barrier postulates that, in multicellular organisms, germ (sex) cells are totally insulated from somatic cells. In this fashion, an occurrence at the somatic level cannot be passed on to progeny. A number of workers are questioning the thesis that the germline is inviolate from the soma. Particles contained in somatic cells, called pangenes, can be influenced by environment and the organs containing them. Pangenes can move via blood to germ cells and influence the course of heredity. Steele (1979) proposes another mechanism inspired by Temin's protovirus hypothesis. He suggests that endogenous retroviruses targeted at the germline may act as vectors for the mutant somatic information by capturing RNAs from somatic cells and transducing them to germ cells. This scenario runs into problems in cases where cells do not divide as often or do not move. Steele offers solutions which need not concern us here.

It has been shown empirically that acquired traits by adults can be inherited in organisms as diverse as the ciliate protozoa and drosophila (Ho and Saunders, 1984, p. 225 ff.). Steele and Pollard (1987) have explained this through the process of reverse transcription. It is similar to Reidl's postulate of the feedback loop from the phenome to genome: 'This feedback information causes to develop, by trial and error, those gene interactions which improve their own adaptive speed or success' (Reidl, 1978, pp. xv–xvi).

The feedback loop for Ho (in Ho and Saunders, 1984, p. 275) is between the cytoplasm (the protoplasm outside the cell's nucleus) and the phenome; the genome only plays a secondary role. She places great emphasis on the cytoplasm since it is actually the whole organism at the zygote stage (Ho, in Ho and Saunders, 1984, p. 280). She conceives the cytoplasm of the ovum as crucial for the instigation and suppression of gene expression and cell differentiation. The cytoplasm registers the experience of the organism, while the genome records the experiences of the species. The experiences of the organism are assimilated and transmitted through the cytoplasm, and indirectly through the genome, to progeny:

> Organisms develop in accordance partly with the assimilated experiences of their forebears and partly with their own experiences. Development evolves through the internalization of new environments. The material link between organism and environment, and development and evolution alike is the hereditary apparatus which realistically includes both cytoplasm and nuclear genes. The cytoplasm registers the somatic imprint of experienced environments which can be transmitted to the next generation independently of the nuclear genes. At the same time, it acts as a true communication channel between the environment and the nuclear genome in the coordination of developmental and evolutionary processes. (Ho, in Ho and Saunders, 1984, p. 284; cf. Pollard, in Ho and Saunders, 1984; Campbell, in Milkman, 1982)

The role she accords to the cytoplasm and non-genetic inheritance complements Webster and Goodwin's structuralist alternative to ND. They provide ways to explain the inheritance of acquired characteristics.

More evidence is being discovered each day that acquired characteristics could be inherited under certain circumstances. This heterodox thesis is no longer on the defensive. It undermines the basic tenet of orthodoxy – Weismann's barrier – and makes it look like a wall with holes. That is, the genetic change of somatic cells can influence the germ cells.

Appendix 3.3 Development and Evolution

Von Baer's Law, after Karl Ernst von Baer, a nineteenth-century embryologist, fosters a developmental view of evolution – which more biologists are recognizing (e.g. Gould, 1977; Marx, 1988). Von Baer's Law stipulates that evolution, like development, is largely a process of differentiation from the general to the more particular. Such a process entails the rise of complexity of biological functions, which were tacitly implied in ancestral forms. That is, evolution is not about adding something totally new, but is rather the elaboration of what already exists – although in a relatively undifferentiated form.

In sympathy with von Baer's Law, Stephen Jay Gould (1977) argues that evolutionary change arises *during* the development of an organism through the change of the rate of reaching adulthood. The rate of unfolding from the general to the particular could be speeded up or retarded, which provides an opportunity for other rates to proceed into new territories. The opportunity to experiment is most crucial in the cases where the environment becomes hostile. According to Gould, the change of rate of development might engender successful species – even a higher taxon.

Gould's view supersedes the biogenetic law, also propagated by a nineteenth-century embryologist, Ernst Haeckel. The biogenetic law relates development to evolution in an opposite fashion to von Baer's Law. Haeckel's biogenetic law stipulates that the development of an organism recapitulates the features of ancestral *adult* forms before adding its own novelty on top (Gould, 1977, pp. 39–45). Advocates of recapitulation usually use the gill slits in a human embryo (see pictures in Sheldrake, 1988, p. 16) as an example of the recapitulation of a feature of adult fish. Such a feature is supposedly pushed back by others added on top of it during evolution. In respect of this example, Gould puts the difference between Haeckel's biogenetic law and von Baer's Law at the outset of his magisterial account:

> Haeckel interpreted the gill slits of human embryos as features of ancestral *adult* fishes, pushed back into the early stages of human ontogeny by a universal acceleration of developmental rates in evolving lineages. Von Baer argued that human gill slits do not reflect a change in developmental timing. They are not adult stages of ancestors pushed back into the embryos of descendants; they merely represent a stage common to the early ontogeny of all vertebrates (embryonic fish also have gill slits, after all). (Gould, 1977, pp. 2–3)

Stated differently, von Baer argues that the human embryo resembles embryos of other vertebrates because they are the most general foundations which give rise to the different lineages. This entails that, according to von Baer's Law, evolution is not a process of adding on totally unrelated features on top of others exhibited by ancestral adults. Rather, evolution is the reworking in new and more complex directions of the *same* general outline which humans, fish, and other schemes share.

Thus, the processes of evolution and development are intricately connected. Both entail the unfolding of the general into the particular. This should weaken the neo-Darwinian theses that mutations are random, and that evolutionary regularities are the outcome of the blind forces of natural selection.

Notes

1. Some prefer to expunge the term 'paradigm' from the English language for its widespread abuse (see Khalil, 1987a). In order to avoid tiresome and lengthy periphrases, however, I use it loosely to mean, what Schumpeter calls, the pre-analytical vision. That is, it should not denote relativistic epistemology.

2. Hollis and Nell (1975) have argued that NC concepts are bogus since positivism, which NC theorists adhere to, stands on shaky grounds. However, first, it has been observed (e.g. Blaug, 1980; Hirsch and de Marchi, 1986) that NC economists in practice are not positivists. Second, NC axioms do not stand or fall with the proclaimed epistemology.

3. It might come as a surprise that mainstream evolutionary theory is ahistorical. Part of the bewilderment stems from the failure to delineate between the *general* theory of evolution, which advocates the reality of the historical change of species, and the *specific* theory of evolution, which proposes an explanation of the general theory. Darwin's mechanism, natural selection, is a specific theory of evolution. The identification of the general theory with Darwinism was not helped by Darwin's popularized writings.

4. The vitalist doctrine submits that life in living organisms is caused and sustained by a vital force. This force is assumed to be distinct from and in addition to all primodial physical and chemical forces. Put differently, the doctrine draws a thick boundary between living and non-living matter.

5. The critics share another platform, the animosity towards the bourgeois ideological underpinning of both orthodoxies, like self-interest, survival of the fittest, *laissez-faire*, and competition. I do not develop this here. It has been attempted by others (Nell, 1972; Kitcher, 1985).

6. Equilibrium, no surplus, and complete market axioms are central to the NC enterprise. Albeit, they are ignored, since the concern of this chapter is with purposeful behaviour and large-scale historical change, while the idea of equilibrium is concerned only with the character of market dynamics. Hence one should deal with the two concerns separately (Khalil, 1990b).

    Some heterodox economists (e.g. Robinson, 1979) have helped convolute the two concerns. She considered the notion of equilibrium to contravene historical thinking. The notion of equilibrium, though, can be defended as an underlying force which need *not* be inconsistent with historical analysis. After all, historical–classical economics upheld the idea of natural price as the centre of gravity of market fluctuation (Eatwell, 1983).

7. Natural selection is the principle agency of evolution according to Darwin. Its modern version espouses the tenet that the genetic frequency of a population changes through time, and so evolves. Evolution occurs for two reasons: first, organisms are heterogenous in regard to hereditary materials. Second, those endowed with traits best fit for survival and reproduction will be overrepresented in the progeny. It is different from genetic drift and random statistical fluctuations.

    Hard-core Darwinians emphasize lower levels of the hierarchy like organisms and genes as the units of selection. Soft-core Darwinians stress that the units of natural selection are higher levels of the hierarchy like species and genus.

    Another related concept is the survival of the fittest, an expression coined by Herbert Spencer to refer to natural selection. Survival of the fittest, though, is no substitute for natural selection since it measures survival *prior* to selection, while natural selection measures fitness *after* the ousting of unfit organisms. Both principles are tautological. This is not necessarily a flaw. Some philosophers argue that theory by definition is a tautology. Thus, I do not entertain this line of criticism.

8. The quantity or property which nature maximizes is more accurately called 'net

reproductive advantage'. The word 'net' indicates that the measurement of fertility, the basis of fitness, makes allowance for mortality.

9. Wilson employs the concept 'inclusive fitness' to explain altruism. An organism supposedly strives for its fitness plus all its influence on the fitness of its relatives other than direct descendants. It is related to kin selection theory. Kin includes brothers, sisters, parents, and cousins. The theory argues that one or more organisms favour the survival and reproduction of relatives who are likely to possess the same genes by common descent.

10. Genotype is the totality of the genetic material of cells; genome is the sum total of genetic material in a fertilized egg. It is supposedly antecedent of phenotype, the external appearance.

11. In another paper (Khalil, 1990b), I show the difference between the phenomena (natural complex) which are organized and require final cause and the phenomena (natural system) which are chaotic and does not require it. The distinction does not run along the traditional separation between living and non-living matter. For example, agents interact in the market chaotically and non-living matter, as quantum mechanics postulates, interact organically (see Khalil, 1989g).

12. The fact that a closed system tends spontaneously towards maximum entropy (maximum melting) has misled many thinkers, notably N. Georgescu-Roegen (1971), to postulate that the entropy law is teleological. Therefore, they have concluded erroneously that the entropy law is the exemplar of, and the impetus behind, social and biological development (Khalil, 1990c, 1991).

13. Bohm conceives matter as a never-ending process of becoming. He postulates an order, called implicate, which gives rise to tangible order, called explicate. While the former is hidden, the latter is accessible to measurements. The philosopher Bhaskar (1978) made a similar distinction between the level of reality (plan of generative structures) and the level of actuality (the place of manifested events).

14. This implies that purposefulness does not necessitate consciousness. The quest to survive is not specifically human. Anyhow, the fact that humans are conscious, not to mention self-conscious, did not stop behaviourist psychologists and NC economists from ignoring purpose and will.

15. Lamarck is also castigated, mostly in Anglo-American circles, for another reason. He is admonished for advocating purposeful behaviour, which he unfortunately equated with 'vital force'. Since classical Greece, philosophers have been divided over whether organs were created for purpose or simply found their purpose after they had been created. Lamarck supported the former position and Darwin the latter one. Lamarck (1984, pp. 355–61) postulated that a trait develops for a purpose as a result of the organism's response to its needs by an appropriate self-modification. This explicitly recognizes the role of will, especially in vertebrate organisms which possess higher nervous systems. Thus, Lamarckianism entails two independent doctrines: the inheritance of acquired characteristics (which may happen for a multitude of reasons) and the more radical notion of will (a particular way of acquiring a characteristic). It is possible to embrace the former and reject the latter radical doctrine – as Darwin did in later editions of *Origin*.

16. A mutation is any physical or functional heritable variation. Two types of mutations are distinguished: *gene mutations* due to changes in the genetic code, and *chromosomal mutations* resulting from modification of the order of the genes (e.g. inversion of a segment).

17. This ecological insensitivity is epitomized by the celebrated Hotelling's (1931) model. Hotelling finds that an exhaustible resource should be used when its present value exceeds its current price. This ignores the needs of future generations.

18. The dwindle of resources is defined by the agency of labour. While the dispersion of heat (greater entropy) is objective, independent of human agency. Thus, the waste

generated by economic organization is conceptually different from the 'waste' generated by the entropy law. The fact that both tendencies are irreversible does not mean they are identical. Otherwise, it would be analogous to the claim that aeroplanes are subject to Newton's law of action and reaction since they rise in the air like rockets (Khalil, 1989b). At the bottom of the confusion of the two kinds of wastes is the failure to view the entropy law as devoid of purposeful agency – as Table 3.2 above shows – and its irreversibility is statistical, not theoretical in nature.

19.   Prigogine's notion of dissipative structure, along with the new science of chaos, is more suited to explain feedbacks, which give rise to the chaotic business cycle and regional polarization (Khalil, 1989c). Albeit, they are outside my concern here, since I investigate purposeful organization.

20.   This distinction between efficiency and productivity also applies to economics: the change of technique is about efficiency, since it involves the production of a greater amount of products with the same inputs; while innovation is about productivity, since it means ability to process a greater amount of inputs (Khalil, 1990c).

21.   The irreversibility of evolution has been widely and erroneously identified with the entropy law – reminiscent of Georgescu-Roegen's fumble. This is taken to extremes by Brooks and Wiley (e.g. in Weber *et al.*, 1988), whose position has come under fire, even from other devotees of the relevance of non-scarcity view of input influx (Weber *et al.*, 1988; Khalil, 1989f).

22.   Thus, Kaldor and other Post-Keynesians conclude that general equilibrium theory is untenable. Arrow (1962), though, shows that learning-by-doing, and its implications, can be accommodated in the general equilibrium framework. This is done, though, with highly contrived assumptions.

23.   This circle would accelerate and the economy would grow faster if innovative activity or productivity gain is mostly occurring in the main sector of the economy, since it has disproportionate weight. This has been empirically established by Verdoon and popularized by Kaldor (1975). It came to be called the Verdoon or Kaldor law (Thirlwall, 1983). It postulates that the rate of growth of GNP would be faster than productivity growth, if the latter is occurring in manufacturing – taken to be the main sector.

24.   This is the story of breakdown of trust (see Khalil, 1993), which is a more plausible explanation of the attenuation of effort expenditure on the part of workers than the explanation that workers simply resent the domination of capitalist bosses (e.g. Gordon *et al.*, in Cherry *et al.*, 1987). One may ask the latter approach, why workers did not question capitalist domination prior to the decline of productivity? Meanwhile, there are many explanations for the abrupt breakdown of trust. One of them is the process of senescence which relations within institutions go through. Marshall (Whitaker, in Black, 1986; cf. Penrose, 1952) and Boulding (1950, p. 34) have supported such a view.

25.   Another suggestion, the 'punctuated equilibria' hypothesis (Gould, in Milkman 1982; Eldredge, 1985a, 1986b; Stanley, 1979), attempts to explain this anomaly without challenging the orthodox dogma that genotype is exogenous. The hypothesis proposes that the unit of selection is mainly the species and higher taxa, rather than the organism. This hierarchical, non-reductionist view jibes with ND, as Buss (1987) shows. Buss views the history of life as a history of changing units of selection from molecules, cells, multicellular organisms, to higher taxa. Although Sâlthe (1985) has given systemic theoretical exposition of the hierarchical perspective, he (1987) admits that it, along with ND, fails to give an account of purposeful behaviour.

26.   Hall (1988) has shown that for bacteria to adapt to a new environment, two independent mutations are required. The chance of both occurring consecutively makes it almost an impossible event.

27. In response, others have tried to explain it away as random mutation (Partridge and Morgan, 1988; Charlesworth *et al.*, 1988; Lenski *et al.*, 1989).
28. This is explained by Grasse (1977, p. 224n) as the result of the holographic nature of 'information': 'The information in an organized being is not at all localized as in a computer. Each cell, i.e. each executant, contains the whole of it. There are as many memories as there are cells.'
29. It has been shown in the past two years that the RNA could be manipulated by variables other than the DNA. Bass and Weintraub (1988) in a serendipitous way found that a double-stranded RNA has been covalently modified by an unwinding activity, without the intervention of the DNA.
30. Waddington departs from ND in this fashion: while he upholds natural selection as the rule which weeds out unfit variations, variations do not originate only from randomness as ND postulates, but are also encouraged by environmental factors.
31. Edelman's work on cell interaction in embryos led to the discovery of cell-adhesion molecule (CAM). CAM and other molecules are complex proteins that regulate interactions among cell surfaces. Such surface interactions influence gene expression, cell shape, movement, and function.
32. The idea of a generative field is reminiscent of Noam Chomsky's (1965) linguistic theory that all languages share a deep structure.
33. In this way, NC theorists can defend marginalism and hyper-rationality without pretending realism. What matters, to Friedman's (1953) brand of positivism, is the predictiveness of assumptions, not their realism.
34. Karl Marx's concept of abstract labour is equivalent to the NC idea of fungibility of technique. For Marx, labour-time is comparable and the basis of exchange value since it has the abstract potential to undertake *any* job. That is, labour-power is a fungible commodity. Thus, job differentiation could be reversed and hence the firm lacks organizational integrity (see Khalil, 1992).
35. The same could be said in respect to advocates of punctuated equilibria, like Gould and Eldredge. They recognize the organism as an integral, imprecise unit, and even view population and higher taxation as individuals, but still cling to the Darwinian apprehension about teleology.
36. The work of Reidl (1978) also advocates teleology and fails to subscribe to organic views of organism. (I owe this note to Stanley Sâlthe.)

References

Alchian, Armen A. (1950) 'Uncertainty, Evolution, and Economic Theory', *Journal of Political Economy*, June, vol. 58, no. 3, pp. 211–21.

Alchian, Armen A. and Harold Demsetz (1972) 'Production, Information Costs, and Economic Organization', *American Economic Review*, December, vol. 62, no. 5, pp. 777–95.

Arrow, Kenneth J. (1962) 'The Economic Implications of Learning by Doing', *Review of Economic Studies*, vol. 29, pp. 155–73.

Artigiani, Robert (1987) 'Revolution and Evolution: Applying Prigogine's Dissipative Structures Model', *Journal of Social and Biological Structures*, July, vol. 10, no. 3, pp. 249–64.

Bass, Brenda L. and Harold Weintraub (1988) 'An Unwinding Activity that Covalently Modifies Its Double-stranded RNA Substrate', *Cell*, 23 December, vol. 55, no. 6, pp. 1089–98.

Battalio, Raymond C. *et al.* (1979) 'Labor Supply of Animal Workers: Towards an Experimental Analysis', *Research in Experimental Economics*, 1, pp. 231–53.

Battalio, Raymond C. *et al.* (1981a) 'Commodity-choice Behavior with Pigeons as Subjects', *Journal of Political Economy*, February, vol. 89, no. 1, pp. 67–91.

Battalio, Raymond C. *et al.* (1981b) 'Income–Leisure Tradeoffs of Animal Workers', *American Economic Review*, September, vol. 71, no. 4, pp. 621–32.

Becker, Gary S. (1976) 'Altruism, Egoism, and Genetic Fitness: Economics and Sociobiology', *Journal of Economic Literature*, September, vol. 4, no. 3, pp. 817–26.

Becker, Gary S. (1981) *A Treatise on the Family* (Cambridge, Mass.: Harvard University Press).

Bergson, Henri (1913) *Creative Evolution* (New York: Holt).

Berry, R. J. (1982) *Neo-Darwinism* (London: Edward Arnold).

Bhaskar, Roy (1978) *A Realist Theory of Science* (Hassocks, Sussex: Harvester Press Atlantic Highlands, NJ: Humanities Press).

Black, R. D. Collison (ed.) (1986) *Ideas in Economics* (Totowa, NJ: Barnes & Noble).

Blaug, Mark (1980) *The Methodology of Economics: Or How Economists Explain* (Cambridge: Cambridge University Press).

Boulding, Kenneth E. (1950) *A Reconstruction of Economics* (New York: John Wiley).

Buss, Leo W. (1987) *The Evolution of Individuality* (Princeton, NJ: Princeton University Press).

Cairns, John, Julie Overbaugh and Stephen Miller (1988) 'The Origin of Mutants', *Nature*, September, vol. 335, no. 6186, pp. 142–5.

Charlesworth, D., *et al.* (1988) 'Origin of Mutants Disputed', *Nature*, 8 December, vol. 336, no. 6199, pp. 525–8.

Cherry, Robert, *et al.* (eds) (1987) *The Imperiled Economy: Book 1* (New York: Union for Radical Political Economics).

Chomsky, Noam (1965) *Aspects of the Theory of Syntax* (Cambridge, Mass.: MIT Press).

Christensen, Paul P. (1989) 'Historical Roots for Ecological Economics – Biophysical Versus Allocative Approaches', *Ecological Economics*, February, vol. 1, no. 1, pp. 17–36.

Coase, R. H. (1937) 'The Nature of the Firm', *Economica*, November, vol. 4, pp. 386–405. (Reprinted in G. J. Stigler and K. E. Boulding (eds) *Readings in Price Theory* (Homewood, Ill.: Irwin, 1952, pp. 331–51).

Daly, Herman E. (1977) *Steady State Economics* (San Francisco: Freeman).

Darwin, Charles (1959) *The Origins of Species*, A Variorum Text, ed. by Morse Peckham (Philadelphia: University of Pennsylvania Press (1859–72).

Dawkins, Richard (1976) *The Selfish Gene* (New York: Oxford University Press).

Depew, David and Bruce Weber (eds) (1985) *Evolution at a Crossroads: The New Biology and the New Philosophy of Science* (Cambridge, Mass.: MIT Press).

Depew, David and Bruce Weber (1989) 'The Evolution of the Darwinian Research Tradition', *Systems Research*, vol. 6.

Dobzhansky, Theodosius (1982) *Genetics and the Origin of Species* (New York: Columbia University Press).

Dosi, Giovanni (1988a) 'Sources, Procedures, and Microeconomic Effects of Innovation', *Journal of Economic Literature*, September, vol. 26, no. 3, pp. 1120–71

Dosi, Giovanni, Christopher Freeman, Richard Nelson, Gerald Silverberg and Luc Soete (eds) (1988b) *Technical Change and Economic Theory* (London and New York: Pinter).

Duijn, J. J. van (1983) *The Long Wave in Economic Life* (London: Unwin Hyman).

Eatwell, John (1983) 'Theories of Value, Output and Employment', in John Eatwell and Murray Milgate (eds), *Keynes's Economics and the Theory of Value and Distribution* (London: Duckworth).

Edelman, Gerald M. (1988) *Topobiology: An Introduction to Molecular Embryology* (New York: Basic Books).

Edelman, Gerald M. (1989) 'Topobiology', *Scientific American*, May, vol. 260, no. 5, pp. 76–88.

Eldredge, Niles (1986a) *Unfinished Synthesis: Biological Hierarchies and Modern Evolutionary Thought* (New York: Oxford University Press).

Eldredge, Niles (1986b) *Time Frames: The Rethinking of Darwinian Evolution and the Theory of Punctuated Equilibria* (New York: Simon & Schuster).

Elster, Jon (1983) *Sour Grapes: Studies in the Subversion of Rationality* (Cambridge: Cambridge University Press)

Englis, Karel (1986) *An Essay on Economic Systems: A Teleological Approach*, trans. by Ivo Moravcik (Boulder, Col.: East European Monographs).

Faber, Malte, Horst Niemes and Gunter Stephen, with the cooperation of L. Freytag (1987) *Entropy, Environment and Resources: An Essay in Physico-Economics*, trans. from the German by I. Pellengahr (New York: Springer).

Fenn, John B. (1982) *Engines, Energy, and Entropy* (San Francisco: Freeman).

Ford, Donald H. (1987) *Humans as Self-Constructing Living Systems: A Developmental Perspective on Behavior and Personality* (Hillsdale, NJ: Lawrence Erlbaum).

Frank, Robert (1989) 'Frames of Reference and the Quality of Life', *American Economic Review*, May, vol. 79, no. 2, pp. 80–5.

Friedman, Milton (1953) *Essays in Positive Economics* (Chicago: University of Chicago Press).

Gadamer H. (1975) *Truth and Method* (New York: Seabury).

Galbraith, J. K. (1958) *The Affluent Society* (Boston: Houghton-Mifflin).

Gambetta, Diego (ed.) (1988) *Trust: Making and Breaking Cooperative Relations* (New York and Oxford: Blackwell).

Georgescu-Roegen, Nicholas (1971) *The Entropy Law and the Economic Process* (Cambridge, Mass.: Harvard University Press).

Ghiselin, Michael T. (1969) *The Triumph of the Darwinian Method* (Berkeley: University of California Press).

Gould, Stephen Jay (1977) *Ontogeny and Phylogeny* (Cambridge, Mass.: Harvard University Press).

Grasse, Pierre-P. (1977) *Evolution of Living Organisms: Evidence for a New Theory of Transformation* (New York: Academic Press).

Hall, Barry G. (1988) 'Adaptive Evolution that Requires Multiple Spontaneous Mutations. I: Mutations Involving an Insertion Sequence', *Genetics*, December, vol. 120, no. 4, pp. 887–97.

Heilbroner, Robert L. (1970) *Between Capitalism and Socialism: Essays in Political Economics* (New York: Vintage Books).

Heilbroner, Robert L. (1986) *The Worldly Philosophers: The Lives, Times, and Ideas of the Great Economic Thinkers* (New York: Simon & Schuster).

Hirsch, Abraham and Neil de Marchi (1986) 'Making a Case When Theory Is Unfalsifiable: Friedman's Monetary History', *Economics and Philosophy*, April, vol. 2, no. 1, pp. 1–21.

Hirshleifer, Jack (1977) 'Economics from a Biological Viewpoint', *Journal of Law and Economics*, April, vol. 20, no. 1, pp. 1–52.

Hirshleifer, Jack (1978a) 'Competition, Cooperation, and Conflict in Economics and Biology', *American Economic Review*, May, vol. 68, no. 2, pp. 238–43.

Hirshleifer, Jack (1978b) 'Natural Economy versus Political Economy', *Journal of Social and Biological Structures*, October, vol. 1, no. 4, pp. 319–37.

Hirshleifer, Jack (1982) 'Evolutionary Models in Economics and Law: Cooperation versus Conflict Strategies', *Research in Law and Economics*, vol. 4, pp. 1–60.

Ho, Mae-Wan and Peter T. Saunders (eds) (1984) *Beyond Neo-Darwinism: An Introduction to the New Evolutionary Paradigm* (London: Academic Press).

Ho, Mae-Wan and Sidney W. Fox (eds) (1988) *Evolutionary Processes and Metaphors* (New York: John Wiley).

Hollis, Martin and Edward J. Nell (1975) *Rational Economic Man: A Philosophical Critique of Neo-classical Economics* (London: Cambridge University Press).

Hotelling, Harold (1931) 'The Economics of Exhaustible Resources', *Journal of Political Economy*, April, vol. 39, no. 2.

Jansson, Ann-Mari (ed.) (1984) *Integration of Economy and Ecology: An Outlook for the Eighties*, Proceedings from the Wallenberg Symposia, Asko Laboratory (Stockholm: University of Stockholm).

Kagel, John H. *et al.* (1975) 'Experimental Studies of Consumer Demand Behavior Using Laboratory Animals', *Economic Inquiry*, March, vol. 13, no. 1, pp. 22–38.

Kagel, John H. *et al.* (1980a) 'Token Economy and Animal Models for the Experimental Analysis of Economic Behavior', in Jan Kmenta and James B. Ramsey (eds), *Evaluation of Econometric Models* (New York: Academic Press).

Kagel, John H. and *et al.* (1980b) 'Consumer Demand Theory Applied to Choice Behavior of Rats', in John E. R. Staddon (ed.), *Limits to Action: The Allocation of Individual Behavior* (New York: Academic Press).

Kaldor, Nicholas (1972) 'The Irrelevance of Equilibrium Economics', *Economic Journal*, December, vol. 82, no. 328, pp. 1237–55.

Kaldor, Nicholas (1975) 'Economic Growth and the Verdoon Law – A Comment on Mr Rowthorn's Article', *Economic Journal*, December, vol. 85, no. 4, pp. 891–6.

Khalil, Elias L. (1987a) 'Kuhn, Lakatos, and the History of Economic Thought', *International Journal of Social Economics*, vol. 14, nos. 3–5, pp. 118–31.

Khalil, Elias L. (1987b) 'Sir James Steuart vs. Professor James Buchanan: Critical Notes on Modern Public Choice', *Review of Social Economy*, October, vol. 45, no. 2, pp. 113–32.

Khalil, Elias L. (1987c) 'The Process of Capitalist Accumulation: A Review Essay of David Levine's Contribution', *Review of Radical Political Economics*, Winter, vol. 19, no. 4, pp. 76–85.

Khalil, Elias L. (1989a) 'A Review of Harvey Leibenstein's *Inside the Firm: The Inefficiencies of Hierarchy*', *Journal of Economic Issues*, March, vol. 23, no. 1, pp. 297–300.

Khalil, Elias L. (1989b) 'A Review of M. Faber, H. Niemes and G. Stephan's *Entropy, Environment and Resources: An Essay in Physico-Economics*', *Journal of Economic Literature*, June, vol. 27, no. 2, pp. 647–9.

Khalil, Elias L. (1989c) 'A Review of P. W. Anderson, K. J. Arrow and D. Pines's (eds) *The Economy as an Evolving Complex System*', *Southern Economic Journal*, July, vol. 56, no. 1, pp. 266–8.

Khalil, Elias L. (1989d) 'Principles, Rules, and Ideology', *Forum for Social Economics*, Spring/Fall, vols. 18/19, nos. 2/1, pp. 41–54.

Khalil, Elias L. (1989e) 'Adam Smith and Albert Einstein: The Aesthetic Principle of Truth', *History of Economics Society Bulletin*, Fall, vol. 11, no. 2, pp. 222–37.

Khalil, Elias L. (1989f) 'A Review of Bruce H. Weber, David J. Depew and James D. Smith's (eds) *Entropy, Information, and Evolution: New Perspectives on Physical and Biological Evolution*', *Journal of Social and Biological Structures*, October, vol. 12, no. 4, pp. 389–91.

Khalil, Elias L. (1989g) 'A Review of B. J. Hiley and F. David Peat's (eds) *Quantum Implications: Essays in Honour of David Bohm*', *Journal of Social and Biological Structures*, October, vol. 12, no. 4, pp. 391–5.

Khalil, Elias L. (1990a) 'Beyond Self-interest and Altruism: A Reconstruction of Adam Smith's Theory of Human Conduct', *Economics and Philosophy*, October, vol. 6, no. 2, pp. 255–73.

Khalil, Elias L. (1990b) 'Natural Complex vs. Natural System', *Journal of Social and Biological Structures*, February, vol. 13, no. 1, pp. 11–31. Reprinted in *General Systems Yearbook* (cap R, vol. 32).

Khalil, Elias L. (1990c) 'Entropy Law and the Exhaustion of Natural Resources: Is Nicholas Georgescu-Roegen's Paradigm Defensible?' *Ecological Economics*, May, vol. 2, no. 2, pp. 163–78.

Khalil, Elias L. (1990d) 'Rationality and Social Labor in Marx', *Critical Review*, Winter/ Spring, vol. 4, nos. 1 & 2, pp. 239–65.

Khalil, Elias L. (1991) 'Entropy Law and Nicholas Georgescu-Roegen's Paradigm: A Reply', *Ecological Economics*, July, vol. 3, no. 2, pp. 161–3.

Khalil, Elias L. (1992) 'Nature and Abstract Labor in Marx', *Social Concept*, vol. 6, no. 2.

Khalil, Elias L. (1993) 'Trust', in Geoff Hodgson, Marc Tool and Warren J. Samuels's (eds) *Handbook on Institutional and Evolutionary Economics*, vol. 2 (Cheltenham, UK: Edward Elgar), in press.

Khalil, Elias L. (n.d.) 'Admiration vs. Respect: A Reformulation of Adam Smith's Theory of Social Rank and Satisfaction', unpublished paper.

Khalil, Elias L. and Kenneth E. Boulding (eds) (1993). *Social and Natural Complexity* (to appear).

Kitcher, Philip (1985) *Vaulting Ambition: Sociobiology and the Quest for Human Nature* (Cambridge, Mass.: MIT Press).

Knight, Frank H. (1971) *Risk, Uncertainty and Profit*, intr. by George J. Stigler (Chicago: University of Chicago Press).

Kohler, Wolfgang (1969) *The Task of Gestalt Psychology* (Princeton, NJ: Princeton University Press).

Kurdas, Cigdem (1988) 'The "Whig Historian" on Adam Smith: Paul Samuelson's Canonical Classical Model", *History of Economic Society Bulletin*, Spring, vol. 10, no. 1, pp. 13–23.

Lamarck, J. B. (1984) *Zoological Philosophy: An Exposition with Regard to the Natural History of Animals*, trans. by Hugh Elliot (Chicago: University of Chicago Press).

Landa, Janet T. and Anthony Wallis (1988) 'Socio-economic Organization of Honeybee Colonies: A Transaction–Cost Approach', *Journal of Social and Biological Structures*, July, vol. 11, no. 3, pp. 353–63.

Langlois, Richard N. (ed.) (1986) *Economics as a Process: Essays in The New Institutional Economics* (Cambridge: Cambridge University Press).

Latsis, S. J. (ed.) (1976) *Method and Appraisal in Economics* (Cambridge: Cambridge University Press).

Leibenstein, Harvey J. (1987) *Inside the Firm: The Inefficiencies of Hierarchy* (Cambridge, Mass.: Harvard University Press).

Lenski, Richard *et al.* (1989) 'Another Alternative to Directed Mutation', *Nature*, 12 January, vol. 337, no. 6203, pp. 123–4.

Levine, David P. (1981) *Economic Theory*, vol. 2: *The System of Economic Relations as a Whole* (London: Routledge & Kegan Paul).

Levine, David P. (1988) *Needs, Rights and the Market* (Boulder and London: Lynne Rienner).

Levins, Richard (1967) *Evolution in Changing Environments* (Princeton, NJ: Princeton University Press).

Lewontin, Richard C. (1984) 'Adaptation', in Elliot Sober (ed.), *Conceptual Issues in Evolutionary Biology: An Anthology* (Cambridge, Mass.: MIT Press), pp. 235–51.

Lotka, Alfred J. (1925) *Elements of Physical Biology* (Baltimore: Williams & Wilkins).

Lotka, Alfred J. (1945) 'The Law of Evolution as a Maximal Principle', *Human Biology*, p. 17.

MacArthur, Robert H. (1972) *Geographical Ecology* (New York: Harper & Row).

Marx, Jean L. (1988) 'Evolution Link to Development Explored', *Science*, 13 May, 1988, vol. 240, no. 4854, pp. 880–2.

Masters, Roger D. (1983) 'The Biological Nature of the State', *World Politics*, vol. 25, pp. 161–93.

Masters, Roger D. (1989) *The Nature of Politics* (New Haven, Conn.: Yale University Press).

Maurice, Marc Francois Sellier and Jean-Jacques Silvestre (1986) *The Social Foundations of Industrial Power: A Comparison of France and Germany*, trans. by Arthur Goldhammer (Cambridge, Mass.: MIT Press).

Mayr, Ernst (1982) *Systematics and the Origin of Species* (New York: Columbia University Press).

Milkman, R. (ed.) (1982) *Perspectives of Evolution* (Sunderland, Mass.: Sinaver Associations).

Mises, Ludwig von (1966) *Human Action: A Treatise on Economics* (Chicago: Contemporary Books).

Monod, Jacques (1972) *Chance and Necessity* (New York: Knopf).

Moorhead, P. S. and M. M. Kaplan (eds) (1987) *Mathematical Challenges of Neo-Darwinian Interpretation of Evolution* (Philadelphia: Wistar Institute Press).

Nell, Edward (1972) 'Economics: The Revival of Political Economy', Robin Blackburn (ed.), *Ideology in Social Science: Readings in Critical Social Theory* (Isle of Man, UK: Fontana), pp. 76–95.

Nell, Edward (1980) (ed.) *Growth, Profits, and Property* (Cambridge: Cambridge University Press).

Nell, Edward (1988) *Prosperity and Public Spending: Transformational Growth and the Role of Government* (London: Unwin Hyman).

Nell, Edward (1992) *Transformational Growth and Effective Demand: Economics After the Capital Critique* (London: Macmillan, and New York: New York University Press).

Nelson, Richard R. and Sidney G. Winter (1982) *An Evolutionary Theory of Economic Change* (Cambridge, Mass.: Harvard University Press).

Noda, H. (1982) 'Probability of Life, Rareness of Realization in Evolution', *Journal of Theoretical Biology*, vol. 95, pp. 145–50.

O'Driscoll, Gerald P. and Mario J. Rizzo (1985) *The Economics of Time and Ignorance* (Oxford: Blackwell).

Odum, Howard T. (1971) *Environment, Power, and Society* (New York: Wiley-Interscience).

Partridge, Linda and Michael J. Morgan (1988) 'Is Bacterial Evolution Random or Selective?' *Nature*, 3 November, vol. 336, no. 6194, p. 22.

Pasinetti, Luigi L. (1966) 'Changes in the Rate of Profit and Switches of Techniques', *Quarterly Journal of Economics*, November, vol. 80, no. 4, pp. 503–17.

Penrose, E. T. (1952) 'Biological Analogies in the Theory of the Firm', *American Economic Review*, December, vol. 42, no. 5, pp. 804–19.

Perrings, Charles (1987) *Economy and Environment: A Theoretical Essay on the Interdependence of Economic and Environmental Systems* (Cambridge: Cambridge University Press).

Polanyi, Michael (1958) *Personal Knowledge: Towards a Post-Critical Philosophy* (New York: Harper & Row).

Pollard, Jeffrey W. (ed.) (1984) *Evolutionary Theory: Paths into the Future* (New York: John Wiley).

Prigogine, Ilya (1980) *From Being into Becoming* (San Francisco: Freeman).

Proops, John L. R. (1989) 'Ecological Economics: Rationale and Problem Areas', *Ecological Economics*, February, vol. 1, no. 1, pp. 59–76.

Ptashne, Mark (1989) 'How Gene Activators Work', *Scientific American*, January, vol. 260, no. 1, pp. 40–7.

Queller, David C., *et al.* (1988) 'Genetic Relatedness in Colonies of Tropical Wasps with Multiple Queens', *Science*, 25 November, vol. 242, no. 4882, pp. 1155–7.

Rapport, David J. and James E. Turner (1977) 'Economic Models in Ecology', *Science*, 28 January, vol. 195, no. 4276, pp. 367–73.

Reidl, Ruppert (1978) *Order in Living Organisms: A System Analysis of Evolution* (New York: John Wiley).

Ricklefs, Robert E. (1979) *Ecology* (New York: Chiron Press).

Robbins, Lionel (1932) *An Essay on the Nature and Significance of Economic Science* (London: Macmillan).

Robinson, Joan (1953) 'The Production Function and the Theory of Capital', *Review of Economic Studies*, vol. 21, pp. 81–106.

Robinson, Joan (1970) 'Capital Theory Up to Date', *Canadian Journal of Economics*, vol. 3, pp. 309–17. (Reprinted in Jesse G. Schwartz and E. K. Hunt (eds), *A Critique of Economic Theory: Selected Readings* (Harmondsworth, Middlesex: Penguin, 1972) pp. 233–44).

Robinson, Joan (1979) 'History Versus Equilibrium', in *Collected Economic Papers*, vol. 5 (Oxford: Oxford University Press).

Rosen, Robert (1985a) 'Organisms as Causal Systems which are not Mechanisms: An Essay into the Nature of Complexity', in Robert Rosen (ed.) *Theoretical Biology and Complexity: Three Essays on the Natural Philosophy of Complex Systems* (Orlando, Flor.: Academic Press).

Rosen, Robert (1985b) *Anticipatory Systems* (Oxford: Pergamon Press).

Rosen, Robert (1987) 'Some Epistemological Issues in Physics and Biology', in Hiley, B. J. and F. David Peat (eds) *Quantum Implications: Essays in Honour of David Bohm* (London and New York: Routledge & Kegan Paul), pp. 314–27.

Rosenberg, Nathan (1976) *Perspectives in Technology* (Cambridge: Cambridge University Press).

Rosenberg, Nathan (1982) *Inside the Black Box* (Cambridge: Cambridge University Press).

Russell, James (1978) *The Acquisition of Knowledge* (New York: St Martin's Press).

Sâlthe, Stanley N. (1985) *Evolving Hierarchical Systems* (New York: Columbia University Press).

Sâlthe, Stanley N. (1987) 'On the Trail of the Unknown in Biology', *The Journal of Heredity*, May/June, vol. 78, no. 3, pp. 213–14. (A book review of Gustafson, Perry J., et al. (eds) *Genetics, Development, and Evolution* (New York: Plenum Press, 1986).

Schoffeniels, E. (1976) *Anti-Chance* (New York: Pergamon).

Schubert, Glendon (1989) *Evolutionary Politics* (Carbondale: Southern Illinois University Press).

Schumpeter, Joseph (1949) *The Theory of Economic Development* (Cambridge, Mass.: Harvard University Press).

Schwartz, Barry (1986) *The Battle for Human Nature* (New York: W.W. Norton).

Shackle, G. L. S. (1970) *Expectations, Enterprise and Profit* (London: Allen & Unwin).

Sheldrake, Rupert (1988) *The Presence of the Past: Morphic Resonance and Habits of Nature* (New York: Times Books (Random House)).

Simon, Herbert A. (1978) 'Rationality as Process and as Product of Thought', *American Economic Review*, May, vol. 68, no. 2, pp. 1–16.

Simpson, George Gaylord (1984) *Tempo and Mode in Evolution* (New York: Columbia University Press).

Smith, Adam (1976a) *The Theory of Moral Sentiments*, ed. by D. D. Raphael and A. L. Macfie (Oxford: Clarendon Press).

Smith, Adam (1976b) *An Inquiry into the Nature and Causes of the Wealth of Nations*, in 2 volumes, general eds R. H. Campbell and A. S. Skinner, text ed. W. B. Todd (Oxford: Clarendon Press).

Smith, Adam (1980) *Essays on Philosophical Subjects*, gen. eds D. D. Raphael and A. S. Skinner, eds W. P. D. Wightman, J. C. Bryce, and I. S. Ross (Oxford: Clarendon Press).

Stanley, Steven M. (1979) *Macroevolution: Pattern and Process* (San Francisco: Freeman).

Steele, E. J. (1979) *Somatic Selection and Adaptive Evolution: On the Inheritance of Acquired Characters* (Chicago: University of Chicago Press).

Steele, E. J. and J. W. Pollard (1987) 'Hypothesis: Somatic Hypermutation by Gene Conversion via the Error Prone DNA → RNA → DNA Information Loop", *Molecular Immunology*, June, vol. 24, no. 6, pp. 667–73.

Stigler, George J. and Gary S. Becker (1977) '*De Gustibus Non Est Disputandum*', *American Economic Review*, March, vol. no. 67, no. 1, pp. 76–90.

Teilhard de Chardin, Pierre (1959) *The Phenomenon of Man*, trans. by B. Wall (New York: Harper & Row).

Thirlwall, A. P. (1983) 'A Plain Man's Guide to Kaldor's Growth Laws', *Journal of Post Keynesian Economics*, Spring, vol. 5, no. 3, pp. 345–59.

Thompson, D'Arcy Wentworth (1961) *On Growth and Form*, ed. by J. T. Bonner. (Cambridge: Cambridge University Press).

Ulanowicz, Robert E. (1986) *Growth and Development: A Phenomenological Perspective* (New York: Springer Verlag).

Ursprung, Heinrich W. (1988) 'Evolution and the Economic Approach to Human Behavior', *Journal of Social and Biological Structures*, April, vol. 11, no. 2, pp. 257–79.

Van Valen, L. (1973) 'A New Evolutionary Law', *Evolutionary Theory*, vol. 1, pp. 1–30.

Varela, F. (1979) *Principles of Biological Autonomy* (New York: Kluwer).

Veblen, Thorstein (1898) 'Why is Economics not an Evolutionary Science?', *Quarterly Journal of Economics*, July, vol. 12, no. 3, pp. 373–97.

Waddington, C. H. (1957) *The Strategy of the Genes* (London: Unwin Hyman).

Walsh, Vivian and Harvey Gram (1980) *Classical and Neoclassical Theories of General Equilibrium: Historical Origins and Mathematical Structure* (New York: Oxford University Press).

Weber, Bruce H., David J. Depew, and James D. Smith (eds) (1988) *Entropy, Information, and Evolution: New Perspectives on Physical and Biological Evolution* (Cambridge, Mass.: MIT Press).

Webster, G. C. and B. C. Goodwin (1982) 'The Origin of Species: A Structuralist Approach', *Journal of Social and Biological Structures*, January, vol. 5, no. 1, pp. 15–47.

Wicken, Jeffrey S. (1986) 'Evolutionary Self-Organization and Entropic Dissipation in Biological and Socioeconomic Systems', *Journal of Social and Biological Structures*, July, vol. 9, no. 3, pp. 261–73.

Wicken, Jeffrey S. (1987) *Evolution, Thermodynamics, and Information: Extending the Darwinian Program* (New York: Oxford University Press).

Williamson, Oliver E. (1985) *The Economic Institutions of Capitalism: Firms, Markets, Relational Contracting* (New York: Free Press).

Wilson, Edward O. (1975) *Sociobiology: The New Synthesis* (Cambridge, Mass.: Harvard University Press).

Wright, Robert (1988) *Three Scientists and their Gods: Looking for Meaning in an Age of Information* (New York: Times Books).

Young, Allyn A. (1928) 'Increasing Returns and Economic Progress', *Economic Journal*, December, vol. 38, no. 152, pp. 527–42.

Part II
Technology and Stages
of History

David Howell, 'Stages of Technical Advance: Industrial Segmentation and Employment'

Early in his career, Heilbroner sketched an analysis of stages of capitalist development, based on fundamental changes in the nature of technology. Although only sketched, these ideas have proved immensely influential, stimulating economic historians and economists both. He returned repeatedly to the theme of stages in development, elaborating and reworking the schema, which reached full flower in the *Nature and Logic of Capitalism*, where, at one point, he presents a 'Historical Schema of the Logic of Capitalist Development'. Howell's chapter focuses on the later periods of Heilbroner's scheme, and explores the issues behind the categories listed as 'technology', 'labour process' and 'organization of capitals'. In particular, he relates these developments to the pressures of competition, while demonstrating how uneven the process is, and how technologies, correctly regarded as belonging to the same stage, can take on different forms in different industries.

4 Stages of Technical Advance, Industrial Segmentation and Employment: Computer-based Automation in Historical Perspective

David R. Howell

At the height of a national debate over automation almost three decades ago, Robert Heilbroner (1962) reviewed some 200 years of debate over the economic and social impact of industrial technology. With his usual ability to identify the most important questions. Heilbroner found in this literature little examination of what he termed their 'historical aspect' and stressed the need to investigate 'whether there is visible a progressive change in the employment-granting possibilities of successive stages of technical advance' (ibid., p. 23). Heilbroner defined these stages as shifts in the pattern of economic development, from agriculture to manufacturing and from the latter to services; he was particularly concerned about the implications of labour-saving technological advances in the service sectors of a service economy (1966, pp. 11–15).

Although the evidence suggests that there is good reason to be concerned over the quality of the jobs being generated in many service sectors, rapid employment growth in these industries in recent years has greatly reduced fears that technological change in a service economy will result in inadequate job growth. But the larger issue that Heilbroner raised – the changing nature of the employment effects of technological change over stages of advance – is one that remains relatively unexplored. This chapter will take up this question for the manufacturing sector, a set of industries that are commonly viewed to lie at the heart of capitalist development.

In brief, the argument of the chapter is that over the last century and a half, the development of production technology can be understood to have taken place in stages, with each stage or technological regime marking a qualitative change in the *scale* (size and specialization), *continuity* (rate of material processing), and *flexibility* (responsiveness to changes in product demand) of the production process. In the transition from one regime to another the production process in most manufacturing industries is transformed by new underlying technologies related to, say, the power source (water, steam, petrol, electricity) or the control mechanism (mechanical, electro-mechanical, microprocessor) used in production. Following Christopher Freeman (1987, pp. 56–7), we can define new technological

75

regimes as 'far reaching and pervasive changes in technology, affecting many (or even all) branches of the economy, as well as giving rise to entirely new sectors . . . Such changes in paradigm make possible a "quantum leap" in potential productivity, which, however, is at first realized in a few leading sectors'. This focus on differences among sectors within technological regimes falls squarely within the Schumpeterian tradition.

With the mechanization of production in the early nineteenth century, three technological regimes can be identified – simple mechanization, based upon mechanical controls and water and steam power; science-based mechanization, based upon fundamental advances in basic science, which provided the technical foundations for increasing the scale and continuity of many processes (e.g. steel, auto, oil refining) and the flexibility of many others (e.g. small batch metalworking firms); and computer-based mechanization, which is founded upon advances in information technologies and microprocessor-based controls and provides the technical capability to increase the flexibility of large-scale processes and the continuity (and flexibility) of operations using smaller-scale, batch methods.

This contrasts sharply with the model put forth by Piore and Sabel (1984), which defines each regime by the near total dominance of *either* flexible craft-type processes or rigid mass production processes, and sees the transition from one to the other as the result not primarily of the *competitive pressures* faced by individual firms to increase efficiency (reduce costs and increase the quality and variety of their products), but rather by the power, and therefore ultimately by the *political choices*, of competing interests in society.

An important consequence of the approach taken here is the emphasis it places on the unevenness of technological development among industries over stages of technical advance. The nature of the transformation varies from one industry to another, depending largely on the kind of materials that are processed, the complexity of the product, and the size and stability of demand. The simple mechanization stage distinguished what I will call the *mechanical* industries (dominated by metalworking) from the *traditional* segment of industries, which process soft materials like cloth, leather and wood. With the transition to science-based mechanization at the end of the nineteenth century, both sets of industries were able to increase flexibility and continuity of production through easier, less costly changes in machine layout and set-up. But in addition, electrification and advances in chemical processes led to the appearance of a third segment of *process* industries, which used inflexible, continuous process methods to produce large volumes of standardized products. The significance of this framework for the debate over the employment effects of technical advances is that they should be viewed as historically unique: the employment effects of technical change are likely to be substantially different in each industry segment within each technological regime.

If we are currently in the midst of a transition to a new technological regime, this framework helps put into perspective Heilbroner's observations on the employment effects of technological change in manufacturing. For example, from the vantage point of the early 1960s the demand for manufactured products seemed to Heilbroner 'elastic enough to provide a kind of stable layer of employment'; further, it was not at all obvious to him that 'modern automation machinery is more labour displacing in the factory than old-fashioned machinery' (1962, pp. 11–12). Two and a half decades later we are presented with a far less optimistic vision of the effects of new technologies: 'a robotic mode of production now seems technically imaginable . . . a partially robotized world is already near enough to raise disturbing questions with respect to the possibilities for employment' (1988, p. 101). These contrasting assessments can easily be reconciled within a stage of advance framework since the improvements in electromechanical automation in the late 1950s and the programmable automation that begins to transform industry in the 1980s reflect, I will argue, two distinct stages of technical development with different implications for the level and skill composition of production worker employment.[1]

The first section considers some issues raised by Piore and Sabel's (1984) influential study of the historical development of production technology. Section 4.2 outlines briefly the competitive advantages of adopting new process technologies. Section 4.3 provides an overview of the three stages of advance in the US and the implications each regime has had for industry segmentation and employment. The first part of section 4.4 outlines some recent employment trends and suggests that the employment effects of the transition to a new computer-based regime that begin to appear in the 1980s are substantially different from those that followed the adoption of mass production methods in the process industries at the turn of the century. The second part of this section considers some lessons that recent Japanese use of industrial robots may have for future employment patterns among production workers.

4.1 SOCIAL CONFLICT AND TECHNOLOGICAL DEVELOPMENT

Piore and Sabel (1984, p. 5) have advanced what might be termed a political, or social conflict, theory of the long-run course of technological development. According to the authors, the divergent interests of 'industrialists, workers, politicians, and intellectuals' lead to social conflicts whose outcomes then determine the course of technological development. Industrial societies must choose one of two 'models' of development: one relies upon flexible craft methods while the other consists of rigid mass production processes. The choice between these alternatives is ultimately determined by the distribution of power in society, and the transition from one technological paradigm to another marks an 'industrial divide'.[2]

The shift from craft to mass manufacturing at the end of the last century marks the one great industrial divide since the Industrial Revolution. This transformation was one in which craft skills, general purpose machinery, and flexible production processes '(gave) way, in almost all sectors of manufacturing, to corporations based on mass manufacturing' (ibid., pp. 5–6). At the source of this divide was the social and political power of certain individuals and corporations; had these actors not chosen aggressively to pursue strategies designed to stabilize demand at the firm, industry and national levels, and had they not dominated the development of the legal regulatory framework governing industries (and industrial relations), this first industrial divide might never have taken place. Craft production, they argue, might well have 'survived as a technologically dynamic, productive form' (ibid., p. 49). The critical policy question that arises out of this view is whether the necessary forces can be mobilized to get firms to revert from the mass manufacturing model to craft forms of production, a development that Piore and Sabel would obviously support.[3]

This chapter departs from the Piore and Sabel view in two important ways. First, technological regimes are defined here by the kinds of technologies that transform production, not by economy-wide shifts between mass and craft models of development. By taking the latter approach, Piore and Sabel are committed to the position that in a new regime, most sectors are impacted in similar ways. Indeed, that is how they portray the 'first industrial divide'. It was, according to the authors, that 'brief moment' at the turn of the last century (1870–1913) when craft production was replaced by mass production methods 'in almost all' manufacturing sectors.[4] This close identification of twentieth-century manufacturing with mass production, and particularly with the motor car industry, has become commonplace. But if the essential features of mass production are the large-scale production of standardized products with special purpose machinery and specialized jobs, then such a complete transformation of the economy never actually took place. Piore and Sabel are clearly aware of this – they note that in recent years about 70 per cent of all the production in the metalworking sectors continues to be carried out with small batch methods with general machinery (ibid., p. 26). Similarly, Ayres and Miller (1983, p. 13) estimate that mass produced durable goods made up only about 26 per cent of total manufacturing value added in 1977. It is worth noting in this regard that it is widely accepted among economic historians that the introduction of electrical power and electro-mechanical controls in the early decades of this century actually increased the flexibility of production in much of the manufacturing sector (see below).

This suggests that 'mass production' is not an adequate characterization of the technological regime that begins in the late 19th century. While the growth of consumer goods, factory size, corporations and industrial unions were all linked closely to mass production, and the impact of these developments on American social life cannot be overstated, mass production methods per se never dominated manufacturing operations in the US, whether measured by output or employment. Perhaps 'mass production' is a good characterization of the industrial culture of the period, but it does not provide a good description of the prevailing production technology in manufacturing – mass production methods have simply never characterized most manufacturing operations in the US, the 'home' of mass production. The point here is that the characteristic features of each regime may affect some industries quite differently from others.

Second, this paper accepts the more traditional view criticized by Piore and Sabel that, given the character of product demand, revolutionary methods of production are adopted for the economic advantages (or efficiency) they offer – lower unit costs, improved product quality, or greater ability to meet changing market demands. The 'resources available to its champions' may help determine the timing of the transition and its particular institutional character, but not the *sequence* of regimes. Powerful individuals and institutions can help facilitate the transformation, but they do not in any meaningful sense 'choose' the regime.

This is not to say that historical experience and institutional characteristics are unimportant – on the contrary. Particularly when world trade is costly, the size and character of demand in a single country is crucial for determining the ultimate profitability of adopting an entirely new production technology, and population growth and the distribution of income appear to be the essential determinants of this demand (Murphy, Shleifer and Vishny, 1989, pp. 537–8). Perhaps the best example of the importance of these underlying structural factors comes from the catalogue of the 1851 London Crystal Palace exhibition:

> The absence in the United States of those vast accumulations of wealth which favor the expenditure of large sums on articles of mere luxury, and the general distribution of the means of procuring the more substantial conveniences of life, impart to the productions of American industry a character distinct from that of many other countries. (Cited in Murphy, Schleifer and Vishny, 1989, p. 538)

It seems more reasonable to attribute the uniqueness of the size and structure of demand in the US to geographic and long-run historical and political differences than to the consequences of contemporary (late nineteenth century) power struggles. Given the character of market demand in the US, it was much more *economically efficient* for US firms than, say, English firms, to develop and adopt the newly available methods of large scale, continuous processing and assembly.

An adequate understanding of the development of production technology and its effects on employment since the first industrial revolution requires a recognition of the differential long-run impact of each new technological regime on industrial sectors – the differences in effects seem quite substantial and systematic. The next section briefly considers the advantages of scale, continuity and flexibility that new technologies may offer to firms aiming to lower unit costs in any historical period. This will help provide a framework for the historical analysis that appears in section 4.3.

4.2   COMPETITIVE ADVANTAGE AND TECHNICAL ADVANCE: SCALE, CONTINUITY AND FLEXIBILITY

Where technically and socially feasible, even firms in imperfectly competitive markets will tend to substitute less costly for more costly factors (capital for labour, unskilled labour for skilled labour) where technically and socially feasible. Somewhat less obviously, firms will also take advantage of new technologies to increase the scale, continuity and flexibility of the production process in order to pursue either a low cost strategy, a product differentiation strategy, or some combination of the two, for gaining competitive advantage.

Much of the recent literature on competitiveness has contended that US firms must 'choose' between a strategy of rigid, high volume processes for the production of standardized goods and a strategy of flexible, low volume methods for differentiated, high quality goods. But the reality is, and has always been, that competitive pressures often leave little real 'choice'. In a given technological regime, flexible unit or small batch processes are clearly most appropriate for some products and sectors, and more rigid capital-intensive continuous flow processes are most appropriate for others. The historical record suggests that costs, quality and responsiveness are objectives for all competitive producers, but the priority accorded to each varies by sector and regime. Indeed, even the specialized rigidity of the early automobile assembly lines had to give way within just two decades to a system of production that could differentiate the product.[5] The relative priority placed on flexibility in production has depended upon such 'structural' factors as the physical nature of the product, the qualities demanded by consumers, and above all by the state of development of industrial technology. In fact, since the mid nineteenth century many new technologies (and organization structures) have been adopted for the explicit purpose of becoming more competitive on all three fronts. The effective use of such pivotal technologies as electricity and microprocessors have shown the potential to lower unit cost and increase both quality and responsiveness for producers in a wide variety of industrial sectors.

Why do producers aim to increase the scale, continuity and flexibility of production? If economies of scale can be realized, producers will increase the size and specialization (machines and jobs) of the process in order to reduce unit costs. With the use of electro-mechanically controlled technologies, large-scale processes tended to require much greater capital-intensity and process rigidity. With computer-based mechanization, however, the benefits of large-scale operations may be achieved without necessarily losing flexibility: large batches may still pay, but the configuration of machinery and workers may now easily be changed.

A more continuous process has the great advantage of raising the rate of materials throughput – the rate at which materials are processed per unit of time. As David Landes (1972, p. 303) has written. 'The basic principle of industrial organization is smooth and direct work flow from start to finish of the manufacturing process; detours, returns and halts are to be avoided as much as possible.' As the rate of throughput increases, the inventory, labour and capital requirements per unit of output will tend to fall.

High rates of throughput require both the integration of various stages of production and the avoidance of work stoppages. Since these goals require careful production scheduling and resource planning, they require predictability – and consequently control – over production. At least since the 1840s, mechanization has served two critical functions in this regard – to reduce the use of direct labour and to limit the control of labour over the pace of work. The following observation in a recent industry trade journal emphasizes the close links between continuity, control and the use of direct labour: 'Reliable, unmanned machining systems . . . can substantially boost machine tool throughput, assure strict adherence to hard-to-meet quality control standards, minimize in-process inventories, and guarantee production rates by eliminating the last major machining variable (the operator)' (Larsen, 1979, p. 64). Thus, while mechanization can make possible higher *potential* rates of throughput, it has also served to help *realize* those rates by limiting the direct use of labour and by controlling the pace and quality of worker effort.

Finally, flexibility, defined as the ability to produce different products in different lot sizes without costly machine set-ups and layout reconfigurations, allows producers to match production capabilities to changes in consumer demand. This can reduce the risk of a narrow market focus and both raise and stabilize capacity utilization. As the next section contends, while the introduction of electro-mechanical technologies in the science-based mechanization stage increased the rigidity of some processes, these technologies increased the flexibility of others. On the other hand, computer-based mechanization has the potential to increase the flexibility of almost all production operations.

4.3 STAGES OF ADVANCE AND SEGMENTATION IN THE US

Over a century ago, Marx identified three 'epochs' of capitalist development: handicraft production, manufacturing production (large-size and systematic division of labour), and modern industry (mechanized production). With the hindsight of the last century, modern industry itself can be viewed as having progressed through a three-stage historical sequence. In the first, *simple mechanization*, advances in factory production techniques were characterized by the systematic application of mechanical and engineering principles (in contrast to the earlier reliance upon of craft workers for technical change) and the growing use of steam-powered machinery in production. By the end of the nineteenth century, the application of advances in the natural sciences (chemistry and physics) ushered in a stage of *science-based mechanization* in which batch operations could be made more continuous and flexible through electrification, and both high throughput assembly (guns, sewing machines, and cars) and continuous flow (steel, petroleum refining and chemicals) operations became technically possible for the first time. Recent advances in the computer sciences have led to micro-processor-based mechanization in the 1970s and 1980s which, like the earlier transition, has the potential to radically alter the production processes of many manufacturing industries, reducing plant size in the process industries and in-creasing flexibility, continuity and control in both mechanical and process segments. The future of manufacturing will take place in this regime of *computer-based mechanization*.

Simple Mechanization

The development of mechanical sciences in the eighteenth century set the stage for the application of steam power to production, which had the effect of greatly expanding factory production and increasing mechanization within the factory. In the United States, the building of canals in the 1820s and 1830s made large supplies of cheap coal accessible to producers for the first time. It was, con-sequently, only in the 1840s that the engineering advances of the preceding century could be widely applied to manufacturing processes. The availability of this critical input determined the timing of the transition to simple mechanization, for which Chandler (1977, pp. 75–7) provides the classic summary:

> The primary constraint on the spread of the factory in the U.S. appears to have been technological; the demand for such volume production existed . . . Coal not only provided the heat so essential for large scale production in foundries and furnace industries and also in the refining and distilling trades, but it also provided an inexpensive and efficient fuel for generating steam power. Cheap coal permitted the building of large steam-driven factories in commercial centers close to markets and existing pools of labor . . . Coal, then, provided the source of energy that made it possible for the factory to replace the artisans, the small mill owners, and putting out system as the basic unit of production in many American industries.

Previously, the use of machinery had been for the most part limited to locations with appropriate water sources – rivers with sufficiently high, stable and strong water flows. With the steam engine came a rapid expansion of factories, their location in urban areas, and the potential for the increasing mechanization of production over time (Landes, 1972, p. 99). Particularly important in this respect was that steam power made possible advances in iron and steel production, which in turn facilitated the replacement of wood with metal parts, providing the tech-nical basis for the take-off of the machine tool industry. The consequence of this dynamic was the production of machines by machines, which dramatically in-creased the productivity of the capital goods sectors and, consequently, the potential for technical change in production. For the first time there were now vast opportunities for capital-embodied technical change, an essential ingredient in industrial growth and development to the present day.

The transformation from handicraft to simple mechanization had the effect of increasing the continuity of and control over production – mechanization increased productivity in part by tying the pace of work to the machine. But in contrast to the transitions to science-based and computer-based methods of production, simple mechanization in the nineteenth century appears to have *reduced* production flexibility. Loss of flexibility was in part simply the result of the increase in the share of fixed costs that followed mechanization. But it was also due to the character of the mechanization: machine layout and the movement of materials were dependent upon an inflexible power transmission apparatus. As Hirschhorn (1986, p. 10) points out, 'Steam power was transmitted vertically through the factory building from the basement to the top floor: primary belting transferred motion to secondary shafts, which in turn transmitted power via pulleys to individual machines.' Once in place, this layout was relatively fixed; product innovation that meant a new layout and new machines required the dismantling of a large and complicated mechanical apparatus.

With the increasing importance of steam-powered machinery, the organization of the workplace shifted from one based on the logic of the division of labour among workers towards one determined by the logic of machine layout. As Cooper (quoted by Clark, 1985, p. 35) has put it:

> The grouping and organisation of detailed labour skills which is the guiding principle of the manufacturing system, is replaced by the grouping and organisation of machines. The technical determinants of the process are no longer the possibilities offered by the division of labour; they are the possibilities of increasing the specialisation and perfection of the machine with its tools. This latter process . . . is subject to far less stringent limitation than was the perfection of the 'instruments of labour' under the manufacturing system – where the physical and mental capabilities of the craftsman set strict limits to the kind of technical advance that can be achieved.

The expansion and mechanization that began to take off in the 1840s had momentous implications for the workplace long before the end of the century. With the 1840s the so-called American System of Manufactures – the use of special purpose machines to produce large volumes of standardized goods with interchangeable parts – took hold in a wide variety of mechanical industries, including guns, watches and clocks, locks, sewing machines, agricultural implements and business machinery. The development of the machine tool industry was critical to the transformation of these industries and led, in the middle decades of this century, to the replacement of hand needles, handlooms and handtools by sewing machines, powerlooms and machine tools. For instance, Rosenberg (1977, p. 20) reports that some 100 000 Lincoln millers, a single variety of milling machine, were built between 1855 and 1880. According to Hounshell (1981, p. 131), in the years prior to 1854 the Wheeler & Wilson Manufacturing Co. had produced only about 300 sewing machines but in 1862 its

Bridgeport factory alone produced 30 000. Just ten years later this factory was producing over 174 000. This kind of growth could not have occurred without substantial changes in the set of tasks and the skills required in production.

New techniques began to transform the non-mechanical industries as well. Printing was transformed by the Adams and Napier presses in the 1840s. In the shoe industry, Ware (1964, p. 47) notes that 'In 1862 the Mckay Machine completely revolutionized the work of the journeymen as the stitching machine [in the early 1850s] had done that of the binders." According to Thompson (1989), three-quarters of total output in the shoe industry was machine bottomed as early as 1873 and the physical productivity of workers (pairs of shoes per worker) almost doubled between 1855 and 1870.

By the 1870s then, it seems safe to say that for a large part of manufacturing – textiles, shoes and the mechanical industries – more than simple proletarianization was taking place; mechanization was transforming the labour process in ways that set the stage for the transition to even larger-scale, mass production methods several decades later.[6] The mechanization also had the effect of distinguishing manufacturing industries into two segments based on the production technology that was employed. While virtually all manufacturing plants saw some mechanization, the use of heavy and complex machinery distinguished the *mechanical* industries, which produced metal parts, tools and machines, from the *traditional* handicraft industries, which produced goods from the fabrication and assembly of easily worked, agricultural and forestry products like cotton, wool, meat, leather and wood.[7]

Science-based Mechanization

With the development of chemistry and physics in the nineteenth century, principles of the natural sciences were for the first time systematically incorporated into the design of plant and machinery. At the end of this century, these advances set the stage for the development of new materials (refined oil), products (the internal combustion engine) and power sources (electricity) that made it technically possible to adopt large-scale, continuous flow methods of production. If the defining characteristic of automation is 'the rationalization of the entire production process . . . based on the conception of work as a continuous flow' (Sultan and Prasow, 1964, pp. 12, 14), there occurred at this time a dramatic increase in the automation of those processing and metalworking industries that could standardize their products – from oil refining and meatpacking to bicycle and motor car assembly.

The ability to achieve high throughout operations was determined by the physical properties of the product (e.g. fluidity and simplicity of assembly) and the size, stability and certainty (product life) of market demand (see Berger and Piore, 1981, chapter 3). Examples of early mass production industries include tobacco, flour, beverages, sugar, oil refining, steel, meatpacking, sewing machines and bicycles and automobiles. In these industries, electrification facilitated a rationalization of production that was a precondition for improving continuity. But the form that this rationalization took was towards inflexible methods because the prevailing technological possibilities and character of consumer demand put a premium on achieving low unit costs through large-scale production processes.[8]

This rationalization also enabled management to increase control over the pace and quality of work by fragmenting jobs, reducing and homogenizing skill requirements, and by adjusting the speed of the line. The effect of this rationalization on the skill mix of the workforce was often substantial. For example, at Ford Motor Company, skilled workers decreased from 31.8 per cent of total production worker employment in 1910 to 21.6 per cent in 1917; over this same period, semi-skilled operatives increased from 29.5 to 62 per cent and unskilled labourers declined from 38.6 to 16.4 per cent (Gordon, Edwards and Reich, 1982, p. 133). The same authors cite research that shows an increase of male semi-skilled operatives and labourers from 38.6 per cent of male manufacturing employment to 55 per cent between 1870 and 1930 (ibid., p. 149).

Probably no less important for the workplace was the effect of the substitution of electricity for mechanical means of transferring power (cranks, gears and pullies) for the low-volume producers of non-standardized products. The use of electrical wires eliminated the major constraint to changes in machine layout; the flow of production could now be redirected to fit the product (Landes, 1972, p. 288; Rosenberg and Birdzell, 1986, pp. 214–15). Machine characteristics were also affected. 'The substitution of electrical for mechanical force in machine design created increasingly flexible and increasingly general-purpose machines' (Hirschhorn, 1986, p. 19). The combination of flexibility in layout and the development of general-purpose machines allowed small firms to become multi product producers whose quicker responses reduced the risk they faced from shifts in demand.

Thus, while achievement of low-unit costs through large-scale production with electro-mechanical (automatic) controls required specialized, rigid processes in some sectors, for the smaller producers using batch methods the electrification of production led to less specialization and more flexibility. Since most goods were produced with small-scale, batch methods, these improvements in flexibility deserve greater recognition than they have received to date. But it should not be forgotten that for most manufacturers, and for most of manufacturing production (in terms of value-added), the so-called mass production period was one of increasing flexibility in production.

This emphasis on the enhancement of flexibility in many batch industries is not meant to minimize the significance of the development of mass methods in many other industries. A variety of statistics from the turn of the century indicate the extent of the transformation that took place in production. While gross capital stock per employee rose from $5066 in 1870 to $6838 in 1890, by 1913 it had almost doubled, to $13 147 (Maddison, 1982, table 3.5, p. 54). That the transformation was well under way by the turn of the century is evident from statistics reported by O'Brien (1988, p. 645). According to his study, about two-thirds of the increase in average factory size from 1869 to 1929 took place before 1890.

Nevertheless, many mechanical and continuous process industries did not take off until the second decade of this century. According to O'Brien, 1988, table 4, p. 648), among the industries with large increases in the average number of wage earners per establishment in the 1909–19 period were paper and allied products (63 to 81), rubber (569 to 968), primary metals (247 to 322), machinery (68 to 112), transportation equipment (62 to 152). In sharp contrast to these dramatic increases in establishment size, there was a decline in average establishment size in the textiles (72 to 50) and apparel (39 to 30) industries, while furniture (33) and leather (54) remained unchanged and lumber and wood products (17 to 19) increased slightly over this same decade. These differences are reflected in the increasing dispersion of industries as measured by the coefficient of variation of wage earners per establishment, which increased from 1.26 in 1899 to 1.33 in 1909 and 1.46 in 1919.[9] These data indicate that industry segmentation based on the technology of production was already solidly established in the first decades of this century.

Of particular interest is O'Brien's finding that technical change in this period was positively correlated with establishment size. Defined by the extent of labour-saving technical change, the most technologically dynamic industries were those with the largest increases in wage earners per establishment (O'Brien, 1988, p. 644). This feature of large-scale mechanization is particularly interesting since it sharply contrasts with the decline in establishment size made possible by programmable automation in the computer-based mechanization stage.

Data from the early 1970s, the end of the science-based mechanization stage, indicate that the labour and industry characteristics of the process, mechanical and light industry segments were quite distinct (Howell, 1989, table 2). For instance, in 1972, the process segment had a capital intensity of 12.5 million dollars per worker, compared to 1.3 million for the mechanical and .3 million for the light industries (differences that are statistically significant at the 1 per cent level). Similarly significant differences among segments existed for profit per worker, establishment size, the share of companies with multiunit operations, the production worker wage, the female share of the workforce, and the quit rate.

Computer-based Mechanization

The widespread adoption of computer-based systems in the office and factory in recent years marks a new, third stage of mechanization. While the early use of computers in production had a limited impact, due mainly to the difficulty of programming complex processes (Hirschhorn, 1986, p. 57), the development of microprocessors and their use in computer-based systems of machines have the potential radically to reduce labour requirements and increase the speed, flexibility, quality and control of operations. Like earlier forms of mechanization, computer-based technologies facilitate substantial reductions in the labour intensity of production. But while capital intensity (the capital to labour ratio) has continued to increase, there is a great deal of evidence suggesting that computer-based mechanization can be capital and energy saving; unlike earlier stages of advance, the ratios of capital and energy to output may decline with this form of mechanization. As Zuboff (1988) has documented, these systems can also reduce the management intensity of production, particularly at the low and middle management levels.

While there are important implications of this transformation for all three industrial segments, probably the greatest effects in the near future will be in high volume processing, metalworking and assembly – the mechanical and process segments. The enhancement of the continuity, control and flexibility of production may be best summarized by example. The following passages (Miller, 1985, pp. 44–5) describe the impact flexible manufacturing systems (FMS) have had at a General Electric plant in the US and a Fanuc plant in Japan.

> The FMS (at G.E.) has one third as many machine tools as the system it replaced. Twenty-nine manually operated machines were replaced by nine automated machining centers. As a result, floor space requirements were reduced by 25% and the typical number of times a part had to be loaded onto a separate machine was cut in half. The total number of people required to support the machining activity over two shifts (material handlers, operators, maintenance workers, schedulers and supervisors) was reduced from 86 to 16 . . . The new system is designed to produce 5600 parts per year, whereas the old system produced about 4100 parts per year . . . The average in-process time was reduced from 16 days to 16 hours.

> This (Fanuc) plant has 29 cell-like work stations. Seven are equipped with robots; 22 are equipped with automatic pallet changers with pallet pools. These stations are connected by unmanned vehicles guided by electromagnetic or optical methods. The plant has two automatic warehouses, one for materials and another for finished parts and subassemblies. The vehicles transport the materials from the warehouse to the unmanned machining stations. Robots or automatic pallet changers load materials onto the stations from the vehicles. Finished parts are transferred again automatically by the vehicles to the second warehouse . . . Every station is equipped with a monitoring device with a TV camera, and one person sits in the control room to monitor all the working stations . . . The monitoring device also records the spindle motor current, calculating the cutting force and time to judge cutting conditions.

These examples suggest not only substantial increases in labour (and total factor) productivity, but also an absolute decrease in the number of workers, the amount of fixed capital, and supervisory and managerial overhead in plants that adopt computer-based methods. These effects can be expected in both process and mechanical industries.

Perhaps the most significant aspect of microprocessor-based operations is the possibility, for the first time, of integrating production operations with product design, purchasing, cost accounting and strategic planning through the generation and feedback of information. Zuboff (1988, pp. 9–10) provides a concise summary of this capability:

> On the one hand, the [information] technology can be applied to automating operations according to a logic that hardly differs from that of the nineteenth-century machine system – replace the human body with a technology that enables the same processes to be performed with more continuity and control. On the other, the same technology simultaneously generates information about the underlying productive and administrative processes through which an organization accomplishes its work . . . Activities, events, and objects are translated into and made visible by information when a technology *informates* as well as *automates*.

The application of microelectronics, therefore, not only offers opportunities for transforming the production process on the shop-floor, but also has revolutionary implications for office processes and for the integration of office, sales and production operations. As Freeman (1986, p. 102) points out, 'The speed, scale, reliability and cost of microelectronics means that the range of industrial and office processes affected by automation can now be greatly expanded'.

The current transformation is characterized by a convergence of manufacturing and service activities – these must be coordinated within the firm to meet customer demands for the timely delivery of high quality, differentiated products. Hirschhorn (1988, p. 380) has written that a defining characteristic of this new 'mode of production' is the shift from mass production with a cost focus to flexible production with a quality focus. This is true for the mass production industries. But the transformation will also take place in the production technologies of small plants producing parts, equipment and machinery with relatively flexible batch methods – what I have termed the mechanical industries. Telecommunications and computer-based production methods have made possible smaller-scale, more flexible operations without sacrificing continuity or control. In all but the most labour-intensive sectors, flexibility and quality can be greatly enhanced with these capital-embodied technologies with little or no increase in unit costs.

To summarize, sections 4.2 and 4.3 have stressed the importance of competitive forces in the 'choice' that firms make about changes in their production technology; making the transition to the new technological regime is necessary to take advantage of new possibilities to greatly increase the flexibility, continuity and control over production. The technological transformation of production from craft work to simple mechanization, to science-based mechanization, and now to computer-based mechanization, reflects the unremitting pressures of the competitive race among firms for profits and survival. The course of this technological development has led to a series of industrial segments, defined by the character of the production technology in use, and has had substantial effects on both the kinds of labour demanded and working conditions in each segment. The next section provides a brief look at the restructuring of employment that appears to be taking place in the current period of transformation to computer-based mechanization.

4.4   COMPUTER-BASED MECHANIZATION AND EMPLOYMENT

Mechanization narrows skills and coerces workers to commit their bodies, if not their minds, to the machine process. Postindustrial technology threatens to throw them out of production, making them into dial watchers without function or purpose . . . Historically, we would then see the worker moving from being the controlled element in the production process to operating the controls to controlling the controls. (Hirschhorn, 1986, pp. 71,73)

While space does not allow a comprehensive discussion of recent changes in the employment and skill requirements in manufacturing, a few observations can be made which will serve to highlight the implications of computer-based mechanization for employment. The second part of this section will consider some of the employment implications of industrial robots, based on their use in Japan in the mid-1980s.

Recent Trends in the Structure of Employment

There appears to have been a substantial growth in the share of operatives and labourers as a share of manufacturing employment between 1900 and 1930, a development that has been interpreted as evidence of 'homogenization' of the workforce by Gordon, Edwards and Reich (1982, p. 149). The increased share of semi-skilled operatives during this period corresponded to an increase in the size of the factory, the specialization and deskilling of jobs, and the enhanced role of machinery as a means to control labour effort (Edwards, 1979).

In contrast to these first decades of the large-scale mechanization, trends in the occupational composition of industrial employment appear to have reversed themselves in recent decades. Manufacturing employment as a whole has fallen in absolute terms since the early 1960s. After rising at an average rate of .15 and .13 percentage points per year in the 1948–57 and 1957–66 periods, hours worked in durable manufacturing decreased by .22 percentage points between 1966 and 1973, and by .22 points again between 1973 and 1979. From 1979 to 1985 the rate of decline more than doubled, to .47 points per year. From 1966 to 1985, durable manufacturing's share of total hours worked declined from 21.4 to 15.7 per cent. The results for non-durables were similar, with large percentage point declines in hours worked per year over the 1966–85 period; the non-durable sector share of total hours worked fell from 14.3 per cent in 1966 to 10.3 per cent in 1985 (Costrell, 1988, table 3-2, pp. 94–5).

There is little evidence that new production technologies, much less program-mable automation, was responsible for the largest part of the job loss and restruc-turing of employment that took place prior to 1980. During this period, much of the employment losses in manufacturing can be attributed to the loss of low skill jobs through import competition and to the outsourcing of labour-intensive opera-tions to foreign sites (Cohen and Zysman, 1987 pp. 196–7). But it should be noted that this process of globalization has been greatly facilitated by advances in computer-based information technologies.

It is not until the late 1970s that computer-based mechanization begins to have an important effect on the plant floor. Indeed, Hirschhorn (1988, table 9-2, p. 383) has shown that in 1980 durable manufacturing had only 20 239 computer systems while non-durable manufacturing had just 15 269 systems, but these increased by more than two and half times in just five years; by 1985 there were 53 490 systems in use in durable and 39 120 systems in non-durable manufac-turing. The growth was even more spectacular in personal computers, which in these five years increased from over 9000 to about 400 000 in durable manu-facturing, and from just under 4000 to 205 000 in non-durables. Data from the Bureau of Economic Analysis (Howell and Wolff, 1987, table 4) indicates that in 1985 the most computer-intensive manufacturing industries were petroleum re-fining, machinery, stone, clay and glass, instruments, and electrical machinery, in that order.[10] In these industries, computer-intensity in 1985 was 2–4 times greater than in 1980.

These data on the diffusion of computers in manufacturing suggest that it is probably not until the early 1980s that we can mark the beginning of the transition to computer-based mechanization. With the transformation of production by programmable automation, technical change in production is likely to become a far more important source of both the occupational restructuring of the workforce and the decline (absolute and relative) in hours worked in manufacturing. Industry case studies lend support to this prediction. Based on their study of technology and employment trends in the electronics industry, Alic and Harris (1986, p. 35) conclude that:

> In U.S. Manufacturing as a whole, however, jobs – at least for production workers – may go down in absolute terms. A major source of decline in employment opportunities will be redesigned production systems utilizing computers and computer networks along with other tools for improving or-ganizational efficiency.

Trends in the aggregate data support both casual observation and case study evidence that we are beginning to see a fundamental change in the production technologies of the mechanical and process industries. Table 4.1 shows changes in employment and employment shares (in parenthesis) for selected occupation groups by industry segment since 1960.

Table 4.1 Changes in the employment composition of selected industries, 1960–85
(thousands of employees; per cent of total employment)

A. *Light Industries*

	1960	1970	1980	1985
Computer Specialists & Engineers				
1. Textiles	3827	8483	9466	8095
	(.40)	(.78)	(.85)	(.91)
2. Apparel	1346	3120	3994	3861
	(.11)	(.28)	(.35)	(.39)
3. Lumber & Wood	1238	2707	3752	4350
	(.17)	(.49)	(.55)	(.63)
4. Furniture & fixtures	1822	3140	4223	5509
	(.48)	(.74)	(.81)	(.93)
5. Leather	614	1290	1182	919
	(.17)	(.46)	(.49)	(.57)
Craft Workers				
1. Textiles	120 222	145 739	201 099	155 027
	(12.5)	(13.5)	(18.0)	(17.4)
2. Apparel	104 227	83 624	105 221	78 600
	(8.4)	(7.6)	(9.2)	(7.9)
3. Lumber & wood	92 770	91 560	127 334	115 727
	(12.8)	(16.7)	(18.6)	(16.9)
4. Furniture & fixtures	98 913	109 892	129 772	131 928
	(26.0)	(26.1)	(24.8)	(22.3)
5. Leather	50 077	38 613	32 548	18 474
	(13.7)	(13.7)	(13.4)	(11.4)
Operatives and Labourers				
1. Textiles	700 230	731 852	675 276	555 941
	(72.9)	(67.6)	(60.5)	(62.4)
2. Apparel	973 183	844 644	848 134	753 605
	(78.3)	(76.7)	(73.9)	(75.6)
3. Lumber & wood	551 963	367 883	431 266	430 785
	(76.0)	(67.1)	(62.8)	(62.8)
4. Furniture & fixtures	212 528	217 552	273 669	313 381
	(55.9)	(51.7)	(52.4)	(53.0)
5. Leather	263 143	191 957	161 871	109 450
	(72.0)	(68.2)	(66.4)	(67.4)

B. *Mechanical Industries*

	1960	1970	1980	1985
Computer Specialists & Engineers				
1. Fabricated metal products	52 360	75 312	65 485	77 131
	(3.94)	(5.23)	(4.45)	(5.42)
2. Machinery	67 361	132 127	193 215	288 967
	(4.17)	(6.7)	(7.08)	(11.11)
3. Electrical machinery	106 242	169 987	189 336	261 201
	(7.0)	(9.03)	(8.46)	(11.39)

4. Other trans. equipment	88 409	124 251	131 435	163 089
	(9.55)	(11.15)	(11.0)	(12.66)
5. Instruments & related prod.	24 284	25 996	39 902	49 643
	(6.68)	(7.09)	(6.93)	(8.17)

Craft Workers

1. Fabricated metal products	323 724	321 252	351 646	320 687
	(24.4)	(22.3)	(23.9)	(22.5)
2. Machinery	482 070	465 337	659 036	558 341
	(29.8)	(23.6)	(24.2)	(21.5)
3. Electrical machinery	251 709	275 870	353 163	326 696
	(16.5)	(14.7)	(15.8)	(14.2)
4. Other trans. equipment	278 643	338 817	346 775	351 353
	(30.1)	(30.4)	(29.0)	(27.3)
5. Instruments & related prod.	72 793	61 977	96 605	95 788
	(20.0)	(16.9)	(16.8)	(15.8)

Operatives and Labourers

1. Fabricated metal products	598 697	646 734	643 288	612 513
	(45.1)	(44.9)	(43.8)	(43.0)
2. Machinery	639 254	775 365	102 650	888 470
	(39.6)	(39.3)	(37.7)	(34.1)
3. Electrical machinery	727 188	852 465	960 110	947 207
	(47.7)	(45.3)	(42.9)	(41.3)
4. Other trans. equipment	303 469	329 494	366 346	384 520
	(32.8)	(29.6)	(30.7)	(29.9)
5. Instruments & related prod.	141 138	139 015	197 402	201 045
	(38.8)	(37.9)	(34.3)	(33.1)

C. *Process Industries*

	1960	1970	1980	1985

Computer Specialists & Engineers

1. Paper & allied products	6882	11 514	13 032	14 187
	(1.16)	(1.79)	(1.93)	(2.17)
2. Chemicals	33 048	47 205	59 719	60 722
	(3.9)	(4.84)	(4.81)	(5.54)
3. Petroleum & coal prod.	12 307	14 730	13 038	13 580
	(4.34)	(7.09)	(6.16)	(7.25)
4. Primary metal industries	22 138	28 616	29 753	22 288
	(1.74)	(2.39)	(2.19)	(2.66)
5. Motor vehicle & equipment	20 945	34 281	48 636	63 562
	(2.39)	(3.42)	(4.15)	(5.31)

Craft Workers

1. Paper & allied products	104 797	118 784	132 635	115 099
	(17.7)	(18.5)	(19.6)	(17.6)
2. Chemicals	146 486	158 115	210 856	156 726
	(17.3)	(16.2)	(17.0)	(14.3)
3. Petroleum & coal prod.	65 735	44 241	49 359	38 557
	(23.2)	(21.3)	(23.3)	(20.6)
4. Primary metal industries	370 500	363 770	382 898	219 717
	(29.0)	(30.4)	(28.2)	(26.2)

5.	Motor vehicle & equipment	200 492	225 476	282 360	276 999
		(22.9)	(22.5)	(24.1)	(23.2)

Operatives and Labourers

1.	Paper & allied products	345 012	341 786	342 570	341 713
		(58.4)	(53.2)	(50.7)	(52.3)
2.	Chemicals	325 108	335 095	410 800	360 813
		(38.4)	(34.4)	(33.1)	(32.9)
3.	Petroleum & coal prod.	93 435	60 280	63 099	56 602
		(32.9)	(29.0)	(29.8)	(30.2)
4.	Primary metal industries	636 319	545 809	630 849	394 731
		(49.9)	(45.6)	(46.5)	(47.0)
5.	Motor vehicle & equipment	477 167	535 306	592 336	594 922
		(54.4)	(53.4)	(50.5)	(49.7)

Source: Derived from the Census of Population's Industry by occupation tables for 1960, 1970, 1980, and *Employment and Earnings* (US Dept. of Labor), January 1986. For details, see Howell and Wolff (1988b).

For the light industries, computer and engineering occupations more than doubled from 1960 to 1985 as a share of total employment, but they began from a tiny base. Not one of these five industries employed enough computer and engineering personnel to reach 1 per cent to total employment in 1985. The restructuring of employment over these twenty five years appears to fall into two periods, 1960–80 and 1980–5: the decline in the share of operatives and labourers in these light industries ranged from 3.5 to 13.2 percentage points between 1960 and 1980, while craft workers increased their shares in three of the five industries, with only slight declines in the other two. In contrast, between 1980 and 1985, the lower skilled occupations increased their shares, while craft workers declined relative to other occupations. These data for the 1980s suggest that the effect of new production technologies on the structure of employment in the light industries has been minimal; if there has been an impact it appears limited to craft workers.

Despite their relatively high base (4–9.5 per cent) of computer specialists and engineers, the mechanical industries show large increases in the shares of these workers over the 1960–85 period. But by far the fastest annual rate of growth has been in the 1980s. This is particularly striking for machinery, electrical machinery and instruments. The absolute increase from 1980 to 1985 in computer and engineering employment was 49.6 per cent, 38 per cent and 24.4 per cent in these three industries, while employment shares grew by 57 per cent, 34.6 per cent and 17.9 per cent. This pattern mirrors the decline in shares of craft workers, which fell substantially in the early 1980s. The share of operatives and labourers has declined in all five mechanical industries since 1960, but most of the decline in low skill employment shares for the two largest industries, machinery and electrical machinery, has occurred since 1970, with the annual rate of decrease rising in the 1980s.

Like the mechanical industries, the annual rate of increase in the share of computer and engineering employment in the process industries was highest in the 1980s, and all five industries showed large declines in the craft share of employment, a tendency that did not characterize the 1960–80 period. Surprisingly, lower skilled production workers have held a fairly stable portion of total employment in four of the five process industries since 1970. (A large portion of the one exception, motor vehicles, consists of parts and equipment and should be classified as a mechanical industry.)

These data document a restructuring of employment in the mechanical and process industries in the 1980s, in which computer and engineering employment has increased sharply while craft workers have declined in importance. In the mechanical industries, particularly machinery and electrical machinery, there were also large declines in the shares of operative and labourer employment. This trend is also apparent for motor vehicles, but did not characterize the other four process industries.

Greater occupational detail for these three decades is reported in Table 4.2. There are several notable results. First, mechanical, chemical and particularly

Table 4.2   Annual employment growth for selected occupations, 1960–85 (per cent)

	Employment 1960	Annual Percentage Change[1]		
		1960–70	1970–80	1980–85
Chemical engineers	43 700	1.67	1.07	2.33
Electrical engineers	187 900	3.97	1.34	10.63
Industrial engineers	115 200	4.63	3.14	1.29
Mechanical engineers	162 200	.81	1.57	6.34
Machine mechanics	1 006 300	4.36	2.80	3.40
Machinists	520 700	–3.28	3.31	–.31
Foreman, n.e.c.	1 186 600	2.87	2.85	–4.31
Inspectors[2]	533 700	1.75	1.29	–.36
Toolmakers	187 700	.67	–.11	–4.59
Welders	388 200	3.15	2.93	–3.90
Assemblers	786 300	1.74	4.52	–2.14
Machine operatives[3]	787 800	2.51	–.04	1.65
Misc. operatives	1 804 000	–1.97	3.90	–.62
Production workers[4]	12 714 900	–.30	1.37	–1.76
Total employment	64 514 400	1.04	3.08	1.61

[1]   The average annual percentage changes were calculated from data for four years (1960, 1970, 1980, and 1985) by taking the difference of the logs and dividing by 10 (1960–70 and 1970–80) or 5 (1980–85).

[2]   The full title is Checkers, Examiners and Inspectors. Data are for manufacturing only.

[3]   Specified machine operatives include drill press operatives, lathe and milling machine operatives, precision machine operatives NEC, and punch and stamping press operatives.

[4]   Manufacturing only.

Source: see Table 4.1.

electrical engineers increased much more rapidly in the early 1980s than in the earlier decades. Second, machine mechanics also increased sharply in the most recent period, as would be expected in a period of rapid technological change. Third, the occupational sources of the decline in craft employment appears to be machinists, foremen,[11] toolmakers and welders. And fourth, unlike the 1970s, three of the four semi-skilled occupations (assemblers, inspectors and miscellaneous operatives) declined in the 1980s. These results are particularly striking since the use of 1980 (a recession year) and 1985 (a peak year) almost certainly has the effect of understating this declining trend for the semi-skilled occupations.[12]

Thus, the 1980–5 data indicate that the relocation of low skill operations offshore and the rationalization and computerization of domestic plants has reduced requirements for assemblers, inspectors, the least skilled operative occupations, and a variety of craft occupations, but has increased the demand for machine maintenance (mechanics) and the engineering occupations. Based on interviews with both managers and workers, a recent series of industry case studies supports these trends. For example, in the machine tool industry, the job content of machinists was found to be in the process of being either downgraded to operative tasks or upgraded to 'manufacturing engineers' – jobs that would require extensive office work and computer and writing skills (Turner and Gold, 1986, pp. 57–8). In the car industry, the same study found that skills are rising gradually since low skill jobs are the easiest to automate and there is an increasing need for repair technicians (ibid., p. 11).

Future Trends: Some Implications of Industrial Robots

Industrial robots are of particular interest for a variety of reasons. They are a key element in the programmable automation of factories, typically being used in conjunction with other computer-based technologies (as part of 'flexible manufacturing systems'). Further, they offer both a precision and an ability to operate under adverse conditions that can result in dramatically improved product quality and reduced occupational health and safety problems. And perhaps most importantly, these 'mechanical' workers offer a solution to the need for management to extract labour effort on the plant floor. They can be used as stand-alone work centres as a strategic means to replace workers who are particularly costly, unreliable or unruly. Or they can be used as part of a larger effort to eliminate the presence of human production labour altogether, a scenario that is no longer simply a possibility.

According to Engelberger, the former head of the largest US robotics firm and among the most prominent advocates of this technology, 'The basic production problem to which robots are addressed is the reduction of cost by eliminating human labor' (quoted by Shaiken, 1984, p. 163). A widely cited Carnegie-Mellon study concluded that industrial robots of 1980 vintage had the technical potential to replace as many as 5.5 million production jobs (Ayres and Miller, 1983).

Due to the absence of comprehensive data, the patterns and determinants of the use of industrial robots in the United States remain largely unexplored. There is currently no national data on the purchases of robots (in either units or value) by type of controlling mechanism (e.g. variable sequence, playback, or numerically controlled), by area of application (e.g. welding, machine loading, or assembly), or by industry. These data are, however, available for Japan from the Japanese Industrial Robot Association (JIRA). Japan is by far the leading user of industrial robots, in absolute number as well as by any measure of intensity. While the US counted under 15 000 robots in use at the beginning of 1985, the stock of Japanese robots exceeded 200 000, or over 70 000 if the simplest robots – manual manipulators and fixed sequence robots – are excluded (Yonemoto, 1985, p. 20).

Table 4.3 presents estimates of the increase in robot purchases necessary for US producers to achieve Japanese intensities (per worker) of robot use. The data are shown for five industries, which account for about 77 per cent of the Level 2 and Level 3 robots purchased for use in Japan from 1978 to 1984 (column 1). Although the availability of US data on robot installations is limited, column 3 presents estimates of the distribution of US robots in 1985 (see Howell, 1988a). Robot use appears to be even more concentrated in these five industries (88 per cent of the total) in the US than they are in Japan. On the basis of robot use per

Table 4.3   US robot stock required to match Japanese intensity levels by industry, 1985

		Stock of robots		
	Japan 1984[1]	*US 1985 equiv.*[2]	*US 1985 actual*[3]	*US require- ments*[4]
1. Plastics	11 513	14 126	2 180	11 946
2. Machinery	4 489	6 428	1 455	4 973
3. Electric machinery	22 855	25 598	1 600	23 998
4. Cars	16 879	36 425	7 275	29 150
5. Instruments	2 568	10 203	290	9 913
Industry subtotal	58 304	92 780	12 805	79 980
% of total deliveries (Level 2 and Level 3)	77.3%		88.0%	

[1] The sum of 1978–84 deliveries of Level 2 and Level 3 robots (variable sequence, playback, numerically controlled, and intelligent robots).
   (A useful life of more than seven years is assumed.)
[2] Based on the application of the 1984 ratio of Japanese robots to value added by industry to US value added for 1985 at 150 yen per dollar. (Japanese value added figures were not available for 1985)
[3] The total stock of US robots comes from the Robot Industry Association (*Robotics News*, June 1985), cited by Flamm (1986). This total is 14 550. The distribution of robots is based primarily on table 5 in Flamm (1986, p. 25a).
[4] The difference between column 2 and column 3.
Source: Howell (1988b, Table 6)

value added in 1984, these five US industries would have had to purchase about 80 000 industrial robots to match Japanese intensity of use in 1984, or more than five times as many as were installed in the US in 1985. This would mean an additional 11 500 in plastics, which had a base of only about 2200 in 1985; the machinery industry would have to increase their use from 1455 to 6428; electrical machinery would increase from 1600 to 25 600 (of which over 60 per cent would be assembly robots); cars would have to add over 29 000 robots; and instruments would have to increase its use from under 300 to just under 10 200, with at least half of this increase made up of assembly robots.

It should be emphasized that these estimates of US requirements are extremely conservative. They exclude the relatively simple fixed sequence robots, which do not fall under the accepted US definition. None the less, as Lustgarten (1982, p. 124) has pointed out: 'Low technology robots can often complete a task as well as the more sophisticated models. The Japanese appear more acutely aware of this and tend to concentrate on implementing existing technology'. (It is of interest, therefore, that the delivery of fixed sequence robots in 1984–5 maintained their 1980–1 level in Japan.) Had these relatively simple robots also been included, these figures would be much larger, particularly in plastics.

What do these results imply for occupations and industries most likely to see extensive robotization? Table 4.4 shows deliveries of robots to the five robot-

Table 4.4   Deliveries of industrial robots to five industries by application area, in Japan, 1978–85 (Levels 1–3)*

Industry	Total		By application area			
	Number	*Per cent of total*	*Application*	*Number*	*Per cent of industry total*	*Changes 1978–9 to 1984–5*
1. Plastics	53 350	29.52	plastic moulding	52 714	98.81	177.1
2. Machinery	15 429	8.54	machine loading	8 188	53.07	160.1
			arc welding	2 487	16.12	3775.7
			assembly	2 096	13.58	587.8
3. Electrical machinery	47 217	26.13	assembly	28 835	61.07	1324.9
			plastic moulding	6 189	13.11	–96.1
			machine loading	4 250	9.00	1974.1
4. Cars	34 769	19.24	spot welding	8 810	25.34	299.3
			machine loading	6 904	19.86	174.2
			arc welding	6 455	18.57	8644.7
			assembly	4 910	14.12	100.9
5. Instruments	8 687	4.81	assembly	4 387	50.50	463.5
			machine loading	1 352	15.56	464
Subtotal	159 452	88.23				
Total domestic	180 719					

* Includes manual manipulators and fixed sequence robots
Source: see Howell (1988a) Table 5.

intensive industries by application area. These data suggest that the occupations most affected by the adoption of industrial robots at Japanese intensity levels would be plastic moulding operators in plastics and electric machinery, machine operator and feeders in machinery, cars, and instruments, welders in machinery and cars, and assemblers in four of the five industries, the exception being plastics (see also Hunt and Hunt, 1983; Howell, 1985, 1988a). From a long-run perspective, the most important result indicated here is that the adoption of Japanese intensity levels of robots by US firms would lead to a considerable shift in staffing patterns away from semi-skilled production jobs in both mechanical (machinery and electrical machinery) and process (cars) industries.

These results are consistent with the general consensus that the future effects of programmable automation (or information technologies) will be a reduction in demand for low and semi-skilled manufacturing workers and an increase in demand for maintenance and engineering skills. In the last transition between technological regimes, the most dynamic industries were those that saw large increases in semi-skilled wage earners. Because the production of machinery and equipment was labour intensive and large-scale mechanization spurred mass consumption (and demand), the installation of labour-saving machinery coincided with absolute employment increases in both supplier and user firms. In contrast, with the transition to computer-based operations, manufacturing employment will probably experience rapid declines that are specifically attributable to technical advances in production.

It is at least plausible that the long-run implications of computer-based mechanization in conjunction with continued outsourcing of labour-intensive operations to lower labour cost nations is the virtual disappearance of low and semi-skilled production workers in US manufacturing. According to Morris-Suzuki (1984, p. 110), 'the development of robots and their incorporation into data-controlled production systems has created a realistic prospect of worker-less factories . . . even in complex assembly processes – including the production of robots themselves'.

As production jobs decline in both absolute and relative terms, the workers who remain will not resemble, in either skills, responsibility or autonomy requirements, the blue-collar workers or previous stages of development. In contrast to the emphasis on specialization of tasks and exclusive management control over (and lack of worker involvement in) the details of production operations that characterized the large-scale mechanization stage, Hirschhorn points out that 'the principle of flexibility creates a conception of work in which the worker's capacity to learn, to adapt, and to regulate the evolving controls becomes central to the machine systems developmental potential' (1986, p. 58; see also Zuboff, 1988). The low education levels of a large part of the US workforce suggest that there is good reason for concern over, as Heilbroner put it, the employment implications of this new 'robotic mode of production'.

4.5   CONCLUSION

With Heilbroner's insight that the employment effects of new technologies should be examined in light of successive stages of technical advance, this chapter has outlined a stage of advance framework and applied it to the long-run course of technological development in US manufacturing. This perspective extends Marx's conception of the three 'epochs' of capitalist development by interpreting 'modern industry' as comprised of three stages of technical advance: simple mechanization, science-based mechanization, and computer-based mechanization.

Since there are leading and lagging industries in each of these technological regimes, this course of development has generated an increasingly differentiated industry structure. By the first decades of this century, three industry segments were already visible: the traditional industries continued to use relatively labour-intensive methods, having failed to advance beyond the use of simple, light machinery largely because of the malleable nature of the product and the variability of demand; the mechanical industries, which required heavier machinery and more extensive mechanization, failed to make the transition to large-scale continuous process methods largely because of the small size and unstable character of their product demand; those that made the transition, such as beverages, chemicals, oil, rubber, flat glass, steel and motor vehicle assembly, comprise a new, third set of industries – the process segment.

This simple framework, one that takes into account stages of technical advance and the effect of this course of technological development on industry segmentation, provides a means to appreciate the complexity of what Heilbroner termed the historical aspect of the effects of technical advances in production. Not only might these effects vary in character and significance across stages of advance, but they may be felt more or less strongly across industry segments.

The close historical link between technological regimes and industry segments raises the question of whether the transition to computer-based production will bring with it a fourth industry segment. In previous work (Howell, 1989), a factor analysis of industry characteristics was conducted in which the first factor was clearly a measure of scale and capital intensity. The second factor, however, appeared to identify industries that were capital intensive but relatively small in average plant size. This would be consistent with what we know of the downsizing potential of new, highly mechanized and computer-intensive plants. With data for the 1980s now becoming available, and with its obvious policy implications, this question should be the focus of future research.

This chapter has also attempted to sketch, very provisionally, the employment effects that can be expected with the transition to a technological regime distinguished by computer-based mechanization, and how these effects may differ from those in earlier regimes. A survey of recent research in this area, and the evidence from the case study of industrial robots presented here, suggests that the introduction of new computer-based technologies in manufacturing will have major effects in most of the mechanical industries and in some process industries – particularly, those that employ high volume assembly lines (e.g. household appliances and motor vehicles). These effects include smaller establishment size, lower dispersion of firm and industry size, decentralized location of production facilities, much lower levels and shares of production worker employment, and a more skilled workforce whose jobs will require considerably more responsibility and the ability to synthesize data and diagnose problems.

These and other implications of computer-based mechanization remain to be conclusively documented, of course, and future research may show other important differences in employment effects between the science-based and computer-based stages. But the historical evidence surveyed here supports a Heilbronian perspective, namely, that the long-run character of technological change and its effect on employment should be examined within a framework which takes into account both the progressive development of production technology through stages of advance and the unevenness of the impact of radical new technologies on industrial sectors within each regime.

Notes

1. Consistent with this perspective, Leontief (1979, p. 49) has expressed his concern that 'we have to face the prospect of technological unemployment's turning from its past benign "voluntary" state into a virulent involuntary stage'.
2. In their own words, industrial divides are

    'brief moments when the path of technological development itself is at issue . . . there is a craft alternative to mass production as a model of technological advance . . . In this model, the triumph of technological breakthrough over competing adaptations depends on its timing and resources available to its champions – rather than on its intrinsic superiority . . . we arrive at a picture of technology as a refractory yet periodically malleable expression of the distribution of power in society'. (Piore and Sabel, 1984, pp. 5, 28, 15, 21).

3. This terminology is unfortunate, since both 'craft' and 'mass production' have fairly clear, concrete and historical meanings, but are used by Piore and Sabel to describe quite general 'models' of development: the use of flexible methods and unspecialized, skilled workers on the one hand, and rigid methods with specialized, low and semi-skilled workers on the other.
4. The recent MIT study of US competitiveness has taken a similar position: 'In its essential elements the system of mass production characterized most of the American manufacturing. Indeed, within the United States the triumph of this system was so complete that other patterns of production were virtually wiped out' (Dertouzos, Lester and Solow, 1989, p. 47).
5. As David Hounshell (1984, p. 13) points out, the motor car market in the 1920s required what he calls 'flexible mass production': 'Automobile consumption in the late 1920s called for a new kind of mass production, a system that could accommodate frequent change and was no longer wedded to the idea of maximum production at minimum cost'.
6. For a somewhat different view, see Gordon, Edwards and Reich (1982) who contend that there was no fundamental technological transformation of US industries until

the late nineteenth century. Growth was based on the 'simple expansion of employ-ment rather than on rising productivity per worker employed' (ibid., p. 81). The result was a 'proletarianized but untransformed labor force'.

7. According to Alfred Chandler (1977, pp. 347, 249):

    Modern industrial enterprise came more slowly and failed to thrive in industries where the processes of production used labor-intensive methods which required little heat, energy or complex machinery . . . Neither the technology nor the organization of the modern factory evolved out of the production processes in the older mechanical industries of textiles, apparel, and other clothing products, of shoes, saddlery, and other leather products, of furniture, wagons and other wooden products.

8. A good example is the production of car engines: 'Except over a very limited range, little flexibility is inherent in the system to accommodate change. Only a single product is made with very limited or minor variations, but under a manufacturing environment that is engineered to turn out the product in large quantities at mini-mum cost (Taylor, quoted by Ayers and Miller, 1983, p.1 4).

9. Calculated from table 4 of O'Brien (1988, p. 648).

10. Computer-intensity is defined as the sum of purchases of office, computer and accounting machinery from 1979–85 per employee in 1985.

11. The increase in the share of foremen in the 1960–80 period is consistent with the view that there was a breakdown of the post-war labour-management 'accord' over the course of this period, requiring an increase in repressive supervision and control (Bowles, Gordon, and Weisskopf, 1984).

12. Lower skill production jobs tend to be the most sensitive to swings in business conditions, rising in share of total employment in good times and declining as the economy slows.

References

Alic, John A. and Martha Caldwell Harris (1989 'Employment Lessons from the Electron-ics Industry', *Monthly Labor Review*, vol. 109, no. 2, February, pp. 27–36.

Ayres, Robert and Steven M. Miller (1983) *Robotics: Applications and Social Implications* (Cambridge, Mass.: Ballinger).

Berger, Suzanne and Michael J. Piore (1980) *Dualism and Discontinuity in Industrial Societies* (Cambridge: Cambridge University Press).

Bowles, Samuel, David M. Gordon, Thomas E. Weisskopf (1984) *Beyond the Wasteland* (New York: Anchor Press).

Chandler, Alfred D. (1977) *The Visible Hand: The Managerial Revolution in American Business* (Cambridge, Mass.: Harvard University Press).

Clark, Norman (1985) *The Political Economy of Science and Technology* (New York: Basil Blackwell).

Cohen, Stephen S. and John Zysman (1987) *Manufacturing Matters: The Myth of the Post-Industrial Economy* (New York: Basic Books).

Costrell, Robert M. (1988) 'The Effect of Technical Progress on Productivity, Wages, and the Distribution of Employment', in Richard M. Cyert and David C. Mowry (eds), *The Impact of Technological Change on Employment and Economic Growth* (Cambridge, Mass.: Ballinger), pp. 73–128.

Dertouzos, Michael L., Richard K. Lester and Robert M. Solow (1989) *Made in America: Regaining the Productive Edge* (Cambridge, Mass.: MIT Press).

Edwards, Richard (1979) *Contested Terrain: The Transformation of Work in the Twentieth Century* (New York: Basic Books, Inc.).

Flamm, Kenneth (1986) 'International Differences on Industrial Robot Use: Trends, Puzzles and Possible Implications for Developing Countries', Report to the World Bank, Washington, DC.

Freeman, Christopher (1986) *The Economics of Industrial Innovation* (Cambridge, Mass.: MIT Press).

Gordon, David M., Richard Edwards and Michael Reich (1982) *Segmented Work, Divided Workers* (New York: Cambridge University Press).

Heilbroner, Robert L. (1962) 'The Impact of Technology: The Historic Debate', in John T. Dunlop (ed.), *Automation and Technological Change* (Englewood Cliffs: Prentice Hall), pp. 7–25.

Heilbroner, Robert L. (1966) 'Automation in the Perspective of Long-term Technological Change', Report of the Proceedings of the Seminar on Manpower Policy and Program, Washington DC, US Department of Labor, December.

Heilbroner, Robert L. (1988) *Behind the Veil of Economics: Essays in the Worldly Philosophy* (New York: W.W. Norton).

Helfgott, Roy B. (1986) 'America's Third Industrial Revolution', *Challenge*, November–December, pp. 41–6.

Hirschhorn, Larry (1986) *Beyond Mechanization: Work and Technology in a Postindustrial Age* (Cambridge, Mass.: MIT Press).

Hirschhorn, Larry (1988) 'Computers and Jobs: Services and the New Mode of Production', in Richard M. Cyert and David C. Mowry, *The Impact of Technological Change on Employment and Economic* Growth (Cambridge, Mass.: Ballinger), pp. 377–415.

Hounshell, David A. (1981) 'The System: Theory and Practice', in Otto Mayr and Robert C. Post (eds), *Yankee Enterprise: The Rise of the American System of Manufactures* (Washington, DC: Smithsonian Institution Press), pp. 127–52.

Hounshell, David A. (1984) *From the American System to Mass Production, 1800–1932* (Baltimore: Johns Hopkins University Press).

Howell, David R. (1985) 'The Future Employment Impacts of Industrial Robots: An Input–Output Approach', *Technological Forecasting and Social Change 28*, pp. 297–310, 1985.

Howell, David R. (1988a) 'The Production and Use of Industrial Robots in Japan: Trends, Determinants and Implications for the United States', Report to the US Department of Labor, Office of International Economic Affairs, September.

Howell, David R. (1988b) 'Changes in the Skill Requirements of the US Labor Force, 1960–85', Report no. 88–26, C.V. Starr Center for Applied Economics, New York University, August.

Howell, David R. (1989) 'Production Technology and the Interindustry Wage Structure', *Industrial Relations*, vol. 28, no. 1, Winter, pp. 32–50.

Howell, David R. and Edward Wolff (1987) 'Skills, Employment Change and the Computerization of US Industries, 1960–85', manuscript, December.

Howell, David R. and Edward Wolff (1991) 'Trends in the Growth and Distribution of Skills in the US Workplace, 1960–1985', *Industrial and Labor Relations Review*, vol. 44, no. 3 (April), pp. 486–502.

Hunt, H. Allan and Timothy L. Hunt (1983) *Human Resource Implications of Robotics* (Kalamazoo, MI: W.E. Upjohn Institute).

Landes, David S. (1972) *The Unbound Prometheus* (Cambridge: Cambridge University Press).

Larsen, Raymond K. (1979) 'Metalcutting: The Shape of Things to Come', *Iron Age*, December.

Leontief, Wassily (1979) "Is Technological Unemployment Inevitable?' *Challenge*, September–October, pp. 48–50.

Lustgarten, Eli S. (1982) 'Robotics and its Relationship to the Automated Factory', in

Exploratory Workshop on the Social Impacts of Robotics Office of Technology Assessment (Washington, DC: US Government Printing Office), pp. 118–35.

Maddison, Angus (1982) *Phases of Capitalist Development* (New York: Oxford University Press).

Miller, Steven M. (1985) 'Industrial Robotics and Flexible Manufacturing Systems: An Overview', in P. Kleindosfer (ed), *The Management of Production and Technology in Manufacturing* (New York: Plenum Press).

Morris-Suzuki, Tessa (1984) 'Robots and Capitalism', *New Left Review*, September–October, pp. 109–21.

Murphy, Kevin M., Andrei Shleifer and Robert Vishny (1989) 'Income Distribution, Market Size, and Industrialization', *Quarterly Journal of Economics*, August, pp. 537–64.

Nelson, Daniel (1981) 'The American System and the American Worker', in Otto Mayr and Robert C. Post (eds), *Yankee Enterprise: The Rise of the American System of Manufactures* (Washington, DC: Smithsonian Institution Press), pp. 171–88.

O'Brien, Anthony Patrick (1988) 'Factory Size, Economies of Scale, and the Great Merger Wave of 1898–1902', *The Journal of Economic History*, September, pp. 639–49.

Piore, Michael J. and Charles F. Sabel (1984) *The Second Industrial Divide* (New York: Basic Books).

Rosenberg, Nathan (1976) *Perspectives on Technology* (Cambridge: Cambridge University Press).

Rosenberg, Nathan (1982) *Inside the Black Box: Technology and Economics* (New York: Cambridge University Press).

Rosenberg, Nathan and L. E. Birdzell Jr (1986) *How the West Grew Rich* (New York: Basic Books).

Shaiken, Harley (1984) *Work Transformed: Automation and Labor in the Computer Age* (New York: Holt, Rinehart & Winston).

Spenner, Kenneth I. (1988) 'Technological Change, Skill Requirements, and Education: The Case for Uncertainty', in Richard M. Cyert and David C. Mowry (eds), *The Impact of Technological Change on Employment and Economic Growth* (Cambridge, Mass.: Ballinger), pp. 131–84.

Sultan, Paul E. and Paul Prasow (1964) *Labour and Automation*, Industrial Labor Organization Bulletin No. 1.

Thompson, Ross (1989) *The Path to Mechanized Shoe Production in the US* (Chapel Hill: University of North Carolina Press).

Turner, Lowell and Jana Gold (1986) 'Perception of Shopfloor Change: Interviews with Business and Labor Leaders in Four Industries', Berkeley Roundtable on the International Economy, Report to the Carnegie Forum on Education and the Economy, 12 December.

Ware, Norman (1964) *The Industrial Worker, 1840–1860* (Chicago: Quadrangle Books).

Yonemoto, Kanji (1985) 'Robotization in Japan: Socio-economic Impacts by Industrial Robots', unpublished paper presented at the International Productivity Forum, 5 June.

Zuboff, Shoshana (1988) *In the Age of the Smart Machine: The Future of Work and Power* (New York: Basic Books).

Part III
Political Economics and Policy

Robert Pollin, 'Budget Deficits and the US Macroeconomy'

Patrick Clawson, 'Managed Capitalism vs. the Small State'

Richard McGahey, 'The Political Economy of Growth and Distribution'

One of Heilbroner's first books on economics, written jointly with Peter Bernstein, was *A Primer on Government Spending*, an outstandingly clear treatment of the impact of government, and government deficits, on the economy. Thirty years later they teamed up again, to write *The Debt and the Deficit*. This is the subject of Pollin's contribution, which carries Heilbroner's approach further, and at the same time suggests some revisions. Clawson takes up a question Heilbroner has often posed – how do we account for the increased role of the state as capitalism developed from the small-scale enterprise of the nineteenth century to modern science-based corporate industry? Is the growth of the state a necessary accompaniment; could accumulation take place without it? Clawson contends that the large state is required by mass production, but that by itself the size of the state neither augments nor constrains growth – which depends not on the size of the state but on its policy stance. McGahey starts by noting the shift from optimism to pessimism in the recent thinking of US policy-makers. Twenty-five years ago the policy community thought in terms of reaching a consensus on policies that could successfully handle our problems and improve our economic well-being. It now no longer expects either consensus or success. Part of this stems from changes in the economy, part from the impact of external events – but both have posed problems that the individualistic philosophy of the US policy-making community cannot handle.

Part III
Political Economics and Policy

5 Budget Deficits and the US Economy: Considerations in a Heilbronerian Mode

Robert Pollin*

5.1 INTRODUCTION

What is the economic impact of federal budget deficits on the US economy? There is no doubt that this is the most widely debated economic issue of our time. Controversy rages all around us – within academic forums, in the press, and even as part of the daily fare of radio call-in shows. The 1988 Presidential campaign elevated the issue to a place of unique prestige: fearing Walter Mondale's 1984 fate, both candidates studiously avoided substantive discussion, even as their brows furrowed rigorously at any mention of the topic.

Contention over this issue, moreover, is nothing new in American economic and political discourse. As James Savage (1988) documents, the question of federal deficits was central to the bitter disputes between Thomas Jefferson and Alexander Hamilton at the time the country was founded. In the twentieth century, the 'fiscal revolution' that Herbert Stein (1969) describes involved a complete overturning of attitudes towards budget deficits and the economy – from the early 1930s when Herbert Hoover sought to counter the Depression through a budget-balancing tax increase, to the early 1960s when John F. Kennedy proposed for his stimulatory tool a deficit-inducing tax reduction. Yet the ink had barely dried on Stein's narrative before a fiscal counter-revolution had begun. At present, the counter-revolution appears to have achieved near total victory, with the majority of US economists supporting the prevailing 1930s view that deficits are either positively pernicious to economic well-being or, at best, irrelevant.

How can one make sense of this confusion? It should not be surprising in this volume dedicated to the work of Robert Heilbroner that one should pose this question. Professor Heilbroner has been an important contributor to the deficit debate through several of its metamorphoses. In 1963, along with Peter Bernstein, he published *A Primer on Government Spending*, a book which presented briefly

* I wish to thank seminar participants at UC-Riverside, Southeast Misourri State University and the 1989 URPE Summer Conference, as well as Gary Dymski, Keith Griffin, John Miller, Tom Weisskopf and especially Ron Blackwell for constructive and enlightening comments on an earlier draft; Sandy Schauer for clerical assistance; and the UC-Riverside Committee on Research for financial support.

and with exceptional clarity the Keynesian defence of deficit spending. Though the majority of the economics profession at that time supported the Keynesian arguments, mainstream public opinion – or more precisely, the 'opinion leaders' at the *New York Times*, in Congress and the like – did not. Despite this, *A Primer* sold well and was widely appreciated, even by President Kennedy, who read it in manuscript form shortly before his assassination. Since then, Heilbroner has written regularly on macroeconomic topics in a range of popular and scholarly forums. More specifically, he has frequently returned to the subject of the deficit itself, including in his recent book, again with Bernstein, *The Debt and the Deficit: False Alarms/Real Possibilities* (1989). Like the *Primer*, this also is a brief and lucid exposition addressed to a non-specialized audience, which again, though now to a generally hostile professional as well as general audience, defends the Keynesian analysis of deficits.

In short, Heilbroner's direct involvement in the deficit debate has been substantial. Nevertheless, I suggest that his most important contribution to understanding the phenomenon of contemporary deficits comes not from these writings, valuable though they are, but rather from Heilbroner's general approach to economic reasoning. As a student of Heilbroner, I was trained to think about economic questions from a historical perspective. This did not mean that we simply took the history of economics seriously, though, of course, there is no more serious student of the history of economics than Professor Heilbroner. But in addition, Heilbroner has long stressed that contemporary economic questions can be adequately understood only when seen as part of an always evolving historical process. More specifically, Heilbroner has written insightfully about dialectical reasoning as a methodology which systematically incorporates a historical perspective in social analysis. In his *Marxism For and Against* (1980) Heilbroner describes a dialectical approach as holding that 'the ultimate and irreducible nature of all reality is motion, not rest, and that to depict things as static or changeless is to disregard or violate the essence of their beings'. Pursuing a historical/dialectical approach, according to Heilbroner, thus 'offers an entrée into the possible nature of things that is blocked to view from a nondialectical perspective' (ibid., pp. 32–3).

I wish to argue that a consciously historical approach is an essential prerequisite for understanding the impact of deficits on the contemporary US macroeconomy, as well as the recent debates on the subject. I would also claim that the absence of such thinking has contributed substantially to the confusion that now surrounds the subject. This is not to say that a historical approach will open a clear pathway to the truth, or even that it necessarily yields a range of answers superior to those advanced by less historically conscious analysts. Indeed, I will argue that some of Professor Heilbroner's own writings on the deficit contain errors similar to those made by more conventional economists. I am making rather a 'necessary but insufficient' type of claim: that without recognizing that the 'irreducible nature' of the US economy is motion, not rest, one will inevitably 'disregard or violate the essence' of the subject, and thus produce analyses – of the deficit in particular but of related topics as well – that are fundamentally flawed. Many economists of varying perspectives are willing to acknowledge that shifting historical circumstances are largely responsible for the changing terms of the mainstream debate over deficits. Few would dispute, for example, that the Depression created the intellectual opening for the Keynesian argument that deficit spending can be a macro stabilizer. It is similarly uncontroversial that the emergence of persistent deficits in the early 1970s, combined with declining real growth and high inflation, encouraged a reversion to pre-Keynesian thinking. Still, what has not been adequately recognized is that the economy's changing conditions have affected not only how economists think about deficits, but have also transformed the relationship between deficits and economic performance itself. That is, the impact of a 1990 deficit is different from that of a 1970 deficit of equivalent magnitude, because the US economy has changed dramatically over these twenty years. This is the historical point that needs to be grasped in order to reach 'the essence' of the deficit question.

I contend, more specifically, that three basic and interrelated changes have occurred in the US economy over the past twenty years. These are: (i) the persistence of stagnationist tendencies; (ii) rising debt dependency by all major non-financial sectors; and (iii) increasing internationalization. These changes have had a decisive impact on the relationship between deficits and economic performance. They have contributed to the growth of deficits over time, weakened the demand-side stimulatory impact of any given-sized deficit, worsened the deficit's negative collateral effects, including its impact on financial markets and the after tax income distribution, and inhibited the Federal Reserve from pursuing more expansionary policies. To say all this does not conflict with the view that deficits, as a first-order effect, continue to be a powerful demand booster. The point rather is that because of stagnation, internationalization and financial fragility, the stimulatory effects of a given-sized deficit are weaker and its negative side effects stronger.

The aim of this chapter is to draw out this perspective on deficits and the economy, and to demonstrate its merits relative to the range of alternative arguments that have been recently advanced. The next section briefly reviews the data on the growth of deficits over the post-war period. Following that, the third section addresses the most prominent views on deficits, including Robert Barro's Ricardian equivalence theorem; the 'crowding out' framework of neo-Keynesians such as Lawrence Summers and Benjamin Friedman; and finally the reconstituted traditional Keynesianism of Robert Eisner. As Heilbroner and Bernstein generously acknowledge, their own recent book largely follows the positions advanced by Eisner. As such, the arguments in *The Debt and the Deficit* will also be considered along with the discussion of Eisner. After identifying some of the basic inadequacies of these positions, the fourth section takes up my alternative framework. Developing this argument will of course require, among other things, that the phenomenon of stagnation, internationalization and financial fragility be clarified in this section.

Throughout the chapter, the wide-ranging contributions of Professor Heilbroner will also be addressed. As noted above, the discussion will be critical of some of his specific formulations. At the same time, my methodological debt to him should be clear throughout.

5.2   DEFICITS AND ECONOMIC PERFORMANCE IN THE POST-WAR US

According to traditional Keynesian reasoning, active macroeconomic management policies involve running deficits during cyclical troughs, when unemployment and unutilized capacity are both substantial; and running surpluses during peaks when 'overutilized' labour and capacity generate significant inflationary pressures on labour and product markets. The logic is familiar: during troughs, deficit spending will increase private incomes. This stimulates aggregate spending, first because consumption spending will rise along with income, but also because incomes and expenditure will be further stimulated through the multiplier effects associated with the initial spending boost. The same mechanism works in reverse when the government runs surpluses. The overall aim is to dampen both the boom and bust extremes of cyclical behaviour. These policies are supposed also to rest on solid financial footing, as deficit and surplus years should roughly balance as the economy stabilizes.

Much of the widespread dissatisfaction with contemporary fiscal policy can be explained by the data in Table 5.1. It shows officially measured US federal deficits as well as real GNP growth between 1950 and 1989. The first point that emerges is that, at least in so far as official deficit figures are meaningful, the

Table 5.1   Post-war budget deficits and economic growth

	1950–9	*1960–9*	*1970–9*	*1980–9*
Number of surplus years	3	2	0	0
Mean size of deficits (billions of current dollars)	1.8	5.7	35.0	156.5
Deficits as percentage of GNP	0.4	0.8	2.0	4.0
Real GNP growth (per cent per annum)	4.0	4.1	2.8	2.6
Fixed investment growth rate, non-financial corporations, (per cent per annum)	3.9	4.3	4.1	2.4

Source: *Economic Report of the President*, 1991, p. 375; US Department of Commerce, *National Income and Product Accounts* (reported in *Citicorp Economic Database*, 1991.2 Edition).

traditional Keynesian strategy of balancing surpluses and deficits has never actually been practised. Rather, the federal government has run surpluses in only five of the thirty-eight years. Fiscal practice did at least vaguely resemble the Keynesian model during the 1950s, when surpluses were run in three years, and the 1960s, when the government ran its last two surpluses (the last one being 1969). From 1970 to the present, deficits have never been offset by surpluses.

Even more striking than the absence of surpluses has been the growth in the size of official deficits. The average deficit from the 1950s was $1.8 billion, and remained a relatively small $5.7 billion for the 1960s. It then grew explosively, from $35 billion in the 1970s to $156.5 billion in the 1980s. Measuring deficits relative to GNP, and thereby controlling for inflation, the growth of deficits over the post-war period is still formidable – from 0.4 per cent in the 1950s to 4.3 per cent in the 1980s.

The final crucial development is shown through the figures for real GNP and fixed investment growth. We see that real GNP growth averaged around 4 per cent over the 1950s and 1960s, but then declined sharply to 2.8 per cent in the 1970s and then 2.6 per cent in the 1980s. Fixed investment growth remained essentially stable at around 4 per cent through the 1970s, but then experienced an even sharper drop, to 2.4 per cent, in the 1980s.

The overall picture, therefore, is one of persistent and rapid growth of federal deficits, accompanied by significant declines in real economic growth. These figures raise a set of important issues. Why have increased official deficits accompanied declining growth? Could increasing deficits be the cause of the GNP growth decline? Are the government's official statistics the appropriate way to measure how budget deficits affect the macroeconomy? Are there deeper problems in the economy causing both budget deficits to grow and GNP to decline? These are the questions raised in the contemporary budget deficit debates, to which we presently turn.[1]

5.3   ALTERNATIVE MAINSTREAM PERSPECTIVES

New Classical Economics and Ricardian Equivalence

New classical economists emerged during the failure of standard Keynesianism to explain the stagnation of the 1970s. It is fundamentally pre-Keynesian in its belief that free market forces inherently generate a harmonious full employment equilibrium. However, it has advanced a novel view of the way government fiscal and monetary interventions create obstacles in the path towards equilibrium. The new classicals argue that activist government policies are unable to reduce unemployment and cyclical fluctuations or encourage economic growth, however much they may seek to do so. At the same time, in their view, activist macro policies absorb resources and distort markets, rendering them not merely impotent but positively harmful to economic well-being.

In reaching these conclusions, the new classicals have placed great stress on the assumption that market participants behave 'rationally', which is to say they behave in ways which will maximize their material well-being. Such a notion of rationality is pervasive in neo-classical economics. But the new classicals have extended the idea dramatically by introducing the notion of 'rational expectations', especially with respect to government policy. Rational expectations in their view implies that private economic agents learn to anticipate the effects of government actions because it is in their self-interest to do so. Their anticipatory behaviour will thus serve to neutralize the government's policy interventions. This is why government interventions become incapable of realizing their economic targets.

In terms of the specific issue of budget deficits, this argument has been expressed most forcefully in the work of Robert Barro. Barro's position, which has been termed the Ricardian Equivalence Theorem, is that budget deficits have no effect on aggregate spending. The reason is that rational individuals realize they will eventually have to pay the principal and interest on the new debt in the form of higher taxes. Further, according to Barro, rational individuals will make current spending decisions based on the expected present value of future tax liabilities. Thus, since they recognize that the budget deficit will have to be paid off in the future, they will not increase consumption in periods of budget deficits, but rather increase savings which will match the future tax liabilities associated with current government borrowing. Barro puts this view succinctly: 'a decrease in government's savings (that is, a current budget deficit) leads to an offsetting increase in desired private saving, and hence to no change in desired national saving' (Barro, 1989, p. 34).[2]

As many economists appear to recognize, this argument strains credulity, as it relies on a set of extremely strong assumptions both about behaviour and the information which guides behaviour.[3] To begin with, it is assumed that people are aware of the size of current budget deficits and are able to calculate accurately what the effects of this will be on their own future taxes. This is most unlikely, given that even professional economists cannot achieve a consensus on the proper way of measuring budget deficits.

But if we accept this assumption about the accounting capacities of US taxpayers, we then face another problem. Such well-informed individuals will surely be aware of the ways in which the real value of their share of the government's liabilities will change with time. Price level fluctuations will change the real value of the outstanding debt and revisions in the tax code will alter an individual's liability. The inflation of the 1970s and tax cuts of the 1980s have demonstrated that both of these factors can bring substantial changes in an individual's real tax liability. Given this history, the well-informed taxpayer would recognize the impossibility of accurately calculating how much any current period deficit will affect their future net liability. They would then be violating the precepts of rational behaviour by presuming they could make such a calculation and, even more, by setting aside a share of their net assets to meet this unknown future liability.

Even if one grants that the future liability of the deficit could be calculated, the Barro argument also makes very strong assumptions about how a rational individual should respond to a federal government deficit. Would it be more rational, for example, for a household to put aside some current income to respond to a future tax liability rather than purchase a new home or car which otherwise would be beyond their present means? If one faces a current debt obligation, would it be more rational to set aside funds for the future tax liability and possibly face delinquency on the present obligation or to pay the debt first? Or even to push the point further, would it be more rational to postpone a European vacation – a pure consumption good – the opportunity for which may not again arise, in order to set aside the requisite funds to pay off one's share of the federal deficit? The point here is that Barro chooses a definition of rationality that is arbitrary, even if it is widespread among economists. Many other scenarios of rational behaviour can be envisioned which would not assign priority to increasing personal savings to meet future tax liabilities. Professor Heilbroner, for example, shows in a recent essay that the Barro-type conception of rational maximizing makes inexplicable a wide range of commonly observed behaviour. Heilbroner writes that 'rationality' in the sense used by Barro 'is a question begging as well as an elucidating term' (1988, p. 26).

Many additional arguments have been made against the Barro hypothesis, and the weight of empirical evidence firmly contradicts his position (Bernheim, 1987). Nevertheless, his position is well known and taken seriously by a large number of economists and in the press.[4] As such, Barro may not simply be engaging in wishful thinking when he predicts that 'the Ricardian approach will become the benchmark model for assessing fiscal policy' (1989, p. 52). One reason why this may be true is that his argument has been politically useful in an era when right-wing governments have created large deficits. The Barro theorem provides legitimacy to the political argument advanced increasingly by Republicans that deficits don't matter. The Barro theorem, more generally, is consistent with the recent thrust of conservative thinking which has newly discovered positive attributes in federal deficits. These attributes include the fact that the deficits have established limits on further growth of government spending while at the same time have distributed income upward. The distributional effects are due to the differential benefits of Reagan's tax cuts flowing to the rich and the interest payments on government debt also flowing to the wealthy, while the cuts in government social spending are suffered disproportionately by the poor and middle class. None of these considerations is mentioned explicitly by Barro. But one would be surprised to find substantial conservative support for his analysis if the distributional impact of contemporary deficits were the reverse.

Neo-Keynesianism and Crowding Out

One of the great ironies of contemporary economic thought is the extent to
which current 'neo-Keynesian' analysis of budget deficits has rejected the ideas
of Keynes and appropriated the ideas of pre-Keynesian and anti-Keynesian
thinkers. According to the current US neo-Keynesian view, the primary determinant of a country's economic growth rate is its saving rate. Lawrence Summers,
a leading neo-Keynesian, puts the case bluntly: 'The rate of savings determines
the rate of economic growth a country can enjoy . . . It can also have an important
influence on a nation's competitiveness in international markets' (1986, p. 65).
Thus – and here the reversion to pre-Keynesian thinking could not be more
apparent – the higher the level of national savings, the greater the rate of investment, and conversely, as national savings declines, so will investment.

In this view, the US federal budget deficit is a net absorber of private savings.
As such, the deficit increases the difficulty or cost for private borrowers to obtain
funds on credit markets, and this in turn inhibits investment. The basic mechanism
works as follows: the availability of funds in the US credit market depends in the
first instance on private savings. When the federal government absorbs a high
level of available savings, this drives up the cost of funds for a given level of
corresponding demand by the private sector. The larger the deficit, the more
prohibitive interest rates become for private borrowers. The high domestic interest rates will attract foreign savings, increasing the availability of credit, but
only at high interest rates. The high rates will discourage private investment by
making borrowing too expensive, and contribute to the country's worsening
competitive position, since it will support a rise in the value of the dollar. As
Benjamin Friedman, another leading neo-Keynesian, writes, 'The heart of the
matter is that deficits absorb saving. When more of what we save goes to finance
the deficit, less is available for other activities that also depend on borrowed
funds' (1988, p. 164). This, according to neo-Keynesians, is the primary way
through which government deficits 'crowd out' domestic private investment
activity, and why, recalling the figures in Table 5.1, we observe a decline in
investment and GNP growth corresponding to the growth of deficits in the 1970s
and especially the 1980s. The neo-Keynesians view the investment growth decline as the fundamental problem in the contemporary macroeconomy; the deficit,
from their perspective, is inflicting great damage on the economy by inhibiting
investment.

This approach gives little credence to the original Keynesian view that deficits
can serve to promote investment by raising incomes and thus stimulating aggregate demand when resources are unemployed. Friedman, for example, concedes
that deficits can be expansionary, but 'only when the economy has room to
expand'. Neo-Keynesians believe that for most of the post-war period, and certainly since recovering from the 1980–2 recession, the economy has not had room
to expand. In their view, the economy must be operating significantly below the
'non-accelerating inflation rate of unemployment', or NAIRU, in order for there

to be room to expand; and neo-Keynesians believe the economy has been operating close to or at NAIRU since the recovery in 1983. When NAIRU is approximated, according to the neo-Keynesians, the additional stimulus from the deficit will generate either 'real' or 'financial' crowding out. Real crowding out refers to the fact that at NAIRU, a federal deficit will not employ idle workers or capacity but will rather accelerate the inflation rate. Deficit spending in these conditions may stimulate nominal income increases, but not real income growth. Financial crowding out means that since real incomes will not increase through deficit spending at NAIRU, savings will not increase either, since savings growth is dependent on income growth. The deficit in this situation thereby becomes a net absorber rather than creator of savings. Interest rates will rise as a result, and this will discourage private borrowers from borrowing.

Overall, according to neo-Keynesians, the deficit acts as both a short- and long-term impediment to investment when the economy approximates NAIRU. In the short run, the deficit absorbs the existing savings supply, and thereby discourages private investors from borrowing and investing. By inhibiting investment, it also prevents the economy's capacity from expanding in the long term. Moreover, as long as capacity does not expand substantially through investment growth, the economy will remain stuck at a low investment NAIRU, and deficit spending will remain an ineffective stimulatory tool.

Finally, according to this approach, to the extent that the economy may require a demand boost, expansionary monetary policy is a perfectly viable substitute for a larger federal deficit. Summers, for example, says: 'The ability of monetary policy to stimulate aggregate demand has been amply demonstrated. Any reductions in demand due to increased government savings can easily be offset by expansionary monetary policy' (1986, p. 73). Again, this position, regardless of its intrinsic merits, represents a striking reversion to pre-Keynesian thinking, ignoring the old Keynesian adage about the intractibility of pushing on a string.[5]

The issue at present, of course, is not whether the neo-Keynesians are faithful to the master, but whether their arguments are valid. Let us consider a few fundamental shortcomings in their approach relating directly to the central issue of crowding out and private investment, leaving until later questions of monetary policy.

A first basic error of the neo-Keynesian position is the assertion that private sector borrowing has been inhibited by the growth of the federal deficit. The relevant evidence, presented in Table 5.2, contradicts this view.[6] It is true, of course, that federal borrowing rises rapidly from the 1970s onward, reaching 4.5 per cent of GNP over 1982–90. But this trend clearly did not prohibit the private sector from also borrowing heavily. Household borrowing for 1982–90, at 5.7 per cent of GNP, was also a post-war peak. Borrowing by non-financial corporations during 1982–90, at 3.0 per cent, was slightly lower than the peak figure of 3.2 per cent during 1970–3. But this figure was still significantly higher than the 2.5 per cent figure for the 1960s, when investment growth was at its peak and federal borrowing was only 0.7 per cent of GNP. The conundrum posed by these data for

Table 5.2   Net borrowing relative to GNP for total non-financial economy and major borrowing sectors (percentages)

Cycles	1953–7	1958–9	1960–9	1970–3	1974–9	1980–1	1982–90
Total non-financial economy	9.1	9.2	9.0	12.0	14.0	12.5	16.1
Households	3.5	3.5	3.6	4.2	5.4	4.0	5.7
Non-financial corporations	1.8	1.9	2.5	3.2	2.6	2.8	3.0
Federal government	0.1	1.7	0.7	1.3	2.8	2.9	4.5

Source: Flow of Funds Accounts of Federal Reserve System, table entitled 'Total Net Borrowing and Lending in Credit Markets'.

the proponents of crowding out are apparent: how could a 3.0 per cent corporate borrowing rate be inadequate to finance private investment in the 1980s, when a 2.5 per cent rate was sufficient to finance rapid growth in the 1960s? Or to put the same question another way: if the government's borrowing inhibited non-financial corporations from borrowing more than 3 per cent of GNP over 1982–90, why, when no such inhibitions existed in the 1960s, did corporations borrow at lower rates?

The neo-Keynesian view of interest rate effects of budget deficits is also erroneous. It is true that real rates of interest have been at historically high levels throughout the 1980s, even though they have fallen considerably from their early 1980s peak. These broad trends are indicated in Figure 5.1, which presents the real prime rate and US Treasury bill rate for the post-war period. Certainly these high interest rates are due partially to the unprecedented level of credit demand during the 1980s. A full explanation, however, would have to incorporate supply-side issues, which we take up later.[7] But even if we consider only the demand side of the market, the data in Table 5.2 make clear that the federal government is not solely responsible for the rise in aggregate credit demand. Indeed, 67 per cent of total borrowing for 1980–90 comes from the private sector. So to explain the demand-side factors exerting upward pressure on interest rates, it is arbitrary to focus solely on the growth of federal government borrowing; one must also inquire as to why, concurrent with rising federal borrowing, the private sector has also sustained high levels of debt financing.

In addition, whatever caused the rise of real interest rates, the evidence shows that this has not significantly weakened private sector credit demand. The 1980–2 phase of extreme monetary restrictiveness did smother private borrowing. But in subsequent years, private sector credit demand has maintained at least the level of the 1970s when real interest rates were low to negative. This means that

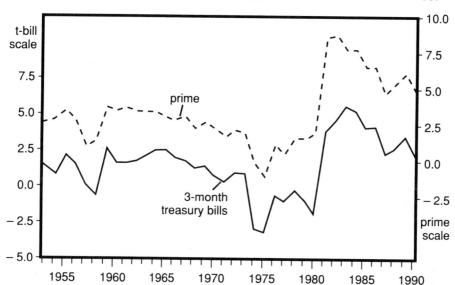

Figure 5.1   Real interest rates in the post-war US economy (real rates are nominal rates minus contemporaneous change in CPI)

Source: Citicorp Economic Database (1991.2 Edition).

the interest elasticity of credit demand, apart from periods of extreme real rate spikes such as 1980–2, is relatively weak.[8]

In sum, we see that the private sector has borrowed heavily along with the federal government during the 1970s and 1980s; that the rise of real rates during the 1980s must be attributed at least partially to this private sector activity if it is to be attributed to demand-side factors at all; and finally, that high real interest rates have not substantially inhibited borrowing in the 1980s. All these points sharply contradict the neo-Keynesian view.

The neo-Keynesians' alarm over the decline in the growth of fixed investment is timely. But their attempt to explain declining investment through the crowding out argument is evidently unsustainable. Benjamin Friedman himself unequivocally (if inadvertently) confirms this in a key passage in his recent book, *Day of Reckoning* (1988). Discussing the failure of the business tax incentives instituted under the Reagan administration to stimulate private investment, Friedman writes as follows:

> With more generous tax breaks, business corporations' after-tax cash flows have represented a larger share of our total income than at any time since World War II . . . And in addition to the growth of their internally generated funds, corporations have also borrowed record amounts . . . But increasing what business has available to invest is not the same thing as increasing what

business actually invests. Despite record internal cash flows and record bor-rowing too, business has used an unusually large part of these funds for purposes other than productive new investment . . . According to plan, our new fiscal policy did increase the funds business had available to finance new investment, but business simply had other plans for how to spend them. (ibid., pp. 264–5)

In other words, says Friedman, business has faced no shortage of investment funds, despite the huge deficits. They were not crowded out; they simply did not utilize the funds available to them in a manner anticipated by neo-Keynesian theory.

One could perhaps construct a real crowding out explanation for these circum-stances, though Friedman himself does not attempt such. The argument would proceed as follows. If one assumes the economy is at NAIRU, firms would then be reluctant to invest in new capacity because the costs of production in tight markets will be too high, and profits will thus be squeezed. As a result, firms would direct their existing financial resources towards leveraged buy-outs, which creates no strain on productive capacity.

There are several problems with this type of argument, however. An initial difficulty would be the need to explain how real crowding out could be so significant a force while, simultaneously, financial crowding out appears negligi-ble. But beyond this, one cannot assume that an economy at NAIRU should discourage investors from creating new capacity. One might just as easily argue that an economy at NAIRU would create incentives for firms to use their 'record levels' of borrowed funds to create new capacity. More specifically, with all else equal, the demand for new capacity should be strong if existing capacity is truly stretched to the limit; and firms should earn high profits from meeting the demand for scarce capacity. At the least, even if firms do not respond to these conditions by building new capacity, the market should reflect this profit potential by valuing the existing real capacity highly.

In fact, however, financial markets have been valuing existing plant and equipment below their replacement cost throughout the 1980s. This can be seen from the behaviour of Tobin's Q ratio, which shows the market value of firms relative to the replacement cost of their physical assets. According to neo-classical theory, the equilibrium value of Q should approach unity, reflecting an equal valuation of firms in two separate markets – the market for equity shares and that for physical assets. As Figure 5.2 shows, the Q ratio never has tended towards an equilibrium value of unity over the post-Second World War era. (Strictly speaking, the ratio reported here is a proxy for Q. Tobin's definition includes the market value of debt and equity in the numerator, but this includes only equity values. Tobin's Q also includes physical assets only in the numerator, while this proxy includes financial assets as well, net of liabilities. For many reasons, an accurate measure of aggregate Q is difficult to construct. At the same time, this more tractable Q proxy accurately reflects the basic movements of Q.)

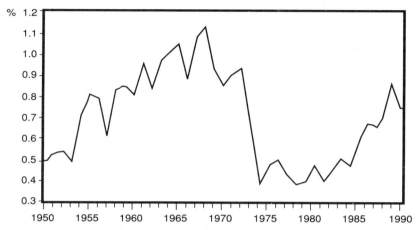

Figure 5.2   Q ratio: market value of non-financial corporate equities/net worth (measured at replacement cost)

Source: Federal Reserve Board, *Balance Sheets for the US Economy, 1945–90* (March 1991).

Most important for our purposes, we see that the ratio has declined sharply from a peak in 1968 of 1.1 to a low in 1974 of .38. As a trend, it has risen since 1974, but never to anywhere near unity; and still, by 1990, remained at approximately .75. This means that despite the 1982–7 stock market boom and post-crash recovery, the financial markets, on average, are still willing to pay only 75 cents for a dollar's worth of physical equipment. If the economy's real resources were indeed strained as the NAIRU/real crowding out argument suggests, one would expect the market to value the economy's scarce real resources more highly.

In short, the neo-Keynesian framework simply cannot explain the concurrence of large deficits, heavy corporate borrowing, and declining real investment growth within either a real or financial crowding out framework. As we see, the approach is too weak to withstand the empirical observations of even such proponents as Professor Friedman.

Beyond these weak empirical foundations, Professor Heilbroner in his recent book with Bernstein (1989), and elsewhere (e.g. 1984), has raised a still more basic problem with the arguments of crowding out proponents: their unexamined assumption that government spending deserves the lowest priority when the economy's financial resources are allocated. If crowding out has to occur, ask Heilbroner and Bernstein (though they basically do not believe it does occur) why should the public sector necessarily be the victim? They emphasize that much of government spending is crucial to economic well-being, while much of private investment is wasteful. Should government borrowing to finance education or infrastructural development be 'crowded out' to make room for leveraged buy outs? Such questions are studiously avoided in the mainstream discussions, but, according to Heilbroner and Bernstein, deserve to be at the centre of concern.

'The issue,' they write, 'turns out to have little to do with deficit spending but a great deal to do with how we feel about the role of government in a capitalist economy. For at its core, crowding out boils down to the relative size of private and public spending. It is as simple – and as complex – as that' (Heilbroner and Bernstein, 1989, p. 110–11).

Robert Eisner and 'Real Budget Deficits'

Probably the most sustained effort to explain why deficits do not work as traditional Keynesian theory would anticipate has been the work of Robert Eisner, an analyst well within the traditional Keynesian framework. His explanation is straightforward. He says deficits *do* still work to raise aggregate demand. The problem, according to Eisner, is that economists have not been measuring deficits in the correct manner. In Eisner's view, this measurement issue is so serious that since the 1970s, what has appeared to be large deficits have actually often been small deficits, inducing a correspondingly small demand booster. What has appeared as moderate deficits have actually been substantial surpluses, which have dampened economic growth. When deficits are measured correctly, his evidence shows that fiscal policy has worked just as anticipated – deficits have been stimulatory and surpluses have been dampening. As Eisner says: 'Mismeasuring deficits, we have confused economic policy and theory alike. We think we have deficits when we do not, and take counteractions that cause recessions. We further see consequences of what we call deficits belying the predictions of economic theory, and question and repudiate our theory' (Eisner, 1986, p. 3). Heilbroner and Bernstein's 1989 book, as noted above and as they fully acknowledge, is largely a popularized version of Eisner's approach. In the present context, this factor alone provides a strong incentive to consider Eisner's work carefully. As we proceed, we will also want to point out where Heilbroner and Bernstein diverge from Eisner's argument.

Eisner contends that the official measurement of deficits contains three basic errors. The first is the fact that the federal government, unlike businesses, makes no distinction between current and capital expenditures. He argues that when the government borrows to finance investment outlays, the liabilities created in this process should not be treated as are the liabilities which finance consumption expenditures. This is because investment financing leads to the creation of assets which yield long-term benefits to the economy. According to Eisner, the growth of government debt during the 1970s was virtually matched by an increase in the government's assets, meaning that the current account deficit was negligible. Even into the 1980s, Eisner says a separate current account deficit would be substantially smaller than the official aggregate current plus capital account deficit.

The second accounting issue that Eisner raises concerns the familiar technique of breaking down the deficit into its 'high employment' and 'cyclical' components. Eisner says that 'the economy affects the deficit perhaps as much as or more than the deficit can be expected to affect the economy' (ibid., p. 81). As a result, official budget deficit figures are not good measures of the impact of fiscal policy. Eisner thus argues that the second necessary adjustment on the official deficit figures is to deduct the cyclical deficit from the total, including only the high employment deficit to measure the impact of the deficit on the economy.

The third and most novel feature of Eisner's approach is his argument that the real size of deficits should be adjusted for the impact of inflation. He writes: 'For deficits to matter they must be real deficits. A real deficit is one which increases the real net debt of the government to the public and hence increases the public's perception of its own real wealth,' (ibid., p. 5).

According to Eisner, inflation reduces the real deficit by lowering the value of the government's outstanding debt associated with a given deficit, thus also lowering the real wealth of the public that holds government debt. More specifically, in Eisner's view, the deficit achieves its primary demand stimulus by increasing the real wealth of government bondholders: the owners of newly issued government bonds will spend more, in Eisner's view, because their wealth has increased. Eisner's position contrasts sharply with the traditional Keynesian perspective that a deficit's primary demand effects will come through the increases in income associated with the rise in government spending and the multiplier. Indeed, this part of Eisner's argument is founded on a neo-classical wealth-based theory of consumption behaviour. In particular, it derives from the real balance, or Pigou, effect which argued, specifically for the case of falling prices, that deflation would stimulate demand by increasing the wealth of government bondholders. Eisner makes it clear that he is fully conscious of his intellectual foundations:

> Now we have married Keynes and Pigou! . . . While Keynesian formulations stress the advantage of budget deficits in contributing to the flow of current after-tax income and purchasing power, the neoclassical, and more fundamental formulation sees *changes in wealth* as affecting current and future demand . . . The neoclassical formulation implies that the budget deficit that will matter for aggregate demand is the one that increases the real net debt of the government to the public. (ibid., p. 173)

Eisner makes two adjustments to account for the inflation-induced depreciation in the real value of government debt. The first is to reduce official deficits by a standard price deflator to reflect the depreciation in the real value of the debt associated with any given deficit. The second is to reduce the real value of the deficit by the difference between the government debt's par and market values. This adjustment is intended to reflect the way higher interest rates drive down the market value of outstanding securities.

Distinguishing cyclical versus high employment, nominal versus inflation-adjusted and capital versus current account deficits – these then are the accounting issues Eisner raises. In *The Debt and the Deficit*, Heilbroner and Bernstein (1989) place equal emphasis on the need to make downward adjustments on the official deficit, but their specific arguments are somewhat different. Like Eisner, they make adjustments based on both the current/capital account distinction and the impact of inflation. But Heilbroner and Bernstein do not pursue Eisner's consideration of cyclical versus high employment deficits. On the other hand, they deduct state and local government surpluses from the deficit total, a point which Eisner neglects. Such differences between these two essentially similar approaches make clear that there can be no single measure of the deficit that will be satisfactory for addressing all relevant analytical questions. Nevertheless, Heilbroner and Bernstein's conclusion that 'today's deficit, by any measure, is far far smaller than we think' (ibid., p. 80) is certainly consistent with all of Eisner's broad findings.

Eisner goes on to develop an econometric model to measure the effects of the 'real' deficit. Here he makes no formal adjustment to account for the distinction between current and capital accounts. But he does perform adjustments to separate the cyclical from the high employment deficit and, most importantly, to control for the effects of inflation. Based on these adjustments, Eisner then measures an 'inflation-corrected high employment deficit'. Through regression analysis, he then seeks to measure the effects of this fully adjusted deficit on the economy. His results are dramatically at odds with mainstream thinking, finding that 'the high employment budget deficit is a substantial predictor of subsequent changes in output and employment' (Eisner, 1986, p. 112). Greater deficits have been associated with more favourable outcomes in gross national product and unemployment, according to Eisner, and the inflation-adjusted high employment deficit is a stronger predictor of changes in output and unemployment than the unadjusted figures. He also finds that the effects of 'real' budget deficits show up in both consumption and investment – the deficits 'crowd in' both consumption and investment. Here then is one answer to the puzzle as to why deficits do not perform as traditional Keynesian theory had suggested. Eisner says they do, but only after one measures the deficit correctly.

Eisner's work, as well as Heilbroner and Bernstein's more popular development of it, has been highly salutary to the general debate on deficits. Their discussions of capital budgeting have, first of all, reminded economists that government spending can serve legitimate functions. More generally, they have also brought accounting questions to the forefront of debate, where they must be placed before generalizations about the impact of deficits can be seriously considered. Finally, they have revived the fundamental, though increasingly moribund, Keynesian argument that the demand effects of deficits can actually promote private investment and consumption spending, although Heilbroner and Bernstein noticeably de-emphasize this point in *The Debt and the Deficit* relative to their 1963 discussion.

Still, given all these valuable contributions, this framework also contains fundamental flaws; we concentrate on Eisner's more fully developed presentation in addressing these. First, with respect to capital budgeting, Eisner is correct to emphasize that the government's debt financed investment spending should be accounted for separately. At the same time, in stressing this point he neglects the equally important issue that the government has relied increasingly on borrowing to purchase its investment as well as consumption goods. This trend towards increased government borrowing to finance both consumption and investment is a legitimate cause for concern, just as when corporations borrow increasingly to finance investments or households assume growing mortgages relative to the value of their homes. In all cases, the growing financing gap carries important implications: the non-financial unit's ability to service debt will decline if income-earning assets are not growing correspondingly; and even if income-earning asset growth is equivalent, growing demand-side stresses will be placed on financial markets. Of course, it is preferable that the government should finance investment spending rather than wasteful consumption. But the composition of government spending, though obviously an important question, needs to be considered separately from the effects of growing deficits to finance both consumption and investment.

Eisner is also correct to distinguish between the cyclical and high employment budgets. But he is again wrong to neglect the fact of growing cyclical deficits. By doing so, Eisner leaves aside the whole issue of structural change in the US economy. The growth of cyclical deficits is an important measure of structural change, indicating most broadly that the economy has become less capable of financing government activities while also allowing after-tax incomes to grow. It also means that the demand-boosting capacities of deficits become less potent: increasing fiscal stimulus becomes necessary to counteract the economy's growing structural weaknesses. In short, by ignoring the question of cyclical deficits – 'how the economy affects the deficit' – Eisner fails to address the basic point that a deficit in one period, even a fully adjusted high employment deficit, may not have the same impact as in another period, because the structure of the economy responding to the deficit has changed.

Eisner's most basic errors are associated with his inflation adjustment. He argues that the only deficit that matters is one that adds to real government debt. In other words, he is contending that the government's borrowing and spending flows associated with a current period deficit are not significant macro variables in themselves, but only as they affect the real stock of government debt. There are several mistakes in this reasoning. The first is that the government's borrowing and spending flows associated with deficits are important factors determining what will be the final change in the real, as well as the nominal, debt stock. The government's spending flows increase aggregate demand, and as such contribute to inflationary pressures, thus influencing the magnitude of Eisner's inflation adjustment. Current period inflation in turn affects nominal interest rates, and interest rate change is the second determinant of Eisner's inflation adjustment.

The government's current period borrowing also has a major impact, operating through financial markets. Among other things, it exerts upward pressure on interest rates and influences the monetary posture of the Fed. As such, the current period borrowing flow associated with the deficit also affects Eisner's inflation adjustment on the debt stock. In short, following Eisner's own accounting, the current period flows of borrowing and spending are major determinants of what real government debt stocks will become in succeeding periods. It is therefore erroneous to regard them as insignificant even within his own theoretical framework.

The theoretical assumptions behind Eisner's inflation adjustment are equally questionable. His entire adjustment has the real balance effect as its foundation. However, he makes no serious effort to explain why he has adopted this position. Eisner, of course, is free to choose a non-Keynesian approach here, but as someone generally in sympathy with Keynes, it would be useful to understand what motivates this departure.

More importantly, in the absence of any development of his theoretical premises, the case for the real balance effect appears weak. One major problem is that the proportion of total households whose demand patterns would be affected by changes in the real value of government bonds is small. This can be seen from the data in Table 5.3, showing ownership shares of federal government debt for 1983, the most recent year for which reliable data are available on household ownership distribution. The table shows, first of all, that individuals who are US residents own only 13 per cent of total outstanding debt. Over half of the government debt is owned by US corporations and financial intermediaries, and the next largest share, 16.3 per cent, is held by foreign institutions and individuals. Changes in the real value of bonds held by corporations, financial institutions and foreigners cannot be expected to affect US aggregate demand directly. Eisner himself never suggests that they will.

Considering then only the 13 per cent of the debt owned by US individuals, we also see in Table 5.3 that ownership is highly skewed towards the wealthiest segment of the population. The richest 10 per cent of households own nearly 80 per cent of all securities held by individuals, and the richest 1 per cent own roughly one-third of all individually held securities. Moreover, ownership is even more concentrated if we consider only larger denomination marketable Treasury securities. Changes in the value of these large denomination securities will have a much larger impact on individual households' real wealth than would revaluations in small denomination savings bonds.

Thus, the demand effects associated with real wealth changes, on which Eisner stakes his argument, would have to emerge from a narrow base of the most affluent US households. Eisner's case is weakened further since, as is well known, affluent households have the greatest latitude in their spending patterns, and the lowest marginal propensity to consume from changes either in income or wealth: the negligible changes in consumption patterns by affluent households induced by the 1987 stock market crash is one dramatic indicator of the weakness of the real balance effect.[9]

Eisner does present econometric evidence to support his position. But in fact, his evidence provides only weak support for his argument. His basic bivariate regression equation is of the following type:

Table 5.3a   Ownership of federal government securities, 1983

Ownership shares by sector	Percentage
Individuals	13.0
State and local governments	14.7
Foreign holdings	16.3
Corporations and financial intermediaries	56.0

[a] A small proportion of this sector includes federal government deposit accounts and government sponsored agencies.
Source: Economic Report of the President, 1988.

Table 5.3b   Concentration of ownership among household

Percentage owned by wealthiest households	All securities	Marketable securities
Top 1%	32.3	37.4
Top 5%	57.2	66.1
Top 10%	78.6	90.3

Source: Federal Reserve Board 1983, 'Survey of Consumer Finances and High Income Supplement'.

$$GNP_t = \alpha + \beta \, HES_{t-1},$$

where *GNP* is the change in real GNP and *HES* is the high employment surplus. He also incorporates other variables, such as monetary growth and interest rate changes, into multivariate specifications. But his main results regarding the impact of deficits emerge clearly with the various specifications of the bivariate case. For that case, a significant negative value for the HES explanatory variable would imply a significant positive impact of high employment deficits on GNP growth. The HES specification changes according to whether Eisner incorporates his price and interest rate adjustments. He then divides the full period for which his data are complete, 1955–84, into two phases, 1955–66 and 1967–84. The first phase, as Eisner explains, represents the years of relatively rapid, non-inflationary growth; and the second phase, the years of stagnation and inflation.

The findings he emphasizes show HES to have substantial inverse explanatory power in tracking changes in GNP. But a careful reading and replication of his regressions presents a less favourable result:

1. For the first post-war phase, his fully adjusted HES variable – including price and interest adjustments – achieves significant explanatory power only when

a two-year time lag is incorporated as an explanatory variable. Its effects are insignificant with either a one-year lag or no lag.

2. For the full period as well, the fully adjusted HES is significant only when specified with a two-year lag. It is also insignificant with no lag or a one-year lag.

3. The results become more robust when one considers only the second phase of his sample. But even these results are unpersuasive. First, he never explains why, for testing the impact of deficits, it is legitimate to divide the full period into two phases, rather than simply examining the period as a whole. Moreover, he never explains why deficit spending should have a substantially greater measured impact during the second post-war phase relative to the first phase or the full period. Eisner's theoretical orientation should probably lead him to anticipate a greater measured impact for deficits during the first post-war period. Such a result would establish a link between the positive impact of deficits that he sees and the superior macro performance of the first phase. But Eisner never addresses this issue.

Overall then, Eisner's econometric findings are not convincing; and this includes the multivariate specifications that follow his basic bivariate equations. Heilbroner and Bernstein's discussion is less technical and therefore is not subject to all the same criticisms. However, given the similarity of their approach to Eisner's, it is likely that their arguments would face comparable difficulties had they developed them further. The fundamental question thus remains: why are growing deficits associated with declining economic performance?

5.4   STRUCTURAL CHANGE AND THE DEFICIT

I now attempt to develop a historical analysis of deficits, one which tries to show how structural changes in the US macroeconomy – specifically the emergence of stagnation, internationalization and debt dependency – have transformed the relationship between deficit spending and macroeconomic activity. We begin by reviewing basic measures of stagnation, internationalization and debt dependency that are relevant for the analysis of federal deficits, then consider some of the interrelationships between these phenomena, again especially as they relate to the growth of federal deficits, and finally try to establish the most important links between deficits and structural macroeconomic change.

Stagnation

In the US and other advanced capitalist countries stagnation a well-known, if insufficiently appreciated, fact of contemporary economic life. One of the earliest diagnoses of the problem was *Beyond Boom and Crash*, a 1978 book by Professor Heilbroner. The book begins by declaring that 'another worldwide crisis of capitalism is upon us' (ibid., p. 11), and proceeds to document the economic sea change between the twenty-five years of buoyant expansion beginning in the early 1950s and the onset in the early 1970s of declining growth for all advanced capitalist countries. Heilbroner also predicted that structural problems of the capitalist world would continue, writing 'of a European community that is fighting demoralization [and] an American economy unable to generate momentum' (ibid., 15). We now know, more than a decade after the publication of *Beyond Boom and Crash*, that Heilbroner's predictions (made without benefit of forecasting wizardry) were prescient. A 1988 essay by Stanley Fischer, for example, describes the continued growth stagnation as 'the most significant macroeconomic development of the last two decades' (ibid., p. 3). Table 5.4 reproduces the data Fischer presented, documenting the declining growth trend for all advanced capitalist countries.

Focusing on the US, we obtain a sharper sense of the stagnation trend in Table 5.5 by observing the behaviour from cycle to cycle of several important indicators: the trend increase in unemployment, and the trend unemployment, and the trend declines in real wages, corporate profitability, and capacity utilization. Note that according to all but the profit indicator, the macro performance for the 1980s is inferior to that even of the latter 1970s – the 'years of malaise'. This is so despite the eight-year expansion of the Reagan–Bush era. Profit rates did recover in 1982–90 from their sharp descent of the 1970s and early 1980s. However, even after having risen fairly steadily for eight years, the average profit rate over 1982–90, at 8.6 per cent, remained well below the level of the 1960s and even the 1950s.

For the purposes of developing the link between stagnation and government deficits, it will not be necessary to pursue an extensive discussion of the causes of stagnation. A substantial and important literature has developed around this question within the Marxian and post-Keynesian traditions, and it will be adequate for our purposes to refer to it selectively below as it relates specifically to the question of deficits.[10]

Table 5.4   Percentage growth of per capita GNP

	1955–73	*1973–86*
United States	2.0	1.3
Japan	8.8	3.1
Germany	4.2	2.0
United Kingdom	2.5	0.9
Italy	4.9	2.0
France	4.6	1.9
Canada	3.0	2.0

Source: Stanley Fischer (1988, p. 4).

Budget Deficits and the US Economy

Table 5.5   Measure of stagnation in the post-war US macro economy

Cycles	1953–7	1958–9	1960–9	1970–3	1974–9	1980–1	1982–90
Pretax Profit Rate[a]	11.1	10.6	12.2	8.1	5.9	6.0	8.6
Capacity Utilization Rate[b]	85.2	78.3	84.9	81.6	80.4	78.8	79.6
Average Weekly Earnings, 1977 dollars[c]	241.2	255.6	284.2	308.2	297.7	272.6	268.6
Unemployment Rate[d]	4.1	5.9	4.6	5.2	6.7	7.3	6.9

[a]   Pretax profits of nonfinancial corporations. Calculation follows methodology in Pollin (1986), data through 1989 only.
   Source: Federal Reserve Board's Flow of Funds Accounts, Department of Commerce, National Income and Product Accounts (1987).

[b]   Manufacturing Capacity Utilization rate, Federal Reserve Board series.
   Source: *Citicorp Economic Database*, 1991–2 edition.

[c]   Average weekly earnings in total private nonagricultural economy.
   Source: *Economic Report of the President*, 1991, p. 336.

[d]   Unemployment rate, all workers.
   Source: *Citicorp Economic Database*, 1991–2 edition.

Debt dependency

We have already reviewed the most important evidence on debt dependency in Table 5.2, showing that the growth of government borrowing has not inhibited non-financial corporations and households from also maintaining high levels of debt financing. What should be emphasized beyond this is that, considering non-financial borrowers in the aggregate, the contemporary rate of debt financing is unprecedented in US history. This can be seen when, following the pioneering work of Gurley and Shaw (1956), we divide twentieth-century US financial activity into 17–19-year-long cycles. Gurley and Shaw found that between 1897 and 1949, the ratio of net borrowing to GNP was remarkably stable at around 9 per cent for each long cycle. This relationship also held between 1950 and 1966. However, over the most recent long cycle, between 1967 and 1986, this figure rose to 14.6 per cent, a 60 per cent increase over the historical average. The federal deficit, as will be discussed below, relates to this trend as both cause and consequence.

Internationalization

There is much controversy as to the causes, extent and implications of internationalization. For our purposes here, we are interested in internationalization only as it relates to the US economy, and specifically the features of internationalization most associated with the impact of federal deficits. To that end, I focus on two key aspects of internationalization – the US trade account and foreign credit flows to the US.

With respect to trade, it is, of course, widely recognized that the US economy has become increasingly integrated in the world market. Table 5.6 presents familiar data, showing US imports and the trade deficit relative to GNP. As we see, both have risen steadily and substantially since the early 1970s.

It is also widely recognized that the US financial market has become increasingly integrated in the world market. This too is readily discernible through basic data on financial flows to the US. Figure 5.3 shows foreign sources of credit as a

Table 5.6   US trade integration

Cycles	1953–7	1958–9	1960–9	1970–3	1974–9	1980–7	1982–90
US Imports/GNP	2.9	3.0	3.2	4.6	7.4	8.9	8.7
US Surplus (+) or Deficit (–)							
Relative to GNP	+0.9	+0.5	+0.7	0.00	–0.7	–0.9	–2.5

Source: *Citicorp Economic Database*, 1991–2 edition.

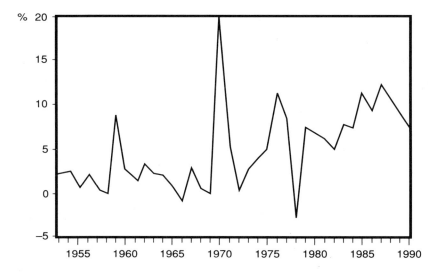

Figure 5.3   Foreign credit sources as a percentage of total funds advanced to US domestic non-financial sectors

Source: *Flow of Funds Accounts of Federal Reserve System*; table entitled 'Total Net Borrowing and Lending in Credit Markets'.

percentage of total US credit market lending. We see that this figure first spiked at nearly 20 per cent in 1971, in association with the growing link between US finance and the Eurodollar market. And while that initial peak has not been equalled, the trend for the ratio over the 1970s and especially the 1980s is strongly upward. The mean figure for 1982–90, for example, was 8.7 per cent, while that for 1960–69 was 1.3 per cent.[11]

As a last step before addressing the relationship between structural macroeconomic change and the deficit, let us briefly consider the connections between stagnation, debt dependency, and internationalization. The links between stagnation and debt dependency, to begin with, are strong. As I have tried to show elsewhere,[12] stagnant household incomes and declining profitability have engendered two types of credit demand. The first is 'necessitous' demand. This refers to the need of households and corporations to become more reliant on borrowed funds in order to sustain expenditure growth in the face of declining revenues. In addition, stagnation has encouraged the growth of 'speculative' credit demand: borrowing to finance purchases of existing assets rather than the creation of new assets, junk bond financing of leveraged buy-outs being the best-known example of speculative credit demand. Below, I try to show how such activity is encouraged through the decline of profitability in productive investments. For now, we can say that debt dependency is a response to stagnation. At the same time, as I will also argue further, the experience of stagnation is transformed through debt dependency. It allows for higher levels of expenditure, but also creates upward interest rate pressure and increasing overall strain on the financial structure.

The stagnation/debt dependency interrelationship can easily be joined to internationalization as well. The major reason why foreign funds moved increasingly into the US credit market is that the demand for such funds had been created through private necessitous and speculative borrowing, as well as the federal deficit. The US trade deficit, moreover, has been instrumental in supplying foreigners with dollars which were then available to be recycled into the US financial market.

Having sketched the main relevant features of stagnation, internationalization, and debt dependency as well as their interrelationships, we can now consider the links between structural change and deficits. I pursue this discussion by attempting to support the following five propositions: (i) structural change has created growing deficits; (ii) structural change has weakened the deficit's demand stimulus; (iii) the deficit has fostered financial fragility; (iv) structural change and the deficit have constrained monetary policy; and (v) servicing the deficit redistributes income upwards. I consider them in turn.

Structural Change Creates Growing Deficits

We addressed this issue briefly in considering Robert Eisner's discussion of the distinction between cyclical and high employment deficits: cyclical deficits, as he puts it, measure the impact of the economy on the deficit, while high employment deficits should be used to gauge the impact of deficits on the economy. As noted, Eisner is correct to distinguish these two components of aggregate deficits, but is mistaken to neglect consideration of why cyclical deficits have grown. For our discussion, it is important to establish the link between deficit growth and stagnation. For one thing, declining pretax profitability and real wage rates have meant that government revenues from corporations and wage earners correspondingly declined. At the same time, declining wages and the rising unemployment trend increased government expenditures on unemployment insurance and other income support programmes. Beyond this – and here perhaps is the single most important factor in explaining the deficit explosion in the 1980s – structural change has also contributed to growing high employment deficits. The channel here is the cuts in tax burdens for both corporations and households during the 1970s and especially the 1980s – indeed the entire 'taxpayers' revolt' of this period. These changes reflected an effort by most sectors of the economy to counteract the stagnation of pretax incomes with a reduction in their tax burdens. Of course, the ultimate beneficiaries of the Reagan era tax cuts were the corporations and the wealthy, not middle-income households. Nevertheless, the origins of the revolt were broadly based.

Structural Change Weakens the Deficit's Demand Stimulus

There are two key elements to understanding this. The first is the impact on the domestic economy of large trade deficits. The second is the relationship between investment, profitability and the deficit.

Impact of trade deficits

It is widely recognized that an important link exists between the trade and budget deficits. What is more controversial is the causal relationship between them. One major connection is clear. As a simple accounting identity, it is necessarily the case that a US trade deficit involves an exporting of domestic aggregate demand. This means that a portion of the budget deficit's demand stimulus will be exported, weakening its multiplier effects on domestic markets and correspondingly on US domestic investment. Frequently, discussions around the trade deficit focus on problems at the microeconomic level associated with the question of US industry's ability to compete with technologically innovative or simply lower cost foreign producers. These problems are real enough, but the macroeconomic problem of losing a share of the deficit's demand stimulus is largely neglected, even though it is analytically straightforward and equally important.

Beyond this basic macroeconomic connection between the trade and budget deficits, analysts within the crowding out framework argue for a further link: they claim that the budget deficit is the *primary cause* of the large trade deficits. In brief, their argument holds that the budget deficit causes US interest rates to rise, which in turn produces a rising value of the dollar. The overvalued dollar, finally, raises US export prices and lowers import prices to the point where a wide range of US products are uncompetitive. But this argument is not supported by the evidence. As we have seen, the budget deficit alone does not cause high interest rates. Rather, continued strong credit demand from the private sector in combination with government borrowing is responsible for the unprecedented demand-side pressure in US credit markets; and this demand-side pressure alone, as we will discuss shortly, is not solely responsible for the high interest rates. Supply-side factors are equally important. Moreover, the value of the dollar has fallen sharply since 1985, even though real interest rates have remained high, and even this, as a final contradiction of the neo-Keynesian position, has not led to a closing of the trade deficit.

In short, we have to look beyond simply the relationship between the trade and budget deficits to explain the causes of the trade deficit. But given the trade deficit, its macroeconomic effect on the budget deficit's demand stimulus is clear enough.

Investment, profitability and the deficit

It is widely argued by economists in the traditions of Marx, Keynes and Kalecki that investment spending is primarily a function of expected profitability. Capitalists, as Marx put it, are driven to investment by their 'werewolf hunger for profits'. As a first approximation, we would expect profit expectations to fall when actual profitability declines over the trend. This is because positive profit expectations, however they are formed, are bound to be disappointed in the aggregate more frequently than negative expectations during a declining profitability trend. The observed decline in investment growth can then be explained, again as a first approximation, as a result of the decline in corporate profitability.[13]

Actual profit expectations are reflected in the behaviour of Tobin's Q ratio, so it will be useful to consider again its movements over the post-war period. We saw in Figure 5.2 that the proxy Q ratio declined sharply from its post-war peak of 1.1 in 1968 to a low of .38 in 1974, has risen over the trend since then, but still, by 1990, remained at approximately .75. This behaviour of the Q proxy closely approximates that of the after-tax corporate profit rate, suggesting that profit expectations do correspond to movements of the actual profit rate.

Beyond this point, the observed decline of Q proxy carries important implications in its own right for investment behaviour. A Q ratio of less than unity means that potential investors can purchase existing assets for less than they would spend to create new assets. Thus as Q remains below unity, the greater the incentive to acquire firms through mergers and acquisitions than invest in building plant and equipment. The 1990 value of the Q proxy implies that one dollar's worth of the average firm's physical assets can be purchased for $.75 on Wall Street. Corporations, in short, can still be bought on the cheap, and this becomes the fundamental basis for the merger and leveraged buy-out frenzy of recent years, as well as the creation of the junk bond market to finance such activities.

With respect to the deficit, the decline of the profit rate and Q has meant an attenuation of the demand stimulus from a given injection of federal deficit spending. As declining profit expectations have dampened animal spirits, larger demand boosters are needed to embolden investors' enthusiasm. And should investors become roused, the low Q ratio creates an incentive for them to direct their funds towards buying existing firms rather than increasing the capital stock. Even substantial deficits thus have diminishing ability to stimulate investment growth via demand.[14]

The Deficit Encourages Financial Fragility

We have already discussed how the historically unprecedented rise of debt financially by the aggregate non-financial sector of the economy has exerted upward interest rate pressure. Here I consider another element of the relationship between deficits and debt dependency: how deficits have encouraged private debt financing and thereby contributed to the deepening fragility of US financial markets.

As we saw, corporations and households since the late 1960s have increased their rates of debt financing both to avoid sharp reductions in their expenditure levels and to pursue speculative investment opportunities. But these factors cannot explain why aggregate debt financing has risen to a historically unprecedented level. Certainly, significant gaps between incomes and expenditure levels have emerged in prior historical phases, as have waves of heavy financial speculation. Yet, as noted earlier, the aggregate debt financing ratio remained highly stable in these previous periods.

Federal deficits have contributed to the contemporary rise in aggregate debt financing in two crucial ways. The first is simply that, unlike previous historical periods, federal borrowing now represents a large component of total borrowing on a permanent basis, not just during wartime. But even more important has been the deficit's short-term counter-cyclical impact. In earlier historical phases, the rise of private debt financing was checked and reversed when credit bubbles were burst by severe debt deflations and widespread defaults, which in turn forced the economy's aggregate rate of debt financing sharply downward. In the contemporary period, cyclical deficits counteract the debt deflation process by increasing the level of aggregate income in the short run. As a result of this intervention, defaults can and do still occur in periods of cyclical decline, but not as severely as would have resulted without the government intervention. When the wave of defaults is avoided, the incipient debt-deflation is thwarted.

Thus, within the financial as well as the product and labour markets, cyclical deficits act to circumscribe the private economy's contractionary tendencies. However, in accomplishing this task, the deficits also necessarily act to nullify the debt deflation process as a financial regulator. In the absence of debt deflations, no automatic mechanism exists for discouraging the sustained growth in private debt financing. This is why the private sector has become increasingly debt dependent in the contemporary period, even as real interest rates have risen and the incomes to service debt have stagnated or declined. As private sector debt dependency increases under these circumstances, greater stresses are created in financial markets – they become more vulnerable to cyclical downturns and random shocks. In short, financial fragility deepens.[15]

Structural Change Constrains Monetary Policy

We have argued that increased debt financing has exerted upward demand-side pressure on US interest rates. But this alone cannot explain the unprecedented levels that US interest rates have since it gives no consideration to supply-side factors. The single most important supply-side influence on interest rates is central bank policy. Conceivably, were the Federal Reserve so inclined, it could fully counteract the strong demand-side pressures through equivalently loose monetary policies, and thereby bring interest rates closer to their historical levels. However, the Fed has been inhibited from pursuing such highly expansionary policies, and the constraints on its behaviour can be best understood within the framework of the economy's structural changes.

Domestic inflationary expectations is the first constraint on Fed behaviour. As is well known, highly accommodative monetary policies do not have the effect of lowering nominal interest rates, especially long-term rates. This is because market participants largely assume the accommodative policies are inflationary. Lenders, as a result, will incorporate an increased inflation premium into nominal rates, to insure that their real returns on loans are protected. If their inflationary expectations are accurate, real interest rates will not be altered by accommodative policies. In any case, the substantial degree of responsiveness of domestic financial market participants to highly accommodative policies inhibits the Fed from pursuing such policies in conditions of strong credit demand.[16]

A second, and equally powerful constraint comes from the trade deficit, which requires that foreigners be willing to hold dollar assets in amounts equal to the cumulative gap in the trade account. This factor is also linked to conditions in the domestic financial market, since the domestic market must attract foreign savings to help meet the credit demand from private US non-financial borrowers and the federal government. Given these conditions, the Federal Reserve recognizes that real yields on US financial assets – taking account of domestic inflation, depreciation of the dollar, as well as nominal interest payments – must be positive and high enough to continue drawing foreign dollar asset holders into the US financial market.

One plausible outcome of allowing interest rates to fall to the low or even negative real levels that prevailed during the 1970s would be a flight from the dollar similar to those of the early and late 1970s. Such a scenario would probably engender a serious financial crisis, greater than those of the 1970s, because of the higher levels at present in aggregate debt financing as well as the continued need to finance the trade deficit. The Federal Reserve, as a result, is unable to pursue highly expansionary policies that could counter the upward interest rate pressure generated from the demand side of financial markets. What is implied, in short, is that two manifestations of structural change – the rise in debt dependency on the demand side and international constraints on the supply side – are together responsible to a large degree for the sustained high real interest rates since the late 1970s.[17]

Financing the Deficit Redistributes Income Upwards

Several factors will determine the net distributive impact of deficit spending. The most important would include: the use to which the funds are put; the extent to which taxation, the alternative means of raising funds, is progressive; and how effective will be the aggregate demand stimulus in generating jobs and income. The net effect of these considerations is difficult (though not impossible) to assess.[18]

Here we ask, more narrowly, what is the distributive impact of *financing* the deficit? To make the question tractable, we have to assume that the distributive effects of the deficit itself are held constant. Working from this *ceteris paribus* condition, it follows from three sets of data that financing the deficit redistributes income upwards. The first set of data, shown earlier in Table 5.3, is the highly skewed ownership pattern of government debt among US households and between households, domestic financial institutions and foreign bondholders. But for unequal ownership of government bonds to have redistributive effect, positive interest return to owners of these bonds must also prevail. This, as we have also seen, was not always the case in the 1970s, but has emphatically been so during the 1980s.

Finally, for the redistribution effect to be significant, interest payments on the bonds must constitute a substantial share of the government budget. This also is the case, as is shown in Table 5.7. This table presents official interest payment figures relative to total government outlays. According to this, interest payments

Table 5.7   Interest share of government budget

	Percentages
1953–7	7.0
1958–9	6.6
1960–9	6.9
1970–3	7.1
1974–9	7.6
1980–7	9.5
1982–90	13.4

Source: US Office of Management and Budget, *Historical Tables, Budget of the US Government, Fiscal Year 1992.*

are a fairly stable proportion of budget outlays through the 1970s, ranging between 6.6–7.6 per cent over the five cycles of the 1950s–70s. Over 1982–9,
however, the interest share basically doubles relative to its historical level, to
13.4 per cent.[19]

Jeffrey Baldini and Thomas Michl (1987) have argued that because of this
redistributive effect, deficits may ultimately serve to weaken, not promote, aggregate demand, since the relative shares of those with the lowest marginal propensities to consume are growing. But two conditions must hold to sustain Baldini
and Michl's argument. The first is that the direct income effects of deficits must
be stronger than the real balance effects. According to Eisner, the stimulative
impact of deficits are greatest when the largest amount of real wealth accrues to
government bondholders. From this perspective, the redistributive impact of
deficits would not dampen, but rather amplify, the deficit's demand stimulus. But
even if one rejects the real balances argument, as I have done earlier, the net effect
of deficits still would not be contractionary if the direct income and multiplier
stimuli from the deficit exceeded the redistributive impact from government
interest payments.

Such relative effects are difficult to compare empirically, but one crude indicator is presented in Figure 5.4 which shows the movements of deficits and
interest payments since 1953. For simplicity, we assume that the total deficit
contributes to the direct income and multiplier stimuli, though, to be more precise,
one might argue that a part of the deficit should be allocated to interest payments.[20] As the figure shows, both the deficit and interest payments rise sharply
in the 1980s. However, through 1986, with its peak deficit of $221 billion, the
deficit's growth was more rapid. But the deficit diminished over 1987–9, while
interest payments, reflecting past obligations, continued to rise despite the deficit's decline. Thus, the two figures became virtually equal, with interest payments
exceeding deficits in 1989. The deficit rose above interest payments again in
1990, and this may have provided some direct stimulus. Still, what becomes clear
is that, unless the Eisnerian real balances argument is correct, then interest
payments are absorbing nearly all the demand stimulus that deficits can provide.
If present trends continue, Baldini and Michl are therefore correct to postulate a
net contractionary effect from government deficit spending in the future.

Structural Change and the Deficit: Summary and Implications

Let us raise the fundamental question one last time: why have growing federal
deficits accompanied declining economic performance in the US since the early
1970s? I believe the historical approach suggested here provides a coherent
framework for answering this otherwise elusive question. More specifically, to
paraphrase Professor Heilbroner, once one identifies structural change in the US
economy as the central focus of the analysis, an entrée into the possible nature of
the deficit is opened that is otherwise blocked from view. This chapter tries to
show several links between structural change – i.e. stagnation, internationaliza-

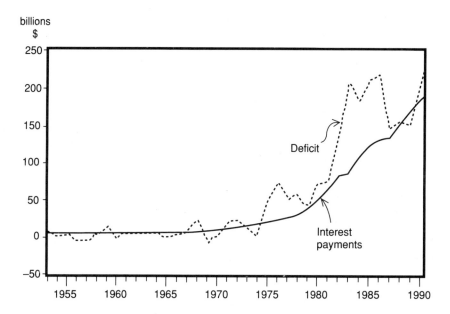

billions
$

Figure 5.4   Federal deficit and interest payments

Sources: See Tables 5.1 and 5.7.

tion, and debt dependency – and the deficit: that structural change has contributed to the growth of deficits over time; that the demand stimulus from a given-sized deficit has diminished because of structural change; and that the negative collateral effects of deficits – increased financial fragility, upward income redistribution, and constraints on monetary policy – have worsened. In the present historical phase, the net impact of deficit spending on growth and employment may still be positive. This is because the direct income and multiplier effects of deficits, taken by themselves, can be so potent. But the conclusion offered here that this net positive impact, if it is still present, is certainly diminishing over time.

Considered from another angle, the conclusion reached here is that, contrary to the 'crowding out' school, deficits are not the cause of declining US macroeconomic performance. Nor, as Eisner would have it, is deficit spending the solution to stagnation. But deficits are not irrelevant to US macroeconomic conditions either, as Barro claims. Persistent and growing deficits, rather, are a consequence of structural change. But they are a major consequence of structural change, and as such, they in turn have become an important determinant of how the on-going process of structural change unfolds.

It is clear then that deficit spending is not an effective tool to counter the consequences of stagnation, internationalization, and debt dependency. However, a resolve to slash and burn federal government spending programmes does not follow from this conclusion. As Professor Heilbroner has repeatedly insisted, the federal government in contemporary US capitalism finances many essential activities – education, housing, infrastructure development, environmental protection, and minority employment. Support for these activities needs to be strengthened, not curtailed, and experience has shown that we cannot hand these functions over to the private market and expect a reasonable outcome. Even from a more narrow perspective, the evidence does not suggest that cutting government spending will promote stabilization and growth. As this chapter has briefly tried to suggest, and others have demonstrated in greater depth, market forces themselves are ultimately responsible for stagnation, internationalization, and debt dependency in the US economy. To gain control over these trends for the benefit of the vast majority will therefore require more democratic control over market forces, not greater market freedom.

This brings us to a dilemma: federal deficits are increasingly ineffective as promoters of growth and stability, yet more public intervention is needed to overcome our economic difficulties. What is implied here is that the *forms* taken by public intervention – or, more fundamentally, by democratic forces in the economy – must change. Fiscal policy interventions and deficit spending are not adequate for promoting growth and stabilization, to say nothing of equity. The next step forward must be towards democratic control over large-scale investment activities – the decisions that give the economy its direction and momentum, and that heretofore remain under the authority of private capital. One evident strength of an investment control strategy is that it removes from private capital the power to determine how fiscal interventions themselves are ultimately absorbed. Under public control, for example, a deficit's demand stimulus would not be dissipated through leveraged buy-outs, since such non-productive activities would evidently be circumscribed under a democratic investment authority.

What is the blueprint for bringing rational public control to the US and other advanced capitalist economies? This question is obviously far beyond the scope of this chapter. But it is also the most basic intellectual and political issue facing the left today. Robert Heilbroner's work, with its broad sweep, eloquence, authority, and most importantly, its insistence on addressing essential questions of human well-being, will remain a wellspring of support as we seek to construct our more rational economic future.

Notes

1. One point of clarification needs to be raised before proceeding. For the most part, the debate over the macroeconomic effects of deficits is conducted at a high level of aggregation, relegating questions over the composition of the government budget to a second order of concern. This approach, of course, was encouraged by Keynes' exaggerated indifference as to whether deficit funds were used to build pyramids, fill holes in the ground, or employed towards more constructive ends. In fact, the

composition of the government budget is of great importance – in terms of its distributional impact, of course, but also for the economy as a whole. The relative employment effects of military versus social spending is only one of the more obvious macroeconomic issues influenced by the budget's composition. However, in the interests of space, I for the most part follow convention here, addressing the issue of the deficit as a whole and putting the question of spending priorities to one side. A recent mainstream work that places prime importance on the composition of government spending rather than simply the size of the deficit is Stein (1989).

2. As O'Driscoll (1977) has pointed out, it is hardly appropriate to associate the work of David Ricardo with Barro's position. In his pamphlet 'Funding System' (1951), Ricardo does explain how one might, in theory, conceive of a taxation/public borrowing relationship. But Ricardo also expresses in the same pamphlet the un-ambiguous view that such an equivalence would not hold in the real world. In considering whether a war should be financed by either taxation or public borrow-ing, Ricardo writes, 'In point of economy, there is no real difference in either of the modes; for twenty millions in one payment, one million per annum for ever, or 1,200,000 pounds for 45 years, are precisely of the same value; but the people who pay the taxes never so estimate them, and therefore do not manage their private affairs accordingly' (ibid., p. 187). In this same passage, Ricardo expands on this point, including some discussion of what now is called the intergenerational transfer issue.

3. For a range of critical views within mainstream discussions, see Bernheim (1987), Eisner (1986), and Summers (1986).

4. For example, a half-page op-ed article in the 2/16/89 *Wall Street Journal* by *Journal* editor Robert Bartley extols the virtues of Barro's theorem. Bartley, an infrequent contributor to his own newspaper or any other publication, emerges from the shadows here to state emphatically that he is 'an unreconstructed supporter of Barro's Ricardian Equivalence Theorem', and to quote Barro's 1989 article at length.

5. Summers and other proponents of this view seem fully conscious of the extent to which their approach represents a departure from Keynes. For example, in another passage of the 1986 article Summers writes despairingly of the 'lingering influence of Keynes' in the US and UK creating undue concern about oversaving-induced stagnation (ibid., p. 69). Despite this, Summers also refers in the same article to his approach as the 'standard Keynesian macro model' (ibid., p. 71). Thus, with perfect Orwellian logic, the legacies of both Ricardo and Keynes are invoked in contempor-ary mainstream macroeconomic discussions to support arguments completely con-trary to those advanced by either of these great figures.

6. The data are grouped by cycles using NBER cycle dates as benchmarks. The NBER's quarterly cycle measures were converted into yearly groupings using the following procedures. When cyclical peaks fall in either the first or second quarters of a given year, that year is defined as the peak year. When the quarterly peaks fall in the third or fourth quarters of a year, the following year is defined as the peak. Peak years are defined as starting points for each cycle.

7. By invoking supply-side considerations within credit markets – specifically the variability of the savings supply and central bank policy – Heilbroner and Bernstein (1989) show clearly the weakness of the crowding out argument which attempts to link budget deficits to high real interest rates. Heilbroner and Bernstein write, 'crowding out is a logical scenario that can easily be confounded by changes in the flow of savings or by changes in monetary policy' (ibid., p. 106).

8. I have done more formal tests of the interest elasticity of US credit demand in Pollin (1986), which considers the case for non-financial corporations and Pollin (1988), which focuses on households. In both these studies, interest elasticity, while gener-

ally statistically significant in econometric testing, emerges as a relatively weak variable in explaining private sector borrowing patterns.

9. Eisner also makes a further, more strictly technical error, in his inflation adjustment. The impact of inflation on a financial instrument is to reduce the real value of its yield, since the nominal yield is fixed. Thus, one way to calculate this fall in real yield is to deflate the nominal values of debt by an appropriate deflation procedure. However, it is also the case that the fall in the real yield is reflected in financial markets when market values of instruments fall relative to par values. One could therefore calculate the impact of inflation by reducing the value of the nominal debt according to the deviation between market and par values. Eisner performs both types of adjustments, and therefore double counts the impact of inflation on the real yields of outstanding government bonds. I have not estimated the extent to which Eisner's overall results are sensitive to this double counting. But in any case this type of error becomes less significant given the more theoretical problems raised in the main text.

10. Within this heterodox tradition, explanations for stagnationist tendencies in the capitalist economies since the mid-1960s have focused on three types of constraints to capitalist growth: the rise of the organic composition of capital due to intracapitalist competition; the inability of demand forces to keep pace with productive capacity; and the sharpening of conflict between capitalist and non-capitalist forces. The best introduction to this literature is Cherry *et al.* (1987). More substantial discussions of various positions within this literature are in *RRPE* (1986) and Nell (1988). One approach which tries to show the theoretical compatibility between these different perspectives is Lipietz (1986).

11. Zevin (1988) argues that world financial markets have not become increasingly integrated. But his conclusion is based on a highly restricted definition of integration, that 'financial assets in different countries be perfect substitutes' (ibid., p. 4). According to Zevin then, one measures integration by the extent to which financial assets of different countries converge to a single price. The alternative definition that I pursue regards the extent of financial flows between countries – and specifically between the US and rest of the world – as a more appropriate measure of integration. From my perspective, international financial flows may increase without there necessarily being any concurrent convergence in financial asset prices. Differential asset prices will persist as long as there are differences in the attributes – the relative risk, return and maturity – of assets; the integration of markets should not necessarily tend to eliminate these differences.

12. See Pollin (1986a), (1987), (1988), (1990).

13. One extensive theoretical and empirical study of the relationship between profits and investment within a Marxian/Kaleckian framework is Gordon, Weisskopf and Bowles (1986).

14. There is one additional point to raise here. This brings us to considering briefly the causes of the profitability decline itself. In a recent paper, Weisskopf (1989) attempts to decompose the causes of the profitability decline into structural and distributional factors. The structural factors are those associated primarily with a declining output–capital ratio (organic composition of capital) and the underutilization of existing capacity. The distributional factor is the relative share of aggregate income flowing to profits and wages within a given economic environment. Weisskopf estimates that for the US environmental factors have been more important than distributional factors in explaining the profitability decline. Of the environmental factors, he identifies the declining output–capital ratio as the most important longterm influence while declining utilization rates are significant in amplifying cyclical profitability declines. What these findings suggest is that unless the declining trend in the output–capital ratio is reversed, any increases in private investment due to

deficit spending will also contribute to the factors exerting long-term downward pressure on the profit rate. In other words, increasing the capital stock when output–capital ratios are declining and utilization rates are low will exacerbate the fundamental causes of the profitability decline. This contradictory effect of deficit spending was recognized early by Kalecki (though this important facet of Kalecki's macro modelling is often overlooked). In a 1945 paper, he finds that 'if effective demand adequate to secure fully employment is created by stimulating private investment, the devices which we use for it must cumulatively increase to offset the influence of the falling rate of profit'.

15.   Professor Heilbroner developed a similar analysis of the impact of large-scale government on contemporary capitalist economies in a 1979 *New Yorker* essay. The article's main contention is conveyed in the following message:

> If the presence of government could somehow be removed, the inherent instability of capitalism might once again vent itself in self-feeding contractions, but these are now blocked by the direct counterforce of government spending and by the indirect effects of government welfare support. But the very measures that place a floor under the downward movement of the economy change expectations in ways that greatly favor its instability upward. (1979, p. 137)

16.   This chapter does not attempt to develop the relationship between inflation and structural change, so it may not be apparent how this inflationary constraint on the Federal Reserve can be linked with structural change. Though the topic is clearly beyond our present scope, suffice it to say that inflation has persistently accompanied stagnationist tendencies, most forcefully in the 1970s – whence the term 'stagflation' – but in the 1980s as well. One manifestation of the persistent inflationary tendencies has been the continued high level of NAIRU, that is, the high levels of actual unemployment that are accepted – indeed favoured – in order to prevent inflation's acceleration. Heilbroner and Bernstein offer some interesting observations on this subject:

> Perhaps the second gravest issue [in the contemporary US economy] is to find some method of controlling the inflationary threat that affects the American economy like a subacute infection – not quite serious but always there, ready to flare up into a really debilitating condition. The problem with this affliction is not so much the damage it does, but that it turns vigorous growth or vigorous public policy into problems rather than solutions. Every time 'good statistics' come out of Washington the market drops, sensing another Federal Reserve massacre around the corner. (1989, p. 134)

17.   A good account of international financial market activity around the dollar in the 1970s is Moffitt (1983). One major concern with respect to prospects of a serious run on the dollar is that such a crisis, unlike the October 1987 stock market crash, could not be contained by Federal Reserve lender-of-last-resort interventions. US authorities, as a result, would not be capable of managing such a crisis on their own, as they had basically done after the 1987 crash. On a more theoretical level, the framework sketched here for understanding interest rate behaviour is highly abbreviated, omitting not only important details but also essential perspective on the manner in which markets and policy interact to determine interest rate levels. I have developed a fuller discussion of these issues within a Post-Keynesian money supply endogeneity perspective in Pollin (1991). The essential conclusion of this study is to affirm the importance of private financial market activity – and in particular the highly flexible methods through which intermediaries manage their liabilities – in

determining market interest rates. It is through such flexible practices, moreover, that the narrow velocity of money has risen over the post-war trend. An important survey discussion of the theory of money supply endogeneity and interest rate determination within it is Rousseaus (1986). A standard modern statement on these themes is Minsky (1957).

18.   A recent standard reference on the overall distributional effects of federal government activity is Page (1983). Within the Marxist literature, an important debate about the distributional effects between classes of federal government activity in the post-war US economy has emerged around the notion of a 'social wage'. Bowles and Gintis (1982) used conventional accounting statistics to find that a significant net social wage does flow via government from capital to labour. Shaikh and Tonak (1987), using Marxian accounting categories, reached the opposite conclusion – that US labour actually pays a 'negative social wage' to capital. Miller (1989) developed a range of measures based on alternative theoretical perspectives, and found, along with Shaikh and Tonak, that the social wage in the post-war US has been consistently negative.

19.   One also needs to consider inflation-adjusted interest payments in this context. The reason for making the adjustment on interest payments would be to account for the fact that in an inflation, a portion of nominal interest payments are effectively principal payments to the government's creditors. This is because financial assets, unlike physical assets, are fixed in monetary terms, and therefore depreciate in real terms relative to physical assets in an inflationary environment. Thus, a portion of interest payments is not a real return to creditors, but simply an offset to the decline in the relative value of their financial asset. This point is similar to that emphasized by Eisner in his discussions of inflationary adjustments on the debt. But Eisner chooses to adjust debt levels rather than interest payments downward. I would argue that interest payments rather than outstanding debt should be adjusted downwards since the effect of inflation is to reduce the real returns to creditors. I have performed downward adjustments on interest payments following the methodology presented in Pollin (1986b), and found that a pattern of interest payments relative to outlays similar to that in Table 5.7 emerges. Of course, with the inflation-adjusted figures, the magnitudes of interest payments are smaller than with the nominal payments. But still, a sharp rise in payments to outlays emerges in the 1980s. Thus, regardless of whether we look at nominal or inflation-adjusted interest payments, it is clear that over the 1980s, a sharp upturn has occurred in the portion of the government's budget going to interest.

20.   But one could also argue that the total of deficit spending be allocated to the direct income effect rather than deducting a share which would go to covering interest payments, on the notion that the deficit finances more variable and marginal expenditures rather than fixed costs such as debt servicing. In any case, this factor will not affect the broad patterns considered here.

References

Baldani, Jeffrey P. and Thomas R. Michl (1987) 'A Balanced Budget Multiplier for Interest Payments', *Journal of Post Keynesian Economics*, vol. 9, no. 3, pp. 424–39.

Barro, Robert J. (1989) 'The Ricardian Approach to Budget Deficits', *Journal of Economic Perspectives*, vol. 3, no. 2, Spring, pp. 37–55.

Bernheim, Douglas B. (1987) 'Ricardian Equivalence: An Evaluation of Theory and Evidence', *NBER Macro Annual*, vol. 2, 263–304.

Bowles, Samuel and Herbert Gintis (1982) 'The Crisis of Liberal Democratic Capitalism:

The Case of the United States', *Politics and Society*, vol. 11, no. 1, pp. 51–93.

Cherry, Robert *et al.* (1987) *The Imperiled Economy, Book I: Macroeconomics From a Left Perspective* (New York: Union for Radical Political Economics).

Eisner, Robert (1986) *How Real Is the Federal Deficit?* (New York: The Free Press).

Fischer, Stanley (1988) 'Symposium on the Slowdown in Productivity Growth', *Journal of Economic Perspectives*, vol. 2, no. 4, Fall, pp. 3–8.

Friedman, Benjamin (1988) *Day of Reckoning: The Consequences of American Economic Policy under Reagan and After* (New York: Random House).

Gordon, David M., Thomas E. Weiskoff and Samuel Bowles (1986) 'A Conflict Model of Investment: The Determinants of US Capital Accumulation in a Global Context', unpublished MS, New School for Social Research, New York.

Gurley, John and Edward Shaw (1956) 'Financial Intermediaries and the Saving–Investment Process', *Journal of Finance*, March, pp. 257–76.

Heilbroner, Robert L. (1978) *Beyond Boom and Crash* (New York: W. W. Norton).

Heilbroner, Robert L. (1979) 'Inflationary Capitalism', *The New Yorker*, 8 October, pp. 121–41.

Heilbroner, Robert L. (1980) *Marxism: For and Against* (New York: W. W. Norton).

Heilbroner, Robert L. (1984) 'The Deficit', *The New Yorker*, 30 July, pp. 47–55.

Heilbroner, Robert L. (1988) *Behind the Veil of Economics: Essays in the Worldly Philosophy* (New York: W. W. Norton).

Heilbroner, Robert L. and Peter L. Bernstein (1963) *A Primer on Government Spending* (New York: Random House).

Heilbroner, Robert L. and Peter L. Bernstein (1989) *The Debt and the Deficit: False Alarms/Real Possibilities* (New York: W. W. Norton).

Kalecki, Michal (1945) 'Full Employment by Stimulating Private Investment?' *Oxford Economic Papers*, March, pp. 83–92.

Lipietz, Alain (1986) 'Behind the Crisis', *Review of Radical Political Economics*, Spring and Summer, pp. 13–32.

Miller, John A. (1989) 'A Negative Social Wage and the Reproduction Crisis of the 1980s', unpublished MS, Wheaton College, Norton, Mass.

Minsky, Hyman P. (1957) 'Central Banking and Money Market Changes', *Quarterly Journal of Economics*, May; reprinted in Minsky (1982) *Can 'It' Happen Again?* (Armonk, NY: M. E. Sharpe) pp. 162–78.

Moffitt, Michael (1983) *The World's Money* (New York: Simon & Schuster).

Nell, Edward (1988) *Prosperity and Public Spending* (Winchester, Mass.: Allen & Unwin).

O'Driscoll, G. P., Jr (1977) 'The Ricardian Nonequivalence Theorem', *Journal of Political Economy*, February, pp. 207–10.

Page, Benjamin (1983) *Who Gets What From Government?* (Berkeley: University of California Press).

Pollin, Robert (1986a) 'Alternative Perspectives on the Rise of Corporate Debt Dependency: The US Postwar Experience', *Review of Radical Political Economics*, Spring and Summer, pp. 205–35.

Pollin, Robert (1986b) 'Corporate Interest Payments and the Falling Rate of Profit in the Postwar US Economy', *Economic Forum*, vol. 15, no. 2, pp. 121–36.

Pollin, Robert (1987) 'Structural Change and Increasing Fragility in the US Financial System', in Cherry *et al.*, *The Imperiled Economy Book I: Macroeconomics from a Left Perspective*, pp. 145–58.

Pollin, Robert (1988a) 'The Growth of US Household Debt: Demand-Side Influences', *Journal of Macroeconomics*, Spring, pp. 231–48.

Pollin, Robert (1990) *Deeper in Debt: The Changing Financial Conditions of US Households* (Washington, DC: Economic Policy Institute).

Pollin, Robert (1991) 'Two Theories of Money Supply Endogeneity: Some Empirical Evidence', *Journal of Post-Keynesian Economics*, vol. 13, no. 3, Spring 1991.

Ricardo, David (1951) 'Funding System', in Piero Sraffa (ed.), *The Works and Correspondence of David Ricardo*, vol. IV, pp. 143–200.

Rousseaus, Stephen (1986) *Post-Keynesian Monetary Economics* (Armonk, NY: M. E. Sharpe).

Savage, James D. (1988) *Balanced Budgets and American Politics* (Ithaca, NY: Cornell University Press).

Shaikh, Anwar and Etrugrul Ahmet Tonak (1987) 'The Welfare State and the Myth of the Social Wage', in Cherry *et al.*, *The Imperiled Economy* (New York: The Union For Radical Political Economics), pp. 183–96.

Stein, Herbert (1969) *The Fiscal Revolution in America* (Chicago: University of Chicago Press).

Stein, Herbert (1989) *Governing the $5 Trillion Economy* (New York: Oxford University Press).

Summers, Lawrence (1986) 'Issues in National Savings Policy', in G. Adams and S. Wachter (eds) *Savings and Capital Formation: The Policy Issues* (Lexington, Mass.: Lexington Books), pp. 65–88.

Review of Radical Political Economics (1986) 'Empirical Work in Marxian Crisis Theory: A Special Double Issue', Spring and Summer, vol. 18, nos. 1 & 2.

Weisskopf, Thomas E. (1989) 'An Analysis of Profitability Changes in Eight Capitalist Economics', *Review of Radical Political Economics*, vol. 20, nos. (2 & 3), Summer and Fall, pp. 68–80.

Zevin, Robert B. (1988) 'Are World Financial Markets More Open? If So Why and With What Effects?', unpublished MS, Conference on Financial Openness, WIDER, Helsinki.

6 Managed Capitalism versus the Small State: Which is the Formula for Capitalist Success?

Patrick Clawson

Heilbroner has argued that capitalism's success has relied, despite the objections of many businessmen, on increasing state intervention. In this century, the government has taken on greater responsibility for aggregate demand management; regulation for purposes ranging from safety and environment to curtailment of oligopoly; and industrial policy. This perspective seems to conflict with the conventional wisdom that growth comes from freeing markets, as evidenced both by the success of the Four Tigers in East Asia and by the better growth record in the US and the UK than in European countries suffering from Eurosclerosis (legislation and customs that inhibit economic flexibility), much less the miserable experience of the Soviets.

This chapter has two aims. The first is to examine the theoretical arguments that increasing state intervention is the inevitable tendency of advanced capitalism. I argue that the foundation for Heilbroner's view is the economies of large-scale business, as contrasted to an explanation such as stagnant demand that can be reversed only through the stimulation of state spending. Some popular arguments about the economic advantages of a small state are then analyzed.

Second, the empirical record of growth in countries with varying sorts of state intervention is examined. The evidence is mixed: some of the countries with the fastest growth have had heavy state involvement, while some nations with a 'light' state have had poor growth records. Government policy has, however, been important for growth; differences in growth cannot be explained by cultural factors or natural resource endowments. The most important issue is not the degree of state intervention but its character, in particular, the extent to which taxation, expenditure, and regulation favour production over consumption. Raising growth rates requires changing the character of state intervention, not reducing the role of the state.[1]

6.1 THE THESIS OF INCREASING STATE INTERVENTION

Heilbroner has argued for more than twenty years that increasing state intervention has characterized modern capitalism.[2] His views in 1966, in *The Limits of*

American Capitalism, were remarkably similar to that in 1988, in *Behind the Veil of Economics*. Markets, he says, are inherently unstable, because 'the output of all firms fails to dovetail with the structure of demand or . . . the production plans of the business community as a whole are not adequate to cope with the independently formulated savings plans of the community at large'.[3] This instability can be accommodated when firms are small, but 'in a milieu of huge enterprises and enormous fixed investments, miscalculations or imbalance carry the potential of a major disruptive impact'. The rigidification of the economy was the underlying cause of the increasingly disruptive crises that climaxed in the Great Depression of the 1930s, 'and it is widely accepted that the growth of the public sector mainly owes its origins to efforts to mitigate the effects of that instability or to prevent its recurrence'.[4] The result is the vast enlargement of the economic role of the state that has been the 'essential aspect' of the change in the post-war social structure.[5]

Heilbroner has been careful to hedge his predictions about the future of capitalism, but he leaves the reader in little doubt about what he sees as the most likely path. In his earlier days, he spoke about 'the necessity of planning',[6] by which he meant increased state intervention. In his seminal theoretical work, *The Nature and Logic of Capitalism*, he warns that the future of capitalism cannot be foretold with the assurance of predictions about the outcome of a chemical reaction, but in all likelihood, 'the trend of capitalist society lies in the increased marshalling and deployment of the powers of the state'.[7] In a 1989 essay, he writes, 'I will place my chips on the political side' in 'the emerging contest between the two realms' of economics and politics.[8]

The Economies of Large-scale Production

Underlying Heilbroner's thesis has been the concept of economies of large-scale production, namely, that larger capitalists are more profitable than smaller. One reason for economies of large-scale production may be technical increasing returns to scale in production, that is, an equal percentage increase in all factors of production produces an increase in output of a greater percentage. Much research has been conducted on whether typical firms operate at a point where increasing or decreasing returns to scale predominate. While undoubtedly an interesting issue from certain perspectives, the debate is quite irrelevant to the thesis at hand. Economies of large-scale production derive from a host of factors other than increasing returns to scale. These can include many of the factors known as monopolistic competition. For instance, larger firms may be able to capture economies of marketing, such as establishing consumer loyalty to a brand name that permits a price higher than needed to cover the extra advertising cost. Or larger firms may gain economies of finance: a large diversified firm may face a lower risk because temporary losses on any one activity can be offset by windfall gains on others, and so the cost of borrowing may be lower.

Certainly, the thesis of economies of large-scale production seems to fit with the stylized facts of economic history through the mid-twentieth century. The typical economic actor in the eighteenth century was the individual producer; the very principle of a limited liability corporation was regarded with suspicion and required complicated procedures to establish. The nineteenth century saw the growth of enterprises that employed scores or more of employees in one location. The turn of the century saw the spread of multilocational enterprises; in the US, this was the era in which the national market was formed. The twentieth century has been the era of the industry-wide trust, of the multinational firm, of the conglomerate (which is still common though the name is not in fashion). To be sure, the evidence is ambiguous as to whether the trend towards bigger and bigger firms has continued in the last twenty years. For instance, in the US, ratio of sales of Fortune 500 to total sales has stagnated. Nevertheless, the general picture has been fully consistent with the thesis that large-scale firms hold an advantage over small.

In the presence of economies of large-scale production, several arguments could be made as to why state intervention will grow. Heilbroner has continually favoured a thesis about the rising cost of firm failure. He argues that with such large-scale firms, permitting failures would entail a tremendous loss of efficiency and, furthermore, that the firms are insulated from market forces to such a degree as to make them sluggish. Therefore, state intervention can mitigate shocks, prevent capacity underutilization, and force more rapid adjustment.[9]

Gerschenkron, in *Economic Backwardness in Historical Perspective*, uses much the same argument of economies of large-scale production to develop a different explanation for increased state intervention.[10] He argues that to mobilize larger and larger sums of capital, more and more coordination is needed. He describes how this was accomplished in the France of the Second Empire through the banking system, which could mobilize and concentrate the savings of many individuals. By the time Russia began its major industrialization push in the 1890s, he writes, the 'supply of capital for the needs of industrialization required the compulsory machinery of government.'[11] This is a theory of late industrialization, that is, industrialization in a world market dominated by more advanced powers. As such, it is particularly relevant to the experience of backward areas, not to the advanced nations themselves. Gerschenkron did not explore the implications of greater capital needs for advanced economies. It is not a great leap from his work, however, to the more general argument that rising minimum capital requirements make use of the state to mobilize that capital more advantageous, for all the same reasons he identifies for backward nations (higher perceived risk, dangers from concentration of funds on a limited number of projects, illiquidity, etc.).

Scitovsky developed another argument for increased state intervention in the presence of economies of large-scale production,[12] though he unnecessarily confined his analysis to economies of scale. He called his concept 'pecuniary external economies', since he saw the phenomenon as similar to traditional external economies which cause social cost–benefit calculation to differ from private – a situation of market failure in which government intervention can increase social welfare. Scitovsky's point was that in order to reap the economies of large-scale production,[13]

The producer must lower his price first and wait for his sales to rise afterwards; but he may not dare to lower price and switch to cheaper mass-production methods without first knowing for certain that a lower price will, indeed, result in sufficiently higher sales. The market's failure consists in its transmitting information only on what is and not on what will (or might) be . . . The deadlock can be broken [through the government] providing the initiative or the guarantees that will assure private initiative, or by the central coordination of interdependent investment plans.

Scitovsky implies that pecuniary external economies prevail only in small markets such as prevail in underdeveloped economies. It could be argued, however, that such pecuniary external economies have become more common because modern technologies require large-scale investments. The start-up costs for high-definition television, a modern airplane, or fifth-generation supercomputers are larger, relative to social income, than was the case for the automobile at the turn of the century or electronics goods at mid-century. The higher the start-up costs, the greater the benefits to be gained from the guarantee of an adequate market. If start-up costs rise through time, then increasing state involvement would permit reaping of pecuniary external economies and therefore raise growth rates.

Arguments that the State must Stimulate Demand

Heilbroner's explanation is hardly the only one that has been offered to explain a tendency for increased state intervention under capitalism. A variety of political arguments has been offered, such as the legitimation provided to capitalism from the benevolent state. This chapter is not the place to explore such theses; the focus here is on economic theory more narrowly defined.

An important strand in economic thinking of the last two hundred years has been that state intervention is needed to stimulate demand. The claim that aggregated demand under capitalism is not self-regulating has been picked up repeatedly, from Malthus via Marx to Keynes. Such a claim may be seen as a call for state intervention to attenuate periodic crises, but it is not in itself sufficient to explain any tendency for continually increasing state intervention. One way to make the link is to argue that advanced capitalism is characterized by more concentrated firms that do not engage in price competition. Therefore, in the face of declining demand, prices remain rigid despite excess capacity problems. Such a world of nominal price rigidity has no place for the mechanism which economic theory says could automatically right the economy, namely, price reductions and restoration of aggregate demand via wealth effects. The most systematic argument along these lines is to be found in Steindl, a work much admired in Marxist circles.[14]

Heilbroner might have been expected to be sympathetic to this view, not least because it is the argument found in the work of Heilbroner's friend and teacher, Adolph Lowe. Lowe's explanation for the transition to 'an organized type of capitalism' was that the steady rise in public demand was needed to overcome 'the slackening of autonomous increases in aggregate demand', which in turn was due to a host of factors.[15] Indeed, Heilbroner originally placed great weight on this explanation. In his 1953 work, *The Worldly Philosophers*, his discussion of the increasing state role was prefaced by an examination of Alvin Hansen's stagnationist theory. Heilbroner then thought, 'most economists felt that the private sector, left to itself, might well fail to generate *enough* purchasing power to absorb the enormous output of our present-day economy . . . [T]here is a need for an important subsidiary stream of public expenditure.' [emphasis in original][16]

Since the 1950s, Heilbroner has been little affected by this argument. He certainly rejects any notion that markets will be physically saturated, arguing that capitalism has been adept at developing new products and at 'expanding its commodity frontiers by moving activities from the sphere of personal life into that of profitable business'.[17] As for lack of purchasing power leading to a shortfall in demand, Heilbroner views the debate as unsettled despite vast amounts of re-search and an immense body of theory.[18] Capitalism clearly creates enough demand for the system to function: it will not fall apart from the weight of its own contradictions, *pace* some Marxist interpretations (though not the master himself, who always thought a political revolution would be needed). But he is not sure that capitalism works well enough by itself that government demand stimulation is undesirable.

The Argument for State Planning

A third economic explanation for the tendency towards increased state inter-vention has been that state planning is needed for coordination because of the decline in competition, due to the increasing size of firms. Much vulgar Marxism echoes this viewpoint, which found its classic statement in Hilferding's *Finance Capital*.[19]

This thesis seems quite unconvincing. The concentration and centralization of firms to which Hilferding refers has been accompanied by the expansion of the market – from the local area to the nation and increasingly to the world. Since market size has grown parallel to or faster than firm size, competition has become, if anything, more intense. For instance, in the current period, the internationaliza-tion of markets has exposed the very largest of US corporations to competition that, in some cases, threatened their very existence.

6.2   THE ARGUMENTS FOR A SMALL STATE

The thesis that the economically most efficient government is the smallest has generally rested on microeconomic grounds. I will consider three of the common arguments, namely, the disincentives from high taxation, the distortionary effect of state regulation, and the inefficiencies of public enterprises.

The Incentive Arguments for a Small State

The first argument has been that the heavy state requires high taxation which is a disincentive to productive effort and, most especially, to the risk taking essential to start up new firms. But this argument is a non-starter for at least two reasons. First, the interventionist state is not necessarily expensive to run. Regulations and guided markets do not require heavy cash expenditures; even their social cost can be relatively small if the state targets its assistance to a small group of priority productive sectors. The more costly measures are to promote social welfare, e.g. transfers to the poor or safety and environmental protection. Worthwhile as they may be, such measures do not promote growth, and as such, they are not motivated by the economic forces under analysis here. Any argument that the state is sure to grow because it is sure to take on additional welfare functions would be a political thesis outside the scope of the present analysis.

Second, taxes can be designed in a way to be neutral to incentives. The extreme example is the head tax. More plausible alternatives are consumption taxes, which are important parts of the tax burden in some industrial nations (petrol taxes, VAT, etc.). The arguments for reduction of high marginal income tax rates are really quite separate from the issue at hand.

The Allocative Efficiency Arguments for a Small State

Another argument against the activist state is that a heavy-handed regulatory environment, as well as social welfare programmes, prevent the flexibility essential to allocative efficiency. The issue of a heavy regulatory environment concerns not only the advanced countries but also the developing nations. De Soto has written a stirring attack on state regulation in Peru, arguing that it constitutes protection for the large modern firms (the formal sector) at the expense of smaller, more flexible producers (the informal sector).[20]

Certainly regulations can ossify an economy, by increasing the cost of shifting productive factors from one activity to another. But regulations may also be a way to improve economic efficiency. The classic argument is that regulations reverse market failure by equalizing social and individual costs and benefits. In the presence of economies of large-scale production, as discussed above, market failure can be a general phenomenon because of external economies. That is, producers could cut costs by producing on a larger scale if they were sure that the markets existed for that extra output, but they would not do so in the absence of some government intervention to assure the existence of the market. A more limited way of making the same argument is the Keynesian defence of spending, namely, that any allocative efficiency losses are much less than the losses due to underutilized capacity.

The debate over market failure has been singularly unsuccessful at reaching agreement on the breadth and depth of the phenomenon. The partisans of free markets reject the notion that market failures are common and argue that alleged market failure is frequently the result of government limitations on the enforcement of property rights; because of those limitations, individuals can impose costs on others without having to pay compensation, which results in the divergence between social and private cost. The counterclaims emphasize the dependence of each firm on the actions of other firms which are outside its control, for example, in the pollution of the environment. Broad agreement on the best economic approach to regulation is unlikely.

The ultimate defence of regulations by their proponents is rarely based on their economic effect. Quite the contrary, the defenders frequently concede the losses in efficiency but say that these are offset by the gains in equity and in non-market benefits. It could be suggested that as societies grow richer, they will spend more to achieve such social goals. That argument would, however, be outside the narrow realm of this chapter, which is limited to purely economic reasons for an increasing state role in the economy.

The Management Efficiency Argument for a Small State

A further argument against the heavy state has been the poor growth record of government-owned enterprises. These enterprises are often said to be lemons that cannot be closed for political reasons. Fair enough, but the problem of state guarantees against failure is not confined to state-owned firms. As market-oriented a government as that of the US has found that some industrial enterprises are too large to fail, e.g. Chrysler. Many governments provide an effective government guarantee against failure to the banking system. It can be argued whether this is economically justifiable to prevent shock waves going through the economy and to limit dead-weight losses, as Heilbroner contends, or whether the guarantee is the by-product of the heavy political influence of a large firm. The arguments are much the same whether the enterprise is state owned or private: the issue is how to conduct policy in an environment of large firms, not how to manage state enterprises.

Public enterprises are said to be inefficient because they have non-economic targets, i.e. targets other than profit-maximizing. In particular, government enterprises are said to serve the interests of their managers and their political sponsors at the expense of economic efficiency. The problem is real, but unfortunately it exists in any large enterprise irrespective of ownership. Berle and Means' classic statement about the character of modern large-scale enterprises was built around the increasing divergence of interest between management and shareholders.[21] The contemporary debate about leveraged buy-outs and hostile take-overs has turned on the issue of self-perpetuating management that has little stake in the performance of the enterprise. Again, the problem of the independent interests of the managers is universal to large enterprises; it is not unique to the state enterprise.

The record of state-owned firms tends to echo the general record of firms in a society: a country in which many firms are heavily indebted and doubtfully solvent is more likely to have parastatals in trouble, and the converse. A government committed to promoting economic growth, like that of Thatcher in the UK, is likely to convert to profitability even the public enterprises that had been the most loss-making previously.

In sum, neither the arguments for nor against the heavy state are self-evidently overwhelming. As so often in economics, a powerful theoretical case can be made for two contradictory theses. Perhaps reference to the empirical record can demonstrate which tendency has been the most important in practice. Even then, the most likely outcome is to show that both positions offer much insight, and that adopting either policy would offer certain advantages, but would entail costs.

6.3   THE RECORD OF THE STATE AND GROWTH

Heilbroner's thesis was based on his analysis of the advanced industrial countries. However, the arguments do not seem confined to those nations, but rather are general to capitalism as a whole. It is therefore appropriate to ask what has been the experience of different types of societies, especially since much of the interest in the 'retreat of the state' has come from the stellar growth record of the East Asian newly industrializing countries that are perceived to have capitalism in its pure, market-driven form.

Liberal Capitalism and Stellar Growth in the Third World

In the Third World, few of the countries with excellent growth records have relied on the three elements proposed by contemporary liberalism (in the nineteenth-century meaning of the term), i.e. (i) entrepreneurs, (ii) free markets, and (iii) export orientation. Taiwan and Hong Kong are certainly the main exceptions. Consider South Korea, where the real GNP per capita rose 275 per cent from 1967 to 1987, an average annual growth of 6.8 per cent.[22] The heart of this growth was in manufacturing.

South Korean industry was certainly not based on entrepreneurship. The government's key role in manufacturing is admitted in a major 1979 study from the World Bank, an agency which would probably rather minimize the contribution of government intervention to growth:

> In the planned subsectors, particularly steel, fertilizer, chemicals and shipbuilding, government identified major projects and ensured their implementation, sometimes to the point of initiating them through the agency of a public enterprise. Even in the unplanned subsectors, such as textiles, there has been active government participation from time to time in establishing programs for modernization and capacity expansion at the enterprise level. Government is currently playing a major direct role in implementing the fourth plan's goals in the machinery and electronics industries.[23]

The heavy hand of the government has resulted in a remarkable concentration of economic activity, quite the reverse of the entrepreneurial model of development. In the mid-1980s, nine firms accounted for 52 per cent of South Korea's manufactured exports. Some thirty companies accounted for 24 per cent of the manufacturing labour force and 31 per cent of manufacturing value added. Indeed, they produced 17 per cent of the total value added in all sectors of the Korean economy. This success was not primarily the result of technical or managerial efficiencies. The World Bank attributes this phenomenon to the government's discovery that 'it was easier to coordinate industrial strategy with a few major producers, rather than a multitude of small ones'.[24]

Nor did South Korea rely on pure market forces. Paul Kuznets describes the benefits to industry of extensive government intervention in pricing, especially by holding down wage costs, providing low-cost credit for export production, and restricting competing imports.[25]

South Korean industry certainly followed the third element of the liberal recipe, namely, export orientation. That orientation is, however, quite possible within the framework of an activist state. Unfortunately, we have an extreme example of this phenomenon: Romania in the late 1980s was one of the most extreme state-controlled economies and at the same time one of the most export-oriented economies, to the point of reducing living standards to wartime levels in order to divert goods to export markets. Nothing inherent in the activist state makes export orientation difficult, nor does a free market approach guarantee that exports will thrive. Export subsidies and directed credit for exports, which have been important spurs to exports in Colombia and South Korea, are examples of distortionary government policies that can promote exports.

The General Experience of the Third World with State Intervention

The data on growth in the decade of 1975–85 show tremendous variation between countries.[26] The obvious question is what is the pattern: what explains how, over a decade, some countries could grow at 7 per cent per annum or more while other countries had falling output? No obvious conclusion leaps out from the data. Certainly some countries reputed to limit state involvement have done well, such as Taiwan (8.4 per cent average annual growth). But others have not: Chile with 3.0 per cent growth, plus African countries like Ivory Coast at 3.0 per cent or Malawi at 2.4 per cent. Some of the world's poorest nations with weak resource bases have done nicely – Bangladesh at 4.5 per cent – while some of the middle income nations with good human and physical resources have done miserably – Argentinan output fell an average 0.6 per cent per annum (see Table 6.1).

The evidence is open to widely differing interpretations. Consider the issue of state intervention in foreign trade prices, using mechanisms like export subsidies and high tariffs or quantitative restrictions to establish systematic differences between domestic prices and those on world markets. The World Bank has had one way of reading the evidence, while the UN University's World Institute for

Table 6.1   Real GNP and its growth for selected developing countries, 1975–85

	Average annual growth in %	GNP in billion 1984 $ 1985	GNP in billion 1984 $ 1975
Taiwan	8.4	60.3	26.3
China	7.6	357.4	172.1
South Korea	7.4	86.6	42.4
Malaysia	6.3	31.4	17.0
Thailand	5.8	41.7	23.8
Tunisia	5.1	8.1	5.0
India	4.5	190.5	123.1
Bangladesh	4.5	14.5	9.4
Cuba	4.0	28.7	19.4
Brazil	3.8	213.8	147.3
North Korea	3.7	23.6	16.4
Colombia	3.5	37.5	26.5
Chile	3.0	18.0	13.4
Peru	0.5	19.5	18.5
Argentina	–0.6	69.4	73.6

Source: World Military Expenditures and Arms Transfers.

Development Economics Research (WIDER) has drawn diametrically opposed conclusions from the same experiences. The World Bank maintains that the average growth in the 1970s of developing countries with low price distortions was 7 per cent compared to 3 per cent for nations with high price distortion.[27] Based on its eighteen case studies, WIDER concluded that price liberalization may force deindustrialization and that anti-liberal policies can have positive effects on output.[28]

Examined without ideological preconceptions, the data on growth in the decade 1975–85 are ambiguous about whether growth is aided by liberal price policies. Theoretically, liberal price policies could be found in a country which had heavy state expenditures and other forms of industrial policy, but in practice the dividing line between liberal and controlled prices runs right along the same fault as that between light and heavy state spending, and between uniform firm treatment and industrial policy. Countries like Chile and Colombia which were on the 'light' state side had rather poor growth rates in 1975–85; both were below such 'heavy' states as India, Cuba or North Korea.

Indeed, the most obvious predictor of growth is geography, not the divide of liberalism versus managed capitalism. The countries at the top of the list, with the fastest growth, were uniformly Asian, while no Asian states are to be found at the bottom. The picture would have been more extreme if the table had included sub-Saharan African states, since their growth record is nearly uniformly abysmal. The geographic dividing line becomes more striking when considering all countries irrespective of state of development. The Asian continent had a growth that was 75 per cent higher than any other continent in 1975–85; 5.1 per cent compared to a world average of 2.9 per cent.

No good explanation has been offered to account for the faster growth of both industrial and developing nations in Asia, compared to the slow growth in Europe (West and East), Latin America, and Africa (Table 6.2). It would be hard to argue that Asia has benefited particularly from favourable external circumstances, given the diversity of experiences. Nor has Asia had uniformly favourable socio-cultural factors, since the attitudes towards work and business vary enormously among countries. Furthermore, favourable external circumstances and socio-cultural factors are not sufficient in themselves to produce growth; look at the experience of Nigeria, where GNP shrank between 1975 and 1985 despite its oil income and a society which encourages entrepreneurialism and hard work.

Thatcherism as the Recipe for Growth?

Perhaps the record is ambiguous for the developing countries, but what about the advanced industrial countries, which Heilbroner had in mind when he formulated his thesis. The popular impression is that the 1980s has been the decade of the entrepreneur: growth has been rapid in the lands that restrained the government to allow free play for the market, while the European nations that have clung to heavy state intervention and expenditure have stagnated.

In fact, the growth record of the US and UK has not been much better than that of countries that relied on heavy state intervention, nor has growth risen under the pro-market governments of Reagan and Thatcher. Impressions about rapid growth in the Anglo-Saxon countries are coloured by the sharper recessions the two nations suffered, which make the recoveries afterwards look more spectacular. The average GNP growth record of the eight Reagan years was identical to that of the Carter years: 3.1 per cent. Similarly, Britain under Thatcher has done little better than in the previous twenty years, despite the impetus of oil income. As for international comparisons, the average annual growth in 1975–85 of the US was 3.0 per cent compared to a weighted average of 2.9 per cent for the rest of the OECD: not a stunning difference. The UK growth in the same period averaged 1.7 per cent per annum.

In the US, there is little to suggest that entrepreneurs have been the engine of growth. Unfortunately, aggregate data about the impact of small firms are

Table 6.2   Real GNP and its growth by continent, 1975–85

	Average annual growth in %	GNP in billion 1984 $ 1985	GNP in billion 1984 $ 1975
World	2.9	14060	10600
Asia	5.1	2531	1536
North America	2.9	4291	2162
Latin America	2.6	684	530
Middle East, Mediterranean	2.5	457	356
Africa	2.0	354	289

Source: World Military Expenditures and Arms Transfers.

hard to come by. Much government data relates to factory size, not firm size; of course, a single firm may have a variety of workplaces. On the other hand, measuring the share of small firms in total output or employment proves little, since this procedure would miss one of the most interesting categories, namely, the small firm that grows to be large. To take anecdotal evidence, consider the computer and software industries, where the stories of entrepreneurs like Steven Jobs are well known. Those most successful in the computer industry have generally been those able to marshall the resources to advertise and gain a distribution network, not the best engineers.

The highest growth by far among the OECD nations during 1975–85 was in Japan, hardly a bastion of unfettered market forces. Japan's average annual real GNP growth rate was 4.7 per cent, 80 per cent above the 2.6 per cent average for the rest of the OECD. Without exaggerating the influence of the Ministry of International Trade and Industry nor the extent of the informal guidance provided by government officials to private firms, it can be safely said that the activist regulatory policy was an important element in Japan's success at increasing output. The current popularity of complaints about Japan's single-minded pursuit of economic growth is in many ways a compliment to the effectiveness of non-market forces; an anti-consumption, pro-production bias at promoting economic growth. Japan's experience is powerful evidence that the issue may not be 'market forces' versus 'the heavy state', but instead the character of state intervention. Anti-consumption, pro-production policies raise growth rates, though not necessarily living standards.

The Soviet Growth Record

A major element in the popular writings about the superiority of free markets was the record of the USSR. Scholars have analyzed the poor performance of the Soviet economy, which the Soviet authorities at first hid and later proclaimed loudly to discredit the previous leadership. Unfortunately, those who did work on the Soviet economy seldom seemed aware that at the same time as Soviet growth took a dive (namely, from the mid-1970s), a similar slowdown hit the OECD and Third World economies. Indeed, while Soviet economic performance has been weak, it surpassed the EEC average (see Table 6.3). What is striking is the similarity in growth performance of Europe, East and West, not the differences among nations.

Applying the general principle of Occam's Razor, the best explanation is the simplest, namely, that a similar problem afflicted Eastern and Western Europe, rather than there being some specifically Soviet or Eastern shortcoming. The problem could, of course, have been the heavy state. Yet it is hard to identify ways in which the state became suddenly heavier in the early or mid-1970s in the Eastern bloc; an argument could be made about the European Community adopting more social regulation, but it would be a weak case since the Community also lightened the burden of inconsistent rules among member nations. In both East

Table 6.3   Real GNP and its growth by bloc, 1975–85

	Average annual growth in %	GNP in billion 1984 $ 1985	1975
World	2.9	14060	10600
OECD	2.9	8435	6329
US	3.0	3867	2903
Japan	4.7	1319	833
EEC	2.1	2347	1904
Other	2.5	862	689
Warsaw Pact	2.1	2928	2367
Soviet Union	2.3	2129	1702
Other	1.6	799	686
Developing nations	3.6	3793	1980

and West, much the same heavy state prevailed during the high growth of the 1950s and 1960s as during the slowdown. That would suggest that the causes of the slowdown lay elsewhere; exactly where is a question well beyond this chapter.

6.4   FINAL THOUGHTS ON THE SHRINKING STATE AND MANAGED CAPITALISM

The theoretical and the empirical evidence is ambiguous: no clear case can be made that the state will expand or contract as capitalism advances. My prejudice is to agree with Heilbroner that the boundary line between the state and the economy has and will keep moving to expand the state's realm. The argument is not that the expansion of the state is desirable for socio-political reasons, but rather that it is likely because of economic forces.

The expansion of the state has no necessary implications for income distribution or welfare of the poor. A frequent but wrong identification is made between the state, the left, and the interests of the common folk. For instance, in the US, a frequent liberal criticism of Reaganism was that the withdrawal of the state was in the interests of an élite that has manipulated the body politic, but it hurt society at large. To paraphrase David Stockman, Reagan's anti-state rhetoric was to justify the hogs feeding at the trough. With regard to developing countries, the usual rhetoric of those on the left is to denounce proposals to reduce the state's heavy hand as reflections of ideological conservatism which are at best mistaken and at worst a cover for policies to aid the rich at the expense of the poor.[29]

A good case can be made for quite the contrary thesis, i.e. that the heavy state serves the interest of a small élite who manipulate the government for their own ends. De Soto provides graphic examples of Peruvian state regulations that did little more than protect a small group of large-scale firms at the expense of a large number of consumers and small producers.[30] As he reminds the reader at length, the liberal tradition in Europe was for the small state, while the activist state was championed by mercantilists who saw the state as the guarantor of the interests of particular sectors.[31] Heilbroner has emphasized the 'conservative political nature'[32] of the state's growing economic role. He may have meant this in the rather narrow sense that the government's intervention is meant to conserve: to restrain or offset the changes brought on by the economy when those changes threaten social peace or orderly economic development. But the same point holds more generally, in that the state's role in impeding change serves the interest of those who hold power and slows the rise of those who are more productive but who lack the political clout that comes with established wealth.

The recent trend has been to emphasize the retreat of the state. Without a doubt, the state has pulled back from economic activity in many countries – both from direct production via privatization of various forms and from regulation. But the retreat of the state has been greatly exaggerated. Two powerful trends work to increase the state's role. First, in the advanced countries, the elasticity of state involvement with respect to income is greater than one: state revenues/ expenditures and sales of state enterprises increase more rapidly than income unless periodic measures are taken to reverse this built-in tendency. Politicians like Thatcher and Reagan may therefore trumpet what they have done to reduce the state's role, while the net effect of their actions may have been little more than to hold steady in the face of an inherent contrary trend. Second, in the Third World, the modern urban economy is expanding at the expense of the isolated rural areas, and the former is the realm in which the state is predominant. De Soto describes the heavy hand of the state in Lima.[33] The tight regulations adopted in the past were administratively more practical because the market being regulated was so small; the vast bulk of the national economy was in the deep countryside (*el Peru profundo*) which effectively escaped state control. A lighter state regulation over a more extensive part of the economy is not by any means proof of the retreat of the state.

Finally, discussion about the growth effect of the heavy versus the light state may be largely focusing on the wrong question. The *character* of state intervention would appear to matter much more than the extent. In particular, excessive consumption has been confused with excessive government. In the Third World, many governments have used intervention to protect consumers, especially import-consuming élites and urban groups that may riot. These policies have clearly hurt growth, as well as often hurting society's poorest, namely, the small farmers. In advanced countries, pro-consumption policies have at times reduced the pool of available savings, thereby raising the cost of capital and reducing the availability of capital for smaller firms and new ventures. A policy of encouraging consumption can therefore reduce growth in an open world economy with markets waiting for the least-cost and most innovative product; the Keynesian strategy of growth via demand stimulation becomes quite counter-productive in such a situation.

Notes and References

1. 'The most successful capitalism of tomorrow will be those that address the difficulties of the present period . . . by new structures that utilize the state in various ways to cope with these problems as best they can managed with a regime of capital' (Robert Heilbroner, *The Nature and Logic of Capitalism* (New York: W.W. Norton, 1985), p. 203).
2. The role of the state in the economy declined steadily for the several centuries during which capitalism was replacing heavily interventionist feudal and mercantilist societies. The discussion here is about the era of modern capitalism, which had begun in Britain by the late eighteenth century.
3. Robert Heilbroner, *The Limits of American Capitalism* (New York: Harpers Books, 1963), p. 89.
4. Robert Heilbroner, *Behind the Veil of Economics* (New York: W.W. Norton, 1988), p. 57.
5. *The Nature and Logic of Capitalism*, p. 172.
6. This argument, in *The Limits of American Capitalism* (New York: Harper & Row, 1966), pp. 117–29, is based in good part on a thesis not found in Heilbroner's later works, namely, that advancing science would create automation so extensive that it would require greater coordination than could be provided by the market.
7. *The Nature and Logic of Capitalism*, p. 201.
8. Robert Heilbroner, 'The Triumph of Capitalism', *The New Yorker*, 23 January 1989, p. 107.
9. In 'The Triumph of Capitalism', he adds the argument that technology is becoming more destructive to the environment. As the gap between social and private cost–benefit calculations grow, the imperative for state intervention increases.
10. Gerschenkron bases his argument (*Economic Backwardness in Historical Perspective* (Cambridge: Harvard University Press, 1962), pp. 10–11) not only on the advantages of 'increases in the average size of the plant', but also on the external economies, by which the progress in one industry accorded benefits to the others.
11. Ibid., p. 20.
12. Tibor Scitovsky, 'Two Concepts of External Economies', *Journal of Political Economy*, vol. 17, 1954, pp. 143–51.
13. Tibor Scitovsky, *Welfare and Competition* (Homewood: Richard D. Irwin, 1971), pp. 283–4.
14. Josef Steindl, *Maturity and Stagnation in American Capitalism* (New York: Monthly Review Press, 1952).
15. Adolph Lowe, *On Economic Knowledge* (New York: Harper & Row, 1965), p. 92.
16. Robert Heilbroner, *The Worldly Philosophers* (New York: Simon & Schuster, 1953), p. 283.
17. Robert Heilbroner, 'The Triumph of Capitalism', *The New Yorker*, 23 January 1989, p. 99.
18. Ibid., p. 100.
19. Rudolph Hilferding, *Finance Capital* (London: Routledge & Kegan Paul, 1981) [German original: 1910], especially pp. 288–300. Hilferding (pp. 366–9) warmly greeted the spread of cartels as a 'socialization of production' which required only

expropriation of the cartels by a workers' state to complete the transition to socialism.

20. Hernando de Soto, *The Other Path* (New York: Harper & Row, 1989).

21. Adolph Berle and Gardiner Means, *The Modern Corporation and Private Property* (New York: Macmillan, 1933).

22. According to the World Bank's *World Tables 1988–89 Edition* (pp. 352–3), South Korea's GNP at 1980 prices went from 12.65 billion won in 1967 to 66.32 billion won in 1987, an average 8.6 per cent increase per annum. GNP per person at 1980 prices went from 420 thousand won in 1967 to 1.58 million won in 1987.

23. Parvez Hasan and D.C. Rao, *Korea: Policy Issues for Long-Term Development* (Baltimore: Johns Hopkins University Press, 1979), p. 104.

24. The World Bank, *Korea: Development in a Global Context* (Washington: The World Bank, 1984), p. 86. The data cited in the text on Korean concentration are from this study, pp. 86 and 232.

25. Paul Kuznets, *Economic Growth and Structure in the Republic of Korea* (New Haven: Yale University Press, 1977), especially p. 107.

26. Many problems exist in making international comparisons of national output for this period, such as valuing output in the then Soviet-style economies or determining the appropriate exchange rate. No data source that covered the whole world, including the Soviet bloc, was particularly good. The least bad was probably the US data, published by the Arms Control and Disarmament Agency in its annual *World Military Expenditures and Arms Transfers*, drawing upon World Bank and CTA data. The major shortcoming of these data was that they exaggerated the weight of the Warsaw Pact nations relative to other countries; however, that does not appear to have affected growth rates much, as the degree of exaggeration was more or less constant.

27. World Bank, *World Development Report 1983*, p. 61. The *World Development Report 1981* (pp. 75–6) argued that countries without distortionary trade policies were typically more successful in adjusting to the external shocks of the 1970s. On a related but by no means identical point, the *World Development Report 1987*, pp. 82–6, argued that outwardly oriented economies grew more rapidly in 1963–85 than did inwardly oriented.

28. Lance Taylor, *Varieties of Stabilization Experience* (Oxford: Oxford University Press, 1988), p. 153.

29. See, for example, the recent UNICEF project on adjustment – Cornia, Jolly, and Stewart, *Adjustment with a Human Face* (Oxford: Clarendon Press, 1987) – or Lance Taylor, *Varieties of Stabilization Experience*, pp. 184–9.

30. Hernando de Soto, *The Other Path*, analyzes the distributional impact of government policies with regard to housing (pp. 17–58), trade (pp. 50–62), and transport (pp. 93–130).

31. Ibid., pp. 201–20.

32. Robert Heilbroner, 'The Triumph of Capitalism', *The New Yorker*, 23 January 1989, p. 106.

33. De Soto, *The Other Path*, pp. 3–14, gives a wonderful description of the reaction of the urban élite to the transformation of the cities from centres of the élite into large concentrations of popular economic activity.

7 The Political Economy of Growth and Distribution: Economics, Public Policy and Politics

Richard McGahey[*]

7.1 INTRODUCTION

[E]vidence of a deep structural challenge can be discerned within the system, but the challenge is more feared and misunderstood than accepted and welcomed, and has progressed only far enough to reveal the limitations of the older structure, not far enough to force a solution for its problems. (Robert Heilbroner (1985), in *The Nature and Logic of Capitalism*)

In 1965, Walter Heller, then chairman of President Johnson's Council of Economic Advisors, presented the Godkin Lectures at Harvard University. Later published as *New Dimensions of Political Economy* (1966), Heller said that the United States had entered 'the age of the economist'. The consolidation of modern macroeconomic theory had been accepted by political leaders, who could use the theory to guide and develop policies leading the United States to new heights of prosperity and social justice.

By the mid-1980s, just twenty years later, this optimistic tone and professional consensus had disappeared from public discussion. A variety of more or less well-developed but incompatible economic theories and policy options were debated in public and professional circles, while the United States struggled with lower economic growth, higher unemployment, and higher inflation than the 1960s. Instead of an optimistic consensus on the policy lessons of economic theory to sustain non-inflationary growth and spread the benefits to all sectors of society, the American debate on economic policy entering the 1990s is fractured and contradictory.

* The views presented here are solely those of the author. Earlier versions of parts of this chapter were presented at the 1985 American Economic Association meetings in New York City and the 1986 Southern History Conference in Charlotte, North Carolina. My thanks to Ron Blackwell and Bob Korstad for helpful comments, and to Joy O'Brien for manuscript preparation. Thanks also to Robert Heilbroner for comments on the earlier AEA paper, and for continuing to provide an exemplary model to economists interested in critical analysis and public policy.

The change in just twenty years is striking. During the 1988 presidential campaign, neither major party offered an economic policy programme that featured greater social equality as a main theme, while both parties made general assertions about their ability to manage and direct the economy. Among politicians and economic analysts, little consensus exists on the causes, possible solutions, or even importance of such problems as the federal budget deficit, America's continuing trade deficit, stagnant productivity growth, and growing poverty and inequality. In 1988, the Democrats offered an admixture of claims to managerial competence, a need to cut the federal deficit and consumption to restore investment, and hesitant concerns about the regional and class distribution of prosperity. The Republicans invoked fears of prior Democratic administrations, whose alleged mismanagement was blamed as the root cause of most US economic problems.

The uncertainty and loss of direction of economic policy is closely tied to the declining performance of the American economy, both absolutely and relative to major international competitors. In a 1982 interview, Robert Heilbroner characterized the American economic policy debate as reflecting 'a position of indecision and blindness, not knowing where we are and not knowing where to go (1988, p. 78)', a characterization that continues to be relevant.

This chapter explores the decline of the American socio-economic policy consensus on issues of growth and equity from the mid-1960s to the 1980s, and offers some speculations on its future direction. The decline can be seen in a variety of ways: the splintering of the political and policy consensus that supported the Democratic Party and Heller's 'new political economy', the analytical and policy confusions that began with the decline of US economic performance in the early 1970s, and the views of leading economic policy thinkers on the relationship of economic growth and equity. The chapter concludes with some speculations on the future of US economic policy. It focuses on the tension between the need for creative economic policy and the barriers posed to such development by changing economic circumstances among the old supporters of the Democratic Party consensus, and by American ideology regarding the proper economic role of government.

The restraining role of ideology is especially important in this regard. Heilbroner (1985, p. 177) once described US economic problems of the late 1970s and early 1980s as 'a crisis of intervention', referring both to the technical problems of economic policy and also 'to the restrictions placed on state intervention as a means of resolving these problems'.

This 'crisis of intervention' is likely to continue and perhaps accelerate in coming years. For the poor performance of the US economy is now giving rise to fears that the United States has entered a period of inexorable decline where it cannot resolve its economic problems in a positive way. Many economists continue to view the problems as narrowly political, charging the political system with an inability or unwillingness to adopt the remedies prescribed by economic theory and policy analysis. But the sharp turns of economic policy analysis and advice between the 1960s and the 1980s, fuelled in part by the declining economy, caution against any assumption that economic theory alone can generate an adequate programme for restoring US economic performance.

These changes in policy analysis also suggest the strong impact of politics on economic analysis, although that impact may not be directly apparent. Any successful programme will be not merely technical (and even here economists cannot agree on the technical issues) but political in the broad sense, building on and being circumscribed by American values, history and political discourse.

The collapse of the American economic policy consensus and the thus far unsuccessful groping for a new vision is a sobering story. It reflects several themes that have animated the work of Robert Heilbroner: the often-unstated influence of economic events and ideology on economic theory and policy, the delay and seeming inability of public institutions and policies to respond effectively to economic change, the continuing confusion over 'public' versus 'private' aspects of economic systems and policies, the long-run trend to greater government involvement in capitalist economies, and the tension between this trend and ideology and public policy in capitalist nations, especially the United States. Unlike the 1960s, there is now widespread scepticism about creating policies that can link economic growth with increases in social equality, much less sustain US growth in a new world of international competition. Creating a new policy and political consensus on these goals will be a task confronting economists and others in the 1990s.

7.2   THE DECLINE OF THE AMERICAN POST-WAR ECONOMIC POLICY CONSENSUS

The link between economic policy and increased socio-economic equality in American public policy was dominated until the 1980s by the New Deal/Great Society consensus that supported the Democratic Party. That consensus emerged in the post-Second World War period with four principal elements:

– aggregate demand management of the economy through fiscal and monetary policy (with a shift to the latter in recent years);

– a growing social safety net in the form of transfer payments such as Social Security, unemployment insurance, Aid for Dependent Children, and government-subsidized medical insurance;

– a commitment to legal, equal access to opportunity, pursued primarily through extended political and legal rights, and education and training for the disadvantaged, especially minorities; and

– a central role for labour unions as representatives of worker interests, as political advocates for labour and broader social legislation, and managers of conflict, especially in the core industries in the economy.

The expectation was that steady non-inflationary economic growth, harmoniously complemented by increasing socio-economic equality, would be achieved by adhering to these four broad policy directions. The consensus developed from the 1930s, but was largely in place by the mid-1960s (Matusow, 1984; Thurow, 1985).

At the macroeconomic level the policies seemed remarkably successful, as the American economy dominated world markets. Although troubled by recessions, the national economy grew fairly steadily, with low rates of inflation and unemployment. The so-called 'Keynesian consensus' in American economic policy relied upon government fiscal stimulus to correct recessions and high unemployment. Arthur Okun characterized the relative stability of the American post-war economy as the 'taming of the business cycle' (1980, p. 163).

But the macroeconomic consensus had another side, one which was always present but came to dominate policy by the early 1980s: holding down aggregate demand and growth to control inflation. Rising price levels throughout the 1970s led to increasing policy interventions to try to hold down inflation, with the deliberate introduction of recessions coming to dominate macroeconomic policy by the late 1970s, even at the expense of economic growth. James Tobin (1986, p. 28) noted the importance of public policy in causing economic downturns: 'All six recessions the United States has suffered in the last 30 years can be attributed to deliberate policies to restrict aggregate demand in order to bring inflation rates down'.

The standard economic view of the business cycle regards expansions and recessions as oscillating swings around a long-term pattern of economic growth, with the timing of recessions due to movements in the private economy. This view is at odds with the history of deliberate policy-induced recessions of the 1970s and 1980s. The recession of the early 1980s was the sixth recession in two decades, and the fourth since 1970.

Each cyclical swing left the United States economy with higher aggregate levels of unemployment. For example, the recession of 1973–5 had an unemployment peak of 9 per cent, the highest in the post-war period until the recession of the early 1980s, when national unemployment reached 10.8 per cent. The average duration of unemployment also rose with each recession and recovery, leaving macroeconomic indicators in succeeding growth periods at levels that would have been considered recessionary in early years. Fear of inflation, exacerbated by the experiences of the 1970s, has virtually eliminated any commitment to high national employment embodied in the Employment Act of 1946 (McGahey and Jeffries, 1984; Tobin, 1986).

After the 1982 recession, the US economy reversed course, at least as measured by conventional indicators of success. By the end of 1988, economic growth, although weak by historical standards, had continued for over five years. Unemployment fell to its lowest level since the early 1970s, and more than 12 million jobs were created since 1981. However, average real wages had barely achieved the levels of the early 1970s, even after five years of economic growth.

Family income grew somewhat, largely due to more two-earner families, and inequality among families and households increased. Inflation settled around 4 per cent annually, an annual rate that would have caused substantial concerns in the 1960s and early 1970s.

But this relatively strong cyclical performance was overshadowed by larger structural concerns. For the growth of the 1980s was not achieved by putting new and sustainable economic and political foundations in place. It was instead driven by sustained increases in most forms of government stimulus – increased military spending, higher direct and indirect government employment in many spheres, and higher transfer payments through Social Security and unemployment insurance. Private demand also rose sharply as regressive tax cuts for households and businesses, especially those in upper-income brackets, were introduced along with continued growth in government expenditures (Friedman, 1988).

Continued growth in public spending coupled with decreasing revenues resulted in the sharp growth of the federal deficit that came to dominate economic policy debates, although not actions, in the late 1980s. With diminished fiscal flexibility, the primary instrument of demand control has become monetary policy. Although a variety of factors has contributed to the shift away from fiscal policy, a major one has been the Reagan administration's policies of sharp tax cuts combined with rapidly increasing military spending and little reduction in non-military appropriations (Eisner, 1986; Tobin, 1986). As fiscal policy became a semi-permanent fiscal stimulus, monetary policy was left as the only instrument of inflation control and macroeconomic adjustment.

So the first element of the New Deal/Great Society consensus – aggregate demand management through a mixture of fiscal and monetary instruments, with a commitment to high employment – has given way to a semi-permanent fiscal stimulus in the form of increased federal deficits and spending, and the use of monetary policy to combat inflation and induce or threaten recession at the expense of higher employment and incomes. The official federal deficit as a percentage of GNP was 7.8 per cent in 1946, as the economy emerged from the Second World War. It never rose above 4.5 per cent after that until 1983, when it climbed to 6.4 per cent. Since then, it has remained above 5 per cent, the highest in the post-war period, and especially high for a period of macroeconomic growth (Eisner, 1986, table 7.8). Annual inflation settled at between 4 and 5 per cent, while national unemployment hovered above 5 per cent.

The second leg of the policy consensus, the social safety net in the form of transfer payments, has also been brought into question in recent years, in part because of the high federal deficit. These programmes have been a major contributor to improved socio-economic equality. In the post-war period, market factors had little or no impact on improving income equality, but they were somewhat offset by government programmes, especially Social Security. Without these programmes, economic inequality would have risen more sharply, especially in the stagnant 1970s (Blinder, 1980; Danziger and Plotnick, 1977; Pear, 1988). (In one of the curious twists of the American policy debate, Social

Security is not viewed as an anti-poverty transfer payment. That role is assigned in public debate to 'welfare', principally Aid for Dependent Children (AFDC) and food stamps.)

The consensus supporting these income transfer policies had been eroding at least since 1968. In that year, the electoral success of George Wallace provided a powerful confirmation of growing antagonism to these programmes, especially within the Democratic Party. The presidential election of 1980 overturned any remaining consensus in favour of more equitable income redistribution and an expansion of the social safety net.

In fact, the 1980s confirmed a trend to reverse progressive income redistribution policies which had appeared during the late 1970s. The loss of political consensus in the Democratic Party and the economic troubles of the late 1970s set the stage for the Reagan administration's attack on social spending, along with tax changes that tilted federal tax policy towards the affluent for the first time since the 1920s. Coupled with the increases in the regressive burden of the Social Security tax on wage earners to finance higher benefit levels for retirees, these tax shifts resulted in net losses for all taxpayers with annual incomes under $75 000, and gains for those in the $75 000 and over category (Edsall, 1984). Even Social Security benefits began to be taxed in the 1980s, in part to meet the fiscal deficit.

The political basis for such a shift appeared during the 1970s. Inflation was pushing many taxpayers into ever-higher marginal brackets, sometimes wiping out any real income gains. Coupled with Social Security tax increases, this increased the federal tax burden on a large number of taxpayers. As Edsall summarizes, 'sharply rising marginal and average tax rates, combined with a progressive rate system that was no longer separating the very rich from the majority of taxpayers but was impinging directly on the well-being of the working and middle classes, created a strong base of deep, anti-tax sentiments' (1984, p. 211). These erupted first not in national debate, but at the state level with anti-property tax movements such as Proposition 13 in California and Proposition 2 1/2 in Massachusetts.

While tax policy in the 1980s tilted towards the affluent, the benefit cuts during the Reagan years landed hardest on those with least income, with the deepest impact on households earning less than $10 000 per year. Discretionary spending programmes, such as AFDC, public job creation, employment and training programmes, food stamps, and school lunches, suffered the brunt of the cuts.

Increasing or even maintaining existing safety net expenditure are now captive to concerns about the deficit and the need to foster economic growth. The political concerns over the federal deficit mean that large new spending initiatives are unlikely in the foreseeable future, no matter which party controls the White House. Of course, the Reagan deficits were built up at a time of economic growth. Economic downturns cause the deficit to grow even faster, leading to calls for further constraints on increased government spending.

The combination of macroeconomic fears of inflation, regressive tax increases, cuts in social programmes for the poor, and the rapid rise in deficit spending and financing all contributed to growing income inequality during the 1980s. During most of the post-Second World War period, economic growth contributed little to greater equality, with some impact at the bottom of the spectrum through lower unemployment rates and higher wages (Blank and Blinder, 1986). But even this slight impact was lost during the 1980s, when the US economy combined weak macroeconomic growth with increasing inequity.

Between 1979 and 1989, the average income of the lowest quintile of US families fell by 4.3 per cent, while it grew by 13.9 per cent among the upper quintile with lesser gains for the next two highest quintile. (US House, Committee on Ways and Means, 1991, table 26, p. 1184). Social Security remained the major anti-poverty transfer programme, but this impact was increasingly purchased by taxes on benefits and continuing increases in highly regressive payroll taxes on current wage earners, not by redistribution from upper income groups. And total government benefits were increasingly concentrated on the elderly, in large part because of the growth of Social Security and medical insurance spending relative to other social programmes. In 1986, the elderly in the US paid 10.4 per cent of federal income and payroll taxes, and received 68.4 per cent of federal transfer benefits (Pear, 1988).

So macroeconomic stimulus policies now are limited by fears of inflation and the size of the budget deficit. And the trends in traditional transfer spending and taxation policies, which in the post-war consensus were tilted towards moderate income redistribution and expansion of transfer payments, were halted or reversed in the 1980s. Any further increase in social equity now is forestalled in a seeming political 'zero-sum' relationship between Social Security and other transfers and social expenditures.

The third leg of the New Deal/Great Society policy consensus – movements towards equality through education and political and legal rights – has also lost support in recent years. Over the past three decades, federal policies to achieve greater equality concentrated on eliminating formal political and legal barriers to socio-economic integration and success. A central component of this strategy has been access to education for achieving socio-economic mobility. Premised in part on a belief in competitive labour markets that reward education and skills, access to education and training became the major consensus element inequity policies. The landmark case of *Brown vs. Board of Education*, the Civil Rights Act of 1964, and later presidential directives, court decisions, laws, and administrative rulings all pointed in this direction.

Government policies towards school desegregation eventually expanded to active redistribution of minority students through busing into predominantly white school districts, in order to achieve higher educational quality. As education is primarily controlled by local governments in the United States, mostly paid for by local property taxes, the stress on educational integration led to attacks on housing segregation. Job training policies, from the earliest efforts of the Manpower Demonstration and Training Act (MDTA) through CETA and the current Job Training Partnership Act (JTPA), concentrated on skill training or other programmes to overcome the presumed lack of occupational expertise and experience held by the disadvantaged (McGahey and Jeffries, 1984, pp. 243 *ff.*).

As with the other elements of the New Deal/Great Society consensus, support for these equity policies became fractured and uncertain through the 1970s and 1980s. Educational spending, especially in elementary and high schools, remains in the control of local and state governments, supported by property taxes. And taxpayer revolts, such as Proposition 13 in California and Proposition 2 1/2 in Massachusetts, severely cut into any expansion of funds for schooling.

These revolts against property taxes were spurred in part by the overall increase in tax burdens during the 1970s which also undercut support for transfer payments, as tax burdens increasingly were borne by moderate income households. Demographics also may have played a role, as older householders without children saw less reason to pay high property taxes to support schools, especially as the school-age population shifted to minority youth. Any effect from the changing demography of the school-age population was exacerbated by busing and other policies launched in pursuit of more educational and economic opportunity for the poor and minorities, which brought working and middle-class whites into sharp conflict with minorities, especially blacks. Squeezed by increasing income, payroll and property taxes, and concluding that government benefits were going mostly to minorities, middle-income whites lost much of their commitment to any agenda for income redistribution and social inequality. (Two excellent cases are found in Lukas (1985) on Boston, and Reider (1986) on Brooklyn.)

The erosion of support for these policies is tied in part to the failing strength of the final consensus element – labour unions. American unions were a critical element in much of the political success of the post-war consensus. Pursuit of higher wages and benefits for members, along with expanded political power at the national level, put unions at the centre of the Democratic Party's debates and policy formation. Union support was critical in implementing such policies as increased environmental and workplace health and safety standards, minimum wage increases, pension rights and regulations, and expanded bargaining obligations under federal law (Dunlop, 1980). Unions also were key supporters of civil rights legislation in the political sphere, although some of them resisted specific programmes like affirmative action and minority contractor set-asides when these seemed to challenge their economic prerogatives.

Union membership declined as a percentage of the total labour force from the mid-1950s, although union political strength remained central to the national policy consensus for much longer. The pattern of declining union membership for this long period is unique to the United States, in contrast to many other industrialized capitalist countries (Freeman, 1980). Demographic and locational shifts in jobs, declining employment in core industrial sectors, the growing active opposition of management, and a changing legal climate in favour of management all played their parts in this decline. By the late 1970s, managers were aggressively contesting union elections, with routine violations of established labour procedures and little effective sanctions from the legal system (ibid.; Weiler, 1983).

Prior to this change, much of the national union leadership had become assured about their central place in the socio-economic picture during the consensus years, leading to less aggressive organizing and talk of new relationships among unions and managers. In 1972, AFL-CIO President George Meany dismissed concerns about declining union membership, stating that 'I used to worry about it [the size of the membership.] But quite a few years ago, I just stopped worrying about it, because it doesn't make any difference. It's the organized voice that counts' (quoted in Edsall, 1984, p. 151).

Meany also speculated that conflicts were coming to an end between managers and large unions. As Edsall (1984, p. 155) notes: 'Just as management was beginning to gear up for a major battle aimed at undermining the base of organized labor, Meany was under the impression that labor's relationship to management in the future would be so cooperative' as to allow conflict resolution through voluntary negotiation. In the 1980s, organized labour's share of the workforce continued to shrink, with public employee unions becoming the major source of union strength. But the anti-tax, anti-government climate of the 1980s made it difficult for public employees to play a leading role in a political movement that could attract workers and taxpayers outside government.

7.3 SOCIO-ECONOMIC CHANGE AND CONFLICT IN THE 1980S

The four major consensus elements that evolved from the New Deal and the Great Society had all eroded and lost their internal cohesion by the 1980s, although most of the fault lines appeared during the 1970s. Macroeconomic policy lost a commitment to high employment, using monetary policy to induce recessions and combat inflation, while fiscal policy lost any flexibility because of the high deficit and political barriers to progressive tax policy. Tax burdens became more regressive and transfer payments slowed, with taxes falling harder on moderate income taxpayers at a time when family and household income was stagnating or actually declining, undercutting support for transfer payments and for educational spending. Diminished transfer payments and educational equality reduced two main approaches for increasing socio-economic equality, especially for minorities. And declining union strength undercut political support for all these policy goals, while it also reduced the positive impact of union membership on wages and incomes.

All these issues were exacerbated in critical ways by racial tensions, as many whites came to feel that disproportionate rewards and benefits from government were going to blacks and other minorities. Pressure for more affirmative action helped to alienate union members, who were at the same time suffering declines in membership, political power, income, benefits and protection for members.

So, by the early 1980s, much of the support for each element of the consensus had eroded or vanished. The internal cohesion that gave the consensus some political stability and strength had also fallen apart, leaving political space for the electoral victories and upwardly redistributive policies of the Reagan years.

The policies of the Reagan years were in some sense the mirror image of the New Deal/Great Society consensus. Macroeconomic policy featured loose fiscal but tight monetary policy, an inversion from the 1960s. Tax policy helped to redistribute income upwards, justified in part by the alleged stimulus to growth that wealthier households would provide. Transfer payments were cut for the non-elderly poor, while Social Security was protected. But benefits were taxed in part for the first time, and sharp increases in Social Security taxes meant that wage earners paid higher taxes that further undercut their earnings. The Reagan years also featured reversals of moves for stronger political rights for minorities and women, increased educational equality, and expanded worker protections and union rights.

The policies that bound the consensus together were premised not only on their mutual compatibility, but also on their contribution to a steadily growing national economy, with high employment and low inflation. With economic stagnation, fault lines appeared among middle-income whites, unionized workers, low-income minorities, and transfer payment recipients, significant political allies in the old consensus. The loss of economic prosperity, with growing economic stagnation and uncertainty, further undercut the policy consensus. The economic policies of the Reagan years were justified in large part by their alleged stimulus to economic prosperity, and the stagnation of the US economy was blamed on the policies stemming from the older consensus.

Despite the fact that a variety of economic factors changed during the period, three seem of critical importance in understanding the fracturing of the consensus: the stagnation of wages and income starting in the mid-1970s, the change in occupational and industrial structure, and the relative position of minorities.

Although the issue of rising inequality began to be widely debated in the late 1970s and the early 1980s with the growth of poverty, growing inequality among Americans in their wage and salary incomes appeared earlier, taking what Harrison and Bluestone have called a 'U-turn' around 1973. During the 1960s, wage and salary inequality declined with some momentary pauses. But in 1973, a long drop began in the growth of wages. Median family income also peaked in that year. Overall earnings became more polarized, and non-labour income also became less equal (Harrison and Bluestone, 1988). Inflation-adjusted family and household incomes have been falling since 1973. After rising by 4 per cent annually between 1947 and 1973 real median family income peaked in 1973 at $28,989. Levels in 1988 had barely reached the 1973 peak, while average real earnings remained stagnant into 1989. Average income per worker fared much worse; average family earnings were maintained by two-earner households, with greater inequality as higher income families also were adding a second income.

Attempts to explain this reversal due to business cycle effects, the entrance of baby-boomers into the labour market, or the effects of the overvalued American dollar all fail to account for most of the inequality. Some of it is due to change in household composition, with real income for single individuals without children rising, while many households (especially those headed by single women) have suffered real income losses, tied both to out-of-wedlock births and from divorce (McGahey and Jeffries, 1984). Of course, the stagnation in real income and rise in income inequality came at a time of high inflation and stagnant economic growth.

One factor that is closely tied to these declining real incomes is the changing occupational and industrial structure of the US economy. The most dominant change is the rise of service employment relative to manufacturing. Manufacturing added 4 million jobs to the US economy between 1958 and 1968. Fewer than 1 million were added in the next ten years, and between 1978 and 1983 nearly 3 million manufacturing jobs were lost, with continuing losses into the late 1980s. By contrast, jobs in service sectors boomed. Health care, legal and business services, finance, insurance, real estate, restaurants – all expanded in terms of total employment (ibid.).

These changes can be seen in patterns of employment growth by industry. Projections of job growth between 1979 and 1990 show absolute gains expected in eating and drinking places, retail trade, hospitals, business services, medical services, wholesale trade, construction, non-profit organizations, doctors' and dentists' services, and banking. In contrast, the ten greatest job losing industries were projected to be agricultural products, dairy products, household services, railways, meat and livestock, motor vehicles, millwork and wood products, food and grain feeds, logging, and bakery products.

Occupational changes show a similar pattern, with percentage growth in employment dominated by office workers such as data processing mechanics, paralegals, computer operators and analysts, office machine repair personnel, aerospace engineers, fast food workers, employment interviewers, and tax preparers. The fastest growing jobs in absolute numbers are janitors, nurses aides, sales clerks, cashiers, waiters and waitresses, office clerks, professional nurses, fast food workers, secretaries, and truck drivers.

Many of the new and fastest growing job categories pay lower wages than older unionized manufacturing positions. A large number of these new jobs are also traditionally female, with their growth linked to the dramatic surge in women's employment and labour force participation during the 1970s and 1980s. Women still receive lower earnings on the whole, tied both to discrimination and occupational segregation, and their increasing share of the labour force is another factor in the shift to greater income inequality.

But sectoral employment shifts are not the entire story. Harrison and Bluestone (1988) attribute the majority of growing wage inequality since 1978 to factors *within* sectors, especially corporate restructuring. Changes include attacks on unionization, changes in investment patterns from increases in productive capacity to more purely financial transactions, and the increased use of 'contingent' (temporary and part-time) workers.

So, starting in 1973, real individual wages fell and family incomes stagnated among many middle-income families, both because of industrial and occupational shifts to non-unionized service employment and internal corporate and sectoral changes. The lack of economic progress for families, declining union strength, and increasingly regressive tax burdens all helped to erode the consensus.

A third factor which fractured the consensus is continuing and increasing poverty, disproportionately concentrated among minorities. Blacks continue to have lower average earnings than whites, but the gap narrowed substantially during the 1950s and 1960s. Blacks and whites both suffered erosions in real income after the early 1970s. There was a strong upward trend in black incomes relative to whites during the 1960s; but stagnation and some reversals in the later 1970s. Among black and white women, incomes are much closer than among black and white men (Blinder, 1980).

Much of America's overall improvement in socio-economic equality was due to transfer payments. Between 1965 and 1985, transfer payments increased for the lowest quintile of the population, while market effects pushed in the other direction. As a result of these countervailing forces, according to Robert Haveman (1988, p. 29), 'poverty today is not markedly lower than its level 25 years ago, and inequality has increased'. Growth in transfers was cancelled out by increasing market inequality.

These income swings, both in relation to real GNP and to relative changes among demographic groups, have important ties to politics and the erosion of the policy consensus. Polling data show that blacks generally reported steady gains in their family economic situation throughout the 1960s until the late 1970s. Whites felt upward movement in their perceived economic situation from 1968 until the late 1970s (Converse *et al.*, 1980).

The stagnation in income and finances felt by whites coincided with increased 'bracket-push' tax burdens and diminished support for equity-oriented social policies, especially policies aimed at improving the position of minorities. For the American debate over socio-economic equality has been tied since the early 1960s to issues regarding racial distributions of prosperity and opportunity. This feature is found in part because the debate over economic justice grew out of the civil rights movement's early emphasis and later dissatisfaction with a focus on legal and political rights to the exclusion of issues of economic distribution.

So several economic forces helped to bring about the decline of the policy consensus. Real earnings and income equality decreased from the mid-1970s onward, with family and household income stagnant and declining from 1973. This stagnation and decline was contemporaneous with the slowdown in US economic growth, the transformation of the employment base towards service jobs, internal corporate and sectoral restructuring, the declining strength of industrial unions, and the loss of support for redistributive and other policies aimed at improving the socio-economic position of minorities. Substantial increases in transfer payments helped to reduce poverty among the elderly, although the aggregate statistics mask a division between the needy and wealthier elderly. But this progress against poverty was offset by growing poverty among children, especially those in single-parent households, who are disproportionately minorities. Economic growth after 1982 did not reverse these trends.

7.4   ECONOMICS IN PUBLIC DISCOURSE: FROM 'GLOWING PROMISE' TO 'RISE AND DECLINE'

Linking economic growth and equality was not just a staple of the post-war policy consensus; it was endorsed and partly rationalized by economic analysis and policy advice. Although economists often act as if their theorizing and policy orientation is largely unaffected by events, shifting analyses from the mid-1960s onward suggests otherwise. An optimistic link between growth and equality characterized economic analysis and advice during the 1960s, but was largely replaced by pessimism in the 1980s.

The tensions in the US economy since the 1960s have been directly reflected in popular writing about economic policy. Although many cross-currents of opinion are reflected in the national debates over socio-economic policy, there has been a profound shift from optimism to pessimism. It is now commonplace for economists, politicians and other citizens to assume that there is a negative relationship between government efforts to increase social equality and economic growth.

This understanding is embodied in much of mainstream economic theory. Increased equity has come to be identified with government redistribution of income, and any such *post hoc* alternation of market incomes is held to be inefficient. But an examination of economic policy writing from the past quarter century shows that the current dominance of this view is relatively new, illustrating how the climate of public debate has shifted since the early 1960s.

Four significant books trace this shift in mood and outlook. The first, Walter Heller's *New Dimensions of Political Economy* (1966), heralded that economics had 'come of age in the 1960's' (ibid., p. 1). Speaking in the Godkin Lectures at Harvard University, Heller claimed that the nation's political leadership had properly accepted responsibility for achieving stable economic growth. Based on the theoretical analysis and policy tools of the Keynesian revolution (principally the use of fiscal and monetary policy) the 1960s represented the 'age of the economist' (ibid., p. 2).

According to Heller, this new era was caused less by theoretical advances, and more by the consolidation of modern macroeconomics and its acceptance by political leaders. This conjuncture was partly responsible for economic growth during the early 1960s, and could help lead the United States to historic levels of prosperity and social justice. 'The significance of the great expansion of the 1960s lies not only in its striking statistics of employment, income, and growth, but in its glowing promise of things to come' (ibid., p. 58). Heller noted that these goals would require the US to 'surmount the economic pressures of Vietnam' (ibid., p. 58).

There is virtually no hint in Heller's analysis that democratic objectives and equality could be opposed to economic growth: 'The promise of modern economic policy in a democracy lies in its capacity to serve our ultimate social objectives in a framework of freedom' (ibid., p. 58). Most macroeconomic theory in this period assumed that gains in areas such as human resources would raise overall productivity, with these human resource gains also leading to higher labour incomes for the disadvantaged. Much of American educational and employment and training policy has been based on this approach, in hopes of achieving both greater economic prosperity and decreased racial differences in income and social standing (McGahey and Jeffries, 1985).

In the late 1960s and early 1970s, the economy entered a period of erratic growth, along with social disruption around civil rights issues and the Vietnam War. The mood of the country was more fragmented. Major new social policy initiatives that would have extended Great Society programmes were postponed or rejected (Matusow, 1984). The Nixon administration surprised many Americans by introducing wage and price controls to check inflation, with a rapid retreat from this policy shortly thereafter. Unlike the early 1960s, economic policy makers seemed less certain about the best course to pursue.

This mood also seemed to influence economic theory. It is captured neatly in Arthur Okun's 1975 volume, *Equality and Efficiency: The Big Tradeoff*. Like Heller, Okun presented Harvard's Godkin Lectures, a significant public platform for the discussion of public policy. But Okun's analysis is very different in tone and outlook. Heller's optimistic cast is gone, replaced by more cautious statements and a generally hesitant tone. For rather than seeing democratic processes and demands for equality as complementary with economic growth, Okun saw them as opposites in many cases.

Okun echoed Heller's general vision of possible prosperity, but in more static and less glowing terms: 'The fulfillment of the right to survival and the eradication of poverty are within the grasp of this affluent nation' (ibid., p 117). Much of Okun's volume is dedicated to a case-by-case weighing of different policies in terms of their relative contributions to efficient growth and greater equality. Like Heller, Okun continued to see labour–market policies such as increased education and training as plus-sum games for the economy and disadvantaged individuals. But plus-sum policies appeared to Okun as the exception rather than the rule. Many other interventionist policies were seen instead as contributors to inefficiency. Okun presented the case for or against particular redistributional policies much more on personal, normative grounds, rather than as stemming from the conclusions of economic theory.

The critical shift between Heller and Okun is a shift of tone. Rather than Heller's optimism, Okun viewed equality and efficiency as antagonistic, although not fatal to each other: 'A democratic capitalist society will keep searching for better ways of drawing the boundary line between the domain of rights and the domain of dollars . . . it will never solve the problem, for the conflict between equality and economic inefficiency is inescapable' (ibid., p. 120). In Okun's view, government exists to balance these two objectives, rather than to lead the economy and society to the promised land glimpsed by Heller.

Economic stagnation continued during the 1970s. Inflation, fuelled by two oil crises, along with declining overall productivity, led to static or declining real economic growth and incomes. This exacerbated political tensions, as did further indecisive economic policies in the Ford and Carter administrations. Carter in particular was viewed as an indecisive leader on a variety of fronts, not only in economic policy. And government policies were seen to be dead-locked and inefficient, incapable of moving the country forward.

Lester Thurow's *The Zero-Sum Society* (1980) concretized this spirit. Thurow argued that economic policies could still be designed to help solve American socio-economic problems, but that rational policies were blocked by structural political barriers. These barriers resulted from the real costs that various economic policies would impose on some groups in society. 'There are solutions for each of our problem areas . . . [but] these solutions have a common characteristic. Each requires that some large group – sometimes a minority and sometimes the majority – be willing to tolerate a large reduction in their real standard of living' (ibid., p. 10). The American political system had generated interest groups that could forestall the costs being placed on themselves, but that were dead-locked with other equally powerful groups over who would bear the costs of adjustment. American society also seemed incapable of equitably rationing out the necessary pains involved in economic change.

In economic terms, Okun's case-by-case problematic regarding equity and efficiency was elevated by Thurow to a more fundamental principle affecting all political allocations of economic costs. In Thurow's view, political decisions about economic disruptions are in fact zero-sum. Someone wins and someone loses and there are few, if any, plus-sum decisions. *Laissez-faire* policies provide no answer, as they only represent one way among many to allocate the gains and losses associated with economic change. Thurow stated his own explicit prefer-ences for policies aimed at increasing socio-economic equity. This would be accomplished through a mixture of tax reform, restructuring of capital and invest-ment incentives, and a national commitment to full employment through a guar-anteed jobs programme.

The *Zero-Sum Society* extended Okun's line of reasoning, but with increasing pessimism about the real possibilities for enlightened political policies. Heller, Okun and Thurow all shared the explicit goal of increasing economic perform-ance along with social equality, but the degree of pessimism about achieving these two goals increases markedly. From the perspective of the early 1970s, Okun saw these goals as trade-offs, although he still envisioned using economic theory as a guide for designing particular programmes. In 1980, Thurow accepted Okun's trade-off in a more stark form, blaming developments in the US political system for the policy deadlock. The policy goals of increased growth and more social equality would necessarily involve painful social and political trade-offs, which the system could not make.

This line of argument completed its trajectory with the 1982 publication of Mancur Olson's *The Rise and Decline of Nations*. Olson elevated Thurow's thesis on American political deadlock to a general theoretical proposition explaining macroeconomic performance in democratic capitalist nations. Olson saw such societies developing 'institutional sclerosis' over time, as political coalitions and interest groups become entrenched and reliant on existing economic policies and distribution patterns. As economic conditions change, such societies cannot adapt and make needed changes.

Although such critiques often are allied to calls for diminished government involvement in the economy, Olson did not offer an optimistic brief for *laissez-faire*. Using microeconomic postulates about self-interested behaviour to ground his argument about the behaviour of interest groups in democratic societies, Olson noted that 'there often will not be competitive markets even if the government does not intervene. The government is by no means the only source of coercion or social pressure in society' (ibid., p. 177). But he viewed self-interested behaviour as directing public and private actions in very similar ways, based on narrow calculations of economic interest.

Olson did take explicit issue with Okun and others who claim that competitive markets generate a substantial degree of inequality that can and should be corrected by government policy (ibid., p. 173). On the contrary, he argued that government policies cannot achieve this goal, and may in fact increase inequality, as more powerful groups will support policies to reward themselves instead of the disadvantaged. Olson viewed special interest coalitions and their effects on economic policy as significantly responsible for widespread problems such as involuntary unemployment, depressions and stagflation, and the general 'development of the macroeconomic problem over time' in different societies. The only solution offered was a general consensus against 'special-interest legislation or regulation' along with the rigorous use of anti-trust laws against cartels or collusions that used their power 'to obtain prices or wages above competitive levels' (ibid., pp. 235–6).

Like Heller, Olson viewed the relationship of growth and equity as embodying general macroeconomic truth. But where Heller saw strong complementarity, Olson saw fatal opposition. The time-span encompassed by these four books is only sixteen years. The profound shifts in their analyses mirror the wide swings in American public and professional economists' debates over socio-economic policy since the early 1960s. Of course, there has been a myriad of other writing on economic policy and theory, but the positions taken in these four books capture much of the spirit of the changing economic policy debate.

Economists' policy positions and analyses often express their results and prescriptions as stemming solely from the theory and attendant empirical analysis. But the changes reflected in these books illustrate that economists and their opinions are as captive to events as politicians or any other groups of citizens. It is quite a journey from Heller's optimistic vision, via Okun's puzzles over specific policies and Thurow's stark posing of the political problems of economic adjustment, to Olson's elevation of this problem to a theoretical statement about social and marcoeconomic reality.

The pronouncements by these four economists closely resemble trends in the economy, and are mirrored in public policy debate. American economic policies since the 1960s trace a similar trajectory, leaving behind any optimism about achieving the twin goals of economic growth along with greater equality. By the late 1980s, economic policy had become divided between a call for sacrifices administered by government, similar to Thurow's analysis, versus a rejection of government's ability to take positive steps in economic management or towards equality, similar to Olson. How American economic policy came to this pass is instructive for considering any future programme to achieve growth and equity together.

7.5   EQUITY, GROWTH AND POLITICS

There has been a mini-boom in the last several years for economic analysis and advice, with a steady appearance of books diagnosing America's economic performance and suggesting possible future policies. This output shows no signs of diminishing, and the details of current and possible future socio-economic policy are widely debated in the media.

One striking feature of this wave of books is the general absence of sustained or serious political analysis. For example, many of the books that are part of the debate over economic policy and its possible future in the United States present elaborately designed economic programmes touching on capital formation, regulation, taxation, infrastructure spending, labour market and educational policies and the like. But the question of how to develop the political support for such programmes is rarely discussed. As a result, many of the volumes have a curiously disengaged tone, sounding more like technical manuals for fixing the economy than guides to new political and economic policy.

This silence on the subject of politics may represent the exhaustion of the various authors. Perhaps it is too much to ask of economists and policy analysts that they provide not only an elaborate plan for the economy, but also a political programme for achieving and implementing that plan. But without such attention to politics, the economic plans do not have much of a future. Most recent writing on alternative future economic policies remains haunted by political questions.

For interventionist programmes, the relationship between economic growth and socio-economic equity is of special importance. Most writing by economists assumes that these two goals must be traded off against each other, but a politics based either on diminished economic growth or on increased inequality is unlikely to command a large enough majority to overcome the traditional American ideology that opposes overt government economic intervention.

There have been attempts to break out of this deadlock, most notably Robert Kuttner's work. In his 1984 volume, *The Economic Illusion*, Kuttner explicitly attacked the idea that increased economic growth and social equity must be opposed. Linking the resurgence of American political conservatism to the 'pseudo-technical claim that equality retards efficiency', Kuttner argues most economic theory and policy analysis fosters the 'illusion of static tradeoffs' rather than seeing that there are many policies that can simultaneously improve equality and efficiency (ibid., pp. 8–9).

Kuttner's work represents a break from the trajectory that runs from Heller, via Okun and Thurow, to Olson. In his view, we are not trapped in a world of zero-sum or static trade-offs. It is not even the traditional New Deal and Great Society world, where growth provides some amount of left-over social surplus that can be spent on social programmes. Rather, much of Kuttner's analysis is dedicated to showing that other advanced capitalist democracies achieved higher levels of equality and economic efficiency during the 1970s and early 1980s, and that 'many models of economic distribution and economic perform-ance are possible' (ibid., p. 265).

The issue of political power and policies was taken up by Kuttner in his 1987 book, *The Life of the Party: Democratic Prospects in 1988 and Beyond*. In that volume, Kuttner argued that the Democratic Party was becoming severed 'both from its principles and from the political logic that connects it to voters' (ibid., p. 151). He criticized much of Democratic policy analyses and politics for failing to blend political realities and the economic needs of traditional constituencies into their overall analysis, with special criticism for economists, 'expert advisors who are congenitally opposed, by professional training, to much of the party philosophy' (ibid., p. 183).

Kuttner asserts that the best strategy for the Democrats is to build on economic issues: 'Democrats can regain their status as majority party only by rebuilding a majority coalition of ordinary, wage- and salary-earning people, whose political and economic interests are not identical to those of the wealthy' (ibid., p. 5). He recommends a modern version of what he calls the 'progressive-populist' tradi-tion, that 'provided redistribution and social justice via inclusion' (ibid., p. 7). By focusing on policies that have broad economic appeal, the Democrats should avoid limiting government programmes to the poor and minorities, which has helped to splinter the broader potential base. Kuttner sketches a programme based on a 'closely interconnected set of issues involving education, labor-market policies, employment opportunities, and related family supports' (ibid., p. 225).

Kuttner's work represents the most sustained attempt to blend an economic analysis linking growth and equity to policies and politics aimed at creating and sustaining electoral majorities. But the difficulties in such a programme should not be underestimated, as Kuttner is well aware. To take just one example, employment opportunities, there is a powerful political tension along racial lines regarding affirmative action programmes that is a continuing source of political fragmentation among diverse parts of the old Democratic coalition. Some craft unions and government employee unions in such areas as police, fire, and transit are in active conflict with advocates of more affirmative action for minorities.

Finding a common base among such groups will not be an easy task as both sides are strongly committed to their positions and the justifications for them. Expanded employment in general might help to relieve some of this pressure, but would not be an automatic solution. Consider the highly unionized construction industry in New York City, which in the late 1980s experienced a five-year boom with record levels of employment, and with Democratic administrations in the City and State governments. Yet the percentage of minorities holding journey-man status overall was declined slightly, and the decline more pronounced when one considers the changing demography of New York's labour force, where the minority percentage increased over the same period. Unions claimed that they could not find qualified minority entrants, and that some affirmative action advocates wanted to curtail union rights, while the advocates suspected the unions of discrimination. No Democratic political leader has taken serious steps to address this problem, probably because of the risks involved relative to the chances of success.

Nevertheless, Kuttner's work offers the most explicit vision of an alternative 'political economy' for the Democrats, although it is one that elected leaders will find quite risky, especially because of their dependence for campaign funding from groups whose economic interests might be challenged by these political trends. Kuttner's explicitly political approach can be contrasted to other policy advisors, such as Lester Thurow in *The Zero-Sum Solution* (1985) or Robert Reich in *Tales of a New America* (1987), where the emphasis is on restoring America's economic competitiveness and global leadership, with policies advanced in pursuit of that goal. Not surprisingly, all these analyses once again make training and education policies central to their recommendations, with economic rationales rather similar to Heller and Okun.

Even with this recent, thoughtful work, the question of how to craft a politics that has a credible programme for achieving economic growth and greater social equality remains elusive. The question remains an important one, especially for those economists who want to advance alternative future policies. The issues of economic growth and social equality remain central in debates over current and future politics, and policies in these areas are likely to play a key role in future American economic performance and social harmony.

One major constraint on the political debate over growth and equity has been the identification of increased equity with the *post hoc* redistribution of labour income through transfer payments. (It is not entirely serendipitous that this formulation is consistent with mainstream economic theory.) But experiences of the 1970s and 1980s suggest that identifying increasing equality solely with the *post hoc* redistribution of income will create substantial political and economic obstacles to short- or long-term policies for greater equality. These problems are especially pronounced at a time of stagnating or declining real income.

For American policies and political culture generally frown upon explicit income redistribution. Even when Americans undertake direct income redistribution, it is called something other than an income transfer to make it politically acceptable, as in the case of Social Security. Instead, greater social equality is pursued sporadically through a variety of indirect means: human resource policies such as early childhood education, labour market programmes of increased training and education, sectoral adjustment policies such as trade adjustment assistance or funds for dislocated workers, interventions for particular groups such as affirmative action plans and minority contractor set-asides, and programmes providing marginal tax benefits to employers and workers to encourage more job creation and work effort.

Although some have advocated a class-based politics of income redistribution, policies aimed at explicit income redistribution and overt economic intervention do not have deep roots in American political culture. American political and economic life is full of specific efforts to aid or retard the interests of one industry, region or income class against another, but the fate of 'industrial policy' in the 1984 Democratic electoral debate illustrates the resistance of American politics to making such efforts more overt and systematic. A similar problem faces any efforts to introduce consciously interventionist race-specific policies.

Schlozman and Verba's research on a sample of the US metropolitan workforce documents these attitudes. Seventy-seven per cent of the sample agreed with the general notion that 'the government should end unemployment'. But only 30 per cent approved government hiring of the jobless, 23 per cent endorsed having the government 'assign jobs', and 47 per cent endorsed taxation to redistribute wealth. (This latter support must be tempered with the 91 per cent dislike of a policy to put an upper limit on incomes.) What is striking in their research is the shared consensus against dramatic economic changes. Attitudes differed very little by occupational or employment status. On the whole, people were very unlikely to endorse radical-sounding changes. A sharp economic downturn, of course, might alter these attitudes, but they are deeply rooted.

Blacks were more willing than whites to endorse sharp changes, but felt that whites were unlikely to support them on black issues. And the perception that explicitly black goals will not draw white support is well founded; many Americans will not endorse race-specific policies even to ameliorate black economic distress. One hoped for result of the civil rights struggles has been a strengthening of belief among all Americans that race and ethnic-specific discrimination is unfair and undesirable. One unanticipated consequence of those victories is a widely held belief that racial discriminatory barriers are no longer an obstacle to black economic progress, and that any race-specific policies are thus 'reverse discrimination', and unnecessary (McGahey, 1984).

American political culture presents a major roadblock to an integrated and interventionist socio-economic policy, a roadblock that is at variance with historical trends. For government continues to take a larger share of GNP each year, and government policy is increasingly intertwined in socio-economic life, regardless of the severe cuts made in social programmes by the Reagan administration. Pressures in the world economy continue to support intervention in a variety of spheres, and welfare state policies, although in substantial turmoil because of their costs, are unlikely to suffer any broad-based reversals. The talk of a 'crisis' in the welfare state, if that is taken to mean its elimination or even substantial reduction, is overblown (Hirschman, 1980).

It seems likely that interpenetration of the economic and political spheres will continue, although the forms of that may change or appear in mutated forms. For example, Robert Reich (1983) has argued convincingly that we already have an industrial policy in the United States for the military, dominated by long-term, non-market spending policies, research and development efforts, labour market and regional adjustment policies, and trade protection.

Like Humpty Dumpty, the old consensus around the New Deal and Great Society policies seems too broken to be put back together. Edsall (1984) makes a strong case that the current national Republican Party ascendency is based on direct service to the interest of wealthier Americans, while the older Democratic coalition has broken apart around questions of economic growth and social equality. Any new majority aiming at socio-economic equality as a goal will have to build on the base established by the New Deal and Great Society consensus, but will also have to move in different directions that are still consistent with American political culture.

Kuttner and others have suggested that a new politics of equality must address issues with a universalistic appeal. Prominent candidates include health care, full employment, and family and child care policies. Leaving aside the question of specific policy ideas and building political coalitions, the broader question posed by many economists and economic theories will still have to be addressed: can a political programme of greater social equality be convincingly linked to a programme of greater economic growth?

In 1984, Kuttner put the issue succinctly: 'I have tried to suggest that injustice is not necessary economics; that the economics of equality can work, and often has worked, when the constituency for it is animated. The *politics* of equality – that is a little harder' (ibid., p. 278, emphasis in original). But in the absence of such a politics, it is hard to imagine any substantive economic engineering at the national, state or local level that will overcome the spectre of special interest politics, and attendant inefficiency.

The political process may instead result in the outcome predicted by Olson: further division of the economic pie by groups with a strong and growing stake in current political economic arrangements, and further stasis in national policy and the economy. In such a world, those with the least power will almost surely bear the brunt of any economic adjustment, as has been the case since the late 1970s.

Avoiding that result will require a political economy that can offer a convincing case for social equality and economic growth as strong complements, or even a programme where equality can lead growth. If growth is to be fuelled at the expense of existing incomes and economic arrangements, the poor and powerless are likely to bear most of that burden.

7.6   ECONOMICS, PUBLIC POLICY, AND POLITICS

These problems pose several challenges to economists and others with an interest in public policy. The issues can be posed at three levels of increasing abstraction. First, can economic policies be designed and implemented that aid both growth and equality, or use increased equality to foster increased growth? For example, can alternative policies be developed that use transfer payments and other government spending in more creative ways, providing actual investments and income for the disadvantaged rather than *post hoc* income transfers?

Second, how can we best understand the relationship between economic growth and social equality in the United States, especially in recent years where growth has been accompanied by increasing inequality? If growth is not linked to overall changes in the distribution of economic well-being, is that an accident of history, or is the lack of a linkage embedded in American demographics, social or economic structure?

Finally, in economic theory, can a convincing theoretical link be made between economic growth and social equality, either positive or negative? Is there something about the process of capitalist economic development that produces inequality? Do market-oriented economies produce more equality than any conceivable political arrangements?

These are large and significant questions that will bedevil the design of specific policies, the analysis and explanation of recent trends in economic performance and social equality, and the development of economic theory. Although Keynes viewed his 'practical men' as influenced by the older ideas of 'defunct economists', it seems clear that much of the current work of economists is equally influenced by political and economic trends of the moment.

There is also a long shadow cast over economics by American political culture, both in terms of implementing new policies, and in terms of basic thinking and conceptualization of problems and policy options. To be accurate and effective, future economic theory and policy analysis will have to take explicit account of political factors as central features of the analysis, not as afterthoughts.

Several policy areas might foster new coalitions that have social equity on their agenda. The rising number of women in the labour force may give rise to greater claims for anti-discrimination efforts or pay equity policies. A related issue that touches many people, especially women, is child care and education. Concerns over health care costs and support for the elderly may also feed into a new coalition. It may be that family and educational issues, coupled with women's increasing importance in the paid economy, will provide a new locus of concern that ties economic issues to equity concerns.

Of course, severe economic downturns may provide the basis for new coalitions. The American economy has been growing in an unstable fashion, fuelled by high and perhaps unsustainable levels of deficit financing with a lack of productive investment. Economic growth continues to stagnate, which will give rise to more calls for policies that free up business spending and support 'capital formation', but may also create room for new labour policies that can raise firm and business productivity, perhaps through greater employee ownership and participation in business operations.

Several key economic trends will continue to dominate the US economy into the 1990s, giving rise to a variety of political responses for managing these problems. In some cases, like the continuing problems of the US trade balance, available political responses are part of the problem (for example, the sterile and academic debate between 'free trade' and 'protectionism'). The successful political response will either recast the issue in new form, or at least avoid the deadlocked polarization that characterizes current national policy debate. With other problems, such as the declining middle class and threats to the American standard of living (which could have been the decisive issue for Democrats in 1988), there is both the opportunity and the necessity to shape the public debate and suggested policy responses.

A major facet of this problem will be finding and building on resources in American historical and political culture that can provide the basis for economic growth along with social equality. The experience of the New Deal and Great Society consensus suggest that they come together in unanticipated ways and break apart when the economic ground shifts underneath them. The issue for the future is what sort of government and public involvement will the American economy have, not whether we will have it. Tying that involvement to efforts for greater socio-economic equality will be a central political issue in coming years.

Creating such a 'new political economy' will have to proceed step by step, especially in the United States. For American political culture and debate continues to see 'government' and the 'economy' as distinctive spheres, with constant tensions over the proper relationships between the two. In a recent essay, Heilbroner restates his analysis locating this division in the historical condition that 'capitalism is unique in history in having not one but two centers of authority, one built around the "economic" prerogatives of the business system, the other around the "political" prerogatives of the government system' (ibid., 1989, p. 102).

In that essay, Heilbroner reaffirms his analysis that the 'political' sphere will continue to increase its reach at the national level: 'The history of every democratic capitalist nation is one of the widening provision of "entitlements", over the nearly universal opposition of business, because from the viewpoint of government these measures have seemed necessary to retain and strengthen the fealty of its citizens' (ibid., p. 108).

The increasing importance of the political sphere is indeed the trend, but the American experience of the 1980s, with upward distribution of wealth in part through direct government policies, cautions that widening entitlements do not necessarily mean greater socio-economic equality. Nor will static redistribution policies solve problems of underinvestment, interna-tional competition, and poverty.

Because of the potential for political tension in conditions of rising inequality, it is hard to imagine a successful political economy that does not improve living standards for at least a politically sustainable majority of its citizens. Again, the ability to divide voters along racial, regional and economic lines should not be overlooked, but such a political strategy does not auger well for economic strength in the future. For example, most commentators accept that a highly trained workforce, forward-looking business management, greater cooperation between business and labour, and improved human resources are all critical elements of future economic success. It is hard to imagine those factors coming together in an economic climate of continuing and growing inequality and stagnating living standards, which are more likely instead to feed divisive and deadlocked politics.

As Heilbroner notes, there will be 'successful and unsuccessful capitalisms', and national variations will succeed or fail in large part on their 'institutional adaptability, ideological pragmatism, and common decency'. Continuing problems with American labour markets, financial, regulatory, and macroeconomic institutions cannot make one confident about America's future prospects. An economically successful United States will require increasing economic growth coupled with social equality, and a variety of new institutions, policies, politics, and eco-nomic analyses that support sustainable economic policies, reinforcing and reinforced by a sustainable political coalition. Economists and others who wish to contribute to those developments will continue to draw substantial in-spiration and intellectual sustenance from Robert Heilbroner's work.

References

Blank, Rebecca M. and Alan S. Blinder (1986) 'Macroeconomics, Distribution, and Poverty', in Sheldon H. Danziger and Daniel H. Weinberg (eds), *Fighting Poverty: What Works and What Doesn't* (Cambridge, Mass.: Harvard University Press).

Blinder, Alan S. (1980) 'The Level and Distribution of Economic Well-Being', in Martin Feldstein (ed.), *The American Economy in Transition* (Chicago: University of Chicago Press).

Carey, Neal (1981) 'Occupational Employment Growth through 1980', *Monthly Labor Review*, August.

Converse, Phillip E., Jean D. Dotson, Wendy J. Hoag and William H. McGee III (1980) *American Social Attitudes Data Sourcebook, 1947–1978* (Cambridge, Mass.: Harvard University Press).

Danziger, Sheldon and Robert Plotnick (1977) 'Demographic Change, Government Trans-fers, and the Distribution of Income', *Monthly Labor Review*, April.

Dunlop, John T. (1980) 'The Changing Character of Labor Markets', in Martin Feldstein (ed.), *The American Economy in Transition* (Chicago: University of Chicago Press).

Edsall, Thomas Byrne (1984) *The New Politics of Inequality* (New York: W. W. Norton).

Eisner, Robert (1986) 'The Federal Budget Crisis', in David Obey and Paul Sarbanes (eds), *The Changing American Economy* (New York: Basil Blackwell).

Freeman, Richard B. (1980) 'The Evolution of the American Labor Market, 1948–80', in Martin Feldstein (ed.), *The American Economy in Transition* (Chicago: University of Chicago Press).

Friedman, Benjamin M. (1988) *Day of Reckoning: The Consequences of American Economic Policy Under Reagan and After* (New York: Random House).

Harrison, Bennett and Barry Bluestone (1988) *The Great U-Turn: Corporate Restructuring and the Polarization of America* (New York: Basic Books).

Haveman, Robert H. (1988) 'New Policy for the New Poverty', *Challenge*, September–October, vol. 31, no. 5.

Heilbroner, Robert L. (1985) *The Nature and Logic of Capitalism* (New York: W. W. Norton).

Heilbroner, Robert L. (1988) *Behind the Veil of Economics: Essays in the Worldly Philosophy* (New York: W.W. Norton).

Heilbroner, Robert L. (1989) 'The Triumph of Capitalism', *The New Yorker*, 23 January 1989.

Heller, Walter W. (1966) *New Dimensions of Political Economy* (Cambridge, Mass.: Harvard University Press).

Hirschman, Albert O. (1980) 'The Welfare State in Trouble: Systemic Crisis or Growing Pains?', *American Economic Review*, vol. 70, no. 2.

Johnson, Clifford M., Andrew M. Sum and James D. Weill (1988) *Vanishing Dreams: The Growing Economic Plight of America's Young Families* (Washington: The Children's Defense Fund).

Kuttner, Robert (1984) *The Economic Illusion: False Choices Between Prosperity and Social Justice* (Boston: Houghton Mifflin).

Kuttner, Robert (1987) *The Life of the Party: Democratic Prospects in 1988 and Beyond* (New York: Viking).

Levy, Frank (1988) 'Incomes, Families, and Living Standards', in Robert E. Litan, Robert Z. Lawrence, and Charles L. Schultze (eds), *American Living Standards: Threats and Challenges* (Washington: Brookings Institution).

Lukas, J. Anthony (1985) *Common Ground: A Turbulent Decade in the Lives of Three American Families* (New York: Alfred A. Knopf).

Marshall, F. Ray (1986a) 'Working Smarter', in David Obey and Paul Sarbanes (eds), *The Changing American Economy* (New York: Basil Blackwell).

Marshall, F. Ray (1986b) 'Reversing the Downtrend in Real Wages', *Challenge*, May–June, vol. 29, no. 2.

Matusow, Allen J. (1984) *The Unraveling of America: A History of Liberalism in the 1960s* (New York: Harper & Row).

McGahey, Richard M. (1984) 'Industrial Policy: Minority Economic Interests and American Political Response', *Review of Black Political Economy*, vol. 13, nos 1 and 2.

McGahey, Richard M. (1987) 'State Economic Development Policy: Strategic Approaches for the Future', *Review of Law and Social Change*, vol. XV, no. 1.

McGahey, Richard M. and John M. Jeffries (1984) 'Equity, Growth and Socioeconomic Change: Anti-Discrimination Policy in an Era of Economic Transformation', *Review of Law and Social Change*, vol. XIII, no. 2.

McGahey, Richard M. and John M. Jeffries (1985) *Minorities and the Labor Market: Twenty Years of Misguided Policy* (Washington: Joint Center for Political Studies).

Okun, Arthur M. (1975) *Equality and Efficiency: The Big Tradeoff* (Washington: Brookings Institution).

Okun, Arthur M. (1980) 'Postwar Macroeconomic Performance', in Martin Feldstein (ed.) *The American Economy in Transition* (Chicago: University of Chicago Press).

Olson, Mancur (1982) *The Rise and Decline of Nations: Economic Growth, Stagnation, and Social Rigidities* (New Haven, Conn: Yale University Press).

Pear, Robert (1988) 'US Pensions Found to Lift Many of the Poor', *New York Times*, 28 December.

Reich, Robert B. (1983) 'An Industrial Policy of the Right', *The Public Interest*, no. 73, Fall.

Reich, Robert B. (1987) *Tales of a New America* (New York: Times Books).

Reider, Jonathan (1986) *Canarsie: The Jews and Italians of New York Against Liberalism* (Cambridge, Mass.: Harvard University Press).

Saks, Daniel H. (1983) *Distressed Workers in the Eighties* (Washington: National Planning Association).

Sawhill, Isabel V. (1988) 'What About America's Underclass?', *Challenge*, May–June, vol. 31, no. 3.

Schlozman, Kay L. and Sidney Verba (1979) *Injury to Insult: Unemployment, Class, and Political Response* (Cambridge, Mass.: Harvard University Press).

Silk, Leonard (1988) 'Now, to Figure Why the Poor Get Poorer', *New York Times*, 18 December.

Thurow, Lester C. (1980) *The Zero-Sum Society: Distribution and the Possibilities for Economic Change* (New York: Basic Books).

Thurow, Lester C. (1985) *The Zero-Sum Solution: Building a World-Class American Economy* (New York: Simon & Schuster).

Tobin, James (1986) 'The Economic Experience', in David Obey and Paul Sarbanes (eds), *The Changing American Economy* (New York: Basil Blackwell).

Tolchin, Martin (1989) 'Richest Got Richer and Poorest Poorer in 1979–87', *New York Times*, 29 March.

US Department of Commerce. Bureau of the Census. Various Years. *Current Population Reports: Consumer Income*, series P-60.

US Department of Commerce (1983) *Statistical Abstract of the United States, 1984* (Washington, DC: US Government Printing Office).

US Department of Commerce. *Historical Statistics of the United States, Colonial Times to 1970* (Washington, DC: US Government Printing Office).

US House. Committee on Ways and Means (1991) *Background Material and Data on Programs Within the Jurisdiction of the Committee on Ways and Means* (Washington, DC: US Government Printing Office).

Weiler, Paul (1983) 'Promises to Keep: Securing Workers' Rights to Self-Organization Under the NLRA', *Harvard Law Review*, vol. 96.

Part IV
History of Thought: Smith, Ricardo and Marx

Robert Urquhart, 'Adam Smith Between Political Economy and Economics'

Richard Castellana, 'History, Human Nature and Justice in Marx'

Martha Campbell, 'The Commodity as "Characteristic Form"'

Adam Smith is perhaps Heilbroner's favourite classic, the epitome of the worldly philosophy. Urquhart explores Smith's concept of the individual, arguing that Smith was poised at a crucial point in the development of this idea, between a Classical conception drawing on Aristotle and Greek tragedy, and a Platonist Christian conception. *The Theory of Moral Sentiments* lay closer to the Classical, while *The Wealth of Nations* moved nearer to the Christian, but adapted to a new guise, in which the Christian (and Platonist) concept of the unitary 'good' was reborn as 'utility', the fruit not of virtue but of rational calculation. Castellana examines Marx, seeking to unearth a concept of justice, implicit in his treatment of human nature, and capable of providing guidelines to actors in the drama of class struggle. This can only be seen, however, by exploring the development of Marx's thought as he moved from philosophical anthropology to historical materialism. Campbell also explores the structure of Marx's thought, showing, by an examination of the concept of the commodity, that capitalist production, based on wage labour, and simple circulation are two mutually dependent aspects of the same unitary system. The argument illustrates Marx's method – the exploration of the inner logic of a system, very much the approach taken by Heilbroner.

8 Adam Smith between Political Economy and Economics

Robert Urquhart

Robert Heilbroner, in his essay 'Behind the Veil of Economics'[1] takes up a fundamental issue – individual motivation and its relation to economic agency. In particular, he explores the psychological underpinnings of exchange behaviour, seeking to understand both how such behaviour contributes to economic order, and how it may be problematic from the standpoint of the ordinary precepts of self-identity and motivation. If one considers, in general terms, what its subject matter requires of economic theory, this hardly seems an unusual inquiry. In the actual practice of economists, however, it is. For the issue has, for the most part, either been ignored, or sidestepped through *a priori* assumptions. The value of Heilbroner's work in this, as in other instances, lies both in his insistence on the existence of a problem for economics, and in his willingness to draw on other disciplines, when the existing resources of economics prove deficient.

The purpose of the present chapter is to explore the issue of individual motivation in another direction, using other resources, and taking Adam Smith as the starting point. We will attempt to show Smith's place between the tradition of eighteenth-century political economy of which he was the end, and the tradition of modern economics of which he is correctly named the inaugurator. In order to understand his place, we will associate each of these traditions with a broad account of the individual and of individuality, which accounts we will name, for convenience, the Classical and the Christian. These accounts are, initially, concerned with ethics, none the less, they come to define the terms of study of human nature and of the actual behaviour of individuals in society. In this light, Smith's importance will lie in his inability to define the economy in terms of one account of individuality alone. But to be able to understand this inability as a *challenge* to modern economics, we must first consider, in very broad terms, the two main traditions of modern economics in relation to Smith, and to each other.

Some terms must be made clear at the outset: throughout this chapter, 'political economy' refers to the project of the eighteenth- (and a few seventeenth-) century predecessors of Smith; and 'economics' to that of his nineteenth-century successors (including those, such as Say, Ricardo and Mill, who took 'political economy' as the name of their subject). Smith, as we shall see, stands between the two. Again, it will be necessary to employ the word 'classical' in two quite normal, but different, usages. One amounts to the assertion of an affinity with Greek, and by extension, Roman, antiquity. The other distinguishes one tradition of economic thought – associated especially with Smith, Ricardo, Mill and Marx – from the so-called neo-classical tradition inaugurated by Menger, Jevons, Marshall and Walras. The context will always distinguish between these usages without confusion.[2]

8.1   SMITH AND THE TRADITIONS OF MODERN ECONOMICS

Two Lines of Thought in the *Wealth of Nations*

In the first three chapters of Book I of the *Wealth of Nations*, Smith presents an extraordinarily compact system composed of the division of labour, the basic human propensity to truck, barter and exchange, the basic human drive of self-interest and the gradual extension of the market. The outcome of this system is the orderly creation of increasing wealth within a self-regulating network of market exchanges, in which the self-interest of each and every participant is furthered to a greater extent – at least in so far as the satisfaction of material needs is concerned – than it would be without the system, and, by implication, than it could be by any other form of social organization. The system operates independently of the intentions of any individual or group of individuals within it, and without any concerted action on their part. It is, in fact, to use a phrase repeatedly used by Smith himself to describe it, 'the natural course of things'.

In the concluding section of Book I, Smith puts forward a rather different picture of the overall order of society. He now describes it in terms of the three great streams of revenue which exhaust the annual product of the nation, one in the form of rents, another in the form of profits, and the third in the form of wages; flowing to, respectively, the landlords, the merchants (and manufacturers), and the labourers. These three form the three great orders of society. They are the ultimate structural outcome of the division of labour. Initially, then, this new picture seems only to add further definition to the earlier one. But it quickly becomes apparent that the structural view poses a serious challenge to the system as first envisaged.

In the original depiction of the market system, the individuals comprising it were simply individuals, each one acting only in pursuit of his or her own individual self-interest. In the new structural version, individuals have become members of classes, with interests held in common with the other members of their class. The spectre of concerted action arises again, threatening the natural course of things. In Smith's account, the problem lies particularly with the merchant class, both because their interests tend to be against the general welfare of the nation, and because their professional skill will allow them to push successfully for their interests against the idleness and ignorance of the landlords, and the powerlessness and ignorance of the labourers. But singling out one class as an especial problem is a secondary matter: Ricardo will argue a formally similar case, but casting the landlords, not the merchants, as the villains. The chief point is that the existence of classes, and so, of *class interests*, must threaten the orderly operation of the market. That class structure itself is a natural outcome of the division of labour only makes the problem the more intractable.

It cannot be said that Smith ever offers us a resolution to the problem he has thus created for himself, though there is a great deal more to his view of the matter. For our present purposes, however, it is sufficient to see that there is a problem, and that it is a serious one.

The Two Main Traditions of Economic Thought

The two main traditions of economic thought are usually given the names Classical and Neo-classical economics. The major figures of the former are usually said to be Smith himself, Ricardo, J.S. Mill, and Marx. The latter begins with Menger, Jevons, Marshall and Walras, and is the foundation of modern economic orthodoxy. For the moment, it is best to set Smith apart from both traditions, though both lay claim to him.

Neo-classical economics is concerned with the efficient allocation of resources through the activities of self-interested individuals in competitive markets. Since the desired outcome is a set of equilibrium prices that will clear all markets, and so complete all desired exchanges, the neo-classical view may properly be thought of as static. Classical economics is concerned with the overall structure of the economy as this is revealed in the structure of classes, their economic functions, and the typical streams of revenue flowing to them. Since the aim of these concerns is to understand the reproduction of the economy over time, its growth, and the changes attendant on that growth, the classical view may properly be thought of as dynamic.

The purpose of setting Smith apart is now obvious, for we see that each of the two main traditions of economic thought does indeed have a claim to Smith, but a claim only to a part of him. Each begins from one of the lines of thought of Book I of the *Wealth of Nations* to the exclusion of the other. Thus, whatever our conclusion may be as to Smith's place in the history of economic thought, that place must at least be distinctive in that his thought embraces two lines, where each major tradition that follows attempts to construct economic theory on the basis of one of these alone.

Important consequences follow from this account of the provenance of classical and neo-classical economics. In the first place, we see that all that distinguishes neo-classical from classical economics comes back to the difference between them in the way each views individuals. Neo-classical theory sees individuals as individuals, acting for themselves, and without any necessary reference to others. Classical theory sees individuals as class members, in the sense that their place and their activities are determined by structures defining their relationships with other individuals in terms of their class position. (The word 'class' here should be treated in a broad functional sense, capable of application equally to Smith's, Ricardo's and Marx's view of class, without exhausting the view of any of them, and especially not that of the last.)

The neo-classical view of the individual, then, is the more abstract. Whatever else individuals are, they have certain formal characteristics by which all are alike, prior to all differences between them; these characteristics and the sharing of them govern the system, and permits its orderly outcome. The classical view does not deny the existence of characteristics in terms of which all individuals are alike. But it asserts that the structures formed by functional differences between individuals are the key to understanding the way in which the economy reproduces itself. We see then, as our use of the words has suggested from the beginning, that one view is particularly concerned with *system*, and the other with *structure*, and that the differing concerns are rooted in the different views of individuals.

Beyond this, however, we see why the neo-classical view is essentially static, and the classical, dynamic. For concentration on a network of exchanges between self-interested individuals all competing on an equal footing (all being alike) will lead us to see the desired outcome as a state of rest, in which all desired exchanges have been completed. It is of the nature of the depiction of self-interest given here that it will have discrete objects, and our view of the network of exchanges will be that of a sum of such discrete objects, each attaching to a single individual, where the completion of all exchanges satisfies each individual in terms of their particular object (and subject to whatever constraints are given). We will indeed expect repetitions of the process, but the end of each will be a state of rest, or, looking ahead, a Sabbath. The classical view, by contrast, concentrates on the functional differences between economic agents, and on the class structures formed by these. The problem then is to see how these structures may be reproduced, and how we are to think of this reproduction: will it always return to the same point or will there be change, quantitative or qualitative? In so far as there is a return, it is not to a state of rest, but to the beginning of a new movement.

A second consequence of this account of the provenance of classical and neo-classical economics is that each necessarily departs from the argument of its source. For whatever the difficulties Smith creates for himself by putting forward two seemingly conflicting accounts, each is equally as grounded in his theoretical starting-point as the other: he must have both of them. But classical and neo-classical economics each takes one side as though it were unconnected to the other. It will not be a surprise, then, to find that in their classical and neo-classical reincarnations, the two lines of Smith's thought are transformed, and transformed because of their separation from each other.

The third consequence which should also cause no surprise is that from Smith's standpoint, whether or not he can solve the problem he has set himself, there *must* be something wrong with both the classical and neo-classical views. Both must be found lacking because each excludes the other.

It is time to look a little more closely at Smith's view of the matter.

Smith and the Incompleteness of Classical and Neo-classical Economics

The great thing to remember about Smith's approach, whether in moral philosophy or in what we call economics, is that he begins with relations between
individuals and not with the individual alone. The individual can only be understood by the context in which it exists; and it only, as it were, becomes human
in the context of relations with other individuals. That this is the case in the
Theory of Moral Sentiments is already obvious from its table of contents.[3] In the
Wealth of Nations, it is established in the starting point – the division of labour.
Smith only begins to tell us things about the individual in itself after he has given
us the division of labour and its effects, its source in the particular relation
between individuals found in the fundamental human propensity to truck, barter
and exchange, and the probably source of *that* propensity in the even more
fundamental (but also relational) human faculties of speech and reason.[4]

The result of Smith's starting point in the *Wealth of Nations* that is of most
immediate significance for us is that it envisions a transformation of individuality
through a process with a strong systematic component, which is none the less
unintended by those through whom it operates. That is to say, the division of
labour finds individuals pretty much alike; its progress differentiates them, creating individuals of different kinds, with different kinds of life, and, ultimately,
belonging to different classes. But while differentiating them it creates a new
bond between them, that of interdependence. Henceforth, the self-interest of
each is necessarily bound up with a specific kind of relation with the others,
the relation of exchange.

The contrast between this view and the neo-classical view of the individual is
obvious. Neo-classical theory begins with the individual defined in terms of strict
behavioural axioms. The relations among individuals are then defined in terms
of these, and as purely external relations. The individuality of the individual is
never engaged in the system of relations in neo-classical theory as it is in Smith.
The individual never changes, it is, quite literally, an atom, and the static character
of the neo-classical system of exchange applies to it also. Its static character
extends also to its purposes in exchange· The neo-classical individual is an
unchanging unity (almost, one might say, a monad, and there is a distinct aura
of pre-established harmony about the system as a whole). It has wants that it
satisfies through quantities of goods, where its wants are capable of rendering
all goods quantitatively commensurate. But its satisfaction through the consumption of these goods is also purely static. *Nothing else* happens than that given
wants are satisfied. There remains an absolute division between the individual,
unchanging, and the objects it consumes for its satisfaction.[5]

It is harder to contrast Smith's view with that of classical economics because
it is less clear what the classical view of the individual is. One crucial distinction
between classical and neo-classical individuals is that the former have *needs*,
while the latter do not. This suggests an openness to the external world from

which a less static conception might be developed. But, on the other hand, the classical individual has very little *individuality*. It is, above all, a member of a class, and its needs are defined in class terms, not individually.[6] If the neo-classical individual has only particular wants, the classical has only general needs. In this way, the classical individual, such as it is, is also statically conceived, in spite of the dynamic character of classical economics. Moreover, uniform behaviour is required of the classical individual as much as of the neo-classical. It turns out, in fact, that whenever the *behaviour* of individuals arises in classical economics, there is very little recourse but to neo-classical categories (especially, that of self-interest defined as rational preference ordering). Any possibility of a dynamic conception of the individual, or of the transformation of individuality, is eliminated. Marx, indeed, does not entirely fit with this account.[7] But it is hardly a surprise, though perhaps regrettable, to find a growing number of modern classical and Marxist economists and political scientists, in the absence of any positive notion of their own, making explicit appeal to neo-classical choice theory, whenever individuals are at issue.[8]

Both the classical and the neo-classical views are prefigured in Smith; even the particular forms they take are prepared in the *Wealth of Nations*. This is most apparent in the way in which Smith narrows and makes more abstract the prevailing eighteenth-century view of self-interest, in order to free his 'natural course' from the disorderliness of historical change.[9] Nonetheless, the separation of the two lines of Smith's thought into two mutually exclusive doctrines works a great change. For it is one of the great merits of Smith's account that in showing the necessary link – in the division of labour – between the two lines, he insists, as his predecessors had insisted, that the individual is a *problem* for theory. In the exclusive treatment of classical and neo-classical economics, the problem largely vanishes.

From Ricardo on, economists (again, with the partial exception of Marx) must choose between individuals as atomic individuals, and individuals as class members.[10] Thus, there is, in a sense, a considerable range of views on the individual and individual motivation in economic thought. But the real situation is that two extreme positions are possible, with no connection between them; although it turns out on closer inspection that the two share a great deal, especially in the narrowness and the static character of their depiction of individual behaviour and its motives. In both cases, all the complexity ordinarily associated with human motivation is eliminated. In the one, this is achieved by imposing on the individual a structure of need determined by class membership, and not by individual motivation; in the other, though the individual is offered choices and told to decide among these purely in terms of self-regard, the prior definition of what an individual is removes any possibility of doubt as to the outcome of the choice.[11]

This state of affairs helps to explain why two other traditions of economic thought – that of Institutionalism and that of Keynes – while almost invariably accorded respectful mention, have had almost negligible influence on economic orthodoxy, neo-classical and classical alike. For by questioning the view shared by both orthodox traditions, that the economy is, in some important sense, a self-ordering system, both of these alternative views raise, at least implicitly, the problem of the depiction of individuals and of individual motivation in economic theory. In so doing, they open up a large abyss just where economists assume their activities to be taking place on solid ground. But economists cannot tolerate any problems with their individuals, they have enough on their hands without that. Therefore, they are passionately committed to the view of the individual as atom – whether it be the atom-monad or the passive member of a stable agglomeration of atoms.[12] In defence of their individuals, they will mount huge arguments, involving formidably elaborate techniques of logic and mathematics. What is more significant, though, is their rhetoric: for a common element of such arguments is their appeal to the supremacy of self-interest, and this appeal has power because it makes the opponent seem so foolish and naive. The trouble is that such an argument will only work on the assumption that self-interest itself can be regarded as unitary and stable, as itself atomic. But there is no particular reason for assuming this to be so; and there is a long and respected tradition of thought that would deny it. In spite of the fact that Smith is one of the founders of the simple, atomic account of self-interest, this other tradition has an important presence in his work.[13]

To proceed, we need a better understanding of what is at stake in the question of the nature of individuality and individual motivation – including the role of self-interest. We will obtain this by giving a very broad depiction of two different accounts seeking to answer the question. We will then consider Smith's thought in terms of the depiction of these two accounts. In so doing, a broader challenge to modern economic theory in general will be discovered in Smith's economics.

Before proceeding, however, it will be worth pausing for a moment to reflect on the meaning of a word of which we have already made use, the word 'atom'. The original meaning of 'atom' is 'uncut'. From this comes its general usage – already in Democritus – as 'indivisible constitutive element'.[14] This usage obtained, in a strict scientific sense, to the end of the nineteenth century. Today, however, one thing that is certain about the atom is not just that it is divisible, but that there is still no end in sight as to the degree of its divisibility. This brings us to the crucial meaning of 'indivisible' when we think of an atom as an indivisible constituent of something else: whatever may happen to the whole of which it is a part, nothing whatever ever happens to the indivisible constitutive element. A whole may be smashed into atoms, each of the atoms is entirely unchanged.[15] It is entirely and completely itself no matter what context it is in. It has no history. Of course, we know now that atoms are not like this: they are *not* indivisible; and this means that they are in some degree vulnerable to their context. There is a continuity between them and what surrounds them; they have a history.[16]

The atom has been a central image in the study of the individual; and in one extremely important line of thought on human nature and moral philosophy, some part of the individual is understood to be *atomic* in the strong sense of the word: that is, indivisible, unchanging and entirely beyond the reach of the world which surrounds it. (This is a view especially associated with the Stoics and with Kant, though for the former, it is an ethical aspiration rather than a constitutional fact. But we will see that Utilitarianism also requires such a view.) It is hardly an exaggeration to say that, in one form or another, this view is the most influential account of the individual of the nineteenth and twentieth centuries. But something similar has happened to the atomic individual as to the physical atom. It becomes harder and harder today – faced, for example, with the views of almost every school of modern psychology – to see the self as unitary, indivisible and beyond the reach of its surroundings. We may still regard the self as an atom in the sense that it preserves, or seeks to preserve, unity and a unique identity; but it is difficult to see ourselves now as completely unitary and indivisible. Instead, we see ourselves as complex, where our complexity both reproduces within us conflicts of the outer world, and creates continuities between ourselves and the outside. Although we seek to preserve our identity, we see ourselves as transferred by our interaction with the world.

Some branches of social thought, however, have largely ignored such challenges to the strong view of the atomic individual, and economics is pre-eminent among these. Thus, as we turn to depict two contrasting accounts of human nature and individuality, we must remember that the strong view is still highly influential – the position of social study is never that of physics. We may also say that one way of putting the difference between the two accounts is that whereas both regard individuals as atoms – unities of unique identity – one sees them as the inviolable atoms of classical physics, the other as the vulnerable, and as yet imperfectly understood atoms of today.

8.2   TWO ACCOUNTS OF INDIVIDUALS AND INDIVIDUALITY

Classical and Christian Accounts of Individuality

We will call the two accounts of individuality the Classical and the Christian.[17] However, we must recognize from the start how imperfect a characterization this is. We could make a substantially similar division within Classical thought itself, between Aristotle and Plato[18] (Coleridge said that everyone was either a Platonist or an Aristotelian, thought the burden of our division is not his); and the Classical view is a major influence on an important tradition of Christian thought. But the line in Plato's thought on which such a division would be based (the line of such dialogues as the *Protagoras*, the *Republic*, and the *Symposium*) can be said to be profoundly anti-Classical.[19] Moreover, though Christianity's debt to Plato can hardly be exaggerated, the specifically Christian version is not only the most perfect statement of the account,[20] it is also the one that has acted most directly on modern thought. Then again, what may be called the Classical, or Aristotelian

Christianity of Scholasticism allows much that is central to Christian doctrine to remain latent, leaving it to post-Reformation theology to follow the implications of such elements to their conclusion. The trend of Classical thought is in one direction, that of Christian thought in another. Nonetheless, we will have occasion to recall how intricate is the relationship which we present now as a simple opposition.[21]

The fundamental ethical framework of the Classical account is that of *virtue* and *vice*, while that of the Christian is *good* and *evil*.[22] Though ethical, both pairs of terms embody conceptions of the actual condition of human nature, and so of individuality and motivation. The basic difference between them is that the opposition of virtue and vice is relative, that of good and evil, absolute. More specifically, a virtue is the mean of two vices (cowardice – courage – rashness), while good and evil are simple antagonists. Virtue and vice, then, are continuous with each other; good and evil are absolutely opposed.[23] The absoluteness of the opposition of good and evil has a further implication. Both are unitary: there is only one good, and only one god; one evil, one devil. There are many virtues, many vices (and many gods, notoriously ready to demonstrate the latter as often as the former).

Everything else follows from this difference, and we must now pursue its major implications. The easiest way to do this is to show, in parallel, how each account emerges from its basic ethical terms. In doing so, we will see how the ethical account defines a conception of individuality and motivation.

For the Classical account,[24] virtue and vice are continuous with each other, and there are many virtues and vices. This ethical claim responds to a view of human nature as complex, and made up of many different components. Any of these may become virtuous or vicious, but they cannot, in the abstract, be defined as one or the other. They will be virtuous or vicious in a particular person, and as a result of the conditions (internal and external) that have led this person to his or her present state. Moreover, the individual is an indissoluble whole made of all these components *together*. It is in their interaction and interpretation that the individual *is* an individual (and loss or dissolution is a loss of individuality); and so it is only in the consideration of this whole, and not through an abstract consideration of each component, apart, that a judgement can be made on the virtuousness or viciousness of the individual. There is, indeed, a hierarchy of these components of human nature: for Aristotle, for example, the soul should rule the body. But this does not imply a strict separation of soul and body. In their proper relationship, they partake of the same virtue and the body is necessary for, and part of the good of, the soul.[25] (Again, Greek polytheism reflects this view of human nature. The frequent absence of virtue in the behaviour of the gods is a fascinating and important subject, but one on which we must, reluctantly, refuse to enter).

Human nature is complex, and any of its components may become virtuous or vicious. We already know the ethical structure answering to this: a virtue is the mean of two vices, one being its excess, the other its deficiency. But this already suggests that virtuous action must take account of its context, it cannot rely on abstract principles alone. We will see the importance of this a little later. Here, the point to stress is that just as human nature is complex, so, decisions about how to behave, so as to be virtuous, are *difficult*. A proper point must be found along the continuum of virtue and vice, or rather, *virtue* must be found along the continuum of *vice* and *vice*. Virtuous behaviour is hard even when only one virtue is at issue. But there are many virtues, and all must receive their due. The *general* situation of the individual, then, is even harder, and harder still when it becomes clear that the claims of different virtues may well conflict. (There is no end of possibilities, but to take a famous example, friendship and love of country – two extremely important virtues – may easily oppose each other.)

To overcome these difficulties, one who wishes to be virtuous must become a *virtuoso*, and the way to virtuosity (like the way to Carnegie Hall) is *practice*.[26] We have noted that the practice of virtue is always in a particular context. Now, we see that the process of becoming practised depends on context as well. This is why education is so important in the Classical account, but it is also why education cannot be simply the teaching of principles, but must be an education in the life of a community and of an individual in it, gained by living in it.[27] Action then is the expression of a practice in which knowledge is embedded; knowledge itself is not an independent state.

Aristotle tells us that moderation is the key to virtue – the mean of two vices. But we must be sure to understand him correctly: moderation is not an average, or a simple cancelling out of extremes. It is the active seeking out and creation of a way of life that is in accordance with the virtues and which is contained within the context of a community. This seeking out requires a skill that is at the same time a love of virtue and good, and which must be learnt as a second nature.

This good life is found through action in a particular setting. The good does not have any other existence than this. It is not something already given and external. In this way, although there can be things like general principles, these are not themselves virtue or good. Good always has an irreducibly concrete, individual dimension.[28] Since this is so, moreover, the good individual is always concerned with the consequences of his or her actions. The good cannot be separated from these any more than it can exist independently of its setting.

Finally, we must note a trio of implications. First, we have seen that human nature, hence virtue, is diverse and complex. The good of human life is to be found in all this diversity. Its components cannot be reduced to each other or measured against each other. They are qualitatively distinct, though inter-connected, parts of life. They must all receive their due; but they must receive their due here, in this world. We know no other, and no other has any meaning for us.[29] Second, this very situation, in which the good is complex, situated within a complex community, and in which we must, as it were, create the good for ourselves, is a vulnerable one. (Since action must necessarily take place within a context – or else what is there to act *on* – it is, of necessity, vulnerable.) Our attempts may be defeated not just in the sense that we will fail to achieve some external goal, but that we will fail to become the self we seek to be. But third, though vulnerable, we are *active*. If our world acts on us, constraining and transforming our selves and our lives; we also act on it, in a measure creating it and transforming it as we create and transform ourselves within it.

The Christian account[30] differs at every point from the Classical. Good and evil are absolutely opposed; there is only one good and one evil. This yields a strict, binary account of human nature, in which its two elements must, in principle and prior to the condition of any particular human being, bear an ethical content. The soul is the locus of good. The body is at best a burden on the soul, at worst, it is a factory of sin and evil. But the soul itself is only good in terms of something external to it and beyond it. The principle of good, to which the soul aspires, is the true reality, the soul only its shadow.

The good is not only unitary, it is simple. There should be no difficulty in knowing the good, provided only that you open your soul to it and to God. Indeed, the *simple* soul is best able to know the good. Skill, virtuosity, are dangers in that they will encourage you to think that you can be good on your own, whereas in truth, good comes only from God. Again, the aim of the soul is founded on the absolute opposition of good and evil. Good must be maximized, evil minimized. Neither has any limit.[31] But goodness is above all a *state*, in itself, it has no necessary connection to any activity at all. The good state is that which is in accordance with the principle of good, which exists prior to all occasions of goodness, apart from them, and which is given to the soul from outside. If the soul is to *be* good, it has no choice, and no rule whatever in determining what *is* good.[32] The standpoint of the Christian account is that of pure knowledge as an independent state, and not that of action as the necessary embodiment of knowledge.

The primary relationship for the individual is that between the soul and God.[33] Any relationship with others in a human community is secondary, and the commanding principle for the individual is to live in accordance with the good as ordained by God. But the good itself is beyond the human community and the world; and so to live in accordance with the good is to live without concern for the consequences, in the world, of such a life.

We may now present a trio of Christian implications parallel to the Classical trio given above. First, the good is unitary and exists independently of all its embodiments in the things of the world (including individuals). These, then, are commensurable in terms of the good, while the good itself is abstract and universal. Not only may things in the world be measured against each other quantitatively in terms of the good, but also any particular thing (including individuals) may be replaced by something else, without loss.[34] Moreover, true good *always* looks beyond this world and beyond its particular manifestations. The world in itself, and communities of human beings in it, are of no intrinsic value. Second, the good soul, with the grace of God, may be invulnerable, and beyond the reach of events in the world. It will be invulnerable by concerning itself entirely with the unchanging good that lies beyond the world, and in so far as it considers them at all, seeing the mutable things of this world, including its own body and other individuals, only as imperfect and disposable means to the life everlasting. But third, this invulnerable soul is passive. It is unchanging, but all its characteristics are given to it from outside. In so far as it is good, it is so only through the grace of God, and not through any effort of its own.[35]

The broad contrasts between these accounts will be obvious enough, but there are a few points worth emphasizing. First, it may be said that it is *difficult* to be good just as it is difficult to be virtuous. But the' two difficulties are of quite different kinds. It is difficult to be virtuous because it is hard to know what the virtuous course is; skill and practice are needed. Being good is difficult because of the temptation to evil, but there is no difficulty in *knowing* what the good is. Thus, here again we encounter the opposition between the standpoint of action and the standpoint of knowledge.

A second point follows from this one. The issue of difficulty accentuates the contrast between the active character of the pursuit of virtue and the passive character of being good. We may go on from this to say that the Classical account is a dynamic one, where the Christian is static. Transformation is a necessary part of the pursuit of virtue, and part of its *good*, even though this makes us vulnerable. But the Christian task is to maintain a *given* state, in so far as transformation occurs, it is through the failure to be good: 'Change and decay in all around I see'. The things of the world are mutable, good is not.

A third contrast involves an actual and important dispute between the two accounts. This is over the possibility of tragic conflict. For the Greek tragedians and for Aristotle, the nature of human life and of the human good allow of the possibility that an individual will be so placed as to have to make a choice between two (or more) courses of action, both of which are, in some serious way, wrong.[36] The official line of the Christian account, subscribed to both by Plato and by Kant, is that this view is simply mistaken. The good *is* simple and unitary, therefore, it is always possible to make an unambiguously good decision between two (or more) courses of action. This opposition between the two accounts is an enormous subject, and we will make no attempt to judge the issue,[37] rather, we will use it first to define the contrast between our two accounts on the subjects of commensurability and vulnerability, and then to dramatize the profundity of the difference between them.

The Christian line on tragic conflict depends on the unity of the good, and thus on the commensurability of all situations and courses of action in terms of the good. It must always be possible to make a calculation as to which course of action yields a greater quantity of good, and is, therefore, the good choice. Alternatively, there cannot be a conflict in principle between two courses of action, in terms of the good; if there is the appearance of conflict, the unity of the good nonetheless prescribes that one is unambiguously superior to the other. (Of course, there is the possibility of each course being equal in amounts of good, in which case, since each replaces the other without loss, nothing turns on the choice.) This in turn serves to emphasize the abstractness of the good in terms of all things of the world, including courses of action. The good itself is always something other than, and beyond, the particular situation; and just as different things – in this case, courses of action – may be measured against each other in terms of the good, so also any particular thing may be replaced by any other that is its quantitative equal. The rejection of tragic conflict is part and parcel of the Christian rejection of the world, and of its insistence that the good, absolute and unchanging, is beyond the world.

That to allow the reality of tragic conflict is to subject human beings to a terrifying kind of vulnerability is obvious. What we need to consider now is what acceptance or rejection of this vulnerability entails. Let us take a well-known example of tragic conflict, which has the added advantage of having been given a brilliant exposition by Martha Nussbaum in her book, *The Fragility of Goodness*: the terrible choice confronting Agamemnon on Aulis when the Greeks are on their way to besiege Troy. The choice comes down to willing the death of the Greek armies, or willing the death of his daughter Iphigenia.[38] Now Kant's view implies that it is not only the case that there is always a right choice, but also that once a person has figured out what the right choice is, he must commit himself to it completely. To have doubts or, after the fact, to feel regret or remorse is, in effect, to doubt the good, and so, wrong.[39] We may add, that it is hard to see how we can fail to be bound by this judgement, *if* we accept Kant's account of the unity of good.

Nussbaum argues (correctly, I think) that Agamemnon's situation on Aulis confronts Kant with a serious, possibly an insoluble, problem (if, that is, he is willing to accept it as a genuine test case[40]). For a strong case can be made that Agamemnon's choice (to sacrifice Iphigenia) is the right one. Yet the sacrifice must be regarded (and must be regarded by Kant) as wrong: it *must* be wrong to kill your own innocent daughter. This is one aspect of the problem, the aspect of the ethical content of the choice. But there is another aspect which better illuminates the present issue, and this is the aspect of Kant's psychological demand on the agent: the demand of absolute commitment to the right choice. Agamemnon (at least according to Aeschylus) does exactly what Kant tells him to do. At first appalled by the choice confronting him, once decided, he accepts, even glories in, his action; and this is what he is condemned for by the Chorus: not for *acting* wrongly – what else could he do? – but for *experiencing* his action wrongly, that is, inhumanly.[41]

To put the matter in this way is not to find in Kant's (the Christian) view a necessary contradiction (which Nussbaum's way, by contrast, convincingly does), but to dramatize the profundity of the gap between the Classical and the Christian accounts, and so to bring us to recognize the need to take seriously our decision as to which we regard as the more adequate in comprehending not merely our individuality, but our humanity.[42] The Classical account (here represented by Aeschylus) tells us that we cease in an important way to be human if we refuse to embrace the particular, and terrible, vulnerability that comes to us as remorse for the consequences of necessary and justified actions. In this, the continuity of our deepest selves with others, and with the world around us is given its most powerful affirmation. The Christian account (here represented by Kant) tells us that we cease in an important way to be good if we allow the consequences of good actions even to move our thoughts by feelings of remorse. The absolute and inviolable barrier between the good individual and the world (including other individuals) cannot be more clearly asserted.

In concluding this presentation of the two accounts, it will be useful to see them in explicit confrontation within a single work. Milton offers us such a confrontation, with the added benefit of reminding us again of the complexities that lie hidden beneath the simple naming of the accounts, one as Classical, the other as Christian. In book IX of 'Paradise Lost', Milton tells us his story of the Fall; and its proximate cause turns out to be the result of an argument between Adam and Eve on the morning of the dread day.[43]

They are about to begin on their daily labours tending the Garden. Eve says that they will get more done if they work separately in different places, because when they try to work together they end up playing with each other instead, 'and th'hour of Supper comes unearn'd'. Adam, who has been warned by the Archangel Raphael of impending danger, is alarmed at this. But he begins by defending their pleasures with each other as of equal value with their work, in God's scheme:

> For not to irksome toile, but to delight
> He made us, and delight to Reason joyn'd.

Only then does he advert to the warning, and says that they would do better to stay together. This angers Eve, however, because she thinks he shows lack of trust in her. Adam, 'with healing words', then offers her an essentially Classical account of their situation, in which he lays stress on his own possible vulner-ability. He says, in effect, that in meeting an enemy it is well to choose your own ground. In this case, they will be far stronger together, and so, for example, if the Enemie should attack him:

> I from the influence of thy looks receave
> Access in every Virtue, in thy sight
> More wise, more watchful, stronger, if need were
> Of outward strength; while shame, thou looking on,
> Shame to be overcome or over-reacht
> Would utmost vigor raise, and rais'd unite.

Eve is still inclined to be resentful, though, and in her resentment, sets forth a lucid statement of Christian ethics.

She challenges Adam's account of their situation:

> If this be our condition, thus to dwell
> In narrow circuit straiten'd by a Foe,
> Suttle or violent, we not endu'd
> Single with like defence, wherever met,
> How are we happier, still in fear of harm?

his account of good:

> . . . what is Faith, Love, Vertue unassaid
> Alone, without exterior help sustain'd?

and she asks what the worth is of a life so ordered:

> Fraile is our happiness, if this be so,
> And Eden were no Eden thus expos'd.

Thus, she says, the individual must always have mastery of the situation, whatever it is, rather than seek to adapt to it. This is possible only if good is internal, alone and invulnerable; and life in any other condition has no value. Adam is impressed by this exposition, though not entirely convinced. Still, he reluctantly agrees to her original suggestion of division of labour. She goes off alone, and alone, meets the Serpent.[44]

Beyond the content of the arguments, the forms in which Milton presents them are significant. The importance of context and consequences is already filled out by Adam's insistence on the inherent value of a rich and multiform life that includes sensual pleasure and desire. The way in which he talks to Eve develops the theme. Fully aware of the danger that threatens their very life, he acts to persuade Eve, framing his words to her liking. The great thing is to find a course that will save them, not to stand on abstract principle. His words and his manner all stress continuity and community with her and with their world.

Eve, by contrast, stresses isolation and purposes beyond life and the world. She is the one who places their work (for God) above their pleasure in each other. Retorting on what she sees as Adam's doubt of her, face to face with the Enemie, she says:

> His violence thou fearst not, being such,
> As wee, not capable of death or paine,
> Can either not receave, or can repell.

The meaning of deathlessness is transformed by the Fall, but this is still the doctrine of all future martyrs and Sidney Cartons, going fearlessly to their deaths, saying under their breath, 'I am the Resurrection and the life . . .'

Milton accentuates the differences between Adam's and Eve's views by the way he introduces their words: 'To whom mild answer Adam thus return'd' is the introduction to Adam's first reply, later, as we saw, he speaks 'healing words'. Always then, Adam's words look not only to consequences, but Milton emphasizes the way in which they seek also to establish relations. Eve, on the other hand, is presented in 'Virgin Majestie', stressing, at the least, *her* sense of her own inviolability, her apartness from any particular setting or situation. (We must remember that Milton is no friend to Eve, persistently seeing her through pagan imagery in which the identification of beauty with sin is already implicit.)[45]

One need hardly be a deconstructionist to be intrigued by these reversals: Eve is, after all, in the wrong, and all human misery stems from her error. Of course, part of Milton's point is to stress the difference in the human condition caused by the Fall. Nonetheless, Eve's views, not Adam's form the basis of future Christian faith. Adam's final argument is, indeed, very much a Christian one. He warns Eve against trusting in reason. Reason can be deceived, and can deceive itself. But Faith and trust in, and obedience to, God will always answer. His final *action,* however, is an absolute affirmation of human life in all its fragility, against obedience to God, and godly invulnerability alike. Eve has tasted the Apple and brought it to Adam. He understands exactly what has happened, and what it means. It is open to him to remain obedient and to allow Eve to fall alone. He does not, and he does not for love of Eve, knowing full well that in this he is denying God. Milton tries to pretend that this is a terrible crime, perhaps the worst of all – God, Messiah and the Archangels discuss it in this light – but it is perfectly obvious that he does not really think so.

We have dwelt on this example, once again, so as to feel the seriousness of the choice with which our two accounts present us. We must now try to bring them closer to the proper subject matter of economics. To do this, we will look first at the presence of the Classical account in eighteenth-century political economy before Smith; and then at the influence of the Christian account on Utilitarianism, and, through it, on neo-classical economics.

The Classical Account in Eighteenth-century Political Economy

One way to characterize eighteenth-century thought in general is as an attempt to create a synthesis of the Classical and the Christian accounts. This is as true of political economy as of other lines of thought.[46] But even from the very brief descriptions given above, it might be expected that the impetus for such a synthesis would be Classical rather than Christian, and this is indeed the case. At least in Britain, which must be our chief concern, the great dynamic of eighteenth-century thought was the attempt at synthesis under the aegis of a Classical Ideal.[47] This is most apparent in literature (for example, in the *Spectator*, in Pope's 'Essay on Man', and in the very form of the novel), and in architecture (almost any of the major buildings of the period will do, but particularly interesting examples are the house and gardens at Stourhead in Wiltshire; the town planning schemes at Bath of the John Woods, father and son; and other town planning derived from these, for example, in Edinburgh). But it is equally present in political, and by extension, in ethical, study.

The general, secularized, form of the synthesis in politics is the recognition of the necessity of a balance between the needs of a political community defining substantial relations between individuals in terms of common values and the claims of individual liberty, including that of the legitimacy of the pursuit of individual self-interest. Political economy emerges as the crucial nexus of these two concerns.

The trajectory of the attempt at synthesis over the course of the eighteenth century is important, however. It emerges out of various lines of thought in the late seventeenth century, some of which appear as explicitly anti-classical. It collapses at the end of the eighteenth century in what is perhaps best described as a Christian *coup d'état*, opening the way for an essentially apolitical view of politics, resting on one or another account of the market economy as the key ordering force in society. Smith, of course, is the chief agent of this *coup* in so far as it is specifically directed against political economy. But we have already hinted that Smith's true position is not nearly as simple as the nineteenth, and for the most part, the twentieth centuries have regarded it.[48]

A word must be said about the late seventeenth century, and Locke is our best example. The beginning of the *Second Treatise of Government* is consciously and deliberately anti-Classical. Not only does Locke insist on the Christian view of the priority of the individual and of the relation of the individual to God over the relations among individuals within a community he also goes to great pains to avoid any possible Classical challenges to his account of property as something inherent to the individual, and not resting on relations with others.[49] But the *Second Treatise* ends a long way from its beginnings. By the time that money has transformed property holding, creating enormous disparities of wealth, and therefore a class society; government has been founded for the safeguarding of life, liberty and estates, that is, *property*, where clearly the safeguarding means most to those with most to safeguard; and individuals lacking property, living by selling their labour, are regarded as servile; Locke has moved a lot closer to a Classical view, and notably, a lot closer to Harrington. (A measure of this – in terms of a restricted class of *active* citizens – is given by Locke's account of how the right of rebellion would actually work.) We have already noted that Locke, like so many other anti-Aristotelians, starts to sound suspiciously like the Philosopher as soon as he begins talking about education.[50] Thus, even in so apparently unpromising a case as Locke's, we see the beginnings of the Classical synthesis.[51]

One other late seventeenth-century author must detain us for a moment, in order to exhibit a typical pattern of thought in political economy. He is the merchant and pamphleteer, Nicholas Barbon. Barbon's *Discourse of Trade* is of real interest in itself, but his views are of particular value here in showing the ordinary perception of broad traditions of thought well below the level of the most articulate and sophisticated theorists. Barbon's purpose is narrow and specific, it is simply to show the vital importance of a flourishing trade to the well-being and power of a nation, and how such a flourishing trade may be achieved and maintained.

Barbon begins by distinguishing between ancient and modern in terms of the absence of discussions of trade in the writings of the former, and even in such modern ancients as Machiavelli. The reason for this absence, he says, is simple: in the ancient world trade did not contribute to the purposes of empire. But in the modern world it does. Having thus seemed to distance himself from the Classical tradition, Barbon immediately enunciates a theme common to all political economy, and to Smith also, though not to all modern economics. This is the pressing need, even from the standpoint of a single interest, to understand trade as a whole, with all the relationships among its component parts. If even a single merchant has an interest in such understanding, how much more necessary it is for the purpose of advancing the wealth and power of the nation as a whole. But this, Barbon says, is just what earlier writers (and he singles out Thomas Mun in particular, if unfairly) have failed to do.[52]

But what chiefly interests us in Barbon is a curious and significant contradiction. He gives clear and unequivocal support to a notion that will be fundamental to modern economics, the limitlessness of human wants. (Much more unequivocal than Locke's almost surreptitious introduction of limitlessness under guise of the rather foolish tendency of human beings to admire and covet little rocks that twinkle.) Now this is a major departure from the Classical view, as exemplified by Aristotle's insistence on the limited character of human nature, and the threat to nature and polis alike of limitless wealth-getting. Moreover, Barbon immediately links unlimited wants with Christianity by an engagingly blasphemous depiction of the Fall as a kind of founding act of trade, with special reference to the clothing industry.[53]

When he comes to the question of how to promote trade, however, he tells a completely different story. In a single sentence – that, even if it were the only thing of interest in it, would make his little pamphlet a vital source for all concerned with the history of economics – he states in full one of the central propositions of political economy: 'The Chief Causes that Promote Trade . . . are Industry in the Poor, and Liberality in the Rich.'[54] The first thing to note about this proposition is that it makes ethical considerations fundamental to Trade, because Industry and Liberality are *virtues*. Moreover, the good to Trade – hence, of the nation – depends on more than one virtue, where each defines the proper life of a social stratum. Finally, just in case we are a bit rusty on our Aristotle, Barbon obligingly reminds us that a virtue is the mean of two vices. So much for limitlessness.[55]

Apart from the unexpected resurrection of the Classical account in this passage, Barbon's juxtaposition of these two contradictory views prefigures the general practice of eighteenth-century political economy. In fact, the attempt to balance something like unlimited wants with a specific ethical framework founded on the virtues, becomes the typical political economic form of the general attempt to balance polity and liberty. As political economy develops, however, another related contrast emerges on the question as to what creates not merely commercial growth, but also commercial *order*. The contrast is between the ethical liberality-in-the-rich-industry-in-the-poor division, and another, purely functional, division usually presented as between farmers and manufacturers, engaged in reciprocal trade.[56] Unlimited wants and the functional division are major forces in the eventual collapse of the political economic synthesis. But here, as we turn from Barbon to eighteenth-century political economy proper, we must recognize them as integral parts of the synthesis; and as showing the eighteenth-century willingness to proclaim accommodation between contradictory elements, on the ground that each is manifestly real.

The importance of the Classical account in eighteenth-century political economy is most apparent in the culminating and greatest work of the tradition, Sir James Steuart's *Principles of Political Economy* (1767). Already in its Preface, Steuart makes clear the basis of his view of individuality:[57]

> Were there but one man upon earth, his duty would contain no other precepts than those dictated by self-love. If he comes to be a father, a husband, a friend, his self-love falls immediately under limitations . . . If he comes to be a judge, a magistrate; he must frequently forget that he is a friend, or a father: and if he rise to be a statesman, he must disregard many other attachments more comprehensive, such as family, place of birth, and even, in certain cases, his native country.

What human nature *is* depends on the fact that there are many different human beings, and different kinds of relation among them. If the species consisted of only one being its *nature* would be different from ours. It is only going a very little way beyond Steuart here, moreover, to say that the fact of many kinds of relation changes each of them. For example, in the relation between parent and child, a part of the parent's feeling is directly *for* the child, but self-love too is present (there need be no contradiction between the two). This self-love, however, will not be quite the same as the self-love that arises when we truly (if we ever can) regard ourselves alone.

Later, Steuart stresses the complexity of human nature in another way: 'Man we find acting uniformly in all ages, in all countries, and in all climates, from the principles of self-interest, expediency, duty, or passion. In this he is alike, in nothing else.' He goes on to say that the same principles of motivation 'produce such a variety of circumstances, that if we consider the several species of animals in the creation, we shall find the individuals of no class so unlike to one another, as man to man'.[58] Not only does man have several different motivating forces (as well as different virtues), but the actual interaction of these in particular circumstances generates a huge diversity of responses, even though these are rooted in the same motivating force. General principles, then, are necessary for understanding human beings and societies, but they do not get us very far. Moreover, they will easily lead us to error if we do not pay very close attention to the limits of their usefulness. Paying such attention then involves us in the concrete study of diverse circumstances, that is, in study of the history of different nations and peoples. In history, the possible varieties of response, on the basis of the same general motivations, are multiplied yet further.

Two dimensions to Steuart's claim as to the nature of political economy must be distinguished. The first has to do with the method of study, and comes down to naming three necessary and interrelated areas of study: that of human nature, that of history, and that of the possibility of social order. Although these may be distinguished conceptually, they depend on each other, and a study that lacks one or another of them will not only be incomplete, it will almost certainly be in error. These three areas form the general framework of eighteenth-century social and political thought.

The second dimension has to do with the content of study undertaken on this basis. It is a study of diversity and transformation in which, as the Classical account claims, good and truth are found only in concrete contexts, to which general or universal principles are only a guide and not themselves the reality. Transformation is both a matter of inescapable contingency and a matter of intention and will. Individuals do not remain always and utterly the same. They are changed by outside events and by their own self-understanding. They are capable of change – both actively and passively – because they exist in continuity with, and not apart from their concrete contexts.

Because this is so, the modern Classical tradition of the eighteenth century is faced with a specific problem concerning individuals that only exists latently in the ancient Classical view (e.g. in Aristotle). Aristotle, writing of a Greek polis, could rest on the idea of what Hegel calls a customary consciousness shared by and binding its constituent individuals. Such a consciousness could be attacked and subverted, but it was, for Aristotle, not merely the norm, but the *natural* state of affairs. With the emergence of modern ideas of individual liberty, and the recognition of the legitimacy of claims for a realm of private self-determination (in particular, a realm of the pursuit of individual self-interest), individuality becomes a social and political problem as it had not been before. This new problem is further aggravated by the general seventeenth- and eighteenth-century view that human nature is itself irremediably imperfect. Thus, the triple structure of social and political thought (concerned with human nature, history, and the very possibility of social order) represents at once a direct confrontation of the difficulty of engaging in such thought, and a commitment to accepting the full complexity of the problem of society in all its dimensions.

The eighteenth-century synthesis thus transforms the Classical account itself, through its probing of the double problem of individuality and social order. This is most apparent in the new idea of history. Neither the simple Aristotelian natural history of the coming to maturity of human communities through the inner principle of human nature nor the exemplary history of Thucydides, and its extension by Polybius to a recurring political cycle are adequate to the new conception of individuality. For individuals and societies can change in kind, through a secular process that is neither a simple process of maturation, nor the simple repetition of a cycle. Above all, modern societies differ in kind from ancient societies, and history is now the measure of the difference, and not the demonstration of proximity. The possibility of social order – recalling the imperfections of human nature – must now be sought rather in the historical transformation of the forms of social interaction, and the unintended consequences of these. The rise of commerce is particularly promising because of the way in which it creates reciprocal bonds of dependency. Moreover, it offers the possibility of a balance between intentional change and unintended consequences. But in adhering to the central Classical idea of the transformation of individuality, even given the alarming increase in the range of uncontrollable circumstances implied by the new idea of history, eighteenth-century political economy insists that social order is necessarily problematic. Commerce can, with proper guidance, be a stabilizing force, but not an elimination of the problem which arises, ultimately, from the nature of individuality itself.

We could trace these themes in many other writers – in Montesquieu, Berkeley, Hume, Tucker and Ferguson, for a start – but I have shown sufficient connection between these others and Steuart elsewhere.[59] We will, then, proceed to consider the contrasting situation of the relation of the Christian account to Utilitarianism and neo-classical economics. Doing so, we will realize that, from the standpoint of the eighteenth-century Classical account, the solutions put forward assume away much of the problem that was to be solved. It will then be time to return to consider Smith's place in all this.

The Christian Account and Utilitarianism

The great and enduring importance of Utilitarianism lies in its single-minded insistence that the happiness of individuals, and through them, of communities, is the sole proper object of science and law. In this, it stands in clear opposition to the Christian account. However, its way of advancing its object belies this opposition.

Nothing like a general account of Utilitarianism is to be attempted here. All that is required is to show how specific elements of the Christian account of individuality appear in Utilitarianism in a secularized form; and then to note that these in turn are adopted by neo-classical economics, forming its intellectual foundation. Fortunately, Jeremy Bentham's obsessive commitment to clarity of expression works to our advantage in this case, allowing us, without prejudice, to base our description of Utilitarianism entirely on the opening chapters of his *Principles of Morals and Legislation*.

An obvious *prime facie* case for Utilitarianism as the foundation of neo-classical economics is already to be seen in the place of *utility* as the central concept of the latter. Beyond this, William Stanley Jevons makes clear in the opening of his *Principles of Political Economy* (in spite of its name, one of the founding works of the neo-classical school) that what he has in mind is the establishment of an actual and determinate quantification of the utilitarian calculus, at least for a crucial range of human activities. That he sees himself as returning to, and defending, the original principles of Utilitarianism is shown by his important, if intemperate, polemic against J.S. Mill, who had, in Jevons's view, subverted the doctrine.[60] Alfred Marshall, to be sure, attempts, in a rather half-hearted way, to show that what he is doing is not *just* Utilitarianism. But this, guarded, aspect of his economics – amounting to an Aristotelian concern not to make the analysis more specific than the subject matter will allow – is precisely that part of his thought that was not taken over by later neo-classical economists (who, against his express directions, skipped the text and went straight to the mathematical appendices.[61]

Virtually every element of the Christian account of individuality, as described above, reappears in secular form in Utilitarianism, and through it, in neo-classical economics. The strict soul/body division becomes the division between the pleasure-maximizing-pain-minimizing individual and *all* external objects, these being the means to pleasure or pain. We will have more to say of this view of the individual in relation to external objects. Here, what is to be understood is that the view of access to pleasure (or pain) requires an individuality apart even from the body, which becomes simply an engine for producing pleasure or pain. The static, passive and unchanging character of the individual in the Christian account is thus reproduced. All the individual does is to receive quantities of pleasure or pain through the consumption of external objects by the body (using 'consumption' in a very broad sense). It is unchanged, its relation to the outside world is purely quantitative, and in this sense even the pleasure and pain it receives are external to it.[62]

These secularizations of the Christian account lead to an obvious analogue of the unity of good. Just as there is only good and evil, so there is only pleasure and pain. The simplicity of the good also is translated. The reduction of all other concerns to the maximizing of pleasure and the minimizing of pain allows us to view our purposes in the simplest way: we need only ask ourselves, simply, and without constraint: what is most pleasurable? and we will know what we want, or, rather, we will know what to want. The answer is as certain as the answer to the Christian question: what is good? Indeed, as with that question, it is as though the answer were given to us.

Pleasure, like good, is abstract and universal. It has a temporary embodiment for us in one or another object. But it is always the pleasure, not the object, that we seek. Pleasure itself is something outside and beyond any object, not limited by, and certainly not receiving any necessary quality from it. In this way, and against Bentham's own view of his doctrine, we may speak of the profound other-worldliness of Utilitarianism.[63]

Pleasure is also, again like good, essentially quantitative. Only as such can it be abstracted from its temporary embodiments; and only as such may they be compared with each other in terms of the quantity of pleasure they yield. None of them has any other intrinsic worth: x Pushpin = y Poetry.[64] More pleasure is better than less, and the central principle of Utilitarianism is to maximize pleasure and minimize pain, just as the central principle of Christianity is to maximize good and minimize evil. It follows that human wants, or, what is the same thing, the desire for pleasure, are unlimited. But in satisfying this desire, any object yielding equal pleasure may replace another without loss; while one that yields more pleasure is unambiguously preferred, and the other may be discarded without regret.

Finally, Utilitarianism, as much as the Christian account of individuality, is based in the individual alone. A community is only an agglomeration of individuals; and the happiness of a community is nothing but the sum of the happiness of the individuals in it.[65] The pleasure, or utility, derived from an object is subjective, and belongs to the particular individual alone. Different individuals will find pleasure in different things, and there is no other comparison between them than that of amounts of utility. Since external objects are only valued in terms of the utility they yield, and since utility is purely subjective, pertaining only to the particular individual, no hierarchy of values in terms of the intrinsic character of external objects is permissible.

But the abolition of an intrinsic or qualitative standard of value must extend to the individuals themselves. Since utility is purely subjective, and the utilities of one individual must be of precisely the same quantitative dimension as that of another, individuals also must be completely interchangeable. Thus, for example, the neo-classical account of individuals is required by its intellectual foundation to abstract from all consideration of class structure (this is not to deny that it may, in addition, be convenient for other reasons to ignore class). But the abstractness and universality of pleasure also extends to the individual. Since only the quantity of pleasure yielded, and not any intrinsic character of the object, is of value; so only the abstract, pleasure-receiving structure of the individual, and not any individual characteristic by which some particular good and not another gives it pleasure (pushpin rather than poetry; or, perhaps, Pushkin rather than pushpin) makes it an individual. Individuality itself is merely the instantiation of a universal principle that is distinct from all particular individuals, but according to which each one may be considered the equivalent of any other.[66]

Relations among individuals in a community, that is to say, the meaning of the community itself, can only be that of summation. Each individual exists apart from the context of the community, and so, not only from other individuals, and external objects, but even from its own body and actions, which themselves become external objects for it. All it does is to receive quantities of pleasure and pain. But it is unchanging in this: only the external objects (including its own body) change. This is made clear by Bentham in the important chapters on 'Pleasures and Pains, their Kinds' and 'Of Circumstances Influencing Sensibility' (chapters V and VI) of the *Principles of Moral and Legislation*. Nowhere in them is there any account of what an individual *is*. The individual is an irreducible given of the inquiry. In other words, it is an atom (in the strong sense), and there is no more to be said. But if this is so, then it must exist apart even from its own body.

J.S. Mill, in his essay on Bentham (pair to the essay on Coleridge), sees this reduction of the individual to a pleasure-seeking atom, virtually indistinguishable from every other such atom – because there can be no external values other than quantitative comparisons of utility – as a deficiency in Bentham's thought. And he explains the deficiency in terms of the limits of Bentham's own personality.[67] Then, in *Utilitarianism*, he attempts to reconcile the utilitarian calculus with a hierarchy of values. But however much one may agree with Mill that there must be some kind of hierarchy of values, it is hard to deny Jevons's claim that in asserting this, Mill is rejecting Utilitarianism. For how else can Utilitarianism possibly make good on its claims without denying all other values than the single measure of pleasure and pain? For the calculus of pleasure and pain to have any coherence, the individual and the sources of pleasure and pain must be entirely independent of each other, the relation between them must be purely quantitative, and the individual must, therefore, be assumed to remain unchanged. There is no room in this for any other evaluation of objects according to any other principle. The intrinsic properties of objects, that have furnished, according to Bentham, the confused and wayward ethical systems of the past, cannot matter. All that can occur is the consumption of external goods, and the receipt of quantities of pleasure (or pain). But this requires a very strict mind/body division; and it reminds us, once again, that Utilitarianism shares with the Christian account a static view of individuality, in which the individual is essentially passive. Individuality is givenness.

Neo-classical economic theory adds one other dimension to the passivity of the Utilitarian individual, and so provides one last analogue to the Christian account.[68] The Utilitarian/neo-classical individual is, also, at least in principle, invulnerable. But the full neo-classical account of the individual's situation could seems quite terrifying (though the neo-classical individual itself, being entirely rational, is above viewing it in such a weak way). This individual exists, with an indefinitely large number of others more or less exactly like it, in a perfectly competitive market. The market gives all external conditions to the individual, who knows that no action of its own can in any way alter these. The individual is free, but since its own individuality is also given in terms of universally binding axioms of behaviour, it never has anything but one choice, one way to act, in any situation. Its choice is determined for it by its character as a rational utility maximizer – a more refined analogue to the Christian simplicity of the good than the simple Utilitarian definition of pleasure. The only way in which neo-classical individuals differ from each other is through the differences in the particular preference orderings which will govern their choices. But these too are given, and in any case they are entirely arbitrary manifestations of the universal utility-maximizing structure which is the only essential component of individuality. The relation of the market to the neo-classical individual is a close approximation of the relation of God to the Christian. Both kinds of individual are utterly helpless.[69]

But this picture of the market immediately brings the phrase 'invisible hand' to mind, signalling to us that it is time to return to Smith. This, accordingly, is what we will do, as soon as we have cited one difference between the utilitarian and neo-classical view, on the one side, and the Christian on the other. The Christian account is, in the first place, normative. For the Christian, it is a fact that God has made the world and man with good and evil in them, and in such a way that the goodness of man depends entirely on the grace of God. That is to say, the main characteristics of the account do indeed have a positive basis. But the problem of being a true Christian is a problem of being what one ought to be, rather than what one is. The true Christian becomes invulnerable, atomic, through God. But it is hard to imagine one more vulnerable, porous, than the sinner: violation, saturation are the dominant images of the Damned in any depiction of the Last Judgement.[70] The problem of the relation of positive to normative in Christian theology is, to say the least, intricate; the prevalence of heresy suggests that it is intractable. The Utilitarian and neo-classical accounts experience no such difficulties. The simplicity of their commitment to their picture of the individual as straightforward, scientifically demonstrable, positive fact is almost endearing; and those more familiar with the latter than with the former version of the position should not imagine that the economists are departing from their forefathers in this: no one can surpass Bentham.

8.3   SMITH'S INDIVIDUALS

An Adam Smith Problem

We have already seen two different lines of thought in the *Wealth of Nations*, and found each to be the basis of one of the main traditions of economics. But the opposition between them is, in itself, rather of conclusions than of premises; both are derived from Smith's account of the division of labour. There is more to it than this. But to understand the more, we must discover another, deeper, opposition in Smith's thought; one which is best described as between the Classical and the Christian accounts of individuality. Such oppositions are the stuff of which Adam Smith Problems are made. The traditional Adam Smith Problem is concerned with the relation between the *Theory of Moral Sentiments* and the *Wealth of Nations*. Recent work has shown that this view is too restricted, but not that there is no problem.[71] Our problem will continue in this line. The opposition will be seen to exist *within* both books, from which it follows that there is no simple relation between the two, whether problematic or not; and no simple development of ideas or simple break, connecting or dividing them. The struggle between Classical and Christian is general to Smith's thought as a whole. But our concern is not so much to discuss this Adam Smith Problem itself, as to use it to illuminate the problem of individuality in economic theory. To do this, we will consider some important passages in the *Theory of Moral Sentiments*, in which the problem will be seen to be present in a way that is significant for Smith's economics. We will then consider the way, or ways, in which Smith presents individuals *in* his economic theory, that is, in the *Wealth of Nations*. Finally, we will conclude by seeing Smith's struggle with the opposition of Classical and Christian as a challenge to modern economics in its entirety.

To arrive at these discussions, however, we must have a general idea of the way in which the opposition of Classical and Christian appears in Smith. Consider these two statements:

> Man was made for action, and to promote by the exertion of his faculties such changes in the external circumstances both of himself and others, as may seem most favourable to the happiness of all.

> It is the interest of every man to live as much at his ease as he can.

It happens that the first is from the *Theory of Moral Sentiments*, and the second from the *Wealth of Nations*,[72] but support for either is easy to find in both books. However, they point to very different ideas of what individuals want, what they do, and, through these, what they are. Following each in turn will not bring us to the same structure of individuality. Of course, an attempt might be made to reconcile them: man, though *born* to act, *wants* to be at ease. The context of the first statement will not really allow of such an interpretation, but leave that aside. There remains a clear contrast of emphasis, the one on action, the other on rest. The action, moreover, is, specifically, one that seeks transformation;[73] while the claim for ease suggests the passive utilitarian consumption of external goods. We will see that there is an important line of thought in Smith that approaches the utilitarian and neo classical views, and which approaches them in the common terms of the Christian account; and we have already seen that it is not so easy to distinguish classical from neo-classical economics on these grounds. On the other hand, in developing the idea of the centrality of action, with all that it entails, Smith places himself equally, or perhaps even more emphatically, within the Classical account of individuality.

Some Ambiguities in the *Theory of Moral Sentiments*

Our concern with the *Theory of Moral Sentiments* is a very limited one. We will not give any general summary of the content or purpose of the book nor even attempt to gauge the relative importance of different lines of thought in it. All we will try to do is to show the important presence of both Classical and Christian views (in the meanings we have given these names) in a couple of passages of fairly evident importance for the book as a whole.

The first passage is from part II, chapter 3, which concerns the utility of the sense of justice implanted in man, since, without justice, society cannot survive, and man cannot survive without society: 'It is thus that man, who can subsist only in society, was fitted by nature to that situation for which he was made.'[74] We will have occasion to discuss Smith's repeated assertions of Nature's benevolence to man. Here, we are interested in his argument for what the sense of justice actually is. There is a common argument, he says, to the effect that our commitment to justice is based on our perception of its social utility (this, for example, is Hume's view).[75] In criticizing this view, he offers an analogy:[76]

> The wheels of the watch are all admirably adjusted to the end for which it was made, the pointing of the hour. All the various motions conspire in the nicest manner to produce this effect. If they were endowed with a desire and intention to produce it, they could not do it better. Yet we never ascribe any such desire or intention to them, but to the watchmaker, and we know that they are put into motion by a spring, which intends the effect it produces as little as they do.

When, however, we argue that human beings adhere to the precepts of justice out of recognition for their social utility we are arguing, in effect, that the wheels of the watch act according to their own intentions.

What is it then that gives justice its power over the human mind? It is that we regard the just as intrinsically good and the unjust intrinsically bad. The sense of the just and the unjust is a part of our humanity (and arises from the necessary sociality of human nature, but that is a somewhat different matter). This seems to be a straightforwardly classical account of justice as a positive value, valued for itself; and of the sense of justice as arising from the love of justice and nothing more. In addition, justice appears here as one virtue among many (although an especially important one, as is clear from the comparison of justice with another virtue, beneficence, earlier in the chapter). Furthermore, the account is presented in explicit rejection of a functional or utilitarian view of justice.

We must recall, however, the point of departure for this account of the sense of justice: the analogy of the wheels in the watch; and we must ask why the operation of the watch is analogous to the operation of the sense of justice. It then becomes clear that what Smith accuses the utilitarian (Humean) view with is giving too much away to the Classical view. For while we may feel the sense of justice as a positive feeling for justice as a good, the reality is that we are the little wheels of a great clock helplessly enacting a purpose entirely beyond our intentions or our powers. Hume's utilitarian view of justice gives too much away because it still allows a central role to human intentions in the actual formation of the bonds of society: in a word, it leaves enthroned the central Classical discipline, politics.[77]

In this passage, we see Smith turning the tables on the Classical synthesis, fitting a classical account into a Christian framework, in a manner that is of obvious importance as a preview of the strategy of the *Wealth of Nations*. We will return to the issues of politics and nature, but we should remember that for all that the overall picture of the sense of justice subverts this, the actual description of the sense as experienced is a Classical one.[78]

The second series of passages offers us a different vantage. It is from part III, chapters 2 and 3.[79] Chapter 2 ends with a comparison, much to the detriment of the former, between the monastic life and the life of action. Action in the world, for the happiness of life in the world, is accorded by 'our natural sense of praise-worthiness . . . the highest merit and most exalted virtue'.[80] Chapter 3 begins with Smith's famous discussion of the limits on the range over which we feel for others: it is our universal experience as human beings that we feel more strongly for those close to us, and, at a certain point, virtually cease to feel for others, at least as individuals, so distant are they from us. This is not only what we do, Smith says, it is what we ought to do.[81]

Having thus endorsed the ordinary behaviour of humanity, he then discusses 'two different sets of philosophers' which have attempted to teach people to balance their feelings for others more equally with their feelings for themselves: 'One set have laboured to increase our sensibility to the interests of others; another, to diminish that to our own.' Both, he says, 'have carried their doctrines a good deal beyond the just standard of nature and propriety'.[82] But the two sets receive very different treatment. The first are given short shrift; they are[83]

> those whining and melancholy moralists, who are perpetually reproaching us with our happiness, while so many of our brethren are in misery, who regard as impious the natural joy of prosperity, which does not think of the many wretches that are every instant labouring under all sorts of calamities . . . Commiseration for those miseries which we never saw, which we never heard of, but which we may be assured are at all times infesting such numbers of our fellow-creatures, ought, they think, to damp the pleasures of the fortunate, and to render a certain melancholy dejection habitual to all men.

Chief among Smith's claims against this view is its uselessness, for its habitual melancholy dejection will never do anything to alleviate the sufferings of those unknowns who are its cause.

The second set of philosophers is quite another matter, having as it does the Stoics as principal members.[84] Smith's treatment of the Stoics, here and else-where, is subtle, interesting and important. We cannot even begin to do justice to it. But one general point should be made: it is unfailingly respectful, gliding backwards and forwards between respectful criticism and the actual adoption of what may be called a moderate Stoical *tone*. We will consider one such move-ment, but it must be remembered that the passage contains a great deal more than we will mention.

Smith criticizes the Stoical claim that even in the worst extremities of pain, the good person ought to preserve a perfect equanimity. One reason why this claim must be wrong, he says, once again concerns Nature's intentions for and bene-volence towards humanity. Nature could not fully compensate the good man for his sufferings:[85]

If it did completely compensate them, he could, from self-interest, have no motive for avoiding an accident which must necessarily diminish his utility both to himself and to society; and Nature, from her parental care of both, meant that he should anxiously avoid such accidents.

That which makes an individual good is necessarily bound up with his ability to act, it is not a mere state. But there is a simpler reason, for Smith, and it is simply that pain and its attendant sufferings are real, and they really do damage to us. For whatever reason, and from whatever intention of Nature, it is a part of our humanity to be vulnerable to pain and suffering, and so to deny them is to deny our humanity. Pain must have its due.[86]

From this denial of the radical Stoical claim, however, Smith goes on to a position of moderate Stoicism on the general issue of which extreme pain is a special case, and that is, what situation is best for a human life. The full Stoical view is that all situations – including that of extreme and unremitting agony – are as one to the good man. Situation has no effect whatever on goodness, and to the good person, being good is the only happiness. Smith demurs, this also is too extreme. But he immediately goes on to say: 'The great source of both the misery and disorders of human life, seems to arise from over-rating the differences between one permanent situation and another.'[87] There is little to choose between in the range of ordinary permanent situations from high to low. The ordinary labourer is as well off as the ordinary king. But it should also be true that the ordinary king is as well off as the ordinary labourer. This is not the impression that Smith leaves us with, however. Perhaps not an ordinary labourer, but the most ordinary of ordinary gentlemen is really better off than the king. For Smith and the Stoics alike, private life is best; and Smith here uses the Stoical view as an underpinning for his own, rather differently motivated, rejection of public life, and especially of politics.

Several of the main elements of our Christian-utilitarian-neo-classical account are, at the least, implicit here: the replaceability of one permanent situation with another suggests the quantitative homogeneity of the good, just as it indicates the abstraction of the good from any particular embodiment. This, in turn, requires the separation of the individual from the objects of which a permanent situation is made. Since one is as good as another, none has any intrinsic value, and any one will do. (But this illuminates a curious paradox in the utilitarian-neo-classical view, as opposed to the Christian-Stoic: pleasure is the all-in-all for the utilitarian, which it certainly is not for the Christian. But the pleasure of the utilitarian, unconnected to any intrinsic value of the concrete pleasurable object, seems a thin lifeless thing. The Christian rejection of the world hangs about it like a 'habitual melancholy dejection'.) Finally, the place of the individual in this ensemble exhibits the simultaneous invulnerability, passivity and helplessness that is so striking a feature of the Christian account and its derivatives: throughout the passage, the *futility* of action is emphasized.[88]

There is something else, however, and which we have already noted: replaceability actually takes place in a more restricted realm than at first appears. The apparent picture is of what may be called a traditional, classical society, divided by rank, and in which an important division is between those who participate in public life and those who do not. The Stoical view recognizes the existence of such divisions, but claims that they have no significance for the good. Smith, implicitly here, but more explicitly elsewhere, goes beyond this. His society is becoming simply an agglomeration of individuals, with no official divisions of rank, or between public and private. In effect, that is to say, all relevant differences are between *private* permanent situations, where public functions are only means for the support of these. Public or political life is not merely no better than private, it has ceased to have any distinctive existence.

The whole discussion of Stoicism, then, seems designed to establish the Stoic *sense*, and while rejecting extreme Stoic doctrine in one direction, actually carries it further in another. But then we turn the page and find ourselves in another world. It is the world of *action* again, and the world of action is where the virtues are at home. Smith now speaks of the kind of man whom we most love and admire. This man possesses to the full two sets of virtues, 'the soft, the amiable, and the gentle virtues [and] the great, the awful, and the respectable'.[89] But virtues do not only express themselves in action, they are the result of practice; and a particular virtue requires practice in a particular context.

The very existence of a multiplicity of virtues necessary for a good and admirable life – and, to insist on the obvious, Smith here asserts their existence and necessity – emphasizes the existence of many distinct aspects of life, of many different kinds of life, and of the distinct value of each aspect and kind. The simple assumption of this view, then, militates strongly against replaceability and the quantitative assessment of the good; and stresses instead the incommensurability of the diverse aspects and kinds of good life. This in turn makes it hard to support the claim for the interchangeability of permanent situations. For the most admirable person will be created and will create himself in a particular kind of life, which must be associated with what is admirable in him – it must be accorded a positive value. Moreover, the great and awful virtues are most likely to be developed in *public* life. Thus, the mere reassertion of the standpoint of the virtues brings the rehabilitation of politics in its train.

These references – they can hardly be called a description – to this passage overlook a problem raised by Smith, but the problem rather increases than diminishes the distance from the modified Stoicism of the previous passage. He tells us that '[t]he person best fitted by nature for acquiring the former of those two sets of virtues [the amiable, etc.], is likewise the best fitted for acquiring the latter [the awful, etc.]'.[90] But, he goes on to say, the *kind of life* that best instills the one set tends to exclude the other:[91]

It is upon this account, that we so frequently find in the world men of great humanity who have little self-command, but who are indolent and irresolute,

and easily disheartened, either by difficulty or danger, from the most honourable pursuits; and, on the contrary, men of the most perfect self-command,
whom no difficulty can discourage, no danger appal, and who are at all times
ready for the most daring and desperate enterprises, but who, at the same time,
seem to be hardened against all sense either of justice or humanity.

Virtue cannot be separated from its practice, and so it cannot be separated from its
context. A virtue cannot simply be learned, as a mathematical formula can be
learned. It must be learned *in action*, where learning is the arduous coming into
being of a second nature which must accept the substantial engagement of the
outside world in its very being.[92] Statement of the problem is, in effect, recognition of the possibility of tragic conflict, and thus denial of the simple unity of the
good. It is, moreover, an assertion of the necessity of action, where the intended
result of action may be defeated, as a condition of a good and admirable life.
'They also serve who only stand and wait' will be at the very least an ancillary
motto for the Stoic, and for Smith when he is adopting the Stoic tone. But when,
as here, he returns to the world of virtue and action it cannot be so.

The passages to which we have alluded here extend over some twenty pages of
the *Theory of Moral Sentiments*. We have not even attempted to summarize the
argument of these pages, let alone to indicate their place in the argument of the
book as a whole. All we have done, and it is enough for our purposes, is to show
the presence in them of both the Christian and the Classical accounts of individuality. We have shown, moreover, the presence of the one view in immediate
juxtaposition with the other. The point of this exercise is not at all to show that
Smith contradicts himself but, in the first place, to emphasize what it means to
say that Smith is *between* political economy and economics. The historical trend
from the eighteenth to the nineteenth century is from the Classical to the Christian
view. Moreover, in the history of the *actual* emergence of economic thought
(that is to say, setting aside the question of its adequacy), it is fair to say that
the coming to dominance of the Christian account is the founding event. But
Smith remains between the two accounts, he needs both of them.

Thus, in the second place, showing the presence of both accounts in Smith
helps us to understand his relation to political economy, on the one hand, and to
economics on the other. In the nineteenth century, the Christian account not only
comes to dominate, it is established in an extreme form which entirely excludes
the Classical. The eighteenth century, by contrast, had committed itself to a
synthesis of the two, albeit under the overall guidance of the Classical. In Smith,
it is probably correct on the whole to say that the Christian comes to the fore.
But his approach remains one of synthesis, though with a new dominant
partner. In relation to nineteenth- (and twentieth-) century economic thought,
this may be expressed by saying that the ambiguities we have found in the
Theory of Moral Sentiments reflect Smith's awareness of the difficulty of doing
social theory in general, and economics in particular, in a way of which the

nineteenth century has become unaware. But to see the relevance of this claim to economics we must turn to the *Wealth of Nations*.

Individuals in the *Wealth of Nations*

It is worth pausing to recall the order of Smith's argument in the opening chapters of the *Wealth of Nations*. He begins with an assertion: improvements in the productive power of labour are chiefly due to the division of labour.[93] He then gives a definition of the term 'division of labour', and offers three reasons in support of his assertion. He concludes his first chapter with a summary of the *results* of an extensive division of labour, the chief of which are an unprecedented increase in the wealth of a nation, which increase reaches to the poorest, hand in hand with an unprecedented growth of bonds of interdependence among all members of the population. Chapter two begins with a discussion of the origins and causes of the division of labour, and, through this, ends with a discussion of its effects which is an extension of the account of results with which the first chapter ends. But whereas the latter is largely concerned with, as it were, *technical* results, the former is concerned with effects on individuals themselves and on the relations between them. (The third chapter discusses the mechanism which relates the progress of the division of labour with the extent of the market.)

Chapter two is our chief concern, but we should bear in mind that by beginning with a technical definition of the division of labour, and of its results, rather than with a historical account of its origins, Smith is not merely departing from eighteenth-century practice. He is asserting that the technical aspects of the system of commerce – that by which it *is* a system – and not its historical and political aspects, are his subjects; and the logic of the assertion is buttressed by the rhetoric of his choice of starting point. Individuals, history, even society, only come in in the second place, in chapter 2, once what is chiefly to be explained has already been asserted as system and as fact.

The purpose of chapter 2 is to provide a preliminary, but decisive, answer to the main challenge that Smith must face from political economy, and especially, from Steuart's political economy. This challenge is contained in the claim that the complexity of human nature in itself, and the diversity of its manifestations in history makes the autonomy of commerce impossible. That is to say, in so far as commerce is a system, it must be one created by the polity.[94] Smith does not take up – here – the question of human nature in general, save for asserting the universal presence in human beings (and in no other species) of the propensity to truck, barter and exchange one thing for another. He does tell us, however, that human beings in nature, in primitive societies, and in modern societies, at birth, are very much alike. The division of labour is the cause, not the effect, of these differences.[95] Moreover, these differences are substantial: different kinds of people are created by the different kinds of life allotted to them by the division of labour.

But these differences are not at all the same as the differences described by political economy. For they are the means to systematic bonds of social inter-dependence. They are a necessary part of what gives order to society, and transforms it from a loose agglomeration of individuals – who, because they are all very much alike and do very much the same sorts of thing, have no particular need for each other – to a functionally differentiated population, each member of which depends, at the limit, on all the others.

Smith's strategy in answering the political economic challenge is an admirably bold one. He takes the claim of political economy – human diversity – and turns it to his own purpose: the demonstration of a self-ordering commercial sphere.

But there is a cost. To use diversity in this way he must emphasize the sociality of the process that creates it. Yet he wants that process to have something very like a natural basis. The propensity which is its root must either be an innate property of human nature or it must be pushed so far back in the natural history of the human race that any group that can be regarded as a human community would exhibit it. The propensity itself and the human drive of self-interestedness to which it is closely allied have a heavy burden to bear. They must be universal for all human communities, and must act in a uniform and constant manner even in those modern communities that have created the greatest differences among individuals. The problem that arises here may be seen as how to respond to the conflicting demands of nature, on the one hand, and of history, on the other; and what is at stake may be discovered by considering the two most obvious altern-atives facing him.

The first is to return to some version of the Aristotelian natural history in which change is the growth of an organism (here the human race) to maturity according to the inner principle of its nature. (This nature does not have to be the same as Aristotle takes it to be. Smith could replace *political* with *economic* as the fundamental characteristic.[96]) Here, history and nature are nicely fused, and failures to arrive at maturity may be put down to contingent events. The second is to treat human beings from the standpoint of science as natural objects, and to discover in them an underlying, unalterable sameness, compared to which all differences are superficial. This is the approach of modern economics.

We can find traces of each alternative in the *Wealth of Nations*, but there are problems with both of them for Smith. The Aristotelian natural history gives an account of growth, and of the gradual emergence of those features which are most human. This will do for the progress of the division of labour, but not for the propensity itself, since Smith insists that we must take it as a given in human beings in all times and places. In offering the Aristotelian alternative to Smith, we begin to see a central theme of the *Wealth of Nations*: that history, far from being the unfolding of nature, tends to interrupt and divert human life from the simple, natural state of affairs in which it functions as it should. Quite apart from this, we have already seen that the Aristotelian natural history is generally regarded, in eighteenth-century thought, as inadequate for the depiction of the historical ori-gins of modern societies; and for Smith to adopt it would be a very large retreat.

The trouble with the scientific reduction of the individual to a natural object is rather the opposite, as may be seen from the common practice of neo-classical economics. The characteristics of the individual are taken to be given and unalterable. There is no place for history or development at all. Economic theory, moreover, must begin from the individual and its given character alone. But this is just what Smith denies, and must deny if he is to make good on his answer to the challenge of political economy. He insists on beginning from relations among individuals, and showing how individuals are transformed by the development of these relations.

Both the alternatives may accommodate an important aspect of Smith's account, his emphasis on the unintended consequences of human actions in creating his system. But this view of unintended consequences is extreme in the orderliness it obtains from them. The actual history of the development becomes entirely secondary, and everything rests on the organizing power of the sum of actions. Thus Smith's use of unintended consequences stands in contrast to that of eighteenth-century historical study in general, which we have already mentioned, in which the actual historical process remains central, and cannot be either the chosen vessel of a pre-established course, or merely a realm of contingency that may or may not impede the coming of order. The entire process, its nature, and its outcome are more vulnerable and less secure. But, in compensation, a role remains for intention and politics. This, however, is just what rules out such a view for Smith.

From these considerations we may give a clearer picture of the general tension in Smith between nature and history. He wants to find a secure social order that is both the result of a process which, at the least, unfolds in history (even if its result is, as it were, predetermined), and which is entirely independent of the intentions of human beings – recall the wheels of the watch. The order, that is, must be akin to a natural, even a mechanical, order; but it must occur within a social and historical process. The individuals constituting this order must, on the one hand, have given characteristics, independent of their relations with each other, through which the order is constituted. On the other hand, they must be, in a sense, created and, at the very least, transformed by the relations formed by the order and the process that it engenders. That is to say, individuals must have, simultaneously, the chief features of the Christian and of the Classical accounts of individuality. So the problem in Smith comes back to the problem of what individuals and individuality are. But it is no simple matter to solve it, because Smith cannot take one side or the other without abandoning vital elements of his theory.

Nonetheless, the weight of demands on the theory do tend to push it in a certain direction. This may be seen in Smith's definite, though unacknowledged, rejection of central aspects of Hume's account of human nature. For Hume, the great defect of human nature is its chronic shortsightedness. Human beings will allow the immediate situation to overwhelm their judgements, at the expense of the future and of careful calculation of the future consequences of their present actions. This shortsightedness, and not depravity or evil, or the unbounded pursuit of self-interest, is the cause of most of the tribulations of human life. Self-interest itself, prudent and calculating as it is, is hardly more of a match for shortsightedness than are benevolence and altruism. But human beings are also by nature active and, in particular, their happiness is found in action, in the pursuit of some goal more than in attainment of the goal itself (Hobbes had said much the same). From these two aspects of human nature, Hume constructs a brilliant representation of the psychology of merchant activity, in which the shortness of the period between engaging in a transaction and receiving profit from it allows for an incessant renewal of activity which, to a degree, suspends the problem of shortsightedness.[97]

Hume's picture of merchant activity serves him well within the general framework of his political economy;[98] but it will not do for Smith. Its basis is far too capricious and arbitrary, most obviously in the strictly cameo role to which it reduces self-interest. For Smith, self-interest must be the star because, in the first place, and in company with virtually all other eighteenth-century writers (including Hume), he sees it as the only possible candidate as a general force for stability, independent of general intentions for social order. In the second place, however, and unlike other writers, he wants to claim that social order will only be achieved independently of intentions. Thus, self-interest has a far greater burden placed on it, and his rejection of Hume's view of shortsightedness and action runs parallel to his rejection of Hume's view of the sense of justice.

Self-interest must be able to overcome shortsightedness. But for this to be so, Hume's view of action must also be denied (even though we have seen Smith himself assert it). We now see why the statement that 'it is in every man's interest to live as much at his ease as he can' is so important. For it separates the individual from his actions, and reasserts the purpose of action as its only value. The individual will have to act at least sometimes, but he will act for a purpose that is now something external to him (because the action itself is no longer a part of him), which, once gained, is to be consumed at his ease. The goods – it would hardly be unfair to say the utilities – of the individual may be calculated by him, apart from himself, and balanced against the effort, in the form of action, required for each of them.

Because the individual is thus separated from his actions and their results, the burden placed on self-interest in Smith's system becomes more plausible, even with the introduction of different kinds of people through the division of labour. For we can now imagine a basic, unchanging self-interest, applying itself in the same way to the complete range of goods, in terms of a good that is abstract and quantifiable. Indeed, if we allow our imagination free rein along this road, it will come before long to such phrases as 'the equilibration of utility and disutility' and 'maximization subject to constraint'. But we can only allow of these developments if we accept the Christian account of individuality, and reject the Classical.

Smith's moderate Stoical account of the good individual in the *Theory of Moral Sentiments* is normative. Moreover, he does not expect that more than a handful of human beings is capable of such goodness. When he speaks of the interest of all men in living as much at their ease as they can, he is making an empirical claim, for all human beings. Whether or not the content of the latter contradicts that of the former (since even the good handful fall within the class of all men), there is certainly a contrast in the image of human beings, just as there is between the levels of the claims – one normative, one empirical. Nonetheless, there is what may be called a *mechanical* affinity between the two, in that both rest largely on the Christian account of individuality, with its strict separation of the individual from the world around it, emphasized by the divorce of the individual even from its own actions. For in the normative case any one of a great range of actions within any one of a great range of permanent situations is as good as any other; and in any case, goodness is apart from any action at all. While in the empirical case, action is always only a means (and a tiresome one at that) to an end distinct alike from it and from the individual it serves. The affinity may also be easily felt by calling up, in contrast, Smith's picture of the good and admirable man of virtue and action.

The affinity of these two very different sides of Smith's thought shows us the beginning of the process of identification of normative and empirical statements that we have already seen completed in utilitarianism and in neo-classical economics. It is also a further indication of the way in which the weight of the argument in the *Wealth of Nations* comes down in favour of the Christian account, at the expense of the Classical. But Smith's problem is not solved. He is still beset by the contrary claims of nature and system on the one hand, and of history and society on the other. What is more, the seriousness of the problem is now already apparent in the first three chapters; we have not even begun to consider it in the light of the problem with which we began, the opposition between these chapters and the conclusion of Book I – the problem of individuals as individuals versus individuals as class members. But it is in regard to the latter – the problem that Smith so clearly sets for himself – that the clearest opposition between history and nature is shown, and on the terrain of Smith's central device, the division of labour.

In the first three chapters, we see the division of labour under the sign of nature and the natural course of things. This course does indeed unfold *for* society *in* history. But the governing force is human nature itself. It creates an orderly system in which different kinds of people are created yet bound together in such a away as to benefit all; and each individual is just one little wheel in the great clock. The power of Smith's vision here comes from his ability to show us the thing from outside; and he can do this because each part, each individual, is negligible in relation to the whole. We *imagine* the whole by thinking of representative relations within it, and then multiplying these beyond all reckoning. We start from a representative individual, and then assume countless others like it. Thus we obtain a sum of individuals in which all differences are, in effect, cancelled out (just as Marshall will explain to us in time to come), leaving only the abstract sameness of the principle of self-interest. The system becomes a natural order open to the scientist's observation. But we do not really see ourselves in it – nor, we suspect, though he tells us that we must, does Smith see himself. The problem with the image of the wheels in the watch is that little wheels do not write books on moral philosophy explaining their passive absence of general intentions.

In the end of Book I, and again, in the later discussion of moral and physical degeneration of labourers, history is the key. We see the specific, and concrete results of the division of labour, not representative examples. The pin-factory and the day-labourer's coat (in chapter 1) can be replaced by any number of other cases, they have no significance in themselves. But rents, profits and wages, and the actual conditions of labour in an advanced division of labour stand only for themselves; and standing for themselves, they threaten the entire vision of a natural order. Now, suddenly, the transformation of individuals, in the creation of different kinds of life, *matters*. It can no longer be set aside by comic paradoxes concerning philosophers and street porters. But if this is so, then the problem of individuals is not solved by the postulation of a natural order.

We can now see why it is the division of labour that holds this problem before us. For division of labour itself has two aspects. On the one hand, it is that which creates, simultaneously, the differences between individuals, and the bonds of dependence through which a self-regulating order is established. It creates, in a word, the conditions of static equilibrium. In this aspect, the division of labour is the inner mechanism of a natural system. On the other hand, the division of labour is also an on-going process, it is a dynamic force driving the linear development of the economy. In this aspect, the division of labour generates change and secular trends; it is a social and historical phenomenon. Thus, the opposition of nature and history is internal to the division of labour itself.

To some extent, the preceding paragraph simply recapitulates the argument of the first section, in which classical and neo-classical economics were associated with the two lines of book I. But we had already seen there the differences between Smith's own versions and their modern economic successors. We can now understand these differences better. For even in the first chapters of book I, the historical and dynamic character of the division of labour is clearly present, even if it seems securely located within a system of natural equilibrium. The system, however, does derive from the division of labour, and so the static result is always related to the dynamic. Neo-classical economics steers clear of the division of labour, and with good reason. For the neo-classical abolition of need at the very best makes the division of labour irrelevant, and the difference between neo-classical goods can never be much more than the difference between flavours of ice cream. Any closer attention to the issue can only lead to embarrassment. Since the root of the problem is the division of labour's insistence on necessary relations *between* individuals, the solution is to replace it with behavioural axioms proper to individuals alone, and say no more on the subject. It almost seems that neo-classical economics learned from Smith's perplexities, and, taking no chances, removed all possible problems of individuals and individuality (arising from starting with relations between individuals, and thus allowing of the possibility of transformation) by assuming them away in its starting point. But Smith might criticize this interpretation just as he criticized Hume's account of the sense of justice: a benevolent Nature watches over neo-classical economics also.

Classical economics maintains the division of labour as a central mechanism, but reduces it to a purely technical function, ignoring Smith's substantial claims as to the meaning of the creation of different kinds of people through the division of labour, and, especially, in the creation of classes. In classical economics the dynamic of history is mechanized.

Smith aimed to eliminate from the study of commerce most of the ethical content regarded as essential by political economy. But he was not prepared to eliminate ethical concerns entirely, and they remain present in his continued insistence on the problem of individuality. Classical and neo-classical economics, however, found a way to do what Smith would not, by treating one line of his thought to the exclusion of the other, and thereby avoiding the problem that lay between them.

Smith's Challenge to Economics

We have, on several occasions, alluded to, and then dismissed, the issue of Smith's appeals to Providence. This must now be addressed. Appeal to providential intent is general to Smith's thought. It recurs as a general theme in all his works. It is not limited to particular, problematic, contexts; and it is certainly not a hastily constructed answer to the problems of economic theory. It is, rather, the central and guiding principle to which all other elements must conform. Moreover, Smith's deployment of the principle in detail is subtle, intricate and fascinating.[99] Providence works through Nature, and Smith sums up its intent in this way:[100]

> In every part of the universe we observe means adjusted with the nicest artifice to the ends which they are intended to produce; and in the mechanisms of a plant, or animal body, admire how every thing is contrived for advancing the two great purposes of nature, the support of the individual, and the propagation of the species.

These purposes are at work in society as in every other part of the universe.

Such a view is not, of course, unique to Smith, but the strength of his assertion of it in moral philosophy and social theory is striking.[101] Furthermore, in this context it may be seen as a sort of naturalized version of the basic political economic problem of achieving balance between the claims of polity and of liberty. But this in turn must be seen as another example of Smith's revision of the synthesis of Classical and Christian, in favour of the latter. (We will return to this point.)

Smith's view of Providence is not unchallenged in his work, however. It exists side by side with a deep historical pessimism which Smith shares with most of his contemporaries, but which is the more bleak in his case just because of his emphasis on Providence. This pessimism is expressed in Smith's judgement that 'the course of human prosperity' rarely runs longer than two hundred years.[102] It is expressed in his dismissals of modern life as degenerate,[103] and in the recurring statement that 'Fortune rules the world'.[104] These are not at all unusual opinions. The first is just run-of-the-mill pessimism; the second receives equal support from Classical or Christian arguments; and the third is a commonplace of Machiavellian civic humanism. But in the setting of Smith's social theory, they reiterate the opposition we have already seen between nature and history, and which now must be seen as implicating Providence itself.

The opposition of Providence and pessimism raises Smith's problem to its highest level, and forces on him the question as to what kind of theory he is advancing. The question, in turn, has at least two main parts: is the theory essentially naturalistic or not? And if it is, what kind of a thing is Nature? As far as the second part is concerned, Smith, for all his emphasis on Providence, wishes to frame his answer strictly in terms of a 'hard' Newtonian science. But it is really the first part of the question that causes the most difficulty. Smith's uncertainty as to its answer appears clearly in his presentation of the propensity to truck, barter and exchange. The propensity may be, he says, simply an innate component of human nature. It is more likely, however, that it is a result of the uniquely human faculty of speech. There is no way of deciding between these possibilities.[105] Now if the second of these is taken according to a straightforward Aristotelian natural history (the parallel with Aristotle in this case has already been noted), the difference between the two possibilities will not be particularly significant. But we have already seen that such an interpretation is hardly acceptable to general eighteenth-century opinions. If, on the other hand, it is taken according to general eighteenth-century opinions, then the difference between the two is between a necessarily naturalistic theory, and one in which an irreducible role is reserved for history; and in the latter case, a necessary categorical distinction must be made between the natural and the social (developing in history).

Smith does not make a clear distinction between these two; and, at least in part as a result of his failure to do so, there is a pervasive confusion in nineteenth-century economic theory between the social and the natural as theoretical categories.[106] But Smith's situation is very different from that of later theorists. In the first place, he is writing within a tradition that did distinguish clearly between the social and the natural,[107] where for the nineteenth century the distinction is largely forgotten. In the second place, and as a result, Smith is well aware of the problem; and, once again, his importance comes from his unresolved grappling with it. We must make one last attempt to describe this.

The name of Aristotle has recurred frequently in our discussion of Smith and his individuals; we will now see that it is possible to describe Smith's approach as a kind of dislocated Aristotelianism. An instance of this is the striking parallel between Smith's account of the propensity to exchange (the foundation of social order), as rooted in the uniquely human faculty of speech, and Aristotle's rooting of justice in the uniquely human faculty of speech, as explanation of the claim that human beings are by nature political.[108] Again, Smith's account of justice, as sensed by human beings as a positive value, but where the true or complete purpose of the sense of justice is not a part of the sense itself, is another instance. More generally, Smith's statement of the twin purposes of nature, which we have already described as a naturalized version of the political economic balance of polity and liberty, is of the same character. What is common to all these instances is the displacement of human intention in the description of the ultimate purposes of human life.

Smith removes human intention from any direct role in the creation of social order because he does not see how an order motivated by conscious human purposes (that is to say, a *political* order) can possibly overcome the known deficiencies of human nature taken as a conscious purposive organism. Nonetheless, he wants an order that is not only systematic but purposive. Since this is so, he must make a far stronger appeal to extra-human (providential) purposes than does eighteenth-century political economy, and insist on a very strong version of unintended consequences as the agents of Providence in history.[109] Just as the Reformation removed the mediation of the priests from the relationship of man and God, so Smith removes the mediation of politics from the relationship of man and Nature. But why, we may ask him, does history do such a bad job, when all that is required of it is to carry out Nature's instructions?

One possible answer to this question is to carry Smith's dislocation of intention a step further. Nature is vulnerable to the obstructions and subversions of history because Providence, the source of Nature's purpose, is like any other individual. It has rational intentions, perfect in form, but these are constantly in danger of being overwhelmed by the passions. For Providence, Nature is reason, History, passion.[110] At the end of all Smith's attempts to establish the primacy of the Christian account, Providence itself appears as a Classical individual: complex, active, vulnerable and changing.

It would be possible to make a strong argument in favour of some version of the Classical account of individuality, or at least of another synthesis, as a superior basis for economic theory to the Christian account alone.[111] But although the tendency of this chapter is clearly in that direction, no such argument will be attempted here. Instead, we will conclude with two more neutral claims. The first is that the Christian account of individuality, quite independently of any discussion of its correctness or incorrectness, is at the least a very extreme view. What is more, its extremity takes the particular form of frequent departures from the ordinary experience of individuality by ordinary individuals.[112] In itself, this claim is clearly not an argument against the Christian account (ordinary experience may very well be mistaken); but it is an argument for the necessity of closely examining the grounds of the account, and with especial reference to the gap between it and ordinary experience. Now modern economics is based on the Christian account (explicitly, in the case of neo-classical economics, implicitly in that of classical). But no such attempt at examination has been made. Quite to the contrary, individuality in economics has been defined by assumption so as to avoid any problems that the individual might pose.[113]

The second claim, then, is that economics needs to engage in such a process of examination, failing which it stands condemned of inadequacy *vis-à-vis* its subject matter. One obvious way to begin this process is to reinstate the Classical account of individuality as a possible alternative to the Christian, and in so doing to admit what ought to be sufficiently obvious: that the individual, motivation and agency *are* problems for economic theory. Smith's challenge to economics is that this is what he has been doing all along.

Notes

I have greatly benefited, in the writing of this chapter, from conversations with Ross Thomson, Martha Campbell, Robert Berman, Nancy Sommerschield, David Levine and Robert Heilbroner. Although I had worked out the general line of argument before reading it, Martha Nussbaum's *The Fragility of Goodness, Luck and Ethics in Greek Tragedy and Philosophy* (1986) was invaluable to me in moving from the general to the final concrete form of the chapter, and in allowing me to think (rightly or wrongly) that I was on the right track.

1. In *Behind the Veil of Economics: Essays in the Worldly Philosophy* (New York: Norton, 1988).
2. For more on the definitions of 'political economy' and 'economics' see Urquhart, *The Problem of the Autonomy of Commerce in Eighteenth Century British Political Economy*, unpublished Ph.D. dissertation, chapter II.
3. Parts I and II are concerned with our judgements of, hence our relations to, others. Only in Part III does Smith take up the question of our judgement of ourselves, arguing that this is only possible *through* living with others in society, judging them, and allowing these judgements to reflect back on ourselves:

   Were it possible that a human creature could grow up to manhood in some solitary place, without any communication with his own species, he could no more think of his own character, of the propriety or demerit of his own sentiments and conduct, of the beauty or deformity of his own mind, than of the beauty or deformity of his own face . . . Bring him into society, and he is immediately provided with the mirror which he wanted before. (*The Theory of Moral Sentiments*, p. 110)

4. There is a striking parallel between Smith's relation of the propensity to speech, and Aristotle's relation of speech to justice in accounting for the political nature of human beings. But Smith's account would make human beings naturally *social*, or *economic*, but not *political*. For more on this subject, see below, pp. 221, 227–8. For the importance of Aristotle's claim, and its difference from the claim of natural sociality, see Gertrude Himmelfarb (1987), 'History with the Politics Left Out', in *The New History and the Old*.

5. For the neo-classical displacement of the division of labour by behavioural axioms as the central mechanism of economic theory, see below, p. 225–6.

6. For a related view of the difference between, and inadequacies of, classical and neo-classical economics on these subjects, see David Levine (1988), *Needs, Rights and the Market*, chapter 1.

7. The question of Marx's place is far too complex and important to be dealt with here. However, one fairly simple point may be made. There certainly is a line of thought in Marx which remains fairly close to that of classical economics. On the other hand, there is much more to Marx than this, and in particular, there is more to his account of economic agency, based as it is on Hegel's concept of the person. But on the one hand, Marx's main *influence* has been (regrettably) through the more primitive, classical line in his thought. On the other hand, that Marx's chief source (in his mature work) for the best of his accounts of economic agency is that part of Hegel's *Philosophy of Right* concerned with abstract right, is telling. For if the account of the individual remains at the level of abstract right, then it is indeed an atomic view. But this is only a part of Hegel's story, which, in its entirety, is the grandest attempt to bring together into a single whole, the two views of individuality to be discussed in the second section of this essay.

8. The school of Analytical Marxism is a chief instance of this development.

9. See Urquhart (1987), *Problem of Autonomy*, pp, 339–40.

10. Ricardo has what may best be called a tragic view of the opposition between the happiness that individuals deserve as individuals, and the inexorable weight of the structure of the economy expressed in the necessary existence of individuals as class members, which must, to an important degree, defeat their attempts at happiness. He sees no resolution to this opposition (and it is not at all inappropriate or exaggerated to compare his view to that of Thomas Hardy). It is important to remember in what follows that Utilitarianism was the *moral philosophy* of the classical economists (though not of Marx). It was only the neo-classical economists, however, who made Utilitarianism the foundation of their economic theory itself. Whether Ricardo would have accepted their strategy in this is very much in doubt; nonetheless, it is important to keep this link between classical and neo-classical economics in mind when considering their respective accounts of individuals. (See below, the third part of section 8.2.)

11. See Levine (1988), *Needs*, chapter 1.

12. The history of 'Keynesianism' is instructive in this regard. The 'Keynesianism' of Samuelson and the neo-classical synthesis is an overt attempt to fit Keynes back into the neo-classical view. The far more substantial and interesting approach of the so-called Post-Keynesians, however, consciously attempting to *rescue* Keynes from the neo-classical synthesis, is, in effect, a parallel effort in favour of the classical view, as is evidenced by their 'improving' on Keynes through appeal to the structural models of Kalecki.

13. Ludwig von Mises's Human Action theory could be seen as a partial exception to the claim that orthodox economics has ignored the *problem* of the individual. But Mises's views, Kantian rather than Utilitarian, exhibit the same failure to understand the individual concretely, rather than through a simple, universal, structure of individuality. (See below, note 66).

14. The chemical elements are atoms.

15. I am, of course, speaking in terms of what the words *mean*, and not of what scientists know or do not know about the existence of indivisible anythings. If something *is* indivisible, then this must be true of it.

16. The last four sentences are based on Victor F. Weisskopf (1961), 'Quality and Quantity in Quantum Physics', an essay of interest well beyond its stated subject; I am grateful to Martha Campbell for drawing it to my attention.

17. That this distinction has a good deal to do with Matthew Arnold's, between the *Hellenic* and the *Hebraic* will be obvious. It is also connected to the distinction between Civic Humanism and Natural Jurisprudence that has been the subject of a stimulating debate involving, among others, J. G. A. Pocock, Quentin Skinner, John Dunn and Donald Winch. However, the issues with which I wish to deal here are on a somewhat different plane from those of that debate. In any case, I am at present working on another essay which takes the latter as its subject. Therefore, I will not employ its terms or consider it further here.

18. For this division, see Martha Nussbaum, *The Fragility of Goodness, Luck and Ethics in Greek Tragedy and Philosophy* (1986, passim).

19. Using the word 'Classical' in a broad sense as for the overall quality of Greek thought: 'Plato versus Homer: That is the complete, the genuine antagonism' (Nietzsche (1967), *Of the Genealogy of Morals*, p. 154). Hannah Arendt (1958) develops this theme in speaking of Plato's inversion of the Greek tradition going back to Homer, for which this world is the world of light, and the other, an underworld of darkness (*The Human Condition*, p. 292).

20. The most perfect, by no means necessarily the most profound. The perfection comes from the roles allotted to God and Salvation, which may well seem evasions from Plato's standpoint. Nietzsche (1973), again, gives a concise, if unflattering statement of the relation: 'Christianity is Platonism for "the people"' (*Beyond Good and Evil*, p. 14).

21. The complexity of the opposition comes, in the first place, from the magnitude of the abyss between the two accounts. This is already obvious in Plato and Aristotle. But today, it comes also from the enormous historical range embraced by the opposition. Each account has undergone many transformations, while the root opposition still remains. But it is perhaps more necessary to remind ourselves of how much the Classical account has changed, than the Christian; both because the former is less well recognized *as* a distinct account, and because the organizing power of Christianity as well as the absolutist structure of the Christian account – both in Christian and non-Christian forms – have proved more resistant to change. Since in the text we will treat the Classical account in largely Antique terms, considering only one major transformation effected by eighteen-century political economy, we will resort to notes in order to remind ourselves of other major transformations which would need to be understood in order to claim some form of the Classical account as of value in addressing questions of *modern* life, economic and otherwise. (See especially, notes 22, 27 and 92.)

22. The word 'good' will be used in describing the Classical account as well as the Christian, and in these contexts it must be understood as the good defined by the schema of virtue and vice. In this connection, it is worth recalling the opposition between 'Good and Bad' and 'Good and Evil' which is the subject of the first essay of Nietzsche's *On the Genealogy of Morals*. For Nietzsche, the former is the standpoint of the good/strong/noble individual, that of the latter, the standpoint of the bad/weak/servile individual. The noble standpoint begins from a strong, affirmative sense of self, and only in the second place a sense of others. The servile standpoint, by contrast, begins from awareness and resentment of the strong, and their identification with evil, only through this does the weak individual come to a sense of itself, defined as good. The importance of Nietzsche's view here is that it is also a version of the same opposition, and which Nietzsche defines as between Ancient Rome on the one hand, and Judaism and Christianity on the other. Yet it is crucially different from the version presented here, in that relation plays a key role in the standpoint of Good and Evil, but not in that of Good and Bad. There is much more to be said about this than can be said here. But the simple explanation of the difference is that Nietzsche's version represents a specific modern tendency, de-

rived from a tradition that he found in Goethe as much as in Schopenhauer, which rejected politics. Nietzsche's sensitivity to classical antiquity is almost unrivalled, and yet this rejection of one of its central concerns always marks it. (See notes 27 and 92 for more on the significance of the transformation of the Classical account through the rejection of politics.)

23. Thus Aristotle's assertion that 'all do all they do thinking it for the good' (*Politics*, 1252a) is impossible in the Christian account. Nonetheless, the absolute opposition of good and evil is an intractable problem for Christianity: did God create evil? Is evil coequal and coeternal with good?

24. Aristotle is a chief source, but his very method of continued appeal to the opinions of the many and of the wise makes him representative. Greek tragedy is also an important source.

25. See, for example, Aristotle's discussions of the relations between body and soul, and reason and desire, in *Politics*, Book I (the context is that of the different relations of master and slave, husband and wife, and parent and child).

26. I borrow (or perhaps 'steal' is a better word) this idea of *virtuosity* from Robert Berman.

27. The centrality of education is already implicit in Aristotle's view of nature as the internal principle by which things (including human beings) grow to maturity. Such growth, though internally guided, requires external means, and it can be stunted or even destroyed by adverse external conditions. The appropriateness of the poetic analogy between human growth and education and the growth of a plant, to this view is obvious. (For the plant image, see Nussbaum, *Fragility* (1986, passim), but, for example, chapter 1; see also, D.S. Carne-Ross (1985), *Pindar*, pp. 35–8, for the *city* as tree.) But here again, modern developments transform the Classical account. The growing plant as image of human growth and education is recreated by the early Romantics: Hölderlin's 'Da ich ein Knabe war' and Wordsworth's 'Three years she grew in sun and shower' both express it with the most perfectly simple beauty, each, in its own way, emphasizing the vulnerability of such perfect growth. But this perfection is only possible in Nature as opposed to Society. The conditions of Society are always adverse and stunting. No *community* can provide the nurturing conditions that perfect growth requires; thus the very possibility of true growth is problematic, as it is not for Aristotle. This opposition between Nature (including the true human nature) and Society comes from the same trend as the rejection of politics. (See notes 22 and 92.)

28. For a discussion of this point in terms of Aristotle's philosophical method, see Nussbaum, *Fragility* (1986, chapter 8). But it may be grasped from the example of one of the greatest works of Greek art. The Doric Order in architecture may seem a very good candidate for an ideal whose truth and beauty is beyond and apart from any particular instantiation. The Parthenon is usually taken as the greatest of all Doric buildings. Thus, one might see it as the closest approximation to the Doric ideal, yet still, the ideal is something *more*. But on closer inspection, the Parthenon itself tells us that this cannot be so. There is not a straight line or a right angle in it; nowhere is it an instantiation of an ideal whose reality is apart from it. It is an incarnation of an ideal, the perfection and truth of which is completely inseparable from the concrete deviation from the Doric Order as a general rule.

29. Not in Utopia, – subterranean fields, –
    Or some secreted island, Heaven knows where!
    But in the very world, which is the world
    Of all of us, – the place where, in the end,
    We find our happiness, or not at all! Wordsworth, 'The Prelude', X, 140–4

30. It is harder to isolate a representative source for this account: Plato, that well-known Christian, is important, as is Kant. But we will feel free to appeal to a general sense of post-Reformation doctrine, as also to Hegel's interpretation of it.

31. Though we recall that evil is a problem for Christianity, see note 23.
32. Education is always a problem for the Christian account: since goodness is a state, and unconnected to the world, how can one *become* good? Indeed, it turns out to be remarkably hard *not* to sound Aristotelian when the subject of education comes up. For the case of Locke, an important upholder of the Christian account, see Urquhart (1988), 'Individuals, Property, and the life of Liberty in the Political Thought of John Locke', section 7. For the problem of education in the Platonic/Kantian scheme, as contrasted to the Aristotelian, see Nussbaum, *Fragility* (1986, pp. 282–7).
33. This relationship can take many forms. It is apparent in the monk or hermit, but is equally realized by the Calvinist who, ceaselessly busy in the activities of this world, is none the less always alone with God.
34. Christianity has an uncanny ability to unite the modern and the archaic: replaceability seems very much an aspect of modern, rational post-Reformation Christianity; yet it is already central to one of the most archaic books of the Old Testament, the Book of Job.
35. Even so moderate a church as the Anglican is very insistent on this; and the churchgoing Anglican will repeat, week after week, the words of the General Confession:

   'Almighty and most merciful Father; We have erred, and strayed from thy ways like lost sheep. We have followed too much the devices and desires of our own hearts. We have offended against thy holy laws. We have left undone those things which we ought to have done; And we have done those things which we ought not to have done; And there is no health in us . . .

36. Agamemnon's choice on Aulis (see below) is an example. There are other possible sources of tragic conflict (see Nussbaum, *Fragility*, 1986, chapters 2 and 3).
37. Nussbaum's book is, in effect, a sustained and eloquent defence of the reality of tragic conflict, against, in particular, the objections of Plato.
38. These events are reported by the Chorus, long after the fact, at the beginning of Aeschylus's *Agamemnon*. For Nussbaum's exposition, see *Fragility* (1986, pp. 32–8).
39. Kant's denial of the possibility of conflicting duties occurs in the Introduction to *The Metaphysical Elements of Justice* (1965, p. 35, which should be read in the context of the entire fourth section of the Introduction, 'Rudimentary Concepts of the Metaphysics of Morals'. The passages on the meaning of the categorical imperative, and on what an individual is doing when acting in accordance with it, in the second and third sections of the *Foundations of the Metaphysics of Morals* are also relevant here). Nussbaum describes Kant's view in *Fragility* (1986, pp. 31–2). Since Kant specifically excludes from his discussions of morals the particular subjective feelings of particular individuals, it might be said that feelings of regret or remorse are simply irrelevant to questions of the good. Still, it is hard to deny that such feelings, irrelevant or not, amount to doubt of the entirety of the good of an action dictated by a categorical imperative, and so of the imperative itself. It is then appropriate to say of Kant's claim that it makes a serious *psychological* demand on the individual.
40. If he is not, others maybe offered to him: Churchill's famous choice, during the Battle of Britain, between allowing a warning of an impending, massive bombing raid on the city of Coventry, and protection of the secret of the breaking of the German military code, springs to mind.
41. Although Nussbaum does not consider Agamemnon's choice in terms of Kant's *psychological* demand, in making this point, I have relied heavily on her interpretation of the *Agamemnon*, and, especially, of the Chorus's reaction.
42. Nietzsche says of the opposing values 'good and bad' and 'good and evil': [T]oday

there is perhaps no more decisive mark of a *higher nature*, a more spiritual nature, than that of being divided in this sense and a genuine battleground of these opposed values' (*On the Genealogy of Morals* (1967), p. 52).

43. All references to, and quotations from, 'Paradise Lost' in what follows are to IX, 11.
44. For an argument between another couple (on the somewhat less portentous topic of amateur theatricals), with equally striking parallels and contrasts with this one, in Jane Austen's *Mansfield Park*, see Urquhart (1987), *Problem of Autonomy*, pp. 203–5.
45. For Milton's hostility to Eve and, more generally, the opposition between Classical and Christian in his poetry, see William Empson (1960), *Some Versions of Pastoral*, chapter 5.
46. Again, the debates of J. G. A. Pocock *et al.*, offer a somewhat different but related picture. See note 17.
47. For a very brief summary, see Urquhart (1987), *Problem of Autonomy*, chapter 1.
48. The course of political economy in the eighteenth century, barely summarized here, is the subject of my *Problem of Autonomy*,.
49. Notably, in the assumption that the original condition on which property is founded is that of a very small number of people, and a huge expanse of land, sea and all their resources – animal, vegetable and mineral – common to all. Scarcity, that is to say, is eliminated. It is instructive to compare Locke's account of property with such a classical account as that of Adam Ferguson, in his *Essay on the History of Civil Society*, where it is the coming into existence of property itself which puts an end to equality.
50. See above, note 32.
51. For an elaboration of this view of Locke, see Urquhart (1988), 'Individuals, Property, etc.'
52. Barbon, Nicholas (1905), *A Discourse of Trade*, Preface.
53. Ibid., p. 14.
54. Ibid., p. 31.
55. Ibid., p. 56. For more on Barbon, in the context of a critique of Joyce Oldham Appleby's *Economic Thought and Ideology in Seventeenth Century England*, see Urquhart (1987), *Problem of Autonomy*, pp. 148–54.
56. Hume's essay 'Of Commerce' is one example among many. The functional division is the precursor of Smith's division of labour, and occupies a middle ground between the two lines in Smith, since, on the one hand, the division is between classes of individuals (farmers, manufacturers), but on the other, the classes are functionally equivalent, and neither the issue of revenue sources nor that of rank arises. The question as to whether the Classical tradition requires a social hierarchy according to which only a few are fully free citizens is an intricate one. (For a brief discussion, see Urquhart (1987), *Problem of Autonomy*, chapter 9. But I will deal with the problem more generally, and at length, in the essay referred to in note 17.) Although the general consensus seems to give an answer in the affirmative, in my opinion, the simple answer is, no, the Classical Tradition, in its eighteenth-century British form, allowed of the possibility of universal citizenship in the full sense. In the language of the Pocock debate, it is not necessary to adopt some version or descendant of natural jurisprudence in order to arrive at an idea of universal citizenship, such an idea is possible within the framework of civic humanism.
57. Steuart, Sir James (1805), *Principles of Political Œconomy*, I, pp. xvii–xviii (references are to the volume number and page number of Steuart's *Works*). For a longer discussion of Steuart, see Urquhart (1987), *Problem of Autonomy*, Part Two.
58. Steuart (1805), *Principles*, I, pp. 7–8.
59. See Urquhart (1987), *Problem of Autonomy*, especially chapter 4.
60. Jevons, William Stanley, 'John Stuart Mill's Philosophy Tested', in *Pure Logic and*

Other Minor Works (1970). See, especially, section 4, 'Utilitarianism'. Jevons's tone is established in the introductory section: '[F]or my part, I will no longer consent to live silently under the incubus of bad logic and bad philosophy which Mill's Works have laid upon us' (p. 201).

61. Marshall, Alfred (1949), *Principles of Economics*, Preface to the First Edition. The so-called 'Hicksian Revolution' has not, for all its claims, altered in any significant way the *structure* of individuality derived by neo-classical economics from Utilitarianism (except insofar as it has rendered that structure even more extreme by the increased formalization of the behavioural axioms). The simple avoidance of the *word* 'utility' is hardly sufficient to count as freeing the theory from its Utilitarian origins, which are, besides, its best claim to conceptual distinction.

62. Bentham argues for the predominance of the physical, to which alone is opposed religion, but, he says, we cannot know anything about the truth or falsity of the claims of religion, and so there is nothing to say about them. Nonetheless, the separation of the individual from the body is a necessary result of his argument.

63. This last point draws attention to the question of the relation of this line of argument to that of Max Weber (1958), in *The Protestant Ethic and the Spirit of Capitalism*. This is an important question, but one that cannot be dealt with here, beyond noting the obvious value, as model, of Weber's account of the secularization of religious principles, and the unresolved nature of the result.

64. John Stuart Mill criticizes Bentham for his famous (or notorious) statement about pushpin and poetry (see below). But, as Jevons retorts against Mill, it follows directly from Utilitarian doctrine.

65. Harriet Martineau, the reforming utilitarian novelist, tells a story that is perhaps more amusing than she realizes, of a visit to Coleridge, in his old age: he said to her, 'You appear to consider society as an *aggregate* of *individuals*'. I replied that I certainly did'. He, she says, then ascended in a 'metaphysical balloon'. (Quoted in W. Jackson Bate (1987), *Coleridge*, p. 232). She went assuming that he could have nothing of value to say to her, but was impressed, though not convinced, in spite of herself; and his eyes were still as fine as they were said to have been.

66. The question as to whether the utilities of different individuals maybe compared, though important, does not really impinge on this point. Comparable or not, the utilities of each individual are of the same kind. Moreover, Marshall who denies comparability between individuals, offers a solution that accentuates the abstraction and universality of the idea of utility. We cannot, he says, compare utilities of two particular individuals, but for a society as a whole, or even a significant part of it, we may construct an average (Marshall (1949), *Principles*, pp. 21–2). A far more important question that arises here is that of the relation of Kantian moral philosophy to Utilitarianism. This is far too difficult to answer in this chapter. But we may note, on this particular point (the individual as instantiation of a universal principle) the criticism of Kant by Hegel in the latter's early work: 'As long as laws are the highest instance . . . the individual must be sacrificed to the universal, i.e. it must be killed'. For an important discussion of the young Hegel's critique of Kant, see Jürgen Habermas (1973), *Theory and Practice*, chapter 4. The quotation from Hegel is given on p. 152.

67. J. S. Mill (n.d.), 'Bentham', in *Dissertations and Discussions*.

68. We should recall that it is only with neo-classical thought that Utilitarianism becomes the basis of *economic* theory, rather than moral theory. See above, note 10.

69. Neo-classical economics may say that it is concerned with only one sphere of activity, and does not deny that individuals do other things and have other ends, in settings other than competitive markets. But, in the first place, its practitioners usually argue for this model of the individual in *all* cases, economic or otherwise, and so the market becomes the model for all other settings. In the second place, *if*

this is the view of the individuals for this important range, it is hard to see how the individual could be otherwise in its other aspects. If individuals are like this in these cases, they must be so in all, and so the market must be a model arena for all human activity. On the helplessness of the neo-classical individual, see William Appleman William's (1961) fascinating interpretation of Poe's 'The Pit and the Pendulum' as an account of the reality of the experience of the free market (*Contours of American History*, pp. 272–4).

70. Of course, it might be said that the Blessed are saturated with Light as the Damned are saturated with Darkness. Such is Dante's Paradise. But here we are back with an opposition which we may loosely define as between Catholic and Protestant Christianities, and which we cannot take up here. However, Weber's comparison between the end of the 'Paradiso' with that of 'Paradise Lost' is of great interest in this regard (*The Protestant Ethic and the Spirit of Capitalism* (1958), pp. 87–9).

71. For a good example of more recent approaches, see Robert Heilbroner (1982), 'The Socialization of the Individual in Adam Smith'. Lawrence Dickey's as yet unpublished work on the development of Smith's thought as exhibited in the successive editions of the *Theory of Moral Sentiments* is also valuable. Placing Smith within eighteenth-century thought as a whole, where before he was treated in lonely isolation, has enormously improved the understanding of his work. The collection of essays discussing the civic humanist and natural jurisprudential 'paradigms' in the understanding of eighteenth-century political economy is an outstanding example of this: Istvan Hont and Michael Ignatieff (eds) (1983), *Wealth and Virtue, The Shaping of Political Economy in the Scottish Enlightenment*.

72. Smith (1976), *Theory of Moral Sentiments*, p. 106; Smith (1976), *Wealth of Nations*, II, p. 760.

73. The transformation of individuality is not involved here, but it is clearly involved elsewhere, as in the progress of the division of labour.

74. Smith (1976), *Moral Sentiments*, p. 85.

75. For references to Hume, and for Smith's association of this view, in another place, with Grotius, see the useful editor's footnote at *Moral Sentiments*, p. 87, fn. 1.

76. Smith (1976), *Moral Sentiments*, p. 87.

77. Whether or not politics is conceived as purely functional, or as serving some positive purpose of its own. Hume's position on this issue is far more ambiguous than is usually allowed; and in understanding it, it is instructive to see, in Smith, quite how far it is possible to go in the elimination of the political.

78. Another example of the continuance of Classical ideas in Smith, though within a new framework, is his frequent use of examples from ancient religion as analogies for, or as rationalizations of, actual characteristics Nature has implanted in us, even while calling them superstitions. (See, e.g. *Moral Sentiments*, pp. 94, 107).

79. The title of Part III is: 'Of the Foundation of our Judgements concerning our own Sentiments and Conduct, and of the Sense of Duty'. The two chapter titles are: 'Of the Love of Praise, and of that of Praise-worthiness; and of the Dread of Blame, and of that of Blame-worthiness', and 'Of the Influence and Authority of Conscience'.

80. Smith (1976), *Moral Sentiments*, p. 134.

81. Smith gives the example of an earthquake swallowing up China and all its inhabitants: whatever our feelings in such an event, they can *do* nothing to mitigate the disaster.

82. Smith (1976), *Moral Sentiments*, p. 139.

83. Ibid. This passage alone should be sufficient answer to those who accuse Smith of humourlessness. It has an almost Dickensian ring.

84. Without entering into detail, it is uncontroversial to say that Stoicism, like Platonism, is an important precursor of Christian thought, and in particular of the Christian account of individuality.

85. Smith (1976), *Moral Sentiments*, p. 148.
86. This discussion of Stoicism bears some similarity to Aristotle's discussion of pre-Stoic views. See Nussbaum, *Fragility* (1986, chapter 11).
87. Smith (1976), *Moral Sentiments*, p. 149.
88. Smith's use of the idea of the *impartial spectator* here powerfully enforces the Stoical line, and creates a kind of psychological analogue to what Hegel calls the killing of the individual (see note 66). For the impartial spectator is constantly requiring us to look at our own concerns *without* any particular, individual interest in or attachment to them, and as if they were the concerns of others (any others), for which our feeling can only be abstract.
89. Smith (1976), *Moral Sentiments*, p. 152.
90. Ibid.
91. Ibid., p. 153.
92. The Aristotelianism of this view is obvious. What is less obvious, but which needs to be emphasized, is the way in which Smith's depiction of the inculcation of virtue is another instance of a modern transformation of the Classical account. The transformation here is related to those considered earlier (see notes 22 and 27): the general characteristic that they share is that of an increasingly negative attitude to society as a locus for human life, associated with a rejection of the core Aristotelian notion of politics as the overarching expression of the human good. But in this case, the specific influence of Christianity, in the transformation, may be seen; and this in turn illuminates a great and central debate, in which ancient and modern join in all possible combinations, on what it is to be good, and what it is to have a good life. The issue focuses on the relative importance in the path to goodness, and in the goodness of a life, of nurturing on the one hand, and adversity on the other. The Classical view – as for example, in the analogy of the plant (see note 27) – stresses nurture and community in the creation of a good, and *strong*, character. The Christian view stresses the benefits of adversity. But Christian adversity is above all important as a *test* of faith, where faith is a given state; and so we are brought back to the static nature of the Christian account and to its difficulties in treating of education (see note 32). Smith's argument in the passage quoted brings the Christian idea of adversity to bear, but in such a way that it is in its turn transformed. For what is suggested here is that adversity may have a true role in education, where the end is not Christian faith but Classical virtue. Adversity has joined nurture as a positive component of growth. We can see a more definite statement of this view, adding to its complexity, in Fielding's *Tom Jones*, where Tom's moral education is not simply one of learning from his mistakes, and learning from adversity, but also of learning from actual moral failure on his own part and that of others. One other more modern example will serve to suggest the range, complexity and importance of the issue. This is to be found in the beautiful passage in which the narrator of Proust's *A la recherche du temps perdu* is told by the painter Elstir of the importance of vulnerability in the particular form of ridiculous or shameful behaviour, as a stage in coming to *be* oneself, in his case, that is, coming to be the greatest painter of his generation; and he emphasizes the necessity of the experience itself, both as action and as something suffered: one cannot learn this 'in principle'. (*A l'ombre des jeunes filles en fleurs*, iii, pp.. 123–6). The importance of these instances is, that unlike the simple Christian idea of the benefit of adversity, they do maintain a truly Aristotelian notion of the individual. But where Aristotle stresses the necessity of nurturing in growth, they have, in effect, taken to heart the Romantic rejection of society (see note 27), and have sought to find, even here, a possibility of growth towards excellence. But by undermining the claim to the possibility of a *community* of excellence (for Proust, especially, the artist is completely alone, to the extent that he sees Elstir's willingness to spend time giving this advice almost as an artistic

failure), these transformations show to what a degree the very idea of the human good has become problematic. (Nussbaum's discussion of Euripides's *Hecuba* is relevant here, see *Fragility* (1986, Epilogue)).

93. For the singularity of this assertion as a point, see Urquhart (1987), *Problem of Autonomy*, pp. 331–2.
94. See above, pp. 208–9.
95. Smith (1976), *Wealth of Nations*, I, p. 28. Contrast Tucker, for whom the division of labour, hence trade, is the natural result of natural inequalities (for Tucker, see *Problem of Autonomy*, chapter 5). This is a place where Smith is directly and deliberately contradicting Steuart but, as always, not naming him.
96. See above, note 4.
97. For short-sightedness, see Hume (1888), *A Treatise of Human Nature*, Book III, Part II, vii; for merchant activity, see 'Of Interest', in Hume (1985), *Essays*, pp. 300–1.
98. For Hume's political economy in general, see *Problem of Autonomy*, chapter 5.
99. As, for example, in his discussion of the value (calculated by Nature) of the human *defect* of judging by results, and not by intentions (Smith (1976), *Moral Sentiments*, p. 105).
100. Ibid., p. 87.
101. Compare Tucker, for example, who, while arguing for Providence in Nature, emphasizes structural defects of human nature to a much greater extent, and *as* defects; where Smith makes defects themselves a part of the Providential scheme. (See note 99; and for Tucker, *Problem of Autonomy*, chapter 5).
102. Smith (1976), *Wealth of Nations*, I, p. 425. See also I, p. 367, where it is said that '[t]he course of human prosperity, indeed, seems scarce ever to have been of so long continuance as to enable any great country to acquire capital sufficient' for all the purposes required for general welfare.
103. Smith (1976), *Moral Sentiments*, p. 77.
104. E.g. Smith (1976), *Moral Sentiments*, p. 104.
105. Smith (1976), *Wealth of Nations*, I, p. 25.
106. Apart from Marx, who criticizes this confusion, and seeks to construct economic theory on the basis of social determinations alone. I am grateful to Martha Campbell for explaining to me the full complexity and importance of this problem, to which we cannot do full justice here.
107. We have seen such a distinction in Steuart, see above, pp. 208–9. Vico is one of the great originators of this distinction, but Montesquieu's direct influence, along similar lines, is stronger in eighteenth-century thought. Steuart, of course, learned from Montesquieu.
108. See above, note 4.
109. In this light, it is hard to agree with John Dunn's identification of Smith with Hume, as having made a crucial step (rightly or wrongly) beyond Locke's 'applied theology' towards 'social analysis'. In this, Dunn follows a common view of Hume and Smith as closely linked, and where, if there are differences, Smith seems more 'advanced'. But we have seen important differences between Smith and Hume, where it might be possible to say that they represent Smith's inclination to turn back towards applied theology, in the face of what he saw as the dangers of Hume's social analysis. Dunn argues that Smith becomes less and less concerned with a religious issues as he gets older. This view is challenged by Lawrence Dickey, in an as yet unpublished work. (John Dunn, 'From Applied Theology to Social Analysis: The Break Between John Locke and the Scottish Enlightenment', in Hont and Ignatieff (eds) (1983), *Wealth and Virtue*.
110. An affinity might be seen between Smith and Rousseau in their dislike of history.
111. David Levine's (1988) *Needs, Rights and the Market* provides a stimulating outline of such an argument.

112. The issue of the gap between normative and empirical claims is of great importance here. For a valuable discussion, in terms of Plato's claims (in the 'Protagoras') for Socrates as the new Prometheus, see *Fragility* (1986, pp. 117–21).
113. It can hardly be said that economics is alone in this failure, but that is another story.

References

Aeschylus (1956–7) *Agamemnon*, in *Aeschylus*, 2 vols, trans. H. W. Smyth, Loeb Classical Library (London: Heinemann).

Arendt, Hannah (1958) *The Human Condition* (Chicago: University of Chicago Press).

Aristotle (1932) *Politics*, trans. H. Rackham, *The Works of Aristotle*, vol. XXI, Loeb Classical Library (London: Heinemann).

Barbon, Nicholas (1905) *A Discourse of Trade*, A Reprint of Economic Tracts (Baltimore: Johns Hopkins University Press).

Bate, W. Jackson (1987) *Coleridge* (Cambridge, Mass.: Harvard University Press).

Bentham, Jeremy (1970) *An Introduction to the Principles of Morals and Legislation: The Collected Works of Jeremy Bentham* (London: Athlone Press).

Carne-Ross, D. S. (1985) *Pindar* (New Haven, Conn.: Yale University Press).

Empson, William (1960) *Some Versions of Pastoral* (New York: New Directions).

Habermas, Jürgen (1973) *Theory and Practice* (Boston, Mass.: Beacon Press).

Hegel, G. W. F. (1952) *The Philosophy of Right*, trans. T. M. Knox (Oxford: Oxford University Press).

Heilbroner, Robert L. (1982) 'The Socialization of the Individual in Adam Smith', *History of Political Economy*, vol. 14, no. 3.

Heilbroner, Robert L. (1988) *Behind the Veil of Economics: Essays in the Worldly Philosophy* (New York: Norton).

Himmelfarb, Gertrude (1987) *The New History and the Old* (Cambridge, Mass.: Harvard University Press).

Hont, Istvan, and Ignatieff, Michael (eds) (1983) *Wealth and Virtue: The Shaping of Political Economy in the Scottish Enlightenment* (Cambridge: Cambridge University Press).

Hume, David (1985) *Essays, Moral, Political, and Literary*, Liberty Classics (N. Shadeland, Ind.: Liberty Fund).

Hume, David (1888) *A Treatise of Human Nature* (Oxford: Oxford University Press).

Jevons, W. S. (1970) *Pure Logic and Other Minor Works* (New York: B. Franklin).

Jevons, W. S. (1965) *The Theory of Political Economy* (Fairfield, NJ: A. M. Kelley).

Kant, Immanuel (1965) *The Metaphysical Elements of Justice*, trans. John Ladd (New York: Bobbs-Merrill).

Kant, Immanuel (1969) *Foundations of the Metaphysics of Morals*, trans. Lewis White Beck (New York: Bobbs-Merrill).

Levine, David (1988) *Needs, Rights, and the Market* (Boulder, Col.: Lynne Rienner).

Marshall, Alfred (1949) *Principles of Economics*, 8th edn (London: Macmillan).

Mill, J. S. (n.d.) *Dissertations and Discussions* (London: Routledge).

Milton, John (1950) *Complete Poems and Selected Prose of John Milton* (New York: Modern Library).

Nietzsche, F. (1967) *On the Genealogy of Morals and Ecce Homo*, trans. W. Kaufman (New York: Vintage).

Nietzsche, F. (1973) *Beyond Good and Evil*, trans. R. J. Hollingdale (Harmondsworth: Penguin).

Nussbaum, Martha C. (1986) *The Fragility of Goodness, Luck and Ethics in Greek Tragedy and Philosophy* (Cambridge: Cambridge University Press).

Proust, Marcel (1919–27) *A l'ombre des jeunes filles en fleurs*, vols 3–5 of *A la recherche du temps perdu*, 15 vols (Paris: Gallimard).

Smith, Adam (1976) *An Inquiry into the Nature and Causes of the Wealth of Nations*, 2 vols (Oxford: Oxford University Press; reprinted by Liberty Classics, 1981).

Smith, Adam (1976) *The Theory of Moral Sentiments* (Oxford: Oxford University Press; reprinted by Liberty Classics, 1982).

Steuart, Sir James (1805) *An Inquiry into the Principles of Political Œconomy*, in *The Works, Political, Metaphisical, and Chronological, of the Late Sir James Steuart of Coltness, Bart.*, six vols (London: Cadell and Davies; reprinted, Fairfield, NJ: A. M. Kelley, 1967).

Urquhart, Robert (1987) *The Problem of the Autonomy of Commerce in Eighteenth Century British Political Economy*, unpublished Ph.D. dissertation, New School for Social Research, New York.

Urquhart, Robert (1988) 'Individuals, Property, and the Life of Liberty in the Political Thought of John Locke', *Social Concept*, vol. 4, no. 1.

Weber, Max (1958) *The Protestant Ethic and the Spirit of Capitalism* (New York: Scribner).

Weisskopf, Victor F. (1961) 'Quality and Quantity in Quantum Physics', in *Quantity and Quality*, ed. David Lerner (New York: The Free Press).

Williams, W. A. (1961) *Contours of American History* (Chicago: World Publishing).

9 History, Human Nature and Justice in Marx

Richard Castellana[*]

> In our times and henceforth, change is upon the world, in large part inspired and guided by Marxism itself. The task now is to understand it.
>
> Robert L. Heilbroner

9.1 THE PROBLEM

Understanding Marx is seldom an easy task, especially when one considers his views on justice. Although he never wrote a treatise on justice, he wrote enough about the topic to generate a lively controversy among Marx scholars.[1] One apparently paradoxical aspect of his thought will be considered here; namely, its affinities to both the natural right and the relativist traditions of justice, traditions which have been in constant opposition to one another. The natural right tradition is based on the premise that principles of justice can be discovered through an examination of the natural attributes of human beings, of human nature in abstraction from the behaviour-shaping properties of historically given social, cultural, economic, and political institutions. In its most rigorous form it holds that there is only one true concept of justice and that it is valid for all times and places. The relativist, on the other hand, denies the possibility that a single, eternal concept of justice can be derived from knowledge of human nature as such. A concept of justice is valid if it is the posit of recognized authorities or if it reflects culturally specific values. A thoroughgoing relativist, therefore, believes it is impossible to find an objective, universal, transcultural, and transhistorical criterion by which to compare, evaluate or rank the normative validity of different concepts of justice.

Marx's affinity with the natural right tradition is especially evident in his early 'philosophical anthropology' with its vision of a communist society whose institutions are more suitable to 'human nature' and, by implication, are 'more just'. As most thinkers in the natural right tradition, he uses his concept of human nature as a standard of evaluation and criticism. For instance, in the *Holy Family* he writes: 'The proletariat . . . is abased and *indignant* at its abasement – feeling to which it is necessarily driven by the contradiction between its *human* nature and

* I would like to thank Robert Berman, Robert L. Heilbroner, Agnes Heller, Reiner Schurmann and especially Ross Thomson and Ron Blackwell for their very helpful comments on earlier versions of this paper. I am also grateful for a summer research grant from Fairleigh Dickinson University.

its situation in life, a situation that is openly, decisively, and comprehensively the negation of that nature' (Marx and Engels, 1845, p. 367).

His affinity with the relativist tradition is most often associated with the 'historical materialism' of his later works, which imply that justice is relative to the mode of production. It must be understood 'that men, who produce their social relations in accordance with their material productivity, also produce *ideas*, *categories*, that is to say the abstract ideal expressions of these same social relations. Thus the categories are no more eternal than the relations they express. They are historical and transitory products' (Marx, 1846, p. 36).[2] 'Human nature', like ideas and categories of thought, is itself also a social product: 'By thus acting on the external world and changing it, he [man] at the same time changes his own nature' (Marx, 1887, p. 177). It is possible to interpret passages such as this to mean that the only immutable 'natural' attribute of the human race – 'the human essence' – is its self-changing character, its *absence* of specific determinations. 'Human nature' as such has no immutable psychic content; instead, all psychic and behavioural attributes are the products of historically specific socio-economic relationships. It would seem that under such an interpretation, human nature can provide no fixed standard whereby the validity of different concepts of justice could be evaluated and/or ranked.

Did Marx simply change his mind, was he truly inconsistent, or are his views only *apparently* inconsistent? Althusser (1969) argues that there is an 'epistemological break' between the early and mature Marx: the mature Marx abandoned the view that an understanding of human nature in abstraction from its social determinations could serve any explanatory purpose; he abandoned his 'philosophical anthropology'. As will become apparent in section 9.5, I agree with the view that Marx's thought underwent a significant development, but I argue that although it is largely speculative Marx's 'philosophical anthropology' has some degree of explanatory value for the late Marx. Even in his mature years, when he was working on the third volume of *Capital*, Marx wrote that socialism would provide people with the 'conditions most favourable to, and worthy of, their human nature' (Marx, 1894, p. 820). Although there is no explicit mention of the term 'justice', it is this sort of 'measurement' with regard to the fitness of institutions to human nature that characterizes natural right theories of justice. Our paradox cannot be fully resolved, therefore, by an appeal to a radical break between the early and late Marx. Marx may well have changed his mind and/or have been inconsistent on a great many important issues, but it will be argued here that the movement from his early to his mature philosophical position is a development towards greater, if not perfect, consistency. In this chapter, an alternative and I believe more satisfactory solution to this paradox will be given.

Section 9.2 argues that it is possible for Marx to combine elements of both the natural right and relativist traditions in a logically consistent manner. Section 9.3 defends the thesis that 'historical materialism' is compatible with the existence of invariant 'truths' regarding human capacities and tendencies. The nature of these invariants – the human capacity for autonomy and self-realization and the innate psychic tendency to find satisfaction in exercising and developing these capacities – is developed in section 9.4. My claim that Marx's 'historical materialism' is a logically consistent development of his 'philosophical anthropology' will be defended in section 9.5. Finally, section 9.6 shows how his views on history and human nature influence his concept of justice.

9.2 AFFINITIES TO THE NATURAL RIGHT AND RELATIVIST TRADITIONS

We shall now take a closer look at how Marx's thought combines elements of both natural right and relativist conceptions of justice.

Consider the following statement written by Engels:

The justice of the Greeks and Romans held slavery to be just; the justice of the bourgeois of 1789 demanded the abolition of feudalism on the ground that it was unjust . . . The conception of eternal justice, therefore, varies not only with time and place, but also with the persons concerned, and belongs among those things of which Muelberger correctly says, 'everyone understands something different'. (Engels, 1872–3 p. 624)

Since it denies the existence of an eternal concept of justice, this statement strongly implies a relativist perspective on justice. One may argue, however, that Engels is not denying that there is an eternal concept of justice; he is only stating that *beliefs* concerning the nature of the 'eternal' vary with time and place. An eternal concept of justice may exist, but we do not yet know what it is. The problem is epistemological, not ontological. In the following statement, however, he also denies the ontological 'existence' of eternal principles: 'We . . . reject every presumptuous attempt to impose on us any dogmatic morality whatever as eternal, final, immutable ethical laws, under the pretext that the moral world, too, has its permanent principles which stand above history and national differences' (Engels, 1877–8, p. 93–4). If these statements are to be taken as genuine reflections of their thought, as I believe they must, then Marx and Engels are not natural right theorists – if, that is, natural right is identified with the belief that there is only one concept of justice which is true for all times and places. I shall call this the 'strong version' of natural right.

Affinities to the Natural Right Tradition

This does not mean, however, that they reject all the principle tenets of the natural right tradition. Consider, for instance, another of Engels' statements: 'That progress in morality, by and large, has been accomplished . . . is not to be doubted' (ibid., p. 94). This statement does not imply the existence of eternal principles of justice but it does suggests that some 'absolute' criterion (or criteria) must exist whereby one can make a judgement as to how far morality and, by implication, justice have progressed. Here, Engels is closer to the natural right than to the relativist tradition. Still, if Engels believed that each nation (or mode of production) has its own concept of progress, this statement would be consistent with a thoroughgoing relativism, since progress itself becomes a relative term. But then the statement would certainly be much weaker than Engels intended it to be. He and Marx certainly believed that communist society will be superior in some fashion to all other societies and will have a cognitively privileged position when it comes to evaluating principles of morality and justice. If Marx believes that this perspective is superior because communist institutions are more suitable to human nature, as I believe he does, then the affinity of his thinking to the natural right tradition re-emerges.

Yet another affinity to the natural right tradition is present in the belief that communist standards of morality and justice, once in existence, will endure. Proletarian moral beliefs, writes Engels, have no 'absolute finality; but that morality is most secure which possesses the most elements promising duration . . . that is to say, the proletarian morality of the future' (ibid., p. 93). The notion of 'durability' resembles Rawls's concept of 'stability' (Rawls, 1971, pp. 454f). A system of justice – the concrete embodiment in laws, institutions, and social practices of a particular concept of justice – is stable, according to Rawls, when people develop a strong sense of justice and voluntarily restrain their behaviour to accord with the principles of justice embodied in their institutions. This occurs when people recognize that justice *promotes their own good* as well as the good of others. A society founded on principles of justice which are congruent with people's idea of the 'good' will therefore be respected and endure; it will be a 'well-ordered' society.

In his *Theory of Justice*, Rawls claimed that a system of justice founded on the principles of justice that he formulated would be both eternally valid and stable because its principles are congruent with basic human attributes and desires.[3] His theory would then belong to the strong version of the natural right tradition as I have defined it. Although Marx does not believe that communist principles of justice are valid in all circumstances, he believes that once embodied in institutions these principles will prove to be *more enduring* than any previously known.[4] If it can be shown (as I will attempt to show in section 9.6) that the reason that communist principles are more enduring is because they are more compatible with fundamental human psychological attributes, then it would be reasonable to say that Marx agrees with a 'weak version' of the natural right tradition. In the weak version, the *validity* of a system of justice is dependent on its compatibility with the historically determined psychic identity of a people, but how long a particular system of justice can remain valid and stable – its *durability* – is dependent on its compatibility with innate human drives which are independent of historical circumstances. In other words, what we are looking for is a concept of human nature which is too variable and too abstract to justify a concept of justice that is valid for all times and places, but sufficiently invariant to provide a standard for ascertaining progress in morality and for evaluating the stability and durability of a system of justice.

Affinities to the Relativist Tradition

Marx's view of justice can also be placed in the relativist tradition, but again only in a weak version of that tradition. To see why, it will be helpful to distinguish three types of relativism: ethical (normative) relativism, metaethical relativism, and cognitive relativism.[5] Marx, I shall argue, is a relativism only with respect to the first.

Ethical relativism holds that what is in reality right or just (not merely what unconsidered, popular opinion holds to be right or just) in one society or culture may be in reality wrong or unjust in a similar situation in another society or culture. It denies, therefore, the existence of a single *substantive* concept of justice that is universally and transculturally valid. *Metaethical relativism* operates at a more abstract level of discourse than does ethical relativism. It is concerned with whether it is possible to discover an objective, rational method or criterion by which the validity of substantive ethical theories can be established. Metaethical relativism denies the possibility of finding a method, a set of standards, or premises whereby the validity – or stability – of ethical norms can be defended or criticized. Clearly, a metaethical relativist would also find it impossible to define an absolute standard of progress in morality or justice. *Cognitive relativism* holds that there are no transcultural, transhistorical, or universally valid standards, methods, or procedures for determining the truth of factual statements, including those about human nature. In other words, scientific concepts and methods are themselves culturally relative. Although it is not directly concerned with normative questions, cognitive relativism has normative significance because it categorically rejects natural right conceptions of justice that are grounded in (non-existent) transcultural conceptions of human nature. Cognitive relativism therefore provides an epistemological basis for ethical and metaethical relativism.

Marx is clearly a normative relativist, but he is neither a metaethical nor a cognitive relativist. He is an ethical relativist because he believes that each socio-economic formation has its own concept of justice. He is a metaethical 'absolutist' since he believes that there is *an objective* method for determining the validity of a concept of justice: the socio-economic structure of society provides, in some fashion we have not yet defined, the objective basis for such an evaluation.[6] He is a cognitive 'absolutist' because he believes in the possibility of progress in the formulation of scientific methods and truths, including truths about the human psyche as such. Marx believes, as I shall soon argue, that communist society will have a better understanding of the innate properties of human nature – its drives and capacities – and thus a better understanding of the socio-economic and political institutions that could promote human happiness.

Marx's 'absolutism' is not inconsistent with ethical relativism. Metaethical 'absolutism' can logically coexist with ethical relativism since each socio-economic formation objectively 'validates' a different (or somewhat different) concept of justice. Cognitive absolutism can logically coexist with ethical relativism since Marx does not believe that the superior understanding of human nature possessed by the future communist society can provide the basis for a *practical*, substantive, transculturally valid concept of justice. Precommunist socio-economic institutions (which like all institutions influence the individual's motives, interests, values, behaviour, and sense of personal identity) create people for whom communist principles of justice are simply inappropriate and consequently invalid. In addition, a communist system of justice would be practical only when labour productivity is extremely high and sufficient leisure time is available to all, so that everyone can fully develop and realize their personal capacities and interests.

As I hope to show, Marx's concept of human nature – a belief in the existence of innate human tendencies towards autonomy and self-realization – has some bearing on his understanding of justice. Marx is ultimately a product of the Enlightenment, and shares the Enlightenment belief in the possibility of moral progress. Although precommunist concepts of justice are valid under appropriate circumstances and can promote a stable and relatively durable social order, they are ultimately inherently unstable and cannot endure because they do not fully recognize the human tendencies to self-realization and autonomy. Since its institutions will encourage these psychic tendencies, communist society will create the conditions for a more stable and enduring system of justice than any previously known. Because Marx believes in the advance of scientific knowledge, he believes that communist society will be in a better position to confirm that self-realization and autonomy are indeed sources of happiness for humans in general. Consequently, it would also possess the sort of knowledge which enables it to make social decisions that promote human happiness even further.

These claims will be defended in subsequent sections. But first we must square Marx's belief in the existence of innate psychic tendencies with 'historical materialism'.

9.3 'HISTORICAL MATERIALISM' AND HUMAN NATURE IN THE ABSTRACT

There can be no doubt that Marx's materialist concept of history is primarily concerned with the differences rather than the similarities among modes of production, but it does not rule out the existence of abstract psychic 'invariants' whose specific character is shaped by socio-economic circumstances. Like Heilbroner's attempt to understand the 'nature and logic' of modern capitalism, Marx's 'historical materialism' is ultimately grounded on a 'science of human nature', on the existence of 'drives and capacities' which constitute the human physical and psychical endowment and which are shaped and channelled by social and economic institutions[7] (Heilbroner, 1985, pp. 20–4). Indeed, the fundamental premises of 'historical materialism' – that political and ideological conflicts reflect more fundamental conflicts involving material interests, and that class struggles will ultimately lead to greater extensions of human freedom – have the status of transhistorical truths that imply the existence of innate drives and capacities. In this section, I shall argue that Marx explicitly recognized the existence of human invariants even after he developed 'historical materialism'. I shall also explain why he belittled their significance, which he surely did.

Nothing seemed to enrage Marx more than philosophers who attributed permanence to what he believed were historically specific attributes of human nature in order to 'eternalize' a concept of justice whose validity was temporal. He attempted to deflate such claims by illustrating their temporality, by showing how ideas and certain apparently common characteristics of human 'nature' originated with historically specific relations of production and were therefore socially rather than naturally determined. As a number of scholars have pointed out, this does not mean that Marx committed the 'genetic fallacy' – he did not believe that the truth or moral value of an idea depends on the motives which bring it into existence.[8] An idea may have a humble, even contemptible origin, it may have been advanced to justify horrendous practices, and still be true or normatively valid when seen in the proper light or when applied to the appropriate circumstances. Although Marx debunked 'bourgeois' ideas of freedom and equality when they were used to serve the interests of capital, he also believed that these ideas were progressive and, when given the proper qualifying conditions, valid and durable. The peasant had to be freed from his feudal bonds in order for the capitalist to have a wage-labourer to exploit, yet the freedom of the wage-labourer marks an advance for humanity even if it is not yet the superior sort of freedom that will be enjoyed by the labourer in communist society.[9]

Marx's 'historical materialism' is not only compatible with the existence of 'eternal' truths regarding human nature, it also suggests that an adequate understanding of them is dependent on the social context and that this understanding can be improved if the social context changes in the 'right' way.

> Bourgeois society is the most developed and the most complex historic organization of production. The categories which express its relations, the comprehension of its structure, thereby also allows insights into the structure and the relations of production of all the vanished social formations out of whose ruins and elements it built itself up . . . Human anatomy contains the anatomy of the ape. The intimation of higher development among the subordinate animal species, however, can be understood only after the higher development is already known. The bourgeois economy thus supplies the key to the ancient, etc. (Marx, 1857–8, p. 105)

Although this passage refers specifically to the insight gained by bourgeois society into earlier societies, it also implies that bourgeois society is in a better position to understand human nature as such because it is in the position of having seen how human relations and structures have developed. After all, as far as Marx is concerned, we humans are social and political animals whose nature undergoes a development as we modify our natural and social environment. Along Aristotelian and Hegelian lines, an object is known best when all its stages of development are revealed to consciousness. Indeed, this passage reminds one of Hegel's representation of the philosopher as the Owl of Minerva who is able to comprehend the 'truth' only after it has become actual.

The more 'highly developed' societies can also achieve a superior understanding of the abstract, common characteristics of human nature, human capacities in particular. Marx attributes this to their complexity and diversity. 'As a rule, the most general abstractions arise only in the midst of the richest possible concrete development, where one thing appears as common to many, to all. Then it ceases to be thinkable in a particular form alone' (ibid., p. 104). In preindustrial societies for example, the *general* source of wealth is commonly identified with those particular activities, such as commerce or agriculture, that are for them the typical source of wealth. Thus Mercantilists attributed wealth to commerce, the Physiocrats to agricultural labour. According to Marx, it is modern capitalist society where wealth accumulates in the hands of industrialists who employ various kinds of skilled and unskilled labour that wealth is properly understood to be the product of labour as such: 'Not only the category, labour, but labour in reality has here [in modern society] become the means of creating wealth in general, and has ceased to be organically linked with particular individuals in any specific form' (ibid., p. 104). Wealth is not the creation of one particular kind of labour, but of labour of various sorts complementing each other in an extensive division of labour. This is a truth about the human *capacity* to create wealth that could not be understood adequately in a society in which most labour took the form of agricultural labour and wealth is measured in cattle or yams rather than that abstract entity, money.

Marx is particularly concerned with understanding how its social relations affect a society's understanding of human capacities. The social relations of the more highly developed societies are more diverse and, therefore, the categories that render this diversity intelligible to the mind are necessarily more abstract. In the 'anatomy of the ape' passage, Marx was referring to economic categories such as abstract labour ('labour as such') and ground rent. These categories arise from the attempt to understand the complex socio-economic relations of bourgeois society, yet because they are more general, they can provide insight into other societies.

An isolated society with a simple, static division of labour and a rigid social structure will have a very limited view of human capacities. Since its understanding of human capacities is severely limited, it will find it nearly impossible to understand that different kinds of social relations can open up different possibilities for their exercise and development. Indeed, Marx appeared to believe that it was not until capitalism developed a labour market, not until all forms of labour power had become 'equally' commodities, that the notion of human 'equality' could become a generally accepted 'fact'. It is not until labour power has itself become a commodity and one is 'forced' to look after one's own interests, that it becomes possible to recognize the fact that normal human beings possess the mental capacity to act as free, self-determining agents. Marx believed that because Aristotle lived in a society based upon slavery he was blinded to the possibility of treating all humans as equals (a blind spot which also prevented him from discovering the source of a commodity's value):

> There was, however, an important fact which prevented Aristotle from seeing that, to attribute value to commodities, is merely a mode of expressing all labour as equal human labour, and consequently labour of equal quality. Greek society was founded upon slavery, and had, therefore, for its natural basis, the inequality of men and of their labour powers. The secret of the expression of value, namely, that all kinds of labour are equal and equivalent, because, and so far as they are human labour in general, cannot be deciphered, until the notion of human equality has already acquired the fixity of a popular prejudice. This, however, is possible only in a society in which the great mass of the produce of labour takes the form of commodities, in which, consequently, the dominant relation between man and man, is that of owners of commodities. The brilliancy of Aristotle's genius is shown by this alone, that he discovered, in the expression of the value of commodities, a relation of equality. The peculiar conditions of the society in which he lived, alone prevented him from discovering what, 'in truth', was at the bottom of this equality. (ibid., 1887, pp. 59–60).

Given the possibility of progress in the understanding of human nature, why does Marx belittle abstract, universal categories and concepts of 'man as such'? There are a number of answers. First and foremost, he believes that their *practical* relevance is historically, socio-economically determined. Although it is *theoretically* true that labour as such produces wealth in all societies, 'abstract labour' is not a category that would enable us to understand the specific nature and dynamics of all societies. We must understand the *specific characteristics* of a society in order to have a *practical* understanding of it – an understanding of the alternatives confronting the members of its various classes, and an understanding of the way its social structure affects their behaviour and personal identity. To understand the forces which govern a society, it is not sufficient to understand the abstract, universal properties of human beings:

> The simplest abstraction, then which modern economics places at the head of its discussions [abstract labour], and which expresses an immeasurably ancient relation valid in all forms of society, nevertheless achieves practical truth as an abstraction only as a category of the most modern society . . . This example of labour shows strikingly how even the most abstract categories, despite their

validity – precisely because of their abstractness – for all epochs, are nevertheless, in the specific character of this abstraction, themselves likewise a product of historic relations, and possess their *full validity* only for and within these relations. (Marx, 1857–8, p. 105, emphasis added)

Although it is invariably true that labour produces wealth, the fact is that in an agricultural society it is farm labour that really produces wealth. If we want to understand its specific character we must investigate the organization of agriculture and observe how this organization affects the actual desires and motives, the actual behaviour of the members of its various classes. *We* understand what they cannot: that the cause of their relative poverty is their limited and frozen division of labour; that their understanding of human capacities is limited by the lack of opportunities available to the majority of its members. This, however, does not enable us adequately to comprehend the 'nature and logic' of a society which may not even desire to accumulate wealth as we understand it.

Marx's 'sociology of knowledge' provides another reason for his belittlement of abstract, general categories. Although Marx believes that progress in the attainment of knowledge is possible – including knowledge of human psychology as such – his sociology of knowledge does not permit one to be absolutely confident of one's conclusions. As long as an essential property of the human species is its ability to change its psychic make-up, even the members of a communist society will have a limited horizon, they too might conflate the particular with the universal. Thus statements regarding human nature as such are highly speculative and must be taken with a healthy dose of scientific scepticism.

Nevertheless, I believe that even with respect to his own theory of history, Marx goes too far in belittling the practical significance of abstract generalities regarding human nature. In the last passage quoted above, for instance, Marx does not deny that the abstract categories can have practical significance, he claims only that whether they do is historically determined. Although 'historical materialism' can be interpreted differently, it is not incompatible with the existence of innate capacities and drives which, if not given an outlet for their realization, can endanger conflict and social change. It may be possible for Marx to explain social change without reference to innate drives and capacities, but not the secular movement towards greater freedom and equality that is also an aspect of his 'historical materialism'.

In Marx's conception of history, the individual's specific abilities, interests, and basic values are primarily shaped by the material conditions of life. This does not preclude the possibility that humans possess 'by nature' a general, unfocused, undirected tendency to realize certain innate capabilities. The level of economic development may not permit everyone to exercise, develop and realise them, and socio-economic and political institutions may repress them – but not without the potential for future conflict. This is the message that comes through in all Marx's works including *Capital* but perhaps most clearly in this passage from the *Grundrisse*:

The recognition of the products as its own and the judgement that its separation from the conditions of its realization is improper – forcibly imposed – is an enormous [advance in] awareness, itself the product of the mode of production resting on capital, and as much the, knell to its doom as, with the slave's awareness that he *cannot be the property of another*, with his consciousness of himself as a person, the existence of slavery becomes a merely artificial, vegetative existence, and ceases to be able to prevail as the basis of production. (Marx, 1857–8, p. 463)

Marx here assumes that once material conditions allow slaves to recognize that they possess the capacity to live independent, autonomous lives characteristic of property owners, the drive to realize that capacity will be irresistible. Similarly, capitalism is doomed once workers recognize that the means of production represent the means for their self-realization through work. Although they can become practical and conscious motive forces only under the appropriate material conditions, Marx, as we shall see, believes that these psychic tendencies operate 'behind people's back' to propel history in the direction of greater freedom and equality.

9.4   MARX'S 'PHILOSOPHICAL ANTHROPOLOGY'

To understand the nature of these innate capacities and tendencies, we must examine Marx's early works in greater detail. I shall argue that, like the classical Greek philosophers, Marx believes that people have a tendency to find fulfilment and derive a sense of self-esteem from the exercise, development, and realization of their inborn mental and physical capacities.[10] In addition, like many modern political philosophers, he believes that people innately want the freedom to choose their own way to the 'good life' and innately want to be treated as morally autonomous individuals. One gains self-respect from being treated as an individual who is not only capable of knowing one's own best interests but of pursuing one's interests in harmony with others. For Marx, however, socio-economic circumstances condition the consciousness of and the value placed on the realization of these capacities. Marx equates the 'truly human life' with their realization and their realization with a particular set of social relationships.

Innate Capacities and Tendencies: Self-realization

From all a species' distinguishing features, Marx singles out the character of its activity as its 'essence'. Since humans have, by nature, no specific identifying activity, the human essence is determinate only in form: 'free, conscious activity . . . is man's species character' (ibid., p. 113). Of course, this freedom is not absolute. Because humans are also social animals an individual's activity is more or less socially determined (alternatively, more or less freely determined by the individual). Although in the abstract we humans have no predetermined activity, our society offers us a limited range of opportunities – a wider or narrower range depending on our social position. One's personal identity, one's individual 'essence', will be defined principally by one's function and activity in relation to the functions and activities of others within the existing social division of labour. One's self-understanding, another aspect of one's personal identity, will also be conditioned by one's objective material circumstances and social relationships.

The specific character of these social relations and thus one's personal identity are, of course, the product of past interactions, the product of history. Thus even in 1844 when his central concern is with human nature and what has happened to it in modern society, Marx makes it clear that in order adequately to understand human nature one must study *history* for 'History is the true natural history of man' (ibid., p. 182). If humans are, like all other species defined by their activity, if their specific activity is by nature indeterminate (free activity, not instinctive activity) and determined (limited) by society, then a proper understanding of human nature – of human capacities and drives – cannot be had in abstraction from society and history:

> As *human nature* is the *true common life* [*Gemeinwesen*] of man, men through the activation of their *nature create* and produce a human *common life*, a social essence which is no abstractly universal power opposed to the single individual, but is the essence or nature of every single individual, his own activity, his own life, his own spirit, his own wealth. (Marx, 1844a, pp. 271–2)

Were this the whole of the young Marx's understanding of human nature (it is not, since we have not yet considered his concept of alienation) then an interesting thought comes to mind: the paradox – that humans both seem to have and not have a fixed essence – that was earlier attributed to the differences between his 'philosophical anthropology' and his 'historical materialism' could be found within the 'philosophical anthropology' itself. If the human essence is created in social life, if self-realization simply meant that 'man makes himself', then it would appear that human nature has no invariant content. Human nature would essentially vary from one social formation to another. Different social formations would have different concepts of human nature. The only 'invariant essence' would appear to be one of *form* only: history reveals that human faculties are malleable and that human activity is conscious and free of natural, instinctive determinations. Even in his early works, therefore, we see the possibility for a relativism in which there would appear to be no mode of social life that is more appropriate to human nature than another. When we examine his early works, however, it is easier to see why this is not so, for Marx clearly believes that unless society permits the individual to choose his or her own life-plans and provides opportunities for self-realization, some unhappy distortion of 'human nature' will inevitably occur.

The malleability of human faculties and the variability of human activity – the formal attributes of human nature – are not the only constants. Marx is saying much more about human drives and what, in general, makes people happy. The following passage from the *The Economic and Philosophic Manuscripts of 1844* shows that the young Marx acknowledged the existence of innately human powers, forces, and tendencies: '*Man* is directly a *natural being*. As a natural being and as a living natural being he is on the one hand endowed with *natural powers of life* – he is an *active* natural being. These forces exist, in him as tendencies and abilities – as *instincts*' (Marx 1844b, p. 181). The list of powers or capacities is familiar: seeing, hearing, feeling, smelling, tasting, acting, thinking, consciousness, and self-consciousness. Although Marx believes that all but the last three are possessed by other animal species, human faculties have a susceptibility to cultural development and refinement. History reveals not only a succession of changes in nature of human activity but progress, for culture can be passed on to and enriched by future generations. This is true not only of activity and mind but of the senses as well: 'The *forming* of the five senses is a labour of the entire history of the world down to the present' (ibid., pp. 137, 141).

Although the specific character of human activity is by 'nature' indeterminate, he believes that activities which exercise, develop, and realize the individual's particular natural endowment – intellectual, sensory, and motor capacities and powers – are by 'nature' more enjoyable, fulfilling, and thus more suitable to 'human nature' than activities that do not. If material and social conditions permit an individual to engage in them, these activities make the individual not only happy but, in a true sense, wealthy: the '*rich* human being is simultaneously the human being *in need* of a totality of human manifestations of life – the man in whom his own realization exists as an inner necessity, as *need*' (ibid., p. 144). Much later, in the *Grundrisse*, Marx reaffirms this when he writes that it is the 'development of all human powers as such [which constitutes the human] . . . end in itself' (Marx, 1857–8, p. 488). Since human activity is conditioned by social arrangements, it follows that there are certain social arrangements which are more suitable for 'human nature' than others because they recognize the innate tendency for people to find satisfaction in exercising, developing, and realizing their natural powers and capacities.

Innate Capacities and Tendencies: Autonomy

The notion that humans possess a capacity for moral autonomy and an innate tendency to exercise it is contained in his concept of humans as 'species being': 'man is not merely a natural being: he is a *human* natural being. That is to say, he is a being for himself. Therefore he is a *species being*, and has to conform and manifest himself as such both in his being and in his knowing' (Marx, 1844b, p. 182). The similarity of the concept of a 'species being' to the concept of moral autonomy is not immediately apparent from this passage, but is implicit in the notion that 'man . . . is a being for himself'. This means that a human being is not only capable of being an 'end in itself' but also capable of being aware that it shares this capability with others. A being who is an 'end in itself' is a being who is 'by nature' *free* to posit its own ends in life, able to choose and lead its own conception of the good life, and who realizes that the 'development of all human powers as such [constitutes the human] . . . end in itself' – it is a being who freely chooses to exercise, develop, and realize a great variety of its natural powers. Thus the human being is a species being – a being for itself – because a human being is capable of recognizing another human being as an autonomous being – a being in itself. If an individual is capable of living an autonomous life, of recognizing this fact, and of recognizing that others are similarly capable, then it is possible for humans to treat – here the moral dimension is added – one another as morally autonomous persons.

However, the notion that the human being is a species being also means that human beings can become conscious of their capacity to live autonomous lives only in their intercourse with others: 'Neither nature objectively nor nature subjectively is directly given in a form adequate to the *human* being' (ibid., p. 182). One gains self-awareness, and awareness of one's human powers, capacities, abilities, and sources of happiness by comparing oneself to others, by discovering that one is *like* others in certain ways and *different* in other ways, and most importantly, by having one's powers affirmed by oneself and by others: one must find in the outside world not only objective signs of one's powers – the products of one's activities – but also the recognition of them by others. To be autonomous in reality, one must be free of the imposition of the will of others to determine one's own life-plans and concept of the good life. This requires a society in which each person respects the autonomy of others.

In general, precommunist societies do not enable everyone fully to 'confirm and manifest' their 'nature'. They block the development of the faculties of the exploited and prevent them from becoming aware that they are capable of living autonomous lives (as in the case of slavery and serfdom) or that self-realization is a source of happiness (as is the case in capitalist society). Thus they can stifle the innate tendency of humans to become autonomous and/or to engage in activities which challenge their capacities. Thus Marx writes of the alienation of the worker in capitalist society:

> The people, though, who do not feel themselves to be men, grow attached to their masters, like a herd of slaves or horses. The hereditary masters are the purpose of this whole society. This world belongs to them. They take it as it is and as it feels. They take themselves as they find themselves, and they stand where their feet have grown, on the necks of these political animals that know of no other destination than to be attached to the masters and subject to them, to be at their disposal. (Marx, 1843a, p. 206)

We see, therefore, that although Marx believes the human 'essence' – its activity – is social and modified by social circumstances, there exist social arrangements which are more or less conducive to human happiness, and thus to 'human nature', because they are more or less oriented towards allowing people to develop their natural endowments and to act autonomously. Thus capitalism is an advance over serfdom because the worker is free to choose, among socially determined alternatives, an occupation which best satisfies his or her natural proclivities. The worker in capitalist society may not actually be happier than the serf because the alternatives are severely limited and the work does not allow for the development of his or her innate capacities, yet the freedom to choose one's activity marks a step forward and would also be valued in communist society. For Marx, communist society would be the most suitable to human nature because it recognizes the individual's autonomy and, to the fullest extent possible with the available resources, consciously aims to develop and realize the human potential. Just as in all societies, the institutions of communist society will shape people's interests and values. But these interests and values will lead people freely to choose to follow their innate tendency to engage in activities, including political activity, which realize their capacities and abilities. In my rather contrary interpretation of Marx, he is a liberal, but a liberal who finds capitalism an obstacle to the full realization of the human potential.

We can now see more precisely the source of the natural right reading of Marx's concept of justice. This early vision of human nature, in which happiness is defined in terms of self-realization and mutual recognition, persisted throughout Marx's life and it is this vision that allowed the Marx of *Capital* to speak of communism as a system which would be more 'favourable to, and worthy of . . . human nature'. However, in order to understand why Marx does not claim that communism is the only just society, but claims only that justice in communist society will be more 'enduring', we must understand how he construes the relationship between justice and autonomy and self-realization. This task will be facilitated, however, if I first defend my claim that the transition from his 'philosophical anthropology' to 'historical materialism' represents a movement towards greater consistency.

9.5 TOWARDS GREATER CONSISTENCY

The focus of Marx's early works was on the contrast between the alienated existence of workers in capitalist society and human existence as it could be in a community which recognizes 'man's' essential nature: 'To say that *man* alienates himself is the same as saying that the *society* of this alienated man is the caricature of his *actual common life*, of his true generic life' (Marx, 1844a, pp. 271–2). Instead of self-realization, the 'need for money is . . . the true need produced by the modern economic system' (Marx, 1844b, p. 147). In his later work, Marx focused his attention on the 'nature and logic' of capitalism. This transition represents a natural evolution in thought towards greater consistency for there is a 'moral' quality in his early writings that belies his message. The moral is that in order to achieve a life 'worthy of man' one must restructure society. In 1843, Marx believed that an 'ideal of man' could motivate the working class to revolution:

> Material force must be overthrown by material force. But theory also becomes a material force once it has gripped the masses . . . The criticism of religion ends with the doctrine that *man is the highest being for man*, hence with the *categorical imperative to overthrow all conditions* in which man is a degraded, enslaved, neglected, contemptible being. (Marx, 1843b, pp. 257–8)

This moral attitude still permeates his work of 1844, but his message has changed. His message is that until people have created an authentic common life they would not fully understand what a life 'worthy of man' really means. Until the 'authentic common life' comes into existence, self-realization could not and would not be life's conscious goal. Even in 1844 he realized that the 'authentic common life' was to arise from life's mundane struggles, not from altruism or high ideals: '*Authentic common life* arises not through reflection; rather it comes about from the *need* and *egoism* of individuals, that is, immediately from the activation of their very existence' (Marx, 1844a, p. 272). This message, however, was not consistent with the idealism that permeated his early work.

If the 'authentic common life' does not arise from altruism or ideals, how exactly could it arise through 'need and egoism'? 'Historical materialism' can be understood as an attempt to answer this question. Marx's answer was in some respects similar to Hegel's 'cunning of reason'. Hegel, according to Marx, believed that human history demonstrated a movement towards increasing freedom, not because people willed it into existence but because the 'concept' of freedom itself worked behind the backs of individuals who were motivated by 'need and egoism'. Marx, following Feuerbach, rejected the idealism of Hegel's thesis that a 'concept' could be an active subject which leads people to an end without their knowing it, yet he looked for a materialist equivalent to this 'cunning of reason'. His study of the 'protohistorical materialists' such as Adam Smith, whose concept of an 'invisible hand' bears a family resemblance to Hegel's 'cunning of reason', led him to find the explanation of historical change in the play of material interests which are tied to *the class structure of economic relations*. Although he recognized even in 1843 that the actual interests of capitalists and workers create a historical dynamic, he had not yet begun to examine this dynamic in concrete detail. He still focused on the contrast between 'human nature' as it is to 'human nature' as it ought to be.

By 1845, with the *German Ideology*, Marx clearly recognized the vanity of the moralistic approach. He is critical of the Young Hegelians (and, implicitly, of himself in his earlier writings) for believing that an ideal of 'man' could be the driving force of history:

[I]ndividuals . . . have been conceived by the philosophers as an ideal, under the name of 'man'. They have conceived the whole process which we have outlined as the evolutionary process of 'man,' so that at every historical stage 'man' was substituted for the individuals and shown as the motive force of history. The whole process was thus conceived as a process of self-estrangement of 'man,' and this was essentially due to the fact that the average individual of the later stage was always foisted on the earlier stage, and the consciousness of a later age on the individuals of an earlier. (Marx, 1845–6, p. 68)

Such an approach is fruitless, for 'the mass of men, i.e. the proletariat . . . theoretical notions do not exist . . . and if this mass ever had theoretical notions, e.g. religious, etc., these have now long been dissolved by circumstances' (ibid., p. 32). Commerce has destroyed not only traditional communities but also the values, moral principles, and ideals which held these communities together. Modern commercial society is pluralistic and tolerant of different systems of belief and values. To appeal to an 'ideal of man' would be fruitless since shared values and ideals originate in shared interests and needs, which are themselves a product of economic life. Marx clearly recognizes now that the only appeal that can motivate workers in modern society is the appeal to existing interests. He appeals to the workers' actual needs and desires, and attempts to show how cooperation and community will be *instrumentally* (extrinsically) valuable in achieving their ends. Their circumstances force them to be concerned with survival, not self-realization. The question Marx poses to them is, 'What is the best means to assure survival – to compete or to cooperate?' They must combine and cooperate in order to save their skins. Yet, cooperation on an equal footing constitutes a step towards a common life which could eventually create the very needs and interests which characterizes Marx's ideal of 'man'. He has an inkling of this in 1844 when he writes that when

communist *artisans* associate with one another, theory, propaganda, etc. is the first end [in his maturity he might have written 'survival is the the first end']. But at the same time, as a result of this association, they acquire a new need – the need for society – and what appears as a means becomes an end. (Marx, 1844b, pp. 154–5)

Despite his early recognition of the importance of actual interests, of 'need and egoism', Marx's early works are rather inconsistently focused on the contrast of these needs and interests to the needs and interests of an ideal of 'man'.

No longer believing that an ideal of 'man' can be a material, historical force, in the *German Ideology* Marx is concerned with identifying more precisely than before the economic preconditions that make progress towards this 'ideal' possible.

> [O]nly with . . . [the] universal development of productive forces is a *universal* intercourse between men established, which produces in all nations simultaneously the phenomenon of the propertyless mass (universal competition), makes each nation dependent on the revolutions of the others, and finally has put world historical, empirically universal individuals in place of local ones. (Marx, 1845–6, pp. 24–5)

The concept of humans as 'species beings' is an empty abstraction until a society comes into existence that creates '*world historical, empirically universal individuals*' – humans who are 'species beings' in actuality because they are in a practical, economic relation to one another. It is the very process of coming together – at first as individuals in the market, then in the work place and, finally, in making the 'revolution' – that creates the precondition for a community in which people are aware of their 'essential' nature: 'Both for the production on a mass scale of their community consciousness, and for the success of this cause itself, the relation of men on a mass scale is necessary, an alteration which can only take place in a practical movement, a revolution' (ibid., p. 69).

Following Smith, Marx recognizes both the universalizing, globe encompassing nature of capital's search for profits and the importance of the 'extent of the market' for productivity and thus the mastery over the forces of nature. Capitalism destroys communities based on traditional modes of production with their stifling social life, fossilized division of labour, stagnant technology, and limited forms of consciousness: 'When men's relations to nature and others is restricted, so is their consciousness' (ibid., p. 20). The world-wide extension of market activities creates channels of communication and a universe of discourse that recognizes no national or cultural boundaries. The development of knowledge is no longer localized and can accumulate rapidly; the wheel does not have to be reinvented in each community.[11] Increases in productivity due to mechanization opens the possibility that *all* individuals will have free time to develop their powers to be in a 'position to achieve a complete and no longer restricted self-activity' (ibid., p. 67), if, that is, they can wrest control of those forces.

Of course, capitalism also breaks up the communal feeling present in these traditional societies and creates instead the alienated, 'abstract individual' (ibid., pp. 64–6). Yet at the same time, it puts 'workers in a position to enter into relations with one another *as individuals*' (ibid., p. 66). The 'same conditions, the same antagonisms, the same interests necessarily [call] forth, on the whole, similar customs everywhere' (ibid., p. 48).[12] Workers, who are universally propertyless, will discover their common interest and create common, global customs. These same themes are echoed years later in the *Grundrisse*:

> Universally developed individuals, whose social relations, as their own communal [*gemeinschaftlich*] relations . . . are no product of nature, but of history. The degree and the universality of the development of wealth where *this* individuality becomes possible supposes production on the basis of exchange

values as a prior condition, whose universality produces not only the alienation of the individual from himself and from others, but also the universality and the comprehensiveness of his relations and capacities. (Marx, 1857–8, p. 162)

Marx thus abandons the appeal to an 'ideal of man' as a motivating force for revolution, but he does not abandon his 'concept of human nature'. His concept of human nature undoubtedly influenced his personal moral beliefs and his advice to the working class: he sides with the working class because he believes its interest will lead it to create the conditions for human self-realization. The concept of human nature elaborated in his early works also provides the theoretical foundation of his 'historical materialism'. In it human self-realization is implicitly posited as an *unconscious* drive, rather than a conscious goal, which propels history on a bumpy road towards mastery over the forces of nature, towards human liberation, and towards greater self-understanding so that eventually self-realization will become the conscious life-goal of the individual and of society. Humans inevitably adapt their goals to the possible, but in their activity, their labour, they also inevitably create new possibilities for the exercise of their faculties, possibilities which awaken their unconscious drive towards autonomy and self-realization. Thus once the slave becomes conscious of the possibility of becoming a person, slavery is doomed; once the worker is aware of the possibility that labour power need not be sold like any other commodity, capitalism is doomed.

9.6   AUTONOMY, SELF-REALIZATION AND JUSTICE

As was noted earlier, Marx's understanding of human nature would seem to provide an invariant standard – an ideal of a person – whereby the validity of a concept of justice could be evaluated. If Marx were a natural right philosopher in the strong sense, that is, if he believed that there is only one eternally valid concept of justice, then the only just society would be the one that recognizes individual autonomy and promotes self-realization. My claim, however, which I am now prepared to defend, is that Marx's 'ideal of man' only provides a standard of measuring progress and for determining the durability of a system of justice; with the exception of communist society, it does not provide the standard for determining the validity of a concept of justice. In order to see why this is so, we must understand the role of justice in society and its relation to autonomy and self-realization.

Marx would not object, I believe, to this 'Humean' characterization of the role of justice in society – all societies: justice is concerned with the peaceful settlement of disputes when resources are moderately scarce and interests conflict. In order for a concept of justice to fulfil this function, its basic principles must be justifiable to those whose interests may come into conflict. As Rawls puts it: 'to justify a conception of justice to someone is to give him a proof of its principles from premises that we both accept . . .' (Rawls, 1971, pp. 580–1). It is this 'proof' that bestows *validity* on a concept of justice. In most theories of justice, Marx's included, the shared premise consists of a set of common interests, values, or goods.[13] Theories of justice can be distinguished from one another by how they construe this shared premise. Natural right theories found the common good on the presumed existence of universal, transhistoric desires, needs, interests, and/or values; whereas relativist theories found the common good on historically or culturally relative desires, needs, etc. With these distinctions in mind our problem can be reformulated as follows: is the shared premise a common interest in autonomy and self-realization that exists independently of socio-economic circumstances, or is it the common interests of individuals as they are at a given time and place?

The answer, I think, is clear. The common good must derive from people as they are. In the *German Ideology*, Marx explicitly states that the constitution of the common good is historically contingent: '. . . the communal interest . . . exists . . . as the mutual interdependence of individuals among whom labour is divided' (Marx, 1845–6, p. 22). For Marx, the common good is not a subjective posit of the individual or community, but has an objective foundation in the structures of economic life. It is their economic life which is the principle force that shapes personal identity and the specific character of people's needs, interests, and values:

> [P]rivate interest is itself already a socially determined interest which can be achieved only within the conditions laid down by society and with the means provided by society; hence it is bound to the reproduction of these conditions and means. It is the interest of private persons; but its content, as well as the form and means of its realization, is given by social conditions independent of all. (Marx, 1875–8, p. 156).

For people whose common life is characterized by alienation, a principle of justice based on autonomy and/or self-realization is an empty abstraction which lacks practical, 'full validity'.

Consider the problem in the light of the nature of justice. The disputes and interests that justice attempts to resolve peacefully arise from the real, practical concerns of material life. Disputes can be peacefully settled in the here and now by appeals to principles of justice which are founded on premises, on a notion of the common good, which are shared by people in the here and now. A concept of justice which was founded on appeals to the interests of Marx's ideal of a person would not constitute a premise with which all could agree and would, therefore, be of no use in settling disputes. If, as we have seen, Marx did not believe that appeals to an ideal of a self-realizing person are of use in motivating workers to make a revolution, he surely could not believe that similar appeals could provide the foundation for an eternal concept of justice. Although he believed that tendencies towards autonomy and self-realization are innate, they can be suppressed or sublimated into socially determined channels. Furthermore, Marx believed that communism, and thus a society which values self-realization for all, is not feasible until the level of economic development is sufficiently advanced to allow everyone enough free time to pursue their interests and develop their powers. Therefore, the *interest* in self-realization cannot form the premise upon which an 'eternal concept of justice is founded, and Marx cannot be said to be a natural right philosopher in the 'strong sense'.

As we have seen, Marx located the origin of the common interest in the division of labour, yet one might have reason to doubt that he really believed that a common good exists in a class society. He focused, after all, on the conflict between classes and rarely mentioned the general interest. Indeed, when he did, he generally referred to it as an 'illusory "general-interest"' (Marx, 1845–6, p. 24). It is only an illusion, however, when compared to the common good as it would be in a communist society. In communist society the division of labour – the system of interdependence which creates the objective foundation of the common good – is supposedly the conscious product of 'freely associated individuals' working in cooperation with one another, whereas in class society the division of labour is usually the result of force and violence and appears as something 'alien' to and imposed on the individual worker (Marx and Engels, 1845–6, p. 22). Nevertheless, in whatever manner the division of labour originates, the 'fact' remains that, once it is in place, it not only shapes human interests and consciousness, it also creates a system of interdependence upon whose reproduction the satisfaction of those interests depend. However unpleasant the reality, unless an alternative mode of allocating labour can be readily established, the existing division of labour must be reproduced if the common interest is to be satisfied. Thus, although a concept of justice favours the particular interests of the ruling class, it is valid if it is able to serve the common good better than any alternative. However, it is the 'fact' that the division of labour is a result of conflict rather than cooperation, it is the 'fact' that the *particular* interests of different classes conflict that makes it impossible for systems of justice that sanction exploitation to endure. Class conflict threatens their stability.

If the *validity* of a concept of justice is based on *rational* argument (do the principles of justice promote the common interest?), the *stability* of a system of justice is based on *affect*, on the voluntary compliance of individuals with the demands of justice. In order for individuals to develop a strong sense of justice they must feel that justice is doing more than simply satisfying the common good, they must feel that it is, all things considered, also promoting their particular interests, their happiness. But justice, since it provides principles for resolving conflicts of interest in which there will be winners and losers, may require great sacrifice from the individual – e.g. from the workers in an exploitative society. One should expect, therefore, that the most stable and enduring system of justice would be the one in which the common good and the conditions for individual happiness overlap to the greatest extent. As Marx envisions it, a communist system of justice is enduring because it is premised on a common interest in autonomy and self-realization. Communist institutions and laws will consciously recognize the innate propensities of the human psyche and allow them expression. In it the particular interest and the common interest are most closely allied; its principles therefore will endure. With respect to the conditions required to produce an enduring sentiment for justice, Marx can be placed in the natural right tradition (in the weak sense): the long-term stability, the durability, of a communist system of justice is decided by its compatibility with 'human nature'.

Indeed, autonomy and self-realization are significant for Marx's concept of justice in three ways: (i) *progress* in justice and morality; (ii) the *common good* in communist society; and (iii) the *stability and durability* of communist principles are all defined with respect to it.

As for Marx's notion of progress, even though Marx believed that each socioeconomic formation has a concept of justice which was most appropriate to it, this did not prevent him from ranking them: 'Right can never be higher than the economic structure of society and its cultural development conditioned thereby' (Marx, 1875, p. 17). If Marx was a relativist in the strong sense – an ethical, metaethical, and cognitive relativist – he could not meaningfully make such a statement. The standards that Marx uses to measure the 'height' to which a given 'system of right' has attained, his criterion of progress, can be none other than the degree to which human powers and individual autonomy have developed. The progression from slavery, through serfdom, through capitalism, and finally to communism represents a movement towards greater autonomy for the individual and greater mastery over nature.

The second way in which autonomy and self-realization enter into Marx's understanding of justice concerns the nature of the common good in communist society. For Marx, communist society will be the first society in which the common good, and thus the common premise upon which a concept of justice is founded, will be consciously identified with individual autonomy *and* the maximization of human powers.[14] It is in the *Critique of the Gotha Programme* that Marx ties the principle of justice in communist society – the principle of need – to the need to develop human powers:

> In a higher phase of communist society, after the enslaving subordination of the individual to the division of labour, and with it also the antithesis between mental and physical labour, has vanished; after labour has become not only a means of life but itself life's prime want; after the productive forces have also increased with the all-round development of the individual, and all the springs of co-operative wealth flow more abundantly – only then can the narrow horizon of bourgeois right be crossed in its entirety and society inscribe on its banners: From each according to his ability, to each according to his needs![15] (Marx 1875, p. 17)

Third, and finally, self-realization is significant because it explains why the principles of justice and morality in communist society will be more enduring than the principles of justice in exploitative societies. As I have already stated, this is because it is based on a premise which is most cognizant of the ultimate source of human happiness: the tendency of people to find fulfilment in leading autonomous lives devoted to realizing their particular capacities and powers. In so far as people are leading fulfilled lives, they will respect the principles of justice which make this possible. If communist principles of justice will endure because people recognize this tendency, societies based on exploitation should be less enduring because they do not. But why should the neglect of self-realization and autonomy be a destabilizing factor? Since people's desires and goals are shaped by the division of labour, it is conceivable that even a society based on slavery could establish a system of justice which engenders stability by permitting the slave to satisfy a limited number of private interests. Why shouldn't societies based on slavery also endure? Of course the slave will have to perform the drudge-work and will have to sacrifice personal ends to the common good. But all societies in which scarcity exists, even communist society, will require individual sacrifice and face problems of stability caused by conflicting private interests – without conflict the need for a system of justice would not exist.

The answer is that not all kinds of conflict are *necessarily destructive* of a system of justice. For Marx, however, class conflicts are. Although class interests are socially and historically determined, all class struggles have something in common: as socio-economic conditions change, the exploited 'discover' that the exploitation of their labour is unjust. A system of justice which legitimizes exploitation cannot endure.

Let us consider the meaning of exploitation in relation to the concepts of autonomy and self-realization. It can be defined as their negation: exploitation exists when one group of people sacrifice control over their activity (the negation of their self-realization) by submitting to the will (the negation of their autonomy) of another class. This is not unjust when society is at a level of economic development which permits only a few people to exercise and develop their capacities or when the requisite sense of personal identity has not yet emerged among the exploited. Nevertheless, because exploitation negates the innate tendencies to self-realization and autonomy, it creates a *perpetual source of conflict* that will eventually destroy the existing mode of production and invalidate its system of justice.

In order to maintain the validity and stability of their system of justice, all societies, be they exploitative or not, must shape the identity of their members in a way that is compatible with the given relations of production. If the given institutional structure – which determines permissible patterns of behaviour, and the specific nature of roles, offices, and duties – of a society is not compatible with the particular (but ever-changing) personal identity of the members of its exploited classes, then the concept of justice which governs its institutions will not be valid and will not be recognized as valid by the exploited classes. Yet it is in the very process of production that people change not only their environment – expanding the limits of the possible through the development of the forces of production – but their 'nature' as well, the specific features of their personal identity. Given these changes in objective and subjective 'nature', the exploited class will discover that their exploitation is no longer appropriate to their 'nature'. They will refuse to submit to the will of the exploiting class or to respect the existing system of justice which justifies this submission.

The problem with exploitative societies, particularly those that deprive individuals of autonomy, is that in order to maintain their validity they require something that Marx believes is 'unnatural': that the historically specific features of individual and group identity remain unchanged. This is to ask that phenomena which are purely historical and have no natural basis become ahistorical and eternal. Although production changes the external environment and, in the process, 'human nature', exploitative societies cannot tolerate such changes:

> The survival of the commune as such in the old mode requires the reproduction of its members in the presupposed objective conditions. Production itself, the advance of population . . . necessarily suspends these conditions little by little; destroys them instead of reproducing them, etc., and, with that the communal system declines and falls, together with the property relations on which it was based. The Asiatic form necessarily hangs on for the longest time. This is due to its presupposition that the individual does not become independent *vis a vis* the community. (Marx, 1857–8, p. 486)

Although the Asiatic mode lasted the longest because it managed to stifle change and individual independence, it could not last forever because its rigid social structure was not appropriate to a being whose nature it is to change itself.

Institutions will endure only if they are compatible with the historically specific *and* the innate properties – both substantive and formal – of 'human nature'. As I have already argued, institutions must allow for self-realization and autonomy (the substantive properties) for all because these are innate, psychic tendencies which are sources of conflict when suppressed. This amounts to saying that institutions and their supporting systems of justice cannot endure if they permit the exploitation of one class by another. What I have not yet argued, however, is that if they are to be compatible with the *formal*, self-changing character of the human species, institutions (social, economic,and political) must be democratic in *form*.

Democracy is required for two reasons. First, it is a procedure for resolving conflicts that is compatible with the changing character of human needs and wants. Indeed, democratic institutions are premised on the notion that a forum must exist whereby people can make their needs and interests known and whereby institutions and laws can be continuously modified order to accommodate change. Those who are in positions of authority are ultimately accountable to those whom they supervise and can be replaced in accordance with established procedures. If the existing laws, institutions, and authorities fail to serve the common good, they can be modified or replaced without destroying the *basic* structure of social relations, relations which are premised on formal (legal) and substantive (absence of economic class) equality. Communist justice is procedural justice operating in an environment with greater substantive equality than exists in a capitalist society.

Second, participation in democratic institutions is in itself an activity that can be a source of self-realization. Participation in political life can develop the individual's moral competence and sense of personal worth.[16] With respect to the democracy of the ancient Greeks, Marx (1843a, p. 206) wrote: 'Freedom, the feeling of man's dignity, will have to be awakened again . . . Only this feeling, which disappeared from the world with the Greeks . . . can again transform society into a community of men to achieve their highest purposes, a democratic state.'

Although capitalism had begun to develop democratic political institutions, Marx believed that this would not be sufficient to establish an enduring capitalist system of justice. The problem he saw with 'bourgeois democracy' was that it did not penetrate the economic base. The capitalist firm is autocratic, concerned with profit not the universal exercise and development of the 'higher' human powers. In a capitalist democracy, human needs are mainly expressed indirectly through 'effective' demand, by dollar 'votes', and are *directly* communicated only through a centralized political system in which few people have the time or inclination to participate. Since the wealth of the capitalists translates into political power, the outcome of the political process would tend to favour the particular interests of the capitalist class, frequently in violation of capital's own principles of justice. In all, the aims and structure of the capitalist firm, the ethos of competition, and the 'accidental', morally arbitrary nature of distribution of labour and goods in a competitive market economy do not engender respect for the capitalist system of justice and threatens its stability.

Although he may be excessively optimistic in this regard, Marx believed distributional problems could best be resolved by means of democratic procedures. In order to develop the necessary human capacity for moral argument, in order for human needs to find a universal forum for expression, and in order to establish a universally shared sense of personal identity 'worthy of human nature' democracy must extend to the economic sphere, all the way down to the workshop floor. Since the division of labour determines which human needs can be satisfied and which powers can be developed, it is only when the division of labour is established through cooperative efforts and rational discourse that the common good should no longer appear as an 'alien' force. Although the division of labour and the distribution of wealth and income which results from democratic decision-making may not be to everyone's satisfaction, a democratic forum (or a system of democratic forums encompassing different levels of decision-making) in which people meet on a *relatively equal socio-economic footing* provides a means whereby needs can be directly expressed and in which the outcome of decisions is less likely consistently to favour one group at the expense of another, as is the case in a class society. Even though particular distributive decisions can go against one's private interest, one would not lose respect for a system of justice that allows one to make one's interests known, encourages the use of resources for individual development, protects one's right to participate in economic decision-making, and enables one to develop a sense of self-respect and dignity.

Notes

1. The controversy has centred on the question: did Marx believe that capitalism is unjust? For a good survey of the literature on this question see Geras, 1985.
2. Although Marx is referring to economic categories in this passage, the thought expressed is also applicable to ethical categories, as many of the passages quoted below in section 9.2 illustrate.
3. Rawls (1985) has subsequently modified his position. He now claims that his concept of justice is valid for a constitutional democracy but leaves it an open question whether it is valid for other political cultures.
4. Robert C. Tucker (1969) and Allen Buchanan (1982) have argued that, as far as Marx is concerned, communism is beyond justice. Obviously, I do not agree. For some of my reasons and for further references see note 14.
5. For a more comprehensive treatment of these various kinds of relativism see Frankena (1963), chapter 6 and Lukes (1977), chapter 8.
6. For an alternative interpretation of Marx that also distinguishes ethical and metaethical levels of discourse, see Shaw, 1981.
7. According to Heilbroner, the science of human nature is premised on the notion that there is a 'vulnerability of human motive and action to the demands of the unconscious' (Heilbroner, 1985, p. 22). Although it may at first sight seem foreign to Marx, I shall argue that his concept of human nature is similarly premised on the existence of innate drives and capacities (quite different from those posited by Heilbroner) which are both channelled by society and at the same time create pressures for social change.
8. See Van DeVeer, 1973 and Panichas, 1981.
9. Marx perceives a historically progressive movement from dependence to greater and greater independence and freedom. Capitalism frees workers from personal dependence, a condition which will endure and be enhanced in the future communist society:

    > Relations of personal dependence . . . are the first social forms, in which human productive capacity develops only to a slight extent and at isolated points. Personal independence founded on *objective* (*sachlicher*) dependence is the second great form, in which a system of general social metabolism, of universal relations, of all-round needs and universal capacities is formed for the first time. Free individuality, based on the universal development of individuals and on their subordination of the communal, social productivity as their social wealth, is the third stage. The second stage creates the conditions for the third. (Marx, 1857–8, p. 158)

10. Rawls calls this the 'Aristotelian Principle', which he defines as follows: 'other things equal, human beings enjoy the exercise of their realized capacities (their innate or trained abilities), and this enjoyment increases the more the capacity is realized, or the greater the complexity' (Rawls, 1971, p. 426). Rawls, it should be noted, also treats this as an innate property of the human psyche. He argues that one reason why a system of justice which embodies his concept of justice would be

stable is because it is concordant with the Aristotelian Principle, that is, it promotes the individual's good as well as the common good. Self-realization plays a similar role in Marx's vision of a just society.

11.   'In primitive history every invention had to be made daily anew and in each locality independently' (Marx 1845–6, p. 49).

12.   Although Marx is speaking of the manner in which a common interest arose among the burghers of different towns during the Middle Ages, I have taken the liberty of using this passage to illustrate a point – a point with which Marx would surely agree – regarding the proletariat.

13.   Although Marx focused on conflicting class interests, as I shall argue below he recognized the existence of a common interest among classes within a given socio-economic formation.

14.   One common interpretation of Marx holds that there will be no necessity for a concept of justice in communist society because scarcity will have been overcome, conflicting interests will be so slight, and/or people will have become so altruistic that an institutional mechanism for resolving disputes will no longer be required. Although there is a great deal of evidence to support it, I do not hold to this view, for there is also evidence to support the opposite view taken here. With communist society in mind, Engels writes that '[t]he struggle for existence – if we here accept this category for the moment – is thus transformed into a struggle for pleasures, no longer for mere means of *subsistence* but for means of *development, socially produced* means of development' (Engels, 1875, p. 284). Clearly this envisions a society in which neither scarcity nor egoism has been overcome, but one in which there is a struggle over the resources necessary for self-realization. Although the textual evidence can support either view, and thus reveals an inconsistency in Marx's thinking, I believe that the interpretation given here is more consistent with his basic theoretical framework. For a more extensive treatment of this issue see Geras, 1985 and Castellana, 1987.

15.   For an argument against the notion that need is a principle of justice for Marx, see Tucker, 1969, p. 48.

16.   According to Elster (1989), Marx does not believe that political activity is a mode of self-realization. This is because, as Elster reads Marx, communist society will be free of conflict and therefore free of the necessity for political activity. Clearly I do not agree with his interpretation of Marx, although I do agree with his notion that politics can be a mode of self-realization.

References

Althusser, Louis (1969) *For Marx*, trans. Ben Brewster (New York: Vintage Books, Random House).

Buchanan, Allen (1982) *Marx and Justice: The Radical Critique of Liberalism* (Totowa, NJ: Rowman & Littlefield).

Castellana, Richard (1987) *Justice and Economic Life: An Interpretation of Marx's Critique of Capitalism*, Ph.D. dissertation, Department of Economics, Graduate Faculty, New School for Social Research, New York.

Cohen, Marshall *et al.* (eds) (1980) *Marx, Justice, and History* (Princeton: Princeton University Press).

Elster, Jon (1989) 'Self-realisation in Work and Politics: the Marxist Conception of the Good Life', in Jon Elster and Karl Ovemoene (eds), *Alternatives to Capitalism* (Cambridge: Cambridge University Press).

Engels, Frederick (1872–3) 'Supplement to the Housing Question', from *The Selected Works of Marx and Engels*, vol. I (Peking: Foreign Languages Publishing House, no date).

Engels, Frederick (1875) Letter November 12[–17]. From *Marx, Engels: Selected Correspondence* (Moscow: Progress Publishers, 1975).

Engels, Frederick (1877–8) *Anti-Dühring* (Peking: Foreign Languages Publishing House, 1959).

Frankena, William K. (1963) *Ethics* (Englewood Cliffs, NJ: Prentice Hall).

Geras, Norman (1985) 'The Controversy About Marx and Justice', *New Left Review*, no. 150.

Heilbroner, Robert L. (1985) *The Nature and Logic of Capitalism* (New York: W. W. Norton).

Lukes, Steven (1977) *Essays in Social Theory* (New York: Columbia University Press).

Marx, Karl (1843a) Letter from the *Deutsch-Franzoesische Jahrbuecher*, from the *Writings of the Young Marx on Philosophy and Society*, ed. and trans. by Loyd D. Easton and Kurt H. Guddat (New York: Anchor Books, 1967).

Marx, Karl (1843b) 'Towards the Critique of Hegel's Philosophy of Law: Introduction', from the Writings of the Young Marx on Philosophy and Society, ed. and trans. by Loyd D. Easton and Kurt H. Guddat (New York: Anchor Books, 1967).

Marx, Karl (1844a) *Excerpt Notes of 1844*, from the *Writings of the Young Marx on Philosophy and Society*, ed. and trans. by Loyd D. Easton and Kurt H. Guddat (New York: Anchor Books, 1967).

Marx, Karl (1844b) *The Economic and Philosophic Manuscripts of 1844*, ed. by Dirk J. Struik, trans. Martin Milligan (New York: International Publishers, 1947).

Marx, Karl (1846) Letter of 28 December, from *Marx, Engels: Selected Correspondence* (Moscow: Progress Publishers, 1975).

Marx, Karl (1857–8) *Grundrisse: Foundations of the Critique of Political Economy*, trans. Martin Nicolaus (Harmondsworth: Penguin Books, 1973).

Marx, Karl (1875) *Critique of the Gotha Programme* (Beijing: Foreign Languages Press, 1972).

Marx, Karl (1887) *Capital*, vol. 1 (New York: International Publishers, 1967).

Marx, Karl (1894) *Capital*, vol. 3 (New York: International Publishers, 1967).

Marx, Karl and Frederich Engels (1845) *The Holy Family*, from the *Writings of the Young Marx on Philosophy and Society*, ed. and trans. by Loyd D. Easton and Kurt H. Guddat (Anchor Books, 1967).

Marx, Karl and Frederich Engels (1845–6) *The German Ideology*, ed. R. Pascal (New York: International Publishers, 1947).

McBride, William L. (1970) 'Marxism and Natural Law', *The American Journal of Jurisprudence*, vol. 15.

Nielsen, Kai and S. C. Patten (eds) (1981) *Marx and Morality, Canadian Journal of Philosophy*, Supplementary vol. VII.

Panichas, George E. (1981) 'Marx's Moral Scepticism' in Neilsen and Patten.

Rawls, John (1971) *A Theory of Justice* (Cambridge, Mass.: Harvard University Press).

Rawls, John (1985) 'Justice as Fairness: Political not Metaphysical', *Philosophy and Public Affairs*, vol. 14, no. 3.

Shaw, William H. (1981) 'Marx and Moral Objectivity' in Neilsen and Patten.

Tucker, Robert C. (1969) *The Marxian Revolutionary Idea* (New York: W.W. Norton).

Van DeVeer, Donald (1973) 'Marx's View of Justice', *Philosophy and Phenomenological Research*, vol. 33, no. 3, March.

Wood, Allen W. (1971–2) 'The Marxian Critique of Justice', *Philosophy and Public Affairs*, vol. 1. Also published in Cohen *et al.* 1980. Page references are to Cohen *et al.*

10 The Commodity as 'Characteristic Form'

Martha Campbell

In his 'Notes on Wagner' Marx describes the commodity as the 'characteristic form' of the product in contemporary society. This description of the commodity, taken together with Marx's claim that 'the determinate character of social man must be the starting point' (Marx, 1975, p. 189), suggests that *Capital* begins with reference to capitalism (with the determinate character of capitalist social man) by beginning with the analysis of the commodity. This interpretation of the beginning of *Capital*, even though suggested by Marx himself, seems, on the face of it, untenable. Because the commodity form is not unique to capitalism, it does not seem possible that an analysis of this form could disclose the determinate character of capitalism.

This chapter will argue that in *Capital* Marx defines all the elements of the capitalist system by the logical implications of and necessary conditions for the commodity form. For this reason, he speaks of the commodity as the 'economic cell form' for bourgeois society (Marx, 1977, p. 90). Because his argument is strictly logical, it demonstrates that the kind of production that is directed by capital and uses wage labour is the necessary condition for simple circulation. This establishes that capitalist production and simple circulation (at least, as Marx presents them in Part I of *Capital*) are mutually requiring subprocesses of one system and, as such, are the two processes that constitute the capitalist system. For Marx's argument to be strictly logical, however, he must begin with a specifically capitalist form. That is, because the commodity, as Marx presents it at the beginning of *Capital*, is specifically capitalist, it implies the other elements of the capitalist system or these other elements can be derived logically from it. On this interpretation, then, Marx's description in the 'Notes' of how *Capital* begins, brings out an aspect of the method of *Capital* that is essential to the logical structure of the argument and to what the argument demonstrates because it is logical.

10.1 THE EXAMPLE OF MERCHANTS' CAPITAL

The first point to establish is that Marx's analysis of the commodity could refer exclusively to capitalism. The idea that it cannot, simply because commodities are present in other circumstances, is based on assumptions that Marx does not share and, accordingly, judges the historical reference of his theory by false criteria. It assumes first that a form must be unique to one historical context to be historically specific. This in turn implies that a form that is common to several contexts remains identical in all of them.

In Marx's theory, the uniqueness of forms is not the only indication of historical specificity and is, in any case, not self-evident (see below p. 279). A form that is common to a variety of historical settings will have different characteristics in each, making the version that belongs to one context distinct from the version that belongs to another. Common forms, therefore, also have a historical character and can be presented in historically specific way.

This may be illustrated by another common form whose specifically capitalist characteristic is more obvious than the commodity's. In Volume III of *Capital*, Marx considers merchants' capital 'merely from the standpoint and within the limits, of the capitalist mode of production' at the same time noting that merchants' capital 'is older than the capitalist mode of production' (Marx, 1967, p. 325). It is obvious that Marx has been referring to merchants' capital in a capitalist context because he has described its interaction with other kinds of capital; in a precapitalist context, merchant capitalists would not be dealing exclusively with other capitalists. There is implicit in Marx's account, however, a more fundamental distinction between capitalist and non-capitalist merchants' capital. Interaction among capitals presupposes that all capitals could realize profits at the same time or that the profits of one do not presuppose another's loss. For this to occur, there must be a net increase in value for all capitals together or the creation of more value than all originally represented. Marx calls this the creation of surplus value and has already established in Volume I that it can result only from the use of wage labour. The Volume III account of the interaction between merchants' and other kinds of capital, therefore, implies a more fundamental feature of capital in a capitalist context, namely, that profits come from wage labour. This is the feature that defines specifically capitalist merchants' capital.

Merchants' capital can be identified as capitalist or non-capitalist, therefore, by the source of its profits. In a precapitalist context, the profits of merchants' capital come from buying at one price and selling at another, i.e. from circulation alone. In a capitalist context, they come from the surplus value generated by the total social capital through the purchase of labour power in circulation and its use in production. Any account of merchants' capital that either explicitly or implicitly attributes profits to this source must refer specifically to capitalism even though merchants' capital, like the elements of simple circulation, can be either precapitalist or capitalist.

If merchants' capital can be presented in a specifically capitalist way, it should be possible to do the same with the commodity. Like merchants' capital, the commodity ought to have some characteristic in capitalism that it has in no other context. The presence or absence of this feature in Marx's account in Part I of *Capital* would indicate whether that account refers to capitalist or precapitalist conditions. To determine whether *Capital* begins with reference to capitalism, therefore, the specifically capitalist feature of the commodity has to be identified.

It is possible to illustrate Marx's view that common forms have distinctive features in capitalism by the example of merchants' capital because his distinction between the capitalist and precapitalist versions of this form is fairly apparent. Even if the distinction seems quite obvious once it is presented, there must be some proof that one definition of capital applies to definite historical circumstances. Marx supplies this proof in the argument of Part II of *Capital*, when he first takes up the topic of capital and identifies what turns out to be its specifically capitalist source of profits. This argument, therefore, illustrates a method for identifying features that distinguish capitalist forms from apparently similar non-capitalist forms. It stands to reason that Marx will have identified the specifically capitalist characteristic of the commodity by the same means. From the method, therefore, it ought to be possible to discover what Marx conceives this characteristic to be. Thus, the argument of Part II of *Capital* will be taken as a model of the way Marx distinguishes capitalist from non-capitalist forms in order to discover the feature that distinguishes the capitalist commodity form.

10.2 SPECIFICALLY CAPITALIST CAPITAL

Marx begins Part II of *Capital* with several observations on the relation between money and commodity circulation – the last topics of Part I – and capital, the new topic to be addressed in Part II (Marx, 1977, p. 247). The first of these observations is historical. The 'modern history of capital' Marx says, begins from 'world trade and the world market of the sixteenth century'. Circulation is the 'starting point of capital', therefore, in the sense that it is the 'historical presupposition' from which capital arises. The second observation brings out an entirely different kind of connection between circulation and capital: 'If we disregard the material content of circulation . . . and consider only the economic forms brought into being by this process, we find that its ultimate product is money. This ultimate product of commodity circulation is the first form of appearance of capital'. This remark can only refer to a conceptual sequence since it indicates that 'we' (the readers of *Capital* and Marx) have adopted a definite standpoint towards circulation and justifies that standpoint as our means of access to the nature of capital. It suggests that, by 'our' disregarding of its material content, circulation has been considered in Part I from the standpoint of form; that this standpoint has been adopted in order to develop the concept of money because money, in turn, as the first appearance form of capital, is the means of access to the concept of capital. The third and final observation elaborates on the appearance form relation between money and capital. Money is both the historically first form of capital, confronting landed property as merchants' and usurers' capital, and the first form in which 'all new capital . . . steps out onto . . . the market' in the present day. That all capital starts as money, suggests that capital by its nature must begin as money (a point confirmed by Marx's subsequent derivation of the circuit of capital – his first, provisional definition of capital – from money as capital's first appearance form). Thus, here both history and the everyday behaviour of capital are called upon to illustrate an inherent property of capital.[1]

These observations form a bridge between Parts I and II because they concern the relation between the topics of each part. By the kinds of relation they establish between these topics, they suggest various principles of transition between the two parts. The first, by pointing to a historical relation, suggests that the sequence of topics in the argument of *Capital* is based on historical sequence. On this principle, for example, Marx would have begun with the commodity because commodities and money are historically prior to capital.[2] The second suggests that content, which has been disregarded in Part I, will come into consideration in Part II. This implies that the transition between the two parts is a conceptual transition from form to content, the rationale for which is that the content of economic relations is disclosed by the examination of their form. Finally, the third observation could suggest that the paths of logic and history coincide: if capital must begin as money, money is a necessary condition for capital; in addition to being historically prior to capital, therefore, money is also logically prior to capital.[3] Alternatively, features of the historical development of capital could be cited solely to illustrate a necessary feature of capital and have no bearing whatsoever on the development of the argument of *Capital*. The historical priority of money is one of the observations that establishes the phenomenon that money is the first form of capital. The subsequent derivation of the concept of capital from this phenomenon shows it to be a necessary feature of capital. As a necessary feature, it would embrace both the historical development and the developed form of capital. This suggests that the nature of capital explains its historical development rather than the reverse. Since money is both the 'ultimate product' of circulation and the first form of capital, the historical relation between circulation and capital could have been cited with the same intent. Marx's historical references, therefore, do not necessarily imply that history is the governing principle of his argument. Thus, while this bridge section suggests several principles of transition (showing why there are several conflicting interpretations of *Capital*), it does not establish which of them is the reigning one. This issue remains to be settled by the path of the argument from this point forward.

The first stage of the argument following the bridge section (chapter 4), is devoted to the definition of capital. The definition that results from this argument, which Marx calls the general formula for capital, follows entirely from capital's beginning as money. Because capital begins as money, it follows that the form of circulation of capital must be MCM. This form of circulation provides the first way of distinguishing money as capital from money as money (money in simple circulation, in the circuit, CMC). Accordingly, Marx first defines capital by its form of circulation: money that describes this course is 'already capital according to its determination' (Marx, 1977, p. 248, retranslated). The 'characteristics of the formal distinctions between the two circuits MCM and CMC' in their turn, reveal 'the distinction in content which lurks behind these formal distinctions' (ibid., retranslated). The replacement of one commodity by another of the same value and a different use value in the circuit, CMC, shows that the content of simple circulation is 'the interchange . . . of different materials in which social labor is embodied' for the sake of 'satisfaction of needs' (ibid., p. 250).[4] By contrast, the return of money to its starting point in the circuit MCM shows that capital 'does not owe its content to any qualitative difference between its extremes' (ibid., p. 251). Its content, therefore, must be due 'solely to quantitative changes', i.e. to an increase in value (ibid.). The original circuit of capital, therefore, is modified into the 'complete form', MCM′, which expresses this content. This is Marx's final definition of the general formula for capital: the movement that converts value (or money, which expresses value) into capital is the addition of more value to the value originally advanced (see ibid., p. 252).

Certain characteristics of capital now become evident from its definition. First, because any given sum of money is limited relative to capital's goal – the expansion of value – the movement of capital is inherently endless. Second, because, as capital, value creates more of itself, Marx speaks of value as the subject (active agent) and substance (that which preserves itself through changes in phenomenal form) of capital. It is now possible to see why the circuit of capital must begin and end with money. In money, value has 'an independent form by means of which its identity with itself may be asserted' as it alternates between the forms of money and commodities in the process of its expansion. The circuit of capital, which was originally introduced simply as an observation, is now explained by the nature of capital. This supplies the foundation for the argument's starting point. Lastly, the completed form MCM' is established as general by the demonstration that it applies to all kinds of capital – merchant, industrial and interest-bearing capital.

This movement from the form of capital's circuit to its content is the path Marx indicated in the second observation of the bridge section. The argument thus far, therefore, does not follow historical sequence, i.e. begin with the earliest forms of capital, merchant's and usurer's capital. On the other hand, there is no conclusive evidence that it refers specifically to capitalism; except that one of the kinds of capital Marx mentions, industrial capital, will turn out to be unique to capitalism. In the next chapter, however, Marx takes up the question: 'how is the creation of additional value possible?' This question has different answers in different historical contexts. The answer given, therefore, necessarily refers to one historical context. It is at this point that Marx explicitly states that he is focusing exclusively on the modern form of capital. He describes his account as the 'analysis of the basic form (*Grundform*) of capital' – the form that 'determines the economic organization of modern society' – and shows, at the same time, why this analysis could not have considered the earliest kinds of capital (ibid., p. 266). This means that the specifically capitalist concept of capital cannot be developed by an argument that proceeds along historical lines (see below pp. 277–80). Instead Marx identifies the specifically capitalist source of additional value from the rules that govern the basic form of capital; that is, the rules to which capital must conform in a capitalist context.

In the order in which Marx considers them, these rules are: (i) that the increase in value represented by surplus value must permit an increase for all capitals at the same time, that is, it must be an increase in value for the economic system as a whole rather than a redistribution of value; and (ii) that exchange is governed by value or is exchange of equal values. The first of these rules, as we have seen, is the condition for interaction among capitals. Thus it is a necessary condition for all economic activity to be subject to capital. The stipulation that surplus value formation conform to this rule, therefore, amounts to the assumption that economic activity could be organized and directed exclusively by capital rather than by capital in combination with other organizing principles. This means that the specifically capitalist basic form is just the general formula for capital as a universal principle. The second rule follows from Marx's analysis of circulation in Part I.[5] Marx argues that wage labour is the necessary condition for an increase in value subject to these rules. On this basis, he shows that the kind of increase in value these rules permit (hence also the kind of capital associated with it) is historically specific because it requires the presence of wage labour.

The argument, in brief, is as follows. Marx addresses the first rule in chapter 5 of *Capital*, showing that, whether or not the second rule is observed, the first rule cannot be satisfied either within circulation by itself or entirely apart from circulation. This means that the formation of surplus value requires both circulation and some other domain, yet to be revealed. With this conclusion, Marx turns to the second rule in chapter 6. By excluding those points in the circuit of capital where an increase in value would violate the rule of exchange of equal values (i.e. changes in value accompanying the changes in the form of value MC or CM), Marx shows that an increase in value can only occur in the consumption of the commodity purchased. For this to be possible, there must be a commodity available for sale that creates value when it is consumed. Since (as Marx argues in Part I of *Capital*) value is the labour objectified in commodities, the consumption of this commodity must be 'an objectification of labor' (ibid., p. 270). From this, Marx concludes that the commodity is labour power. On the assumption that the relation involved in the purchase of labour power is defined solely by the implications of commodity exchange, or as Marx says, 'implies no other relations of dependence than those that result from [the] . . . nature' of commodity exchange (ibid., pp. 270–1), Marx concludes that labour power as a commodity is wage labour.[6]

This demonstration that additional value can be created subject to the rules governing the basic form of capital only by the use of wage labour, establishes that wage labour is the necessary condition for surplus value. Since the basic form of capital is capital as a universal principle, wage labour, as the necessary condition for the basic form of capital, must be the universal form of labour. The other domain required for the formation of surplus value turns out to be consumption, which, because of the nature of the commodity labour power, is productive consumption. This means that wage labour is the connecting link between the visible domain of circulation and the 'hidden abode of production' to which Marx will turn in Part III of *Capital* (ibid., p. 279). The creation of surplus value requires both circulation and production because the capacity to work must be purchased as the commodity labour power in circulation, be consumed in production and its products returned to circulation. Finally, the rule of exchange of equal values is observed wherever it applies, i.e. at those points where the process of value creation enters circulation, both in the purchase of labour power and the sale of products.

Wage labour is also the first characteristic in the argument of *Capital* that is unambiguously historically specific. Commodities, exchange, money and even capital are present in precapitalist as well as capitalist conditions; wage labour, as a universal form of labour comparable to the basic form of capital, is present only in capitalism.[7] The proof that wage labour is unique to a definite historical period will consist in the demonstration of the condition necessary for its presence. For the moment, Marx sets this aside. Having established that wage labour is the necessary condition for the creation of surplus value, he proceeds directly to production, on the assumption that wage labour is present.[8] He does remark, however, that since the 'relation [of owners of money and commodities to men possessing nothing but their own labour power] has no basis in natural history, nor does it have a social basis common to all periods of human history' it must be 'the result of a past historical development' (ibid., p. 273).

When Marx does address the necessary condition for the presence of universal wage labour at the end of Volume I of *Capital*, it is, as indicated earlier, a historical development. This is the separation of labour power from the means of production which Marx calls the original accumulation. The original accumulation establishes definite relations to the necessary elements of all production: privately owned labour capacity with no direct connection to the material means of production on one side, and its counterpart, privately owned material means of production, on the other. The demonstration that this relation is the result of a historical development establishes that all production prior to this development could not have been based on this kind of relation to the elements of production. It is, in other words, the proof of Marx's earlier claim that wage labour is neither natural nor common to all periods of history, i.e. that wage labour and its counterpart, capital as the private ownership of the material means of production, are historically specific.

Once universal wage labour is shown to be historically specific by the argument of the original accumulation, it becomes the means for establishing the historical specificity of surplus value. Since surplus value (as defined by the rules that govern the basic form of capital) cannot be created without wage labour and wage labour belongs to a definite historical context, surplus value must belong to the same historical context as wage labour. Thus, the demonstration that wage labour is the necessary condition for the creation of surplus value (Part II of *Capital*), together with the demonstration that wage labour is the result of a historical development (Part VIII of *Capital*), prove that surplus value is uniquely capitalist. Surplus value, in its turn, is the necessary condition for the basic form of capital. By the dependence of the basic form on surplus value, of surplus value on wage labour and of wage labour on the original accumulation, the basic form of capital is shown to be historically specific.

10.3 THE DISTINCTIVE CHARACTERISTIC OF CAPITALISM

In the case of capital, therefore, Marx has presented the specifically capitalist version of capital (the basic form) and proven that it is historically specific by showing its logical dependence on wage labour. From the basic form of capital, it can be seen why all elements of a capitalist system do require wage labour and therefore could be identified by this method. The basic form of capital was defined by the rules that would have to be observed for all economic activity to be organized by capital. By definition, therefore, it is the form capital would have to assume to be the sole organizing principle of an economic system. The demonstration that this form can exist only in the presence of wage labour establishes that such a system is different in kind from all previous economic orders. On this basis capitalism can be distinguished from all precapitalist economic orders as a system in which economic activity can be organized exclusively by capital.[9] All other economic orders, by contrast, would require some organizing principle other than capital, although the form, capital, could be present in conjunction with this other principle. It follows that the characteristics that distinguish capitalist forms are those that result from the absence of any other organizing principle than capital.

Capital, however, is value that realizes the goal of accumulating more value (by Marx's definition of the complete form, see above p. 273). All elements of a capitalist system, therefore, must have the characteristics necessary for value creation to be the exclusive goal of economic activity. (The non-capitalist versions of common forms would lack these characteristics but would have characteristics necessary for the realization of other goals – such as the institution of relations of status or kinship – since in the absence of wage labour, value creation cannot be the exclusive goal of economic activity.) By these characteristics, each capitalist form shows itself to be an element of a pure value system and implies that value must be created. Since wage labour is the necessary condition for the creation of value, all such characteristics ultimately depend on wage labour.

This dependence of all other capitalist economic forms on wage labour is shown by the structure of the argument of *Capital*.[10] From the demonstration that wage labour is necessary, Marx proceeds on the assumption that it is present (see note 8). All forms after wage labour in the argument of *Capital*, therefore, depend on wage labour because Marx assumes wage labour in order to define them. On the other side, all the forms before wage labour depend on it because Marx derives wage labour from them as their necessary condition. It has already been shown, for example, that the basic form of capital requires surplus value which in turn requires wage labour. This sequence of forms, all of which ultimately depend on wage labour, goes back to the beginning of *Capital*. When Marx gets to wage labour in the argument of *Capital*, he points out that the commodity also has a characteristic that requires wage labour. This is universality: 'it is only from this moment [when labour power takes on the form of wage labour] that the commodity form of the products of labour becomes universal' (ibid., p. 274, n.4). The universality of the commodity form fulfils the criterion that has been established for distinguishing capitalist forms. For all economic activity to be devoted to the creation of value, all products would have to be commodities, since the commodity is the only form of product that is exchanged and therefore has value. In other words, the presence of products that are not commodities implies that economic activity has some other goal besides value creation; the absence of any products but commodities implies that value is the exclusive goal. Marx shows this by establishing that the universality of the commodity (and its logical consequences, the universality of money and circulation) requires the basic form of capital and, therefore, wage labour. As will be shown by the explanation of the transition from Part I to Part II, the argument of *Capital* from the commodity to wage labour demonstrates the dependence of all prior forms on wage labour and by this means, proves them to be specifically capitalist. This will establish that *Capital* begins with reference to capitalism.

It has yet to be established before leaving Part II why, as noted earlier, Marx does not include the earliest forms of capital in his account of the basic form. As will be shown next, Marx's explanation for excluding these forms shows why the argument of *Capital* could not have begun either with precapitalist forms or with common characteristics by themselves (i.e. apart from a specifically capitalist form which has other characteristics besides those it shares with precapitalist forms). The elimination of these alternatives complements the demonstration that the commodity, as considered in Part I, is specifically capitalist.

10.4 AN ALTERNATIVE ARGUMENT BASED ON HISTORICAL SEQUENCE

The opening paragraphs of Part II indicate the course the argument would have taken had it been based on historical sequence. If the reference to the historical relation between circulation and capital is meant to indicate that circulation is considered before capital because it is historically prior to capital, the argument would proceed on this principle from circulation to the earliest forms of capital (identified in this passage as merchants' and usurers' capital), and from these to the later form, industrial capital. The reasons Marx gives for excluding the earliest forms of capital show why the argument of *Capital* could not proceed historically at this or any other point.

Both merchants' and usurers' capital, as Marx points out, run their course without leaving the sphere of circulation (see ibid., p. 266). A theory that took these forms as the model of capital, therefore, would have to attribute surplus value to circulation. From his demonstration that 'circulation creates no value' (ibid.), Marx argues that attributing surplus value to circulation has two other consequences: (i) that an increase in the total amount of value would have to be held to be impossible, so that surplus value would be conceived as the result of a redistribution of value; and (ii) that this redistribution would be conceived to result from unequal exchange.

This account has its shortcomings as an explanation of capital surplus value. It rules out the possibility of the kind of surplus value required for interaction among capitals and presents a notion of value while maintaining at the same time that exchange violates the law of value. If these shortcomings were not sufficiently apparent to begin with, they need not become apparent in the attempt to extend this account to industrial capital. By reversing Marx's ranking of the various kinds of capital, for example, industrial capital (rather than merchants' and usurers' capital) could be conceived as the derivative form and its profits explained as a share of the surplus value extracted from circulation by merchants' capital.

From this point forward the argument of *Capital* would be transformed in quite significant ways. With profits explained by unequal exchange and value creation ruled out, the need for wage labour cannot be established. Without wage labour, there is no way of establishing a connection between circulation and production, and therefore that production of a definite kind is required by circulation. This rupture between production and circulation leaves two possibilities, both of which are represented in economic theory before (and after) Marx: either (i) all economic relations, including relations of production, will be conceived as if they were relations of circulation, since circulation is what is immediately visible (as in vulgar theory, see e.g. Marx, 1973, pp. 249–50), or (ii) production and circulation will be conceived to be completely unrelated (as in J. S. Mill's scheme, where production is conceived to be governed entirely by natural laws and circulation – because it depends on a historically form of appropriation, private property – is conceived to be socially determined, see ibid., p. 87).

This alternative line of argument shows why the sequence of the argument of *Capital* could not have been historical. It shows, first, that merchants' and usurers' capital do not require wage labour. This explains why they can exist without it; that is, why they can be precapitalist forms of capital. It also explains why the argument that begins with them cannot establish the necessity for wage labour. As the development of this argument illustrates, forms that do not require wage labour imply other forms that do not require wage labour. The definitions that follow from merchants' and usurers' capital, therefore, are also independent of wage labour. From the perspective of Marx's theory, these definitions can be classified into two groups. The forms that are common to precapitalist and capitalist society (i.e. forms that can exist without wage labour but whose capitalist version requires wage labour, such as capital and profits) will be defined in their precapitalist version. The forms that are unique to capitalism (i.e. forms that cannot exist without wage labour, such as production based on wage labour) will be completely misconceived. They will lack the characteristics necessary to be elements of a system that creates value but will not be given determinacy by any other principle, since no other principle follows from the analysis of capital.[11] There is no logical connection, however, between forms that do not require wage labour and forms that do.

The idea that theory would arrive at an account of capitalism simply by following the course of history, therefore, must rest on the presumption that the observation of capitalist forms will override the logical implications of precapitalist forms. This amounts to the hope that capitalist forms will announce themselves as obviously different in kind from precapitalist forms. The difference between capitalist and precapitalist forms proves to be much more difficult to recognize than this view implies and to be just as much a problem with forms that are unique to capitalism as with common forms. Capitalist and precapitalist capital, for example, resemble each other to the extent that both conform to the general formula for capital. The inappropriateness of the precapitalist concept of capital to capitalist capital does not become obvious simply from the observation of industrial capital. The distinguishing features of the basic form of capital are consequences of the universality of capital. One of these consequences is that if capital is universal, production must be subject to capital. Industrial capital, like the basic form of capital, requires production. The direction of production by capital, however, which occurs with all industrial capital, does not necessarily imply the basic form or the universality of capital (i.e. some production could be subject to capital).

Even if capitalist forms could be recognized easily (and if they could be, this second problem would be more obvious), it remains the case that there is no reason for a theory of capitalism to include an account of precapitalist forms. For example, the account of capital that is modelled on merchants' and usurers' capital is simply irrelevant to Marx's account of capitalist capital. A theory that began with the historically earlier forms would have to discard the account that follows from them and begin again to account for capitalist capital. This being the case, it might as well have started with specifically capitalist capital in the first place.

The same would be true of a theory that began with characteristics common to precapitalist and capitalist society. The reason that precapitalist and capitalist forms are different (and the analysis of one irrelevant to the other) is that they belong to social orders that are organized by different principles; precapitalist social orders are organized by some principle other than value, capitalist society is the only social order that creates value and is therefore the only social order that can be organized exclusively by value. The manifestation of this difference, therefore, is that all precapitalist forms do not and all capitalist forms do require wage labour, which, according to Marx, is the ultimate source of value creation. Common characteristics manifest their difference from capitalist forms in the same way and the analysis of these characteristics by themselves is irrelevant to the theory of capitalism for the same reason. Characteristics common to capitalist and precapitalist society do not require wage labour any more than precapitalist forms, since if these characteristics can be present in precapitalist society they cannot require wage labour. The analysis of such characteristics, therefore, cannot lead to the demonstration of the necessity for wage labour or to definitions of forms that depend on it.[12]

Both the simple and general commodity production interpretations of *Capital*, therefore, are open to the objection that, if capitalism is a distinct form of social organization, as Marx maintains, nothing is to be gained towards the understanding of capitalism from the analysis either of precapitalist forms or of common characteristics. The general commodity production interpretation is open to the additional objection of inconsistency. It claims that *Capital* begins with common characteristics and proceeds logically from these to specifically capitalist forms. There is no logical connection between common characteristics and capitalist forms, however, and therefore no way of proceeding logically from one to the other.

10.5 THE SEQUENCE OF THE ARGUMENT OF PART II: AN EXAMPLE OF AN APPEARANCE FORM TRANSITION

What has been shown about the method of *Capital* may be summarized by re-evaluating the bridge section from the standpoint of Part II as a whole. Marx's references to the historical relations between circulation and capital and between money and capital are compatible with the idea that the argument proceeds historically and therefore, on a first reading, seem to justify it. If this idea were manifestly inconsistent with the text, it would never have been proposed. On the other hand, however, it is conclusively refuted by Marx's exclusion of merchants' and usurers' capital. The principle illustrated by the exclusion of these forms is that all but specifically capitalist forms are irrelevant to the theory of capitalism. It follows that the argument would have been set on the wrong course had forms that are not specifically capitalist been taken into account. This shows that historical sequence neither determines the course of the argument nor coincides with the principle that does.

Apart from their historical relation, the only other relation ascribed to money and capital is that money is the first appearance form of capital. The elimination of history as a principle of sequence shows that the transition from money to capital must be based exclusively on their appearance form relation. From this case, therefore, the general outlines of an argument sequence based on a relation of this sort can be established.

The sequence starts with something that is immediately apparent, that is, with a phenomenon; in this instance, that money is the first form of capital. The object of the first phase of the argument is to establish what the phenomenon expresses. This is accomplished by working out the logical implications of the starting phenomenon, as, for example, the argument of chapter 4 establishes the general formula for capital by showing that it is logically implied by the phenomenon that capital begins as money. In the second phase, the argument returns to the starting phenomenon, presenting it as the result of what it expresses, as, e.g. once the general formula for capital is established, Marx shows why capital must begin as money (see p. 273). In this return, the starting phenomenon is revised to include the features that have been discovered; in this case, MCM is revised into MCM'.[13] The function of the historical references can now be identified relative to the overall form of the argument. Marx's observations that circulation precedes capital historically and that monetary wealth is the historically first form of capital introduce the phenomenon from which the transition to the general formula for capital begins.

The transition from money to capital is the only transition of its kind that both begins and ends in Part II of *Capital*. Thus it is the only illustration Part II offers of this form of argument in its entirety and, by sheer good luck, happens to be among the simplest and clearest illustrations of the form. From the model this case provides, the signs of the same form of argument can be recognized in other cases. In particular, Marx speaks of circulation as a 'surface' in contrast to production as a 'hidden abode' (Marx, 1977, p. 279). This together with the points established in Part II, first, that circulation requires something other than itself, and second, that this other something is wage labour used in production, suggest that circulation is the appearance form of capitalist production. If this is true, the appearance form relation between circulation and production would provide the basis for an argument of the same form as the transition from money to capital and back. It would follow also that Marx begins with the commodity form because this form implies circulation which, in turn, is the phenomenon that provides access to the nature of capitalist production. Since specifically capitalist forms cannot be derived from forms that are not specifically capitalist and the concept of production that Marx begins to define in Part III of *Capital* must be specifically capitalist because it involves the use of wage labour, the starting phenomenon in this transition would have to be specifically capitalist circulation.

10.6 THE SPECIFICALLY CAPITALIST COMMODITY

Following the same procedure with the commodity as with capital, Marx assumes the commodity in its specifically capitalist form (just as capital was assumed in its basic form) and demonstrates that this form is specifically capitalist by showing that it depends on the presence of wage labour. He is not in a position to prove what the specifically capitalist characteristic of the commodity is, however, until the argument of *Capital* reaches wage labour. At this point, as already noted, Marx states that the commodity does not become the universal form of products until labour takes the form of wage labour. This means that capitalism is the only economic order in which all products could be commodities (and would be commodities in capitalism in its pure form). By contrast, commodities could be present in non-capitalist societies but, if they were, there would have to be other forms of products as well.

The difference between some and all products being commodities, being only a difference in extent, does not immediately seem to translate into a difference in kind that would distinguish the commodity in capitalism from the commodity in any other context. The difference between capitalist and precapitalist capital, however, also first appears as a difference in extent (the basic form of capital being the general formula for capital as universal) and does develop into a difference in kind. The same is true in the case of the commodity. The universality of the commodity form has certain implications which do not follow simply from some commodities. It will be shown, first, that Marx draws implications in Part I of *Capital* which depend on the universality of the commodity form. This will establish that the commodity is assumed to be universal from the beginning of *Capital*. It will then be shown that the universality of the commodity form presupposes the basic form of capital, and therefore wage labour. This will establish that the universality of the commodity form is specifically capitalist.

The Analysis and Universality of the Commodity Form

Marx begins *Capital* by observing that, where the capitalist mode of production dominates, 'wealth . . . appears as an immense collection of commodities' (ibid., p. 125). This rather guarded statement commits Marx neither exclusively to capitalism nor exclusively to the commodity form. As the argument develops, however, Marx shows that the commodity form implies a definite structure of commodity relations (rather than just a 'collection' of commodities) and that this structure, which Marx calls the commodity world, is both uniform and unified. Further, he takes the characteristics of commodities within this world to define the characteristics of economic activity, or social labour. It will be shown here that the definition of social labour solely by the implications of the commodity form rests on the assumption that the commodity form is universal. Since the characteristics of social labour are derived from the characteristics of commodities within the commodity world, the first step is to show the structure of the commodity world.

The commodity world: exchange value and value

The characteristics of the commodity world emerge from Marx's examination of exchange value because exchange value is the relation of commodities. There are two accounts of exchange value in chapter 1. In the first, value is derived from the phenomenon of exchange value. In the second, the section on the form of value, the phenomenon exchange value is reconstructed from value. From the model provided by the transition from money to the general formula for capital, these two accounts can be recognized as the two phases of an argument based on an appearance form relation. Since they together form one argument, they will be considered together here.[14]

The derivation of value from exchange value begins with the observation of the simplest kind of exchange relation (just as the concept of capital was derived from the observation that capital always begins as money). As Marx says, this is the way exchange value first appears (see ibid. p. 126) or is exchange value as a pre-theoretical phenomenon. The introduction of more complex kinds of exchange relations brings out additional features of exchange value until exchange value appears distinct from value.

Exchange value first appears in: (1) *the relation of any one commodity to a second commodity of a different kind* (i.e. a commodity with a different use value). In this exchange relation, the exchange value of a given quantity of one commodity appears as the quantity of a second commodity that is equal to the quantity of the first in exchange. This relation brings out exchange value's character as a relation of commodities, but also confines its character to their relation, and so precludes the possibility that commodities have intrinsic value.

Marx's observation that any given commodity is exchangeable for many (implicitly all) other commodities, introduces exchange relation: (2) *the relation of any one commodity to every other commodity in turn*. The exchange value of a given quantity of one commodity now appears as the set of quantities of all other commodities that are equal in exchange to the quantity of the first commodity. The multiplicity of the first commodity's exchange values shows the homogeneity of commodities. Since the exchange values of the first commodity are all equal in exchange to the given quantity of the first commodity, they must all be equal to each other (they are 'replaceable by each other or equally large exchange values' ibid., p. 127). Since they are all equal to each other, something remains the same in all the relations between the first commodity and every other commodity. This shows, first, that the exchange value of a commodity does not depend on that commodity's relation to another commodity (i.e. is not purely relative) and second, that the exchange relations between one commodity and every other imply some property common to all commodities (hence that commodities are homogeneous in terms of this property). Since exchange relations imply a common property of commodities, it follows that exchange value is distinct from value: exchange value is the relation in which the common property, value, appears or the 'appearance form of a content distinct from it' (ibid.).

Having established that value is distinct from exchange value, Marx leaves value as an abstraction which he makes from exchange relation (2). It should be noted, however, that although value may be inferred from this relation, the relation itself does not present commodities as instances of their common property, hence is not the relation of commodities to each other as values. To be presented as instances of their common property, for example, commodities would have to be presented as different quantities of that property. This means that the values of different commodities would have to be comparable in quantitative terms. For the values of different commodities to be quantitatively comparable, they would all have to be measured in the same unit. Since value can only appear in the relation of commodities, if the values of all commodities are to be measured in the same unit, one commodity would have to be set aside to express the values of all others. Thus the exchange relation necessary to present commodities as values is: (3) *the relation of all commodities but one to the remaining one other commodity*. The exchange values of definite quantities of all commodities but one would appear as different quantities of one and the same commodity, therefore as different magnitudes of the same property. By representing commodities to be related to values, Marx tacitly assumes relation (3). Thus the derivation of value implies, but does not show, one definite structure of commodity relations. This structure is made explicit in the second account.

Reversing directions, exchange value can be derived from value by the terms of its relation to value as value's appearance form. This is simply the converse of the original derivation of value from exchange value. Originally value appeared through the phenomenon of exchange value or an exchange relation of commodities. It follows that exchange value must be that phenomenon which has the capacity to make the nature of value manifest. With value given, therefore, exchange value is defined by the requirement that exchange value, as value's appearance form, must express value.

The exchange relations considered earlier in the derivation of value are all possible candidates for exchange value since value appeared from them in the first place. These are now reconsidered as possible (appearance) forms of value (and therefore labelled *provisionally* as forms of value) which means that their capacity to express value is evaluated.[15] From this standpoint, any aspect of value that a form cannot express is a defect of that form as a form of value. Once the defect of a given form is identified, it can be corrected to make the next form a more adequate expression of value. The process of correcting defects ultimately leads to a form that has no defects or brings out all aspects of value. This form is, by definition, the appearance form of value and therefore exchange value. The process by which Marx arrives at this form may be summarized as follows:

Form (1) relation of any one commodity to a second commodity of a different kind: expresses relation (therefore also poles of a relation and since the relation is being considered as an expression of value, the function of each pole in the expression of value can be defined).
Defect: does not express a commodity's 'qualitative equality with all other commodities' (ibid., p. 154). As a result of this defect, this relation presents value as if the value of a commodity arises from its relations to other commodities (see ibid., p. 149) – which is the view held by those who consider this form to be exchange value (see ibid., 153). 'Our analysis [i.e. the derivation of value] has shown' however 'that the form of value [or relation of commodities] . . . arises from the nature of commodity-value' (ibid., p. 152).

This defect is corrected if the form is expanded from one to all possible relations of this kind, yielding:

Form (2) the relation of any commodity to every other commodity in turn: expresses the qualitative equality (or homogeneity) of all commodities as values because it brings each commodity into relation with 'the whole world of commodities' (ibid., p. 155). Therefore, shows that commodity relations are based on the values of commodities (see ibid., p. 156).
Defect: does not give value a 'single unified form of appearance' (ibid., p. 157), therefore does not present commodities as different quantities of the same content.

This defect is corrected if the relation of one to every other one is reversed yielding:

Form (3) the relation of all commodities but one to the one remaining commodity: expresses the quantitative comparability of commodities as values because the values of all commodities but one are presented in terms of one and the same commodity (i.e. in terms of the same unit). On one side of this relation, all commodities but one differ only in magnitude and are therefore presented as magnitudes of the same content. On the other side, the one remaining commodity stands for this content and shows it to be one property common to all commodities.
Defect: lacks social validity.

Form (4) associates the one remaining commodity in form (3) with a specific kind of commodity by custom or law: makes one commodity the 'socially recognized equivalent form' (ibid., 180) so that all economic agents can bring the commodities they own into relation as values by relating them to the same money commodity. This is the aspect of the appearance of value that is determined by social stipulation.

In the derivation of value, Marx's deduction that 'the exchange values of a particular commodity express something equal' (ibid., 127) took the place of form (3) and form (4) did not come into consideration because exchange value seems at first to be only a relation among commodities and to have nothing to do with the members of society. Apart from these differences, since the forms of value are just other names for the original exchange relations, each one brings out the same features as before. The sequence of forms is also the same but, since the content which the forms are supposed to express is already defined (i.e. value is established by the first analysis), the logic behind the sequence becomes apparent. The forms are arranged so that each one brings out a single aspect of value which the subsequent forms continue to express and each new form brings out an additional aspect of value which the previous forms failed to express. Thus the examination of inadequate forms (i.e. forms that are not exchange value) is a device for considering each of the constituent aspects of value separately so that they can be made explicit and the process of correcting defects, a device for bringing these aspects together so that value is conceived as their unity.[16] In retrospect, the same can be seen to be true in the derivation of value, except that there, value is originally and to a large extent remains an implication drawn by the analyst rather than a content that exchange value expresses.

This reveals the principal difference between the two accounts. All the characteristics brought out by 'our analysis' in the first account are transformed, in the second account, into properties of commodities in their relations to each other (ibid., p. 143, see also p. 141). This process concludes with the twin results of the universal form of value (form 3 or 4): (i) that value, which was previously only an abstraction, assumes a material shape as the money commodity,[17] and (ii) that other commodities are presented as different quantities of value by their relation to money rather than by 'our' abstraction from their differences. Marx must have had this structure of commodity relations in mind from the beginning; by   his own account, no form but the universal form of value expresses value, therefore value could not have been derived from any other form. The universal form of value must be what Marx means by the commodity world. Only in the second account, however, does he show what this structure is or, in other words, identify exchange value explicitly as one kind of relation.

The identification of exchange value as the universal form of value shows the commodity world to be homogeneous (because each commodity is equivalent to every other commodity) and unified (because all ordinary commodities relate to the same money commodity). The homogeneity and unity of the commodity world are logical consequences of the definition of the commodity (the structure of the commodity world, therefore, is directly implied by the commodity form). Since the commodity is a product that is exchanged (i.e. converted into money), it is tautologically true that all commodities are homogeneous and linked by exchange. Similarly, money is by definition the universal equivalent in the sense that it is the equivalent for all products that assume the commodity form. If this were all Marx claimed to show by his analysis of the commodity form, that analysis, being completely tautological, would apply to all circumstances where commodities are present, whether the commodity form were universal or not.

The commodity world, congealed labour and the organization of labour activity

Marx does not confine himself to these tautological meanings of money and the commodity world, however. Before he defines the universal equivalent explicitly, he draws two connections between commodity relations and labour. He argues, first, that the labour that has been spent to produce commodities (or, as Marx calls it, congealed labour) is the substance of commodity values and the basis of the exchange relation among commodities. He argues, second, that commodity production entails a definite organization of labour activity; products become commodities, Marx maintains, only on the condition that they are 'products of mutually independent acts of labour performed in isolation' (ibid., p. 132).[18]

The implication of the first connection is that congealed labour, as the substance of value, has the same characteristics as commodities in their relation money. Accordingly, Marx presents the labour congealed in commodities as homogeneous, because it is equated by the equation of commodities, and unified into 'one . . . mass of human labour power' (ibid., p. 129) by the relation of all ordinary commodities to money. The implication of the second connection is that the labour activities that produce commodities are related only indirectly by the exchange relation of their products (see e.g. ibid., p. 165). The exchange value relation of commodities, therefore, is the means by which commodity producing labour activities are associated. To put the two together, congealed labour becomes an objective property of products (or products become commodities) because the relation of products is the only connection among labour activities.

On the other side of the exchange value relation, therefore, money, as the equivalent for all commodities, has the properties that follow from these connections between commodity relations and labour. It follows from the first, that money is the 'appearance form' or 'visible incarnation' of the labour congealed in commodities. Because different kinds of commodities are equated with money, money presents the labour congealed in commodities as 'undifferentiated labour'. It follows from the second connection that the relation of all commodities to money links all commodity producing labour activities, i.e. that money integrates the private and independent labour activities of commodity producers.

When Marx does define money, therefore, he attributes these properties to it. He modifies them, however, by incorporating an additional assumption. He presents money (i) as the expression of congealed labour *per se* ('the visible incarnation . . . of all human labour', alternatively, the 'appearance form of undifferentiated human labour', ibid., p. 159) and (ii) as the means of integrating all labour activities into one network of social labour (once some commodity becomes the 'incarnation of all human labour . . . men are . . . related to each other in their social process of production in a purely atomistic way, ibid., 187). This concept of money does not follow tautologically from the definition of the commodity form. For money to be the appearance form of undifferentiated human labour, the commodity form must be universal. Similarly, relations in production can be 'purely atomistic' only if all labour activities are linked indirectly by the relation of products, that is, only if all labour is devoted to producing commodities.[19] The properties Marx attributes to money, therefore, depend on the assumption that the commodity form is universal. Although this assumption is more evident in Marx's account of money than in his earlier arguments, it has, in fact, been made all along.

For example, it underlies Marx's claim that commodities as values 'are merely congealed quantities of homogeneous human labour' (ibid., p. 128). While commodities are homogeneous by definition, congealed labour is homogeneous only if all products are equated in exchange, i.e. only if all products are commodities. Limited exchange, or a limitation in the extent of the commodity form, would not equate congealed labour itself, but only some particular branch of labour. The exclusion of any products from exchange excludes some congealed labour from equalization, so that congealed labour does not transcend the heterogeneity of products. For human labour without qualification to be equated by exchange, therefore, every product must, in principle, be equal to (i.e. exchangeable for) every other product. In other words, the homogeneity of labour means nothing if it does not refer to the total labour of society, and if it is to refer to the total labour of society, the commodity form must be universal.

Moreover, as will be shown next, Marx intends homogeneity in this sense. In the argument on socially necessary labour time, Marx attributes all the characteristics of commodities as values (i.e. unity, quantitative comparability, homogeneity) to congealed labour. As in the argument on the form of value, homogeneity and quantitative comparability are presented as consequences of unity. Since Marx conceives congealed labour to be homogeneous because it is unified by the relation of all commodities to money, he must mean homogeneity to encompass all labour.

Since the argument on socially necessary labour time can prove rather elusive, we will begin with Marx's simplest and clearest conclusion. This is that any given commodity contains the average amount of labour required to produce commodities of its kind. The justification Marx presents for this conclusion is that each unit of congealed labour power 'is the same as any other' (ibid., p. 129). The argument, in other words, is that once labour has been spent on commodities, it counts as labour that has had the same effect in the same amount of time in the production of any product. Then, on the grounds that all commodities (of the same or of different kinds) count as products of 'equal human labour' (ibid.), Marx argues that all units of the same kind of commodity contain the same amount of labour, i.e. the average amount of labour required for that kind of commodity. In turn, Marx's justification for maintaining that all units of congealed labour are equal is that 'the total labour power of society . . . counts as one homogeneous mass of human power' (ibid.). Lastly, the total labour power of society counts as one homogeneous mass because this is the way it is 'manifested in the values of the commodity world' (ibid.). The expression of the values of all commodities in one commodity (form 3) is here presented as the manifestation of all congealed labour – the total labour power of society – as one. This unity of congealed labour is the basis Marx presents for the quantitative equality and homogeneity of all units of congealed labour (just as, in the argument on the form of value, Marx shows that the relation of all commodities to money presents commodity values as quantitatively comparable and qualitatively homogeneous). The unity of congealed labour, then, is the ultimate basis for Marx's case that value magnitude is determined by socially necessary labour time. For all congealed labour to be unified by the relation of commodities to money, all products must be commodities.

As both the arguments on money and socially necessary labour time show, Marx is taking the characteristics of labour that are implied by the commodity form (the unity, quantitative equality and homogeneity of congealed labour and the purely atomistic character of labour activity) to be all-encompassing characteristics of social labour, i.e. of the total labour of society. By this, he is tacitly equating commodity producing labour with all labour activity or assuming the universality of the commodity form.

If the commodity form were limited, for example, and the total social product composed of some other kind of product besides commodities, social labour (in the sense of labour as a whole) would have to have other characteristics besides those that are implied by the commodity form. By Marx's argument that labour is the substance of value, the labour congealed in commodities would be homogeneous because commodities are equated by exchange. Social labour could not be homogeneous, however, because the total social product includes products that are not commodities, and these are not exchanged either with each other or with commodities. Similarly, labour activities devoted to commodities could be independent of each other but labour activity devoted to the other kind of product would have to be directly associated in some way. Moreover, on the assumption that the commodity and non-commodity producing sectors form one network of social labour (otherwise there would not be one social product composed of commodities and some other kind of product but two social products, one composed entirely of commodities, the other, of some other kind of product), the commodity producing sector as a whole would have to be integrated with the non-commodity producing sector by some principle of direct association, since the two are not linked by exchange. Labour activity as a whole, therefore, could not be private and independent.

In summary, Marx's derivation of the characteristics of social labour from the commodity form presupposes the universality of the commodity form. Because Marx assumes the commodity form to be universal, his account of social labour (and the conclusions he draws from it, e.g. with respect to money) does not follow tautologically from the definition of the commodity and does not apply to all circumstances in which commodities are present. The reason that social labour is defined solely by the implications of the commodity form is that the argument is an analysis of this form. As such, it can consider only what the commodity implies.

The reason Marx gives for analyzing the commodity, in turn, is that, as he observes in the first sentence of *Capital*, the wealth of capitalist societies 'appears as an immense collection of commodities' (ibid., p. 125). The analysis of the commodity is informed by the observation that the commodity is the dominant (i.e. virtually universal) form of wealth. That analysis, therefore, presupposes the commodity's dominance. By assuming the commodity to be universal, Marx has simply expressed the commodity's dominance in its pure form.

The universality of the commodity form, as already shown, implies that the characteristics of social labour follow exclusively from the commodity form. In the same way, it implies that the characteristics of 'social material interchange' (ibid., p. 198, or the distribution of the social product) follow exclusively from this form. The kind of material interchange implied by the commodity form is exchange. As Marx shows in chapter 2 of *Capital*, in exchange, the members of society relate to each other as individuals by means of their relation to commodities as their private property. Since it has already been shown that Marx is assuming the commodity form to be universal, his account of exchange will be considered very briefly, noting only those features of it that are presupposed in the argument of Part II of *Capital*.

First, exchange 'transfers commodities from hands in which they are non-use values to hands in which they are use values' (ibid., p. 198), hence realizes the goal of satisfying needs. This means also that commodities do not satisfy needs until after they are exchanged. The members of society must participate in exchange, therefore, in order to satisfy their needs by commodities. Second, where the commodity is the universal form of product, all economic needs are satisfied by commodities.[20] This makes exchange the necessary means of satisfying needs or makes participation in exchange a prerequisite for satisfying needs. Since exchange is a prerequisite for satisfying needs, all members of society must participate in exchange. It follows that all members of society must be commodity owners and relate to each other as individuals. In short, the universality of the commodity form implies that all members of society have the characteristics required for the material interchange of commodities, just as it implies that all labour has the characteristics of commodity producing labour.

The demonstration, to be presented next, that universal circulation presupposes the basic form of capital, will identify capitalist production as the second sphere of interaction that is necessary for this first one. By this demonstration, the individuals in simple circulation are further defined as wage labourers and capitalists in production and private and independent labour activity is further defined as the activity of wage labourers under the direction of capital.

10.7 THE BASIC FORM OF CAPITAL AS THE NECESSARY CONDITION FOR UNIVERSAL CIRCULATION

In Part I of *Capital* Marx shows that the universal commodity form implies value, money and universal circulation as the form of social material interchange. In Part II, he shows that the basic form of capital implies surplus value and wage labour. The connecting link between these two logical sequences is the transition from universal simple circulation to capital.

Marx presents two other versions of this transition in the *Grundrisse* and in the *Urtext*. In these versions, Marx presents the transition. as a logical progression and explains its basis: 'The general concept of capital can be derived from the consideration of simple circulation because, within the bourgeois mode of production, simple circulation itself exists only as the presupposition of capital and presupposing capital' (Marx, 1974, p. 945).[21] In a similar account, which brings out another aspect of simple circulation, Marx states that 'simple circulation is an abstract sphere of the whole bourgeois production process, which proves by its own determinations that it is the mere appearance form of a deeper process lying behind it . . . which process both results from it and produces it' (ibid., pp. 922–3). The transition from simple circulation to capital based on this account would involve the demonstration, first, that simple circulation is a 'mere appearance form', which is supposed to become evident from the consideration of simple circulation itself (just as exchange value was shown to be an appearance form by its analysis) and, second, that simple circulation is the appearance form of capital, which would follow from the demonstration that simple circulation presupposes capital or that capital is the necessary condition for simple circulation.

Marx does not present this explanation in *Capital*, however, and there are grounds for thinking that it does not apply to the argument of *Capital*. First, Marx opens Part II of *Capital* by establishing the phenomenon that capital begins as money. Because this phenomenon is foreign to simple circulation, the topic of Part I, it seems to mark a break with the argument before it and hence a new beginning. Marx does point to a link between this phenomenon and simple circulation: money, which was shown in Part I to be the product of simple circulation, is considered in Part II as the first form of capital, and, although this is not apparent from the beginning of Part II, capital will turn out to be money's (or value's) relation to itself. This link, however, does not seem to provide the basis for a logical progression from circulation to capital, i.e. does not seem to establish that capital must be present because money and universal circulation are present. The circuits MCM and CMC then seem to coexist side by side, coincidentally; which is also suggested at times by Marx's language: 'alongside this form [CMC], we find another form that is quite distinct from the first . . . MCM' (Marx, 1977, p. 248). Second, there is no reason to think that the transition is logical unless it involves specifically capitalist forms. If universal circulation is specifically capitalist, it should imply specifically capitalist capital because both are elements of the same economic system. Universal circulation is proven to be specifically capitalist, however, by the demonstration that it presupposes specifically capitalist capital (and ultimately, wage labour), i.e. by the logical character of the argument. In other words, to see the logical character of the argument it must be recognized that the forms in the argument are specifically capitalist and to see that the forms are specifically capitalist it must be recognized that the argument is logical. To break out of this circle, universal circulation may be assumed, provisionally, to be specifically capitalist on the strength of Marx's claim that the universality of the commodity form requires wage labour. These problems certainly obscure the logical basis of the transition but they do not rule out the explanation Marx gives in the *Urtext*.

Although capital is introduced by a new phenomenon, simple circulation is still under consideration in the contrast between CMC and MCM. The transition really occurs only by means of this contrast rather than at the beginning of Part II. The demonstration that capital is the necessary condition for simple circulation (i.e. the explanation given in the *Urtext*) is implicit in the conclusions drawn from this contrast. The characteristics of the CMC circuit show that simple circulation cannot sustain itself. When the commodity form is universal (as assumed in Part I), however, simple circulation must be an ongoing process or established sphere of interaction. Since simple circulation cannot sustain itself but is sustained, it must be sustained by some other process (this is what Marx means by saying that simple circulation proves by its own determinations that it is a mere appearance form). The characteristics of the process that is required to sustain simple circulation prove to be the characteristics of the MCM' circuit.

As shown above (p. 272), Marx first contrasts the forms of the two circuits and from the difference in their form derives the difference in their content or goal. Under each rubric, CMC is shown to lack and MCM' to possess, some characteristic necessary for the renewal of simple circulation. The demonstration that capital is the necessary condition for simple circulation need not have taken the form of a contrast, however, and since it is only for the sake of this contrast that the concept of capital is introduced by a new phenomenon, capital need not have been introduced this way. The deficiencies of CMC as a self-renewing process could have been identified from the consideration of CMC by itself. These deficiencies could have shown the characteristics that would be required of the process that does support simple circulation. From these character-istics, this process could be shown to be MCM'. Transformed into a sequence from CMC to MCM', the argument is more evidently a logical progression. Since the object here is to bring out the logical basis of the transition, the conclusions Marx draws from the contrast will be rearranged into a sequence.[22]

On the formal side, CMC lacks the character of a continuous process because the end of one circuit is not immediately the beginning of another. The end and the beginning of each circuit are both commodities but because they are necessar-ily different commodities there is no 'identity of the real point of departure and the point of return' (Marx, 1973, p. 261). Instead each circuit is finite because it has a definite starting point and a definite end: 'The whole process begins when money is received in return for commodities, and comes to an end when money is given up in return for commodities' (Marx, 1977, p. 249). Moreover, each circuit involves a separate nexus of transactions because the commodity that ends one circuit does not begin a new circuit but leaves circulation. Simple circulation, therefore, is the sum of finite and separate circuits rather than a continuous movement.[23]

To be self-renewing, circulation would have to be continuous. Since simple circulation is not itself continuous, but is present on a continuous basis, it must be sustained by some other process. To be capable of sustaining simple circulation, this other process must involve the same components as simple circulation (i.e. the forms, money and commodities, the relations between these forms, purchase and sale, and the dramatis personae, buyers and sellers, see ibid., pp. 248–9) but must arrange these components into the form of a continuous movement. The inversion of sale and purchase into purchase and sale yields the continuous process MCM: 'in buying in order to sell . . . the end and the beginning are the same, money or exchange-value, and this very fact makes the movement an endless one' (ibid., p. 252, see also p. 253). On the formal side, therefore, MCM fulfils a condition for self-renewal which CMC lacks. Since continuity is a necessary rather than a sufficient condition for self-renewal, MCM could be the process that supports CMC. This is confirmed by the consideration of the content of CMC.

With regard to its content, CMC lacks the capacity to restore the forms of simple circulation (i.e. commodities) to circulation because the goal of simple circulation does not require these forms. The goal of simple circulation is to satisfy needs (see above p. 290, and ibid., p. 250). Where the commodity form is universal, therefore, it is the renewal of need that is responsible for the repetition of the CMC circuit (see ibid., p. 252).

Need satisfaction, however, is a goal that 'lies outside circulation' (ibid., p. 253) or is 'irrelevant' to the forms of circulation (see e.g. Marx, 1973, pp. 251, 269). Need satisfaction, in other words, has nothing to do with the form of products as commodities. The commodity satisfies needs not by virtue of its form as a commodity (i.e. not by virtue of being a product that has value) but by virtue of its use value (i.e. simply by virtue of being a product). The proof of this is that the commodity only satisfies needs once it 'falls out of circulation' (Marx, 1977, p. 250) and loses 'its quality as form' (Marx, 1973, p. 263), i.e. is no longer a commodity.

That commodities satisfy needs by virtue of their use value, or the characteristic they share with all other kinds of products, shows that need satisfaction is a goal common to all kinds of products. Each different kind of product is associated with a different process of material interchange or satisfies needs in a different way. The process of material interchange, therefore, always has a definite form (just as 'there is no production in general' (ibid., p. 86), there is no need satisfaction in general). As a common goal, however, need satisfaction does not determine the specific manner in which needs are satisfied by any one kind of product, i.e. does not determine the specific form of the process of material interchange. While universal circulation has yet to be shown to be specifically capitalist, it can be recognized as a specific form of material interchange because it involves commodities, a specific form of product, and money, a specific form of relation of products. The ongoing nature of need insures the repetitions of CMC subject to the condition that circulation is the necessary means of satisfying needs, i.e. on the condition that the commodity form is universal. The goal of satisfying needs, however, does not explain why products take the form of commodities. Because the goal of satisfying needs can be realized by any form of product, products do not take the form of commodities, hence, material interchange does not take the form of circulation, for the sake of realizing this goal. The continuous presence of circulation, therefore, cannot be attributed to need satisfaction, the goal of CMC.

This shows, on the other side, that what would establish circulation as the specific way of satisfying needs is a goal that can be realized only through circulation. The presence of circulation as the specific form of material interchange, therefore, presupposes a goal for which circulation is a necessary condition. For circulation to be necessary for realizing some goal, the goal must pertain to the features that distinguish circulation from other kinds of material interchange. These are value, which distinguishes commodities from other kinds of products, and money, the necessary appearance form of value and the product of circulation (see Marx, 1977, p. 247). Because value and money are purely quantitative, this goal must be to realize an increase in their amount. In the circuit CMC, however, 'the equivalence of the values [of the two extremes] is a necessary condition for its normal course' (ibid., p. 252).[24] Realizing an increase in value, therefore, requires a different process than CMC, but, since this process establishes CMC as the form of material interchange, it must take place through circulation and involve the same components, money and commodities. Money, which is the means in the process CMC, is the goal of this other process, and commodities, which realize the goal of CMC, must be the means in this other process for converting one quantity of value into a larger quantity. Since the inversion of the phases of CMC transforms its goal into a means and its means into a goal, this other process is MCM, or, taking into account the increase in value, MCM'. Since the process MCM' is required to establish CMC as the specific form of material interchange, the presence of simple circulation presupposes capital. CMC and MCM' are therefore simultaneous aspects of circulation: circulation satisfies needs because it is the distribution of products; the distribution of products assumes the specific form, circulation, in order to realize an increase in value.

The demonstration that universal circulation requires capital could be stated more simply if reference were made to production. The argument could then be summarized as follows: universal circulation is the distribution of products of the commodity form. As such it presupposes production and production of a kind that must create commodities. Since all production satisfies needs, the goal of satisfying needs does not determine that products assume the form of commodities. Universal commodity production, therefore, must realize a specific goal in addition to the common goal of satisfying needs. This specific goal is identified by asking: 'What is achieved by the production of commodities that cannot be achieved by the production of any other kind of product?' Since value is the distinguishing feature of commodities, and is purely quantitative, this goal must be the expansion of value or capital. Since the expansion of value can be realized only by commodities, it is the goal that insures that products take the form of commodities, hence accounts for the presence of universal circulation.

It should be noted that the demonstration that capital is the necessary condition for circulation applies only to universal circulation (i.e. circulation as it is presented in Part I of *Capital*). If circulation is universal, it is the necessary form of material interchange (or participation in exchange is a precondition for satisfying needs, see above p. 290). If circulation is necessary, it must be necessary for something. That is, as necessary, circulation presupposes a goal for which circulation is a necessary condition. The demonstration that the expansion of value is the only goal for which circulation could be necessary, establishes that circulation is necessary for capital, therefore, presupposes capital. In other words, since capital explains why circulation is necessary, capital accounts for the presence of circulation only on the condition that circulation is necessary. Since circulation is necessary when it is universal, universal circulation presupposes capital.

If circulation is limited in extent, however, capital need not be present at all. A limitation in the extent of circulation indicates that there are other ways of satisfying needs besides circulation. The goals realized by these other ways (and each way realizes some specific goal besides the common goal of satisfying needs) can have nothing to do with circulation, and therefore with value, since they do not require circulation.[25] Such circulation as exists may be completely subservient to these other goals. That is, circulation may not be necessary at all but simply a convenient way of realizing some goal that is unrelated to value. As long as circulation is present to the extent that it has given rise to money, the form, capital may also be present. If capital is present, however, it must be present in conjunction with other goals. Under conditions of limited exchange, therefore, capital cannot be the specifically capitalist basic form. Circulation, in other words, is a necessary (but not sufficient) condition for capital because capital, in any context, is the transformation of one amount of money into a larger amount and money is the product of circulation. Capital, however, is not a necessary condition for circulation unless circulation is universal. When circulation is universal, capital must be the only goal of economic activity. Universal circulation, therefore, presupposes specifically capitalist capital.

To state this conclusion in the terminology of the *Urtext* (see above p. 291), under all circumstances circulation is merely a phenomenon because it cannot sustain itself. Circulation may be a phenomenon in either of two ways, however: it may be the means of access to (or expression of) the process that sustains it or it may be incidental to (or give no indication of the character of) that process. In the first case, the phenomenon is an appearance form, in the second, it is a semblance or mere show.[26] The difference between the two may be illustrated in terms of the analogy drawn earlier between an appearance form and the symptom of a disease (see note 1). The same phenomenon, a flushed complexion, may be produced either by a fever or by lighting conditions. In the first case, it is the sign of an underlying disorder, hence an appearance form, in the second, it has no connection to an underlying condition and is a semblance or mere show. To return to the phenomenon, circulation: under conditions of limited exchange, circulation is not the manifestation of the process that underlies it because the goal of economic activity may have nothing to do with value, the distinguishing feature of circulation. Universal circulation, by contrast, presupposes value creation as the exclusive goal of economic activity or the basic form of capital. In this case, therefore, circulation expresses the character of the process that sustains it because the distinguishing feature of circulation, value, is the goal of the underlying process. Universal circulation, therefore, is the appearance form of specifically capitalist capital.

As argued earlier, the remainder of the argument of Part II of *Capital* establishes that the basic form of capital requires wage labour, hence capitalist production. The demonstration that universal circulation requires the basic form of capital links all the forms considered in Part I to wage labour and shows them to be specifically capitalist. This connection between Parts I and II of *Capital* establishes that universal circulation is the appearance form of capitalist production.

10.8 SUMMARY AND CONCLUSION

Capitalist and precapitalist societies share many of the same forms; the commodity, the elements of simple circulation, and even capital. One obvious and indisputable difference between them, however, is that exchange is more prevalent in capitalism than in historically earlier societies. Because this is only a difference in extent, it suggests that capitalism is simply a more developed version of precapitalist economic relations rather than a distinct kind of economic organization. By developing the logical consequences of this one, immediately apparent distinguishing characteristic of capitalism, the prevalence of exchange, Marx shows that capitalism is a kind of economic system whose sole regulating principle and goal is value. Further, by showing that the condition for the existence of such a system is the result of a historical development, Marx establishes that precapitalist relations could not have constituted a system of this kind.

As this chapter has argued, all the forms Marx defines in *Capital* are implications of or necessary conditions for the universality of the commodity form (the dominance of exchange in its pure form). In Part I of *Capital*, Marx argues that the universal commodity implies value, money and universal circulation or circulation as the social form of distributing products. In Part II, he argues that the basic form of capital is the necessary condition for universal circulation, that surplus value, in the sense of a system-wide net increase in value, is the necessary condition for the basic form of capital, and that universal wage labour is the necessary condition for surplus value. Although it has not been examined here, in Part III Marx turns to production organized by the relation of wage labour to capital. Because Marx's argument from the universal commodity form to capitalist production is one continuous logical development, it establishes that universal circulation presupposes capitalist production. Capitalist production, therefore, is the process that underlies the starting phenomenon, the universal commodity form.

As other instances of this kind of argument show, the argument in its complete form would return to the starting phenomenon, demonstrating that this phenomenon is the result of the process that underlies it. In this case, the return would involve the demonstration that universal circulation is the result of capitalist production. Marx merely mentions the return in Volume I of *Capital* (ibid., p. 709).[27] It is evident, however, that capitalist production must create commodities in order to realize its goal, the expansion of value. If all production is under the direction of capital (i.e. if capital is the basic form of capital), therefore, all products must be commodities. The completed argument, then, shows both that universal circulation presupposes capitalist production and that capitalist production presupposes universal circulation. This establishes that universal circulation and capitalist production are completely integrated, mutually requiring subprocesses of one system.

Once a system of this kind exists, each subprocess restores the other. Capitalist production continually creates products, in the form of commodities, hence restores distribution of the social product in the form of circulation and perpetuates the relation of members of society to each other in exchange as private owners of commodities and, therefore, as individuals. The realization of surplus value in circulation, in turn, continually restores the separate private ownership of material means of production and labour capacity, hence perpetuates the relation of members of society to each other in production as wage labourers and capitalists. Since, according to Marx's argument, circulation can be universal only if all production is capitalist, all production must be capitalist before circulation can be universal. This means that the separate private ownership of material means of production and labour capacity, on which capitalist production is based, must be established, for the first time, by some process other than universal circulation. Marx's demonstration that this other process is historical, establishes that the capitalist system is historically specific. That is, it establishes that all economic orders prior to the original accumulation must have involved other relations besides those that constitute a capitalist system and other goals besides the expansion of value. Although many forms are common to capitalist and precapitalist society, these forms can be universal only in capitalism. Capitalism, as distinct from all historically earlier economic orders, therefore, is a system of 'value in its purity and generality' (Marx, 1973, p. 252, see also p. 776).

From Marx's definition of the capitalist system and his proof that this system is historically specific, it is clear why he conceives the commodity form to be characteristic of capitalism, even though, as he is well aware, commodities are present in other economic orders. First, the commodity is characteristic of capitalism in the sense that the prevalence of commodities in capitalism is immediately apparent. Because the prevalence of the commodity form is immediately apparent, it is the first identifying feature of capitalism. Second, the commodity is the 'economic cell form' for capitalism because the commodity form implies the process of simple circulation. Universal simple circulation, in turn, presupposes capitalist production and is, therefore, the appearance form of (or means of access to) capitalist production. Thus, the capitalist system as a whole can be defined by developing the logical consequences of the commodity form. Finally, capitalist production must produce products of the commodity form. Where all production is directed by capital (i.e. in a pure capitalist system), therefore, the commodity must be the universal form of products. This accounts for the initially observed prevalence of commodities.

Notes

I thank Ron Blackwell and Ross Thomson for their very helpful comments on an earlier draft of this paper and Robert Berman and Robert Urquhart for countless discussions of the issues it addresses. The responsibility for any remaining mistakes is, of course, solely mine.

1.   Marx's term 'appearance form' refers to a phenomenon understood as the expression of something else that is not phenomenal or immediately apparent. For example, a symptom, when correctly understood, expresses the presence of a disease and, on the other side, the disease, or underlying disorder, manifests itself through the phenomena it gives off, or its symptoms. In this way, phenomena are the means of access to what is not phenomenal. Appearance form relations will be discussed in more detail below in connection with the transition from money to capital, the relation between exchange value and value, and the relation between universal circulation and capitalist production.

2.   This is the simple commodity production interpretation. According to this view, *Capital* begins with reference to relations that antedate capitalism and proceeds historically from these to specifically capitalist relations. One of the clearest exponents of this view is R. Meek (1973, see p. xv). The general commodity production interpretation, proposed by DeBrunhoff, also maintains that *Capital* does not begin with reference to capitalism. According to this view, *Capital* begins with characteristics that are common to all commodity producing societies and proceeds logically from these to specifically capitalist characteristics (see DeBrunhoff, 1976, pp. xiii, 19–25). The differences between these two views turn out to be quite superficial; both are open to the same objection (see below pp. 277–80).

3.   This is the interpretation proposed by Rosdolsky (1977, p. 115) who maintains that Marx's method is logico-historical. This interpretation at first appears to be a nice compromise between the purely historical versus purely logical alternatives proposed respectively by the simple and general commodity production interpretation. The demonstration that historical sequence cannot play any role in the sequence of the argument in *Capital*, which rules out the simple commodity production interpretation, rules out this view as well.

4.   By content, therefore, Marx means purpose or goal. See also Marx (1977), pp. 248, 250 and 251, where Marx says that MCM would be without content or purposeless if it involved two equal sums of money.

5.   The demonstration, to be presented below, that capital as universal organizing principle is a necessary condition for the commodity relations presented in Part I will establish that the first rule is also derived from Marx's analysis of the commodity.

6.   As Marx goes on to explain, by this assumption, he excludes slavery (or the purchase of the labourer rather than labour power) as a possible source of surplus value because slavery is a 'relation of dependence' that is not inherent in exchange. As Marx shows in Part I of *Capital*, exchange entails the relation of members of society to each other as individuals (see Marx, 1977, p. 178). The assumption that the purchase of labour power involves no other relations of dependence than those

that follow from commodity exchange, means not only that both parties to the exchange are individuals, but also that there are no human beings involved in the transaction who are not individuals, i.e. there are no slaves.

The justification for this assumption is that the entire argument of *Capital* is the development of the implications of and necessary conditions for the commodity form. On this basis, Marx defines all members of society as individuals in part I of *Capital* (see p. 290 below) and shows that this relation entails their 'all-sided material dependence' (Marx, 1977, p. 203). As will be shown below (pp. 290–6), in Part II of *Capital*, Marx develops the necessary conditions for the relations he has defined in Part I. Because Marx is developing the necessary conditions for commodity exchange, he excludes all characteristics that are not inherent in commodity exchange. On this basis, Marx defines the commodity labour power as wage labour and shows that the relation of wage labour to capital is a second relation of dependence that results from the nature of commodity exchange.

7. When Marx says that capital 'announces . . . a new epoch' in contrast to commodities and money, which are 'common to many economic social formations', he means the kind of capital that requires universal wage labour (Marx, 1977, pp. 273–4). The justification for equating capital with the basic form of capital is that Marx has not discussed any other kind of capital.

8. 'Why this free worker confronts him in the sphere of circulation is a question which does not interest the owner of money, for he finds the labour market in existence as a particular branch of the commodity market. *And for the present it interests us just as little. We confine ourselves to the fact theoretically*, as he does practically' (Marx, 1977, p. 273, emphasis added).

9. Economic activity organized exclusively by capital would be capitalism in its pure state, which, as Marx says in the Preface to the first edition (Marx, 1977, p. 90), is the subject matter of *Capital*. This definition of capitalism does not preclude the possibility that other principles besides capital could be present in a real capitalist system. It merely states that the capitalist system could function without any other principles, i.e. that other principles are unnecessary.

10. This point is made by John Wetlaufer (1977) on which the present discussion of the role of wage labour in the argument of *Capital* is based. By this account, the function of the original accumulation argument is to demonstrate the historically specific character of the capitalist system as a whole. This identifies one of the functions of historical reference in Marx's argument.

11. In Marx's account, capitalist production is defined by the goal of expanding value; this is why wage labour is necessary. Precapitalist production is defined by some goal that has nothing to do with value (and therefore does not follow from the examination of any kind of capital) such as the institution and preservation of relations of status or kinship. All production has some specific goal besides the provision of use value, the goal common to all kinds of production (or, as Marx says in the *Grundrisse*, 'there is no production in general' (1973, p. 86)) because all production involves some definite relation of the members of society to the means of production and to each other by means of their relation to the means of production.

12. An account of the characteristics common to capitalist and precapitalist forms, such as the account given above of merchants' and usurers' capital, does not include either the additional characteristics these forms have in capitalism (i.e. the consequences of the universality of capital) or the other goals that would have to be present in a precapitalist situation. Developing the logical implications of common characteristics, therefore, would yield pseudo-precapitalist, rather than capitalist relations.

13.   The revision of the starting phenomenon, therefore, is not accidental but is inherent
       in Marx's method. The reason for the revision is that the starting phenomenon is a
       pretheoretical conception (that is, something that is immediately obvious) while the
       concluding phenomenon is the phenomenon as it is explained by theory. The two
       other appearance form transitions that will be discussed below are exchange value
       as the appearance form of value and universal circulation as the appearance form of
       capitalist production. By the first, the notion that the commodity is a use value and
       an exchange value is revised to the notion that the commodity is a use value and a
       value (see Marx, 1977, p. 152). By the second, the notion that exchange is 'a relation
       between owners of commodities in which they appropriate the produce of the labour
       of others by alienating the produce of their own labour' (ibid., 203) is revised to the
       notion that all normal commodities (commodities that are products) are owned by
       capitalists.

14.   Marx seems to have considered the two accounts so similar as to make the form of
       value argument redundant: 'I present the *same thing* [and this could only mean the
       same as the first account, the derivation value] as simply and as pedagogically
       as possible' giving 'each new division of the text *its own title*' (letter to Engels
       22/6/1867, Marx and Engels, 1975, p. 177). The two accounts are the same in that
       they consider the same set of different exchange relations and are based on the
       appearance form relation between exchange value and value. Only in the second
       account, however, is it made explicit that value has only one appearance form.

15.   It should be noted that 'form' does not have the same meaning in the term 'appear-
       ance form' as it has, for example, in the statement that the commodity is a form of
       product. The notion of a phenomenon as an appearance form presupposes that the
       phenomenon is the only way a given content can appear, i.e. that the phenomenon
       is the only adequate expression of that content. By contrast, when Marx says that the
       commodity is a form of product, he means that the commodity is one kind of product
       and that there are other kinds.

16.   Thus the argument on the form of value (and its counterpart, the derivation of value)
       is an example of the movement from simple to complex, which Marx (1973,
       pp. 100–5) describes in the *Grundrisse*. By this movement, elements of the complex,
       which have been isolated from each other by thought, are brought together to
       reconstitute the complex. By this means, the complex is understood as the unity of
       all its aspects. In reality, however, the elements of the complex do not exist in
       isolation from each other. Thus, in this case, Marx's real starting point is the final
       form which is 'reduced [into its constitutive elements] by working backwards'
       (Marx, 1977, p. 163) through the sequence of forms: the quantitative commensura-
       bility of commodities (in forms (3) and (4)) implies their qualitative equivalence
       (which is considered independently of quantitative commensurability in form (2)
       and qualitative equivalence is manifested by the relation of commodities (which is
       considered independently of quantitative or qualitative equivalence in form (1)).

       The movement from simple to complex *may* correspond to a historical sequence
       but is not guided by historical sequence. In this case, for example, exchange relation
       (1) could exist without (2) and (2) could exist without (3) but (3) does not exist
       without both (1) and (2) because they are already present in (3) as its constitutive
       aspects ((2) cannot exist without (1) for the same reason). Thus relation (3) cannot
       be historically prior to relations (2) and (1) and relation (2) cannot be historically
       prior to relation (1). To this extent, the sequence of forms produced by the process
       of correcting defects in the expression of value could be the same as the sequence
       in which these forms appear independently of each other historically. Even if the
       two sequences do correspond, however, the relations within each sequence express
       different things. If relation (1) or (2) were present without (3), the characteristics it
       expresses would be isolated in reality (rather than in thought) from those expressed

by relation (3) (for this reason, historically earlier relations can provide examples of some single aspect of value by itself). In that case, relation (1) would not express value in any respect since value is the unity of all aspects expressed in form (3). Marx speaks as if, for example, relation (1) expresses certain features of value, because he has already established what value is and is looking for a form that expresses it adequately.

17. Thus Marx speaks of the equivalent commodity as a 'value thing' or a 'value body' (see Marx, 1977, pp. 141–4). As the material commodity that expresses the abstract aspect common to all commodities, the money commodity is a concrete universal.

18. It is not the intention here to justify either of these connections, but simply to point out that Marx makes them and to show, from what he makes of them, that he is assuming the commodity form to be universal.

19. Marx attributes the concept of non-social labour activity (i.e. the concept of completely dissociated labour activities) to the way commodity producing labour appears. Commodity producing labour activities do not seem to be connected at all because the only connection among them is indirect. See, for example, Marx (1977), p. 168: 'the money form . . . conceals the social character of private labour and the social relations between the individual workers by making those relations appear as relations between material objects'.

20. The definition of economic need as need satisfied by products is implicit in *Capital* because use value (and therefore, need) is considered only as an aspect of the commodity. When Marx speaks of need, therefore, he means only those needs that are satisfied by commodities (or, later on in the argument, needs that are generated by the implications of and necessary conditions for the commodity form, such as the need for a commodity that creates value when it is consumed). Since the commodity is a form of product, needs satisfied by commodities are, in general terms, needs satisfied by products. This definition of need is also implied by Marx's response to Bastiat's notion that the ancient Greeks and Romans lived by plunder alone (see Marx, 1977, p. 175, note 35).

21. The other versions of the transition are Marx (1973), pp. 239–320 and Marx (1974), pp. 919–47, see also Marx (1973), 790. For the transition to be logical it would have to show that simple circulation 'presupposes' and, in this sense 'produces' capital. The reverse argument, that simple circulation is the result of capital, appears in the 'Results'.

22. It is not entirely clear why Marx chose to present the transition as a contrast rather than a sequence. The contrast form does seem quite intentional since it becomes progressively more pronounced in each successive version of the transition. The advantage of the contrast form is that it allows Marx to present a multifaceted argument with great simplicity. It shows very clearly that the goal of capital is to increase value. The movement from money as the product of circulation to money as goal continues the line of development in Part I, chapter 3, in which the functions of money are arranged so that money is progressively more independent of circulation. The form – content – form movement in chapter 4, which is a clear example of an appearance form transition, depends on beginning chapter 4 with a new phenomenon. The disadvantage of the contrast form, however, is that the logical basis of the transition all but disappears. The sequential alternative to Marx's contrast is presented with the hope that, between the two versions, the basis of the argument will be made clear.

23. See also Marx (1973) p. 790: 'Simple circulation regarded in itself is not bent back into itself but consists of an infinite number of indifferent and accidentally adjacent movements'.

24. Alternatively, Marx shows in chapter 5 of *Capital* that CMC cannot realize an increase in value.

25. These other goals are not purely economic. Examples are, the institution of relations of status or kinship for their own sake or those goals of the state that are not intended as means for the effective operation of capital, for example, national security, public education, social welfare. Capitalism in its pure form, therefore, is unique in being an economic system. No precapitalist social order has an economic system in the sense of a system that is directed towards a purely economic goal.

26. This illustration of a semblance or mere show and the analogy between an appearance form and the symptom of a disease are both taken from Heidegger (1962), pp. 50–4.

27. Marx never quite completes this movement. In Volume I of *Capital*, he presupposes the return to circulation (see Marx, 1977, pp. 709–10). Although the 'Results' mark one attempt to accomplish this return, it seems that Marx decided in favour of delaying the return to circulation until he could specify all the factors that influence capitalist circulation. These include the specifications that arise from the circulation of capital (Volume II) and the specifications that arise from the relation among capitals (competition) and between capital and land ownership (Volume III). Volume III however, remains unfinished.

References

DeBrunhoff, Suzanne (1976) *Marx on Money*, transl. Maurice Goldbloom (New York: Urizen Books).

Heidegger, Martin (1962) *Being and Time* (New York: Harper & Row).

Marx, K. (1967) *Capital*, vol. III (New York: International Publ.).

Marx, K. (1973) *Grundrisse*, transl. Martin Nicolaus (New York: Vintage Books).

Marx, K. (1974) *Urtext*, in *Grundrisse* (Berlin: Dietz Verlag).

Marx, K. (1975) 'Notes on Wagner', in *Texts on Method*, transl. and ed. Terrell Carver (Oxford: Basil Blackwell).

Marx, K. (1977) *Capital*, vol. I, transl. Ben Fowkes (New York: Vintage Books).

Marx, K. and F. Engels (1975) *Selected Correspondence*, ed. S. W. Ryazanskaya, transl. by I. Lasker, 3rd edn. (Moscow: Progress Publishers).

Meek, Ronald (1973) *Studies in the Labour Theory of Value*, 2nd edn. (London: Lawrence & Wishart).

Rosdolsky, Roman (1977) *The Making of Marx's 'Capital'*, transl. Pete Burgess (London: Pluto Press).

Wetlaufer, John (1977) 'The Original Accumulation and the Concept of Capital', Graduate Faculty Philosophy Journal, vol. 6, no. 2, Fall, pp. 241–92.

Part V
Contemporary Theory in the Light of the Classics

Steven Pressman, 'Quesnay's Theory of Economic Growth and Decline'

Tom Michl, 'Adam Smith and the New Economics of Effort'

Chidem Kurdas, 'Classical Perspectives on Investment'

Frank Roosevelt, 'Marx and Market Socialism'

Heilbroner has always insisted that the classics should be read, not as historical curiosities, but as attempts to cope with real problems; each of these papers shows the relevance of classical texts to current issues. Pressman first reconstructs Quesnay's static Tableau, showing it to be free of the errors and problems commonly attributed to it. Following the same method, he then reconstructs the dynamic Tableau, moving a little beyond what Quesnay actually said, perhaps. But this enables him to argue that Quesnay's main points concern a very modern problem, one evident in the work of Kaldor, and relevant to contemporary policy issues, namely, the relation between the size and growth of a dynamic sector, and the productivity growth of the economy as a whole. Tom Michl takes up an important but seldom carefully studied aspect of Smith – his account of the labour market, which contains some surprises. There is a clear statement of what today is known as the theory of 'efficiency wages', and Michl relates this carefully to Smith's treatment of incentives and technology. Kurdas first contrasts Ricardo and Malthus on the determinants of investment, then considers Marx's account, in the light of the criticisms advanced by Schumpeter and Blaug, concluding that while neither Malthus nor Ricardo had more than an embryonic vision of investment, Marx had a sophisticated but underdeveloped idea. The propensity to save out of profits would adapt to the stimulus to invest, rising and falling according to the opportunities and new markets available. Finally, very much in Heilbroner's spirit, Roosevelt re-examines the functioning of markets in a socialist economy, contrasting their obvious utility in promoting economic objectives with their serious deficiencies in the light of socialist values, as highlighted by Marx. For socialism to flourish, it cannot reject the market, but it cannot simply rely on it either. Markets must be circumscribed or adapted in the light of socialist goals.

303

11 Quesnay's Theory of Economic Growth and Decline

Steven Pressman

11.1 INTRODUCTION

Beginning with Adam Smith, historians of economic thought have had high regard for Quesnay and the Physiocrats. The same, however, cannot be said of their economic model – the *Tableau Economique*. Well known is Eugen Duhring's opinion that the *Tableau* is a mathematical fantasy comparable to squaring the circle.[1] More recently, Paul Samuelson has equated the *Tableau* to 'mystification and abracadabara'.[2]

Such criticism was directed primarily at versions of the *Tableau* showing simple reproduction. Even more complicated and difficult to comprehend are the dynamic *Tableaux* showing economic growth and decline. Because few people understood the static *Tableau*, very few have attempted to understand Quesnay's more complex model.

This is unfortunate, for the dynamic *Tableaux* are the truly interesting ones. These are models of real economies that can be used to explain the causes of stagnation and develop policies for promoting economic growth. Lack of interest in the dynamic *Tableau* is also unfortunate because, like the static *Tableau*, the model does make sense – it is a logically consistent model based upon a reasonable set of assumptions.

Section 11.2 of this chapter lays out the mechanics of the static *Tableau*, and argues that Quesnay's model is not a mathematical fantasy. Section 11.3 does the same for the dynamic *Tableau*. Section 11.4 then examines the relevance of this model for understanding contemporary problems of stagnation.

11.2 RECONSTRUCTING THE STATIC *TABLEAU*

The famous zigzags of Quesnay's static *Tableau* should be familiar to most historians of economic thought. Table 11.1 reproduces the first edition of the *Tableau*, which has a base of 400 lives.[3] These zigzags, however, represent only a small portion of Quesnay's model. A set of assumptions and explanatory remarks accompanies each edition of the *Tableau*. These provide the overarching assumptions upon which the construction and operation of the table are based.

Table 11.1   The first edition of the *Tableau*

Productive class	Proprietor revenues	Sterile class
Annual Advances		Annual Advances
400^1 produce net	400^1	200^1
200 reproduce net	200	200
100 reproduce net	100	100
50 reproduce net	50	50
25 reproduce net	25	25
12^1 10^s reproduce net	12^1 10	12 10^s
6^1 5^s reproduce net	6^1 5	6^1 5^s
3^1 2^s 6^d reproduce net	3^1 2^s 6^d	3^1 2^s 6^d
1^1 11^s 3^d reproduce net	1^1 11^s 3^d	1^1 11^s 3^d
15^s 7^d reproduce net	15^s 7^d	15^s 7^d
8^s reproduce net	8^s	8^s
4^s reproduce net	4^s	4^s
2^s reproduce net	2^s	2^s
1^s reproduce net	1^s	1^s

Nine assumptions turn out to be critical for understanding the workings of the static *Tableau*.

Class assumptions

(1) Society is composed of three classes: a productive class of agricultural workers, a class of proprietors or landlords, and a manufacturing class. The productive class produces food and raw materials; the manufacturing class, manufactured goods; and the proprietors produce nothing – at least nothing of economic significance.

(2) The productive class is the only class which generates a surplus. The manufacturing class is thus 'sterile'.

(3) The productive class must pay a rent every year to the proprietors. This rent is the price equivalent of the surplus generated by the productive class for the year.

Population assumption

(4) The proprietors constitute one-quarter of the entire population; the manufacturing class comprises another quarter of the population; and the productive class consists of the remaining half of the population.

Consumption assumptions

(5) The rent payments received by the proprietors are all used for consumption. Likewise, incomes of productive and manufacturing class workers are all spent. Thus there is no savings.[4]

(6) All classes divide their consumption equally between food and manufactured goods. These are the only goods consumed by members of society.

(7) Per capita consumption for the manufacturing class is equal to per capita consumption for the productive class which is equal to one-half per capita consumption of the proprietors.[5]

Input–output assumptions

(8) $X of inputs yield $2X worth of products in the agricultural sector. In addition, in the productive sector, food and manufactured goods are the only inputs, and they are to be used in equal amounts. In the manufacturing sector three inputs are required – food, raw materials, and manufactured goods. These are needed as means of consumption for the worker (clothing, shelter, etc.) and as means of production (tools and equipment). Following Quesnay, we suppose that $X of food, $X of manufactured goods, and $2X of raw materials are needed to produce $4X of manufactured goods.

Endowments assumption

(9) The original holdings of each class following production by both the agricultural and manufacturing sectors are as follows:

Productive class	*Proprietors*	*Manufacturing class*
$2000 money	($2000 in rent claims)	$2000 manufactured goods
$1000 raw materials		
$3000 food		

It can now be postulated that the following six stages of exchange and production take place.

Step 1:   The productive class pays $2000 to the proprietors as rent.

Productive class	*Proprietors*	*Manufacturing class*
$3000 food	$2000 money	$2000 manufactured goods
$1000 raw materials		

Step 2:   The proprietors purchase $1000 food from the productive class and $1000 manufactured goods from the manufacturing class. This will enable the proprietors to consume equal amounts of food and manufactured goods as required by assumption (7). They also spend all their rental receipts, as stipulated by assumption (5). The situation now becomes:

Productive class	*Proprietors*	*Manufacturing class*
$2000 food	$1000 food	$1000 manufactured goods
$1000 raw materials	$1000 manufactured goods	$1000 money
$1000 money		

Step 3:   The manufacturing class buys $1000 raw materials from the productive class, which results in:

Productive class	*Proprietors*	*Manufacturing class*
$2000 food	$1000 food	$1000 manufactured goods
$2000 money	$1000 manufactured goods	$1000 raw materials

Step 4:   The manufacturing class sells $1000 manufactured goods to the productive class, and then buys $1000 food with the money it receives. These two transactions represent the sum total of all the zigzag transactions in the *Tableau*. This gives us the following class holdings:

Productive class	*Proprietors*	*Manufacturing class*
$1000 food	$1000 food	$1000 food
$2000 money	$1000 manufactured goods	$1000 raw materials
$1000 manufactured goods		

Step 5:   The manufacturing class exports $500 food and imports $500 foreign manufactured goods. This is needed because by assumptions (4), (6) and (7) total food consumption of the manufacturing class must be one-half the total food consumption of the productive class. Such trade is also consistent with Quesnay's calls for exporting agricultural goods and for balanced trade.[6] Finally, since trade is a sterile economic activity it must take place within the manufacturing sector. Foreign trade leads to the position shown below:

Productive class	*Proprietors*	*Manufacturing class*
$1000 food	$1000 food	$500 food
$2000 money	$1000 manufactured goods	$1000 raw materials
$1000 manufactured goods		$500 manufactured goods

Step 6: Production and consumption take place in accord with assumption (8), and, by assumption (3), the proprietors receive $2000 in rent claims. We have now returned to our original situation:

Productive class	*Proprietors*	*Manufacturing class*
$2000 money	($2000 in rent claims)	$2000 manufactured goods
$1000 raw materials		
$3000 food		

The above reconstruction does not fall prey to the ambiguities of Quesnay's zigzags. Foreign trade, class holdings, the exchange of money for commodities, and commodity input requirements are all clearly shown. None of the assumptions made by Quesnay is violated. Thus, all the mechanisms of the *Tableau* are laid out in a coherent and easily understood fashion, and there should be no complaints about mystification or obscurity regarding the static *Tableau*.

11.3 RECONSTRUCTING THE DYNAMIC *TABLEAU*

In various works Quesnay set forth *Tableaux* showing economic growth and decline. Four causes of economic decline stand out in these works. First, if proprietors hoard their revenues there will be less spending in the economy and output will fall.[7] Second, if the agricultural class receives lower prices for their goods, this will reduce profits, making less money available for investment in more efficient technologies. Also, when profits decline in the agricultural sector, proprietor rents fall (though possibly with a lag due to long-term rental contracts). This in turn will lead to less spending by the proprietary class, and thus to lower output.[8] Third, Quesnay argued that faulty tax policies cause economic decline. For example, taxes on the productive sector of the economy reduce the means of production available in that sector, reduce the agricultural surplus of the economy, and slow down economic growth.[9] Finally, Quesnay argued that structural changes in the economy can cause stagnation.[10] If the sterile sector of the economy grows at the expense of the productive sector, output will eventually fall in *both* sectors. Since the first three sources of decline have become part of the conventional economic wisdom, this section focuses on the fourth source of decline as it attempts to explain the dynamic *Tableau*.

As we saw, in the static *Tableau* all classes spend one-half of their income on manufactured goods and one-half on agricultural goods. Under this assumption the economy reproduces output valued at $6000 ($4000 agricultural goods – half of which goes to the proprietors – plus $2000 manufactured goods) each year.

This assumption can be relaxed. If classes were to spend three-fifths on manufactured goods and two-fifths on food, the manufacturing sector would grow at the expense of the productive, agricultural sector. The consequences of this is depleted in Table 12.2. Total output falls from $6000 to $5579 ($3368 agri-

Table 11.2   The dynamic *Tableau* in decline

Productive class annual advances	Proprietors revenue	Manufacturing class annual advances
2000	2000	1000
800 ⸺reproduces net	800	1200
480 ⸺reproduces net	480	480
192 ⸺reproduces net	192	288
115 ⸺reproduces net	115	115
–	–	–
–	–	–
–	–	–
1684	1684	2211

cultural goods + $2211 manufactured goods). Since agricultural output has de-clined, so too must the surplus of this sector. Because this surplus goes to the proprietary class, proprietor revenues must fall also.

For succeeding years the decline in proprietor incomes causes further declines in output and incomes. In fact, the very next production period sees manufactur-ing output drop below its original figure of $2000 (see Table 11.3), and total output drops to $4697. For all subsequent periods proprietor revenues will con-tinue to decline, further reducing their spending on agricultural and manufactured goods, and also reducing the output of each sector.

In contrast, if spending favours the agricultural sector, proprietor revenues rise. This leads to greater spending and output in the future. Here the economy grows, and it will continue to grow as long as spending is primarily on agricultural goods.

The major difficulty in understanding these *Tableaux* can be stated succinctly.[11] Quesnay maintained that when the effective demand for a commodity increases, the output of that commodity increases. His model, however, is one of the production of commodities by commodities. Inputs are necessary for production. Increased sales, though, reduce the inputs available to a sector. How then can output increase? Making matters worse, Quesnay assumed that the manufactur-ing sector of the economy was sterile, and so the value of inputs must equal the value of the output produced. A change in the price of manufactured goods then cannot explain the increased value of manufacturing output in Table 11.2. Nor can falling prices explain the decline in Table 11.3.

What must be explained is how output can increase when demand increases. This mechanism must explain how a sector can produce more when it sells more

Table 11.3   Second period decline in the dynamic *Tableau*

Productive class annual advances	Proprietors revenue	Manufacturing class annual advances
1684	1684	1105.5
674 reproduces net	674	1010
404 reproduces net	404	404
162 reproduces net	162	242
972 reproduces net	97	97
–	–	–
–	–	–
–	–	–
1418	1418	1861

and has fewer inputs available for production. It must also be a mechanism that Quesnay recognizes.

Population changes constitute such a mechanism. Changes in spending propensities cause sectoral changes in the population. People find employment in those sectors of the economy experiencing growing demand, and leave sectors for which effective demand is declining.

This mechanism was clearly recognized by Quesnay. In 'Corn', he wrote: 'Population increases much more through revenue and expenditure than it does through the propagation of the nation itself. Revenue increases expenditure, and expenditure attracts men who seek gain.'[12] And in 'Men', where Quesnay was most concerned with population, it is again revenue, or demand generated by the spending of revenue, that determines population. 'The population of a state increases in the proportion that the nation's revenue increases, because the revenue procures well-being and gains by which men are maintained and attracted.'[13]

In these passages Quesnay's concern is the entire population. He seems to envision the influx of foreign labourers and the migration of excess labour to foreign nations as the cause of changes in the total population of a country. However, the principle proffered applies as well to the distribution of the population within the domestic economy. When demand for the goods produced by one sector increases, employment opportunities in that sector increase, and men are attracted to that sector. The sector experiencing a reduction in demand needs fewer workers. Workers who cannot find employment there will seek jobs in that sector experiencing increased demand.

Quesnay incorporated this idea into the *Tableau*. All editions of the *Tableau* calculate a sector's population, given revenues. In the first edition, explanatory notes compute the population that can subsist, given proprietor revenues.

> The proprietor, who spends the revenue of 400 livres, draws his subsistence from it. The 200 livres distributed to each expenditure class can support one man in each; thus 400 livres of revenue enable three heads of families to subsist. On this basis 400 millions of revenue can enable three million families to subsist, estimated at three persons above the age of infancy per family.[14]

Similar calculations are carried out in the 'Economic Maxims of M. de Sully',[15] which was appended to the second and third editions.

Population changes are necessary, but not necessary and sufficient conditions, for explaining the working of the dynamic *Tableau*. For population changes do not explain how output can change by the amounts stated by Quesnay when demand changes. Two things must occur in addition. The transfer of inputs or means of subsistence must accompany the migration of workers; and there must be changes in agricultural sector productivity.

Quesnay recognized both these consequences of changes in the composition of the population. 'If [farmers] are harassed into abandoning the countryside and withdrawing to the towns, they take their fathers' wealth which used to be employed in cultivation.'[16] Reduced capital in the agricultural sector will then reduce agricultural productivity. Quesnay's static *Tableau* always assumed that 'The advances of the farmers are sufficient to enable the expenses of cultivation to reproduce at least 100 percent; for if the advances are not sufficient, the expenses of cultivation are higher and produce little net revenue.'[17]

In Table 11.2 manufacturing output increases to $2211. Only if annual advances accompany new workers to the manufacturing sector is it possible for the manufacturing sector to begin with inputs of $2000 and end the circulation and production process with $2211 manufactured goods while creating no surplus. Capitalist farmers, moving to the manufacturing sector become capitalist merchants, manufacturers and traders. Their wage fund becomes the new manufacturing advances. More workers can be hired now in the manufacturing sector, and manufacturing output will rise.

For manufactured output to increase by $221, inputs worth $221 must be transferred from the agricultural to the manufacturing sector. If agricultural advances continue to reproduce 100 per cent, agricultural output would decline by $422 ($211 × 2). But agricultural production declines by $632 according to Table 11.2. The explanation for this additional decline can only be a change in agricultural sector productivity. As capital is removed from agriculture, less efficient means of productions are employed in the agricultural sector. 'Petite' agriculture replaces 'grande' agriculture, and average productivity declines.[18]

The two mechanisms described above are integral aspects of the dynamic *Tableau*. Using a sequence of Meekian tables, we now look at the dynamic *Tableau* in decline. The growth case, of course, will follow along similar lines. As before, each class begins with the following holdings:

Productive class	*Proprietors*	*Manufacturing class*
$3000 food	$2000 money	$2000 manufactured goods
$1000 raw materials		

The proprietors spend three-fifths of their incomes on manufactured goods and two-fifths on food. When other classes do likewise, this will result in the production of $3368 agricultural goods and $2211 manufactured goods in the next period. We will see how circulation, exchange, population changes, and productivity changes in agriculture generate this result. Proprietor spending gives us the following:

Productive class	*Proprietors*	*Manufacturing class*
$2200 food	$800 food	$800 manufactured goods
$1000 raw materials	$1200 manufactured goods	$1200 money
$800 money		

The manufacturing class purchases $884 food from the agricultural class. This represents one portion of the *Tableau*'s zigzags, and results in:

Productive class	*Proprietors*	*Manufacturing class*
$1316 food	$800 food	$800 manufactured goods
$1000 raw materials	$1200 manufactured goods	$316 money
$1684 money		$884 food

The manufacturing sector purchases $316 manufactured goods from abroad. There is no return sale, so a trade deficit results. The deficit is necessary to meet the greater demand for manufactured goods of the agricultural class. Also, it reduces the domestic money supply by the amount that the agricultural surplus will be reduced, so in future periods the money supply will be just sufficient to facilitate domestic exchanges. This transaction makes holdings:

Productive class	*Proprietors*	*Manufacturing class*
$1316 food	$800 food	$1116 manufactured goods
$1000 raw materials	$1200 manufactured goods	$884 food
$1684 money		

The manufacturing class sells $1011 manufactured goods to the productive class. This completes the *Tableau*'s zigzags, and gives us:

Productive class	*Proprietors*	*Manufacturing class*
$1316 food	$800 food	$105 manufactured goods
$1000 raw materials	$1200 manufactured goods	$1011 money
$673 money		$884 food
$1011 manufactured goods		

We now consider the effect of these expenditures on the population. The new spending propensities shift people and their means of subsistence from agriculture to manufacturing. As we have seen, $211 in inputs must move from the agricultural to the manufacturing sector. To simplify the analysis, I will assume that this is done in the form of $105.5 manufactured goods and $105.5 food. This migration makes holdings:

Productive class	Proprietors	Manufacturing class
$1210.5 food	$800 food	$210.5 manufactured goods
$1000 raw materials	$1200 manufactured goods	$1011 money
$673 money		$989.5 food
$905.5 manufactured goods		

At this point the manufacturing sector purchases raw materials from the productive class. It requires $1011 raw materials. If the productive sector produced more raw materials and less food in the preceding period this would be possible. If not, the manufacturing class can purchase $1000 raw materials and $11 food and obtain additional raw materials by foreign trade. Since we show the productive class with only $1000 raw materials, the latter transaction will take place. This results in:

Productive class	Proprietors	Manufacturing class
$1199.5 food	$800 food	$1000 raw materials
$905.5 manufactured goods	$1200 manufactured goods	$210.5 manufactured goods
$1684 money		$1000.5 food

The manufacturing sector exports $447.75 food, and imports $105.5 raw materials and $342.25 manufactured goods. This gives us:

Productive class	Proprietors	Manufacturing class
$1199.5 food	$800 food	$1105.5 raw materials
$905.5 manufactured goods	$1200 manufactured goods	$552.75 manufactured goods
$1684 money		$552.75 food

The manufacturing sector now has the inputs it needs to produce $2211 manufactured goods in accordance with Quesnay's input-output assumptions.[19] The agricultural sector has $2005 of inputs. For Quesnay, equal amounts of food and manufactured goods must be employed when producing agricultural goods. Food worth $194 is thus wasted and goes to produce no agricultural goods. Inputs of $1811 – $905.5 food and $905.5 manufactured goods produce $3368 agricultural goods rather than $3622. Advances no longer reproduce 100 per cent. The transfer of men and capital to the manufacturing sector has lowered agricultural productivity. Finally, rent payments, production and consumption bring us to:

Productive class	*Proprietors*	*Manufacturing class*
$3368 food and raw materials	$1684 money	$2211 manufactured goods

The first cycle of decline is complete. Exchange and production can continue each year along these lines. Each year output, surpluses and proprietor revenues will fall. Inputs will find their way to the class which needs them. More workers will find employment in the manufacturing sector, and agricultural productivity will continue to decline. Economic decline will occur following the schema laid out by Quesnay.

It is doubtful if Quesnay saw the *Tableau* in terms of the above steps. The mechanisms employed, however, are all his. Indeed, for Quesnay population was a function of effective demand, and productivity in agriculture was a function of capital employed. He assumed these two principles would determine growth and decline in the *Tableau*, although he did not work out the process in detail.

11.4 POLICY IMPLICATIONS OF THE MODEL

Without doubt, Quesnay made some very peculiar assumptions about economic surpluses and productivity in different sectors of the economy. His position that manufacturing was sterile has been criticized numerous times, beginning with Adam Smith in the *Wealth of Nations*.[20] Excessive focus on this easy target, however, has diverted attention from the important policy implications of the dynamic *Tableau*.

The critical point is not whether manufacturing is productive. Nor is it whether agriculture is more productive than manufacturing. Quesnay's key insight is a more general one – when spending favours less productive sectors, an economy will stagnate; in contrast, when spending favours more productive sectors, an economy will grow and prosper.

This insight provides the foundation for understanding the real world process of growth and stagnation. It also provides a plausible explanation for the deterioration of the US economy over the past twenty years. Moreover, it is consistent with several contemporary analyses of US economic decline.

Economist Lester Thurow has argued that the decline in US productivity growth 'can be traced to a shift in the mix of goods and services being produced'.[21] The service sector (including retail trade), where productivity is low and growing slowly, is the growing sector of the American economy in terms of both output and jobs. Manufacturing, with high and more rapidly growing productivity, is becoming a smaller portion of total output and employment. Because production and employment are shifting towards low productivity sectors, Thurow maintains that economy-wide productivity is falling. Falling productivity is then held responsible by Thurow for a stagnating economy and for falling standards of living in the United States.

Thurow's argument here is a simple mathematical one, involving weighted averages. Although this point is consistent with the dynamic *Tableau*, Quesnay actually moves one step beyond Thurow. Productivity is not a static notion for Quesnay. Rather, it changes with changing economic circumstances. Growth raises productivity and economic stagnation causes productivity to decline. Quesnay would thus add to the argument of Thurow the point that as **production** shifts away from manufacturing, productivity growth in the manufacturing sector should fall. This important fact about the actual US productivity slowdown is left unexplained by Thurow.

This also leads us to the second contemporary parallel with the dynamic Tableau – the growth laws of Nicholas Kaldor.[22] Tony Thirlwall[23] has identified several propositions which constitute the core of Kaldor's theory:

(i)   The faster the growth of the manufacturing sector, the faster overall economic growth.

(ii) The faster the growth of the manufacturing sector, the faster the growth of productivity in manufacturing. This is due to economies of scale or increasing returns.

(iii) The faster the growth of the manufacturing sector, the faster the growth of productivity outside manufacturing, and thus the faster the growth of productivity in the economy as a whole.

(iv) The growth of manufacturing is not constrained by the supply of labour, but is determined by demand from the agricultural and foreign sectors of the economy.

Juxtaposition of Kaldor and Quesnay on these four propositions is quite illuminating.

First, and most obvious, both Kaldor and Quesnay argue for the special status of one economic sector. It is agriculture that possesses dynamic features for Quesnay and manufacturing that is dynamic for Kaldor. Yet, for both of them, the growth of that dynamic sector causes overall economic growth. Moreover, this relationship does not work in reverse. The growth of other sectors does not spur economic growth according to Kaldor's laws. For Quesnay, as we have seen, relative growth of the sterile sector actually causes economic contraction.

Second, increasing returns provides a key mechanism in the growth theories of both Kaldor and Quesnay. Following the argument of Allyn Young, Kaldor maintains that the growth of manufacturing leads to economies of scale from increased differentiation and the process of 'learning by doing'.[24] For Quesnay, faster growth permits the transition from 'petite' to 'grande' agriculture. 'Grande' agriculture is large-scale farming. It employs horses rather than oxen to plough the land, and requires ploughs and other equipment to exploit the power of these horses. This is possible only when the demand for agricultural goods is high, thus justifying the additional investment as well as providing the additional resources to purchase horses and equipment.[25]

Third, the major difference between Kaldor and Quesnay concerns the impact of dynamic growth on the productivity of other economic sectors. Kaldor held that the productivity of other sectors would increase. In general, 'industrialization tends to accelerate the rate of change of technology, not just in one sector, but in the economy as a whole'.[26] Quesnay, of course, held that the manufacturing sector was always sterile. Shifts from 'petite' to 'grande' agriculture fail to have any positive consequences for manufacturing sector productivity. Manufacturing remains sterile in the face of all improvements in the agricultural sector.

Fourth, both Quesnay and Kaldor see the dynamic sector constrained by demand factors rather than by supply factors. We saw above that according to the *Tableau* increased demand for agricultural goods reallocate inputs to the agricultural sector. One potential economic problem for Quesnay is that spending, especially by wealthy proprietors, is likely to favour luxury manufactured goods. Similarly, Kaldor argued that economic growth would increase the demand for goods produced by the tertiary sector of the economy. For both Kaldor and Quesnay these spending tendencies will reduce overall economic growth unless something is done to raise demand for goods produced by the dynamic sector of the economy. Quesnay favoured taxes on wealthy proprietors and state spending on agricultural goods. Kaldor's solution, encouraging the export of manufactured goods, brings us to the third area where Quesnay's dynamic *Tableau* dovetails with contemporary analyses of US economic decline.

Beginning in the early 1980s a number of American economists have written about the loss of manufacturing jobs as a critical component of US economic decline.[27] To halt and reverse this decline, many analysts have called for a US industrial policy, paralleling the industrial policy employed in Japan.

As explained by Chalmers Johnson, industrial policy refers to government activities designed to develop various industries and enhance the global competitiveness of national industries. 'It involves the specific recognition that all government measures – taxes, licenses, prohibitions, regulations – have a significant impact on the well-being or ill-health of whole sectors. Industries and enterprises in a market economy.'[28] Industrial policy thus moves beyond the broad concerns of fiscal and monetary policies, which are indifferent to which sectors or parts of the economy receive economic stimulus.

Advocates of a US industrial policy have called for government support of high value-added industries. It is thought that development of these industries would create jobs that pay more to American workers, thus raising their standard of living, and also make America more competitive internationally.[29] As noted by Chalmers Johnson in the quotation above, this support can take many forms.

Several forms of industrial policy are evident in the dynamic *Tableau*. Most obvious is the need for government support for dynamic economic sectors. Although the dynamic *Tableaux* presented in section 12.3 had no government sector, this was merely a simplifying assumption of the exposition. For Quesnay, the state was part of the proprietary class. Therefore, the distribution of government expenditures between agriculture and manufacturing affects the distribution of proprietary class spending on these two sectors. Quesnay also assumed that spending propensities by those in the agricultural and manufacturing sectors would basically follow the lead of the proprietary class. As such, spending decisions by the government can affect economic growth both directly and indirectly.

A second form of industrial policy in the *Tableau* involves pricing. Quesnay consistently argued for high prices for agricultural goods. As early as his *Encyclopedia* article 'Corn', Quesnay noted the harmful effects of a low price for corn. Workers became lazy; farmers had difficulty finding workers; and servants served badly.[30] In contrast, high prices compensate the cultivator for his costs and prevent the agricultural sector from declining.[31]

An identical position is presented in all three editions of the static *Tableau*,[32] where Quesnay begins with the assumption of low and stable prices. He then assumes a change in economic policy – free trade, both foreign and domestic, becomes the new policy of the French government. Its implementation results in high and stable prices for all goods. Quesnay identified other policies having the same effect. Encouragement of trade; abolition of privileges, prohibitions and taxes; and increased communications would also tend to stabilize prices at high levels.[33] These policies all increase surplus of the dynamic agricultural sector, generate additional economic growth, and lead to a new equilibrium at a higher level of output.

Taxation constitutes a third sort of industrial policy in the dynamic *Tableau*. One of the most famous policy prescriptions of the Physiocrats was their call for a single tax on the agricultural surplus received by the proprietors. Imposing taxes elsewhere would reduce necessary inputs in agriculture or manufacturing. This, in turn, would lower output from these sectors.

The doctrine of the unique tax first appeared in Quesnay's *Encyclopedia* articles. The theme running through these pieces is that the cultivator ought not to be taxed.

If the sovereign imposes taxes on the cultivator . . . there is a decline in cultivation and a diminution in the proprietor's revenue, whence follows an inevitable retrenchment which affects hired people, merchants, workers and servants. The general system of expenditure, work, gain and consumption is thrown out of gear; the state grows weaker; and the tax comes to have a more and more destructive effect.[34]

Instead, Quesnay argues, taxes should be placed on the proprietor's revenue. This is the true wealth of the nation, and the only income that can be taxed without causing economic decline. Each edition of the static *Tableau* contains a maxim that makes a similar point – to obtain the high level of economic activity taxes must be laid directly on the proprieties.[35]

Quesnay's dynamic *Tableau* can therefore be regarded as the first use of tax policy for encouraging economic growth. This view is consistent with industrial policies that call for reduced tax rates, or tax incentives, for the high value-added sectors of the economy. In fact, the Physiocrats should be regarded as the first advocates of a tax-based industrial policy.

Finally, contemporary arguments for an industrial policy suffer from one serious flaw – they lack rigorous theoretical justification. Traditional economic analysis, which combines utility theory with Walrasian general equilibrium models, provides support for *laissez-faire* economic policies. Any government intervention distorts the allocation of resources, lowers economic efficiency, reduces the utility of members of society, and pushes economic growth below its potential.[36] Traditional theory thus views industrial policy as hindering economic performance.

To be taken seriously, industrial policy requires its own theoretical backing. One avenue of support can be found in the rich economic model of the *Tableau Economique*. The *Tableau* shows how government support for more productive sectors can improve economic efficiency and increase production. It also demonstrates how intelligent economic policy by the state contributes to dynamic economic growth, and how in the absence of appropriate policies economies can come to stagnate at very low levels of production. These lessons are as important today as they were more than 200 years ago.

Notes and References

1.   These remarks are reported in Fredrich Engels, *Herr Eugen Duhring's Revolution in Science* (New York: International Publishers, no date), p. 276.
2.   Paul A. Samuelson, 'Quesnay's "Tableau Economique" as a Theorist would Formulate it Today", in Ian Bradley and Michael Howard (eds), *Classical and Marxian Political Economy* (New York: St Martin's Press, 1982), p. 47.
3.   Marguerite Kuczynski and Ronald L. Meek (eds) *Quesnay's Tableau Economique* (New York: Augustine M. Kelley, 1972), Appendix A, no page number. The second and third editions of the *Tableau* are basically the same as edition one. However, they employ a base of 600 rather than 400 livres; thus all figures are 50 per cent greater in these latter versions of the *Tableau*.
4.   This proposition is expressed in Remarks 1, 5 and 6 which accompany the first edition of the *Tableau*. The theme running through these three remarks is that 'the whole of the 400 millions of revenue enters into the annual circulation and runs through it to the full extent of its course; and that it is never formed into monetary fortunes, which check the flow of a part of this annual revenue of a nation . . . to the detriment of the reproduction of this revenue and the well-being of the people',

Ronald L. Meek, *The Economics of Physiocracy* (Cambridge, Mass.: Harvard University Press, 1962), p. 109.

5. Quesnay's marginal notes at the left of the *Tableau* contain a few assumptions about population and per capita consumption. Revenue of 400 livres enables the proprietor to purchase the food and manufactured goods to live on. Quesnay maintains that his expenditures – 200 livres on agricultural goods and 200 livres on manufactured goods – can support one person in each of the producing classes. So while proprietors live on 400 livres, workers in the manufacturing and agricultural sectors subsist on 200 livres apiece. Per capita consumption of the proprietors is thus twice the per capita consumption of the producing classes. See Kuczynski and Meek, *Quesnay's Tableau Economique*, Appendix A.

6. This proposition is expressed in Remarks 2, 3, 4 and 10 which accompany the first edition of the *Tableau*. These all stipulate that the trade account of the economy must be in balance. Quesnay's most forceful call for exporting agricultural goods resounds in his article 'Corn', written between 1756 and 1757 for Diderots's *Encyclopedia*. This article was a polemic for free trade, and argued that with free trade France would export corn and import manufactured goods. See Ronald L. Meek, *The Economics of Physiocracy*, pp. 72–87.

7. Victor de Riquetti, Marquis de Mirabeau and François Quesnay, *L'Ami des Hommes* (Avignon, 1762), vol. V, pp. 92–101.

8. François Quesnay, 'The "First Economic Problem"', reprinted in Ronald Meek, *The Economics of Physiocracy* (Cambridge, Mass.: Harvard University Press, 1963), pp. 168–85.

9. Mirabeau and Quesnay, *L'Ami des Hommes*, vol. V, p. 118; vol. I, p. 348; and vol. II, p. 270; and François Quesnay, 'The "Second Economic Problem"', reprinted in Ronald Meek, *The Economics of Physiocracy* (Cambridge, Mass.: Harvard University Press, 1963), pp. 186–202. Also see Luigi Einaudi, 'The Physiocratic Theory of Taxation', in *Economic Essays in Honour of Gustav Cassel* (London: Frank Cass, 1967).

10. François Quesnay, *Philosophie Rurale* (Amsterdam: Chez Les Libraires Associes, 1764), vol. III, p. 29ff and vol. II, p. 45ff.

11. This problem plagues all attempts to reconstruct the dynamic *Tableau* such as Robert V. Eagly, *The Structure of Classical Economic Theory* (New York: Oxford University Press, 1974), chapter 2; Ronald L. Meek, 'Problems of the Tableau Economique', in Ronald L. Meek, *The Economics of Physiocracy*, pp. 265–96; and Henri Woog, *The Tableau Economique of François Quesnay* (Bern, Switzerland: A. Francke A. G. Verlag, 1950), pp. 82–98. For a more detailed explanation of the problems with these reconstructions see Steven Pressman, *Quesnay's Tableau: A Critique and Reconstruction* (New York: Augustus M. Kelley, forthcoming), chapter IV.

12. Meek, *The Economics of Physiocracy*, p. 84.

13. Ibid., p. 88.

14. Ibid., p. 110.

15. For calculations in the second edition of the *Tableau* see Meek, *The Economics of Physiocracy*, p. 120; for population calculations in the third edition of the *Tableau* see Marguerite Kuczynski and Ronald L. Meek (eds) *Quesnay's Tableau Economique* (New York: Augustus M. Kelley, 1972), p. 1f.

16. Meek, *The Economics of Physiocracy*, p. 112.

17. Ibid.

18. See Ibid., pp. 81, 131; François Quesnay, *François Quesnay et la Physiocratie* (Parls: Institut National d'Etudes Demographiques, 1958), pp. 450–2; and Joseph J. Spengler, 'Mercantilist and Physiocratic Growth Theory', Bert Hoselitz *et al.*, *Theories of Economic Growth* (Glencoe: Free Press, 1960), p. 60f.

19. Quesnay assumed that in the manufacturing sector $X food + $X manufactured goods + $2X raw materials would always yield $4X manufactured goods. In the agricultural sector, Quesnay assumed that equal values of food and manufactured goods were necessary to produce agricultural goods. The value of agricultural output varied, however, depending on agricultural productivity, but was always greater than the value of agricultural inputs.

20. Adam Smith, *The Wealth of Nations* (New York: Modern Library, 1937), p. 638ff.

21. Lester C. Thurow, *The Zero-Sum Society* (New York: Basic Books, 1980), p. 86. Also see Lester C. Thurow, *The Zero-Sum Solution* (New York: Simon & Schuster, 1985), chapter 3 – 'Slow Productivity Growth'.

22. Nicholas Kaldor, *Strategic Factors in Economic Development* (Ithaca: Cornell University Press, 1967). Also see the symposium on Kaldor's growth laws in the Spring 1983 Issue of the *Journal of Post Keynesian Economics* and Thomas R. Michl, 'International Comparisons of Productivity Growth: Verdoon's Law Revisited', *Journal of Post Keynesian Economics*, vol. VII (Summer, 1985), pp. 472–92.

23. Anthony P. Thirlwall, 'A Plain Man's Guide to Kaldor's Growth Laws', *Journal of Post Keynesian Economics*, vol. 5, no. 3 (Spring, 1983), pp..345–58.

24. Kaldor, *Strategic Factors in Economic Development*, p. 14.

25. Gianni Vaggi, *The Economics of François Quesnay* (London: Macmillan, 1987), p. 49; and Meek, *The Economics of Physiocracy*, p. 248.

26. Kaldor, *Strategic Factors in Economic Development*, p. 23.

27. See Barry Bluestone and Bennett Harrison, *The Deindustrialization of America* (New York: Basic Books, 1982); The Business Week Team, *The Reindustrialization of America* (New York: McGraw Hill, 1982); Robert Relch, *The Next American Frontier* (New York: Times Books, 1983); and Chalmers Johnson (ed.) *The Industrial Policy Debate* (San Francisco: Institute for Contemporary Studies, 1984). For an argument that the decline of the manufacturing sector caused the decline of the British economy see John Eatwell, *Whatever Happened to Britain?* (New York: Oxford University Press, 19820.

28. Johnson, *The Industrial Policy Debate*, p. 7.

29. Relch, *The Next American Frontier*, especially chapters I and XII; and Lester C. Thurow, *The Zero-Sum Solution* (New York: Simon & Schuster, 1985).

30. Meek, *The Economics of Physiocracy*, p. 86.

31. Ibid., p. 76.

32. See Remarks 12 and 13 of the first edition of the *Tableau* and Maxims 12 and 13 of the second and third editions.

33. See Woog, *The Tableau Economique of François Quesnay*, p. 90 and the references cited there.

34. Meek, *The Economics of Physiocracy*, p. 82.

35. This is usually Maxim 7. See Meek, *The Economics of Physiocracy*, pp. 112 and 121; and Kuczynski and Meek, *Quesnay's Tableau Economique*, p. 4f.

36. For arguments to this effect see Robert Z. Lawrence, *Can America Compete?* (Washington, DC: Brookings Institution, 1984).

12 Adam Smith and the New Economics of Effort

Thomas Michl

I

Neo-classical economists pay implicit tribute to Adam Smith by their continuing adherence to his view of the labour market. 'Of the many ideas of Adam Smith that have stood the test of time,' writes Albert Rees (1975, p. 336), 'few have weathered better or are still more relevant than the idea of compensating wage differentials.' Yet Smith's theory that a competitive labour market rewards workers for skills that are costly to acquire and for the disamenities associated with their work has stubbornly defied empirical verification. One explanation for this resistance to empirical tests, the efficiency wage theory, holds that the moral hazard involved in eliciting labour effort imposes a distorting layer of rents on the structure of pay.

In this chapter, I propose to examine Smith's labour market doctrines with special attention to the issues raised by this new view of the labour market. Surprisingly, Smith's thinking about the labour exchange anticipates the new view in several ways. He was, for example, mindful of the moral hazard involved in labour requiring trust, and he was aware that higher wages can increase the efficiency of labour. But historical limitations prevented him from combining these elements into an embryonic version of the efficiency wage model.

II

With characteristic economy, Adam Smith explains his theory of the inequalities of wages in the celebrated chapter X of the *Wealth of Nations*, thus,

> The five following are the principal circumstances which, so far as I have been able to observe, make up for a small pecuniary gain in some employments and counter-balance a great one in others: first, the agreeableness or disagreeableness of the employments themselves; secondly, the easiness and cheapness, or the difficulty and expence of learning them; thirdly, the constancy or inconstancy of employment in them; fourthly, the small or great trust which must be reposed in those who exercise them; and fifthly, the probability or improbability of success in them. (Smith, 1937, p. 100)

To these five factors, Smith adds qualifications. Employments must be 'well-known and long established', in their 'natural state' with respect to demand, and the 'principal employments of those who occupy them'. Even then, only under conditions of 'perfect liberty' will the labour market establish compensating wage differentials, and indeed, Smith devotes the second half of the chapter to the distortions in these produced by the 'policy of Europe'.

This account, with some minor emendations, conforms closely to the views of modern neo-classical economists. Two bicentennial tributes to Adam Smith as a labour economist, Rees (1975) and Brown (1976), follow Smith's logical structure by simply adding new items to the list of conditions which violate perfect liberty. A somewhat deeper modification, hedonic wage theory, formalizes the heterogeneity of tastes towards disamenities and the ability of firms to vary, at a cost, the amount of a disamenity offered; neither of these aspects were emphasized by Smith. But beneath the mathematical shell of the hedonic wage theory lies a kernel which is recognizably Smithian.

Recent efforts to verify the neo-Smithian theory have failed in two distinct dimensions. First, the Smithian theory predicts that, controlling for the skills which workers have acquired through investments in human capital, disamenities should receive a compensating differential. Yet aside from the risk of death or serious injury, little evidence exists that workers are so compensated. Second, the theory predicts that controlling for variations in the agreeableness or disagreeableness of work, industries should pay wages which reflect the skills and training costs required of their workers. Although there is obviously a high correlation between education and earnings, the industrial structure of wages contains a very large component that does not reflect the classical determinants. Two otherwise identical workers employed in similarly disagreeable jobs located in different industries do not, as a rule, earn equal wages.[1]

One class of efficiency wage models proposes that some of the inequality observed among industries originates from employment rents which arise where the moral hazard inherent in the labour exchange is acute.[2] A moral hazard exists whenever economic agents can take action to the detriment of other contracting agents, and avoid the consequences because, for example, information about their actions is costly to obtain. Moral hazard is a broad encompassing category, and efficiency wage models exploit one particular instance of it. An employer can hire only the worker, not her labour itself, which must be elicited or 'extracted' from the worker during her time under the employer's supervision. If information about worker performance is costly to obtain, workers can shirk with some chance of avoiding the consequences, this being the moral hazard faced by the employer. Conditions are ripe for an efficiency wage solution, to wit, pay workers a rent or wage premium which raises the cost of job loss since workers forfeit the rent should they shirk and be discovered. Because under some conditions raising wages can reduce labour costs by eliciting greater worker effort, these theories have come to be called efficiency wage theories.

A classic case in point is Henry Ford's five-dollar day, which, said Ford, was 'one of the finest cost cutting moves we ever made' (cited in Raff and Summers,

1987, S59). In 1913, Ford's plant suffered a 370 per cent annual turnover rate, a 10 per cent daily absenteeism rate, and was plagued by disciplinary problems. In 1914, he more than doubled wages, to five dollars a day, in the midst of a recession. In principle, the five-dollar day could have been compensation for the unpleasant conditions on the new assembly line. Raff and Summers (ibid.) present circumstantial evidence that it was not; Henry Ford paid efficiency wages.

Two groups of economists have simultaneously 'discovered' the efficiency wage idea, much like collective Merton twins. Each has its interpretation of the idea and, following Samuel Bowles (1985), it is useful to distinguish between the Marxian and the neo-Hobbesian interpretations. The Marxian interpretation identifies the antagonistic social relations inherent in private and unequal ownership of productive assets as the root of the problem of effort elicitation, or in Marx's terminology, extracting labour from labour power. The neo-Hobbesian interpretation identifies opportunistic individualism as a human condition, and the problem of effort elicitation is seen as inherent in any institutionalized system of social production. We can begin to appreciate his relationship to the new view of the labour market by asking if either school (or both) can rightfully claim Adam Smith as intellectual antecedent.

The Hobbesian firm is essentially a Leviathan in microcosm that creates benefits for all members of the firm by overcoming the free rider problem created by shirkers. It is very difficult to speculate on Smith's hypothetical view of such a firm. Smith rejects the Hobbesian doctrine on the origin of the State without at the same time rejecting that doctrine's emphasis on the benefits that the State confers upon citizens by lifting them out of a state of savagery.[3] For Smith, it is not the utility of civil authority which recommends it to us, but rather that we are constituted by our nature, particularly by our propensity to sympathize or emphathize with our fellows, to accept the restrictions imposed by a social order. This, among others, is a prominent and familiar theme in his *Theory of Moral Sentiments*. It is doubtful that Smith would accept the assumption of opportunistic individualism attached to the Hobbesian view of the firm.[4]

Yet Smith's more charitable view of human nature does not qualify him by default as a predecessor of the Marxian view. His views on the necessity for government to hold in check the envy of the poor for the private property of rich, and his reduction of distinctions of rank to expressions of human nature both betray a strong and instinctual conservatism.[5] Still, Smith comes very close to the position that the problem of motivation is endemic to capitalist social relations. 'A poor independent workman will generally be more industrious,' he writes, 'than even a journeyman who works by the piece. The one enjoys the whole produce of his own industry; the other shares it with his master' (Smith, 1937, p. 83).

III

Adam Smith recognizes the moral hazard problem in its general form by the inclusion of trust among the factors influencing wage inequality, and in his views of slavery, improvements on rented land, and the efficacy of joint stock companies (we would say corporations).

As Jevons (1964) first pointed out, Smith's theory of compensating wage differentials expanded on ideas of Richard Cantillon, who tells us that

> The Arts and Crafts which are accompanied by risks and dangers like those of Founders, Mariners, Silver miners, etc. ought to be paid in proportion to the risks. When over and above the dangers skill is needed they ought to be paid still more, e.g. Pilots, Drivers, Engineers, etc. When Capacity and trust-worthiness are needed the labour is paid still more highly, as in the case of Jewellers, Bookkeepers, Cashiers and others. (Cantillon, 1964, p. 21).

Smith extended and deepened these primitive thoughts, for example by adding the factors constancy of employment and probability of success, and by recognizing that the return to special training is likeable in principle to the return on any investment. His appropriation of trustworthiness appears in the following pas-sages, which retain the example of jewellers but add, somewhat confusingly, two of the 'liberal professions':

> The wages of goldsmiths and jewellers are every-where superior to those of many other workmen, not only of equal, but of much superior ingenuity; on account of the precious materials with which they are intrusted . . . We trust our health to the physician; our fortune and sometimes our life to the lawyer and attorney. Such confidence could not safely be reposed in people of a very mean or low condition. Their reward must be such, therefore, as may give them that rank in the society which so important a trust requires. (Smith, 1937, p. 105)

These passages have been the source of some confusion. Cannan, for example, notes Smith's apparent inconsistency here, for while the opening section of the chapter 'requires an allegation that it is a disadvantage to a person to have trust reposed to him . . . no such allegation is made' (ibid., note 15). It is difficult to see why working with valuables would impose a hardship on a goldsmith or jeweller, yet Hollander adopts this interpretation, writing that this 'element appears to be present in the argument' (Hollander, 1973, p. 131). Cannan's instinct that trust does not represent a disamenity appears to me correct, and some alternative explanation of the mechanism by which it does its work would seem to be required.

John Stuart Mill interprets the liberal reward for trustworthiness as a 'kind of monopoly price' (Mill, 1904, p. 208). Integrity is a scarce resource. A more plausible and less *ad hoc* interpretation is that, as regards the example of gold-smiths and jewellers at least, Smith recognizes a sort of moral hazard problem, for these workers receive a bonus or rent to dissuade them from embezzling the 'precious materials' with which they work. Sans the modern jargon (moral hazard, etc.), this is Paul Douglas's interpretation. The higher wages of goldsmiths and jewellers are 'insurance policies against theft' (Douglas, 1952, p. 119). 'Since men do not believe that virtue is its own reward, it is necessary to furnish more tangible incentives' (ibid.).

Can the same reasoning be applied to lawyers and doctors? Because these professions involve specialized information, their practice creates a moral hazard for the recipient of legal and medical services. How does a lay person know when his lawyer's or doctor's advice is sound and responsible? He who is willing to part with a substantial fee, or more precisely, a bribe, can be more confident of being well served by a professional unwilling to risk losing such business by providing slipshod service. Yet there are problems applying this formula to lawyers and doctors, and Douglas prefers to believe that these trades require pay commensurate with the 'lavish personal expenditure' that is a 'necessary competitive advertising expense which is required if one is to secure prestige and consequently public patronage' (ibid., p. 120). Brown (1976, pp. 249–50) more recently suggests simply that trust requires high status, and high status, in turn, requires high pay; but, he notes that in other places, Smith (1937, p. 100) was keen to show that status itself is a form of compensation ('Honor makes a greater part of the reward of all honourable professions') and that the liberal professions are partly on this account under-rewarded in pecuniary terms.

There remains one other reference to trust which has gone unnoticed in this connection. Smith denies that the wages of 'inspection and direction' are part of the profits of stock. Rather, they represent the value of the manager's labour, and are a return 'not only to his labour and skill, but to the trust which is reposed in him' (ibid., p. 49). Smith clearly has in mind a hired manager ('In many great works, almost the whole labour of this kind is committed to some principal clerk'), and seems to refer to a type of moral hazard problem. The manager is responsible for the capital which the owner has entrusted to him, and should he fail to oversee the labour process with due diligence, the owner faces a (morally hazardous) loss of yield or principal on his capital advance.

In at least three other settings, Smith refers to a recognizable moral hazard problem. First, the labour of slaves, 'though it appears to cost only their maintenance, is in the end the dearest of all. A person who can acquire no property, can have no other interest but to eat as much, and to labour as little as possible' (ibid., p. 365). Second, under leases of short or insecure term (an imperfect contract in modern terminology), farmers are discouraged from improving the land, lest they be dispossessed before such investments are recovered with the expected profit. The relatively favourable conditions under which English farmers rent, however, remove this barrier to modernization. 'There is, I believe, no-where in Europe, except in England, any instance of the tenant building upon the land of which he has no lease, and trusting that the honour of his landlord would take no advantage of so important an improvement' (ibid., pp. 368–9).

Third, Smith's strictures against joint stock companies stand as perhaps the *locus classicus* of the moral hazard literature.

The directors of such companies, however, being the managers of other people's money then of their own, it cannot well be expected, that they should watch over it with the same anxious vigilance with which the partners in a private copartnery frequently watch over their own . . . Negligence and profusion, therefore, must always prevail, more or less, in the management of the affairs of such a company. (ibid., p. 700)

Despite the modern flavour of his evident appreciation of the existence of the moral hazard problem in these special cases, Smith does not apply it consistently to the elicitation of labour effort. To gain an appreciation of his views of this problem, I turn to his eighteenth-century economic milieu, as represented by that 'trifling manufacture', the pin factory.

IV

'What characterizes him as the political economist par excellence of the period of Manufacture,' Karl Marx says of Adam Smith, 'is the stress he lays on the division of labour' (Marx, 1967, p. 348). Here, manufacture denotes a system of division of labour erected on the foundation of traditional artisanal techniques of production, and organized around domestic shops, sheds, and small manufactories – 'proto-industry' is the term in currency among historians. Smith's relative silence on the system Marx termed Modern Industry, organized around the factory and machino-facturing techniques, is the subject of the final section. Since Smith's views of the labour market must have been heavily influenced by the manufacturing system as it reached its zenith in the late eighteenth century, let us consider the nature of work and of the worker in this period.

Adam Smith's choice of the pin factory (we might now say manufactory) to illustrate the effects of the division of labour affords a handy expositional strategem. Although he claims to have actually visited such a factory, his description appears to have been drawn from the *Encyclopedie*, and it focuses entirely on the technical side of things.[6] Ashton (1925) describes a pin manufactory in Warrington, around 1814–21, which is probably representative of late eighteenth-century conditions. From his description, we can flesh out some of the interesting institutional details of such an operation.

With one exception, all work was piecework (ibid., p. 283). Nor was this exceptional in the period. 'Almost all master manufacturers now find it to their interest to pay their workpeople by the piece or the great,' wrote a pamphleteer in 1757 (quoted in Ashton 1954, p. 217). Under piecework, it is fair to say that there is no moral hazard problem deriving from effort elicitation, for workers are paid by results. Such payment systems must have been effective under static technical conditions. With technical change, payment by results creates incessant disputes over rates, such as the rate fight which first inspired Frederick Taylor to conceive his philosophy of scientific management in the late nineteenth century.

In the pin factory, whitening and tinning were assigned to the foreman, who received a fixed wage of 25s per week. There is no record of whether he paid helpers or assistants out of this stipend (during the plant's first months of operation, the process was done by two or three men), but subcontracting was a common arrangement elsewhere in the operation. Heading, for example, was primarily put out to women, who ran home shops in which children were employed and paid out of the piecewages that the women received. Subcontracting, a common practice in the manufacturing system as well as in later factories, resolves a problem of supervision; more precisely, this 'was not a method of creating factory discipline, but of evading it' (Pollard, 1963, p. 264). In cases like the home shops of headers, the adult workers saw to it that their young charges pulled their weight. In cases of group payment like the butty system, where the subcontracting group was made up more nearly of equals, each worker had an interest in monitoring his mates.

While many operations were performed on premises, a substantial amount was put out. Wire drawing, straightening, pointing and cutting were performed on premises, by men. Twisting and cutting heads were done in home shops, with tools provided by the firm, by men and women. As noted above, some heading and all whitening and tinning were done on premises. The final stage, papering, was homework performed by women and children.

Outwork carries with it a danger of embezzlement and adulteration that dogged the putters-out of the eighteenth century. Spinners might return yarn moistened with oil or water to compensate for light weight; small pebbles woven into coarse fabrics might serve the same purpose. The spoils of such activity might find an outlet on a black market. That these abuses were more than episodic is shown by the progressive increase of penalties from 1700 to 1770 against purloining goods, and the reduction in the legally mandated limit to the term during which put-out goods were to be returned, from twenty-one days in 1749 to eight in 1777 (Ashton, 1954, p. 210). In many cases, the risk of recovering adulterated or mishandled produce must have been a powerful force in urging a workshop or proto-factory form of organization upon the master, as in the West Country, where 'high-grade wool was too expensive to be entrusted to scattered cottagers' (ibid., p. 115). One might speculate that the mosaic of outwork and shopwork in the pin factory, and others like it, may in part reflect differences in the need for close supervision of materials and tools at different stages of the production process. It is legitimate to criticize Adam Smith, as has Stephen Marglin (1974) for failing to recognize the import of this particular moral hazard problem in the genesis of the manufactory.

For the worker, the eighteenth century lay at the cusp of a change from the task orientation of preindustry to the timed labour of modern society, as E. P. Thompson (1967) reminds us. The task orientation of much outworking encouraged the habit of alternate spells of hard labour and idleness so well captured by a popular late eighteenth-century song.

How upon a good Saint Monday
Sitting by the smithy fire,
Telling what's been done o't Sunday
And in cheerful mirth conspire
    Soon I hear the trap-door rise up,
    On the ladder stands my wife;
    Damn thee, Jack, I'll dust my eyes up,
    Thou leads a plaguy drunken life;
                'The Jovial Cutlers'
              (in Thompson, 1967, p. 73)

The cutler's wife was not without company in her complaints. Prominent in writings of the eighteenth century was disapproval of the short weeks, drunken weekends, holidays, and desultory work habits of the labouring classes. Many writers endorsed the view of Arthur Young, that 'everyone but an idiot knows that the lower classes must be kept poor or they will never be industrious' (cited in Furniss, 1920, p. 118). In *Lectures on Jurisprudence*, Smith himself repeats this deprecating attitude towards the working poor. In elaborating his well-known qualification that the division of labour has as its drawback that it stupifies the worker, he adds this stricture against neglecting education by apprenticing a child too young:

When he is grown up he has no ideas with which he can amuse himself. When he is away from his work he must therefore betake himself to drunkenness and riot. Accordingly we find that in the commercial parts of England, the tradesmen are for the most part in this despicable condition: their work thro' half the week is sufficient to maintain them, and thro' want of education they have no amusement for the other but riot and debauchery. So it may very justly be said that the people who cloath the whole world are in rags themselves. (Smith, 1978, p. 540)

The latter half of the century witnessed a sea change in the attitudes of writers on the habits of workers, as exemplified in Smith's own writing.[7] Thus, in the *Wealth of Nations*, Smith writes, volte-face:

The liberal reward of labour, as it encourages the propagation, so it increases the industry of the common people . . . Where wages are high, accordingly, we shall always find the workmen more active, diligent, and expeditious, than where they are low . . . Some workmen, indeed, when they can earn in four days what will maintain them through the week, will be idle the other three. This however, is by no means the case with the greater part. (Smith, 1937, p. 81)

Smith advances two analytically distinct mechanisms for the economy of high wages by which increased pay encourages industry. First, he makes clear the role which payment by results has in producing such activism.

> Workmen, on the contrary, when they are liberally paid by the piece, are very apt to over-work themselves, and to ruin their health and constitution in a very few years. A carpenter in London and in some other places, is not supposed to last in his utmost vigour above eight years. Something of the same kind happens in many other trades, in which the workmen are paid by the piece; as they generally are in manufactures . . . Excessive application during four days of the week, is frequently the real cause of the idleness of the other three, so much and so loudly complained of. (ibid., 81–2)

Far from begrudging the worker his or her relaxation, Smith now treats it as an entitlement, a well-deserved break, and he does not hesitate to pronounce upon the motives of those who complain 'so much and so loudly'. 'Masters of all sorts, therefore, frequently make better bargains with their servants in dear than in cheap years, and find them more humble and dependent in the former than in the latter . . . They naturally commend the former as more favorable to industry' (ibid., p. 83).

Second, and here the argument takes a strange twist, he now invokes the very different principle that 'in years of plenty, servants frequently leave their masters and trust their subsistence to what they can make by their own industry' (ibid., p. 83). Recall that independence is conducive to greater effort ('A poor independent workman will generally be more industrious'). It is a curious argument that the industriousness of the labouring population should rise in years of prosperity because these 'increase the proportion of independent workmen to journeymen and servants of all kinds' (ibid., p. 84). Smith may have had outworkers in mind, for what else would a poor independent workman do in the eighteenth century?

It is notable that Adam Smith here comes closest to embracing the central insight of modern efficiency wage theories precisely by referring to two conditions which render the efficiency wage theory nugatory. The economy of high wages in one instance derives from the ability of workers to escape from the labour exchange. And in the case of payment by results, where the efficiency wage theory does not apply even though other varieties of moral hazard may be present, he simply judges the workers' supply elasticity of effort with respect to piece rates to be positive and large. At any rate, his ideas have clearly been conditioned by his location at the height of manufacturing but before there arose the very different problems of labour discipline associated with the factory.

V

As the scale of enterprises grows, so too does the classic problem of taming the refractory hand of labour. In small manufactories and workshops, the presence of the owner or his manager permits close supervision and monitoring. But in larger enterprises, surveillance becomes more difficult. Modern efficiency wage theorists have suggested that the tendency for large establishments to pay higher wages, controlling for levels of human capital, may reflect the greater acuteness of the effort elicitation and monitoring problems in large organizations.

Of the labour of inspection and direction, recall that Smith writes that in 'many great works' it is 'committed to some principal clerk'. Were the special problems of management in such enterprises unknown to him? There are two explanations for his silence on the matter. First, it has been argued that Smith ignored the many hints of technological change that snowballed into the Industrial Revolution; his silence could be merely a species of the same indifference to current economic developments. But Koebner (1959), who introduced this opinion, argues that it was not ignorance of recent changes but the fact that spectacular breakthroughs by 'projectors' (as Smith called them) did not jibe with Smith's own project of warning of the potentially deleterious influence of the merchants and manufacturers.

Second, Smith could have been genuinely uninformed about the factory. Hollander, who dissents from Koebner's opinion by stressing the importance of technical change in Smith's thought, concedes that Smith failed to appreciate the development of integrated factories, especially in the cotton trades (Arkwright's Cromford mill opened in 1771), but implies this is the result of the insignificance of the cotton industry in comparison to woollens (Hollander, 1973, p. 240). Perhaps large-scale factories, with their new discipline problems, were too rare an occurrence to have attracted Smith's attention. Ashton reports that around 1780, there were only twenty water driven factories in the whole of England, but that ten years later the number had risen to 150 (Ashton, 1954, p. 117).

Yet Smith was definitely not unaware of the iron works of the Carron Company. Its proximity to Kirkaldy (where the company maintained a warehouse even as Smith was there working on the *Wealth of Nations*), its fame across Europe, and its novelty in a relatively backward Scotland would have made it an object of curiosity. Smith was a personal friend of one of the founding partners, John Roebuck; surviving correspondence (Roebuck, 1977) from 1775 from Roebuck suggests they were well acquainted. Hume wrote to Smith, in 1772, that 'The Carron Company is reeling' and asked if this, together with the financial panic of that year, 'will occasion the Revisal of any Chapters' (Hume, 1977) in the forthcoming magnus opus. But Smith's only mention in the *Wealth of Nations* of the works is when he notes that 'there has lately been a considerable rise in the demand for labor about Glasgow, Carron, Ayr-shire, etc.' (Smith, 1937, p. 76), which has caused an elevation of pay levels. Finally, in 1784, Smith toured the Carron works with Edmund Burke (Campbell and Skinner 1982, p. 202).

Tours of the Carron works illustrate, in an unexpected way, the nature of indiscipline in these early factories. The works was quite large by contemporaneous standards, employing over 600 workers at its opening, and never under 300

(Campbell, 161, p. 65). As the fame of such a large and technically advanced operation spread, it became a routine call for visitors to Scotland. In 1772, the company served notice to the public that tours would only be provided upon presentation of a ticket, apparently because the workers themselves were running their own concessions. The plant manager, writing to the secretary, assured him that with this notice, 'we have taken every opportunity of showing disapprobation of our Servants and Workmen receiving money from strangers under pretence of showing the Works. We therefore hope that the Nobility and Gentry, who may please to command Tickets will give no money at the Gates or in the Works' (in Campbell, 1961, p. 39). None the less, unauthorized visits for other purposes continued, and 'pilfering, great as well as small, continued on an extensive scale almost daily' (ibid., p. 40). By 1780, the plant had been secured by the erection of a fence and the employment of watchmen.

The early history of the works is punctuated by frequent incidents of conflict between management and labour. The plant's first manager, William Cadell, complained of the drunkenness and inefficiency of even the most skilled workers, who had been imported from England for their knowledge of furnace keeping, and he resorted to dismissals in 1761 to promote order (ibid., pp. 52–3). There were strikes, usually by the colliers employed by the company but there were also episodes of unrest involving the furnace keepers (ibid., pp. 64–9). The following passage, which includes mention of the company's response to the 1772 crisis, reveals that the problems of ordinary indiscipline were endemic:

> At work men were often careless so that their workmanship was defective – in 1772 the managers were instructed to deduct an appropriate amount from wages for all defective goods produced – and timekeeping was bad. In sum, for all the harsh measures, or perhaps simply because of them, industrial discipline was really nonexistent. After the 1772 crisis Gascoigne and Thomas Roebuck tried to implement a major reorganization of their labour force to try to prevent any underemployment. They began at the top by ordering William Lowes and the other clerks in the office to be there from eight to two and from three to seven in summer and from nine to two and from three to seven in winter, and to have all letters written by twelve o'clock and copied by four. Attempts were made to extend this new code of industrial discipline downwards, but with little success. (ibid., pp. 70–1)

What can account for Adam Smith's apparent indifference to the problem of discipline in the early factory? His closeness to the principals and to the plant of the Carron Company and the evident degree to which indiscipline was a problem there suggest to me that ignorance is not a likely candidate. Rather, I submit, one needs to keep in mind the power that Smith's vision of the manufacturing system had in shaping his thoughts, and in this case, in filtering the raw data drawn from economic life. From this angle, the Carron works and others like it might have appeared as curiosities that did not demand incorporation into economic theory.

And it is important to recall that the problem of management was being solved by the practical men – Wedgwood, Arkwright, and the like – who faced it. Systematic *thinking* about the problem of management would await the arrival of Andrew Ure, Charles Babbage and Frederick Taylor. Despite the absence of even the beginnings of a theory of labour discipline under Modern Industry, arguably so necessary to the efficiency wage model, Smith's thought richly anticipates other key elements of the new view of the labour market.

Notes

1. While these generalizations remain contentious, they are supported by a substantial empirical literature. For evidence about returns to disamenities, see Brown (1980); for evidence on interindustry wage differentials, see Krueger and Summers (1987).
2. The model described here is sometimes called the shirking model. Other efficiency wage models do exist, based on alternative ways in which the efficiency of labour can depend upon the wage such as through turnover costs or adverse selection.
3. For Smith's discussion of this issue, see (Smith, 1976, pp. 499–502).
4. This claim plays a central role in the controversy on the alleged inconsistency between the *Wealth of Nations* and *Theory of Moral Sentiments*; see Heilbroner (1982) and references therein for further discussion. In short, I would agree with the position taken by Heilbroner and others that the 'prudent man' of *Theory of Moral Sentiments*; whose behaviour is deeply social albeit self-interested, is the economic agent of the *Wealth of Nations*.
5. Heilbroner (1982) brings into sharp relief that Smith's conservatism on the issue of social ranks required a curiously asymmetric application of the principle of sympathy, namely, that we sympathize (or empathize) with our social superiors with greater intensity and effect than we do with the poor.
6. Foley (1974) discusses Smith's sources of information about the division of labour in some detail.
7. See Coats (1958) for an important discussion of this change.

References

Ashton, T. S. (1925) 'The Records of a Pin Manufactory, 1814–21', *Economica*, vol. 15, November, pp. 281–92.

Ashton, T. S. (1954) *An Economic History of England: The 18th Century* (New York: Barnes & Noble).

Bowles, S. (1985) 'The Production Process in a Competitive Economy: Walrasian, Neo-Hobbesian, and Marxian Models, *American Economic Review*, vol. 75, no. 1, March, pp. 16–36.

Brown, C. (1980) 'Equalizing Differences in the Labour Market', *Quarterly Journal of Economics*, vol. 94, February, pp. 113–34.

Brown, E. H. Phelps (1976) 'The Labour Market', in T. Wilson and A. S. Skinner (eds), *The Market and the State: Essays in Honour of Adam Smith* (Oxford: Clarendon Press), pp. 243–59.

Campbell, R. H. (1961) *Carron Company* (Edinburgh: Oliver & Boyd).

Campbell, R. H. and A. S. Skinner (1982) *Adam Smith* (New York: St Martin's Press).

Cantillon, R. (1964) *Essai sur la nature du commerce en generale*, ed. by H. Higgs (New York: Augustus M. Kelley).

Coats, A. W. (1958) 'Changing Attitudes to Labour in the Mid-eighteenth Century', *Economic History Review, Second Series*, vol. 11, no. 1, August, pp. 35–51.

Douglas, P. H. (1952) 'Smith's Theory of Value and Distribution', in H. W. Spiegel (ed.), *The Development of Economic Thought* (New York: John Wiley).

Foley, V. (1974) 'The Division of Labour in Plato and Smith', *History of Political Economy*, vol. 6, pp. 220–42.

Furniss, E. (1920) *The Position of the Labourer in a System of Nationalism* (New York: Houghton Mifflin).

Heilbroner, R. L. (1982) 'On the Socialization of the Individual in Adam Smith', *History of Political Economy*, vol. 14, no. 3, pp. 427–39.

Hollander, S. (1973) *The Economics of Adam Smith* (Toronto: University of Toronto Press).

Hume, D. (1977) 'Letter to Adam Smith, 27 June 1772', in E. C. Mossner and I. S. Ross (eds), *The Correspondence of Adam Smith* (Oxford: Clarendon Press)., pp. 161–63.

Jevons, W. S. (1964) 'Richard Cantillon and the Nationality of Political Economy', in H. Higgs (ed.), *Essai sur la nature du commerce en general* by Richard Cantillon (New York: Augustus M. Kelley).

Koebner, R. (1959) 'Adam Smith and the Industrial Revolution', *Economic History Review, Second Series*, vol. 11, no. 3, 381–91.

Krueger, A. and L. H. Summers (1987) 'Reflections on the Inter-industry Wage Structure', in K. Lang and J. Leonard (eds), *Unemployment and the Structure of Labor Markets* (New York: Basil Blackwell).

Marglin, S. A. (1974) 'What Do Bosses Do?', Part I, *Review of Radical Political Economics*, vol. 6, Summer, pp. 60–112.

Marx, K. (1967) *Capital, volume I* (New York: International Publishers).

Mill, J. S. (1904) *Principles of Political Economy* (New York: D. Appleton).

Pollard, S. (1963) 'Factory Discipline in the Industrial Revolution', *Economic History Review, Second Series*, vol. 16, no. 2, pp. 254–71.

Raff, D. M. G. and L. H. Summers (1987) 'Did Henry Ford Pay Efficiency Wages?', *Journal of Labor Economics*, vol. 5, no. 4, Part 2, October, pp. S57–S86.

Rees, A. (1975) 'Compensating Wage Differentials', in A. S. Skinner and T. Wilson (eds), *Essays on Adam Smith* (Oxford: Clarendon Press), pp. 336–49.

Roebuck, J. (1977) 'Letter to Adam Smith, 1 November 1775', in E. C. Mossner and I. S. Ross (eds), *The Correspondence of Adam Smith* (Oxford: Clarendon Press), pp. 182–4.

Smith, A. (1937) *An Inquiry into the Nature and Causes of the Wealth of Nations*, ed. E. Cannan (New York: Modern Library).

Smith, A. (1976) *Theory of Moral Sentiments* (N. Shadeland, Ind.: Liberty Fund/Liberty Classics).

Smith, A. (1978) *Lectures on Jurisprudence*, ed. by R. L. Meek, D. Raphael, and P. Stein (Oxford: Oxford University Press).

Thompson, E. P. (1967) 'Time, Work-discipline, and Industrial Capitalism', *Past and Present*, vol. 38, December, pp. 56–97.

13 Classical Perspectives on Investment: An Exegesis of Behavioural Assumptions

Chidem Kurdas

> We all wish to add to our enjoyments or to our power. Consumption adds to our enjoyments – accumulation to our power . . . D. Ricardo, 1952, vol. VI, pp. 134–35

There is a mechanistic view of investment commonly attributed to classical writers, from Smith to Marx. Josef Schumpeter summarizes this view: 'the important thing was to have something to invest: the investment itself did not present additional problems either as to promptness – it was *normally* sure to be immediate – or as to direction – it was sure to be guided by investment opportunities that were equally obvious to all men' (Schumpeter, 1954, p. 572; italics in original). The purpose of this chapter is to qualify the image of investment as automatic reaction. The discussion focuses on classical statements as to the motives behind the act. The first two sections are on the role this question plays in the 'general glut' debate between Ricardo and Malthus. The other two sections are on Marx's explanation of investment. The common theme is that the various perspectives on investment rest on different assumptions as to what motivates individuals, and these assumptions fall beyond the conventional subject matter of economics.

Perhaps the most fundamental lesson one can get from classical writings with regard to the determinants of investment is from the *Wealth of Nations*. It is a lesson that points to the crucial role of the larger political and social environment. The Chinese economy, according to Adam Smith, has long been stationary. What accounts for the lack of accumulation in China? The country, Smith observes, 'had probably long ago acquired that full complement of riches which is consistent with the nature of its laws and institutions'. These riches are less than what it could achieve, with its natural resources, under different laws and institutions (Smith, 1976, p. 111). Foreign trade is frowned upon and constrained in China. Small business people have no security, and can be 'pillaged and plundered at any time by inferior mandarins'. Hence they are discouraged from accumulating capital. The rich and powerful monopolize all trades and make high profits. They do not need to save and invest since they can already appropriate so large a share of the social product. Legal, political and social structures of the Empire thus discourage investment. The wealth of China could be much larger, according to the central message of the *Wealth of Nations*, if it became a society of 'perfect liberty'.

13.1 PROFIT AND ACCUMULATION: RICARDO VERSUS MALTHUS

There are three issues that relate to investment in the exchange between Malthus and Ricardo:

(1) Whether aggregate demand can fall short of a country's potential output – the nub of the general glut controversy.
(2) If it does, whether this can affect the long-run rate of profit.
(3) The consequence of a fall in the rate of profit.

The second issue does not directly impinge on the subject of investment. It is concerned not with why there may be a general glut, but with the distributional impact of deficient aggregate demand. By contrast, the replies to questions one and three depend on the determinants of investment spending. In question one, investment is a possible *cause* of general glut, while in question three it is the *effect* of falling profitability. Following this logical schema I will first deal with number two, then turn to one and three, which are more fully explored in the next section.

In his 1824 review of McCulloch's *Essays*, a year after Ricardo's death, Malthus gave an uncharacteristically clear statement of the conclusion he wanted to draw from the general glut argument.

> Of the truths which Mr. Ricardo has established, one of the most useful and important, is that profits are determined by the proportion of the whole produce which goes to labor . . . It is, however, one important step in the theory of profits, which of course cannot be complete till we have ascertained the cause which, under all circumstances, regulates this proportion of the whole produce. (Malthus, 1963, p. 189)

For a given wage, Ricardo shows how to determine the corresponding rate of profit. Malthus proposes, in effect, to close Ricardo's system, by adding an explanation of the real wage.[1] The problem is that the system is already closed. Ricardo assumed a subsistence wage rate, which is enforced by the population mechanism described in Malthus's early *Essay on Population*. There is no degree of freedom with regard to the rate of profit – it is determined by the subsistence wage rate.[2]

Malthus does not explicitly confront the conflict between his later supply and demand explanation of income distribution and his earlier, population-based view. But he does indirectly try to resolve it. The productiveness of labour on land has been supposed to regulate the share of labour, he writes. In his opinion 'improvements in agriculture' suspend the operation of this effect. The fertility of land sets a limit on the profit rate, and the 'state of demand and supply' regulate profit-ability within this limit. As less fertile lands come into cultivation, the ceiling on the profit rate comes down. Malthus is confused here: given any 'ceiling', i.e. given any degree of land fertility, it is the subsistence living standard of workers[3] that determines the 'normal' profit rate in the Ricardian schema. If the 'proportion in which the produce . . . is divided between labor and profits' depends on the supply of and demand for total output, then the real wage must be capable of staying above subsistence without being endangered by population growth. Malthus asserts that the 'ordinary state of profits' depends on the 'ordinary state of demand', evidently meaning by 'ordinary' what Ricardo meant by 'normal'. This implies that the long-term wage rate will not be brought down to a socially given minimum by an increase in numbers.[4]

Leaving aside the weakness of his attempt to get around the population-based subsistence wage that Ricardo took from his own *Essay on Population*, Malthus argues that the level of demand relative to productive capacity affects the general price level. Through this effect it has the power to change the real wage rate, since the money wage is relatively sticky. Hence when there is a strong demand for commodities compared to the amount that can be supplied, prices will go up, the real wage down, and profitability will improve. Conversely, when demand is weak, prices fall, workers will get a larger share of the product, and profitability will decline. The second sequence is what happens in slumps.[5] The similarity between Malthus's argument and the 'widow's cruse' idea in Keynes's *Treatise* is worth noting. There, too, profits vary directly with aggregate demand. The difference is that for Keynes what causes the variation is investment demand, while Malthus does not clarify the distinction between the induced and autonomous components of aggregate demand. Post-Keynesian growth theory, following Keynes's lead, also argues that the growth rate of capital stock, through its impact on the price level, conditions profitability – investment spending generates profit, like the biblical 'widow's cruse' (Pasinetti, 1974). The common element with Malthus is the link between aggregate demand and income distribution.

For Malthus, an economy with substantial productive capacity, like England's, has a tendency to deflation. He and Ricardo conduct part of their discussion in the context of the post-Napoleonic war slump. Ricardo does not deny that there was some dislocation at the end of the war; what he denies is Malthus's contention that the slump is economy-wide and will have lasting ramifications. According to Ricardo there is a temporary mismatch between demand and the composition of output, due to the enlargement of sectors catering to wartime demand during the previous years. The mismatch is in the process of resolving itself as the overgrown industries shrink by discharging part of their labour force and those catering to regular peacetime demand increase employment and production. This readjustment process should have no long-term effect on income distribution.

The use of the post-war slump as illustration implies that the controversy is about cycles. But in linking the level of aggregate demand to distribution, Malthus goes beyond an explanation of recession. He argues that low profitability will depress investment not just temporarily but along a growth path. An economy subject to frequent slumps will have a low rate of capital formation, and in a historical perspective will become impoverished, even though the recessions themselves are due to demand lagging behind productive capacity. Malthus envisages accumulation facing the opposed dangers of too low a savings rate, as a result of which 'wealth must be gradually destroyed from the want of power to produce', and too high a savings rate, creating an economy where 'the motive to accumulate and produce must cease from the want of effectual demand' (Malthus, 1951, pp. 6–7).

A basic difference between Ricardo and Malthus reappears in later literature in various guises, and has an important bearing on the understanding of investment motivations. This is the difference in the time dimensions of their respective arguments. Ricardo's well-known statement that he is interested in long-run effects while Malthus is discussing short-term disturbances is specifically about the effect of demand on income distribution. By Ricardo's reasoning this can only be temporary, since in the long run the profit rate is a function of the cost of obtaining sufficient food to keep workers at subsistence level, and changes only as diminishing returns set in on land due to accumulation and population growth. Interestingly, critics of the later post-Keynesian version of the relationship between demand and distribution also discount it as a 'temporary' mechanism (Vianello, 1985).

Malthus (1951, p. 250) hotly denies that the effects he envisages are temporary, by asserting that the level of 'ordinary' demand determines 'ordinary' profitability, in contrast to an 'accidental state of the supply compared to the demand'. The latter is indeed temporary, but the 'ordinary' state of demand is supposed to be a persistent force. In his examples Malthus refers to historical experience and differences between countries. Thus England's high level of wealth is traced to foreign commerce from the time of Edward I onwards (*Notes* in Ricardo, 1951, p. 359). The country is now in danger of impoverishment since demand is not keeping up with capital accumulation. South American economies cannot grow 'while the extreme inequality of landed property continues, and no sufficient vent is found for the raw produce in foreign commerce' (ibid., p. 340). It is curious that Malthus, with landed interests close to his heart, decries 'extreme' inequality in land distribution. His point is that a large number of affluent farmers will form a mass market for manufactures, while a few grand landlords will not. He writes, 'A very large proprietor, surrounded by very poor peasants, presents a distribution of property most unfavorable to effectual demand' (Malthus, 1951, p. 373). Similarly, Ireland lacks the middle class that constitutes a domestic market for manufactured goods, and its exports have been restricted in the past by English protectionism (ibid., pp. 348–9n). Lacking both foreign and domestic markets, Malthus argues, even if Ireland had the capital, there would be nowhere to invest it. By contrast, the United States has grown rapidly thanks to its egalitarian land tenure system.

It would seem that Malthus thinks in terms of a succession of actual historical stages, not notional positions. He starts with a high rate of capital accumulation, such as that experienced in England prior to his own time. Fast growing export markets have kept demand and profits up for British manufactures, and as a result investment has been brisk. But this accumulation eventually produces a volume of commodities that cannot be sold at the original price level on which the investment calculations were based. The larger amount of output can be sold only at a lower price, and this causes profitability to fall below what was expected by the investors. At the next stage accumulation is weaker, but still with sufficient drive to cause the same situation again in the future. Through this sequence of deflations emerges a gradually weakening trend of growth. The reason why aggregate demand should fall chronically short of productive capacity at the original price level is a separate matter, to which we now turn.

13.2 THE INDUCEMENT TO INVEST

Both Malthus and Ricardo expect that a fall in profitability, due to whatever cause, will discourage accumulation. Ricardo consistently espouses the simple explanation of investment expressed in the following passage.

> The farmer and manufacturer can no more live without profit, than the labourer without wages. Their motive for accumulation will diminish with every diminution of profit, and will cease altogether when their profits are so low as not to afford them an adequate compensation for their trouble, and the risk they must necessarily encounter in employing their capital productivity. (Ricardo, 1951, p. 122)

The implication is that above the minimum necessary to cover the investor's 'trouble' and risk, investment is simply proportional to profitability – the mechanical view described by Schumpeter.

Malthus concurs that diminished profits lead to slower accumulation. But he cannot stop at this view of investment, given that he wants to provide an affirmative answer to the first question. He suggests that there may be a weakness in the incentive to invest prior to a fall in profit. In other words, in order to establish the possibility of a general glut, and answer the first question posed above, Malthus tries to qualify the automatic investment mechanism. But in terms of the consequences of falling profits, he envisages the same investor reaction as Ricardo.

Ricardo, like Malthus, forecasts declining profitability. But he attributes this to an altogether different reason, namely, the increase in the prices of foodstuffs with the real wage held constant at subsistence. Referring to Say's law, Ricardo argues that profitability cannot fall due to deficiency of demand, 'because demand is only limited by production' (Ricardo, 1951, *Principles*, p. 290). Adam Smith had written that 'the desire of the conveniences and ornaments of building, dress, equipage, and household furniture, seems to have no limit'. In that case, 'there can be no limit to the capital that may be employed in procuring them' (ibid., pp. 293–4). Smith is not consistent with his own view when he maintains that accumulation will increase the 'competition of capitals' and thereby reduce the profit rate; since markets grow at the same rate as capital, there can never be more 'capital' than 'market', so to speak. The same logic, of course, shows the error of Malthus's view that a deficiency of demand can lower the rate of profit. 'In response Malthus tries this track: You constantly say that it is not a question about the motives to produce. Now I have certainly intended to make it almost entirely a question about motives' (Ricardo, 1951, vol. VII, pp. 10–11). The question of motive arises with respect to both consumption and investment. In the context of consumption, Malthus tries to illustrate the point about aggregate demand by using examples of individual commodities: 'If we could not export our cottons, it is quite certain that, though we might have the power, we should not have the will, to consume them ourselves at such prices as would pay the producers' (Malthus, 1951, p. 359).

On occasion, Malthus and Ricardo distinguish the motivation behind investment from the availability of savings to be invested. Given the classical assumption that savings come from profits alone, of course, the division of the product between wages and profits is the crucial issue in growth. But they separate two aspects of accumulation: the 'power' to accumulate, meaning the availability of profits, versus the 'will' to accumulate. The distinction is not always clear, as 'power' and 'will' move together, i.e. when profitability falls, both the ability to finance investment and the desire to invest are reduced. However, Malthus seems to emphasize a possible failure of the *motivation* in the face of declining profitability, while for Ricardo the spirit is always willing provided the funds are there. Malthus argues: 'The demand for capital depends, not upon the abundance of *present* produce, but upon the demand for the future products of capital, or the power of producing something which shall be more in demand than the produce actually employed' (Ricardo 1951, vol. VI, p. 117; italics in original). The motive to accumulate, then, stems from a belief that the future output 'shall be more in demand', and according to Malthus such a belief is erronous, since demand will not rise at the same rate as the social product. Investors with 'rational expectations' formed in accordance with the Malthusian view of aggregate demand would know this, and therefore not invest. But in a world obeying Say's law it is irrational for investors to expect a falling off of future demand; there is no reason for them to hesitate to invest to the extent that profits allow, as Ricardo tirelessly points out. Malthus can only assert that investment will not be made because demand will be insufficient to buy the products of *future* capacity, which of course says nothing about why this is going to be the case. To explain how demand can fall off, he would have had to recast the expectation of 'demand for future products' as an independent force, so that when capitalists expect demand to lag behind and cut down their investments accordingly, their expectation becomes self-fulfilling.

Ricardo, for his part, cannot conceive a failure in both the motivation to invest and to consume. He reasons that if one goes down the other will go up sufficiently to compensate. In a letter Ricardo expresses this view:

We agree that effectual demand consists of two elements, the *power* and the *will* to purchase, but I think the will is very seldom wanting where the power exists – for the desire of accumulation will occasion demand just as effectually as the desire to consume . . . tho' it appears natural that the desire of accumulation should decrease with an increase of capital, and diminished profits, it appears equally probable that consumption will increase in the same ratio . . . In short I consider the wants and tastes of mankind to be unlimited. We all wish to add to our enjoyments or to our power. Consumption adds to our enjoyments – accumulation to our power, and they equally promote demand. (ibid., vol. VI, pp. 133–5; italics in original)

Thus Ricardo finds it plausible that the desire for both pleasure and power, on an individual and collective level, will exceed the capacity to produce. Obviously he assumes, as modern economists do, non-satiation in consumption. There is no reason for the two motives to add up to less than total income, leading to deficient effective demand. Malthus hints at a failure of motivation on both fronts, but he cannot say why the population should not be as voracious in pursuing pleasure and power as Ricardo supposes it to be.

What Malthus tries to argue is that a weakening of the pleasure motive would also destroy the potential for gaining future power. 'If the richer portion of society have to forego their accustomed conveniences and luxuries with a view to accumulation', they could invest a large share of national income for 'necessaries' for the whole population (Malthus, 1951, pp. 315–6). The hypothetical example Malthus sets up can be expressed in algebra:

$$P = L + I$$
$$W = N$$

Where P is total profits, L total luxury consumption, I investment, W the wage bill, and N worker consumption consisting of 'necessities'. Aggregate income is:

$$P + W = L + I + N$$

Now, Malthus reasons, suppose L went down. The funds can then be shifted to investment. Since the consumption of luxuries has gone down, this investment will have to be for the increased production of consumer goods for workers. Taking the total labour force as constant, there will be a shift of workers from industries catering to the rich to those provisioning the poor.

All very well, but workers can buy these additional consumer goods only if the wage bill is proportionally larger. With the size of the labour force constant, only a real wage increase provides them with the additional purchasing power. This can come about from a fall in the price level, or from a rise in the money wage. Presumably there will be no general glut if wages become high enough to create demand for the increased supply of necessaries.

But such investment 'could not possibly happen', concludes Malthus, because it would not be profitable. As we have seen, he accepts Ricardo's argument that there is an inverse relation between the wage rate and the profit rate. The higher wage rate, which creates demand for subsistence goods, means a lower profit rate. Malthus's reasoning requires that the individuals who are in a position to invest know that the profitability of investment has gone down. On these premises it is possible that the fall in investment will cause aggregate demand to fall short of capacity, in spite of greater consumption by workers.

This hypothetical example makes no sense whatsoever from Ricardo's perspective. It artificially assumes that the affluent citizens will not consume in spite of their decision not to invest. If they cannot use their income to extend their power, that is, if I remains low, why do they not use it for current enjoyment, i.e. put it back into L? Ricardo thus had the last word.

Perhaps, within his own framework, Malthus could have outflanked him. The merchants and manufacturers are a distinct social group in their savings behaviour. It is their excessive savings in particular that is supposed to cause deficiency in aggregate demand, since the landlords are not motivated to save. Whatever human beings in general feel about the pleasure of consuming, it is clear that for Malthus this specific group is very much into frugality. In fact, its members may enjoy saving at least as much as they enjoy consumption, and engage in it in spite of their pessimistic expectations with respect to future profitability. Malthus does not go in this direction, though it is implicit in his description of merchants and manufacturers (ibid., p. 400). They may save even if they lack the inducement to invest. The corollary is that investment does not necessarily take place just because savings are available.

In conclusion, there is a disagreement about basic motives in the general glut debate. In his objection to Say's law, Malthus hints that wealthy individuals may lack the motivation both to consume and to invest. Ricardo assumes that consumption is so desirable that this possibility is precluded. The non-satiation postulate is usually taken to be intuitively obvious. Certainly Ricardo regards it this way. Neither he nor modern economists defend it on more substantive grounds. Indeed, such a defence would go beyond the purview of mainstream economics, since it involves social and psychological factors. We shall see that this line of thought is a critical element in Marx's analysis of accumulation.

13.3 MARX ON SAVINGS AND INVESTMENT

It is tempting to inquire no further into Marx's investment mechanism than the image of accumulation as Moses and the prophets. As Schumpeter (1954, p. 750, n29) put it, for Marx capitalists are always in a hurry to invest and that they will do so can be taken for granted. This view is not strictly incorrect, but it is incomplete. The conventional classical notion that whatever is saved is invested is not an accurate representation of Marx, although an automatic investment impulse is part and parcel of his picture of capitalist dynamics. I will start by inquiring into the motives behind this impulse, then sketch out the other dimensions that have to be added on to this general frame to get a full view of the Marxian accumulation process.

Mark Blaug's (1985, p. 254) interpretation of the investment issue makes an interesting starting point. The deepest problem in the Marxian system, according to Blaug, is 'precisely what . . . govern(s) the willingness to invest'. Blaug reasons that the central classical notion of surplus depends on the investment question:

> If there is any economic sense in giving the name 'surplus value' to the incomes of capitalists and landlords, it must be because such payments, unlike the wages of workers, are not necessary to call forth the services of capital and land . . . The only condition under which the supply price of capital is always zero . . . is when neither savings nor investment is in any way connected with the interest rate or the profit rate. (ibid., p. 244)

Furthermore, Blaug concludes, Marx foresaw this objection: 'There is no problem of inducement to invest in Marx and if the theory of surplus value is really taken seriously there cannot logically be any problem of investment incentives. Unfortunately, this view destroys Marx's theory of business cycles and, indeed, his whole conception of the 'breakdown' of capitalism' (ibid., p. 245). Marx's writings do contain passages that indicate the motivation to invest is not lacking in capitalist society; it will be forthcoming in doses large enough to match available profits. But for him the motivation to accumulate is a different animal from the neo-classical motivation to sacrifice current consumption.

A number of relevant statements are to be found in Marx's attack on the abstinence theory of profits (section 3, chapter XXIV of *Capital*, volume I). Marx starts by distinguishing the two uses to which surplus product is put: 'One portion is consumed by the capitalist as revenue, the other is employed as capital, is accumulated . . . Given the mass of surplus value, then, the larger the one of these parts, the smaller is the other. *Ceteris Paribus*, the ratio of these parts determines the magnitude of accumulation' (Marx, 1954, pp. 554–5). The question is how this important ratio is determined. This is where most Marxian models stop, assuming investment is a residual – the profits left over from capitalist consumption, determined by the profit rate and the capitalist propensity to consume. Marx's comments in fact point in the opposite direction. Consumption is incidental since the capitalist as such is motivated by the prospect of augmenting his wealth as an end in itself. As 'personified capital' he is not interested in use values. It is 'exchange value and its augmentation that spur him into action'. These comments do not explain why this is the case, but in the subsequent text and in other writings Marx does suggest why he thinks capitalist wealth is an end in itself.

In his attempt to rebut the abstinence view, Marx asserts that luxury consumption is merely one of the means to achieving wealth, undertaken to assure the world of the capitalist's financial solvency. This is not a new idea for Marx, who propounded it long before he came to political economy and the writing of *Capital*. In the 1844 manuscripts he contrasts the old-fashioned 'spendthrift landowner' to the '*hard working, sober, economical, prosaic* industrialist who is enlightened about the nature of wealth' (italics in original). The latter 'also has his pleasures . . . but his enjoyment is a secondary matter; it is recreation subordinated to production and thus *a calculated, economic* enjoyment, for he charges his pleasures as an expense of capital' (Marx, 1963, p. 178; italics in original). The young Marx thinks that as industrial capitalism advances, 'the pleasure-loving individual is subordinated to the capital-accumulating individual, whereas formerly the contrary was the case'. Everybody, including the landlord, has to subordinate his consumption to the needs of capital, or face ruin (ibid., pp. 178–9). (This subordination obviously includes three martini lunches that can be charged 'as an expense of capital'.) As for economists who argue about the conflict between luxury and savings, they are 'still burdened with romantic, anti-industrial memories' of an earlier era (ibid., p. 180).

The accumulative urge rests on two separate rationales, one sociological, the other purely economic. These are described succinctly in the aforementioned chapter of *Capital*:

> Only as personified capital is the capitalist respectable. As such, he shares with the miser the passion for wealth as wealth. But that which in the miser is a mere idiosyncracy, is, in the capitalist, the effect of the social mechanism, of which he is but one of the wheels. Moreover, the development of capitalist production makes it constantly necessary to keep increasing the amount of the capital laid out in a given industrial undertaking, and competition makes the immanent laws of capitalist production to be felt by each individual capitalist, as external coercive laws. It compels him to keep constantly expanding his capital, in order to preserve it. (Marx, 1954, p. 555)

The word 'moreover' in the middle of this passage separates the social inducement to accumulate from the economic one. The first shows up as social pressure stemming from capitalist society's criterion of respectability. This is what Blaug refers to as 'conspicuous accumulation for its own sake' (Blaug, 1985, p. 254). Marx's sociological explanation runs deeper than the acquisition of prestige through wealth. He explicitly attributes the accumulative drive to the quest for power: 'To accumulate, is to conquer the world of social wealth, to increase the mass of human beings exploited by him, and thus to extend both the direct and the indirect sway of the capitalist.' A footnote elaborates this idea with a quotation from Martin Luther. Marx thus introduces the quote: 'Taking the usurer, that old-fashioned but ever renewed specimen of the capitalist for his text, Luther shows very aptly that the love of power is an element in the desire to get rich' (Marx, 1954, p. 555n). The passage cited includes the sentence: 'Therefore is there, on this earth, no greater enemy of man (after the devil) than a gripe-money, and usurer, for he wants to be God over all men.'

The point can be extended by referring to the increasing commodification of all aspects of life, which makes money the ultimate embodiment and symbol of all that is desirable. The young Marx had philosophized: 'What I as a *man* am unable to do, and thus what all my individual faculties are unable to do, is made possible for me by *money*' (Marx, 1963, p. 192; italics in original). The development of capitalist relations presumably reduces the importance of non-monetary goals inherited from earlier social orders. For this reason most individuals seeking prestige and power are bound to do so through capital accumulation, pointing to a systemic tendency in capitalism to invest whatever surplus is available. In this light Ricardo seems right that the 'will' to invest, of itself, should not constitute a limit to accumulation; businessmen will automatically invest profits to expand their status and realm of control. They can no more stop investing than medieval warlords could stop fighting. Or to put it slightly differently, just as a class of warlords who stop fighting have ceased being warlords, capitalists who break the MCM' circuit cease being capitalists. Furthermore, the economics of the market place reinforce the sociological drive. Competition forces each and every capitalist to strive to expand his capital for fear of being squeezed out by faster growing rivals. In brief, combined economic and social forces dictate the motto, 'Accumulate, accumulate! That is Moses and the Prophets!' (Marx, 1954, p. 558). So far we have only confirmed Blaug's conclusion that 'capitalists automatically re-invest all profits regardless of prospective returns' (Blaug, 1985, p. 245).

But of course they do not reinvest *all* profits; part of the surplus becomes 'revenue' used for capitalist consumption. The capital part of surplus is not a residual, since consumption in itself, as Marx emphasizes again and again, is not the capitalist goal. Neither the generalized social goad to save and invest, nor the pressure of competition, explains the share of capitalist consumption in profits. These social and competitive mechanisms indicate that in the long run invest they must – but what determines the fraction of profits to be saved? Interestingly, Marx states that the propensity to save will be adjusted if new opportunities for investment arise:

Under special stimulus to enrichment, such as the opening of new markets, or of new spheres for the outlay of capital in consequence of newly developed social wants, etc., the scale of accumulation may be suddenly extended, merely by a change in the division of surplus-value or surplus product into capital and revenue. (ibid., p. 575; italics added)

This sounds like the kind of stimulus Marx and Engels described in the Communist Manifesto as being responsible for the upsurge of capitalism in the first place: 'The discovery of America, the rounding of the Cape, opened up fresh ground for the rising bourgeoisie. The East-Indian and Chinese markets, the colonisation of America, trade with the colonies . . . (Tucker, 1978, p. 474). The opening of new markets goes on, leading to the rise of modern industry: 'Meantime the markets kept ever growing, the demand ever rising. Even manufacture no longer sufficed. Thereupon steam and machinery revolutionised industrial production' (ibid.). Presumably the waves of world-wide market expansion continue under advanced capitalism, and present, at times, 'special stimulus to enrichment' for capitalists. The propensity to save out of profits then adjusts to the increased propensity to invest. Marx does not mention a rising rate of profit in these circumstances, it seems that the new opportunities encourage expectations of profitability, whether or not the actual rate of return is higher.

The above passage on the adjustment of the savings propensity is consistent with the other statements on the unimportance of consumption to the capitalist, and has to be taken seriously. However, with this additional dimension, the Marxian savings and investment story appears to be both contradictory and indeterminate. Contradictory, since on the one hand there is an inherent tendency to invest to the limit, on the other, more can be easily invested by curtailing consumption if a 'special stimulus' comes around. Indeterminate, since investment opportunities determine savings, but investment was supposed to be constrained only by the availability of surplus. This impression is 50 per cent accurate. Indeterminacy is indeed a characteristic of the Marxian accumulation mechanism. But the two strands can be reconciled by considering the social need to accumulate as the normal state of things, defined with respect to a given savings propensity.

The 'normal' operation of the capitalist economy, above the minimum rate of profit necessary for there to be any accumulation at all, is

$$g = s \cdot r$$

This schedule is shown in Figure 13.1 as $s_1 \cdot r$. Investment stops altogether at r_{min}, for the same reason that Ricardo thought it would stop, namely, because the risk and trouble is no longer covered by the return. When new internal and/or external markets open up, the savings propensity changes, and the 'normal' relationship shifts, say to $s_2 \cdot r$, corresponding to the higher savings rate. The two types of movement, i.e. along the schedule and shifts of the schedule, are not logically contradictory, but the exact nature of the changes in the savings propensity is far from clear.

New markets provide the 'stimulus' to increase the fraction of profits saved; the stimulus must work through expectations of future profits. The idea is similar to what Keynes would describe as an upward shift of the marginal efficiency of capital schedule. The difference is that in the Keynesian context the effect of the shift is not on the propensity to save but on income and secondarily on the absolute amount of savings. For Marx, as for Keynes, businesses do not invest whatever they happen to save, but rather save what they want to invest, in

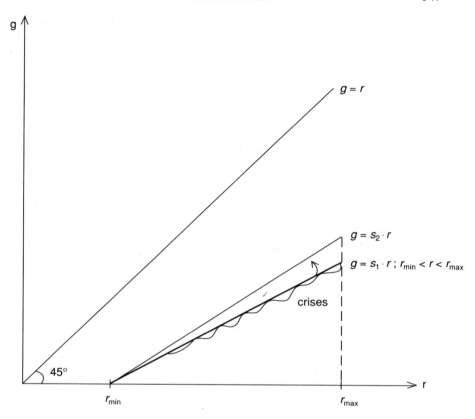

Figure 13.1   Marxian growth scenario

accordance with their perception of investment opportunities under given circumstances. The 'special stimulus to enrichment' could be labelled a certain state of long-term expectations. Capitalist consumption is the endogenous variable that comes out of the wash.

The ideas are similar in their ambiguity as well. Marx's notion of 'stimulus' is as indeterminate as Keynes's discussion of the state of expectations. Its vagueness becomes especially apparent when the idea is applied in the opposite direction. By inference, the lack of new markets and needs must cause capitalists to settle down to consuming more of the surplus. But new markets are in some measure due to accumulation; 'newly developed social wants' tend to be developed by businesses.[6] If capitalists will only invest, thus playing that 'most revolutionary' part attributed to them in the Communist Manifesto, new markets may follow. In this light Marx's remark can be seen as describing a virtuous circle of accumulation–market expansion–accumulation. However, this sequence of mutual feedbacks can be reduced to an extreme version of the Keynesian expectations view, a view expressed thus by Kaldor (1951): 'an economy is likely to grow at the rate at which its business men expect it to grow'. If business men think new markets can be created, and on this basis expand their operations, they may lift themselves up by their bootstraps. The 'new markets' and 'newly developed social wants' may be the cause of accumulation, but may also be its effect. The most that can be said unambiguously is that in an environment of rapid change in tastes and technology, and of commercialization of existing needs, capitalists are likely to perceive 'special stimulus', and accumulate at a higher rate.

There is yet another, a third, aspect to the convoluted story of the Marxian investment function. As Blaug and others (Laibman, 1983) have recognized, there is also a cyclical explanation of investment. In his discussion of crises Marx does consider the inducement to invest to be dependent on the profit rate. Thus on the 'tendency of the rate of profit to fall' Marx (1967) agrees with Ricardo and Malthus that accumulation falls with the rate of profit, not just because there are less profits to be invested, but because the 'motivation' to invest is eroded:

> The rate of profit is the motive power of capitalist accumulation. Things are produced only as long as they can be produced with a profit . . . What worries Ricardo is the fact that the rate of profit, the stimulating principle of capitalist production, the fundamental premise and driving force of accumulation, should be endangered by the development of production itself. (ibid., p. 259)

Blaug notes that accumulation as Moses and the prophets, and accumulation as determined by profitability, have different time dimensions. The check to accumulation due to a lower rate of profit breeds crises of 'overproduction' and unemployment (ibid., p. 242), but 'permanent crises do not exist' (Marx, 1968, p. 497n), so this is a temporary effect. What we have, then, is a cyclical mechanism, a simple economic explanation of fluctuations in investment, superimposed on the unconstrained social drive to accumulate. Marx sees the profit rate influencing investment not only because profits provide the finance, but because investors expect to make the same rate of return in the future as they made in the past. The profit rate does condition the willingness to invest, but only when it changes, and then temporarily – a steady rate of profit does not affect the *motivation* to invest, although it does condition the ability to finance the investment. Thus at a given, constant profit rate, investment is a point on the $(s_1 \cdot r)$ schedule in Figure 13.1. If there is a fall in the rate of return on investment, however, as Marx expects there to be due to mechanization, accumulation does not follow along the $(s_1 \cdot r)$ schedule. It temporarily fluctuates below it.

Changes in profitability influence capitalists' view of investment by disappointing their expectations. With a falling rate of return, expectations based on past rates are not borne out and this disrupts the accumulation process, feeding the crisis. But the disruption is temporary; expectations adjust to the new profit rate and accumulation resumes. Expectations adjust precisely because the underlying need to accumulate overcomes disappointment: 'once capitalists grow accustomed to a new, lower rate, accumulation resumes, no matter how low the new rate may be' (Laibman, 1983, p. 376). After all, within the Marxian frame of reference there is no long-term alternative to capital formation: what else can capitalists do?[7]

Marx, of course, does not make the case that capitalists consume more when profitability falls. That would contradict his understanding of what happens in crises. If capitalists switched from investment to consumption there would be no 'overproduction and surplus capital'.

We now have the three separate elements that constitute the Marxian approach to investment, summarized in Figure 13.1:

(1) The $s_1 \cdot r$ shows the 'normal' process, under given circumstances, both domestic and international, which underlie the savings propensity. It maps a steady rate of profit to a growth rate.

(2) The economy does not move down along $s_1 \cdot r$ when there is a fall in profitability (this being the only option Marx considers as a long-term trend). Instead, it dips below the schedule, to the shaded area of 'crises' (What sets off this crisis, i.e. what causes the rate of profit to fall, is not important to the crisis dynamics. It could be falling due to any reason, not necessarily the rising organic composition of capital Marx envisages.) The economy eventually makes its way back to $s_1 \cdot r$, with a lower growth rate to match the lower profit rate.

(3) When the underlying circumstances change, an increased 'stimulus' shifts $s_1 \cdot r$ up to $s_2 \cdot r$. At the same rate of profit, more is saved and invested.

13.4 IMPLICATIONS OF THE ACCUMULATION MODEL: SURPLUS VERSUS ABSTINENCE

Mark Blaug's comments on the notion of surplus can be evaluated in view of the three-point scenario summarized above. For Blaug, the independence of investment from profitability[8] is a logical requirement of the surplus view of profit. Even with this independence, Blaug implies that the idea of surplus is weak, since in any and all societies there is a real cost to saving. Hence 'the institutions of capitalism actually disguise the nature of interest as an index of the cost of "waiting", and it would seem that a satisfactory theory of the rate of interest must begin by abstracting from the specific sociological characteristics of capitalism', writes Blaug (1985, p. 255). Marx, obviously, does the opposite; the nature of capitalist society is in the forefront of his explanation of intent.

Schumpeter levies a different sort of accusation on this score. He characterizes the section on abstinence in volume I of *Capital* as 'unfortunate', and suspects that Marx's vehement but 'empty' rhetoric is a cover-up. It then turns out that

Marx is trying to sweep under the carpet, with all his vicious invectives against the virtuous Senior, no less than the presence of abstinence in the Marxian system itself. Schumpeter infers this from the treatment Marx gives to different durabilities of capital in his value theory – that Pandora's box we will not open here. Schumpeter writes: 'We need not trouble either Moses or the prophets in order to see capitalists "abstain" with Marx quite as much as they do with Senior' (1954, p. 661, n35).

Between the two of them, Schumpeter and Blaug have Marx in what looks like a nasty dilemma. On one side is the Scylla of recognizing that interest is due to 'waiting', as Schumpeter thinks Marx does on the sly. Profits then appear as the necessary payment to elicit the factor of production, 'waiting' services. As a part of the cost of production, profit cannot be meaningfully considered a surplus, and this central concept of Classical–Marxian economics evaporates. Then there is the Charybdis of giving no quarter to abstinence. But if 'waiting' does indeed underlie the return on capital as Blaug reasons, Marx has misunderstood, of all things, the one phenomenon he sought most to elucidate: capital.

The general validity of the notion of abstinence, and of its modern version, waiting, in comparison to the surplus approach, is well beyond the scope of this study. All that is attempted here is to spell out some implications of the Marxian accumulation scheme outlined above. Fundamental assumptions are the issue, not only about social arrangements, but also about what Robert Heilbroner describes as 'human nature', for lack of a more precise term. However, there is a surface resemblance between the Marxian view of the role of capital, and the 'waiting' theory of profit. Marxian capitalists do 'abstain' from withdrawing their capital from social use as long as their terms are met. This similarity obscures the fundamental disagreement and leads Schumpeter to see Marx as a closet abstinence theorist.

Neither Schumpeter nor Blaug take the sociological aspect of Marx's perspective seriously. Indeed, Blaug considers precisely this aspect irrelevant for the subject. Abstinence pertains to the act of saving, not to investment. We have seen that Marxian capitalists save because they want to invest, not the other way around. But from what has been described, the ever present Marxian goad to investment is the quest for power and prestige. Consider the exact nature of the power of owners of capital. The power consists of the right to withdraw the capital, or to deny other members of society the use of means of production, thereby depriving them of their livelihood (Heilbroner, 1988). Profit, then, is the payment exacted by those who monopolize the means of production, and is paid so that they allow others to use these. Profit is like a bribe – the payers let owners appropriate, in order not to be deprived of access to capital. The last sentence sounds very much like a Marxian version of the abstinence explanation. Here, then, is some justification for Schumpeter's indictment.

However, the rest of the Marxian story belies this resemblance. The payment is necessary only within the context of given ownership rights. Indeed, for Marx, 'capital' comprised these rights, the dissolution of which would vitiate the rationale for profit. Once the ownership of the means of production is considered a variable instead of a given, interest does not appear as universally necessary. It is tied to specific institutional rights and abstinence alone would not generate it. Blaug acknowledges that 'waiting' theory does not justify private ownership of property, but then points out the obvious: any society, capitalist or not, faces the question of how much of its annual product to consume. At a *given* level of output, investment is by definition foregone consumption. But in the Marxian story interest is *not* the microcosmic expression of social scarcity; capitalists could appropriate a payment even if their incomes were so high that they made no sacrifice by not consuming their capital, that is, even if there was no opportunity cost. Two positions, which for expositionary convenience we may refer to as Marshallian versus Marxian, can be thus summarized:

(1) Rational economic agents save now in order to consume later. What they do not consume is invested. Savers are rewarded for sacrificing their power to consume, and for continuing to do so.
(2) Investors save because they want to protect their socio-economic status and expand their power over others. What they do not want to invest is consumed. They appropriate a surplus by virtue of the power of ownership.

The two types of reasoning can also be applied to other resources and other social settings. As an illustration consider a society of landlords and landless peasants. In the Marshallian picture the former provide the latter with 'rental services', and in return receive a payment. Presumably, there is something else they can do with their land – turn it into hunting ground or enclose it for raising sheep. The rent then is the opportunity cost of peasant cultivation in terms of the utility of hunting, or of the return on sheep farming. In the Marxian script the landlord class does not really have such choices *within the given historical frame*. If land were to be used for hunting rather than cultivation, we would be looking at a different sort of society altogether, in which we would observe not landlords and peasants but hunters, organized around different institutions. If the land is consolidated into large commercial enterprises, again that would not be a society of landlords and peasants, but one of capitalists and workers. Obviously, land has been put to these different uses, but not within the same institutional setting. Marx sees such changes as irreversible historical events that usher in new epochs, and therefore as irrelevant within the existing epoch; transposing the different uses as alternatives to one another in one time and place appears as a form of anachronism.

Within the broad institutional parameters of what Marx knew as capitalism, there is no alternative use to capital. Accumulation is the dominant way for the individual to achieve success. Consuming one's capital may perhaps bring a temporary halo of glamour, but for 'human nature' moulded and channelled by the capitalist imperative, that is a shallow and transient pleasure. If, somehow, religious devotion and philanthropy replaced the ownership of capital as the means to status and power, then indeed giving one's capital away to religious foundations would be a real alternative, and the opportunity cost of accumulation would be the loss of religious satisfaction and social approbation. But that would be a social formation to which Marx's analysis of capitalism would not apply. To emphasize, *given* his view of how human nature is shaped in contemporary society, and the institutional parameters of the capitalist setting, there is no real alternative to accumulation, and therefore no opportunity cost to the amassing of capital.

A thinker who makes institutional distinctions is likely to reason in this way, without necessarily following Marx. Thus the institutionalist John R. Commons, in discussing the concept of opportunity cost, accuses Carey and Bastiat of the 'fallacy of non-concomitant alternatives' (Commons, 1934, p. 318). This, according to him, is

> a fallacy respecting the human will. The will is limited to here and now. Bastiat's laborer does not choose between the cost of food now and the cost a thousand years ago . . . He does not choose between an accessible and an inaccessible alternative in space, nor an alternative that has disappeared in time past and one that is here in time present. (ibid.)

That would be, Commons claims, 'no choice'. Similarly, Marx denies that consuming one's capital is an option within the capitalist worldview; individuals moulded by capitalist institutions will not consider it an alternative, because it does not provide the power they seek through investment. If there is no choice, then, there is no meaningful 'abstinence'.[9]

There is a connection to the general glut controversy here. As pointed out in section 13.2 above, Malthus might have had a somewhat stronger case against Ricardo's inexorable logic had he used the institutional argument that capitalists have a different goal from other social groups, that they consider frugality in itself a 'pleasure'. This is not the same as Marx's view, where it is investment that is the goal. But it would have made it possible to argue that individuals may save without investing.

The Marxian vision of society and the individual may seem altogether wrong. It can be pointed out that consumption *is* the primary goal of individuals in all modern societies, capitalist or not. But the rejection is on sociological or psychological grounds that lie beyond the realm of conventional economics. 'Human nature' is not what Marx thought it was, and capitalism does not make of it 'personified capital'. Therefore, there is an opportunity cost to saving, and investment is conditioned by the willingness to sacrifice consumption. The difference between the abstinence and Marxian views stems from supra-economic premises, on whether individuals are motivated by their desire for consumption or their quest for social power. The issue is to what extent the choice as to allocating material resources is subject to a universal optimization calculus and to what extent it is conditioned by institutional factors.

Hence one of the viewpoints cannot imply anything for the internal consistency of the other. As the commentators note, Marx does not tackle the logic of Senior's argument, he simply berates the latter for his worldview. On the other side, Blaug applies Marshallian reasoning to a system resting on antithetical premises as to the foundations of economic behaviour. In fact Blaug is not commenting on the internal consistency of Marx's economic argument, but on his view of social arrangements and the way these work through individual motivation. Behind the different viewpoints looms the integrated nature of social phenomena studied in separate compartments. The supposedly distinct set of behaviour studied by economists rests on implicit assumptions made about non-economic forces. We tend to forget these premises and their reflection in economic discourse.

Notes

1. In formal terms, the Ricardian system with n commodities can be expressed as n price equations. Given the wage rate, these determine $n-1$ relative prices and the profit rate (Sraffa, 1960, chapter 1). Malthus thinks aggregate supply and demand close this system by determining the wage rate.
2. Costabile and Rowthorn (1985), like Malthus himself, seem to miss the conflict between the Malthus of the *Essay on Population* and the Malthus of the *Principles*.
3. Needless to say the 'subsistence' standard can be a social rather than biological variable.
4. In technical terms, Malthus confuses the trade-off between the profit rate and wage rate along a schedule based on *given* productivity with shifts in the profit–wage trade-off schedule due to diminishing returns on land.
5. This argument has been formalized by Costabile and Rowthorn (1985).
6. Historically, needs previously supplied within the household have been transformed into market demand as capitalist relations spread. Craft production is driven out of the market as capital expands (Dobb, 1963; Nell, 1988, 1992). Capitalists themselves do the commercializing, destroying the other forms of production in their quest for markets.
7. The cyclical movement described in this paragraph is depicted as fluctuations below the $s_1 \cdot r$ schedule in Figure 13.1. It should be noted that the accumulation scenario sketched here is *not* a description of how a capitalist society actually functions. It is only meant to clarify Marx's approach.
8. Interest and profit are not differentiated in the general discussion given here since interest was seen by Marx as a subset of profit, itself a subset of the larger category, surplus. The neo-classical 'return on waiting' explanation, and the earlier abstinence argument, are about interest, but of course have implications for profit and surplus as well, if these are the genus to which the species interest belongs.
9. Commons, not taking the same view as Marx of what motivates individuals, does not reach the same conclusion. The common ground is their distinction between ownership and the physical means of production. In Commons' jargon, this is the difference between the 'legal activity' of ownership on the one hand, and the technical issue of efficiency and the physical delivery of commodities on the other. Profit is due to the former, not the latter. Commons, following Hume, thinks that scarcity is the necessary condition of property; but what he considers 'scarcity' is merely the existence of use value (Commons, 1934, passim).

References

Bharadwaj, Krishna (1986) *Classical Political Economy and Rise to Dominance of Supply and Demand Theories* (London: Sangam Books).

Blaug, Mark (1985) *Economic Theory in Retrospect*, 4th edn (Cambridge: Cambridge University Press).

Bleaney, Michael (1976) *Underconsumption Theories: A History and Critical Analysis* (New York: International Publisher).

Bronfenbrenner, Martin (1965) 'Das Kapital for the Modern Man', *Science and Society*, Fall, Vol. 29, No. 1.

Commons, John R. (1924) *Legal Foundations of Capitalism* (New York: Macmillan).

Commons, John R. (1934) *Institutional Economics* (New York: Macmillan).

Costabile, Lilia and Bob Rowthorn (1985) 'Malthus's Theory of Wages and Growth', in *Economic Journal*, June, Vol. 95, No. 378.

Dobb, Maurice (1963) *Studies in the Development of Capitalism* (New York: International Publishers).

Eltis, W. A. (1984) *The Classical Theory of Economic Growth* (New York: St Martin's Press).

Garegnani, Pierangelo (1984) 'Value and Distribution in the Classical Economists and Marx', *Oxford Economic Papers*, Vol. 36, No. 2.

Goodwin, Richard M. (1967) 'A Growth Cycle', in C. H. Feinstein (ed.), *Socialism, Capitalism and Economic Growth* (Cambridge: Cambridge University Press).

Harcourt, G. C. (1982) *The Social Science Imperialists* (London: Routledge & Kegan Paul).

Heilbroner, Robert L. (1980) *Marxism: For and Against* (New York and London: W. W. Norton).

Heilbroner, Robert L. (1985) *The Nature and Logic of Capitalism* (New York and London: W. W. Norton).

Heilbroner, Robert L. (1988) *Behind the Veil of Economics: Essays in the Worldly Philosophy* (New York and London: W. W. Norton).

Hollander, Samuel (1962) 'Malthus and Keynes. A Note', *Economic Journal*, June, Vol. 72, No. 286.

Hollander, Samuel (1969) 'Malthus and the Post-Napoleonic Depression', *History of Political Economy*, Vol. 1–2.

Hollander, Samuel (1979) *The Economics of David Ricardo* (Toronto: Toronto University Press).

Hollis, M. and E. J. Nell (1975) *Rational Economic Man* (Cambridge: Cambridge University Press).

Jones, Hywel G. (1976) *An Introduction to Modern Theories of Economic Growth* (New York: McGraw-Hill).

Kaldor, Nicholas (1951) 'Mr Hicks on the Trade Cycle', *Economic Journal*, Dec., Vol. 61, No. 244.

Keynes, John Maynard (1964) *The General Theory of Employment, Interest and Money* (New York and London: Harcourt Brace Jovanovich).

Keynes, John Maynard (1971) *The Treatise on Money* (London: Macmillan).

Laibman, David (1983) 'Capitalism and Immanent Crisis: Broad Strokes for a Theoretical Foundation', *Social Research*, Vol. 50, No. 2.

Lowe, Adolph (1976a) *The Path of Economic Growth* (Cambridge: Cambridge University Press).

Lowe, Adolph (1976b) 'Adam Smith's System of Equilibrium Growth', in Skinner and Wilson (1976).

Malthus, Thomas R. (1951) *Principles of Political Economy, Considered with a View to Their Practical Application*, 2nd edn. (New York: Augustus M. Kelley).

Malthus, Thomas R. (1963) 'Review of Essay on Political Economy', first published in the *Quarterly Review*, 1824; reprinted in Semmel (ed.), *Occasional Papers of T. R. Malthus* (New York: Burt Franklin).

Marglin, Stephen A. (1984) *Growth, Distribution and Prices* (Cambridge, Mass.: Harvard University Press).

Marglin, Stephen A. (1987) 'Investment and Accumulation', in Eatwell, Milgate and Newman (eds), *The New Palgrave: A Dictionary of Economics* (New York: Stockton Press).

Marx, Karl (1954) *Capital: A Critical Analysis of Capitalist Production*, vol. I (Moscow: Progress Publishers).

Marx, Karl (1963) *Early Writings*, transl. and ed. by T. Bottomore (New York: McGraw-Hill).

Marx, Karl (1967) *Capital: A Critique of Political Economy*, vols II and III (New York: International Publishers).

Marx, Karl (1968) Theories of Surplus-Value, parts II and III (Moscow: Progress Publishers).

Nell, Edward J. (ed.) (1980) *Growth, Profits and Property* (Cambridge: Cambridge University Press).

Nell, Edward J. (1987) 'Accumulation of Capital', in Eatwell, Milgate and Newman (eds), *The New Palgrave: A Dictionary of Economics* (New York: Stockton Press).

Nell, Edward J. (1988) 'Say's Law, Artisan Technology and Early Capitalism', *New School Series in Political Economy* (New York: New School for Social Research).

Nell, Edward J. (1992) *Transformational Growth and Effective Demand* (London: Macmillan and New York: New York University Press).

Palley, Thomas (1989) 'Neo-Classicism, Neo-Keynesianism and Under-Consumption', New School For Social Research.

Pasinetti, Luigi L. (1974) *Growth and Income Distribution. Essays in Economic Theory* (Cambridge: Cambridge University Press).

Ricardo, David (1951 onwards) *The Works and Correspondence of David Ricardo*, P. Sraffa (ed.) (Cambridge: Cambridge University Press).

Rosenberg, Nathan (1960) 'Some Institutional Aspects of the *Wealth of Nations*', *Journal of Political Economy*, December, Vol. 68, No. 6.

Schumpeter, J. A. (1950) *Capitalism, Socialism and Democracy* (New York: Harper & Row).

Schumpeter, J. A. (1954) *History of Economic Analysis* (New York: Oxford University Press).

Sen, Amartya (ed.) (1970) *Growth Economics* (Harmondsworth: Penguin).

Skinner, A. S. and T. Wilson (eds) (1976) *Essays on Adam Smith* (Oxford: Oxford University Press).

Smith, Adam (1976) *An Inquiry into the Nature and Causes of the Wealth of Nations*, R. H. Campbell and A. S. Skinner (eds) (Oxford: Oxford University Press).

Sraffa, Piero (1960) *Production of Commodities by Means of Commodities: Prelude to a Critique of Economic Theory* (Cambridge: Cambridge University Press).

Steindl, Josel (1976) *Maturity and Stagnation in American Capitalism* (New York and London: Monthly Review Press).

Sylos-Labini, Paolo (1984) *The Forces of Economic Growth and Decline* (Cambridge, Mass.: MIT Press).

Tucker, Robert C. (ed.) *The Marx–Engels Reader*, 2nd edn. (New York and London: W. W. Norton).

Vianello, Fernando (1985) 'The Pace of Accumulation', *Political Economy. Studies in the Surplus Approach*.

West, E. G. (1982) 'Ricardo in Historical Perspective', in *Canadian Journal of Economics*, May, Vol. 15, No. 2.

14 Marx and Market Socialism

Frank Roosevelt[1]

Karl Marx went on record as ruling out any role for the market in a socialist economy. 'Within the cooperative society based on common ownership of the means of production', he wrote, 'the producers do not exchange their products' (Marx, 1938' p. 8). Marx's collaborator, Frederick Engels, stated their position even more bluntly: 'The seizure of the means of production by society puts an end to commodity production . . . [and at that point the market is to be] replaced by conscious organization on a planned basis' (Engels, 1939, p. 309). Clearly, neither Marx nor Engels saw any role for markets in a socialist society.

Today, however, socialists around the world are moving, both in theory and in practice, towards assigning a larger role to the market as a means of organizing, coordinating, and motivating economic activities. 'Market Socialism' (Brus, 1987) is coming to be seen by a growing number of progressives as a way to implement socialist values within an efficient economic system and, hence, as a chance to revive the socialist project in the face of nearly universal disenchantment with the orthodox model of central planning and state ownership. I count myself among those who believe that the development of a workable model of market socialism is both necessary and desirable.

But the movement towards the market is not without some real problems for socialists. Most importantly, there is the possibility that an increased role for the market will make it difficult or impossible to achieve many of the defining goals of socialism.[2] In this paper, I first set forth a number of arguments in favour of utilizing markets in a socialist economy – presenting them as a critique of Marx – and I then examine Marx's reasons for wanting to abolish the market. In my conclusion, I argue that, although Marx's abolitionist position must be rejected, his insights into the way markets work and his ultimate objectives for socialism remain valid.

14.1 THE MARKET SOCIALIST CRITIQUE OF MARX[3]

Markets *vs*. Political Allocation

Perhaps the most general criticism that has been levelled against Marx is that he seems not to have paid attention to the fact that there are only two known ways, broadly speaking, in which the economic activities of any society can be organized and coordinated – these being, on the one hand, the market and, on the other, some form of political process (i.e., planning of one kind or another). Before one recommends the elimination of one of these options, one should be reasonably certain that the other one will work (i.e., will accomplish the objectives one has in mind). That Marx did not engage in this necessary thought process may be seen in a well-known passage in *The German Ideology*, in which he and Engels criticized the capitalist division of labour and contrasted it with their view of the way economic life would be organized in communist society:

> For as soon as the distribution of labour comes into being, each man has a particular, exclusive sphere of activity which is forced upon him and from which he cannot escape. He is a hunter, a fisherman, a shepherd, or a critical critic, and must remain so if he does not want to lose his means of livelihood; while in communist society, where nobody has one exclusive sphere of activity but each can become accomplished in any branch he wishes, *society regulates the general production* and thus makes it possible for me to do one thing today and another tomorrow, to hunt in the morning, fish in the afternoon, rear cattle in the evening, criticise after dinner, just as I have a mind, without ever becoming hunter, fisherman, shepherd or critic. (Marx and Engels, 1970, p. 53, italics added.)

Leaving aside the pastoral setting of this passage – hardly an appropriate context for recommendations concerning a post-capitalist society – the key phrase here is the one in which Marx and Engels blithely assert that, under communism, the division of labour can be eliminated because, at that point, 'society regulates the general production'. They neglect to explain *who* is to represent 'society' and *how* the 'regulation of production' is to be accomplished in a way that allocates resources efficiently.

A great many writers over the years have pointed out the difficulty – or even impossibility – of effectively organizing a modern economy without relying on markets. Rather than reviewing the voluminous literature, I will simply reproduce David Belkin's list of the more common problems that have been observed in many of the (former) Communist countries that have tried to eliminate the market (Belkin, 1991, p. 1):

- bureaucratic domination of production and social life;
- resources tied up in obsolete investments;
- prices unrelated to costs, hence distorted allocation of resources;
- goods and services in chronic short supply;
- slow growth in real incomes;
- disguised unemployment (e.g., people holding unproductive jobs);
- poor motivation and work discipline;
- little reward for attending to environmental considerations.

While many of these problems can also be observed in capitalist countries, the point is that these problems have occurred in societies that claimed to have found an economic system superior to capitalism. My own view is that we need to recognize that at least part of the reason why socialism has not yet outperformed capitalism is that the first attempts to create socialist societies were based on the mistaken idea, inspired by Marx, that the market can simply be abolished.

Scale and Complexity

A more specific criticism of Marx's vision of a communist economy is that, while it might be applicable to a small and relatively simple society, it is not an effective way to organize and coordinate the economic activities of a large and complex nation (much less the whole world).

 The problem here arises from the fact (noted above) that, once the market is eliminated, the allocation of economic resources has to be accomplished through some form of political process. When the society in which such an experiment is attempted is relatively small and simple (e.g., an Israeli *kibbutz*), the political process can also be simple. Everyone can be included, decisions can be made democratically and, conceivably, most members of the community will be satisfied with the results. More significantly, decisions about what to produce, how to produce it, and so on, can be arrived at without reference to market-determined prices because everyone involved in the decision-making process can have direct knowledge of the relative costs of producing different things, and the preferences of the members of the community for the various possible outputs will also be known. Under these conditions, it is a relatively easy task to decide (a) how much of each output to produce and (b) how to distribute the various goods and services within the community for consumption. Assigning various tasks to specific people – achieving an acceptable 'division of labour' – and motivating everyone to do their tasks well can also be accomplished. Thus, in small communities Marx's vision of unalienated 'production for use' is a feasible option.

 Unfortunately, it is otherwise with large and complex societies. The collection of essential information becomes more difficult, motivation becomes a problem, and the political process necessarily becomes more complex as direct democracy ceases to be an option. Inevitably, a sub-set of the population is selected by some method to gather information and to make production and resource-allocation decisions. Mechanisms are put in place to motivate people to perform necessary tasks and to distribute the output of the economy. The information gathered may be closely held or widely shared, and the procedures for making decisions at various levels may be more or less democratic. But the fact remains that, in a large and complex economy, not everything can be done by everybody. The selection of those who perform the more vital tasks and the methods by which this selection is accomplished necessarily become important issues. The question also arises as to what social interests those selected – the planners, politicians, bureaucrats, etc. – will actually represent. Is it likely that these 'agents' will be able to, or even wish to, represent the interests of the population ('principals') as a whole? If not, how will the goals of socialism be achieved in a marketless society?

None of these difficult questions were seriously considered by Marx. In the same sentence in the *Critique of the Gotha Program* in which he banished commodity exchange from communist society he went on to assert that 'now, in contrast to capitalist society, individual labour no longer exists in an indirect fashion but [exists] directly as a component part of the total labour' (Marx, 1938, p. 8). The meaning and implications of this brief statement had been elaborated in some detail by Marx in the first chapter of the first volume of *Capital* and it is worth quoting most of a paragraph from this chapter in order to show just how over-simplified his concept of a socialist economy was.

> Let us now picture to ourselves . . . a community of free individuals, carrying on their work with the means of production in common, in which the labour-power of all the different individuals is consciously applied as the combined labour-power of the community. All the characteristics of Robinson [Crusoe]'s labour are here repeated, but with this difference, that they are social, instead of individual. Everything produced by him was exclusively the result of his own personal labour, and therefore simply an object of use for himself. The total product of our community [in contrast] is a social product. One portion serves as fresh means of production and remains social. But another portion is consumed by the members as means of subsistence. A distribution of this portion amongst them is consequently necessary . . . We will assume . . . that the share of each individual producer in the means of subsistence is determined by his labour-time. Labour-time would, in that case, play a double part. Its apportionment in accordance with a definite social plan, maintains the proper proportion between the different kinds of work to be done and the various wants of the community. On the other hand, it also serves as a measure of the portion of the common labour borne by each individual, and of his share in the part of the total product destined for individual consumption. The social relations of the individual producers, with regard both to their labour and to its products, are in this case perfectly simple and intelligible, and [this is also true] with regard not only to production but also to distribution. (Marx, 1967, pp. 78–9)

The first flaw in the argument of this passage is the notion that we can consider the economic tasks of a socialist society in essentially the same way that we think about those of a single, isolated individual – Robinson Crusoe – only 'with this difference, that they are social, instead of individual'. It seems that Marx's bias in favour of 'production for use' (exemplified in the purest form by the Robinson Crusoe story) blinded him to the many difficulties involved in moving from the analysis of a one-person economy to the modelling of complex socialist economy. Although he begins to introduce some complexity when he notes that the output of a socialist community must be consciously divided between investment and consumption, he skirts several more difficult issues when he suggests that labour-time can be used both as the basis for resource allocation and as the principle for distributing consumer goods.

Indeed, Marx alludes to one of the central problems of a socialist economy when he asserts that the 'apportionment [of labour-time] in accordance with a definite social plan, maintains the proper proportion between the different kinds of work to be done [on the one hand] and the various wants of the community [on the other]'. It is clear that the effectiveness of *any* economic system can be evaluated with regard to how well it achieves this 'proper proportion'. However, the question being asked today is: can a centrally-planned socialist economy – one that attempts to minimize the role of markets – actually allocate the 'different kinds of work to be done' in such a way as to provide effectively for the 'various wants of the community' (both in the present and in the future)? Judging from the widespread dissatisfaction with centrally-planned economies and the pronounced movement away from planning and towards the market, the answer would appear to be: no – or, not very effectively.

Information and Incentives

So what is the problem? Why is it not possible for a socialist economy to replace the market with planning? Part of the answer to this question is supplied by Alec Nove in his discussion of 'the *ex ante* illusion' (Nove, 1983, pp. 39–42). The *ex ante* illusion, as explained by Nove, is the idea that the needs and wants of the community can somehow be determined *before* production takes place, thereby allowing production itself (the apportionment of labour-time) to be undertaken in a precise way ('in accordance with a definite social plan') to provide exactly the goods and services that the community wants. If things could actually be done this way, and done effectively, it would certainly eliminate a good deal of the waste that occurs in a market economy – with some resources employed to produce things that nobody buys, and other resources used just to persuade people to buy things that they may not need.

However, as Nove points out, there is a fundamental problem – or several fundamental problems – with this conception of a planned economy. One problem has to do with the task of collecting the necessary information from the population regarding the preferred design and size of shoes, etc., in advance of production. Some people (myself included) do not know exactly what style and size shoe they want until they actually go into a shoe store, look around, and try on a number of different pairs. But this way of allowing consumers to express (and form) their preferences is only available in a market economy, and the validation of the allocation of social labour only occurs *ex post*. In other words, one can only know whether or not society's labour-time was allocated in the 'proper proportion' *after* consumers have made their purchasing decisions – and, inevitably, the shoes (and other items) that do not get purchased will represent resources wasted.

Another problem with the *ex ante* planned economy approach is that, even if all of the necessary information about consumers' preferences could somehow be collected in advance of production, it is far from a sure thing that exactly the desired quantities and qualities of products will be produced. If, for some reason, producers do not turn out exactly the number and quality of goods and services that the community wants, what recourse does the community have – either individually or collectively – to bring about a correction in the production process so that what is desired is what is actually produced?

Whatever its deficiencies may be – and, as will be noted later, they are many a market economy does provide consumers with choices, and it can also give producers incentives to produce what consumers (or other producers) want. As Herbert Gintis (1989) has pointed out, the 'power to switch' is the basis of whatever 'sovereignty' consumers have in any economic system. And in providing consumers (and producers) with choices, a market economy necessarily involves competition among producers. Since one of the aims of socialism is to foster cooperation in place of competition, we are faced with a trade-off: more choice and more responsive production along with more competition *vs* less choice, less responsive production but also less competition and more cooperation. Unfortunately, there are no simple choices in this world – but many people in the existing socialist countries seem to be so dissatisfied with the way their planned economies have been working (or not working) that they are now inclined to move towards more markets and more competition even though this will result in less cooperation.

The argument for relying more on markets than on planning in large and complex economies is rooted ultimately in issues concerning information and incentives. As economists from von Mises to Nove (and from as wide a range of political positions) have pointed out, it simply is not feasible for a central planning authority to gather with sufficient accuracy the quantity and quality of information regarding consumer preferences and production possibilities that would be needed in order to allocate resources efficiently. Even if this could be done, there would remain the problem of inducing or motivating the individual production units to carry out their tasks effectively. And, most significantly, there are the broader questions regarding the compatibility of a planned economy with democratic participation and individual liberty at the various levels and in the different spheres of society (from family to workplace to local, regional and national governments).

The chief virtue of a market economy – again, without brushing under the rug its very real defects – is that it allows prices to be established which, however roughly and imperfectly, reflect the relative scarcities of the available resources both in relation to each other (e.g., land, labour, and machinery; wood, coal, and water-power) and in relation to the multitude of consumer preferences for all of the goods and services that can be produced. If there is a workable degree of competition in the economy (i.e., relatively little monopoly or monopsony power), these prices can serve as signals which *both* transmit information about relative scarcities, production possibilities and consumer preferences *and* provide the incentives that will induce individual enterprises to carry out production to meet the needs of the community in as effective a way as possible.

Marx saw the market and its corresponding money relations as having predominantly negative and mystifying effects on people. He believed that only in a marketless society would everything be transparent and thus amenable to human control. Unfortunately, he neglected to consider all of the possible consequences of eliminating – or attempting to eliminate – the market. Although he wrote about the dangers of bureaucracy in his youth (Marx, 1977a), he did not imagine that some of his followers who would later act on his desire to abolish the market would end up creating monstrous bureaucracies. What Marx failed to see is that markets are (among other things) a necessary condition for popular sovereignty because only with access to the information presented in prices can the citizens of highly complex modern societies evaluate alternative policies or development strategies.[4]

Scarcity and Abundance

There is one assumption which, if made at the outset, would consign to irrelevance all of the reasons for relying on markets, prices and competition in a socialist economy – and that is the assumption of abundance (Nove, 1983, pp. 15–20). For if everything were plentiful (including natural resources and capital goods) and if – as a result of advances in technology – human labour were many times more productive than it is today, then we would not have to worry about priorities or concern ourselves with allocating scarce resources effectively in production to meet as many human needs as possible. Rather, we would enjoy a state of affairs where efficiency would not be very important and virtually all social needs could be easily satisfied.[5]

As implausible as it may seem, Marx appears to have made such an assumption. In *The Communist Manifesto*, he and Engels observed that '[t]he bourgeoisie cannot exist without constantly revolutionizing the instruments of production', and went on to note with admiration that, 'during its rule of scarce one hundred years, [it] has created more massive and more colossal productive forces than have all preceding generations together' (1948, pp. 12–14). In Marx's view of history, it was the specific mission of the bourgeoisie to raise productivity to such a high level that humanity could look forward to an age of abundance – an age in which scarcity and its attendant conflicts over goods and resources could be left behind. Indeed, in *The German Ideology*, which Marx wrote with Engels shortly before they wrote the *Manifesto*, there was an explicit reference to 'a great increase of productive power, a high degree of its development' as a precondition for communist society:

[T]his development of [the] productive forces . . . is an absolutely necessary practical premise [for the communist revolution] because without it *want* is merely made general, and with *destitution* the struggle for necessities and all the old filthy business would necessarily be reproduced. (Marx and Engels, 1970, p. 56)

In Marx's mind there was clearly a connection – and a logical one – between the achievement of abundance and the possibility of doing away with 'want' and 'all the old filthy business' associated with competition, markets, prices, and capitalism. In his view, communist society would not have to wrestle with 'the economic problem' but could reach its goals in an environment of plenty. But how realistic is this assumption in a world in which most of the population is still poor, and bringing everyone's standard of living up to the level of the average person in the already industrialized countries is probably not ecologically feasible?

Given present realities, Marx's assumption of abundance seems naïve at best and, if one takes into account ecological constraints on further industrialization, irresponsible. A more realistic/responsive view would accept the continued presence of scarcity and would explore ways in which socialist societies might share the burden of this scarcity and at the same time pursue growth in ways that would be both equitable and ecologically sustainable.

Individual Development

The final criticism of Marx to be discussed here is the argument that there is an inconsistency between his abolitionist position on the market and his view of capitalism as a progressive stage in history. As David Miller has pointed out in his recent book, *Market, State, and Community* (1989, pp. 208–19), Marx praised capitalism for having liberated individuals from their pre-capitalist entrapment in fixed positions in production and society but failed to explain how this achievement was to be sustained and expanded in a marketless communist society.

Having initially praised the progressive character of capitalism in *The Communist Manifesto*, Marx went on at greater length in the chapter on 'Machinery and Modern Industry' in the first volume of *Capital* to explain how the development of capitalist production within a framework of market competition had led to the emergence of what he called 'the fully developed individual':

> Modern Industry never looks upon and treats the existing form of a process as final. . . . [I]t is continually causing changes not only in the technical basis of production but also in the functions of the labourer and in the social combinations of the labour-process. At the same time, it thereby also revolutionizes the division of labour within the society and incessantly launches masses of capital and of workpeople form one branch of production to another. . . . [B]y its very nature, therefore [it] necessitates variation of labour, fluency of function, [and] universal mobility of the labourer . . . But if, on the one hand, variation of work at present imposes itself after the manner of an overpowering natural law, and with the blindly destructive action of a natural law that meets with resistance at all points, Modern Industry, on the other hand, . . . imposes the necessity of recognizing, as a fundamental law of production, variation of work, consequently fitness of the labourer for varied work, consequently the greatest

possible development of his varied aptitudes. It becomes a question of life and
death for society to adapt the mode of production to the normal functioning of
this law. Modern Industry, indeed, compels society, under pressure of death, to
replace the detail-worker of today, crippled by life-long repetition of one and
the same operation, and thus reduced to a mere fragment of a man, by the fully
developed individual, fit for a variety of labours, ready to face any change of
production, and to whom the different social functions he performs are but so
many modes of giving free scope to his own natural and acquired powers.
(Marx, 1976, pp. 487–8)

The question that Miller raises in connection with this passage is the following:
why did Marx, having credited the market with such positive effects in its
oppressive capitalist integument, decide to banish it altogether in his vision of
socialist (communist) society? Did Marx even consider the possibility that eliminating the market might open the way for a reversion to the kind of static and
limited life that individuals had led in pre-capitalist societies? After exploring two
possible ways in which Marx might have responded to this question, Miller finds
both of them unsatisfactory and concludes that retaining markets and at least some
competition within a socialist institutional framework is the best way to achieve
Marx's own goal of 'free individuality, based on the universal development of
individuals' (1973, quoted in Miller, 1989, p. 213). Through this line of reasoning, Miller is able to argue that one can interpret Marx's analysis of capitalism as
being not incompatible with the case for market socialism.

14.2 MARX'S CRITIQUE OF THE MARKET

If all – or even a few – of the above arguments in favour of retaining the market
in a socialist economy are valid, why would Marx have been so set on seeing it
disappear along with capitalism? Was he simply naïve, or did he really not
understand the workings of an institution that he spent his life attempting to
understand? In this part of the paper, I explain how Marx's stance against the
market emerged directly from his critique of capitalism as a system that generates
inequality, operates with increasing instability, turns everything into a commodity, spreads human alienation, and prevents people from achieving true freedom.

A key issue for market socialists is whether Marx's critique of the market,
formulated in the context of his critique of capitalism, is limited by its historically
specific focus on the capitalist market economy or whether it applies more
generally to markets in whatever institutional framework they are embedded. I
will show that within Marx's historically specific critique there is a general
critique of market relations *per se*. Thus, although market socialists may well be
able to remedy certain defects of a market economy by altering its existing
capitalist framework, they will still have to find ways of counteracting certain
undesirable tendencies that are inherent in the operation of markets themselves.

Inequality

One of the criticisms Marx levels against capitalism is that it is a system that exacerbates economic inequalities and pits people against each other in social classes. Anyone familiar with his analysis of the origins of capitalism will recall his account of how, in Britain, the modern division of society into capitalists and workers occurred as a result of the historical process of 'primitive accumulation' (Marx, 1967, Part VIII). There is, however, another argument in *Capital* which holds that 'commodity production, *in accordance with its own inherent laws*, develops further [as soon as some people begin selling their productive capacities to others] into capitalist production' (Marx, 1967, p. 587, italics added). According to this argument, even if we could (somehow) start with an equal distribution of economic resources, the normal operation of markets themselves would sooner or later lead to increasing inequality, to class divisions and thus to the well-known capitalist forms of domination, exploitation, and alienation. If Marx is correct – and if the socialist goal of a classless society is to be retained – the advocates of market socialism will have to devise institutional mechanisms to counteract the tendency of markets to generate inequality.

Instability

Marx's second argument against markets has to do with the inherent instability of a market economy. As is well known, he devoted much effort to explaining why capitalist economies are increasingly likely to experience economic crises. However, the reason why *any* market economy will be unstable, in Marx's view, is that production decisions are made by individuals or firms without social coordination. This leaves the economy vulnerable to swings in expectations about the future. When there is an optimistic mood in the air, firms will tend to expand production, hire more workers and use more inputs until, for one reason or another, the optimism is replaced by pessimism and output rates are cut, workers laid off, and so on. Thus, the macroeconomic variables – total output, investment, employment, and the like – will tend to fluctuate because of the way in which the microeconomic decisions are made. As a result, a market economy will fail to utilize its human and material resources consistently over time and will not produce the amount of output that might otherwise be produced and consumed. With resources often idle at the same time as there are unfulfilled human needs, a market economy can be said to be both irrational and wasteful. This is another problem that market socialists will have to deal with.

The two arguments presented so far – those having to do with the inequality and instability of a market economy – may be characterized as primarily *economic* in their focus. The other objections lodged by Marx against markets are essentially *moral* arguments. Indeed, as we proceed we will see that, departing from his commitment to 'scientific socialism', Marx here engages in a profoundly utopian exercise. Much more than was the case with the first two points, each of the following arguments for abolishing markets was closely connected in Marx's mind with his vision of how things ought to be in a future communist society.

Commodification

Running through the whole of Marx's critique of capitalism is the idea that markets gradually turn everything into a commodity and, in the process, corrode traditional values, corrupt social morality, and undermine community.[6]

At the most basic level, Marx's desire to abolish the market was rooted in a profound communitarian impulse, a desire to get back to – or, rather, to achieve on a higher level – the kind of social solidarity, based on a commonly accepted social ethic, that had prevailed in simpler societies before the appearance of class divisions, the state, and the market (with its arms-length, impersonal relations of commodity exchange). This is not an entirely new idea – or one put forward only by Marx. It had been a central concern of his predecessors whom he labelled 'utopian socialists' and, in one form or another, it was part of the thinking of Aristotle (the human being as a 'political animal'), Rousseau (the political 'association' consciously created by a social contract), and Ferdinand Tönnies (*gemeinshaft* vs *gesellschaft*).

Here is the way in which the still youthful Marx set forth his ethical critique of the market in the course of his (1847) polemic against Proudhon:

> [With the spread of markets] there came a time when everything that men had considered as inalienable became an object of exchange, of traffic, and could be alienated. This is the time when the very things which till then had been communicated, but never exchanged; given, but never sold, acquired, but never bought – virtue, love, conviction, knowledge, conscience, etc. – when everything, in short, passed into commerce. It is the time of general corruption, of universal venality, or, to speak in terms of political economy, the time when everything, moral or physical, having become a marketable value, is brought to market to be assessed at its truest value. (Marx, 1963, p. 34)

The same point was also made in the famous passage in *The Communist Manifesto* in which Marx and Engels note that the development of capitalism 'has left remaining no other nexus between man and man than naked self-interest, than callous "cash payment"' (Marx and Engels, 1948, p. 11). While the general thrust of such passages is not hard to discern, the important point is that Marx's position here is quite similar to that adopted by moral philosophers from Immanuel Kant to Martin Buber: they all condemn any behaviour which uses others in an instrumental fashion or treats other human beings as means rather than as ends.

Alienation

Whereas I have used the term 'commodification' to refer to Marx's analysis of the socially corrupting effects of market *exchange*, the term 'alienation' (or 'alienated labour') was used by Marx to indicate the various ways in which social relationships are distorted by commodity *production*. The conclusion he drew from his analysis of alienation was that 'production for use' (rather than for exchange) is the only possible foundation for fully human relationships.

In the *Economic and Philosophic Manuscripts of 1844* Marx elaborated four dimensions of alienation, showing that in capitalist production workers are alienated from (1) the work-processes; (2) the product; (3) other people; and (4) their own human nature (Marx, 1964, pp. 120–4). The first of these dimensions of alienation is attributable to the specifically capitalist organization of the labour-process, but the last three may be seen as operating in any form of market economy. This is evident in the *1844 Manuscripts*, but the argument is set forth more explicitly in the notes 'On James Mill' that Marx wrote at the same time he was writing the better-known *Manuscripts* (Marx, 1977a). In these notes he begins from the following premise:

> Since human nature is the true communal nature of man, [people] create and produce their communal nature by their [own] natural action; . . . but so long as man has not recognized himself as man and has not organized the world in a human way, *this communal nature appears in the form of alienation*. (Marx, 1977a, p. 115, italics added)

From this starting point, Marx launches into a critique of classical economics as both a reflection of and a rationalization for a world that has not yet been organized in a 'human', i.e., communal, way:

> Economics conceives of the communal nature of man . . . under the form of exchange and commerce. Society . . . is a series of mutual exchanges. . . . Society, says Adam Smith, is a commercial society and each of its members is a tradesman.
>
> We can see how economics rigidifies the *alienated form of social intercourse* as [if it were] the original form that corresponds to man's nature. Marx, 1977a, p. 116, italics added)

The point of Marx's argument in these notes 'On James Mill' is that 'production for exchange' is necessarily an 'alienated form of social intercourse' while 'production for use' – either directly for one's own use or for the use of people in one's immediate community – is the only truly human way of producing things.

However, the most significant thing about this text is that, although it is billed as a commentary on James Mill, what it really is is a radical critique of the philosophical assumptions of Adam Smith. Recall the following familiar passage from *The Wealth of Nations*:

> In civilized society [the individual] stands at all times in need of the cooperation and assistance of great multitudes . . . But . . . it is in vain for him to expect

it from their benevolence only. He will be more likely to prevail if he can interest their self-love in his favour, and show them that it is for their own advantage to do for him what he requires of them. Whoever offers to another a bargain of any kind, proposes to do this. Give me that which I want, and you shall have this which you want, is the meaning of every such offer; and it is in this manner that we obtain from one another the far greater part of those good offices which we stand in need of. It is not from the benevolence of the butcher, the brewer, or the baker, that we expect our dinner, but from their regard to their own interest. We address ourselves, not to their humanity but to their self-love, and never talk to them of our own necessities but of their advantages. (Smith, 1937, p. 14)

In what appears to be a direct response to this passage, Marx comments:

I have produced for myself and not for you, as you have produced for yourself and not for me. You are as little concerned by the result of my production in itself as I am directly concerned by the result of your production. That is, our production is not a production of men for men as such, that is, social production. . . . Each of us sees in his own product only his own selfish needs objectified, and thus in the product of another he only sees the objectification of another selfish need independent [of] and alien to him. (Marx, 1977a, pp. 119–20).

Whereas Adam Smith believed that egoistic market relations and the division of labour derived from 'a certain propensity in human nature . . . the propensity to truck, barter and exchange one thing for another' (Smith, 1937, p. 13), Karl Marx held a radically different view, both of 'human nature' and of the way an economy should be organized. In what is perhaps the most utopian paragraph he ever wrote – it appears near the end of his notes 'On James Mill' – he provided a description of *unalienated* production in a truly human, and totally marketless, community:

Supposing that we had produced in a human manner; each of us would in his production have doubly affirmed himself and his fellow men. (1) I would have objectified in my production my individuality and its peculiarity and thus both [a] in my activity enjoyed an individual expression of my life and [b] in looking at the object have had the individual pleasure of realizing that my personality was objective [and] visible to the senses . . . (2) In your enjoyment or use of my product, I would have had the direct enjoyment of realizing that I had both satisfied a human need by my work and . . . fashioned for another human being the object that met his need. (3) I would have been for you the mediator between you and the species and thus been acknowledged and felt by you as a completion of your own essence . . . and have thus realized that I am confirmed both in your thought and in your love. (4) In my expression of my life, I would have fashioned your expression of your life, and thus in my own activity have realized my own essence, my human, my communal essence. (Marx, 1977a, pp. 121–2)

This passage makes clear the reason why Marx placed such a high priority on 'production for use' as opposed to 'production for exchange'. However, the question that inevitably arises is: how relevant is this conception of unalienated production to the achievement of a feasible socialism – or is it even reconcilable with Marx's own vision of a global communist society?

Limited Freedom

The last of Marx's arguments for abolishing the market springs from his desire to promote human freedom. He believed that reliance upon the market to coordinate economic activities prevents a society – and the individuals in it – from achieving freedom in the fullest sense of the word. In order to grasp the complexity of his argument on this point, it is necessary to refer to his theory of 'commodity fetishism' (Marx, 1967, Ch. I, Section 4).[7]

Marx's argument here can be summarized as follows: first, people begin to exchange their products (commodities) in markets. Before long, the exchange of products takes on a life of its own and comes to be seen by the people who do the exchanging as something that is independent of and superior to themselves. Using an analogy to the process in which 'primitive' people carve a tree into a totem pole and then turn it into an object of worship, Marx called the modern tendency to reify the market 'commodity fetishism'. It was his view that, once people begin to attribute objective power to 'the forces of supply and demand' (forgetting that they themselves set the process of exchange in motion, that it did not fall from the sky), the 'market mechanism' becomes an autonomous power and people lose control over certain very important social decisions (e.g., what is to be produced, by what methods, where, and for whom). Indeed, people lose control over the direction in which their society is moving and, although not realizing that they are doing this, allow crucial social choices to be made without society as a whole (or any representative bodies) having a chance to deliberate on or decide them in a conscious way. Examples of such choices might include the process and pace of urbanization, choices among alternative technologies, priorities for developing energy sources, and the degree of inequality in the distribution of income and wealth.

Marx's analysis of commodity fetishism was first elaborated at length in Volume I of *Capital*, but it was anticipated more than twenty years earlier in one striking sentence in *The German Ideology*:

[As the market develops] . . . trade, which after all is nothing more than the exchange of products of various individuals and countries, rules the whole world through the relation of supply and demand – a relation which, as an English economist says, hovers over the earth like the fate of the ancients, and with *invisible hand* allots fortune and misfortune to men, sets up empires and wrecks empires, causes nations to rise and to disappear – whereas with the abolition of the basis [of trade], private property, with the communist regulation of production (and, implicit in this, the abolition of the alien attitude of men to their own product), *the power of the relation of supply and demand is dissolved into nothing*, and men once more gain control of exchange, production and the way they behave to one another. (Marx and Engels, 1976, p. 44, italics added)

From the perspective of Marx's analysis of commodity fetishism, it is clear that his conception of freedom went beyond the classical liberal definition that focused on the rights of individuals to express themselves and to make choices without being interfered with or constrained by the state. For Marx, free individual choice and expression do not give a person freedom if he or she has an 'alien attitude' toward the market mechanism and is without any power to influence important social decisions. It was Marx's view that freedom in the fullest sense would only come with the abolition of the market and its replacement by 'the communist regulation of production'.

14.3 CONCLUSION

What, finally, is the bearing of the preceding discussion on the contemporary push for market socialism? First, the reader should be convinced, for the reasons set forth in the first part of the paper, that Marx's abolitionist position on the market must be rejected. Under today's (or any foreseeable future) conditions, it is simply not possible – and probably not desirable – to construct a socialist economy without markets. This being said, however, we should take care not to throw the proverbial baby out with the bathwater.

It is clear to the present writer, at least, that Marx's specific criticisms of the workings and social implications of markets remain valid. Moreover, if one believes that Marx's value-judgements are consistent with the aspirations of contemporary socialism, then it follows logically that there will always exist certain tensions between our socialist values and the tendencies of markets that Marx so astutely elucidated.[8] To illustrate this point, I will end with a set of brief suggestions as to how market socialists might attempt to counteract some of the inherent tendencies of markets and work towards the achievement of Marx's fundamental objectives.

(1) *Equality* Reduce inequality and chip away the economic basis of class power by promoting one or another variant of social ownership of the means of production. While allowing market-determined labour incomes, this would provide for a more equal pre-tax distribution of income, thereby lightening the burden on government tax policies and income transfer programmes to equalize

incomes. Social ownership could also eliminate the economic basis of differential influence on the political process. Models of market socialism which provide for private banks and capital markets have to be seriously questioned, as these institutions tend to increase inequality and reinforce class power.

(2) *Stability* Attenuate economic fluctuations and promote stable and ecologically sustainable growth by using 'indicative planning' and 'industrial policy'. This would achieve some degree of social coordination of production without risking the harmful effects of central planning.

(3) *Decommodification* Clearly locate and defend the boundary between market and non-market realms with a conscious effort to slow down, and then reverse, the 'commodification' process. Decommodify certain goods and services which serve people's basic needs – e.g., education, health care, infrastructure, public amenities. (The selected goods and services could be provided 'free' through the public sector.) Ultimately, labour-power itself could be 'decommodified' by gradually expanding the workers' cooperative sector. By establishing limits on the reach of market relations (the 'cash nexus'), community life can be strengthened, social responsibility can be extended, and cooperation can gradually be substituted for competition.

(4) *Overcoming alienation* This central objective could be pursued, if not by organizing the whole economy on the basis of 'production for use', at least by promoting workers' cooperatives, encouraging workplace democracy and self-management, and strengthening those regulations and workers' rights which ensure safer and more humane working conditions.

(5) *Freedom* Implementation of 'indicative planning' and 'industrial policy' on the basis of democratically-determined priorities would give people a degree of collective control over the direction of their social development. 'Commodity fetishism' would be less prevalent in a society which viewed the market as an instrument for the achievement of social objectives rather than as a sacrosanct mechanism for equilibrating 'the forces of supply and demand'.

The most important lesson we might learn from Marx would be to take seriously his 'materialist conception of history'. As he himself once said, 'Men make their own history, but they do not make it just as they please; . . . [rather, they make it] under circumstances directly encountered, given, and transmitted from the past' (Marx, 1954, p. 10). Thus, rather than attempting to abolish the market – which would surely qualify as an effort by people to make history 'just as they please' – we should try to devise ways of incorporating the market within a framework that will allow us simultaneously to achieve economic efficiency and to advance socialist values.

Notes

1.   I would like to express my gratitude to Robert Heilbroner whose 1969 course on Comparative Economic Systems at the New School for Social Research sparked my interest in market socialism. He has continued to be a source of intellectual stimulation and personal support in the years since then. Among Heilbroner's many writings on the issues, his 'Reflections on the Future of Socialism' (1969) still stands as a remarkably prescient and insightful survey.
2.   For my earlier views on this point, see Roosevelt (1969).
3.   Several of the criticisms elaborated in this part of the paper have been cogently set forth in Nove (1983), Part 1, 'The Legacy of Marx'.
4.   I am indebted to Deborah Milenkovitch for this point.
5.   For an appealing projection of such a state of affairs, see Keynes (1963).
6.   On this point, Marx was actually in accord with Adam Smith. See Cropsey (1957).
7.   For an extended treatment of this topic, see Roosevelt (1975).
8.   There will also exist certain tensions among various socialist values themselves. See Miller (1991) and Roosevelt (1991).

References

Belkin, David (1991) 'Politicizing the Economic', unpublished paper presented at the Ninth Annual Socialist Scholars Conference, New York City, April 6th.

Brus, Wlodzimierz (1987) 'Market Socialism', in *The New Palgrave: A Dictionary of Economics*, John Eatwell, Murray Milgate, and Peter Newman (eds), Vol. 3, (London: Macmillan) pp. 33–42.

Cropsey, Joseph (1957) *Polity and Economy: An Interpretation of the Principles of Adam Smith* (The Hague: Martinus Nijhoff).

Engels, Frederick (1939) *Anti-Düring* (New York: International Publishers).

Gintis, Herbert (1989) 'The Power to Switch: On the Political Economy of Consumer Sovereignty', in, *Unconventional Wisdom*, Samuel Bowles, Richard C. Edwards and William G. Shepard (eds) (Boston: Houghton Mifflin) pp. 65–79.

Heilbroner, Robert L. (1969) 'Reflections on the Future of Socialism', *Commentary*, November. Reprinted in Robert L. Heilbroner, Between Capitalism and Socialism (New York: Random House, 1970) pp. 79–114.

Keynes, J. M. (1963) 'Economic Possibilities for our Grandchildren', in, *Essays in Persuasion* (New York: Norton & Company) pp. 358–73.

Marx, Karl (1938) *Critique of the Gotha Program* (New York: International Publishers).

Marx, Karl (1954) *The Eighteenth Brumaire of Louis Bonaparte* (Moscow: Progress Publishers).

Marx, Karl (1963) *The Poverty of Philosophy* (New York: International Publishers).

Marx, Karl (1964) *Early Writings* T. B. Bottomore (trans. and ed.) (New York: McGraw-Hill).

Marx, Karl (1967) *Capital*, Vol. I (New York: International Publishers).

Marx, Karl (1973) *Grundrisse* (New York: Random House).

Marx, Karl (1977a) 'On Bureaucracy (a section of the Critique of Hegel's 'Philosophy of Right'), in, *Selected Writings*, David McLellan (ed.) (Oxford: Oxford University Press) pp. 30–2.

Marx, Karl (1977b) 'On James Mill', in, *Selected Writings*, David McLellan (ed.) (Oxford: Oxford University Press) pp. 114–22.

Marx, Karl and Frederick Engels (1948) *The Communist Manifesto* (New York: International Publishers).

Marx, Karl and Frederick Engels (1970) *The German Ideology* (New York: International Publishers).

Marx, Karl and Frederick Engels (1976) 'Feuerbach. Opposition of the Materialist and Idealist Outlooks, new publication of Chapter I of *The German Ideology* (Moscow: Progress Publishers).

Miller, David (1989) *Market, State, and Community: Theoretical Foundations of Market Socialism* (Oxford: Clarendon Press).

Miller, David (1991) 'A Vision of Market Socialism', *Dissent*, Summer, pp. 406–14.

Nove, Alec (1983) *The Economics of Feasible Socialism* (London: George Allen & Unwin).

Roosevelt, Frank (1969) 'Market Socialism: A Humane Economy?', *Journal of Economic Issues*, Vol. III, No. 4, pp. 3–20.

Roosevelt, Frank (1975) 'Cambridge Economics as Commodity Fetishism', *Review of Radical Political Economics*, Vol. 7, No. 4, pp. 1–32.

Roosevelt, Frank (1991) 'Questions about Market Socialism', *Dissent*, Fall, pp. 580–2.

Smith, Adam (1937) *An Inquiry into the Nature and Causes of the Wealth of Nations*, Edwin Cannan (ed.) (New York: Modern Library).

Epilogue

For most economists, at least in the US, economics is a science, at once technical and mathematical, abstract yet empirical – although 'empirical' has a very special meaning. Empirical studies are conducted in armchairs, with computers and data banks; no empirical investigator, say of production, ever has to visit a factory or construction site. And no serious economist ever has to think about history or the changing meaning of the activities under investigation, any more than the physicist or chemist has to worry about the history of the atoms or molecules being studied. This may be economics, but it is not worldly philosophy.

Heilbroner recognizes a place for technical economics; it is important to get the technical questions right – but it is even more important to know what those questions mean! Heilbroner's very first publication, in the *American Economic Review*, concerned the technicalities of the saving–investment relationship. But, characteristically, he also dealt with the place and significance of the problem in regard to Keynesian theory.

Technical issues, in Heilbroner's view, must be set in historical and philosophical perspective, that is, related to the evolution of social and economic systems. Economics concerns the material foundation of society; but each social order develops its own inner dynamics. To understand this is to grasp the nature and logic of the system, and that comprises the larger picture in which technical questions must be placed. But once that picture is established, technical analysis can be very useful.

The classics understood this better than present-day neo-classical economists. They saw economics, not as a science, but as a branch of the philosophy of history and society. Re-examining them, then, is not a matter of tracing the early anticipations of our present state of advanced knowledge; it is instead a matter of recovering from a wrong turning, going back to the source for inspiration, and towards a method of thought capable of encompassing the whole society, rather than one that tries to separate the 'economic' from the rest. And, besides inspiration, we may look to them even for clues to the answers to today's problems. Thus we have Smith suggesting what today are known as 'efficiency wages' – but on grounds that lead to a different and arguably superior understanding; Marx leads us to think in terms of variable saving ratios, and provides a critique of the institution of the market, which every serious social thinker – and especially socialists – ought to confront; Keynes and Kalecki provide a framework for understanding debt and the deficit; Quesnay provides a way of looking at leading sectors, suggesting an approach to technical change; and the classics in general suggest that economic history be conceived in terms of stages of historical development.

Economics understood as the analysis of markets – in the conventional wisdom – is important. 'Real world socialism' collapsed, at least in part, because it failed to understand the functioning of markets. Not that 'planning got the prices wrong', as conventional economists sometimes say; 'inefficiencies' due to 'misallocation' are not that important, and prices are probably just as 'wrong' in the West, as a consequence of regulations, monopoly power, price leadership, trade barriers, etc. etc. But the system of real world socialism failed to set up adequate incentives for workers, managers, firms, bureaucrats – indeed, for any-body. Nobody had an incentive to innovate, few had incentives to work hard or to improve their effectiveness on the job, or to suggest how the job or product could be redesigned to perform better. The system failed to encourage either innovation or productivity, and this failure lies at the basis of its collapse. The most important feature of markets is the way they generate and channel incentives. But, remark-ably, innovation and developing or failing to develop productivity are matters that mainstream economics cannot explain, even though technical progress is among the chief successes of modern capitalism.

Yet just as the system of market capitalism celebrates its greatest success, it confronts its greatest challenge. Not only has present-day capitalism fallen into its worst recession in a generation, after a decade of stagnant or falling real standards of living, surrounded by decaying public infrastructure, but the impact of indus-trial wastes on the environment has become unsustainable. As Heilbroner points out in his gloomiest work, *The Human Prospect*, capitalism cannot continue on its present course without running the risk of destroying the world as we know it. The environment simply cannot stand another generation of industrialization. This implies not only that we cannot grow further along the same path, but, even more problematically, that the Third World can never be brought up to the present standard of living of the First. How are we to meet this challenge? As was once asked in another context, what is to be done? Can industrialization be curbed? How could material incentives be restrained or re-channelled? How will the relationship of governments to markets change under the impact of these prob-lems? To understand these economic issues historically as well as politically, and to explain our predicament in ways that will enable us to see how to overcome it, is the task Heilbroner has bequeathed us, not as economists, but as worldly philosophers.

The Writings of Robert L. Heilbroner

(as of 28 January 1992)

(each category in order of publication)

Books and Pamphlets

The Worldly Philosophers (New York: Simon & Schuster, 1952) revised editions, 1961, 1967, 1972, 1980, 1986, 1992 (update).

The Quest for Wealth (New York: Simon & Schuster, 1956).

The Future as History (New York: Harper & Bros., 1959, 1960).

The Making of Economic Society (Englewood Cliffs, New Jersey: Prentice Hall, 1962) revised editions, 1968, 1970, 1972, 1975, 1980, 1985, 1989, 1992 (forthcoming).

The Great Ascent (New York: Harper & Row, 1963).

A Primer on Government Spending (with Peter L. Bernstein) (New York: Random House, 1963) revised edition, 1970.

The Limits of American Capitalism (New York: Harper & Row, 1965, 1966).

Automation in the Perspective of Long-Term Technological Change, US Department of Labour, 1966 (pamphlet).

Understanding Macroeconomics (Englewood Cliffs, NJ: Prentice Hall, 1965) revised editions, 1968, 1972; (with Lester Thurow) 1975, 1978, 1981, 1984; (with James Galbraith) 1987, 1989.

Understanding Microeconomics (Englewood Cliffs, NJ: Prentice Hall, 1968) revised edition, 1972; (with Lester Thurow) 1975, 1978, 1981, 1984; (with James Galbraith) 1987, 1989.

The Economic Problem (Englewood Cliffs, NJ: Prentice Hall, 1968) revised editions, 1970, 1972; (with Lester Thurow) 1975, 1978, 1981, 1984; (with James Galbraith) 1987, 1989.

Between Capitalism and Socialism (New York: Random House, 1970).

Business Civilization in Decline (New York: W. W. Norton & Co., 1976).

An Inquiry into The Human Prospect (New York: W. W. Norton & Co., 1974) revised editions, 1980, 1991.

The Economic Transformation of America (with Aaron Singer) (New York: Harcourt Brace Jovanovich, 1976) revised edition, 1984.

Beyond Boom and Crash (New York: W. W. Norton & Co., 1978).

Marxism: For and Against (New York: W. W. Norton & Co., 1980).

Five Economic Challenges (with Lester Thurow) (Englewood Cliffs, NJ: Prentice Hall, 1981).

Economics Explained (with Lester Thurow) (New York: Simon & Schuster, 1982) revised editions, 1987, 1993 (forthcoming).

The Nature and Logic of Capitalism (New York: W. W. Norton & Co., 1985).
The Act of Work, Library of Congress, Washington, 1985.
The Essential Adam Smith (with Laurence J. Malone) (New York: W. W. Norton, 1986; also London: Oxford University Press, 1986).
Behind the Veil of Economics (New York: W. W. Norton & Co., 1988).
The Debt and the Deficit: False Alarms, Real Possibilities (with Peter Bernstein) (New York: W. W. Norton, 1989).

Edited books

Economic Means and Social Ends: Essays in Political Economics (Englewood Cliffs, NJ: Prentice Hall, 1969).
In the Name of Profit (Garden City, NY: Doubleday, 1972).
Corporate Social Policy: Selections from Business and Society Review (with Paul London) (Reading, Mass.: Addison-Wesley Publishing, 1972).
Is Economics Relevant? (with Arthur Ford) (Pacific Palisades, Cal.: Goodyear Publishing Co., Inc., 1971) revised edition, 1976.

Essays in books (partial listing)

'The American Poor', *Man and Modern Society*, K. De Schweinitz and K. W. Thompson (eds) (New York: Holt, 1953).
'Communicating Economic Research: As a Writer Sees It', *Report on the Conference on Communicating Economic Research* (Hanover, New Hampshire: Amos Tuck School, 1957).
'The Impact of Technology', *Automation and Technological Change* (American Assembly, Englewoods Cliffs, NJ: Prentice Hall, 1962).
'The View from the Top: Reflections on a Changing Business Ideology', *The Business Establishment*, E. Cheit (ed.) (New York: Wiley & Sons, 1964).
'Which Goals for the Future?', *Manpower Policies for Youth*, National Committee on Employment of Youth, E. Cohen and L. Kapp (eds) (New York: Columbia University Press, 1966).
'Counter-revolutionary America', *A Dissenter's Guide to Foreign* Irving Howe (ed.) (New York: Praeger, 1968) and 'Rebuttal', *op. cit.*
'On the Limited Relevance of Economics', *Capitalism Today*, Daniel Bell and Irving Kristol (eds) (New York: Basic Books, 1971).
'The Roots of Social Neglect in the United States', *Is Law Dead?*, E. V. Rostow (ed.) (New York: Simon & Schuster, 1971).
'Do Machines Make History?' *Technology and Culture*, M. Kranzberg and W. H. Davenport (eds) (New York: Schocken Books, 1972). Also reprinted in (See listing under "Technological Determinism Revisited", below).
'Adam Smith', *Encyclopedia Britannica*, 1974.
'Economic Systems', *Encyclopedia Britannica*, 1991.
'The Paradox of Progress: Decline and Decay in the Wealth of Nations', *Essays*

on Adam Smith, A. S. Skinner and T. Wilson, (eds) (New York: Oxford, 1975, 1976).

'Was Schumpeter Right?', *Schumpeter's Vision*, A. Heertje (ed.) (New York: Praeger, 1981).

'What is Socialism?', *Beyond the Welfare State*, Irving Howe (ed.) (New York: Schocken, 1982).

'John D. Rockefeller', *Historical Viewpoints*, John Garraty (ed.) (New York: Harper & Row, 1983).

'Capitalism as Gestalt: A Contrast of Visions', *Free Market Conservatism*, Edward Nell (ed.) (London: George Allen & Unwin, 1984).

'The Nature and Logic of Capitalism According to Adam Smith', *Beschaftigung, Verteilung und Konjunctur* (Festschrift für Adolph Lowe, Bremen: Universita Bremen, 1984).

'Economics and Political Economy: Marx, Keynes, and Schumpeter', *Marx, Schumpeter and Keynes*, Suzanne Helburn and David Bramhall (eds) (Armonk, NY: M. E. Sharpe, 1986).

'Realities and Appearances in Capitalism', *Corporations and the Common Good*, Robert B. Dickie and Leroy S. Rouner (eds) (Notre Dame, Ind.: University of Notre Dame Press, 1986).

'Wealth', *The New Palgrave*, John Eatwell, Murray Milgate, and Peter Newman (eds) (New York and London: Macmillan, 1988).

'Capitalism', *The New Palgrave*, *supra cit.*

'Rhetoric and Ideology', *The Consequences of Economic Rhetoric*, Klamer, McCloskey and Solow (eds) (New York: Cambridge University Press, 1988).

'Economics as Ideology', *Economics as Discourse*, Warren Samuels (ed.) (Boston: Kluwer, 1990).

'Economic Systems', *Encyclopedia Britannica*, (1991).

'Socialism', *The Fortune Encyclopedia of Economics*, David Henderson (ed.) 1993 (forthcoming).

'The Future of Capitalism', in *Sea-Changes: American Foreign Policy in a World Transformed*, Nicolas X. Rizopoulos (ed.) (New York: Council on Foreign Relations Press, 1990).

'Technological Determinism Revisited', in a book edited by Merrit Roe Smith, MIT Press, forthcoming.

'The Economic View of Progress', in *The Idea of Progress Revisited*, Leo Marx and Bruce Mazlish (eds), (forthcoming).

Articles

(partial listing, not including shorter, miscellaneous articles in *The Commercial and Financial Chronicle* (1946); in *American Business Magazine* (1946–1950); and on the Op Ed page of the *New York Times*, 1980–1991; also in *Challenge, The Nation*, The New School *Commentator*, The *New York Times* business section and special supplements, other).

'Saving and Investment: Dynamic Aspects', *American Economic Review*, December 1942.

'Labour Unrest in the British Nationalized Sector', *Social Research*, March, 1952.

'Epitaph for the Steel Master', *American Heritage*, August 1960.

'The Revolution of Economic Development', *American Scholar*, Autumn, 1962.

'The Share-the-Tax Revenue Plan', *New York Times Sunday Magazine*, December 27, 1964.

'Is Economic Theory Possible?', *Social Research*, Summer, 1966.

'Rhetoric and Reality in the Struggle Between Business and the State', *Social Research*, Autumn, 1968.

'The Multinational Corporation and the Nation State', *New York Review*, February 11, 1971.

'A Radical View of Socialism', *Social Research*, Spring, 1972.

'Ecological 'Balance' and the 'Stationary' State (with Jack Allentuck), *Land Economics*, August 1972.

'Growth and Survival', *Foreign Affairs*, October 1972.

'The Paradox of Progress: Decline and Decay in the Wealth of Nations', *Journal of the History of Ideas*, April 1973.

'Economic Problems of a 'Post-Industrial' Society', *Dissent*, Spring 1973.

'Economics as a 'Value Free' Science', *Social Research*, Spring 1973.

'The Clouded Crystal Ball', American Economic Association, *Papers and Proceedings*, May 1974.

'What Is The Human Prospect?', *New York Review*, January 24, 1976.

'Marxism, Psychoanalysis and the Problem of a Unified Theory of Behaviour', *Social Research, Autumn, 1975*.

'Homage to Adam Smith', *Challenge*, March–April, 1976.

'Boom and Crash', *The New Yorker*, August 28, 1976.

'Middle Class Myths; Middle Class Realities', *Atlantic*, October, 1976.

'Inescapable Marx', *New York Review*, June 29, 1978.

'Modern Economics as a Chapter in the History of Economic Thought', History of Political Economy, Vol. 11, No. 2, 1979; also included in Mark Blaug (ed.) *The Historiography of Economics* (London: Elgar, 1991).

'Inflationary Capitalism', *The New Yorker*, October 8, 1979.

'Adolph Lowe', *Journal of Economic Issues*, June 1980.

'The Demand for the Supply Side', *New York Review*, June 11, 1981.

'The Socialization of the Individual in Adam Smith', *History of Political Economy*, Vol. 2, 1982.

'The Problem of Value in the Constitution of Economic Thought', *Social Research*, Summer 1983.

'Economic Prospects', *The New Yorker*, August 29, 1983 (first prize, Gerald R. Loeb Awards for Distinguished Financial and Business Journalism).

'Perceptions and Misperceptions: How Economists and the Public See Economics – and Each Other', *Journal of Economic and Monetary Affairs*, Middlebury,

Vt., International Institute for Economic Advancement, July 1987.

'Hard Times', *New Yorker*, September, 1987 (first prize, Gerald R. Loeb Awards).

'The Coming Meltdown of Traditional Capitalism', *Ethics and International Affairs*, No. 2, 1988.

'The Deficit', *New York Times*, September 4, 1988.

'The Triumph of Capitalism', *The New Yorker*, Sept. 23, 1989.

'Rereading the Affluent Society', *Journal of Economic Issues*, Fall, 1989.

'Seize the Day', *New York Review of Books*, Feb. 15, 1990.

'After Communism', *New Yorker*, Sept. 10, 1990.

'Rethinking the Past, Re-hoping the Future', *Social Research*, Fall, 1990.

'The World After Communism', *Dissent*, Fall, 1990 (adapted in *Harper's*, Jan. 1991).

'Analysis and Vision in the History of Modern Economic Thought', *J. Econ. Lit.*, Sept., 1990.

'Economics as Universal Science', *Social Research*, Summer, 1991.

'Economic Predictions', *New Yorker*, July 22, 1991.

'Thoughts on The Triumph of Capitalism', *The American Prospect*, Fall, 1991.

'Lifting the Silent Depression', *New York Review of Books*, October 23, 1991.

'Thedeficit', *Nation*, Jan. 27, 1992.

Reviews and Review Articles
(partial listing by author and volume, not by title of review)

Joseph Schumpeter, *History of Economic Analysis*, *The Nation*, n.d. (1953).

Edmund Stillman and William Pfaff, *The Politics of Hysteria*, *New York Review*, Feb. 20, 1964.

Kenneth Boulding, *The Meaning of the 20th Century*, *Book Week*, January 17, 1965.

Seymour Melman, *Pentagon Capitalism*, *New York Review*, July 23, 1970.

W. W. Rostow, *Politics and the Stages of Growth*, *New York Times Book Review*, August 1, 1971.

Bertell Ollman, *Alienation: Marx's Conception of Man in Capitalist Society*, and Walter Weisskopf, *Alienation and Economics*, *New York Review*, March 9, 1972.

'Radical Economics: A Review Essay', *American Political Science Review*, September, 1972.

Barrington Moore, *Reflections in the Causes of Human Misery*, *New York Review*, October 5, 1972.

David P. Calleo and Benjamin Rowland, *America and the World Political Economy*, *New York Review*, November 29, 1973.

Harry Braverman, *Labour and Monopoly Capital*, *New York Review*, January 23, 1975.

'Kenneth Boulding, Collected Papers: A Review Article', *Journal of Economic Issues*, March, 1975.

Charles E. Lindblom, *Politics and Markets*, New York Times Book Review, February 19, 1978.

Milton and Rose *Friedman, Free to Choose: A Personal Statement*, New York Review, April 17, 1980.

Alfred Eichner, *A Guide to Post Keynesian Economics*, New York Review, February 21, 1980.

Albert Hirschman, *Essays in Trespassing and Shifting Involvements*, New York Review, June 24, 1982.

Michael Piore and Charles Sabel, *The Second Industrial Divide*, New York Times Book Review, January 6, 1985.

Guy Routh, *Economics: An Alternative Text*, Journal of Economic Literature, March, 1986.

Donald N. McCloskey, *The Rhetoric of Economics*, New York Review, April 24, 1986.

Robert Skidelsky, *John Maynard Keynes*, Vol. I, New York Times Book Review, May 11, 1986.

Eli Sagan, *At the Dawn of Tyranny*, Monthly Review, September, 1986.

John Kenneth Galbraith, *Economics in Perspective*, New York Review, November 5, 1987.

Friedrich Hayek, *The Fatal Conceit*, The Nation, April, 1989.

The New Palgrave: A Dictionary of Economics, (eds) John Eatwell, Peter Newman, and Murray Milgate, New York Review, March 3, 1988.

Herbert Stein, *Governing A $5 Trillion Dollar Economy*, Challenge, Aug/Sept, 1989.

Michael Harrington, *Socialism, Past and Future*, Dissent, Fall, 1989.

John Donahue, *The Privatization Decision*, New York Times Book Review, Dec. 17, 1989.

Alfred Chandler, *Scale and Scope: The Dynamics of Industrial Capitalism*, New York Review, October 11, 1990.

Robert Kuttner, *The End of Laissez-Faire*, National Purpose and the Global Economy After the Cold War, Dissent, Summer, 1991.

Patricia Werhane, *Adam Smith and his Legacy for Modern Capitalism*, Journal of Economic Studies, 1992 (forthcoming).

Interviews and Profiles (partial listing)

Business Week, September 30, 1972.

Bill Moyers' Journal, *WNET* interview, April 23, 1974.

Science, August 16, 1974.

Psychology Today, February, 1975.

A Biographical Dictionary of Dissenting Economists, ed. Philip Arestis and Malcolm Sawyer (Edward Elgar, 1992).

Hearings before the Subcommittee on the Environment, House of Representatives, Serial No. 93–55, pp. 33–51.

Current Biography, H. H. Wilson Co., June, 1976.

World Authors, 1980–1985, H. H. Wilson Co., 1991 pp. 402–5.

US News and World Report, March 8, 1976.

Chronicle of Higher Education, October 16, 1978.

Public Opinion, April/May, 1980.

Challenge, October/November, 1982.

Arnold Heertje, *The U.S.A. in the World Economy* (San Francisco, Freeman, Cooper & Co., 1984) pp. 58–67.

Loren J. Okroi, *Galbraith, Harrington, Heilbroner: Economics and Dissent in an Age of Optimism* (Princeton, N. J., Princeton Univ. Press, 1988).

New Perspectives Quarterly, Fall, 1989.

Forbes Magazine, May 27, 1991.

Index

Index 385

Blinder, A. S.   165, 167, 172
Bluestone, B.   170, 171–2, 321
body, individuality and   210
Bohm, D.   30, 63
borrowing, deficits and   115–17, 130,
    139–40
    see also debt dependency
Boulding, K. E.   64
bourgeois society   247–8
Bowles, S.   101, 140, 142, 324
Bradley, I.   319
breakdown of trust   64
Brown, C.   333
Brown, E. H. Phelps   323, 326
Brus, W.   356
Buchanan, A.   266
budget constraints   30–1, 31–2
budget deficits, US   107–38, 166
    Eisner and 'real'   120–6
    growth of   111, 130–1, 165
    neo-Keynesianism and crowding
        out   114–20
    new classical economics and Ricardian
        equivalence   111–13
    post-war economic performance
        110–11
    structural change and   126–38; debt
        dependency   128–9; demand
        stimulus   131–3; financial
        fragility   133–4; income
        redistribution   135–6;
        internationalization   129–30;
        monetary policy   134–5;
        stagnation   126–8
bureaucracies   362
business tax incentives   117–18
Business Week Team   321
Buss, L. W.   64

Cadell, W.   332
Cairns, J.   47
Campbell, R. H.   331–2
Cantillon, R.   325
capacities, innate   251–5
    see also autonomy; self-realization
capital
    accumulation see accumulation
    basic form and universal
        circulation   290–6
    consumption of   351–2
    industrial   278
    merchants'   269–71, 277, 278

money first form of   271–2, 280–1
    specifically capitalist   271–6;
        defining   272–3
    usurers'   271, 273, 277, 278
capital budgeting   120, 122–3
capitalism   376
    democracy and   265
    Heilbroner and see Heilbroner
    Marx and see Marx
    self-realization and   251, 258–9
    Smith and   2
    and state intervention   145–59; liberal
        capitalism and growth   152–3;
        shrinking state and managed
        capitalism   157–9; Thatcherism and
        growth   155–6
    see also commodity
Carne-Ross, D. S.   232
Carron Company   331–2
Carter, J.   175
Castellana, R.   267
cell-adhesion molecule (CAM)   65
Chandler, A. D.   82, 101
Charlesworth, D.   65
Cherry, R.   43, 64, 140
China   335
choice see preferences
Chomsky, N.   65
Christensen, P. P.   38
Christian account of individuality
    compared with classical account
        196–204, 231, 232, 233;
        adversity   237
    Locke   205
    Smith   213–29 passim
    and Utilitarianism   209–13
Churchill, W. S.   233
circulation   4, 271, 280–1
    defining capital   272–3
    production and   278
    universal   290–6, 296–7, 297, 300
Clark, N.   83
class   191
    conflict   261, 263
    markets and   4–5, 190–1
    Quesnay's Tableaux   306–7
classical account of individuality   189
    compared with Christian
        account   196–204, 231, 232, 233;
        path to goodness   237
    18th-century political economy   204–9
    Smith   213–29 passim